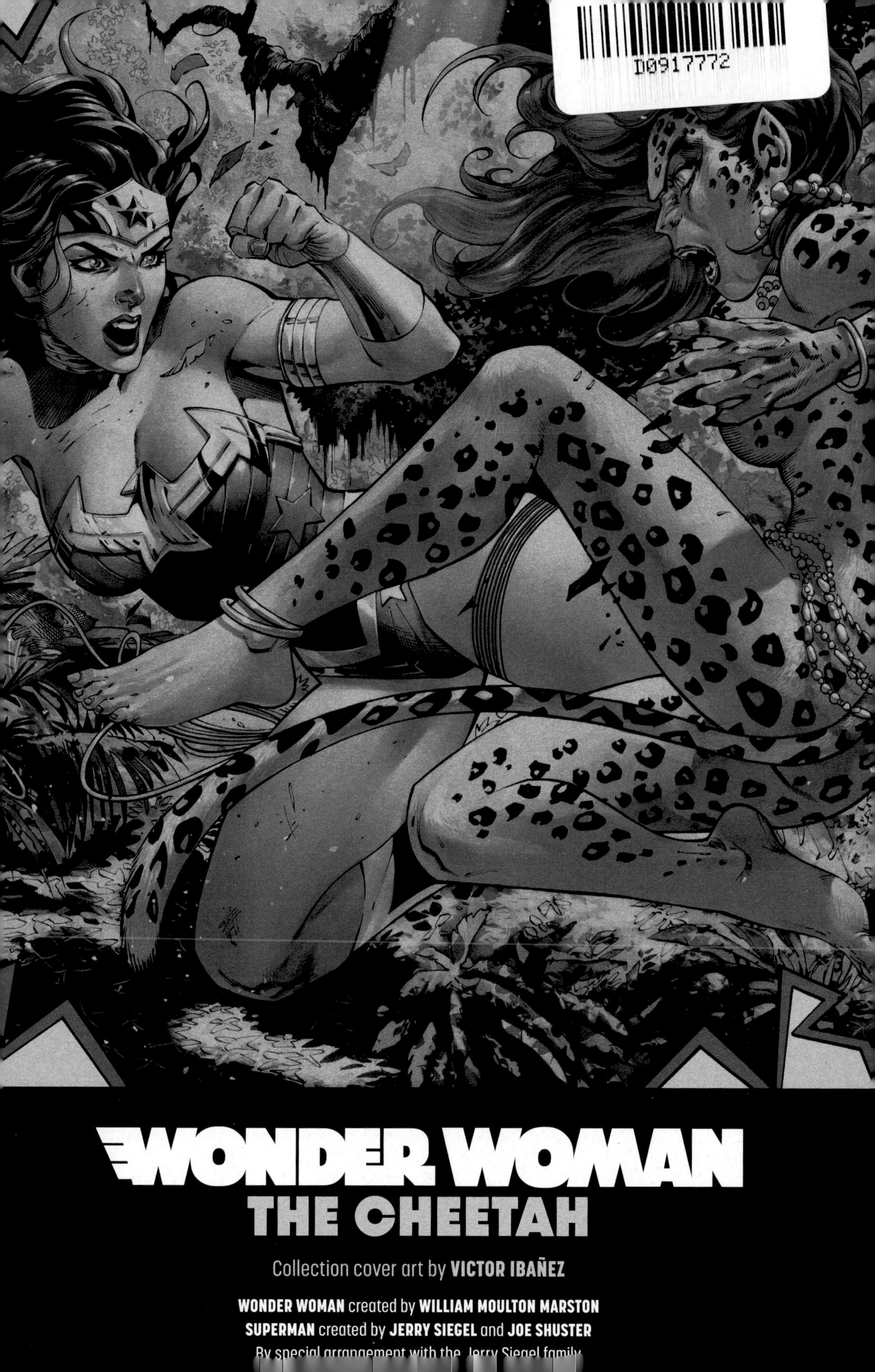

WONDER WOMAN
THE CHEETAH

Collection cover art by **VICTOR IBAÑEZ**

WONDER WOMAN created by **WILLIAM MOULTON MARSTON**
SUPERMAN created by **JERRY SIEGEL** and **JOE SHUSTER**
By special arrangement with the Jerry Siegel family

TABLE OF CONTENTS

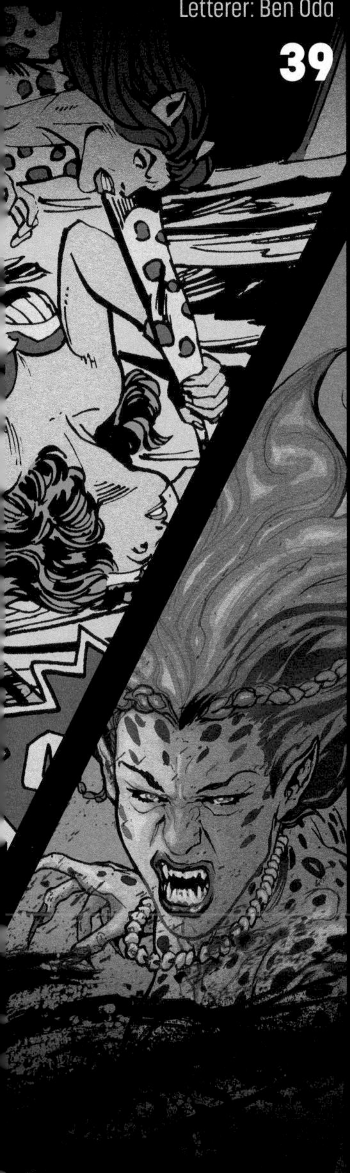

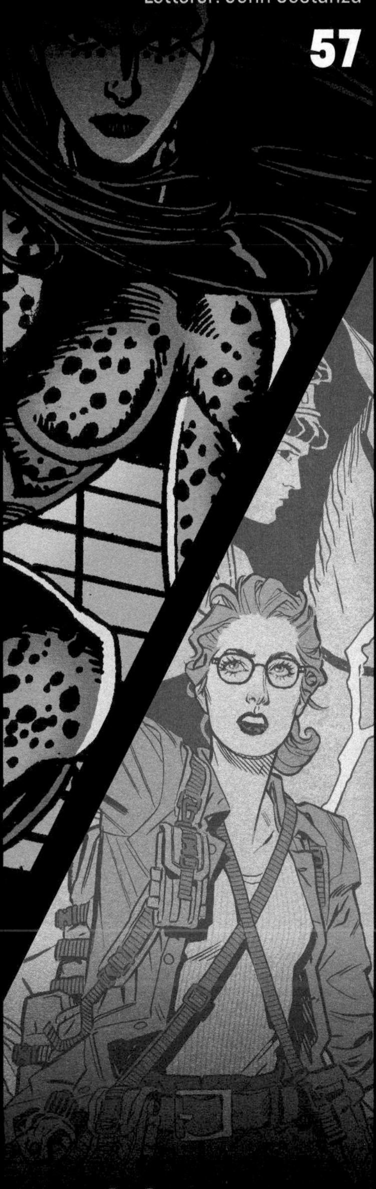

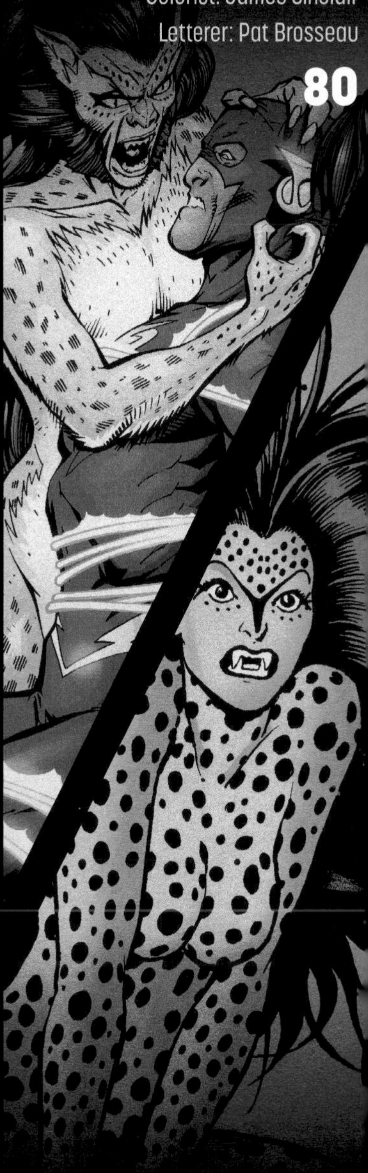

WONDER WOMAN: THE CHEETAH

Published by DC Comics. Compilation and all new material Copyright © 2020 DC Comics. All Rights Reserved. Originally published in single magazine form in *Wonder Woman* 6, 274-275, *Wonder Woman* 9, *The Flash* 219, *Wonder Woman* 214, *Justice League* 13-14, *Wonder Woman* 23.1, *Wonder Woman* 8, *Who's Who in the DC Universe* 4. Copyright © 1943, 1980, 1981, 1987, 1990, 2005, 2012, 2013, 2016 DC Comics. All Rights Reserved. All characters, their distinctive likenesses, and related elements featured in this publication are trademarks of DC Comics. The stories, characters, and incidents featured in this publication are entirely fictional. DC Comics does not read or accept unsolicited submissions of ideas, stories, or artwork. DC - a WarnerMedia Company.

DC Comics, 2900 West Alameda Ave., Burbank, CA 91505
Printed by LSC Communications, Kendallville, IN, USA. 2/7/20. First Printing.
ISBN: 978-1-4012-9166-2

Library of Congress Cataloging-in-Publication Data is available.

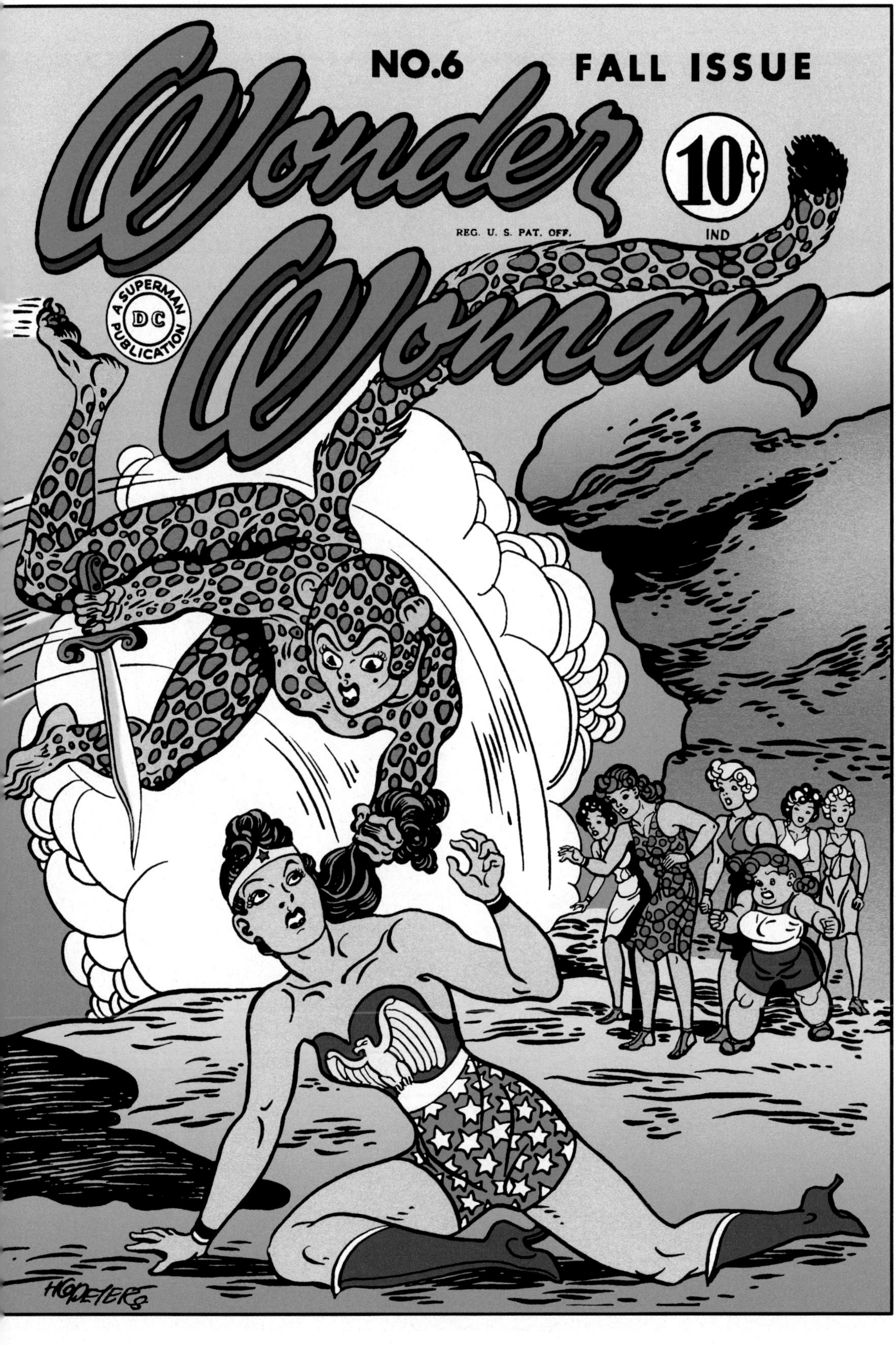

NO.6
FALL ISSUE
Wonder Woman
10¢
REG. U. S. PAT. OFF.
IND
A SUPERMAN DC PUBLICATION

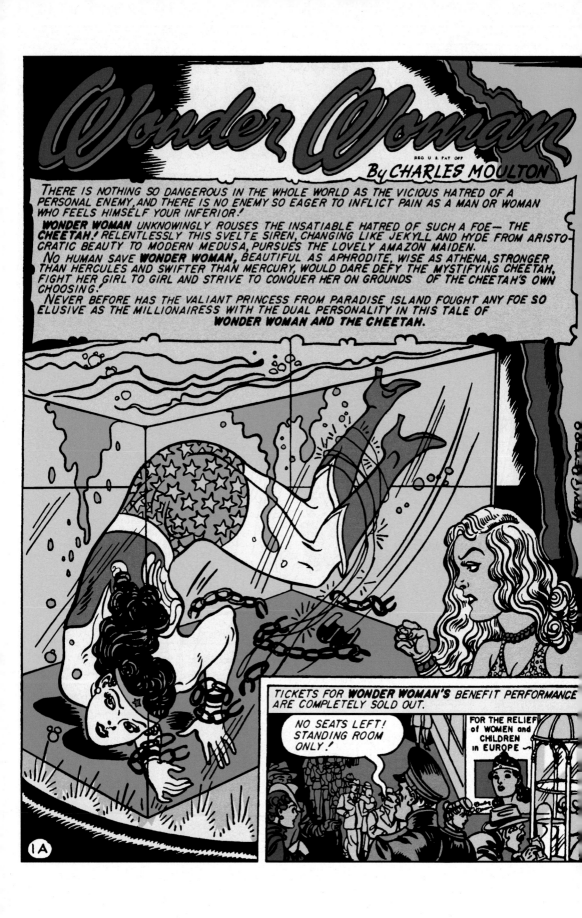

Wonder Woman

REG. U.S. PAT. OFF.

By CHARLES MOULTON

THERE IS NOTHING SO DANGEROUS IN THE WHOLE WORLD AS THE VICIOUS HATRED OF A PERSONAL ENEMY, AND THERE IS NO ENEMY SO EAGER TO INFLICT PAIN AS A MAN OR WOMAN WHO FEELS HIMSELF YOUR INFERIOR!

WONDER WOMAN UNKNOWINGLY ROUSES THE INSATIABLE HATRED OF SUCH A FOE— THE CHEETAH! RELENTLESSLY THIS SVELTE SIREN, CHANGING LIKE JEKYLL AND HYDE FROM ARISTO-CRATIC BEAUTY TO MODERN MEDUSA, PURSUES THE LOVELY AMAZON MAIDEN.

NO HUMAN SAVE WONDER WOMAN, BEAUTIFUL AS APHRODITE, WISE AS ATHENA, STRONGER THAN HERCULES AND SWIFTER THAN MERCURY, WOULD DARE DEFY THE MYSTIFYING CHEETAH, FIGHT HER GIRL TO GIRL AND STRIVE TO CONQUER HER ON GROUNDS OF THE CHEETAH'S OWN CHOOSING!

NEVER BEFORE HAS THE VALIANT PRINCESS FROM PARADISE ISLAND FOUGHT ANY FOE SO ELUSIVE AS THE MILLIONAIRESS WITH THE DUAL PERSONALITY IN THIS TALE OF WONDER WOMAN AND THE CHEETAH.

TICKETS FOR WONDER WOMAN'S BENEFIT PERFORMANCE ARE COMPLETELY SOLD OUT.

NO SEATS LEFT! STANDING ROOM ONLY!

FOR THE RELIEF of WOMEN and CHILDREN in EUROPE —

1A

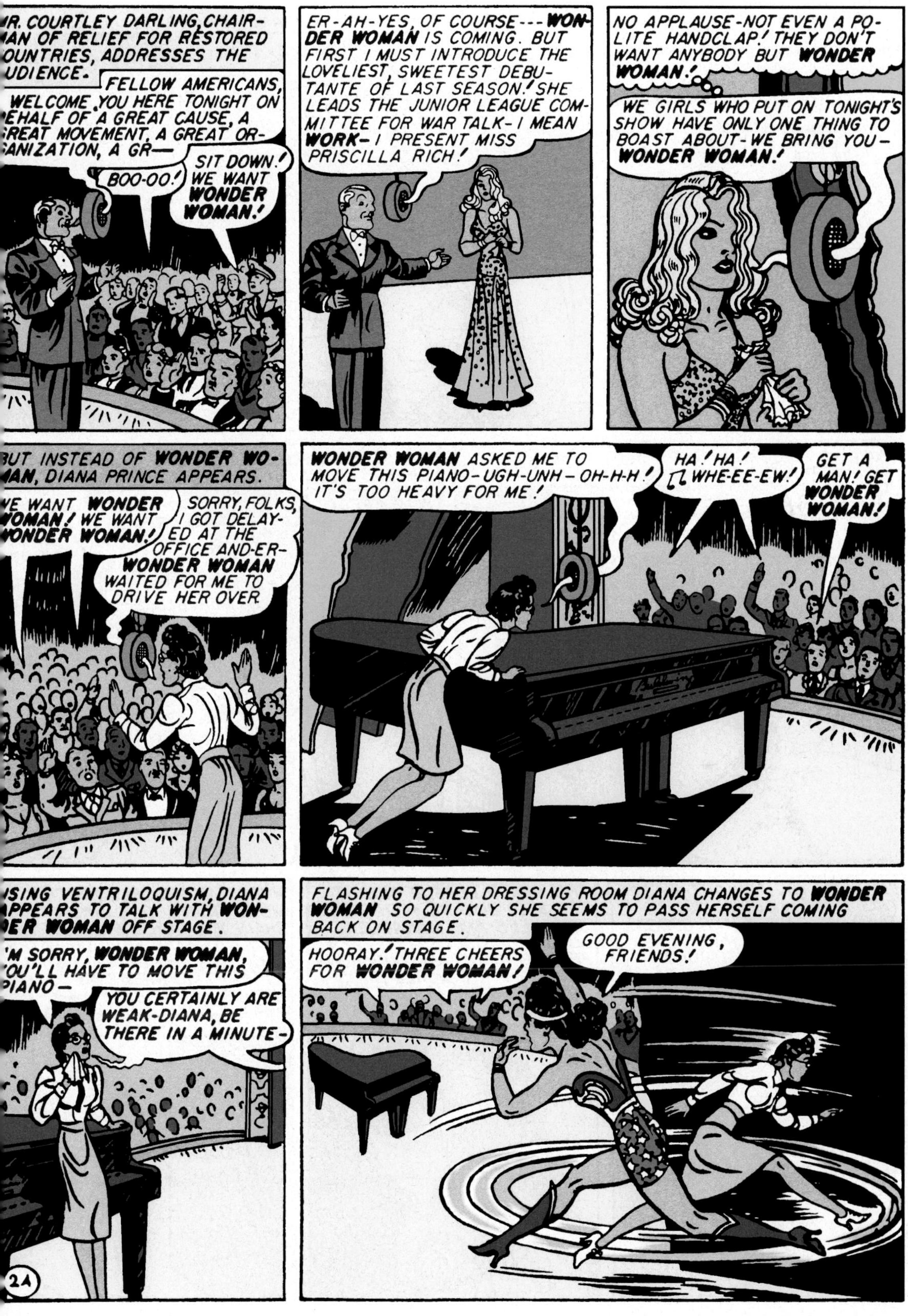

R. COURTLEY DARLING, CHAIRMAN OF RELIEF FOR RESTORED OUNTRIES, ADDRESSES THE UDIENCE.
FELLOW AMERICANS, WELCOME. YOU HERE TONIGHT ON EHALF OF A GREAT CAUSE, A REAT MOVEMENT, A GREAT OR-ANIZATION, A GR—
BOO-OO!
SIT DOWN! WE WANT WONDER WOMAN!
ER-AH-YES, OF COURSE---WONDER WOMAN IS COMING. BUT FIRST I MUST INTRODUCE THE LOVELIEST, SWEETEST DEBUTANTE OF LAST SEASON! SHE LEADS THE JUNIOR LEAGUE COMMITTEE FOR WAR TALK- I MEAN WORK- I PRESENT MISS PRISCILLA RICH!
NO APPLAUSE-NOT EVEN A POLITE HANDCLAP! THEY DON'T WANT ANYBODY BUT WONDER WOMAN!
WE GIRLS WHO PUT ON TONIGHT'S SHOW HAVE ONLY ONE THING TO BOAST ABOUT-WE BRING YOU-WONDER WOMAN!
UT INSTEAD OF WONDER WOMAN, DIANA PRINCE APPEARS.
E WANT WONDER OMAN! WE WANT ONDER WOMAN!
SORRY, FOLKS, I GOT DELAYED AT THE OFFICE AND-ER-WONDER WOMAN WAITED FOR ME TO DRIVE HER OVER
WONDER WOMAN ASKED ME TO MOVE THIS PIANO-UGH-UNH-OH-H-H! IT'S TOO HEAVY FOR ME!
HA! HA! WHE-EE-EW!
GET A MAN! GET WONDER WOMAN!
SING VENTRILOQUISM, DIANA PPEARS TO TALK WITH WONDER WOMAN OFF STAGE.
'M SORRY, WONDER WOMAN, OU'LL HAVE TO MOVE THIS PIANO—
YOU CERTAINLY ARE WEAK-DIANA, BE THERE IN A MINUTE-
2A
FLASHING TO HER DRESSING ROOM DIANA CHANGES TO WONDER WOMAN SO QUICKLY SHE SEEMS TO PASS HERSELF COMING BACK ON STAGE.
HOORAY! THREE CHEERS FOR WONDER WOMAN!
GOOD EVENING, FRIENDS!

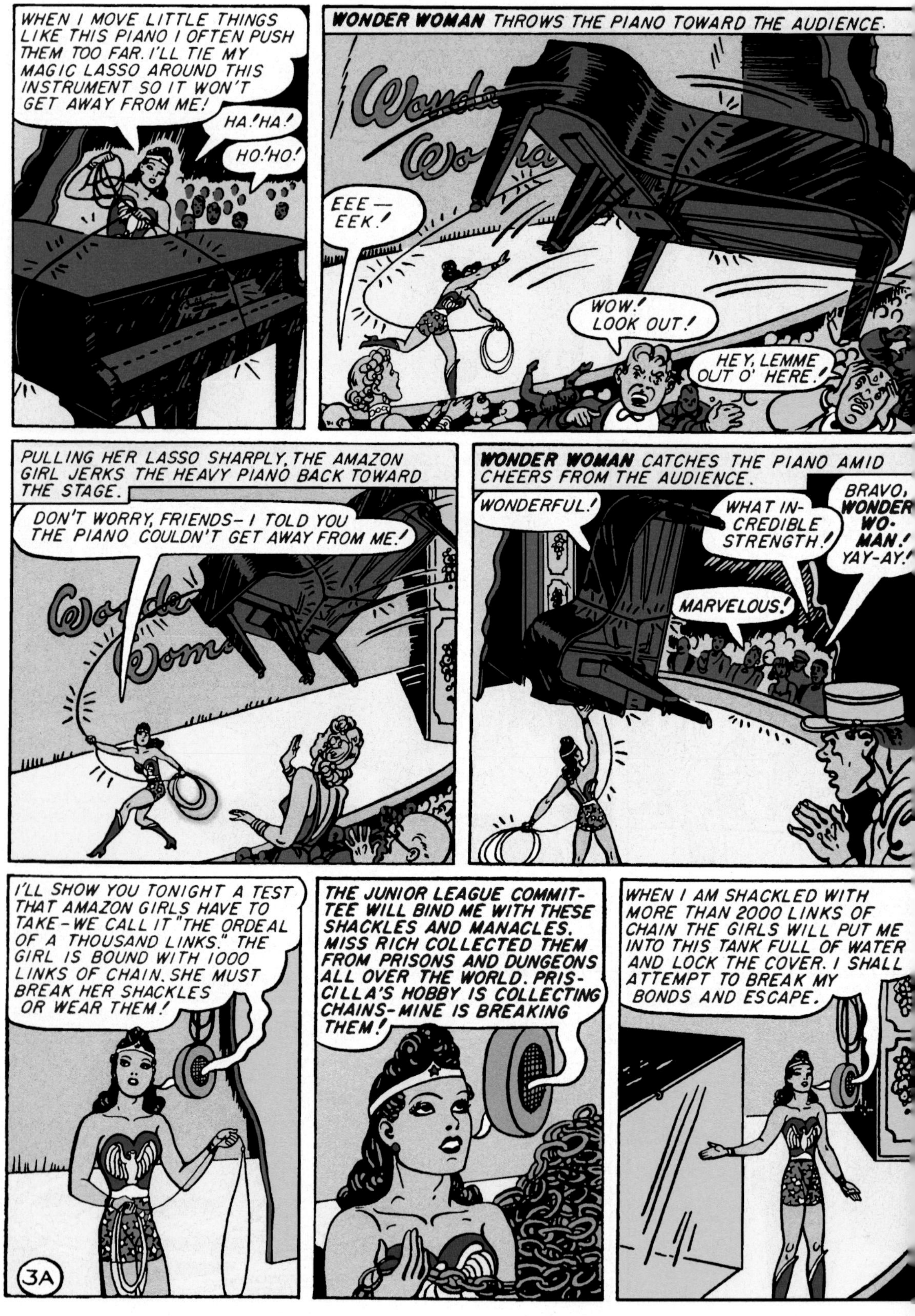
WHEN I MOVE LITTLE THINGS LIKE THIS PIANO I OFTEN PUSH THEM TOO FAR. I'LL TIE MY MAGIC LASSO AROUND THIS INSTRUMENT SO IT WON'T GET AWAY FROM ME!
HA! HA!
HO! HO!
WONDER WOMAN THROWS THE PIANO TOWARD THE AUDIENCE.
Wonder Woman
EEE—EEK!
WOW! LOOK OUT!
HEY, LEMME OUT O' HERE!
PULLING HER LASSO SHARPLY, THE AMAZON GIRL JERKS THE HEAVY PIANO BACK TOWARD THE STAGE.
DON'T WORRY, FRIENDS— I TOLD YOU THE PIANO COULDN'T GET AWAY FROM ME!
WONDER WOMAN CATCHES THE PIANO AMID CHEERS FROM THE AUDIENCE.
WONDERFUL!
WHAT IN-CREDIBLE STRENGTH!
BRAVO, WONDER WO-MAN! YAY-AY!
MARVELOUS!
I'LL SHOW YOU TONIGHT A TEST THAT AMAZON GIRLS HAVE TO TAKE—WE CALL IT "THE ORDEAL OF A THOUSAND LINKS." THE GIRL IS BOUND WITH 1000 LINKS OF CHAIN. SHE MUST BREAK HER SHACKLES OR WEAR THEM!
3A
THE JUNIOR LEAGUE COMMIT-TEE WILL BIND ME WITH THESE SHACKLES AND MANACLES. MISS RICH COLLECTED THEM FROM PRISONS AND DUNGEONS ALL OVER THE WORLD. PRIS-CILLA'S HOBBY IS COLLECTING CHAINS—MINE IS BREAKING THEM!
WHEN I AM SHACKLED WITH MORE THAN 2000 LINKS OF CHAIN THE GIRLS WILL PUT ME INTO THIS TANK FULL OF WATER AND LOCK THE COVER. I SHALL ATTEMPT TO BREAK MY BONDS AND ESCAPE.

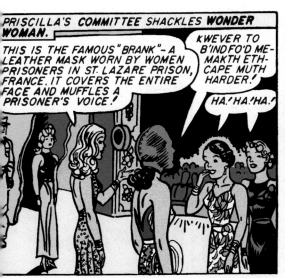

PRISCILLA'S **COMMITTEE** SHACKLES **WONDER WOMAN.**

THIS IS THE FAMOUS "BRANK"— A LEATHER MASK WORN BY WOMEN PRISONERS IN ST. LAZARE PRISON, FRANCE. IT COVERS THE ENTIRE FACE AND MUFFLES A PRISONER'S VOICE!

KWEVER TO B'INDFO'D ME—MAKTH ETH-CAPE MUTH HARDER!

HA! HA! HA!

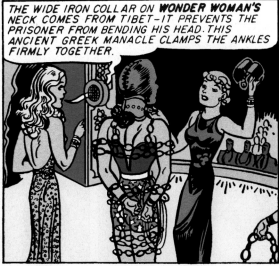

THE WIDE IRON COLLAR ON **WONDER WOMAN'S** NECK COMES FROM TIBET—IT PREVENTS THE PRISONER FROM BENDING HIS HEAD. THIS ANCIENT GREEK MANACLE CLAMPS THE ANKLES FIRMLY TOGETHER.

WHILE **WONDER WOMAN**, COMPLETELY SHACKLED, WAITS FOR THE TANK TO BE MADE READY, STEALTHY HANDS REACH FROM THE WINGS AND STEAL HER MAGIC LASSO.

WEIGHTED WITH SHACKLES, **WONDER WOMAN** CANNOT FEEL THE LIGHT TOUCH OF MYSTERIOUS FINGERS LACING HER ARM CHAINS TOGETHER WITH THE UNBREAKABLE GOLDEN LARIAT.

I'VE A HUNCH SOMEONE'S TRYING MONKEY BUSINESS— I WISH I WEREN'T BLINDFOLDED!

WONDER WOMAN IS LOWERED INTO THE TANK.

WOW! SHE SURE IS HEAVY!

THEY GOT A TON OF CHAINS ON HER.

4A

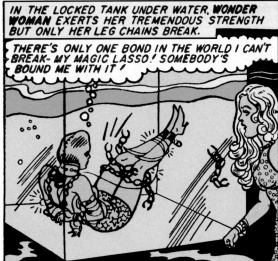

IN THE LOCKED TANK UNDER WATER, **WONDER WOMAN** EXERTS HER TREMENDOUS STRENGTH BUT ONLY HER LEG CHAINS BREAK.

THERE'S ONLY ONE BOND IN THE WORLD I CAN'T BREAK— MY MAGIC LASSO! SOMEBODY'S BOUND ME WITH IT!

TO FREE HER MOUTH, **WONDER WOMAN** BITES THROUGH THE TOUGH LEATHER OF THE BRANK.

THE FRENCH GIRLS WHO WORE THIS CONTRAPTION MUST HAVE HAD WEAK TEETH— IT'S EASY TO TEAR OFF!

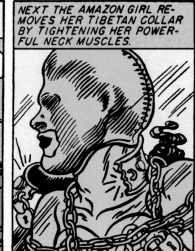

NEXT THE AMAZON GIRL REMOVES HER TIBETAN COLLAR BY TIGHTENING HER POWERFUL NECK MUSCLES.

WONDER WOMAN TRIES TO SEIZE THE MAGIC LASSO IN HER TEETH, BUT WITH HER EYES STILL BOUND, THE GOLDEN CORD ELUDES HER.

WHERE *IS* THAT LASSO LOOP? I CAN'T HOLD MY BREATH FOREVER!

THE AUDIENCE, MEANWHILE, BECOMES FRANTIC WITH FEAR FOR ITS IDOL.

WONDER WOMAN CAN'T BREAK LOOSE!

SHE'LL DROWN!

OPEN THAT TANK!

SMASH THAT GLASS! FREE WONDER WOMAN!

PRISCILLA RICH TRIES IN VAIN TO PREVENT SPECTATORS FROM INTERFERING.

OUT OF OUR WAY! RELEASE **WONDER WOMAN**!

PLEASE, EVERYBODY, KEEP BACK! YOU'LL SPOIL **WONDER WOMAN'S** ACT! SHE CAN BREAK ANY BONDS!

HA! EXCEPT THE MAGIC LASSO!

WONDER WOMAN, HER LUNGS BURSTING, TRIES AN ACROBATIC TRICK.

THAT'S BETTER—NOW I CAN SEE WHAT I'M DOING!

5A

GRIPPING THE MAGIC LASSO IN HER TEETH, **WONDER WOMAN** TEARS OFF THE GREEK FETTERS FROM HER ANKLES.

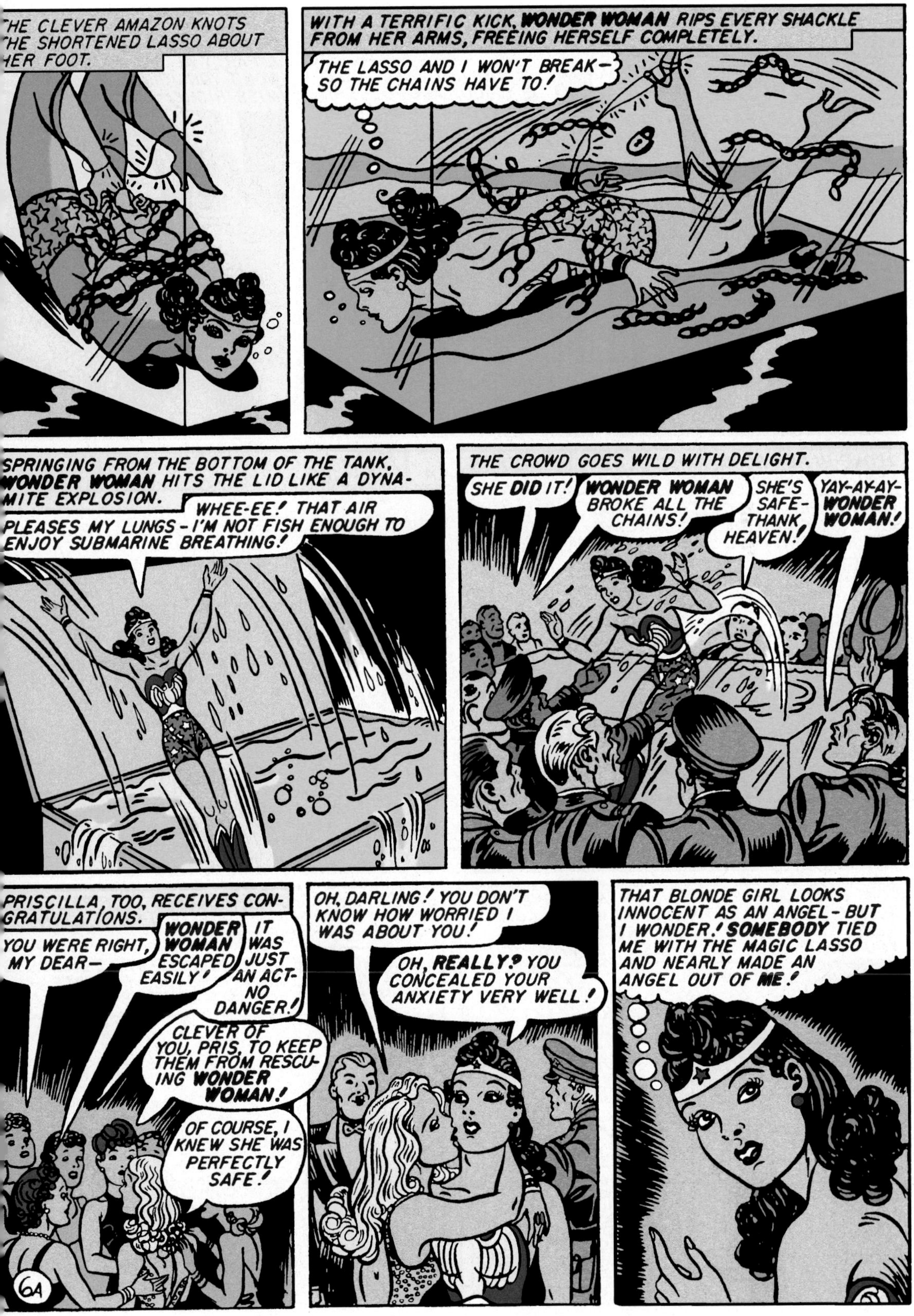

THE CLEVER AMAZON KNOTS THE SHORTENED LASSO ABOUT HER FOOT.
WITH A TERRIFIC KICK, WONDER WOMAN RIPS EVERY SHACKLE FROM HER ARMS, FREEING HERSELF COMPLETELY.
THE LASSO AND I WON'T BREAK– SO THE CHAINS HAVE TO!
SPRINGING FROM THE BOTTOM OF THE TANK, WONDER WOMAN HITS THE LID LIKE A DYNAMITE EXPLOSION.
WHEE-EE! THAT AIR PLEASES MY LUNGS – I'M NOT FISH ENOUGH TO ENJOY SUBMARINE BREATHING!
THE CROWD GOES WILD WITH DELIGHT.
SHE DID IT!
WONDER WOMAN BROKE ALL THE CHAINS!
SHE'S SAFE– THANK HEAVEN!
YAY-AY-AY– WONDER WOMAN!
PRISCILLA, TOO, RECEIVES CONGRATULATIONS.
YOU WERE RIGHT, MY DEAR–
WONDER WOMAN ESCAPED EASILY!
IT WAS JUST AN ACT– NO DANGER!
CLEVER OF YOU, PRIS, TO KEEP THEM FROM RESCUING WONDER WOMAN!
OF COURSE, I KNEW SHE WAS PERFECTLY SAFE!
6A
OH, DARLING! YOU DON'T KNOW HOW WORRIED I WAS ABOUT YOU!
OH, REALLY? YOU CONCEALED YOUR ANXIETY VERY WELL!
THAT BLONDE GIRL LOOKS INNOCENT AS AN ANGEL– BUT I WONDER! SOMEBODY TIED ME WITH THE MAGIC LASSO AND NEARLY MADE AN ANGEL OUT OF ME!

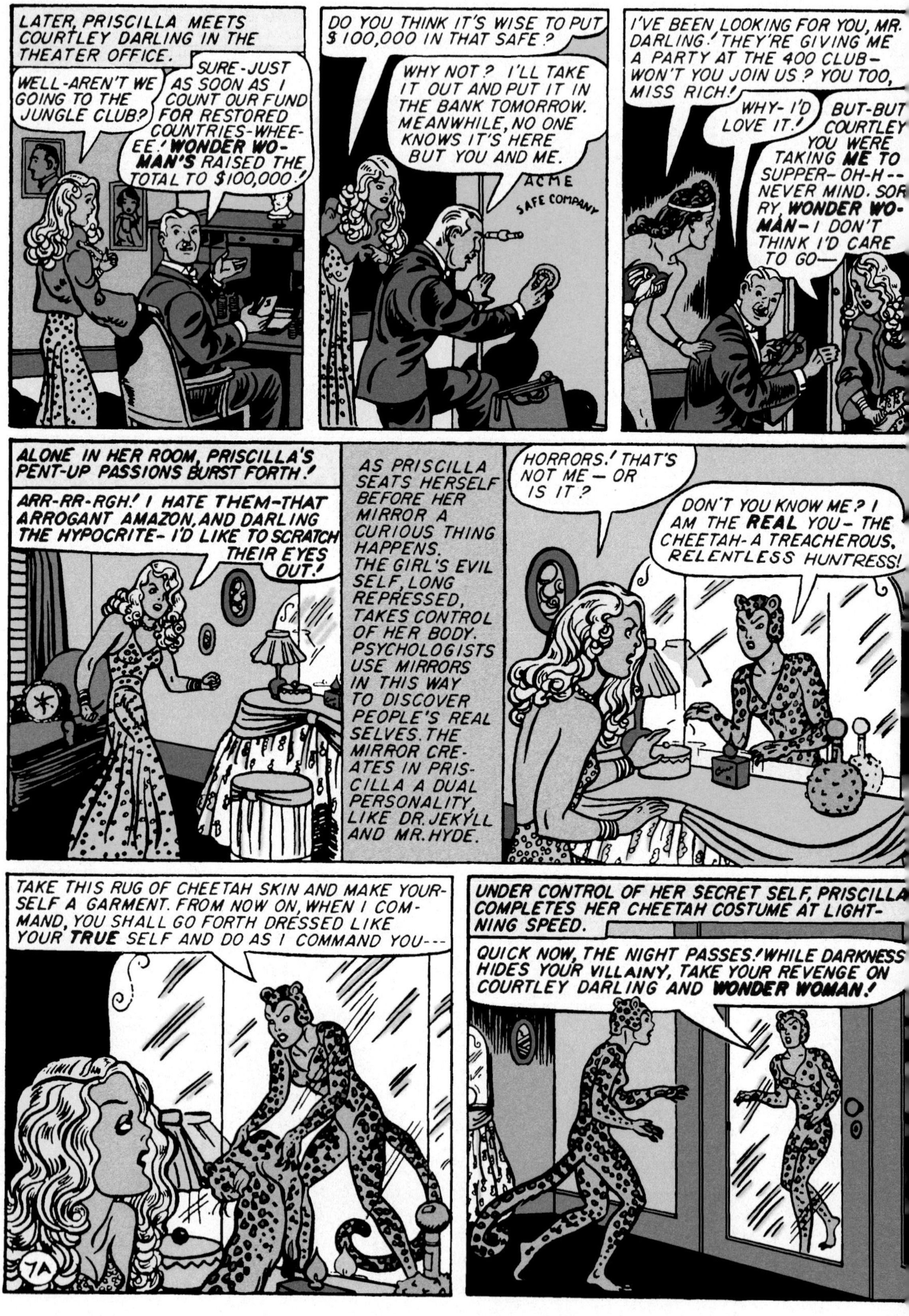
LATER, PRISCILLA MEETS COURTLEY DARLING IN THE THEATER OFFICE.
WELL-AREN'T WE GOING TO THE JUNGLE CLUB?
SURE-JUST AS SOON AS I COUNT OUR FUND FOR RESTORED COUNTRIES-WHEE-EE! WONDER WOMAN'S RAISED THE TOTAL TO $100,000!
DO YOU THINK IT'S WISE TO PUT $100,000 IN THAT SAFE?
WHY NOT? I'LL TAKE IT OUT AND PUT IT IN THE BANK TOMORROW. MEANWHILE, NO ONE KNOWS IT'S HERE BUT YOU AND ME.
ACME SAFE COMPANY
I'VE BEEN LOOKING FOR YOU, MR. DARLING! THEY'RE GIVING ME A PARTY AT THE 400 CLUB-WON'T YOU JOIN US? YOU TOO, MISS RICH!
WHY- I'D LOVE IT!
BUT-BUT COURTLEY YOU WERE TAKING ME TO SUPPER- OH-H -- NEVER MIND. SORRY, WONDER WOMAN- I DON'T THINK I'D CARE TO GO—
ALONE IN HER ROOM, PRISCILLA'S PENT-UP PASSIONS BURST FORTH!
ARR-RR-RGH! I HATE THEM-THAT ARROGANT AMAZON, AND DARLING THE HYPOCRITE- I'D LIKE TO SCRATCH THEIR EYES OUT!
AS PRISCILLA SEATS HERSELF BEFORE HER MIRROR A CURIOUS THING HAPPENS. THE GIRL'S EVIL SELF, LONG REPRESSED, TAKES CONTROL OF HER BODY. PSYCHOLOGISTS USE MIRRORS IN THIS WAY TO DISCOVER PEOPLE'S REAL SELVES. THE MIRROR CREATES IN PRISCILLA A DUAL PERSONALITY, LIKE DR. JEKYLL AND MR. HYDE.
HORRORS! THAT'S NOT ME — OR IS IT?
DON'T YOU KNOW ME? I AM THE REAL YOU- THE CHEETAH- A TREACHEROUS, RELENTLESS HUNTRESS!
TAKE THIS RUG OF CHEETAH SKIN AND MAKE YOURSELF A GARMENT. FROM NOW ON, WHEN I COMMAND, YOU SHALL GO FORTH DRESSED LIKE YOUR TRUE SELF AND DO AS I COMMAND YOU---
7A
UNDER CONTROL OF HER SECRET SELF, PRISCILLA COMPLETES HER CHEETAH COSTUME AT LIGHTNING SPEED.
QUICK NOW, THE NIGHT PASSES! WHILE DARKNESS HIDES YOUR VILLAINY, TAKE YOUR REVENGE ON COURTLEY DARLING AND WONDER WOMAN!

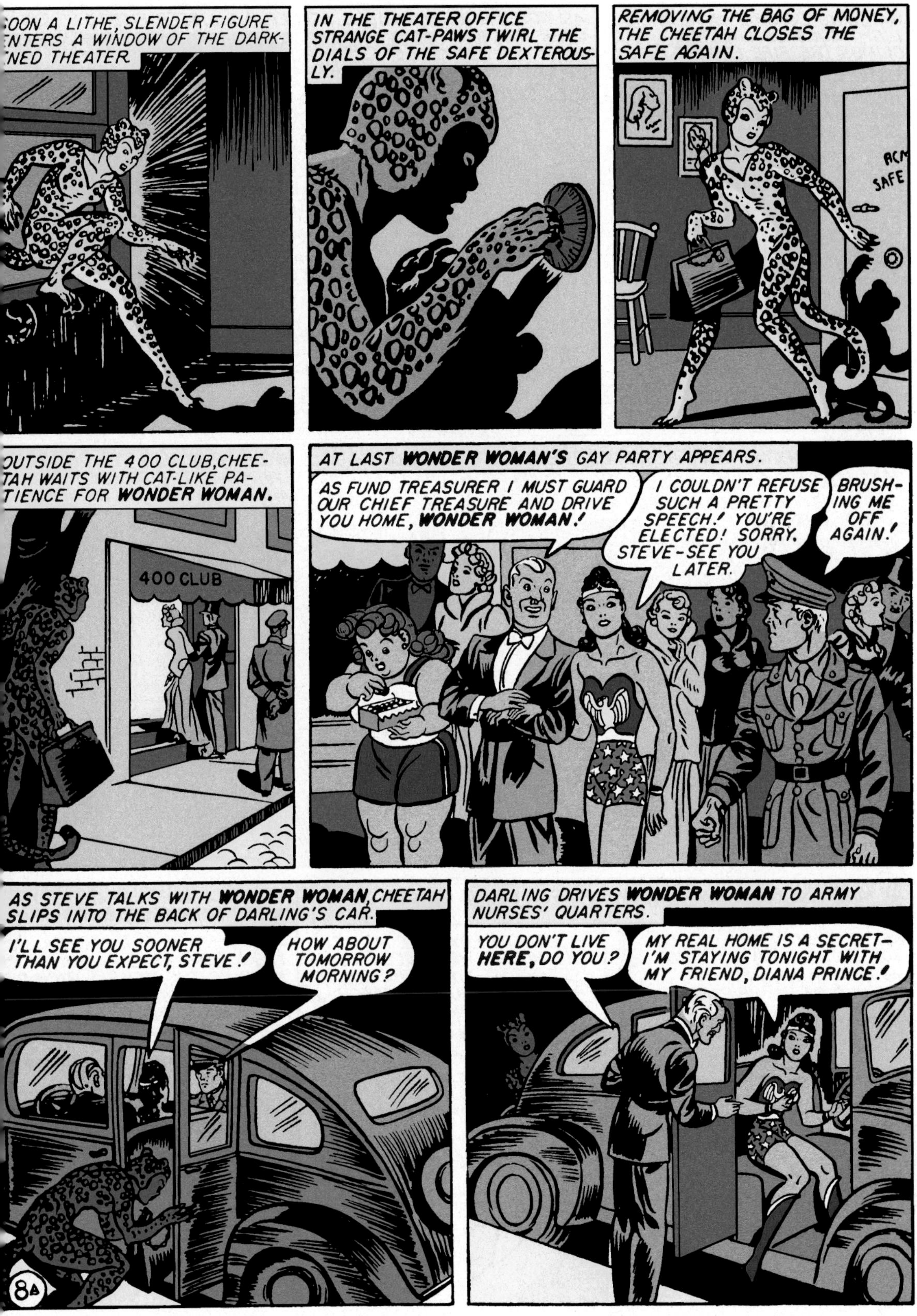
SOON A LITHE, SLENDER FIGURE ENTERS A WINDOW OF THE DARKENED THEATER.
IN THE THEATER OFFICE STRANGE CAT-PAWS TWIRL THE DIALS OF THE SAFE DEXTEROUSLY.
REMOVING THE BAG OF MONEY, THE CHEETAH CLOSES THE SAFE AGAIN.
SAFE
OUTSIDE THE 400 CLUB, CHEETAH WAITS WITH CAT-LIKE PATIENCE FOR WONDER WOMAN.
400 CLUB
AT LAST WONDER WOMAN'S GAY PARTY APPEARS.
AS FUND TREASURER I MUST GUARD OUR CHIEF TREASURE AND DRIVE YOU HOME, WONDER WOMAN!
I COULDN'T REFUSE SUCH A PRETTY SPEECH! YOU'RE ELECTED! SORRY, STEVE-SEE YOU LATER.
BRUSHING ME OFF AGAIN!
AS STEVE TALKS WITH WONDER WOMAN, CHEETAH SLIPS INTO THE BACK OF DARLING'S CAR.
I'LL SEE YOU SOONER THAN YOU EXPECT, STEVE!
HOW ABOUT TOMORROW MORNING?
8A
DARLING DRIVES WONDER WOMAN TO ARMY NURSES' QUARTERS.
YOU DON'T LIVE HERE, DO YOU?
MY REAL HOME IS A SECRET-I'M STAYING TONIGHT WITH MY FRIEND, DIANA PRINCE!

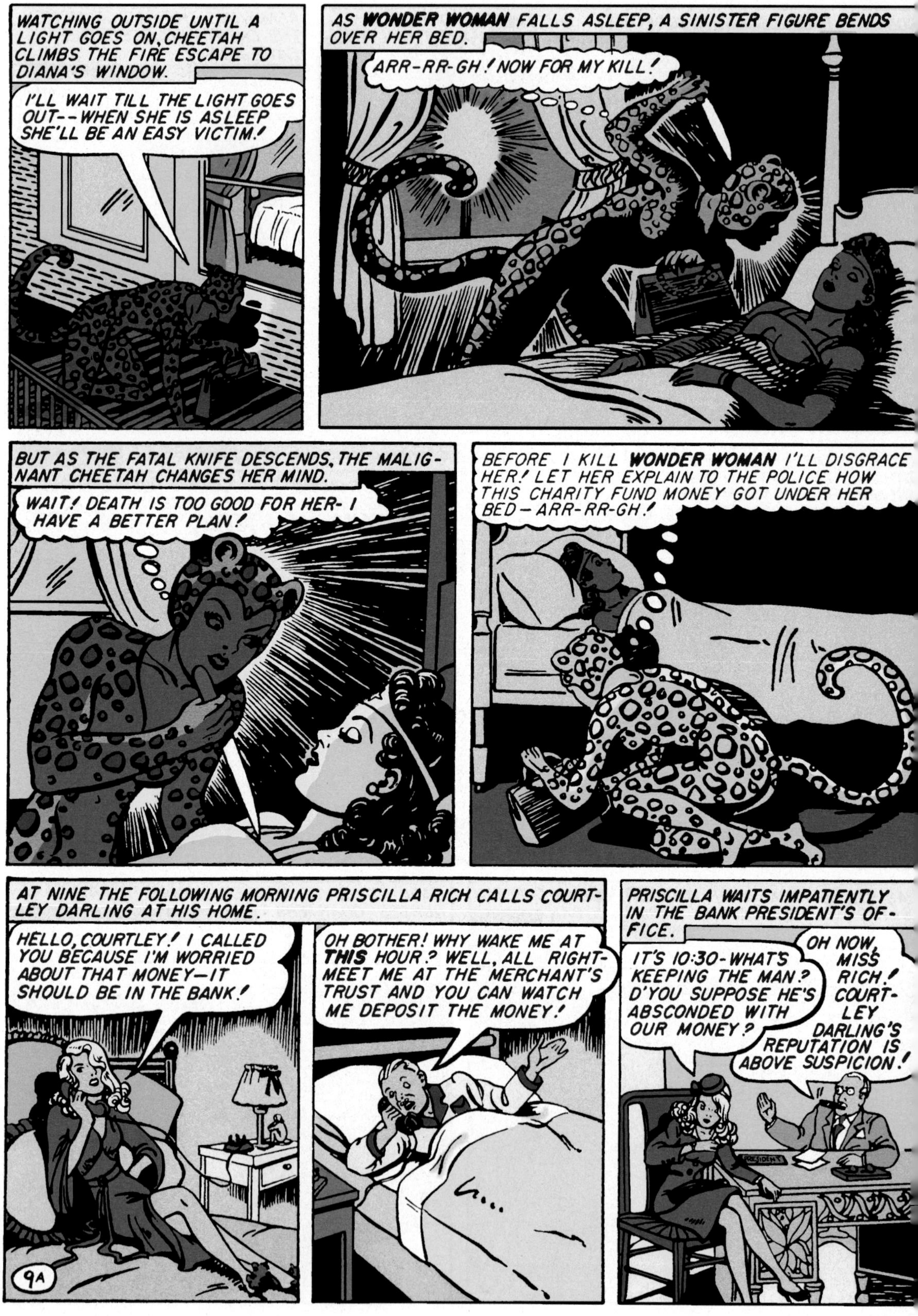
WATCHING OUTSIDE UNTIL A LIGHT GOES ON, CHEETAH CLIMBS THE FIRE ESCAPE TO DIANA'S WINDOW.
I'LL WAIT TILL THE LIGHT GOES OUT--WHEN SHE IS ASLEEP SHE'LL BE AN EASY VICTIM!
AS WONDER WOMAN FALLS ASLEEP, A SINISTER FIGURE BENDS OVER HER BED.
ARR-RR-GH! NOW FOR MY KILL!
BUT AS THE FATAL KNIFE DESCENDS, THE MALIGNANT CHEETAH CHANGES HER MIND.
WAIT! DEATH IS TOO GOOD FOR HER- I HAVE A BETTER PLAN!
BEFORE I KILL WONDER WOMAN I'LL DISGRACE HER! LET HER EXPLAIN TO THE POLICE HOW THIS CHARITY FUND MONEY GOT UNDER HER BED—ARR-RR-GH!
AT NINE THE FOLLOWING MORNING PRISCILLA RICH CALLS COURTLEY DARLING AT HIS HOME.
HELLO, COURTLEY! I CALLED YOU BECAUSE I'M WORRIED ABOUT THAT MONEY—IT SHOULD BE IN THE BANK!
9A
OH BOTHER! WHY WAKE ME AT THIS HOUR? WELL, ALL RIGHT- MEET ME AT THE MERCHANT'S TRUST AND YOU CAN WATCH ME DEPOSIT THE MONEY!
PRISCILLA WAITS IMPATIENTLY IN THE BANK PRESIDENT'S OFFICE.
IT'S 10:30-WHAT'S KEEPING THE MAN? D'YOU SUPPOSE HE'S ABSCONDED WITH OUR MONEY?
OH NOW, MISS RICH! COURTLEY DARLING'S REPUTATION IS ABOVE SUSPICION!
PRESIDENT

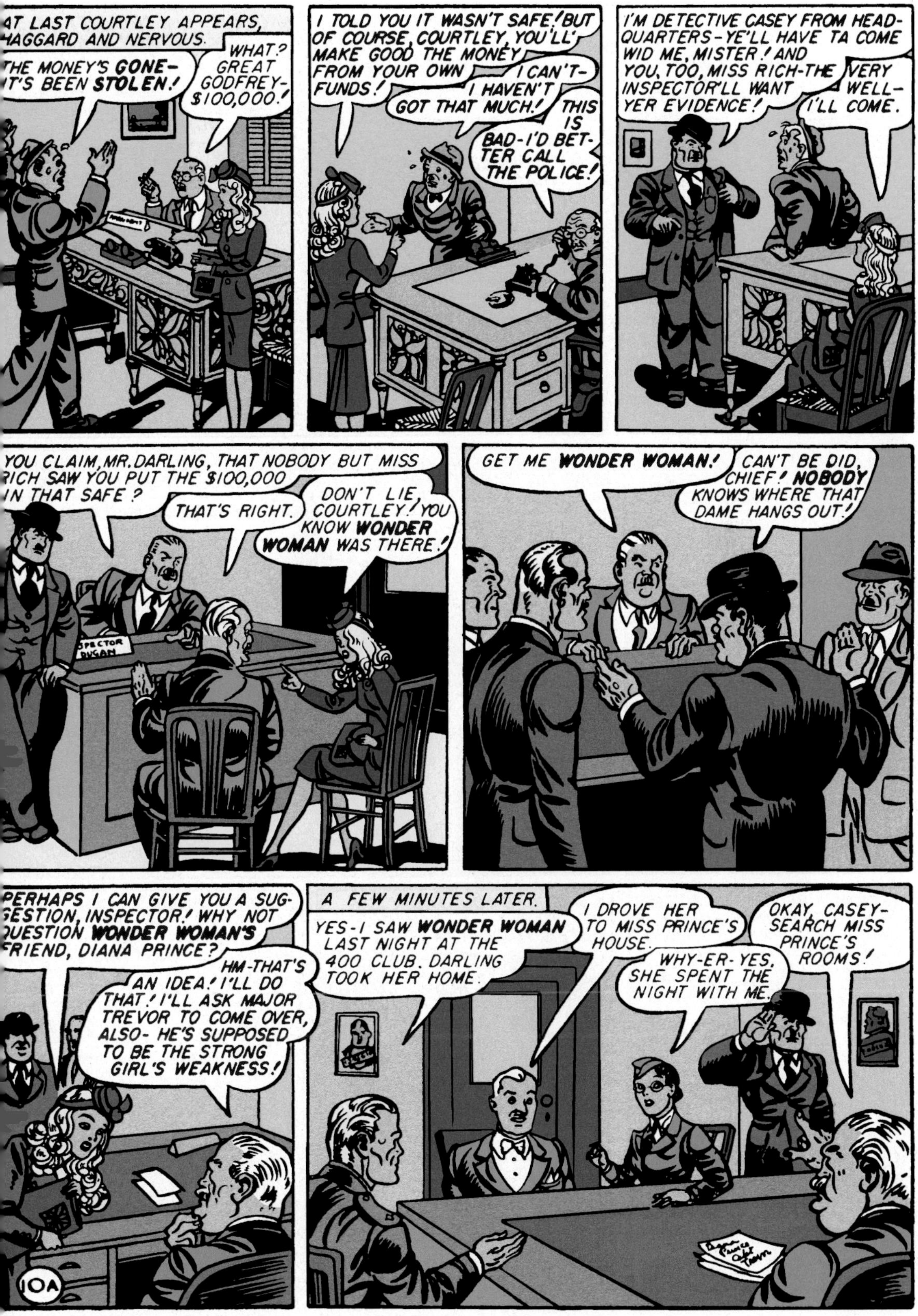
AT LAST COURTLEY APPEARS, HAGGARD AND NERVOUS.
THE MONEY'S GONE-IT'S BEEN STOLEN!
WHAT? GREAT GODFREY-$100,000!
I TOLD YOU IT WASN'T SAFE! BUT OF COURSE, COURTLEY, YOU'LL MAKE GOOD THE MONEY FROM YOUR OWN FUNDS!
I CAN'T-I HAVEN'T GOT THAT MUCH!
THIS IS BAD-I'D BETTER CALL THE POLICE!
I'M DETECTIVE CASEY FROM HEADQUARTERS-YE'LL HAVE TA COME WID ME, MISTER! AND YOU, TOO, MISS RICH-THE INSPECTOR'LL WANT YER EVIDENCE!
VERY WELL-I'LL COME.
YOU CLAIM, MR. DARLING, THAT NOBODY BUT MISS RICH SAW YOU PUT THE $100,000 IN THAT SAFE?
THAT'S RIGHT.
DON'T LIE, COURTLEY! YOU KNOW WONDER WOMAN WAS THERE!
GET ME WONDER WOMAN!
CAN'T BE DID, CHIEF! NOBODY KNOWS WHERE THAT DAME HANGS OUT!
PERHAPS I CAN GIVE YOU A SUGGESTION, INSPECTOR! WHY NOT QUESTION WONDER WOMAN'S FRIEND, DIANA PRINCE?
HM-THAT'S AN IDEA! I'LL DO THAT! I'LL ASK MAJOR TREVOR TO COME OVER, ALSO- HE'S SUPPOSED TO BE THE STRONG GIRL'S WEAKNESS!
10A
A FEW MINUTES LATER.
YES-I SAW WONDER WOMAN LAST NIGHT AT THE 400 CLUB. DARLING TOOK HER HOME.
I DROVE HER TO MISS PRINCE'S HOUSE.
WHY-ER-YES. SHE SPENT THE NIGHT WITH ME.
OKAY, CASEY-SEARCH MISS PRINCE'S ROOMS!

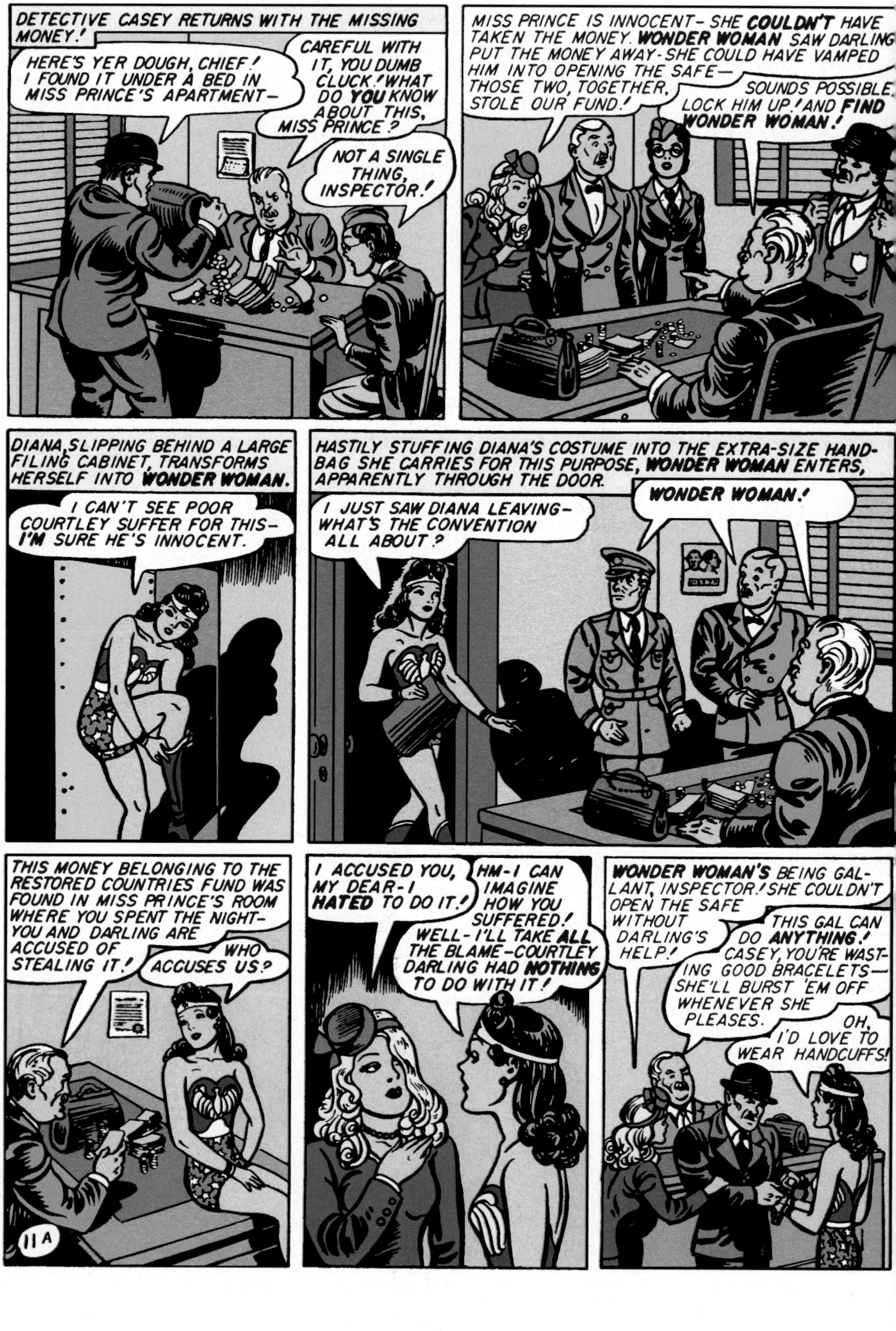
DETECTIVE CASEY RETURNS WITH THE MISSING MONEY!
HERE'S YER DOUGH, CHIEF! I FOUND IT UNDER A BED IN MISS PRINCE'S APARTMENT—
CAREFUL WITH IT, YOU DUMB CLUCK! WHAT DO YOU KNOW ABOUT THIS, MISS PRINCE?
NOT A SINGLE THING, INSPECTOR!
MISS PRINCE IS INNOCENT—SHE COULDN'T HAVE TAKEN THE MONEY. WONDER WOMAN SAW DARLING PUT THE MONEY AWAY—SHE COULD HAVE VAMPED HIM INTO OPENING THE SAFE— THOSE TWO, TOGETHER, STOLE OUR FUND!
SOUNDS POSSIBLE. LOCK HIM UP! AND FIND WONDER WOMAN!
DIANA, SLIPPING BEHIND A LARGE FILING CABINET, TRANSFORMS HERSELF INTO WONDER WOMAN.
I CAN'T SEE POOR COURTLEY SUFFER FOR THIS—I'M SURE HE'S INNOCENT.
HASTILY STUFFING DIANA'S COSTUME INTO THE EXTRA-SIZE HAND-BAG SHE CARRIES FOR THIS PURPOSE, WONDER WOMAN ENTERS, APPARENTLY THROUGH THE DOOR.
I JUST SAW DIANA LEAVING—WHAT'S THE CONVENTION ALL ABOUT?
WONDER WOMAN!
THIS MONEY BELONGING TO THE RESTORED COUNTRIES FUND WAS FOUND IN MISS PRINCE'S ROOM WHERE YOU SPENT THE NIGHT—YOU AND DARLING ARE ACCUSED OF STEALING IT!
WHO ACCUSES US?
11 A
I ACCUSED YOU, MY DEAR—I HATED TO DO IT!
HM—I CAN IMAGINE HOW YOU SUFFERED! WELL—I'LL TAKE ALL THE BLAME—COURTLEY DARLING HAD NOTHING TO DO WITH IT!
WONDER WOMAN'S BEING GALLANT, INSPECTOR! SHE COULDN'T OPEN THE SAFE WITHOUT DARLING'S HELP!
THIS GAL CAN DO ANYTHING! CASEY, YOU'RE WASTING GOOD BRACELETS—SHE'LL BURST 'EM OFF WHENEVER SHE PLEASES.
OH, I'D LOVE TO WEAR HANDCUFFS!

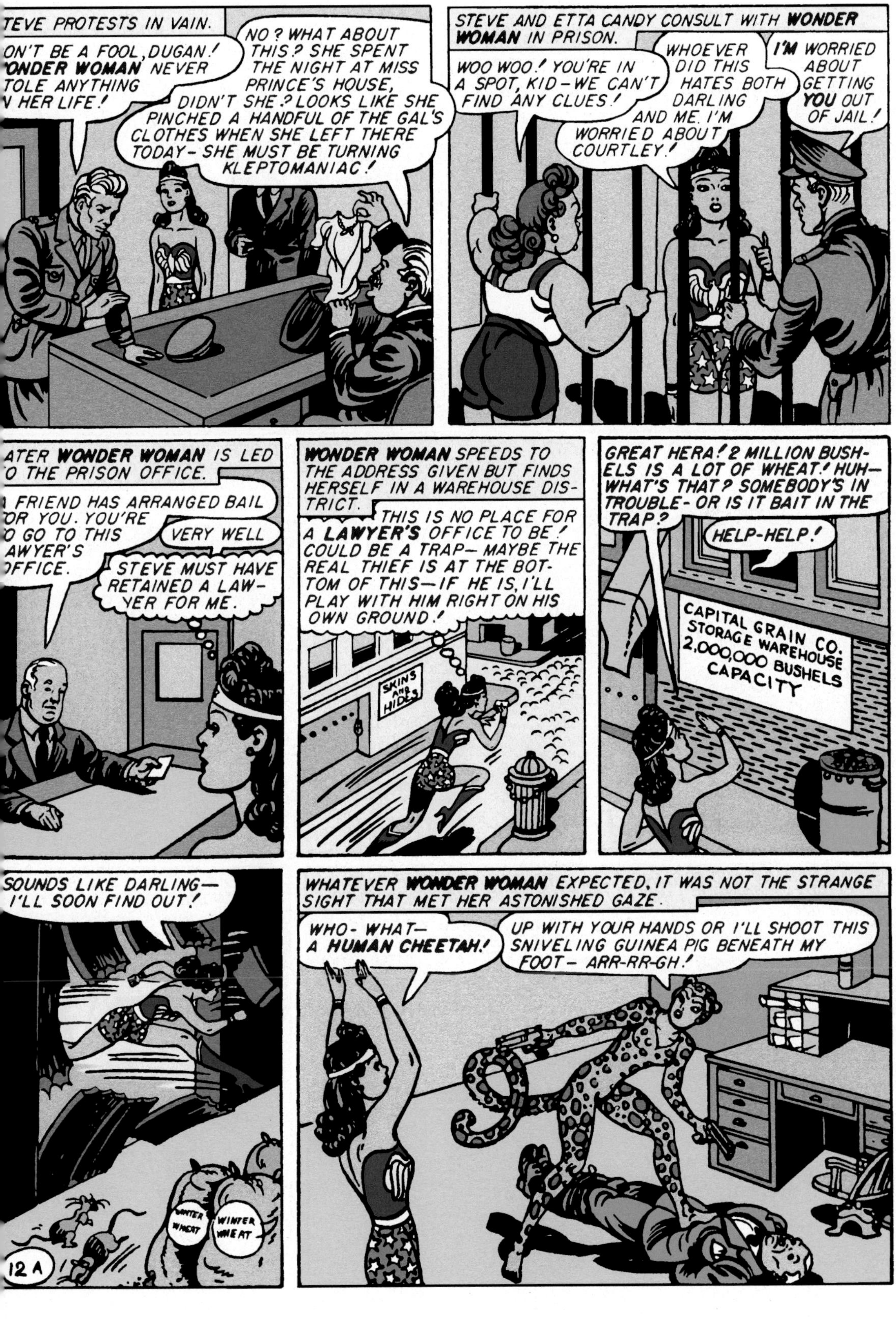
STEVE PROTESTS IN VAIN.
ON'T BE A FOOL, DUGAN! WONDER WOMAN NEVER TOLE ANYTHING N HER LIFE!
NO? WHAT ABOUT THIS? SHE SPENT THE NIGHT AT MISS PRINCE'S HOUSE, DIDN'T SHE? LOOKS LIKE SHE PINCHED A HANDFUL OF THE GAL'S CLOTHES WHEN SHE LEFT THERE TODAY- SHE MUST BE TURNING KLEPTOMANIAC!
STEVE AND ETTA CANDY CONSULT WITH WONDER WOMAN IN PRISON.
WOO WOO! YOU'RE IN A SPOT, KID - WE CAN'T FIND ANY CLUES!
WHOEVER DID THIS HATES BOTH DARLING AND ME. I'M WORRIED ABOUT COURTLEY!
I'M WORRIED ABOUT GETTING YOU OUT OF JAIL!
ATER WONDER WOMAN IS LED O THE PRISON OFFICE.
A FRIEND HAS ARRANGED BAIL OR YOU. YOU'RE O GO TO THIS AWYER'S OFFICE.
VERY WELL
STEVE MUST HAVE RETAINED A LAWYER FOR ME.
WONDER WOMAN SPEEDS TO THE ADDRESS GIVEN BUT FINDS HERSELF IN A WAREHOUSE DISTRICT.
THIS IS NO PLACE FOR A LAWYER'S OFFICE TO BE! COULD BE A TRAP— MAYBE THE REAL THIEF IS AT THE BOTTOM OF THIS—IF HE IS, I'LL PLAY WITH HIM RIGHT ON HIS OWN GROUND!
SKINS AND HIDES
GREAT HERA! 2 MILLION BUSHELS IS A LOT OF WHEAT! HUH— WHAT'S THAT? SOMEBODY'S IN TROUBLE- OR IS IT BAIT IN THE TRAP?
HELP-HELP!
CAPITAL GRAIN CO. STORAGE WAREHOUSE 2,000,000 BUSHELS CAPACITY
SOUNDS LIKE DARLING— I'LL SOON FIND OUT!
WINTER WHEAT
WINTER WHEAT
12 A
WHATEVER WONDER WOMAN EXPECTED, IT WAS NOT THE STRANGE SIGHT THAT MET HER ASTONISHED GAZE.
WHO- WHAT— A HUMAN CHEETAH!
UP WITH YOUR HANDS OR I'LL SHOOT THIS SNIVELING GUINEA PIG BENEATH MY FOOT- ARR-RR-GH!

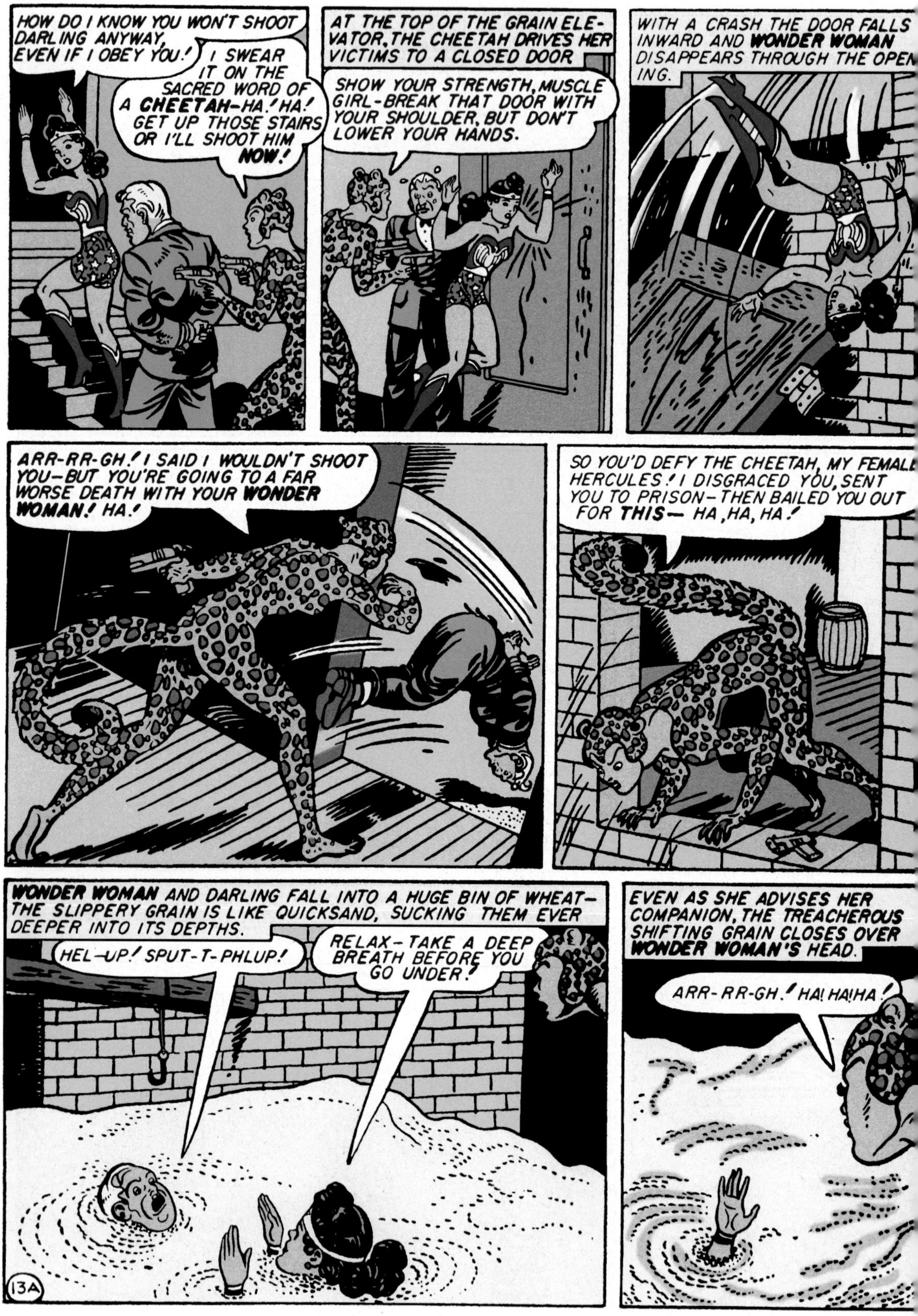
HOW DO I KNOW YOU WON'T SHOOT DARLING ANYWAY, EVEN IF I OBEY YOU!
I SWEAR IT ON THE SACRED WORD OF A CHEETAH-HA! HA! GET UP THOSE STAIRS OR I'LL SHOOT HIM NOW!
AT THE TOP OF THE GRAIN ELEVATOR, THE CHEETAH DRIVES HER VICTIMS TO A CLOSED DOOR
SHOW YOUR STRENGTH, MUSCLE GIRL-BREAK THAT DOOR WITH YOUR SHOULDER, BUT DON'T LOWER YOUR HANDS.
WITH A CRASH THE DOOR FALLS INWARD AND WONDER WOMAN DISAPPEARS THROUGH THE OPENING.
ARR-RR-GH! I SAID I WOULDN'T SHOOT YOU-BUT YOU'RE GOING TO A FAR WORSE DEATH WITH YOUR WONDER WOMAN! HA!
SO YOU'D DEFY THE CHEETAH, MY FEMALE HERCULES! I DISGRACED YOU, SENT YOU TO PRISON-THEN BAILED YOU OUT FOR THIS- HA, HA, HA!
WONDER WOMAN AND DARLING FALL INTO A HUGE BIN OF WHEAT- THE SLIPPERY GRAIN IS LIKE QUICKSAND, SUCKING THEM EVER DEEPER INTO ITS DEPTHS.
HEL-UP! SPUT-T-PHLUP!
RELAX-TAKE A DEEP BREATH BEFORE YOU GO UNDER!
13A
EVEN AS SHE ADVISES HER COMPANION, THE TREACHEROUS SHIFTING GRAIN CLOSES OVER WONDER WOMAN'S HEAD.
ARR-RR-GH! HA! HA! HA!

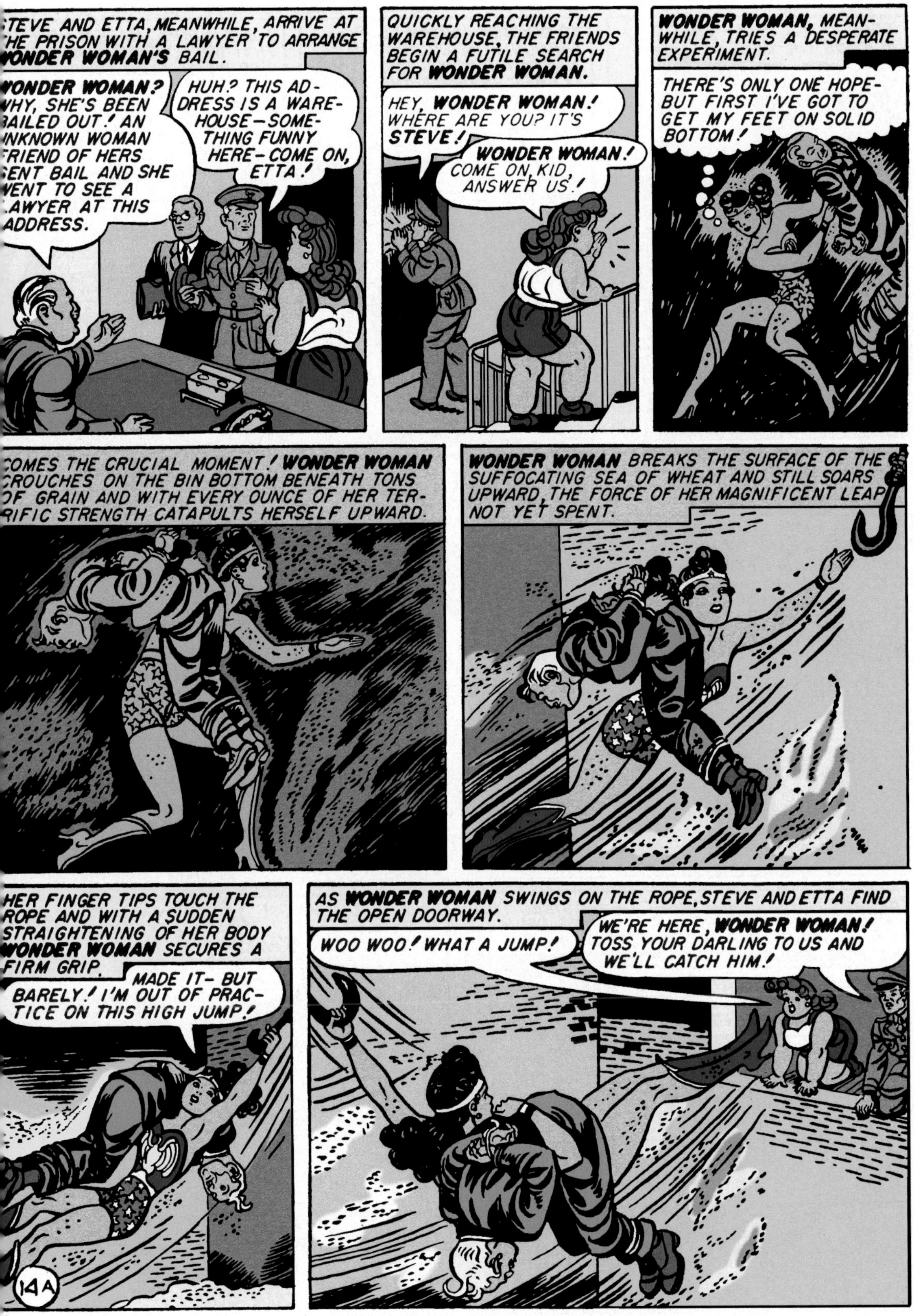
STEVE AND ETTA, MEANWHILE, ARRIVE AT THE PRISON WITH A LAWYER TO ARRANGE WONDER WOMAN'S BAIL.
WONDER WOMAN? WHY, SHE'S BEEN BAILED OUT! AN UNKNOWN WOMAN FRIEND OF HERS SENT BAIL AND SHE WENT TO SEE A LAWYER AT THIS ADDRESS.
HUH? THIS ADDRESS IS A WAREHOUSE—SOMETHING FUNNY HERE—COME ON, ETTA!
QUICKLY REACHING THE WAREHOUSE, THE FRIENDS BEGIN A FUTILE SEARCH FOR WONDER WOMAN.
HEY, WONDER WOMAN! WHERE ARE YOU? IT'S STEVE!
WONDER WOMAN! COME ON, KID, ANSWER US!
WONDER WOMAN, MEANWHILE, TRIES A DESPERATE EXPERIMENT.
THERE'S ONLY ONE HOPE—BUT FIRST I'VE GOT TO GET MY FEET ON SOLID BOTTOM!
COMES THE CRUCIAL MOMENT! WONDER WOMAN CROUCHES ON THE BIN BOTTOM BENEATH TONS OF GRAIN AND WITH EVERY OUNCE OF HER TERRIFIC STRENGTH CATAPULTS HERSELF UPWARD.
WONDER WOMAN BREAKS THE SURFACE OF THE SUFFOCATING SEA OF WHEAT AND STILL SOARS UPWARD, THE FORCE OF HER MAGNIFICENT LEAP NOT YET SPENT.
HER FINGER TIPS TOUCH THE ROPE AND WITH A SUDDEN STRAIGHTENING OF HER BODY WONDER WOMAN SECURES A FIRM GRIP.
MADE IT—BUT BARELY! I'M OUT OF PRACTICE ON THIS HIGH JUMP!
14A
AS WONDER WOMAN SWINGS ON THE ROPE, STEVE AND ETTA FIND THE OPEN DOORWAY.
WOO WOO! WHAT A JUMP!
WE'RE HERE, WONDER WOMAN! TOSS YOUR DARLING TO US AND WE'LL CATCH HIM!

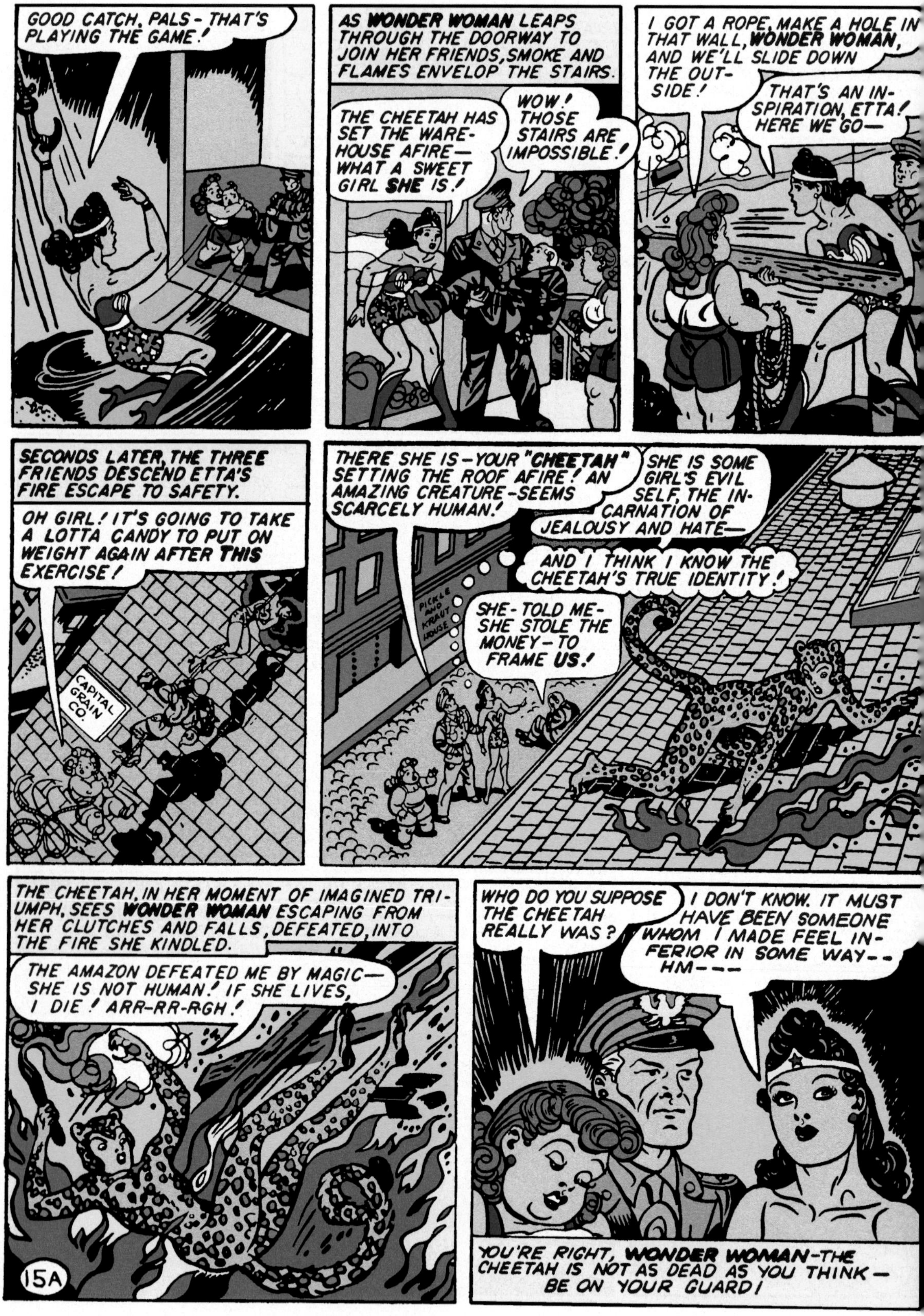
GOOD CATCH, PALS - THAT'S PLAYING THE GAME!
AS WONDER WOMAN LEAPS THROUGH THE DOORWAY TO JOIN HER FRIENDS, SMOKE AND FLAMES ENVELOP THE STAIRS.
THE CHEETAH HAS SET THE WAREHOUSE AFIRE— WHAT A SWEET GIRL SHE IS!
WOW! THOSE STAIRS ARE IMPOSSIBLE!
I GOT A ROPE, MAKE A HOLE IN THAT WALL, WONDER WOMAN, AND WE'LL SLIDE DOWN THE OUTSIDE!
THAT'S AN INSPIRATION, ETTA! HERE WE GO—
SECONDS LATER, THE THREE FRIENDS DESCEND ETTA'S FIRE ESCAPE TO SAFETY.
OH GIRL! IT'S GOING TO TAKE A LOTTA CANDY TO PUT ON WEIGHT AGAIN AFTER THIS EXERCISE!
CAPITAL GRAIN CO.
THERE SHE IS—YOUR "CHEETAH" SETTING THE ROOF AFIRE! AN AMAZING CREATURE—SEEMS SCARCELY HUMAN!
SHE IS SOME GIRL'S EVIL SELF, THE INCARNATION OF JEALOUSY AND HATE—
AND I THINK I KNOW THE CHEETAH'S TRUE IDENTITY!
PICKLE AND KRAUT HOUSE
SHE- TOLD ME- SHE STOLE THE MONEY—TO FRAME US!
THE CHEETAH, IN HER MOMENT OF IMAGINED TRIUMPH, SEES WONDER WOMAN ESCAPING FROM HER CLUTCHES AND FALLS, DEFEATED, INTO THE FIRE SHE KINDLED.
THE AMAZON DEFEATED ME BY MAGIC— SHE IS NOT HUMAN! IF SHE LIVES, I DIE! ARR-RR-RGH!
15A
WHO DO YOU SUPPOSE THE CHEETAH REALLY WAS?
I DON'T KNOW. IT MUST HAVE BEEN SOMEONE WHOM I MADE FEEL INFERIOR IN SOME WAY-- HM---
YOU'RE RIGHT, WONDER WOMAN-THE CHEETAH IS NOT AS DEAD AS YOU THINK— BE ON YOUR GUARD!

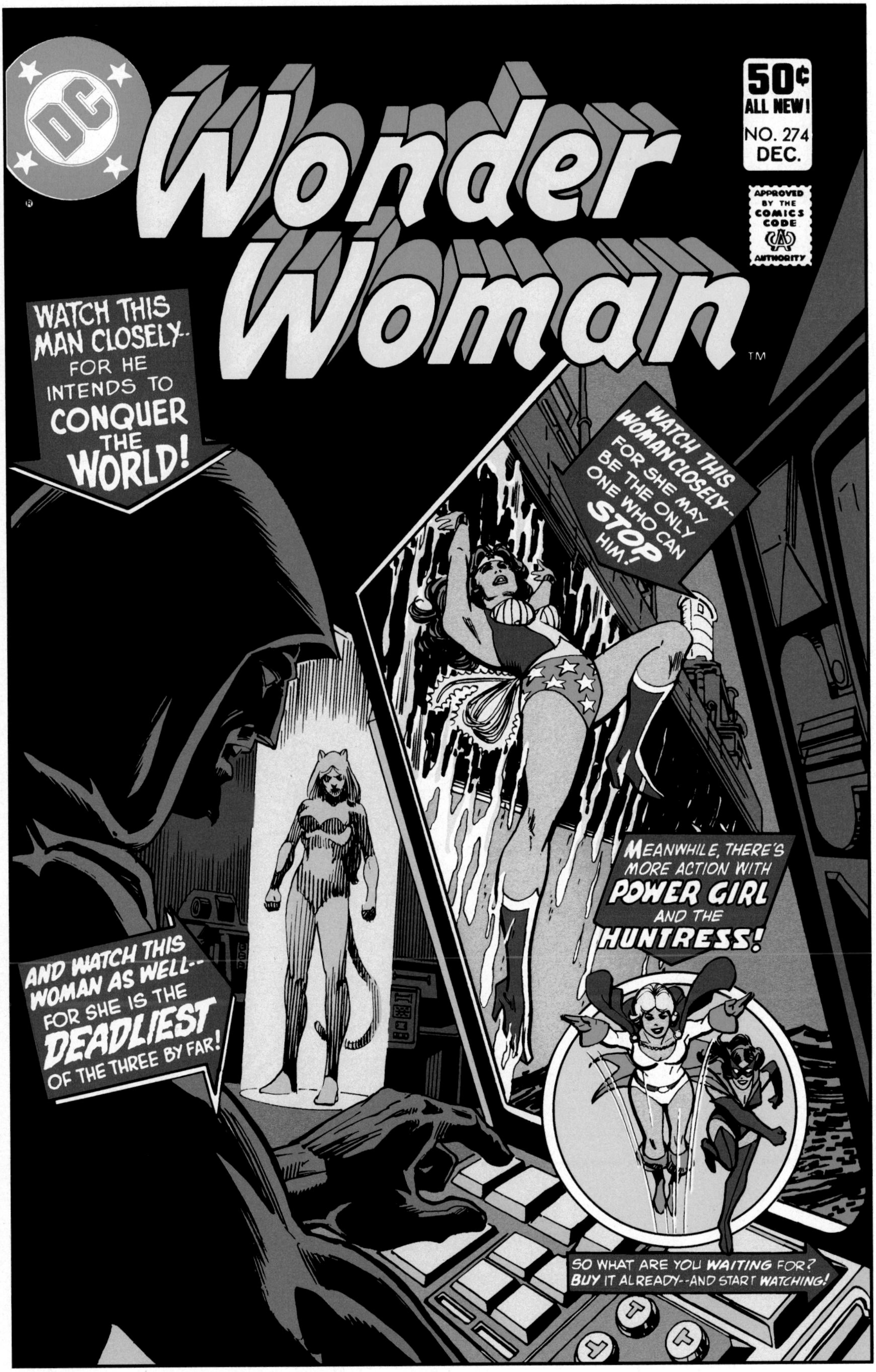
DC
Wonder Woman
50¢
ALL NEW!
NO. 274
DEC.
APPROVED BY THE COMICS CODE AUTHORITY
WATCH THIS MAN CLOSELY-- FOR HE INTENDS TO CONQUER THE WORLD!
WATCH THIS WOMAN CLOSELY-- FOR SHE MAY BE THE ONLY ONE WHO CAN STOP HIM!
MEANWHILE, THERE'S MORE ACTION WITH POWER GIRL AND THE HUNTRESS!
AND WATCH THIS WOMAN AS WELL-- FOR SHE IS THE DEADLIEST OF THE THREE BY FAR!
SO WHAT ARE YOU WAITING FOR? BUY IT ALREADY--AND START WATCHING!

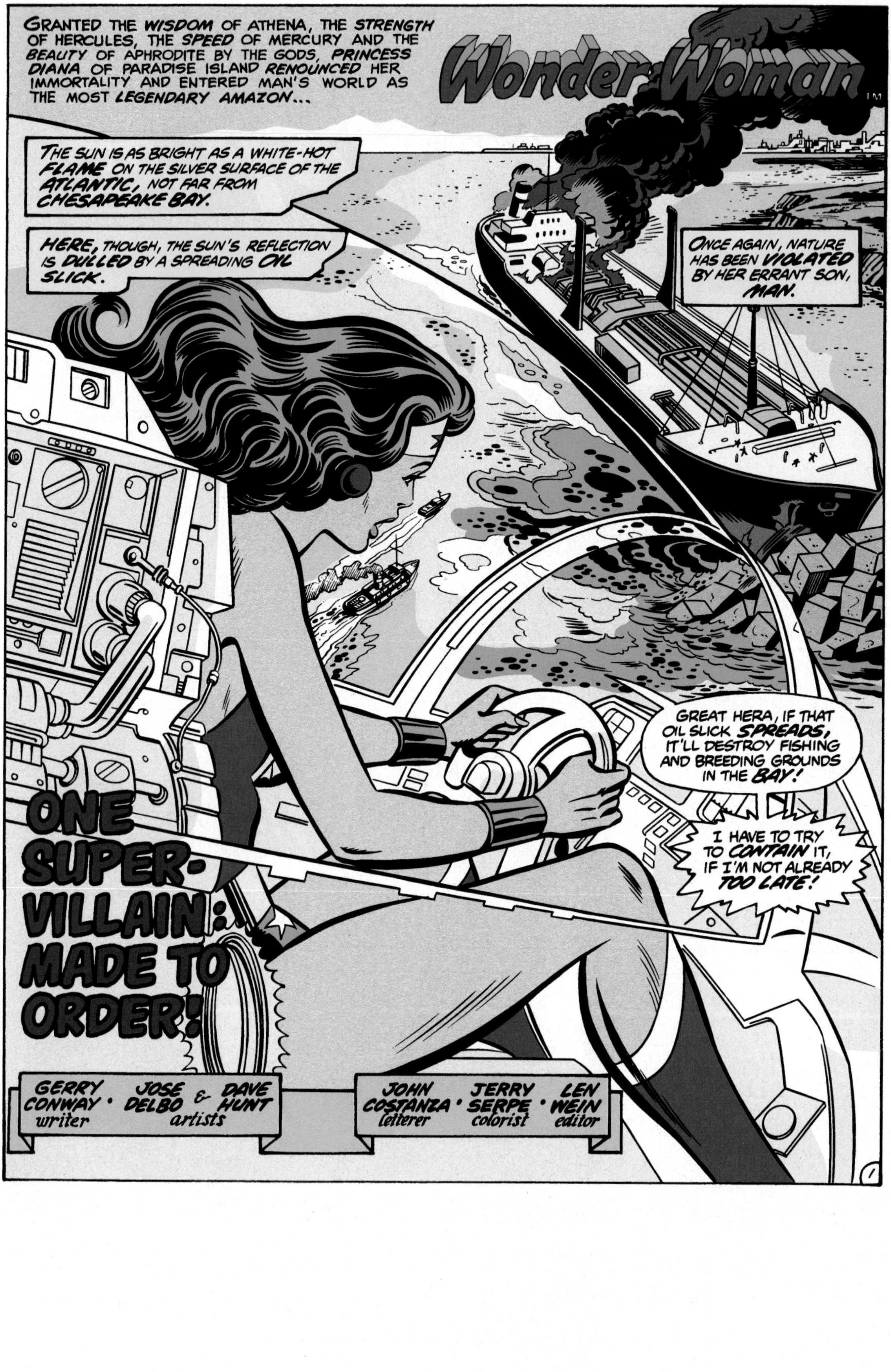
GRANTED THE WISDOM OF ATHENA, THE STRENGTH OF HERCULES, THE SPEED OF MERCURY AND THE BEAUTY OF APHRODITE BY THE GODS, PRINCESS DIANA OF PARADISE ISLAND RENOUNCED HER IMMORTALITY AND ENTERED MAN'S WORLD AS THE MOST LEGENDARY AMAZON...
Wonder Woman
THE SUN IS AS BRIGHT AS A WHITE-HOT FLAME ON THE SILVER SURFACE OF THE ATLANTIC, NOT FAR FROM CHESAPEAKE BAY.
HERE, THOUGH, THE SUN'S REFLECTION IS DULLED BY A SPREADING OIL SLICK.
ONCE AGAIN, NATURE HAS BEEN VIOLATED BY HER ERRANT SON, MAN.
GREAT HERA, IF THAT OIL SLICK SPREADS, IT'LL DESTROY FISHING AND BREEDING GROUNDS IN THE BAY!
I HAVE TO TRY TO CONTAIN IT, IF I'M NOT ALREADY TOO LATE!
ONE SUPER-VILLAIN: MADE TO ORDER!
GERRY CONWAY writer · JOSE DELBO & DAVE HUNT artists
JOHN COSTANZA letterer · JERRY SERPE colorist · LEN WEIN editor
1

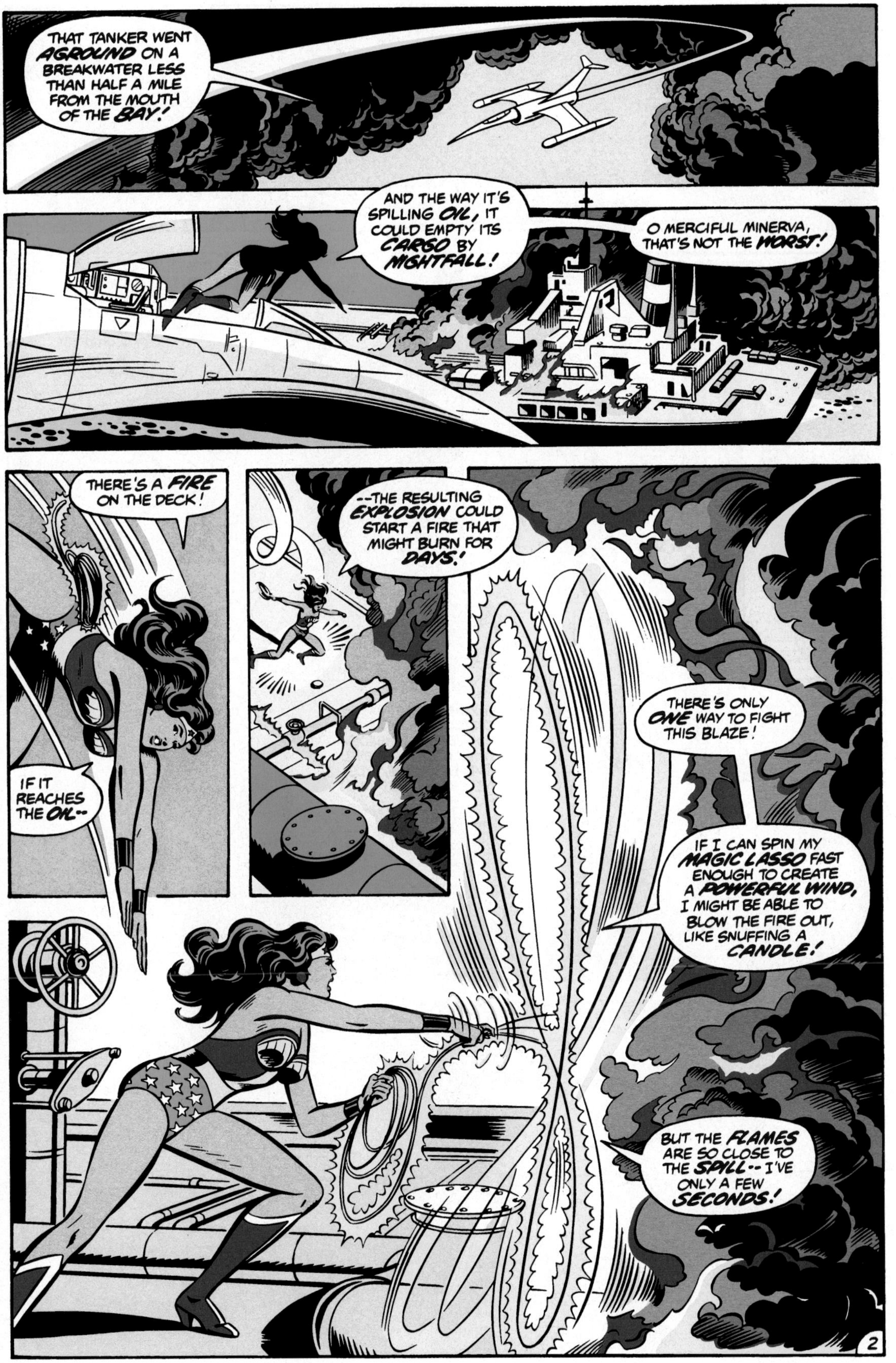
THAT TANKER WENT AGROUND ON A BREAKWATER LESS THAN HALF A MILE FROM THE MOUTH OF THE BAY!
AND THE WAY IT'S SPILLING OIL, IT COULD EMPTY ITS CARGO BY NIGHTFALL!
O MERCIFUL MINERVA, THAT'S NOT THE WORST!
THERE'S A FIRE ON THE DECK!
IF IT REACHES THE OIL--
--THE RESULTING EXPLOSION COULD START A FIRE THAT MIGHT BURN FOR DAYS!
THERE'S ONLY ONE WAY TO FIGHT THIS BLAZE!
IF I CAN SPIN MY MAGIC LASSO FAST ENOUGH TO CREATE A POWERFUL WIND, I MIGHT BE ABLE TO BLOW THE FIRE OUT, LIKE SNUFFING A CANDLE!
BUT THE FLAMES ARE SO CLOSE TO THE SPILL-- I'VE ONLY A FEW SECONDS!
2

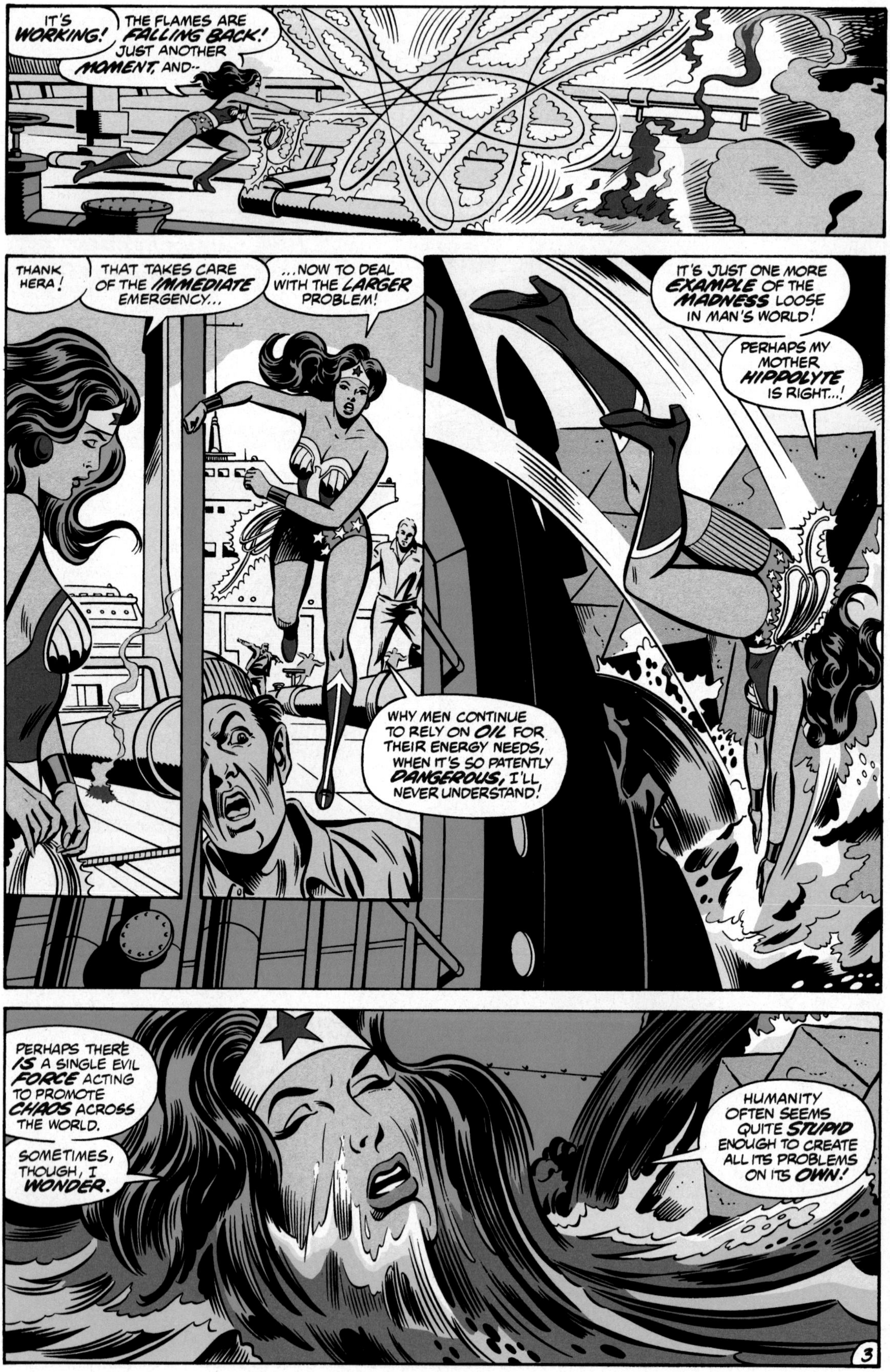
IT'S WORKING!
THE FLAMES ARE FALLING BACK! JUST ANOTHER MOMENT, AND--
THANK HERA!
THAT TAKES CARE OF THE IMMEDIATE EMERGENCY...
...NOW TO DEAL WITH THE LARGER PROBLEM!
WHY MEN CONTINUE TO RELY ON OIL FOR THEIR ENERGY NEEDS, WHEN IT'S SO PATENTLY DANGEROUS, I'LL NEVER UNDERSTAND!
IT'S JUST ONE MORE EXAMPLE OF THE MADNESS LOOSE IN MAN'S WORLD!
PERHAPS MY MOTHER HIPPOLYTE IS RIGHT...!
PERHAPS THERE IS A SINGLE EVIL FORCE ACTING TO PROMOTE CHAOS ACROSS THE WORLD.
SOMETIMES, THOUGH, I WONDER.
HUMANITY OFTEN SEEMS QUITE STUPID ENOUGH TO CREATE ALL ITS PROBLEMS ON ITS OWN!
3

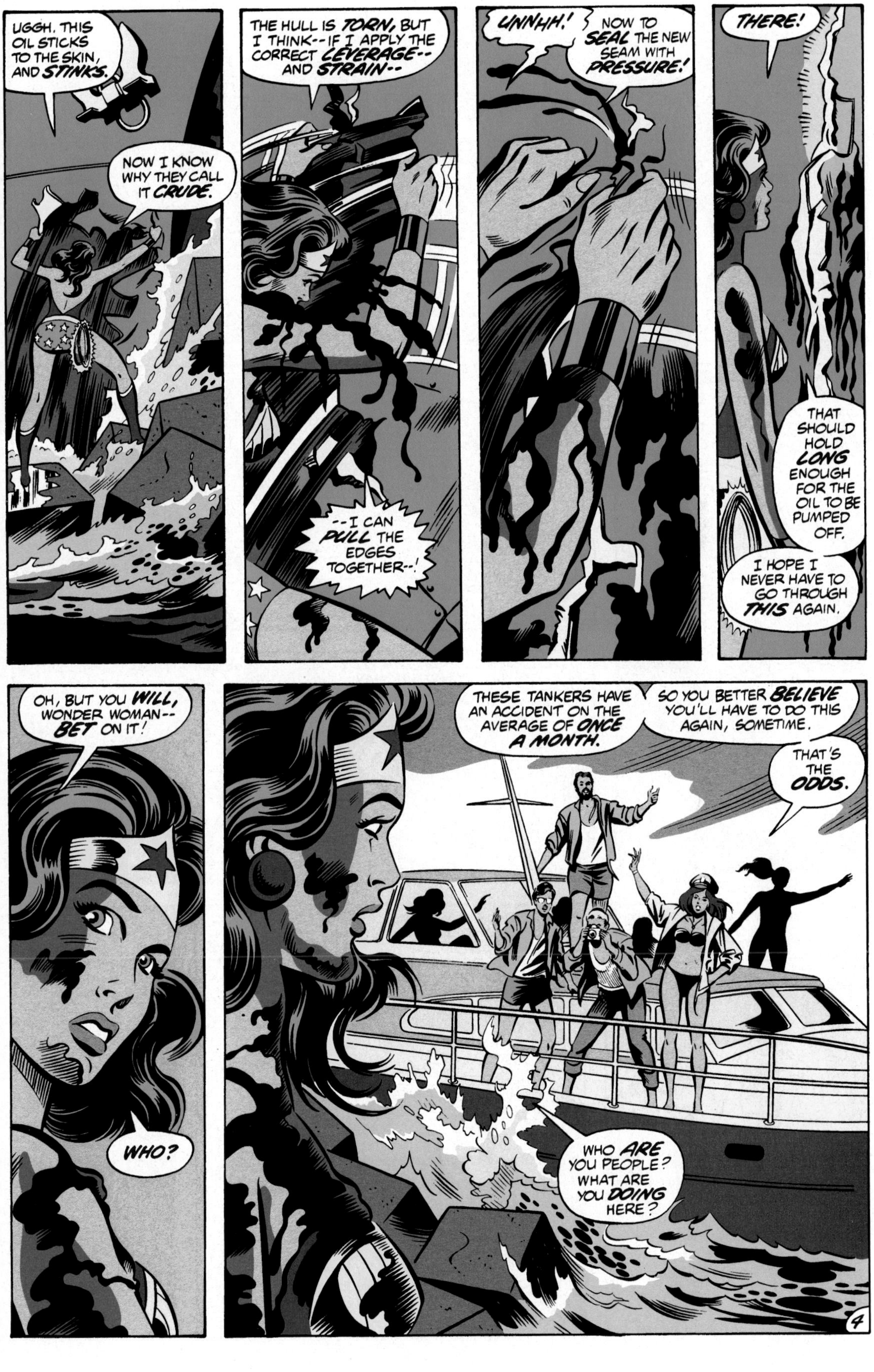
UGGH. THIS OIL STICKS TO THE SKIN, AND STINKS.
NOW I KNOW WHY THEY CALL IT CRUDE.
THE HULL IS TORN, BUT I THINK--IF I APPLY THE CORRECT LEVERAGE--AND STRAIN--
--I CAN PULL THE EDGES TOGETHER--!
UNNHH!
NOW TO SEAL THE NEW SEAM WITH PRESSURE!
THERE!
THAT SHOULD HOLD LONG ENOUGH FOR THE OIL TO BE PUMPED OFF.
I HOPE I NEVER HAVE TO GO THROUGH THIS AGAIN.
OH, BUT YOU WILL, WONDER WOMAN--BET ON IT!
WHO?
THESE TANKERS HAVE AN ACCIDENT ON THE AVERAGE OF ONCE A MONTH.
SO YOU BETTER BELIEVE YOU'LL HAVE TO DO THIS AGAIN, SOMETIME.
THAT'S THE ODDS.
WHO ARE YOU PEOPLE? WHAT ARE YOU DOING HERE?
4

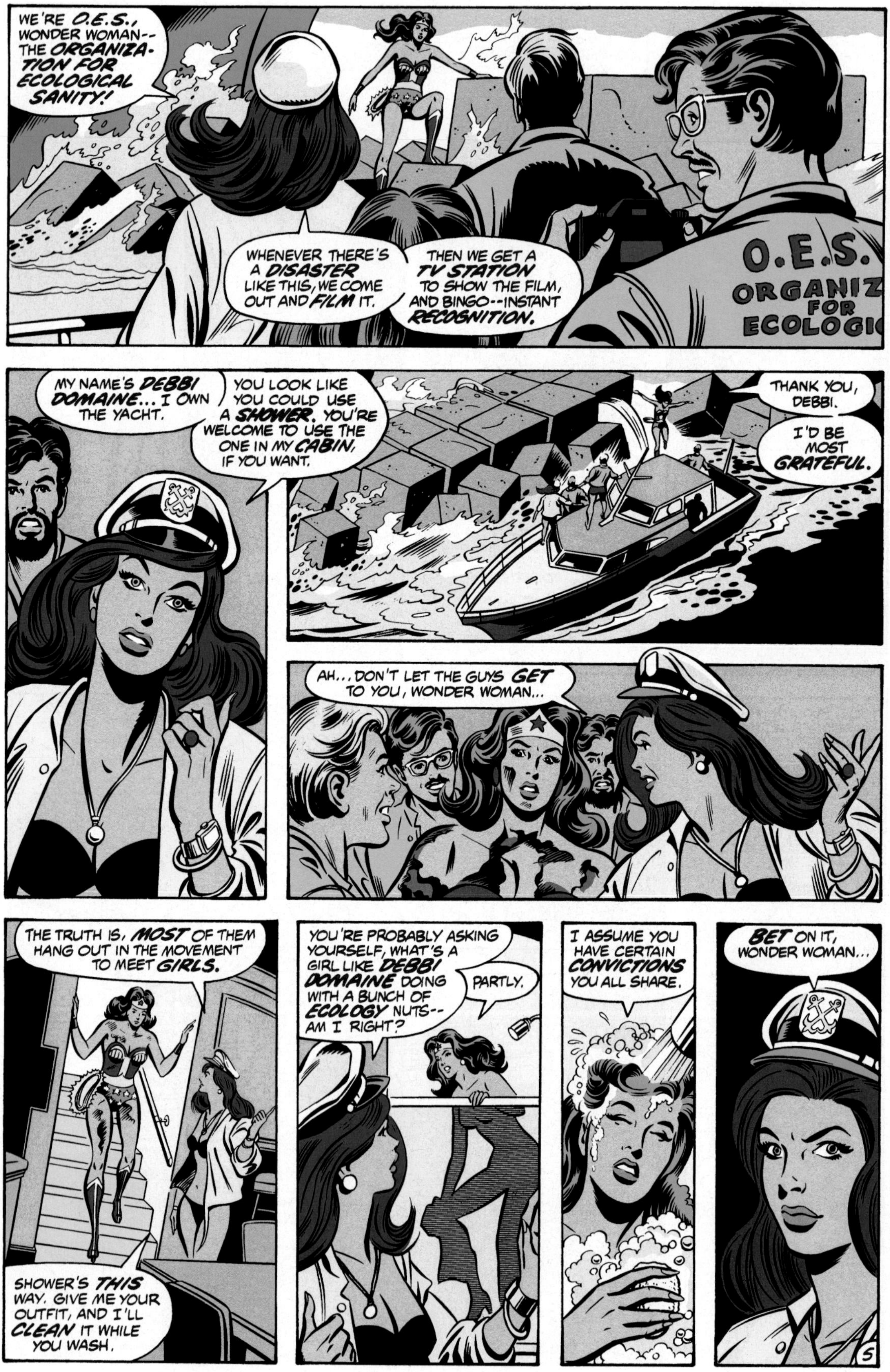
WE'RE O.E.S., WONDER WOMAN-- THE ORGANIZATION FOR ECOLOGICAL SANITY!
WHENEVER THERE'S A DISASTER LIKE THIS, WE COME OUT AND FILM IT.
THEN WE GET A TV STATION TO SHOW THE FILM, AND BINGO--INSTANT RECOGNITION.
O.E.S.
ORGANIZ
FOR
ECOLOGI
MY NAME'S DEBBI DOMAINE... I OWN THE YACHT.
YOU LOOK LIKE YOU COULD USE A SHOWER. YOU'RE WELCOME TO USE THE ONE IN MY CABIN, IF YOU WANT.
THANK YOU, DEBBI.
I'D BE MOST GRATEFUL.
AH... DON'T LET THE GUYS GET TO YOU, WONDER WOMAN...
THE TRUTH IS, MOST OF THEM HANG OUT IN THE MOVEMENT TO MEET GIRLS.
SHOWER'S THIS WAY. GIVE ME YOUR OUTFIT, AND I'LL CLEAN IT WHILE YOU WASH.
YOU'RE PROBABLY ASKING YOURSELF, WHAT'S A GIRL LIKE DEBBI DOMAINE DOING WITH A BUNCH OF ECOLOGY NUTS-- AM I RIGHT?
PARTLY.
I ASSUME YOU HAVE CERTAIN CONVICTIONS YOU ALL SHARE.
BET ON IT, WONDER WOMAN...
5

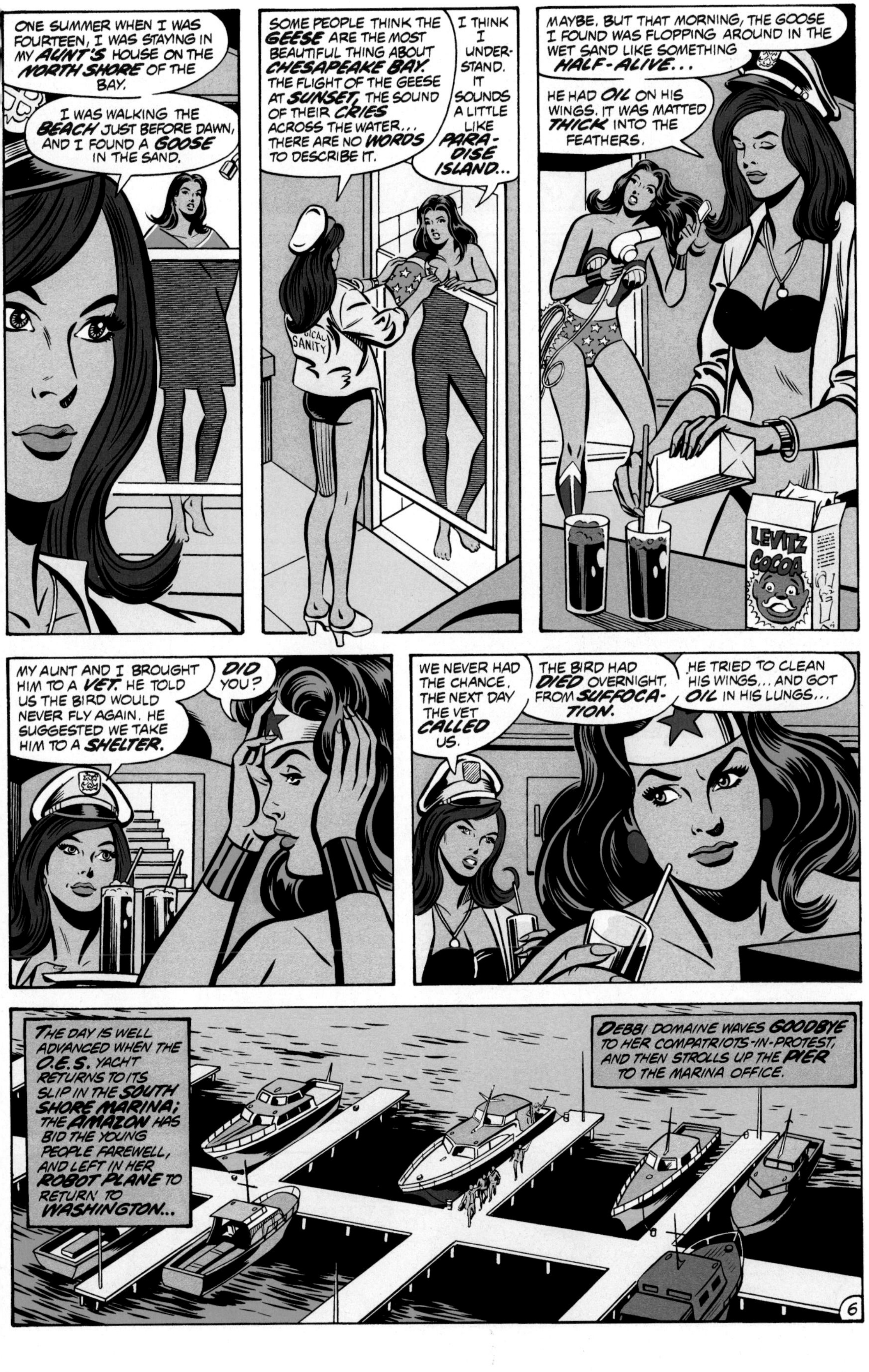
ONE SUMMER WHEN I WAS FOURTEEN, I WAS STAYING IN MY AUNT'S HOUSE ON THE NORTH SHORE OF THE BAY.
I WAS WALKING THE BEACH JUST BEFORE DAWN, AND I FOUND A GOOSE IN THE SAND.
SOME PEOPLE THINK THE GEESE ARE THE MOST BEAUTIFUL THING ABOUT CHESAPEAKE BAY. THE FLIGHT OF THE GEESE AT SUNSET, THE SOUND OF THEIR CRIES ACROSS THE WATER... THERE ARE NO WORDS TO DESCRIBE IT.
I THINK I UNDERSTAND. IT SOUNDS A LITTLE LIKE PARADISE ISLAND...
MAYBE. BUT THAT MORNING, THE GOOSE I FOUND WAS FLOPPING AROUND IN THE WET SAND LIKE SOMETHING HALF-ALIVE...
HE HAD OIL ON HIS WINGS. IT WAS MATTED THICK INTO THE FEATHERS.
LEVITZ COCOA
MY AUNT AND I BROUGHT HIM TO A VET. HE TOLD US THE BIRD WOULD NEVER FLY AGAIN. HE SUGGESTED WE TAKE HIM TO A SHELTER.
DID YOU?
WE NEVER HAD THE CHANCE. THE NEXT DAY THE VET CALLED US.
THE BIRD HAD DIED OVERNIGHT, FROM SUFFOCATION.
HE TRIED TO CLEAN HIS WINGS... AND GOT OIL IN HIS LUNGS...
THE DAY IS WELL ADVANCED WHEN THE O.E.S. YACHT RETURNS TO ITS SLIP IN THE SOUTH SHORE MARINA; THE AMAZON HAS BID THE YOUNG PEOPLE FAREWELL, AND LEFT IN HER ROBOT PLANE TO RETURN TO WASHINGTON...
DEBBI DOMAINE WAVES GOODBYE TO HER COMPATRIOTS-IN-PROTEST, AND THEN STROLLS UP THE PIER TO THE MARINA OFFICE.
6

MAIL'S IN, SAY... NOW ISN'T *THIS* A COINCIDENCE?

I WAS TELLING *WONDER WOMAN* ABOUT MY *AUNT* JUST A FEW HOURS AGO, AND NOW HERE'S A *LETTER* FROM-- OH, *NO!*

WHY DO THE *GOOD* PEOPLE ALWAYS HAVE TO DIE? *WHY?*

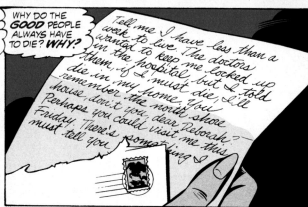

Tell me I have less than a week to live. The doctors wanted to keep me locked up in the hospital, but I told them, if I must die, I'll die in my home. You remember the north shore house, don't you, dear Deborah? Perhaps you could visit me this Friday. There's something I must tell you.

AS THE HEARTSTRICKEN DEBBI DOMAINE READS ON THROUGH HER TEARS, SOME MILES AWAY, OUTSIDE THAT SET OF BUREAUCRATIC BUILDING BLOCKS KNOWN AS THE PENTAGON--

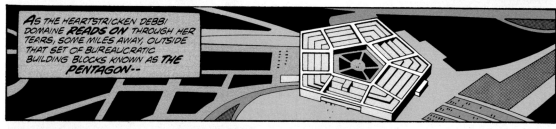

-- A HURRYING AMAZON MAKES A SWIFT TRANSFORMATION FROM WOMAN WARRIOR TO AIR FORCE CAPTAIN:

I'M *LATE* FOR A BRIEFING ON THE CORP'S NEW SOLAR-POWERED AIR BASE *PROJECT!*

IT TOOK WEEKS OF MANUEVERING TO GET BOTH *STEVE TREVOR* AND *GENERAL DARNELL* TO THIS BRIEFING -- I *CAN'T* LET IT ALL FALL APART NOW!

7

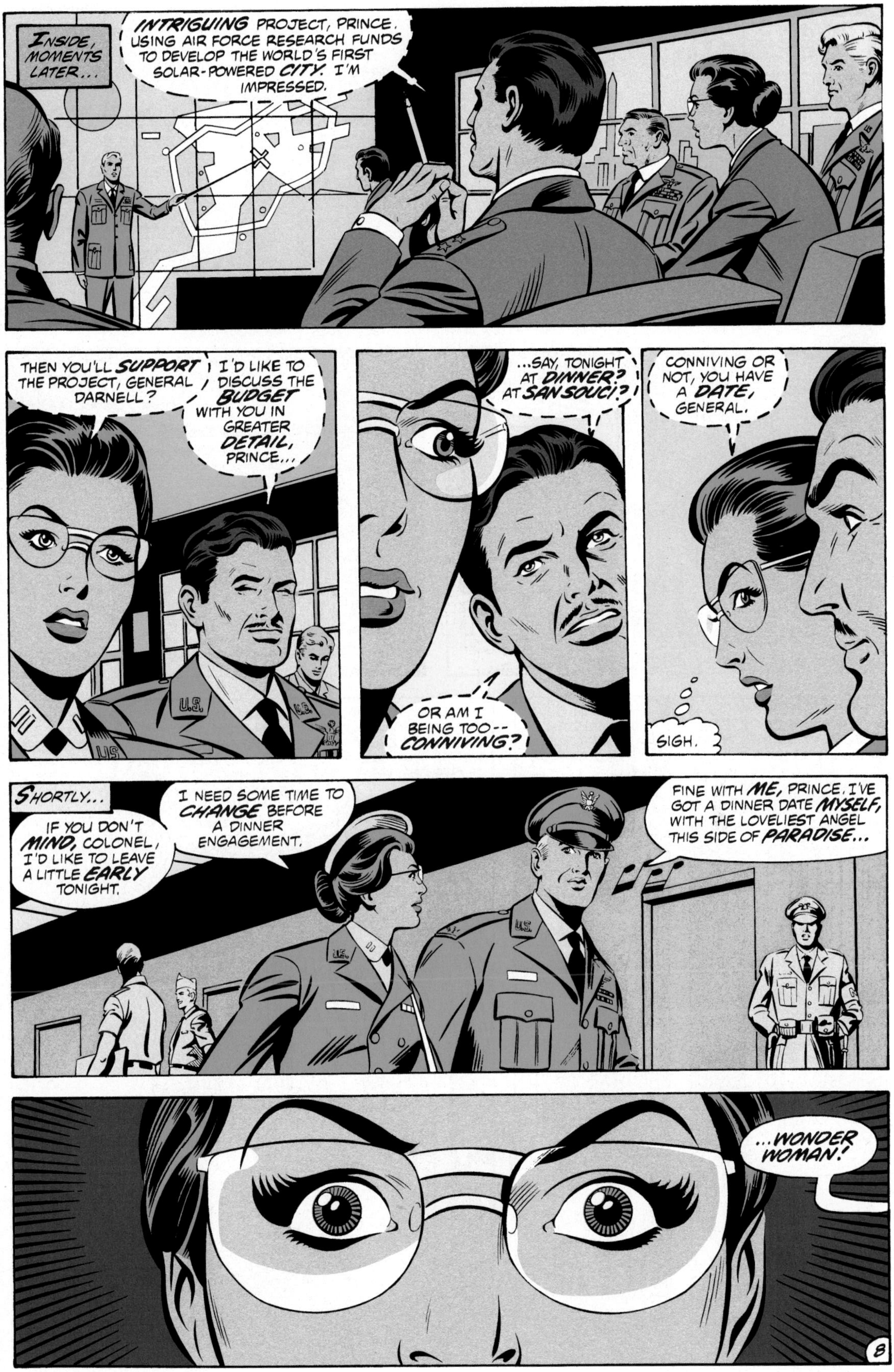

INSIDE, MOMENTS LATER...
INTRIGUING PROJECT, PRINCE. USING AIR FORCE RESEARCH FUNDS TO DEVELOP THE WORLD'S FIRST SOLAR-POWERED CITY. I'M IMPRESSED.
THEN YOU'LL SUPPORT THE PROJECT, GENERAL DARNELL?
I'D LIKE TO DISCUSS THE BUDGET WITH YOU IN GREATER DETAIL, PRINCE...
...SAY, TONIGHT AT DINNER? AT SAN SOUCI?
OR AM I BEING TOO--CONNIVING?
CONNIVING OR NOT, YOU HAVE A DATE, GENERAL.
SIGH.
SHORTLY...
IF YOU DON'T MIND, COLONEL, I'D LIKE TO LEAVE A LITTLE EARLY TONIGHT.
I NEED SOME TIME TO CHANGE BEFORE A DINNER ENGAGEMENT.
FINE WITH ME, PRINCE. I'VE GOT A DINNER DATE MYSELF, WITH THE LOVELIEST ANGEL THIS SIDE OF PARADISE...
...WONDER WOMAN!
8

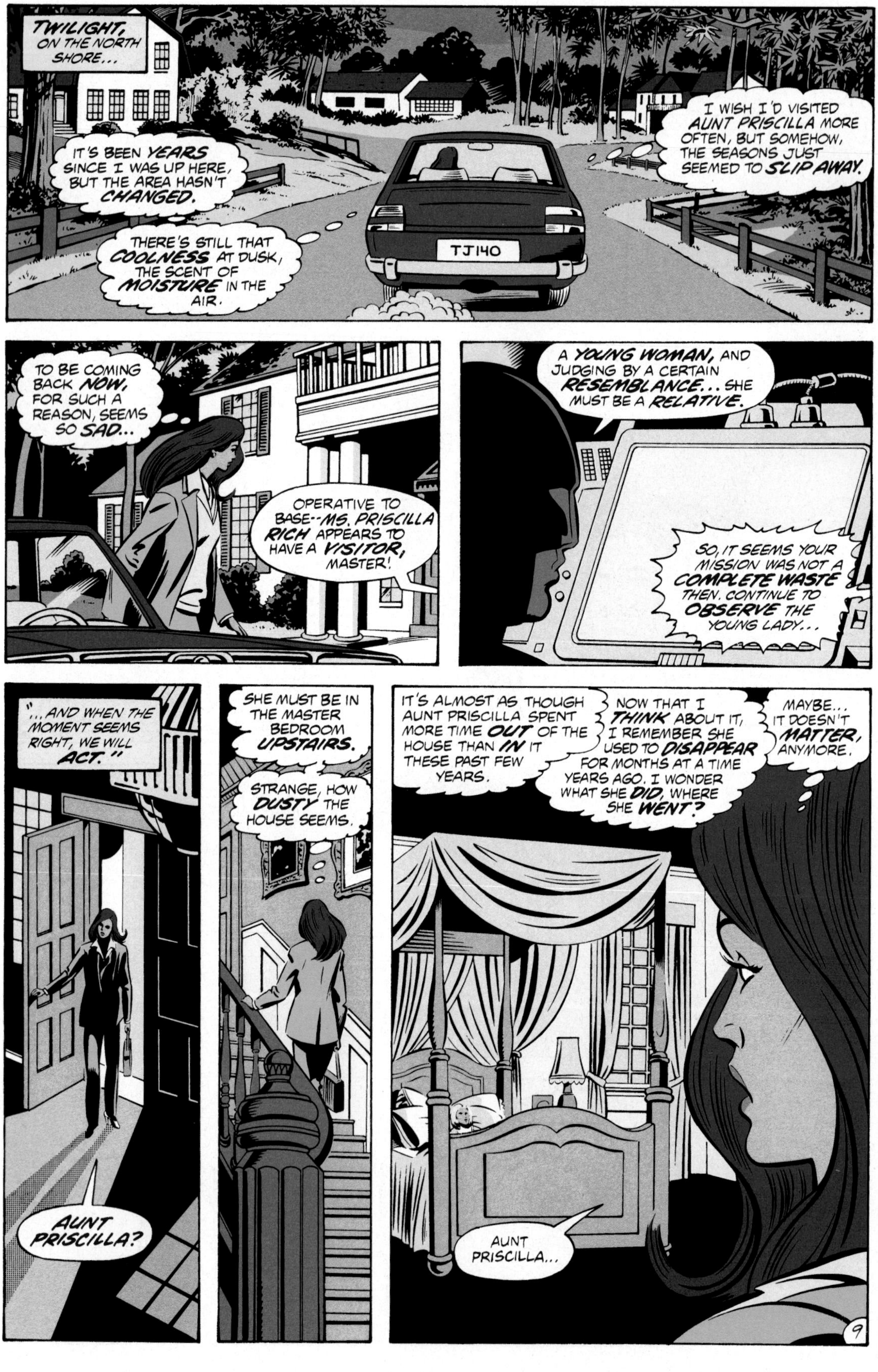
TWILIGHT, ON THE NORTH SHORE...
IT'S BEEN YEARS SINCE I WAS UP HERE, BUT THE AREA HASN'T CHANGED.
THERE'S STILL THAT COOLNESS AT DUSK, THE SCENT OF MOISTURE IN THE AIR.
I WISH I'D VISITED AUNT PRISCILLA MORE OFTEN, BUT SOMEHOW, THE SEASONS JUST SEEMED TO SLIP AWAY.
TJ140
TO BE COMING BACK NOW, FOR SUCH A REASON, SEEMS SO SAD...
OPERATIVE TO BASE--MS. PRISCILLA RICH APPEARS TO HAVE A VISITOR, MASTER!
A YOUNG WOMAN, AND JUDGING BY A CERTAIN RESEMBLANCE... SHE MUST BE A RELATIVE.
SO, IT SEEMS YOUR MISSION WAS NOT A COMPLETE WASTE THEN. CONTINUE TO OBSERVE THE YOUNG LADY...
"...AND WHEN THE MOMENT SEEMS RIGHT, WE WILL ACT."
AUNT PRISCILLA?
SHE MUST BE IN THE MASTER BEDROOM UPSTAIRS.
STRANGE, HOW DUSTY THE HOUSE SEEMS.
IT'S ALMOST AS THOUGH AUNT PRISCILLA SPENT MORE TIME OUT OF THE HOUSE THAN IN IT THESE PAST FEW YEARS.
NOW THAT I THINK ABOUT IT, I REMEMBER SHE USED TO DISAPPEAR FOR MONTHS AT A TIME YEARS AGO. I WONDER WHAT SHE DID, WHERE SHE WENT?
MAYBE... IT DOESN'T MATTER, ANYMORE.
AUNT PRISCILLA...
9

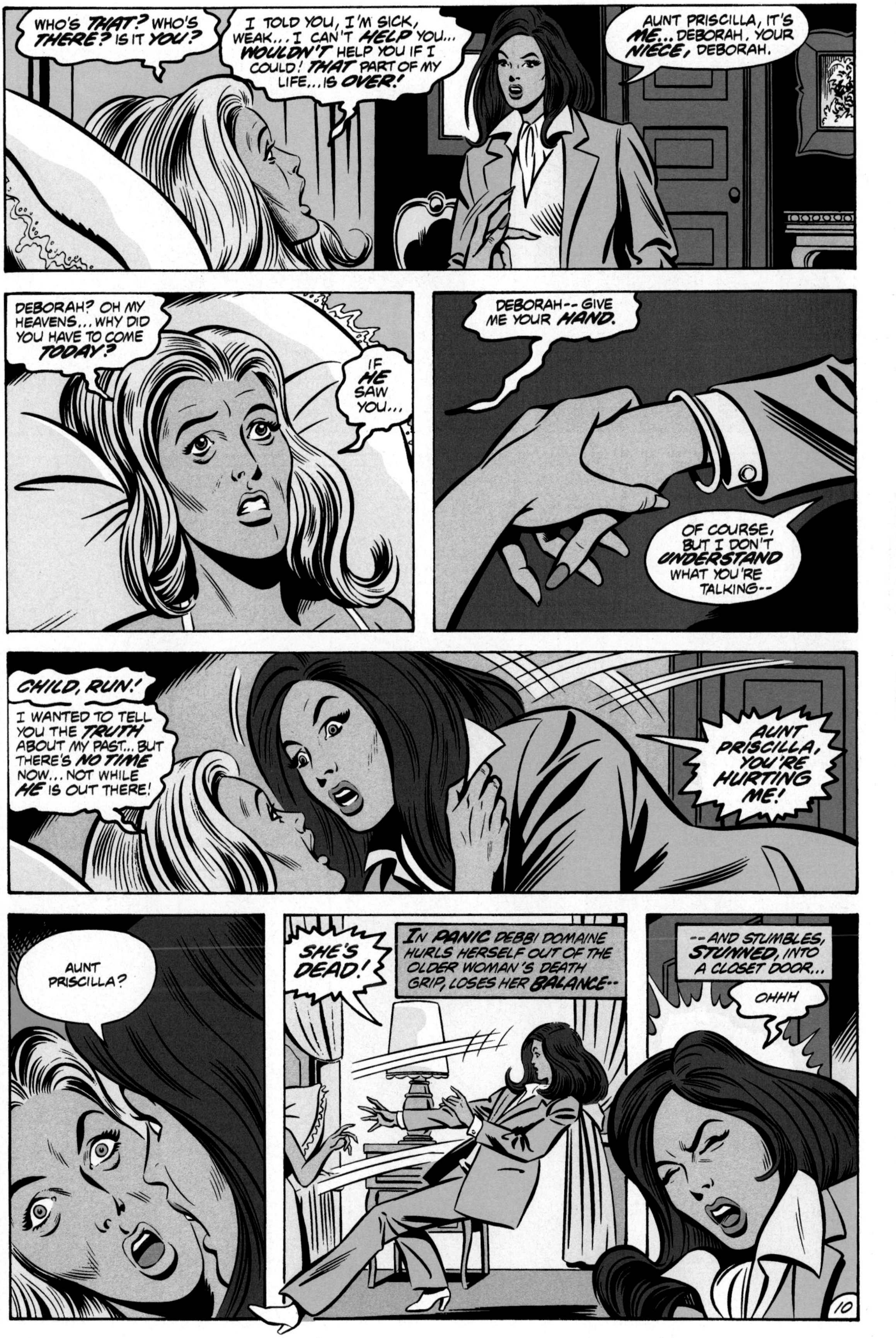
WHO'S THAT? WHO'S THERE? IS IT YOU?
I TOLD YOU, I'M SICK, WEAK... I CAN'T HELP YOU... WOULDN'T HELP YOU IF I COULD! THAT PART OF MY LIFE... IS OVER!
AUNT PRISCILLA, IT'S ME... DEBORAH, YOUR NIECE, DEBORAH.
DEBORAH? OH MY HEAVENS... WHY DID YOU HAVE TO COME TODAY?
IF HE SAW YOU...
DEBORAH-- GIVE ME YOUR HAND.
OF COURSE, BUT I DON'T UNDERSTAND WHAT YOU'RE TALKING--
CHILD, RUN!
I WANTED TO TELL YOU THE TRUTH ABOUT MY PAST... BUT THERE'S NO TIME NOW... NOT WHILE HE IS OUT THERE!
AUNT PRISCILLA, YOU'RE HURTING ME!
AUNT PRISCILLA?
SHE'S DEAD!
IN PANIC DEBBI DOMAINE HURLS HERSELF OUT OF THE OLDER WOMAN'S DEATH GRIP, LOSES HER BALANCE--
--AND STUMBLES, STUNNED, INTO A CLOSET DOOR...
OHHH
10

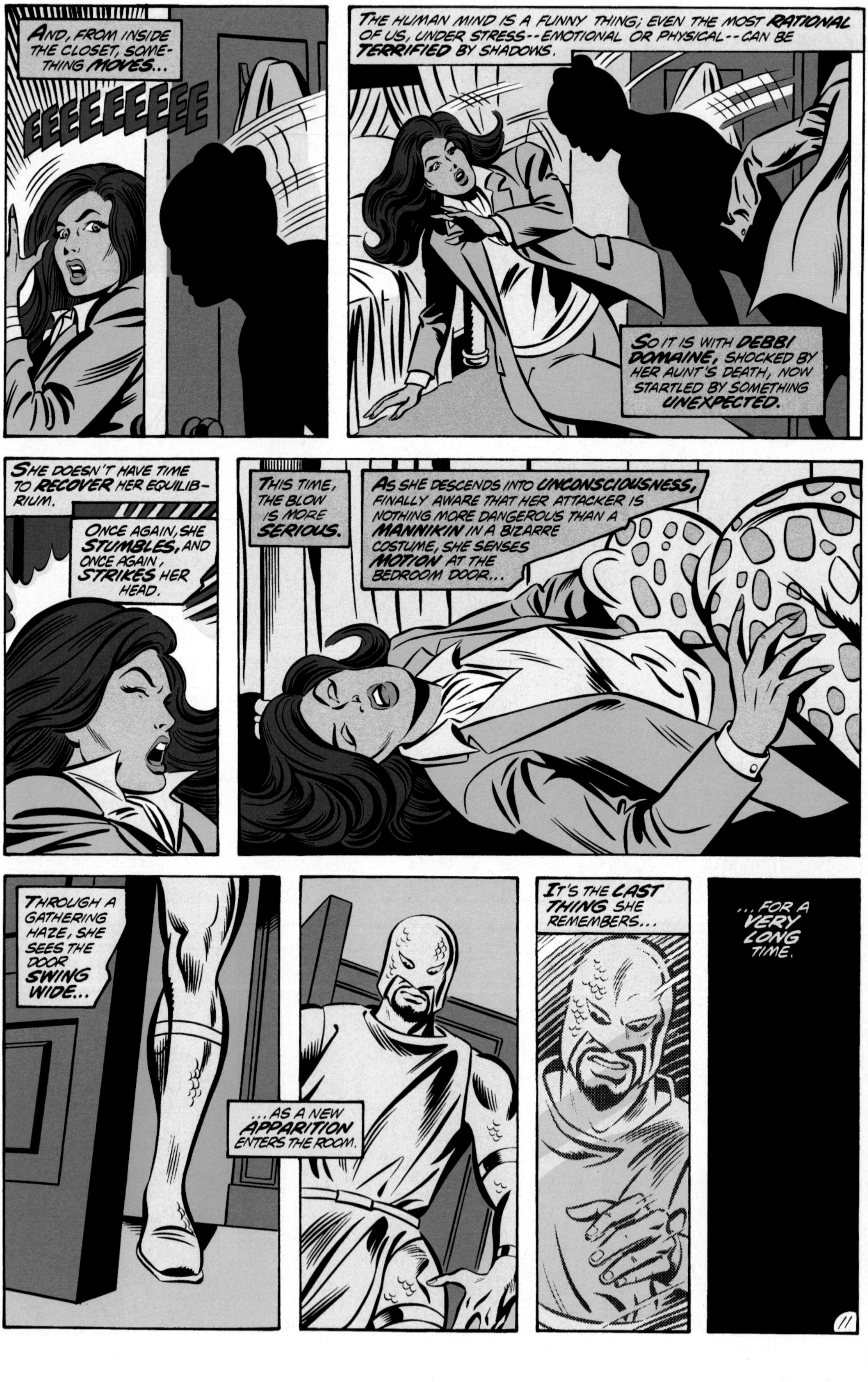

AND, FROM INSIDE THE CLOSET, SOMETHING MOVES...
EEEEEEEEE
THE HUMAN MIND IS A FUNNY THING; EVEN THE MOST RATIONAL OF US, UNDER STRESS--EMOTIONAL OR PHYSICAL--CAN BE TERRIFIED BY SHADOWS.
SO IT IS WITH DEBBI DOMAINE, SHOCKED BY HER AUNT'S DEATH, NOW STARTLED BY SOMETHING UNEXPECTED.
SHE DOESN'T HAVE TIME TO RECOVER HER EQUILIBRIUM.
ONCE AGAIN, SHE STUMBLES, AND ONCE AGAIN, STRIKES HER HEAD.
THIS TIME, THE BLOW IS MORE SERIOUS.
AS SHE DESCENDS INTO UNCONSCIOUSNESS, FINALLY AWARE THAT HER ATTACKER IS NOTHING MORE DANGEROUS THAN A MANNIKIN IN A BIZARRE COSTUME, SHE SENSES MOTION AT THE BEDROOM DOOR...
THROUGH A GATHERING HAZE, SHE SEES THE DOOR SWING WIDE...
...AS A NEW APPARITION ENTERS THE ROOM.
IT'S THE LAST THING SHE REMEMBERS...
...FOR A VERY LONG TIME.
11

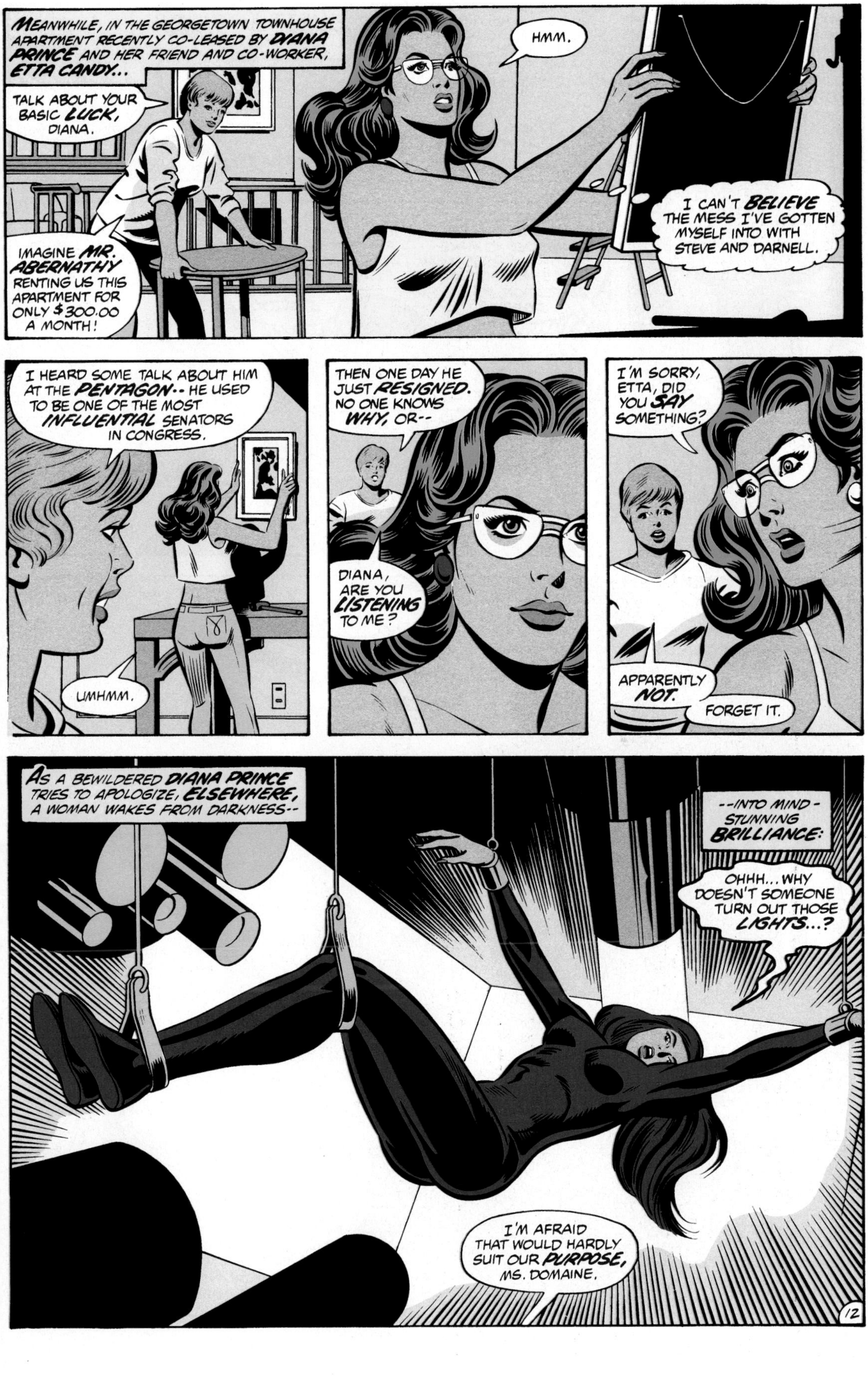

MEANWHILE, IN THE GEORGETOWN TOWNHOUSE APARTMENT RECENTLY CO-LEASED BY DIANA PRINCE AND HER FRIEND AND CO-WORKER, ETTA CANDY...
TALK ABOUT YOUR BASIC LUCK, DIANA.
HMM.
IMAGINE MR. ABERNATHY RENTING US THIS APARTMENT FOR ONLY $300.00 A MONTH!
I CAN'T BELIEVE THE MESS I'VE GOTTEN MYSELF INTO WITH STEVE AND DARNELL.
I HEARD SOME TALK ABOUT HIM AT THE PENTAGON-- HE USED TO BE ONE OF THE MOST INFLUENTIAL SENATORS IN CONGRESS.
UMHMM.
THEN ONE DAY HE JUST RESIGNED. NO ONE KNOWS WHY, OR--
DIANA, ARE YOU LISTENING TO ME?
I'M SORRY, ETTA, DID YOU SAY SOMETHING?
APPARENTLY NOT.
FORGET IT.
AS A BEWILDERED DIANA PRINCE TRIES TO APOLOGIZE, ELSEWHERE, A WOMAN WAKES FROM DARKNESS--
--INTO MIND-STUNNING BRILLIANCE:
OHHH... WHY DOESN'T SOMEONE TURN OUT THOSE LIGHTS...?
I'M AFRAID THAT WOULD HARDLY SUIT OUR PURPOSE, MS. DOMAINE.
12

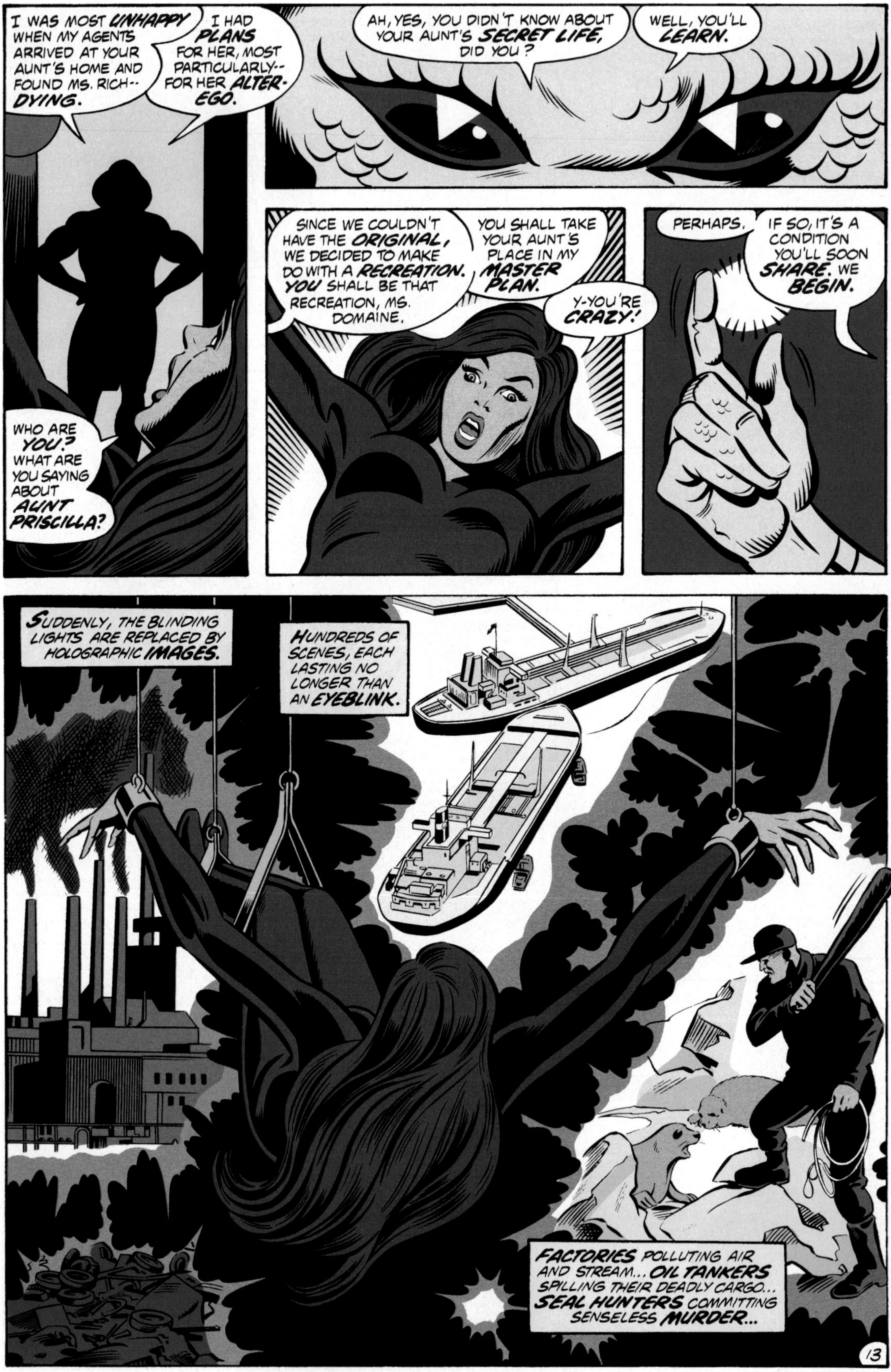
I WAS MOST UNHAPPY WHEN MY AGENTS ARRIVED AT YOUR AUNT'S HOME AND FOUND MS. RICH-- DYING.
I HAD PLANS FOR HER, MOST PARTICULARLY-- FOR HER ALTER-EGO.
AH, YES, YOU DIDN'T KNOW ABOUT YOUR AUNT'S SECRET LIFE, DID YOU?
WELL, YOU'LL LEARN.
WHO ARE YOU? WHAT ARE YOU SAYING ABOUT AUNT PRISCILLA?
SINCE WE COULDN'T HAVE THE ORIGINAL, WE DECIDED TO MAKE DO WITH A RECREATION. YOU SHALL BE THAT RECREATION, MS. DOMAINE.
YOU SHALL TAKE YOUR AUNT'S PLACE IN MY MASTER PLAN.
Y-YOU'RE CRAZY!
PERHAPS.
IF SO, IT'S A CONDITION YOU'LL SOON SHARE. WE BEGIN.
SUDDENLY, THE BLINDING LIGHTS ARE REPLACED BY HOLOGRAPHIC IMAGES.
HUNDREDS OF SCENES, EACH LASTING NO LONGER THAN AN EYEBLINK.
FACTORIES POLLUTING AIR AND STREAM... OIL TANKERS SPILLING THEIR DEADLY CARGO... SEAL HUNTERS COMMITTING SENSELESS MURDER...
13

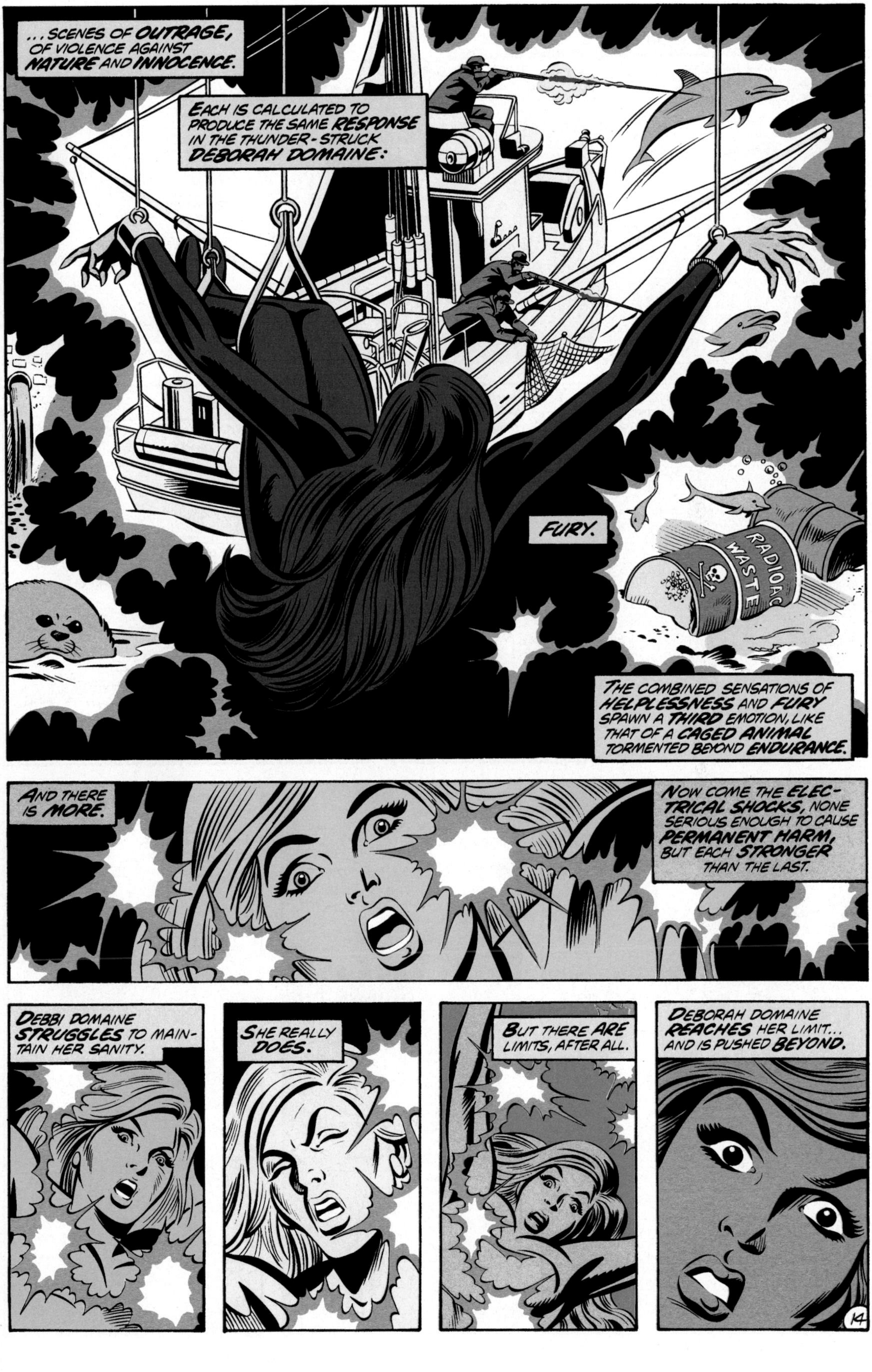

...SCENES OF OUTRAGE, OF VIOLENCE AGAINST NATURE AND INNOCENCE.
EACH IS CALCULATED TO PRODUCE THE SAME RESPONSE IN THE THUNDER-STRUCK DEBORAH DOMAINE:
FURY.
RADIOACTIVE WASTE
THE COMBINED SENSATIONS OF HELPLESSNESS AND FURY SPAWN A THIRD EMOTION, LIKE THAT OF A CAGED ANIMAL TORMENTED BEYOND ENDURANCE.
AND THERE IS MORE.
NOW COME THE ELECTRICAL SHOCKS, NONE SERIOUS ENOUGH TO CAUSE PERMANENT HARM, BUT EACH STRONGER THAN THE LAST.
DEBBI DOMAINE STRUGGLES TO MAINTAIN HER SANITY.
SHE REALLY DOES.
BUT THERE ARE LIMITS, AFTER ALL.
DEBORAH DOMAINE REACHES HER LIMIT... AND IS PUSHED BEYOND.
14

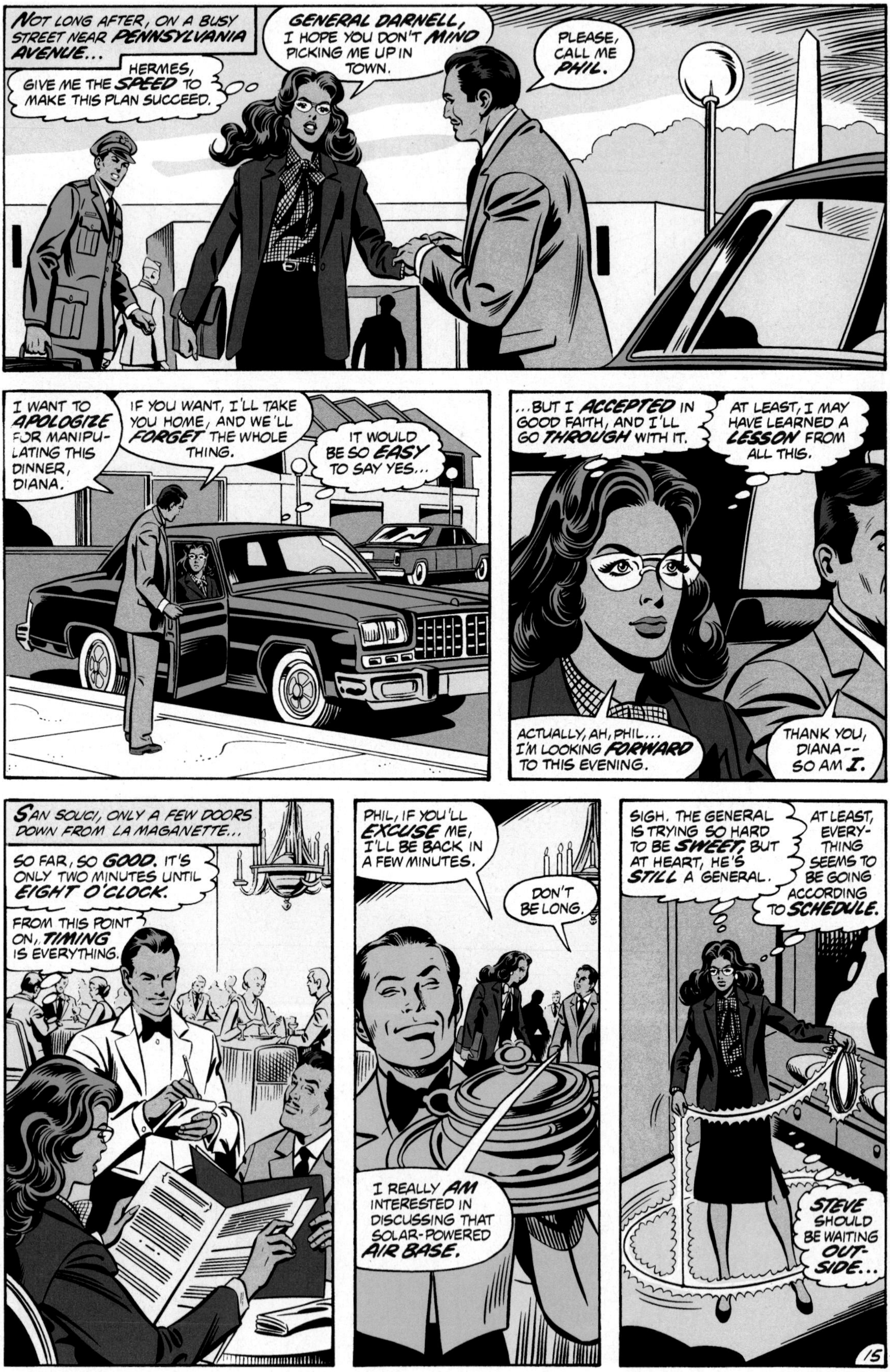
NOT LONG AFTER, ON A BUSY STREET NEAR PENNSYLVANIA AVENUE...
HERMES, GIVE ME THE SPEED TO MAKE THIS PLAN SUCCEED.
GENERAL DARNELL, I HOPE YOU DON'T MIND PICKING ME UP IN TOWN.
PLEASE, CALL ME PHIL.
I WANT TO APOLOGIZE FOR MANIPULATING THIS DINNER, DIANA.
IF YOU WANT, I'LL TAKE YOU HOME, AND WE'LL FORGET THE WHOLE THING.
IT WOULD BE SO EASY TO SAY YES...
...BUT I ACCEPTED IN GOOD FAITH, AND I'LL GO THROUGH WITH IT.
AT LEAST, I MAY HAVE LEARNED A LESSON FROM ALL THIS.
ACTUALLY, AH, PHIL... I'M LOOKING FORWARD TO THIS EVENING.
THANK YOU, DIANA -- SO AM I.
SAN SOUCI, ONLY A FEW DOORS DOWN FROM LA MAGANETTE...
SO FAR, SO GOOD. IT'S ONLY TWO MINUTES UNTIL EIGHT O'CLOCK.
FROM THIS POINT ON, TIMING IS EVERYTHING.
PHIL, IF YOU'LL EXCUSE ME, I'LL BE BACK IN A FEW MINUTES.
DON'T BE LONG.
I REALLY AM INTERESTED IN DISCUSSING THAT SOLAR-POWERED AIR BASE.
SIGH. THE GENERAL IS TRYING SO HARD TO BE SWEET, BUT AT HEART, HE'S STILL A GENERAL.
AT LEAST, EVERYTHING SEEMS TO BE GOING ACCORDING TO SCHEDULE.
STEVE SHOULD BE WAITING OUTSIDE...
15

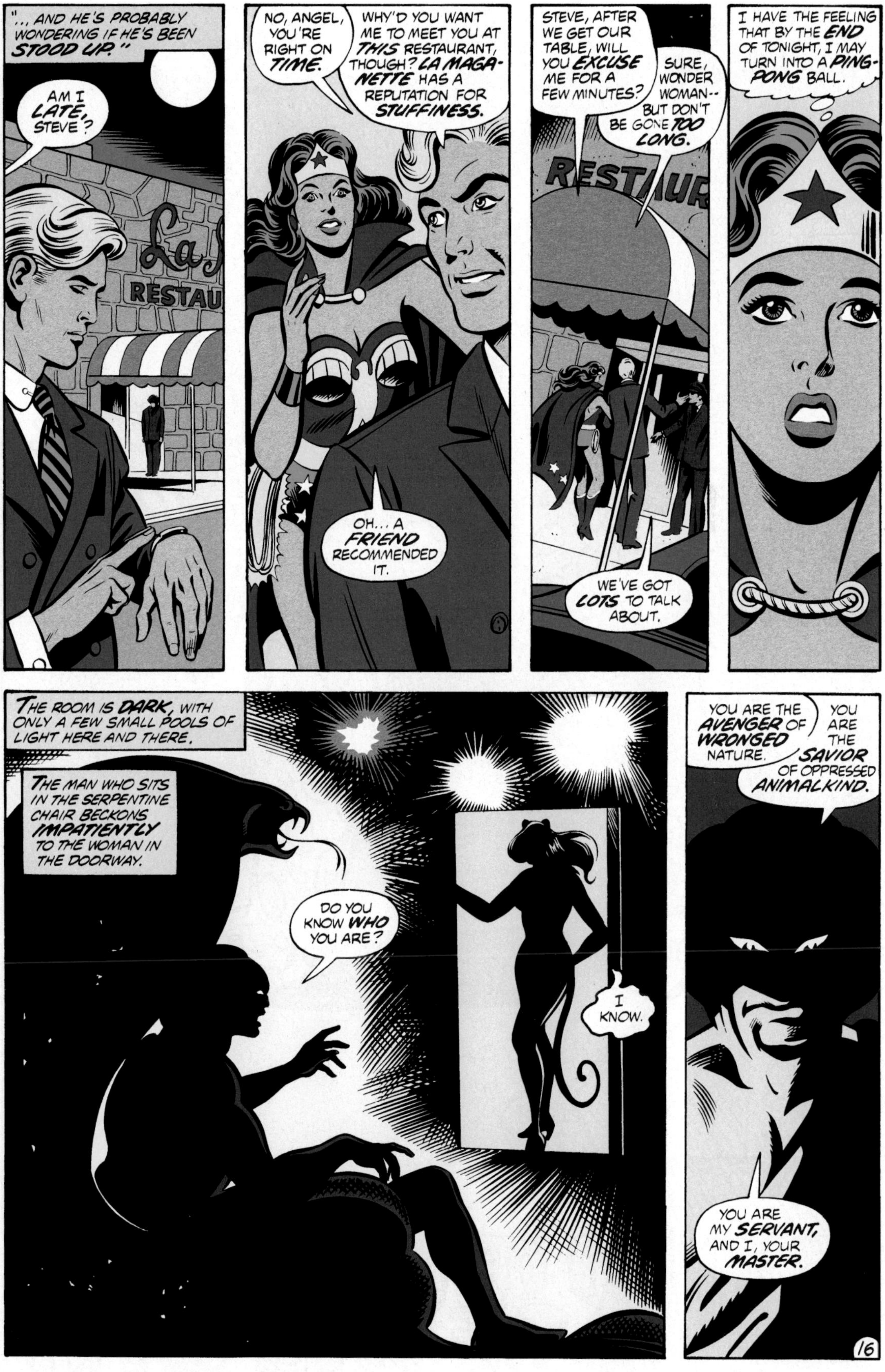
"... AND HE'S PROBABLY WONDERING IF HE'S BEEN STOOD UP."
AM I LATE, STEVE?
NO, ANGEL, YOU'RE RIGHT ON TIME.
WHY'D YOU WANT ME TO MEET YOU AT THIS RESTAURANT, THOUGH? LA MAGA-NETTE HAS A REPUTATION FOR STUFFINESS.
OH... A FRIEND RECOMMENDED IT.
STEVE, AFTER WE GET OUR TABLE, WILL YOU EXCUSE ME FOR A FEW MINUTES?
SURE, WONDER WOMAN-- BUT DON'T BE GONE TOO LONG.
WE'VE GOT LOTS TO TALK ABOUT.
I HAVE THE FEELING THAT BY THE END OF TONIGHT, I MAY TURN INTO A PING-PONG BALL.
THE ROOM IS DARK, WITH ONLY A FEW SMALL POOLS OF LIGHT HERE AND THERE.
THE MAN WHO SITS IN THE SERPENTINE CHAIR BECKONS IMPATIENTLY TO THE WOMAN IN THE DOORWAY.
DO YOU KNOW WHO YOU ARE?
I KNOW.
YOU ARE THE AVENGER OF WRONGED NATURE.
YOU ARE THE SAVIOR OF OPPRESSED ANIMALKIND.
YOU ARE MY SERVANT, AND I, YOUR MASTER.
16

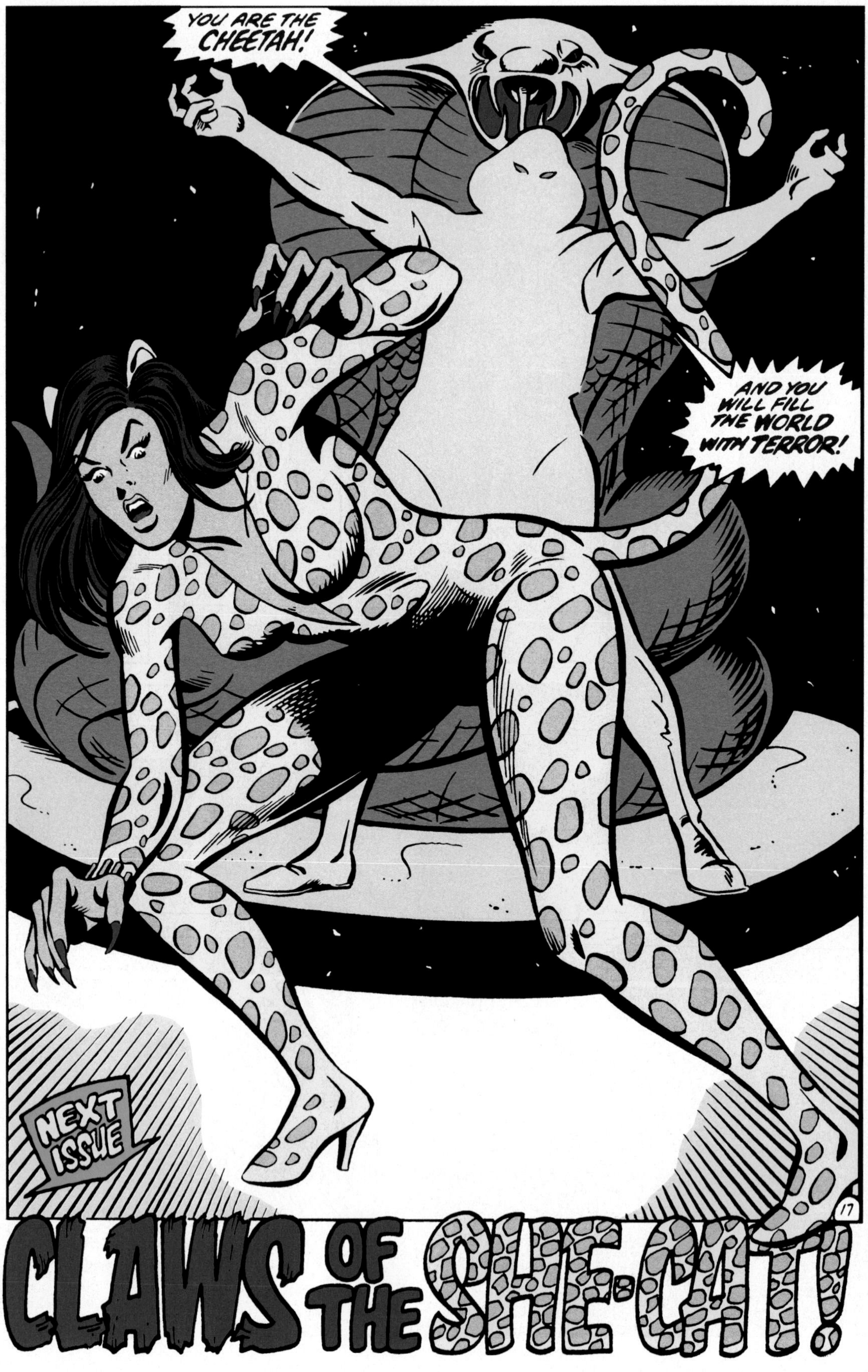
YOU ARE THE CHEETAH!
AND YOU WILL FILL THE WORLD WITH TERROR!
NEXT ISSUE
17
CLAWS OF THE SHE-CAT!

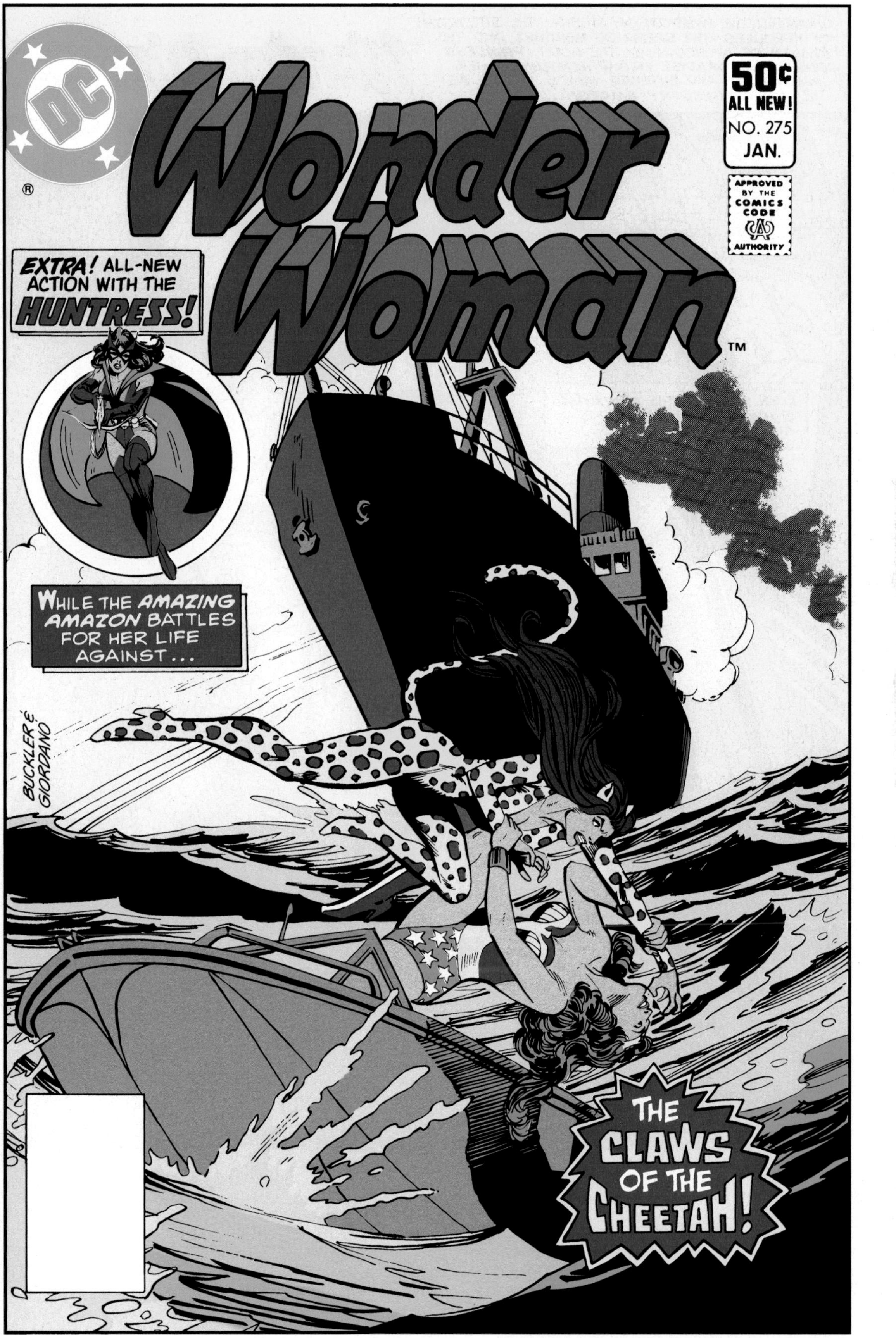
DC
Wonder Woman
50¢
ALL NEW!
NO. 275
JAN.
APPROVED BY THE COMICS CODE AUTHORITY
EXTRA! ALL-NEW ACTION WITH THE HUNTRESS!
WHILE THE AMAZING AMAZON BATTLES FOR HER LIFE AGAINST...
BUCKLER & GIORDANO
THE CLAWS OF THE CHEETAH!

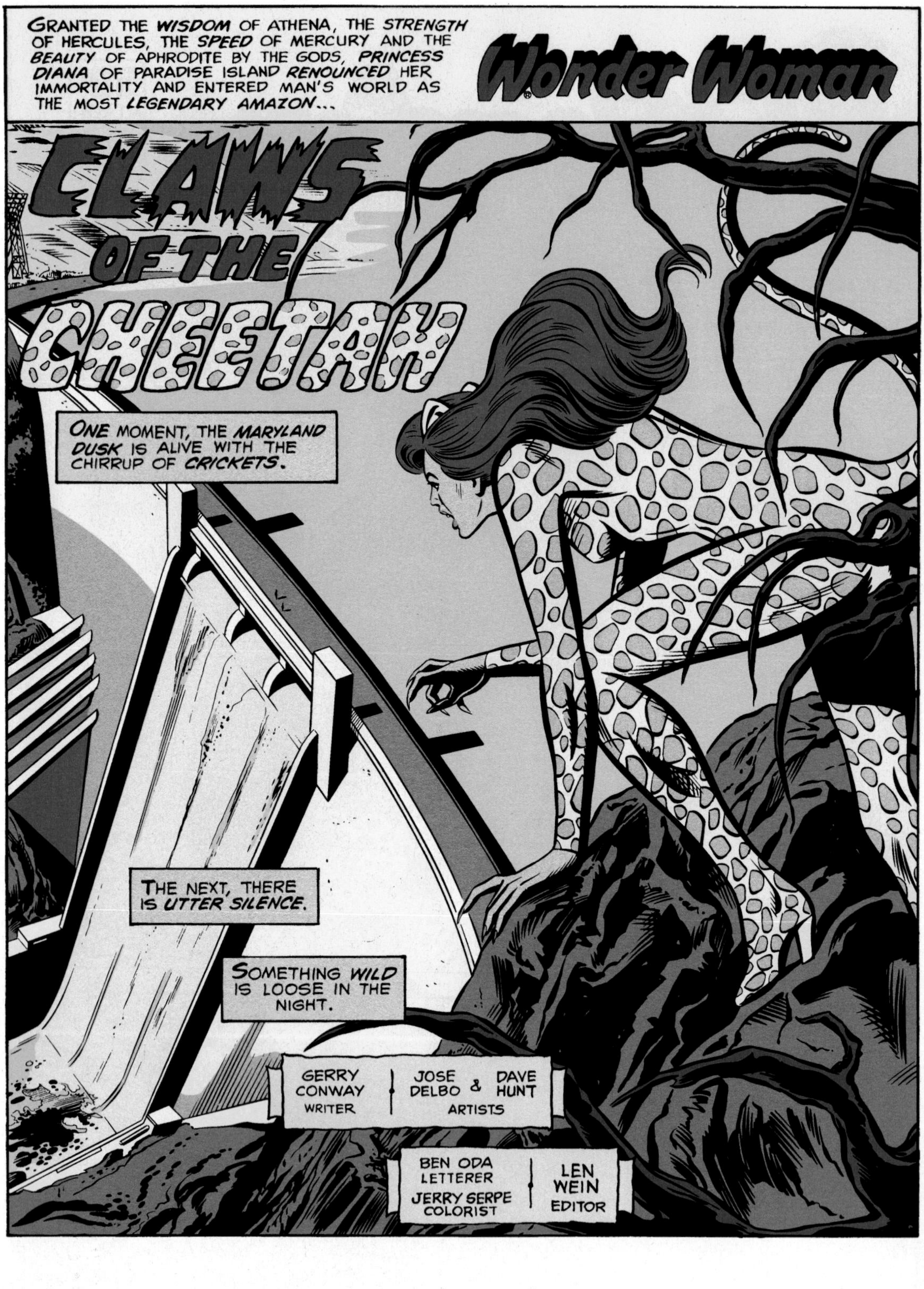
GRANTED THE WISDOM OF ATHENA, THE STRENGTH OF HERCULES, THE SPEED OF MERCURY AND THE BEAUTY OF APHRODITE BY THE GODS, PRINCESS DIANA OF PARADISE ISLAND RENOUNCED HER IMMORTALITY AND ENTERED MAN'S WORLD AS THE MOST LEGENDARY AMAZON...
Wonder Woman
CLAWS OF THE CHEETAH
ONE MOMENT, THE MARYLAND DUSK IS ALIVE WITH THE CHIRRUP OF CRICKETS.
THE NEXT, THERE IS UTTER SILENCE.
SOMETHING WILD IS LOOSE IN THE NIGHT.
GERRY CONWAY WRITER
JOSE DELBO & DAVE HUNT ARTISTS
BEN ODA LETTERER
JERRY SERPE COLORIST
LEN WEIN EDITOR

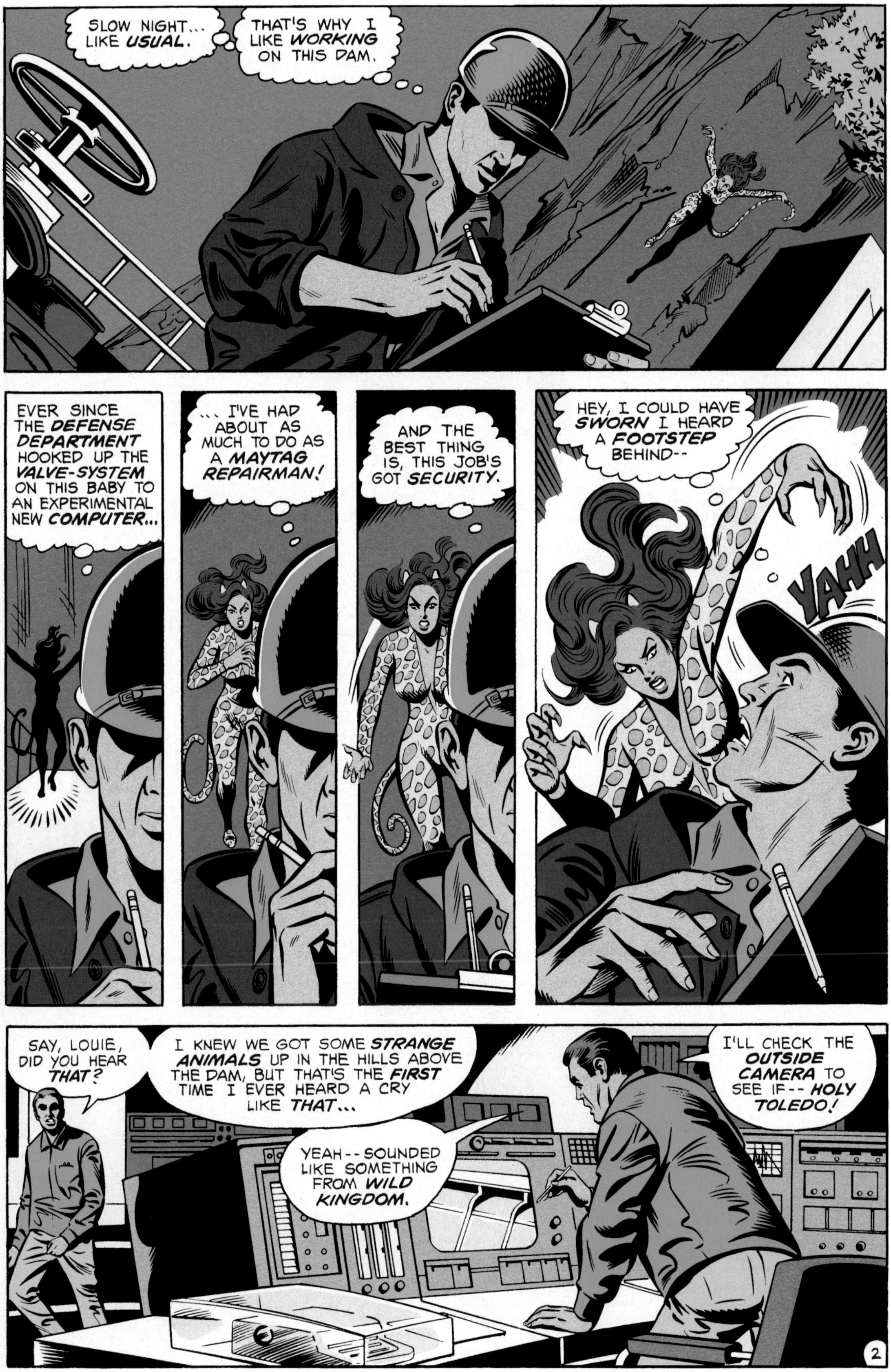
SLOW NIGHT... LIKE USUAL.
THAT'S WHY I LIKE WORKING ON THIS DAM.
EVER SINCE THE DEFENSE DEPARTMENT HOOKED UP THE VALVE-SYSTEM ON THIS BABY TO AN EXPERIMENTAL NEW COMPUTER...
... I'VE HAD ABOUT AS MUCH TO DO AS A MAYTAG REPAIRMAN!
AND THE BEST THING IS, THIS JOB'S GOT SECURITY.
HEY, I COULD HAVE SWORN I HEARD A FOOTSTEP BEHIND--
YAHH
SAY, LOUIE, DID YOU HEAR THAT?
I KNEW WE GOT SOME STRANGE ANIMALS UP IN THE HILLS ABOVE THE DAM, BUT THAT'S THE FIRST TIME I EVER HEARD A CRY LIKE THAT...
YEAH--SOUNDED LIKE SOMETHING FROM WILD KINGDOM.
I'LL CHECK THE OUTSIDE CAMERA TO SEE IF-- HOLY TOLEDO!
2

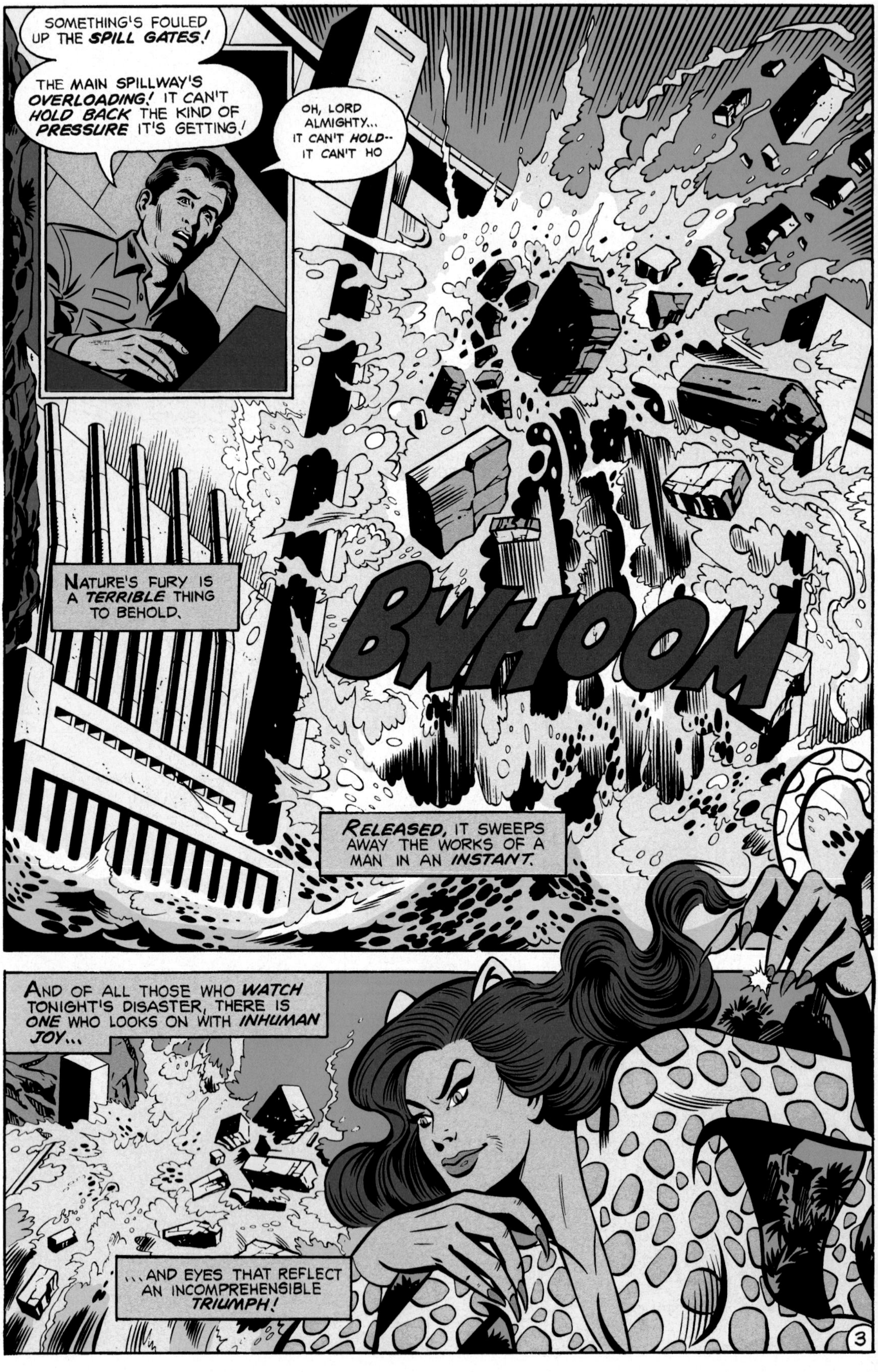
SOMETHING'S FOULED UP THE SPILL GATES!
THE MAIN SPILLWAY'S OVERLOADING! IT CAN'T HOLD BACK THE KIND OF PRESSURE IT'S GETTING!
OH, LORD ALMIGHTY... IT CAN'T HOLD-- IT CAN'T HO
NATURE'S FURY IS A TERRIBLE THING TO BEHOLD.
BWHOOM
RELEASED, IT SWEEPS AWAY THE WORKS OF A MAN IN AN INSTANT.
AND OF ALL THOSE WHO WATCH TONIGHT'S DISASTER, THERE IS ONE WHO LOOKS ON WITH INHUMAN JOY...
...AND EYES THAT REFLECT AN INCOMPREHENSIBLE TRIUMPH!
3

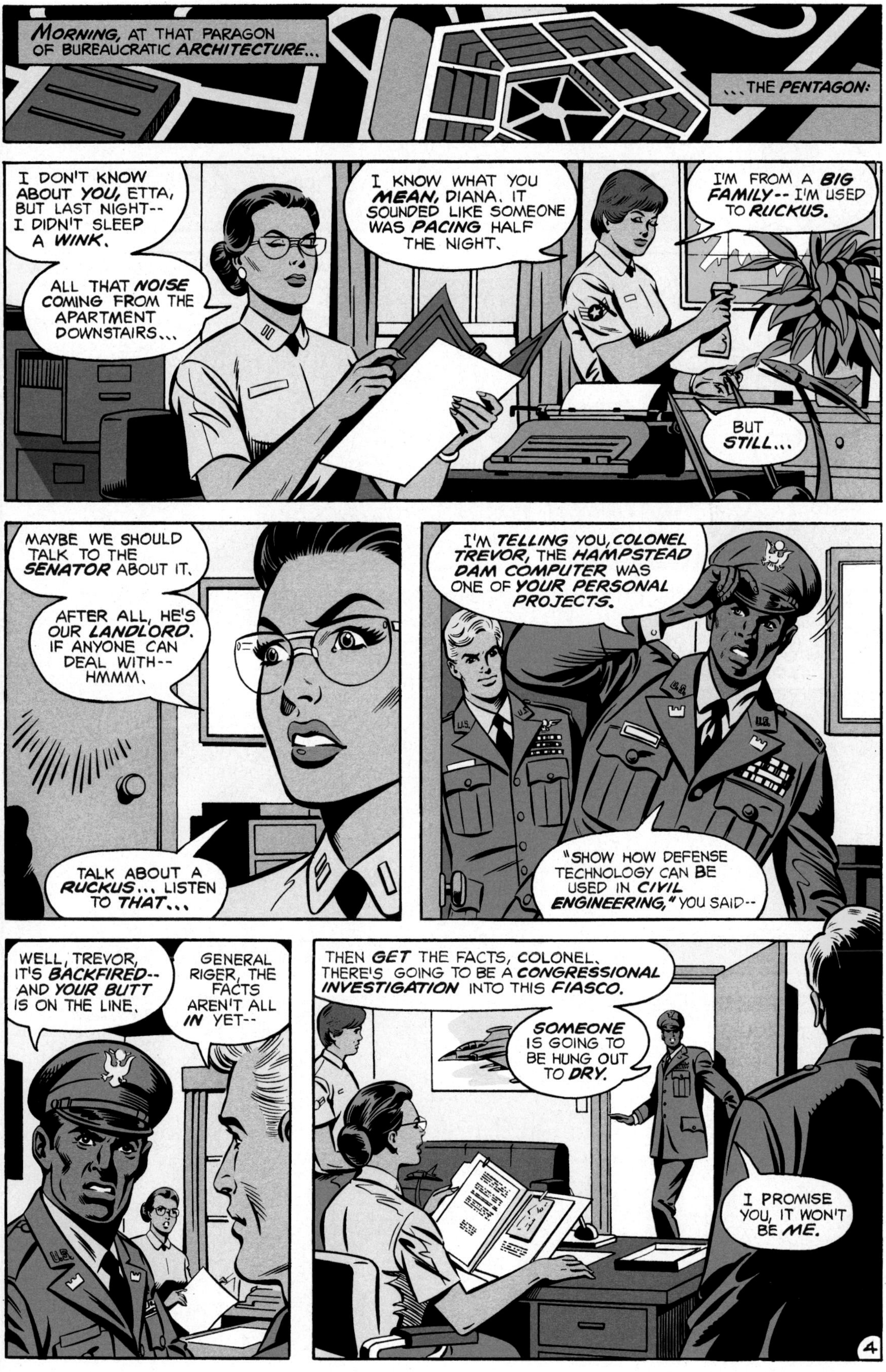
MORNING, AT THAT PARAGON OF BUREAUCRATIC ARCHITECTURE...
...THE PENTAGON:
I DON'T KNOW ABOUT YOU, ETTA, BUT LAST NIGHT-- I DIDN'T SLEEP A WINK.
ALL THAT NOISE COMING FROM THE APARTMENT DOWNSTAIRS...
I KNOW WHAT YOU MEAN, DIANA. IT SOUNDED LIKE SOMEONE WAS PACING HALF THE NIGHT.
I'M FROM A BIG FAMILY-- I'M USED TO RUCKUS.
BUT STILL...
MAYBE WE SHOULD TALK TO THE SENATOR ABOUT IT.
AFTER ALL, HE'S OUR LANDLORD. IF ANYONE CAN DEAL WITH-- HMMM.
TALK ABOUT A RUCKUS... LISTEN TO THAT...
I'M TELLING YOU, COLONEL TREVOR, THE HAMPSTEAD DAM COMPUTER WAS ONE OF YOUR PERSONAL PROJECTS.
"SHOW HOW DEFENSE TECHNOLOGY CAN BE USED IN CIVIL ENGINEERING," YOU SAID--
WELL, TREVOR, IT'S BACKFIRED-- AND YOUR BUTT IS ON THE LINE.
GENERAL RIGER, THE FACTS AREN'T ALL IN YET--
THEN GET THE FACTS, COLONEL. THERE'S GOING TO BE A CONGRESSIONAL INVESTIGATION INTO THIS FIASCO.
SOMEONE IS GOING TO BE HUNG OUT TO DRY.
I PROMISE YOU, IT WON'T BE ME.
4

GENERAL RIGER CERTAINLY LIVES UP TO HIS *REPUTATION* AS A *FIREBRAND*.

MAY I ASK WHAT ALL *THAT* WAS ABOUT, COLONEL?

LIEUTENANT CANDY, *THAT* WAS ABOUT THE *HAMPSTEAD FLOOD*.

THE *WHAT*--?

IT HAPPENED *LAST NIGHT*, A HUNDRED MILES NORTH-WEST OF WASHINGTON.

A *DAM* BURST...

... A DAM USING *DEFENSE DEPARTMENT* TECHNOLOGY, ON *MY* RECOMMENDATION.

RESCUE OPERATIONS ARE STILL BEING CARRIED OUT.

PRINCE, CALL *ANDREWS AIR FORCE BASE*--

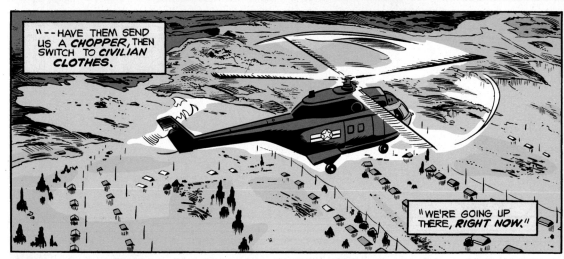

"--HAVE THEM SEND US A *CHOPPER*, THEN SWITCH TO *CIVILIAN CLOTHES*."

"WE'RE GOING UP THERE, *RIGHT NOW*."

...TERRIBLE, SUCH SUFFERING AND *DEVASTATION*.

HOW COULD IT *HAPPEN*?

IT *COULDN'T*, DIANA--UNLESS THERE WAS *SABOTAGE*.

"*SABOTAGE*"-- YOU MEAN, SOMEONE DELIBERATELY *CAUSED* THIS?

5

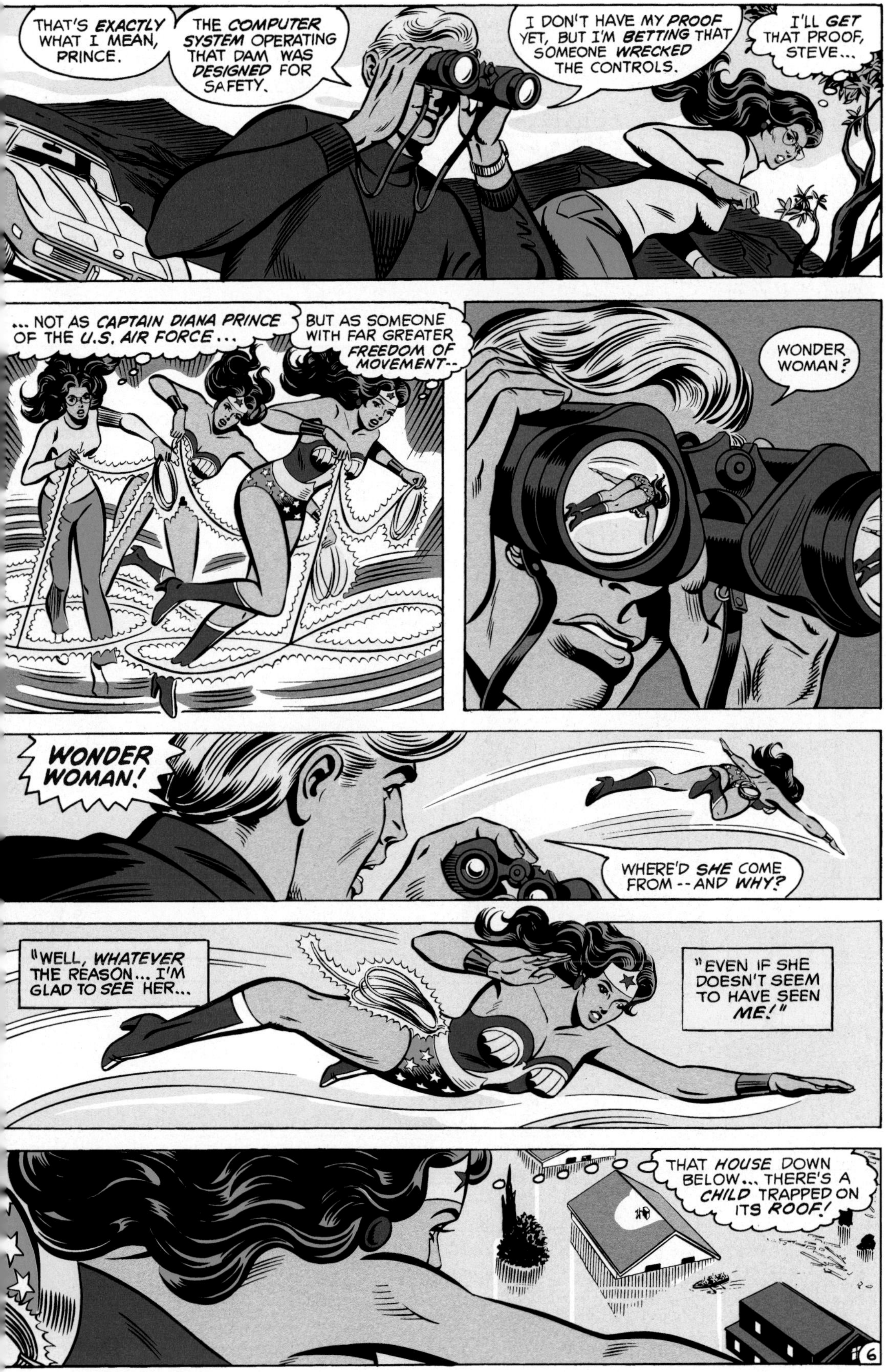
THAT'S EXACTLY WHAT I MEAN, PRINCE.
THE COMPUTER SYSTEM OPERATING THAT DAM WAS DESIGNED FOR SAFETY.
I DON'T HAVE MY PROOF YET, BUT I'M BETTING THAT SOMEONE WRECKED THE CONTROLS.
I'LL GET THAT PROOF, STEVE...
... NOT AS CAPTAIN DIANA PRINCE OF THE U.S. AIR FORCE...
BUT AS SOMEONE WITH FAR GREATER FREEDOM OF MOVEMENT--
WONDER WOMAN?
WONDER WOMAN!
WHERE'D SHE COME FROM -- AND WHY?
"WELL, WHATEVER THE REASON... I'M GLAD TO SEE HER...
"EVEN IF SHE DOESN'T SEEM TO HAVE SEEN ME!"
THAT HOUSE DOWN BELOW... THERE'S A CHILD TRAPPED ON ITS ROOF!
6

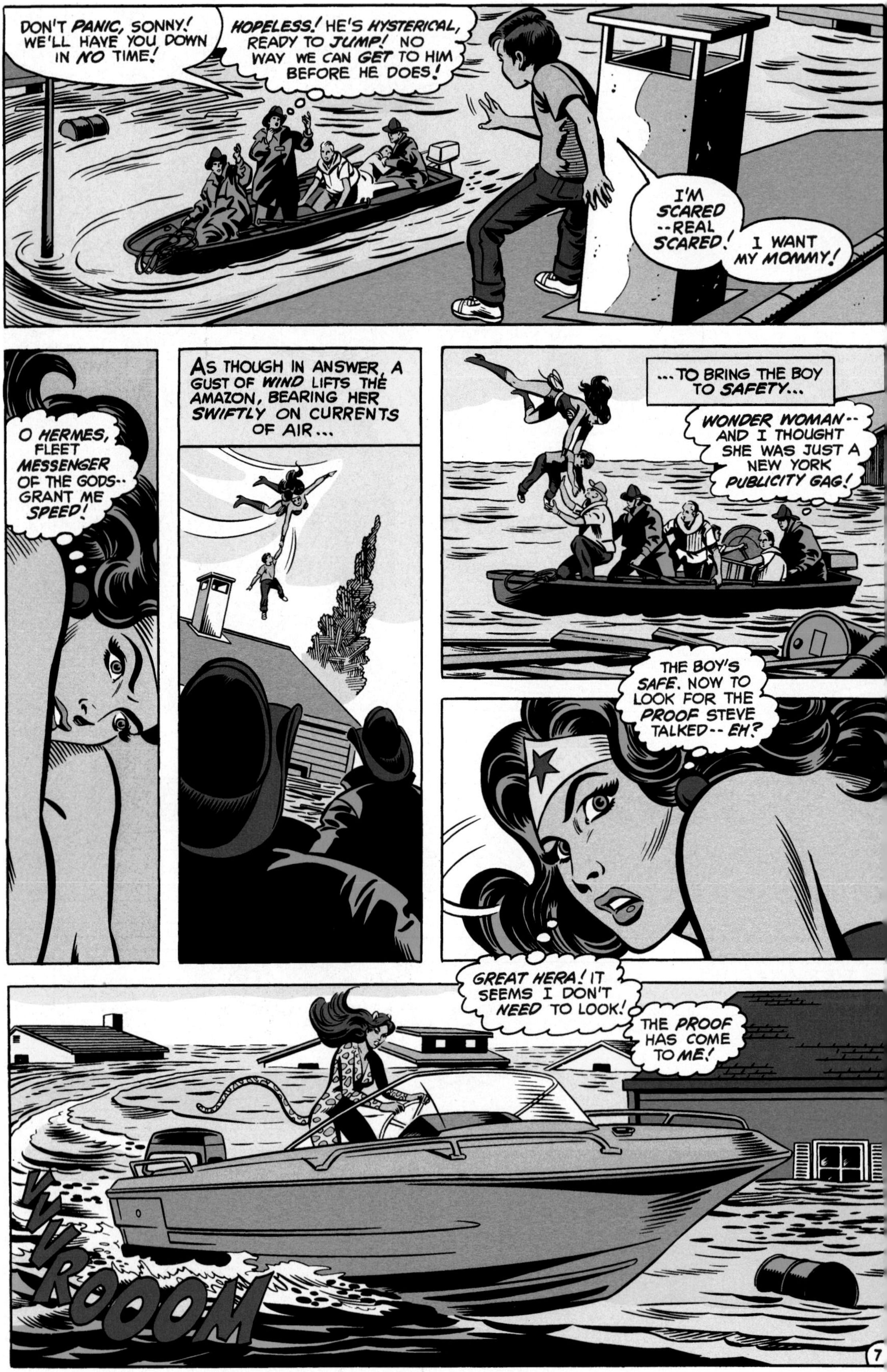

DON'T PANIC, SONNY! WE'LL HAVE YOU DOWN IN NO TIME!
HOPELESS! HE'S HYSTERICAL, READY TO JUMP! NO WAY WE CAN GET TO HIM BEFORE HE DOES!
I'M SCARED --REAL SCARED!
I WANT MY MOMMY!
O HERMES, FLEET MESSENGER OF THE GODS-- GRANT ME SPEED!
AS THOUGH IN ANSWER, A GUST OF WIND LIFTS THE AMAZON, BEARING HER SWIFTLY ON CURRENTS OF AIR...
...TO BRING THE BOY TO SAFETY...
WONDER WOMAN-- AND I THOUGHT SHE WAS JUST A NEW YORK PUBLICITY GAG!
THE BOY'S SAFE. NOW TO LOOK FOR THE PROOF STEVE TALKED-- EH?
GREAT HERA! IT SEEMS I DON'T NEED TO LOOK!
THE PROOF HAS COME TO ME!
VVROOOM
7

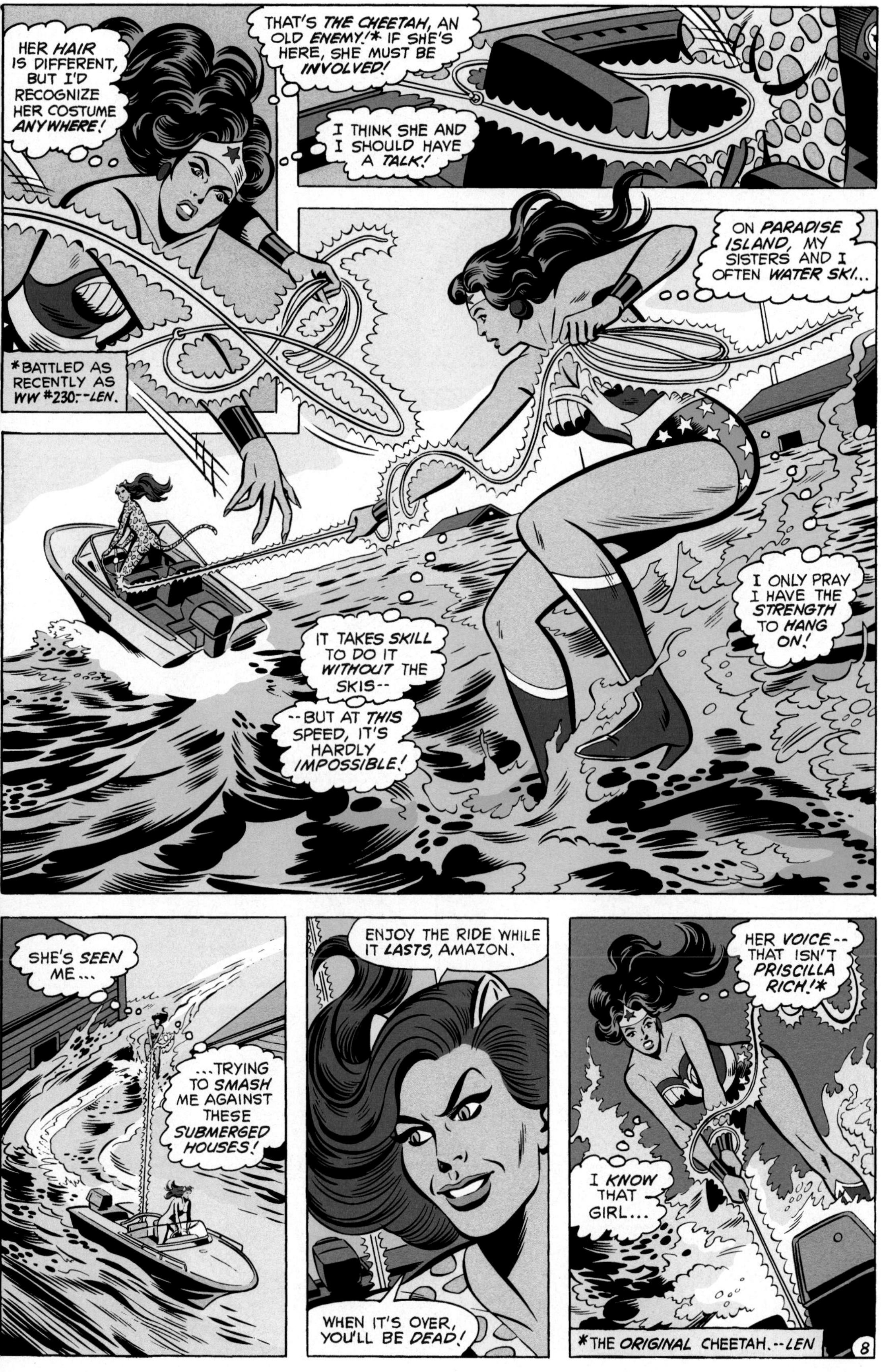
HER HAIR IS DIFFERENT, BUT I'D RECOGNIZE HER COSTUME ANYWHERE!
THAT'S THE CHEETAH, AN OLD ENEMY!* IF SHE'S HERE, SHE MUST BE INVOLVED!
I THINK SHE AND I SHOULD HAVE A TALK!
*BATTLED AS RECENTLY AS WW #230.--LEN.
ON PARADISE ISLAND, MY SISTERS AND I OFTEN WATER SKI...
IT TAKES SKILL TO DO IT WITHOUT THE SKIS--
--BUT AT THIS SPEED, IT'S HARDLY IMPOSSIBLE!
I ONLY PRAY I HAVE THE STRENGTH TO HANG ON!
SHE'S SEEN ME...
...TRYING TO SMASH ME AGAINST THESE SUBMERGED HOUSES!
ENJOY THE RIDE WHILE IT LASTS, AMAZON.
WHEN IT'S OVER, YOU'LL BE DEAD!
HER VOICE--THAT ISN'T PRISCILLA RICH!*
I KNOW THAT GIRL...
*THE ORIGINAL CHEETAH.--LEN
8

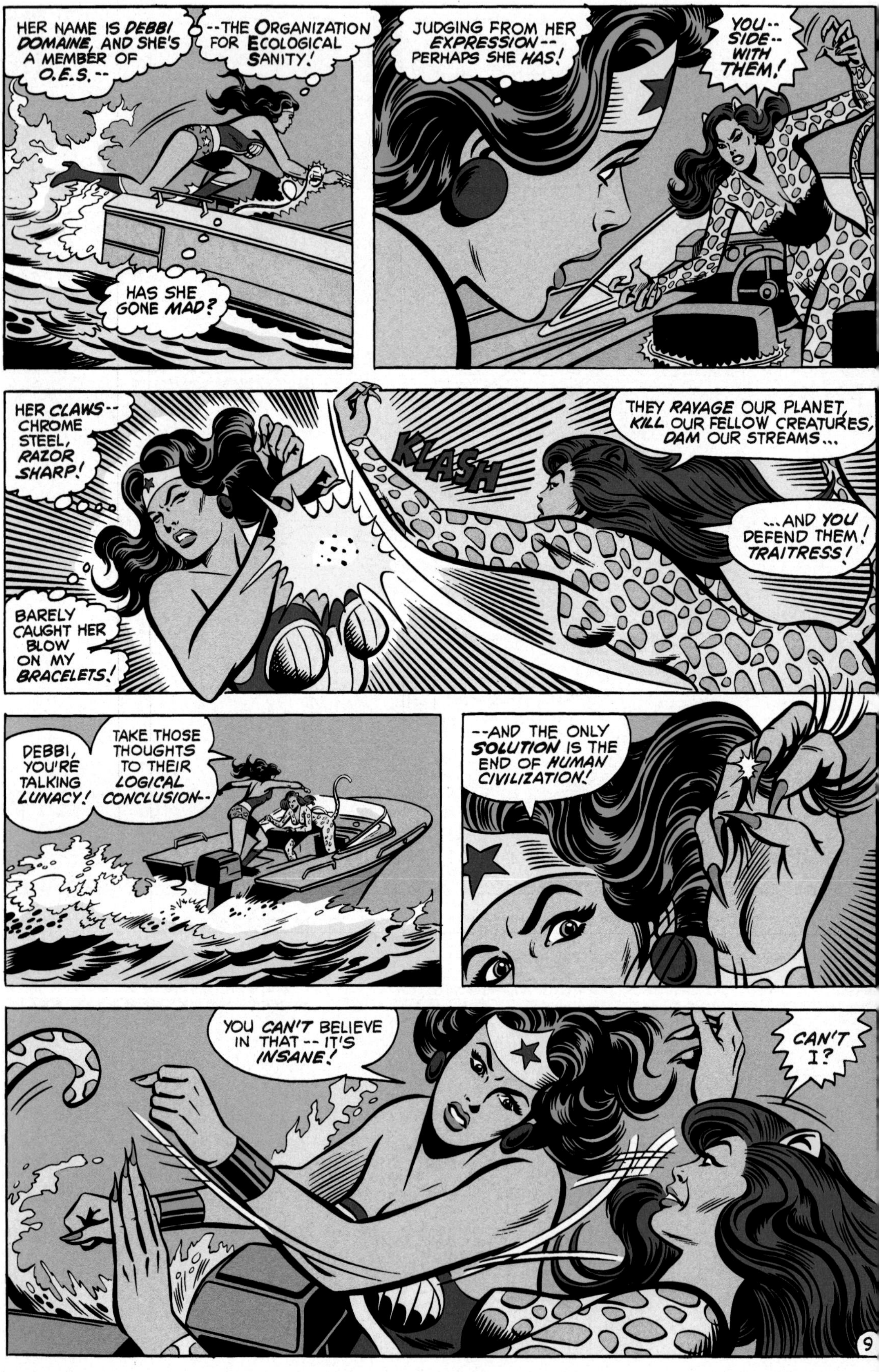
HER NAME IS DEBBI DOMAINE, AND SHE'S A MEMBER OF O.E.S.--
--THE ORGANIZATION FOR ECOLOGICAL SANITY!
HAS SHE GONE MAD?
JUDGING FROM HER EXPRESSION-- PERHAPS SHE HAS!
YOU-- SIDE-- WITH THEM!
HER CLAWS-- CHROME STEEL, RAZOR SHARP!
KLASH
THEY RAVAGE OUR PLANET, KILL OUR FELLOW CREATURES, DAM OUR STREAMS...
...AND YOU DEFEND THEM! TRAITRESS!
BARELY CAUGHT HER BLOW ON MY BRACELETS!
DEBBI, YOU'RE TALKING LUNACY!
TAKE THOSE THOUGHTS TO THEIR LOGICAL CONCLUSION--
--AND THE ONLY SOLUTION IS THE END OF HUMAN CIVILIZATION!
YOU CAN'T BELIEVE IN THAT -- IT'S INSANE!
CAN'T I?
9

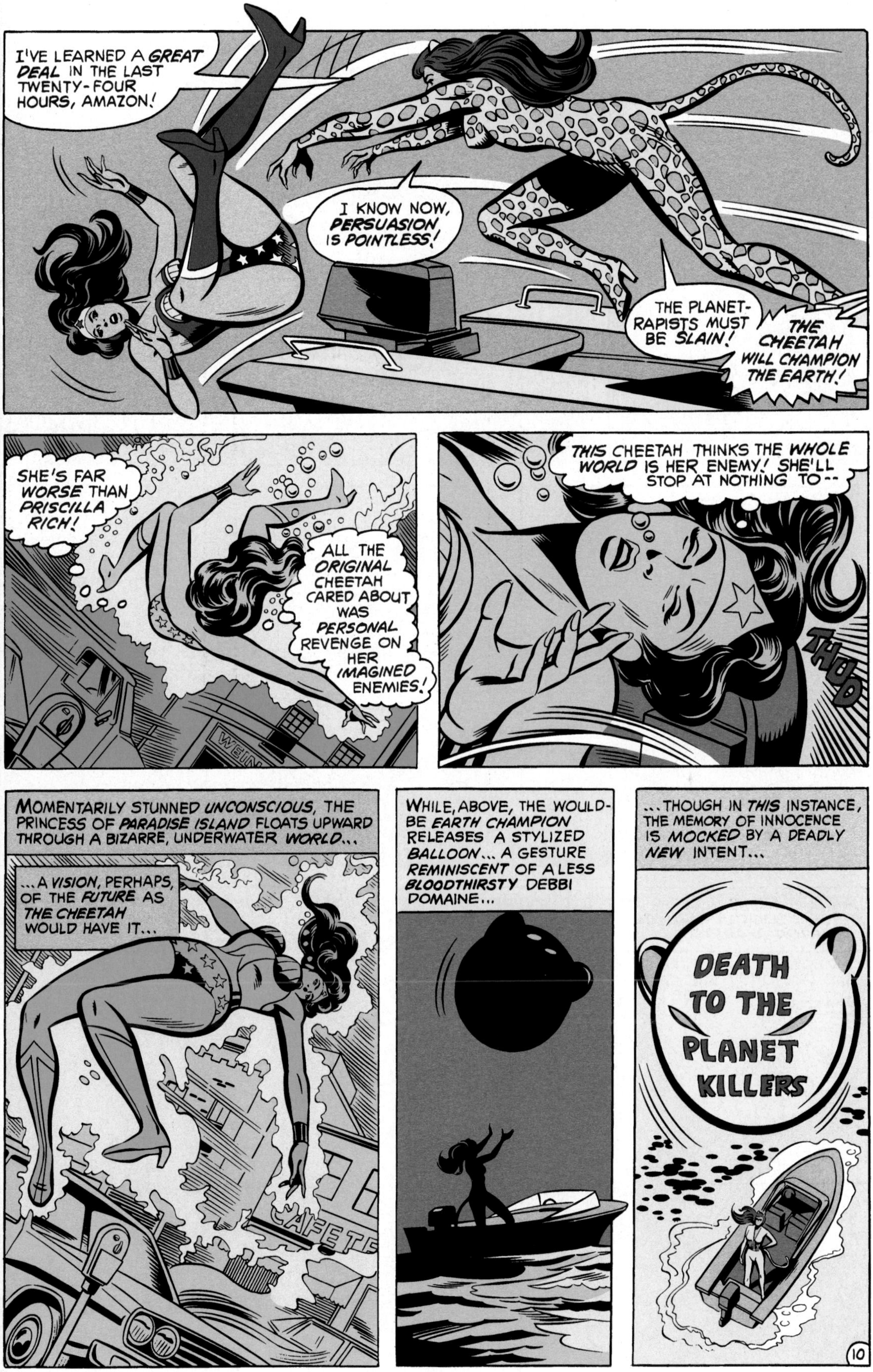
I'VE LEARNED A GREAT DEAL IN THE LAST TWENTY-FOUR HOURS, AMAZON!
I KNOW NOW, PERSUASION IS POINTLESS!
THE PLANET-RAPISTS MUST BE SLAIN!
THE CHEETAH WILL CHAMPION THE EARTH!
SHE'S FAR WORSE THAN PRISCILLA RICH!
ALL THE ORIGINAL CHEETAH CARED ABOUT WAS PERSONAL REVENGE ON HER IMAGINED ENEMIES!
THIS CHEETAH THINKS THE WHOLE WORLD IS HER ENEMY! SHE'LL STOP AT NOTHING TO--
THUD
MOMENTARILY STUNNED UNCONSCIOUS, THE PRINCESS OF PARADISE ISLAND FLOATS UPWARD THROUGH A BIZARRE, UNDERWATER WORLD...
...A VISION, PERHAPS, OF THE FUTURE AS THE CHEETAH WOULD HAVE IT...
CAFETE
WHILE, ABOVE, THE WOULD-BE EARTH CHAMPION RELEASES A STYLIZED BALLOON... A GESTURE REMINISCENT OF A LESS BLOODTHIRSTY DEBBI DOMAINE...
...THOUGH IN THIS INSTANCE, THE MEMORY OF INNOCENCE IS MOCKED BY A DEADLY NEW INTENT...
DEATH TO THE PLANET KILLERS
10

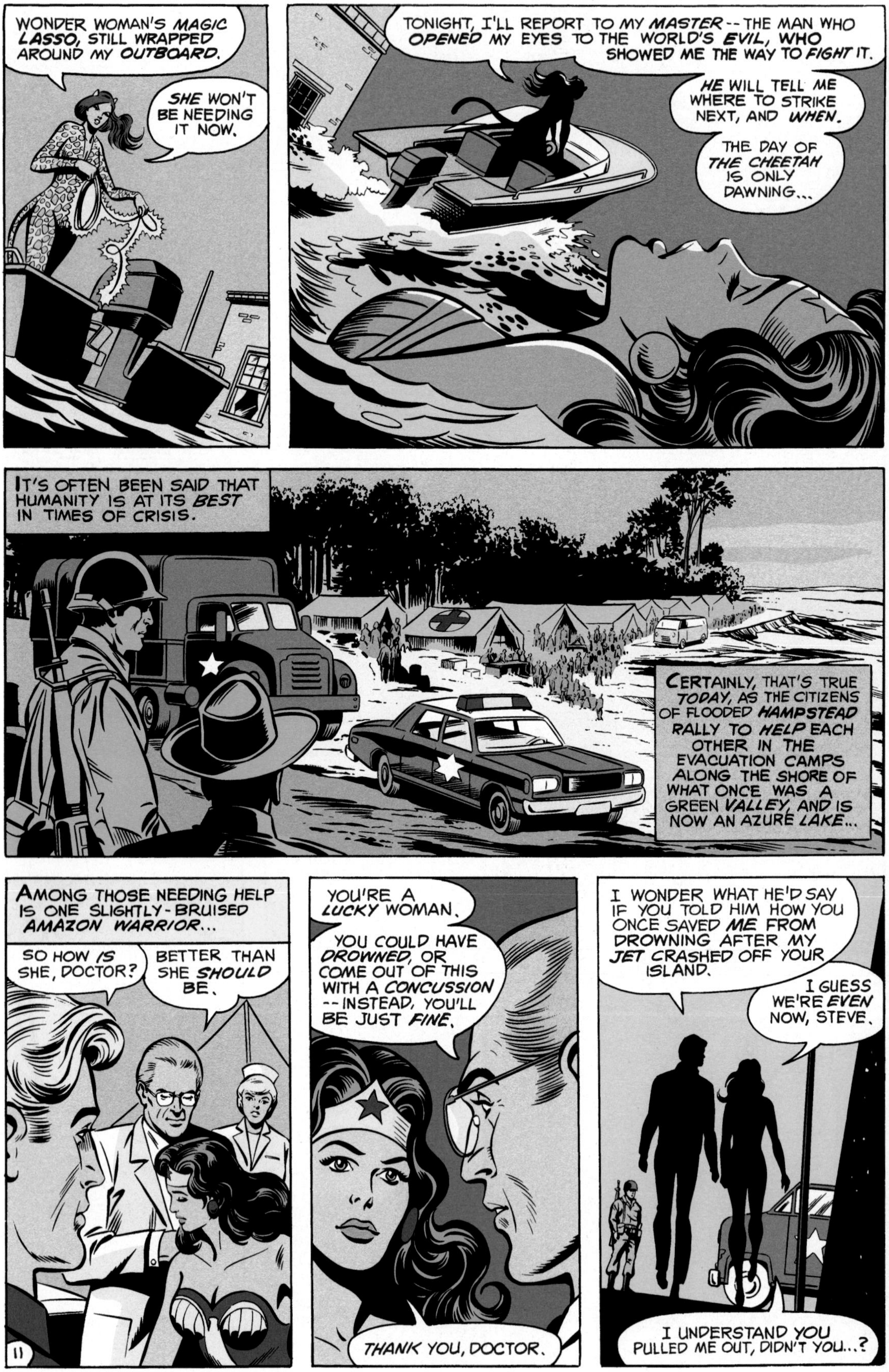

WONDER WOMAN'S MAGIC LASSO, STILL WRAPPED AROUND MY OUTBOARD.
SHE WON'T BE NEEDING IT NOW.
TONIGHT, I'LL REPORT TO MY MASTER -- THE MAN WHO OPENED MY EYES TO THE WORLD'S EVIL, WHO SHOWED ME THE WAY TO FIGHT IT.
HE WILL TELL ME WHERE TO STRIKE NEXT, AND WHEN.
THE DAY OF THE CHEETAH IS ONLY DAWNING...
IT'S OFTEN BEEN SAID THAT HUMANITY IS AT ITS BEST IN TIMES OF CRISIS.
CERTAINLY, THAT'S TRUE TODAY, AS THE CITIZENS OF FLOODED HAMPSTEAD RALLY TO HELP EACH OTHER IN THE EVACUATION CAMPS ALONG THE SHORE OF WHAT ONCE WAS A GREEN VALLEY, AND IS NOW AN AZURE LAKE...
AMONG THOSE NEEDING HELP IS ONE SLIGHTLY-BRUISED AMAZON WARRIOR...
SO HOW IS SHE, DOCTOR?
BETTER THAN SHE SHOULD BE.
11
YOU'RE A LUCKY WOMAN.
YOU COULD HAVE DROWNED, OR COME OUT OF THIS WITH A CONCUSSION -- INSTEAD, YOU'LL BE JUST FINE.
THANK YOU, DOCTOR.
I WONDER WHAT HE'D SAY IF YOU TOLD HIM HOW YOU ONCE SAVED ME FROM DROWNING AFTER MY JET CRASHED OFF YOUR ISLAND.
I GUESS WE'RE EVEN NOW, STEVE.
I UNDERSTAND YOU PULLED ME OUT, DIDN'T YOU...?

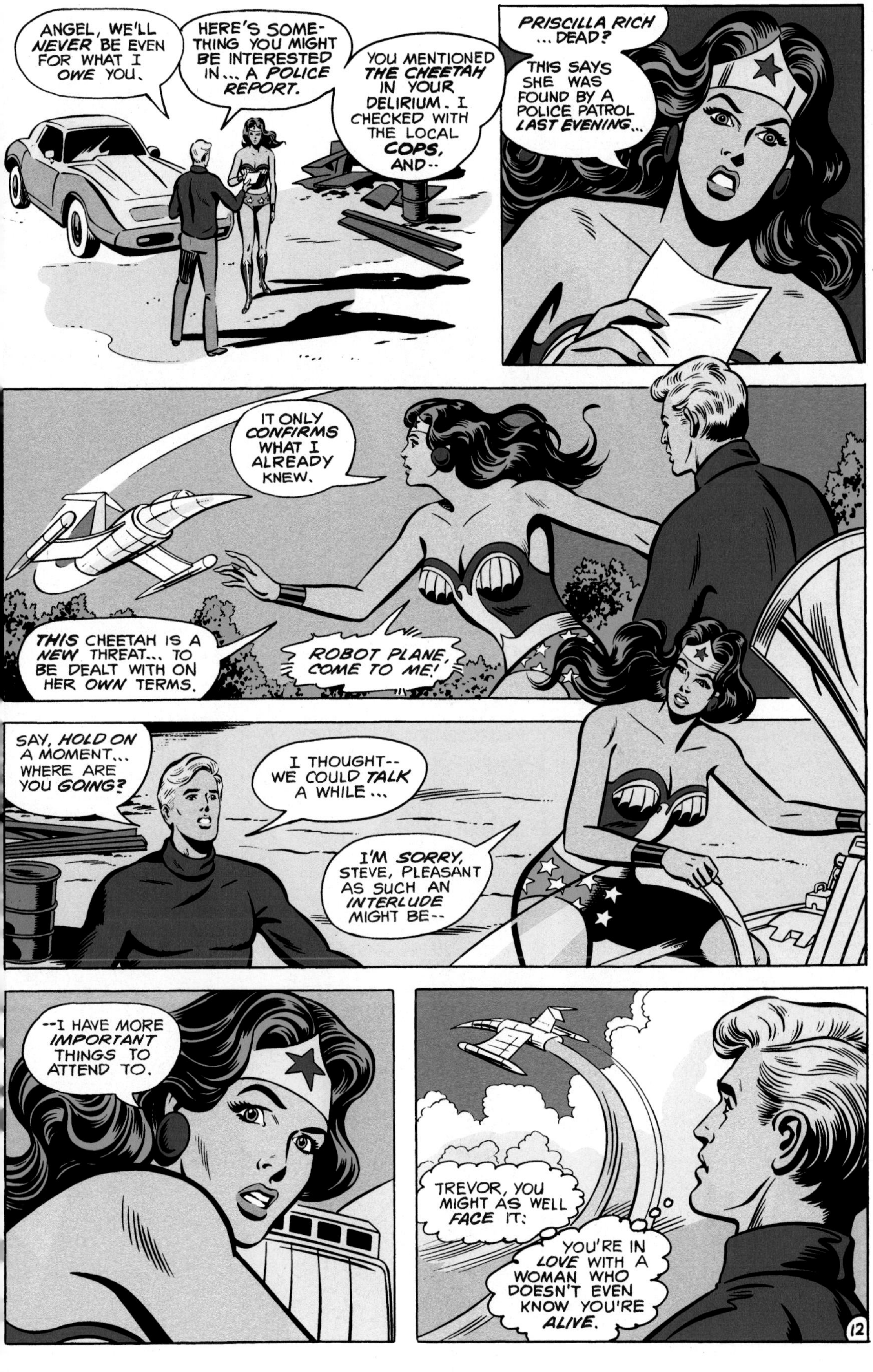
ANGEL, WE'LL NEVER BE EVEN FOR WHAT I OWE YOU.
HERE'S SOMETHING YOU MIGHT BE INTERESTED IN... A POLICE REPORT.
YOU MENTIONED THE CHEETAH IN YOUR DELIRIUM. I CHECKED WITH THE LOCAL COPS, AND--
PRISCILLA RICH ...DEAD?
THIS SAYS SHE WAS FOUND BY A POLICE PATROL LAST EVENING...
IT ONLY CONFIRMS WHAT I ALREADY KNEW.
THIS CHEETAH IS A NEW THREAT... TO BE DEALT WITH ON HER OWN TERMS.
ROBOT PLANE, COME TO ME!
SAY, HOLD ON A MOMENT... WHERE ARE YOU GOING?
I THOUGHT-- WE COULD TALK A WHILE...
I'M SORRY, STEVE, PLEASANT AS SUCH AN INTERLUDE MIGHT BE--
--I HAVE MORE IMPORTANT THINGS TO ATTEND TO.
TREVOR, YOU MIGHT AS WELL FACE IT:
YOU'RE IN LOVE WITH A WOMAN WHO DOESN'T EVEN KNOW YOU'RE ALIVE.
12

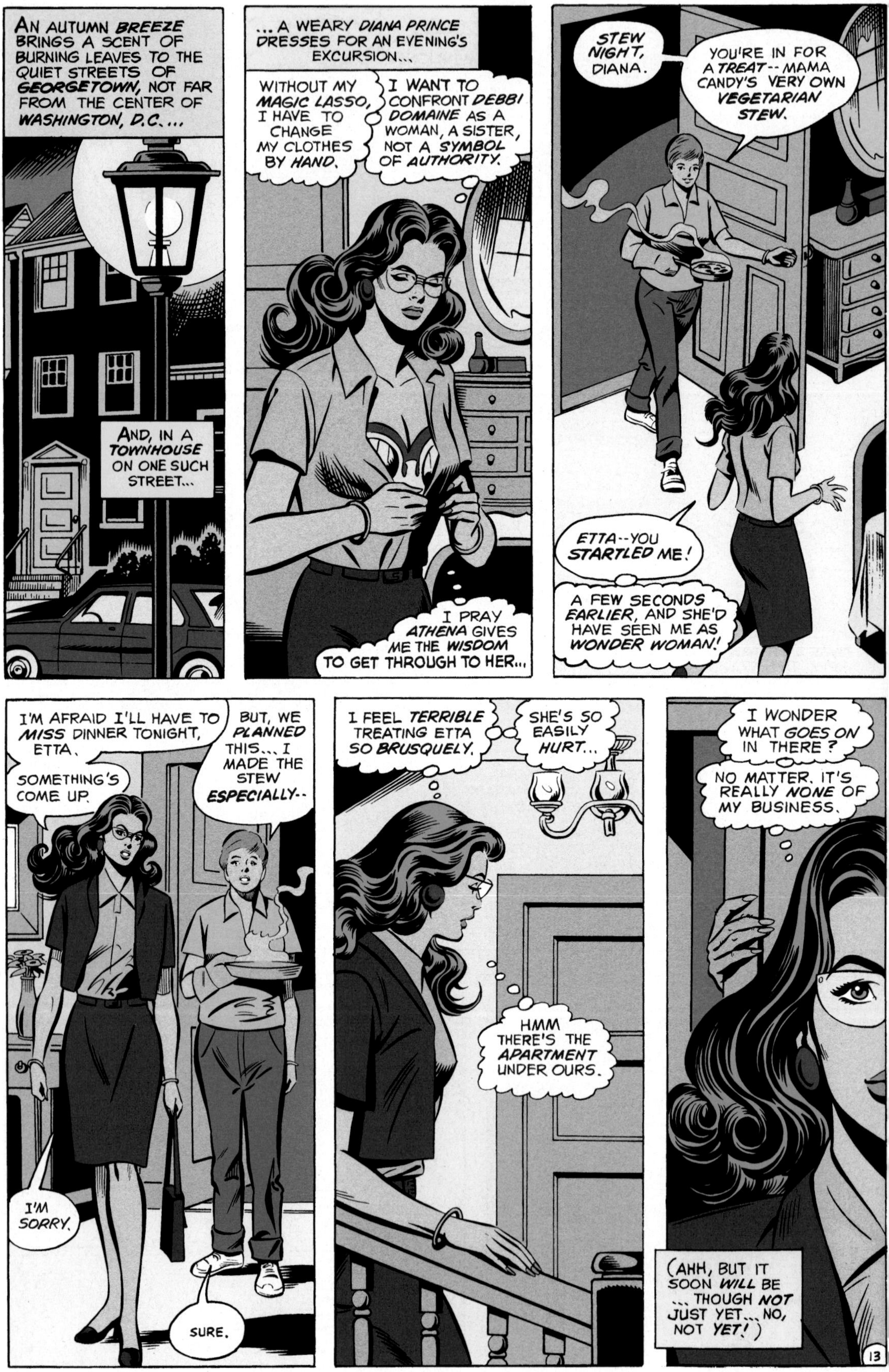
AN AUTUMN BREEZE BRINGS A SCENT OF BURNING LEAVES TO THE QUIET STREETS OF GEORGETOWN, NOT FAR FROM THE CENTER OF WASHINGTON, D.C....
AND, IN A TOWNHOUSE ON ONE SUCH STREET...
...A WEARY DIANA PRINCE DRESSES FOR AN EVENING'S EXCURSION...
WITHOUT MY MAGIC LASSO, I HAVE TO CHANGE MY CLOTHES BY HAND.
I WANT TO CONFRONT DEBBI DOMAINE AS A WOMAN, A SISTER, NOT A SYMBOL OF AUTHORITY.
I PRAY ATHENA GIVES ME THE WISDOM TO GET THROUGH TO HER...
STEW NIGHT, DIANA.
YOU'RE IN FOR A TREAT-- MAMA CANDY'S VERY OWN VEGETARIAN STEW.
ETTA--YOU STARTLED ME!
A FEW SECONDS EARLIER, AND SHE'D HAVE SEEN ME AS WONDER WOMAN!
I'M AFRAID I'LL HAVE TO MISS DINNER TONIGHT, ETTA.
SOMETHING'S COME UP.
BUT, WE PLANNED THIS... I MADE THE STEW ESPECIALLY--
I'M SORRY.
SURE.
I FEEL TERRIBLE TREATING ETTA SO BRUSQUELY.
SHE'S SO EASILY HURT...
HMM THERE'S THE APARTMENT UNDER OURS.
I WONDER WHAT GOES ON IN THERE?
NO MATTER. IT'S REALLY NONE OF MY BUSINESS.
(AHH, BUT IT SOON WILL BE ... THOUGH NOT JUST YET... NO, NOT YET!)
13

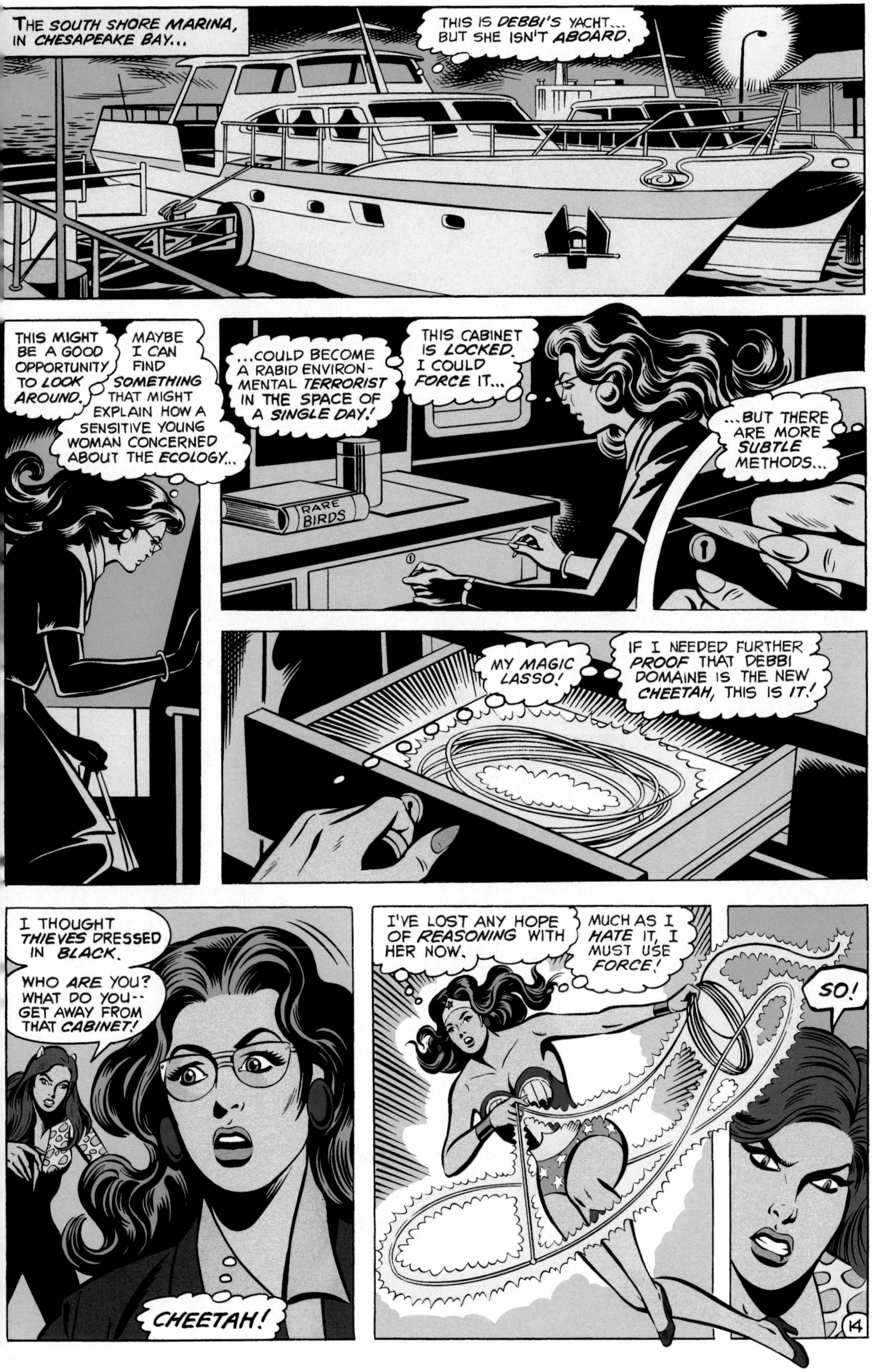
THE SOUTH SHORE MARINA, IN CHESAPEAKE BAY...
THIS IS DEBBI'S YACHT... BUT SHE ISN'T ABOARD.
THIS MIGHT BE A GOOD OPPORTUNITY TO LOOK AROUND.
MAYBE I CAN FIND SOMETHING THAT MIGHT EXPLAIN HOW A SENSITIVE YOUNG WOMAN CONCERNED ABOUT THE ECOLOGY...
...COULD BECOME A RABID ENVIRONMENTAL TERRORIST IN THE SPACE OF A SINGLE DAY!
THIS CABINET IS LOCKED. I COULD FORCE IT...
...BUT THERE ARE MORE SUBTLE METHODS...
RARE BIRDS
MY MAGIC LASSO!
IF I NEEDED FURTHER PROOF THAT DEBBI DOMAINE IS THE NEW CHEETAH, THIS IS IT!
I THOUGHT THIEVES DRESSED IN BLACK.
WHO ARE YOU? WHAT DO YOU-- GET AWAY FROM THAT CABINET!
CHEETAH!
I'VE LOST ANY HOPE OF REASONING WITH HER NOW.
MUCH AS I HATE IT, I MUST USE FORCE!
SO!
14

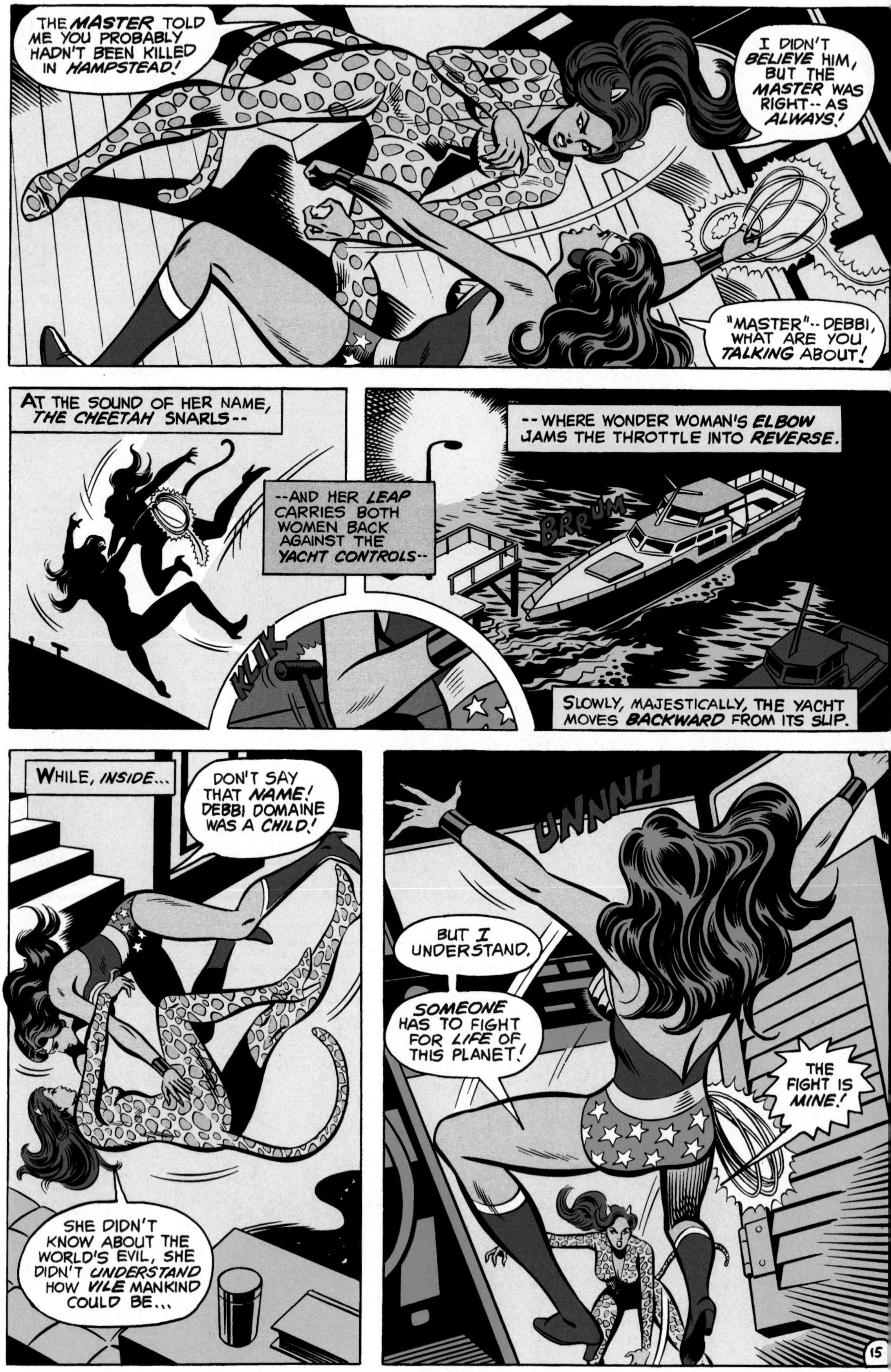
THE MASTER TOLD ME YOU PROBABLY HADN'T BEEN KILLED IN HAMPSTEAD!
I DIDN'T BELIEVE HIM, BUT THE MASTER WAS RIGHT-- AS ALWAYS!
"MASTER"-- DEBBI, WHAT ARE YOU TALKING ABOUT!
AT THE SOUND OF HER NAME, THE CHEETAH SNARLS--
--AND HER LEAP CARRIES BOTH WOMEN BACK AGAINST THE YACHT CONTROLS--
KLIK
--WHERE WONDER WOMAN'S ELBOW JAMS THE THROTTLE INTO REVERSE.
BRRUM
SLOWLY, MAJESTICALLY, THE YACHT MOVES BACKWARD FROM ITS SLIP.
WHILE, INSIDE...
DON'T SAY THAT NAME! DEBBI DOMAINE WAS A CHILD!
SHE DIDN'T KNOW ABOUT THE WORLD'S EVIL, SHE DIDN'T UNDERSTAND HOW VILE MANKIND COULD BE...
UNNNH
BUT I UNDERSTAND.
SOMEONE HAS TO FIGHT FOR LIFE OF THIS PLANET!
THE FIGHT IS MINE!
15

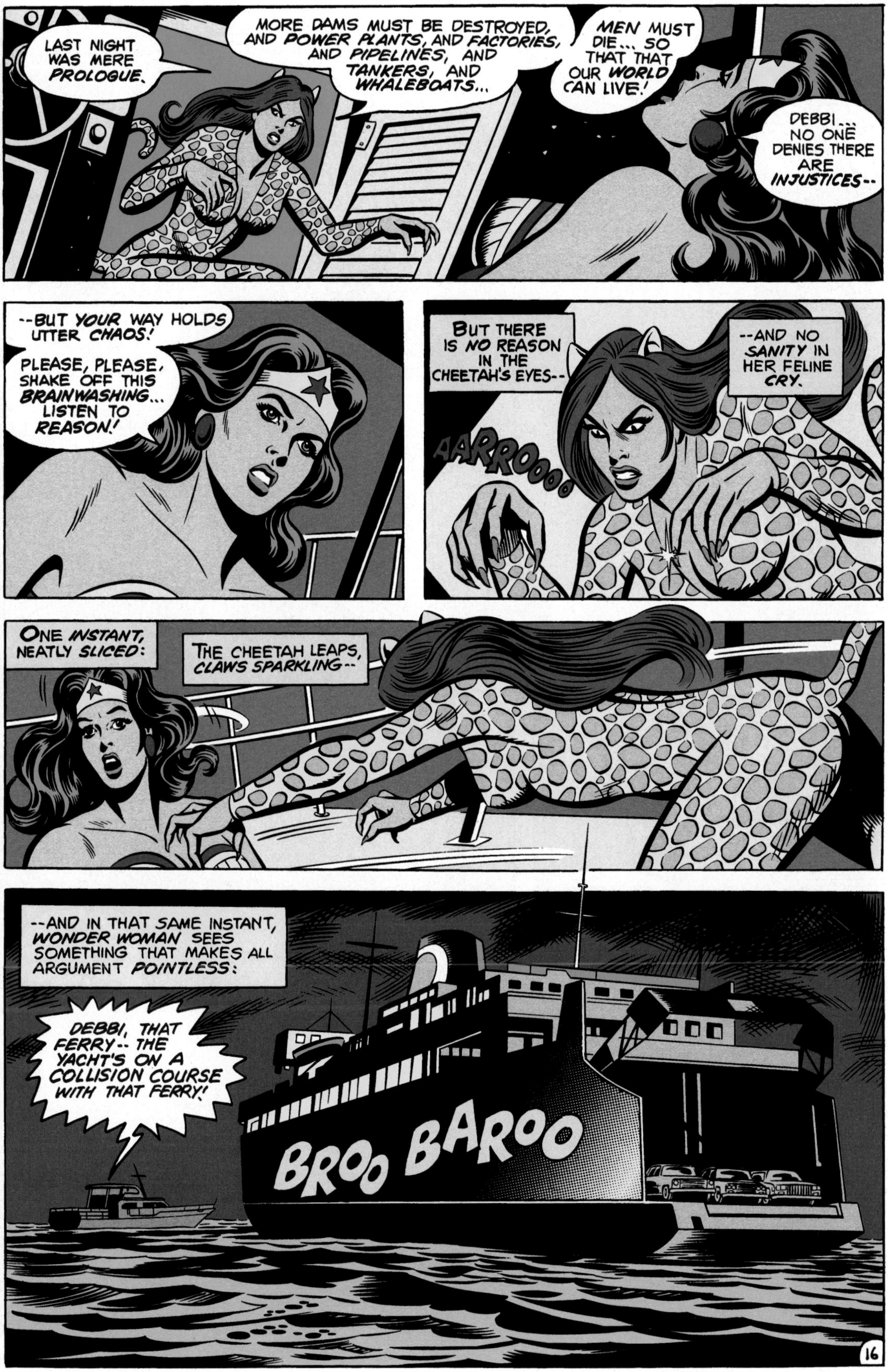
LAST NIGHT WAS MERE PROLOGUE.
MORE DAMS MUST BE DESTROYED, AND POWER PLANTS, AND FACTORIES, AND PIPELINES, AND TANKERS, AND WHALEBOATS...
MEN MUST DIE... SO THAT THAT OUR WORLD CAN LIVE!
DEBBI... NO ONE DENIES THERE ARE INJUSTICES--
--BUT YOUR WAY HOLDS UTTER CHAOS!
PLEASE, PLEASE, SHAKE OFF THIS BRAINWASHING... LISTEN TO REASON!
BUT THERE IS NO REASON IN THE CHEETAH'S EYES--
--AND NO SANITY IN HER FELINE CRY.
AARROOOO
ONE INSTANT, NEATLY SLICED:
THE CHEETAH LEAPS, CLAWS SPARKLING--
--AND IN THAT SAME INSTANT, WONDER WOMAN SEES SOMETHING THAT MAKES ALL ARGUMENT POINTLESS:
DEBBI, THAT FERRY-- THE YACHT'S ON A COLLISION COURSE WITH THAT FERRY!
BROO BAROO
16

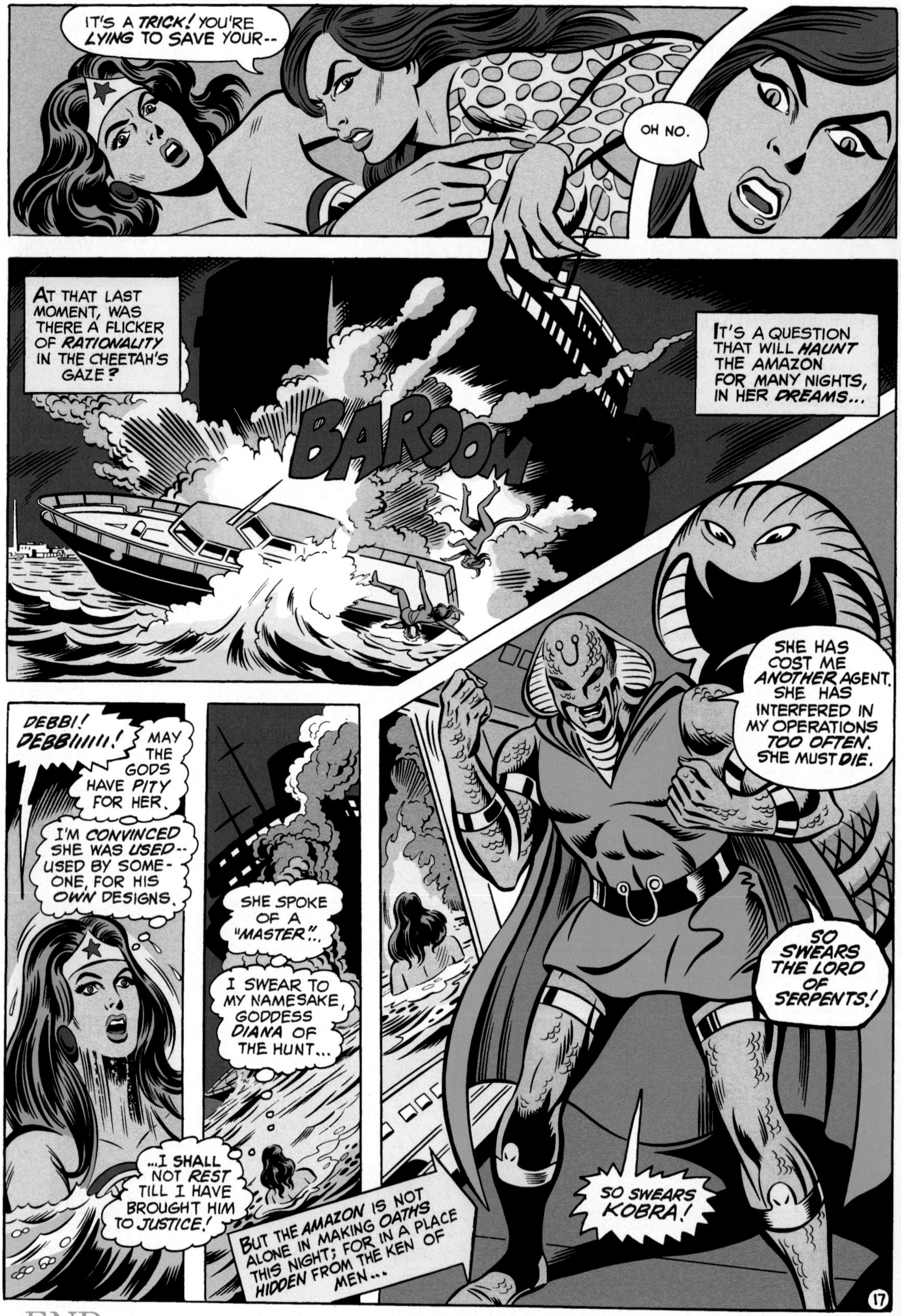
IT'S A TRICK! YOU'RE LYING TO SAVE YOUR--
OH NO.
AT THAT LAST MOMENT, WAS THERE A FLICKER OF RATIONALITY IN THE CHEETAH'S GAZE?
BAROOM
IT'S A QUESTION THAT WILL HAUNT THE AMAZON FOR MANY NIGHTS, IN HER DREAMS...
DEBBI! DEBBI!!!!!!!
MAY THE GODS HAVE PITY FOR HER.
I'M CONVINCED SHE WAS USED-- USED BY SOMEONE, FOR HIS OWN DESIGNS.
SHE SPOKE OF A "MASTER"...
I SWEAR TO MY NAMESAKE, GODDESS DIANA OF THE HUNT...
...I SHALL NOT REST TILL I HAVE BROUGHT HIM TO JUSTICE!
BUT THE AMAZON IS NOT ALONE IN MAKING OATHS THIS NIGHT; FOR IN A PLACE HIDDEN FROM THE KEN OF MEN...
SHE HAS COST ME ANOTHER AGENT. SHE HAS INTERFERED IN MY OPERATIONS TOO OFTEN. SHE MUST DIE.
SO SWEARS THE LORD OF SERPENTS!
SO SWEARS KOBRA!
17

END

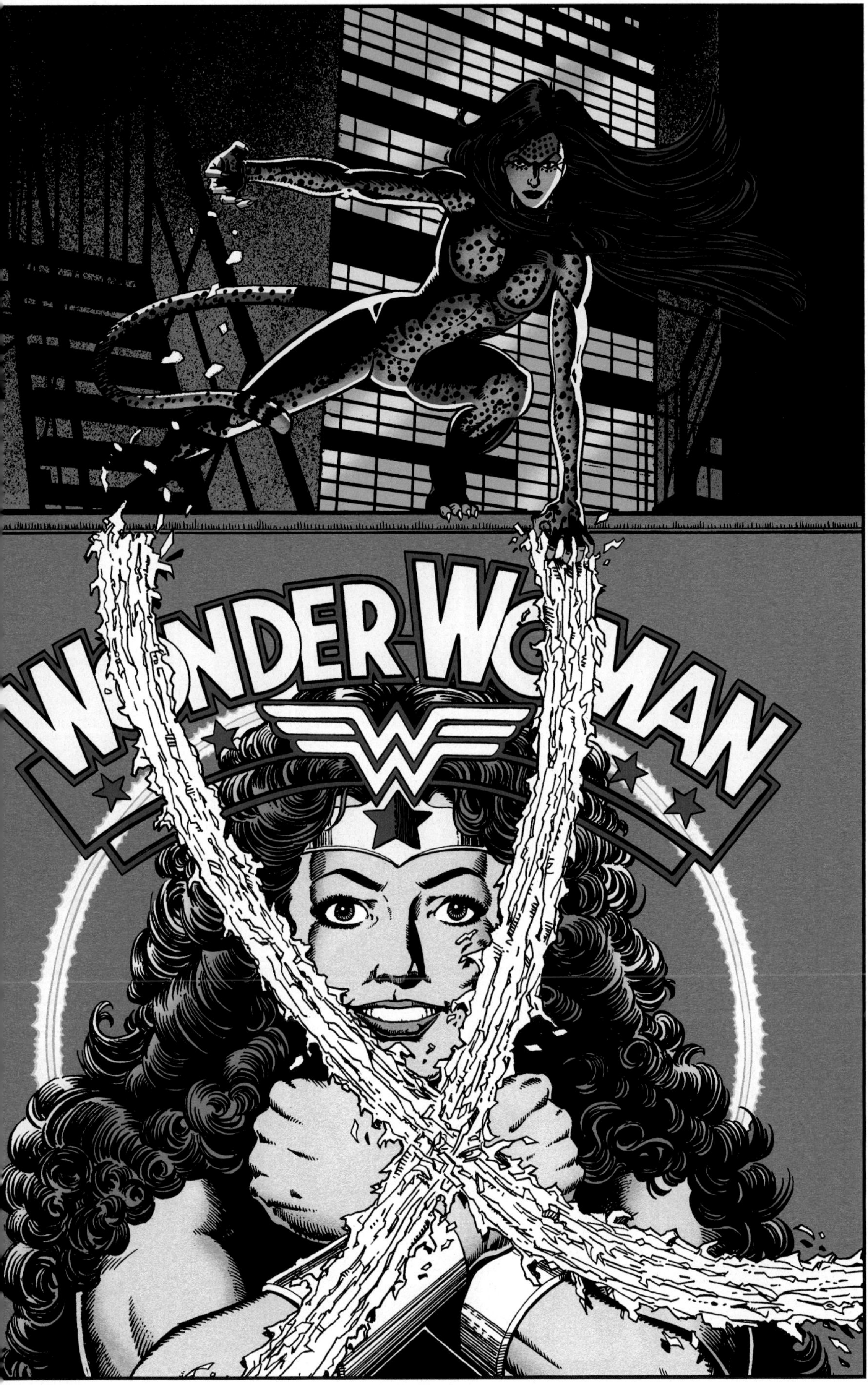

LISTEN! CAN YOU HEAR IT?

ABOVE THE RUMBLE OF THE TRAFFIC AND THE NEON'S CRACKLING HUM?

THERE ARE DRUMS IN THE NIGHT!

AND, TO THE RHYTHM OF THE DRUMS, THERE IS CHANTING!

THE OLD MAN STANDS ON THE BALCONY, HIS WEATHERED FACE AWASH WITH MOONLIGHT--

--AND RAZORED DEATH GLEAMS BRIGHTLY IN HIS HAND!

HE TURNS, AND THE DRUMS GROW LOUDER--

--AS IF KNOWING WHAT IS NEXT TO COME...

MORE OFTEN THAN HE CARES TO REMEMBER, THE OLD MAN HAS PERFORMED THE SACRED RITUAL--

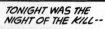

--AND HE PRAYS EACH TIME WILL BE THE LAST!

TONIGHT WAS THE NIGHT OF THE KILL--

-- THE NIGHT OF THE HUNGER--

--THE NIGHT WHEN THE DRUMS ARE ONE WITH HER HEART--

-- AND HER HEART BEATS QUICK AND STRONG...

TONIGHT IS THE NIGHT OF THE BLOODFEAST!

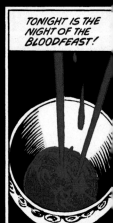

1

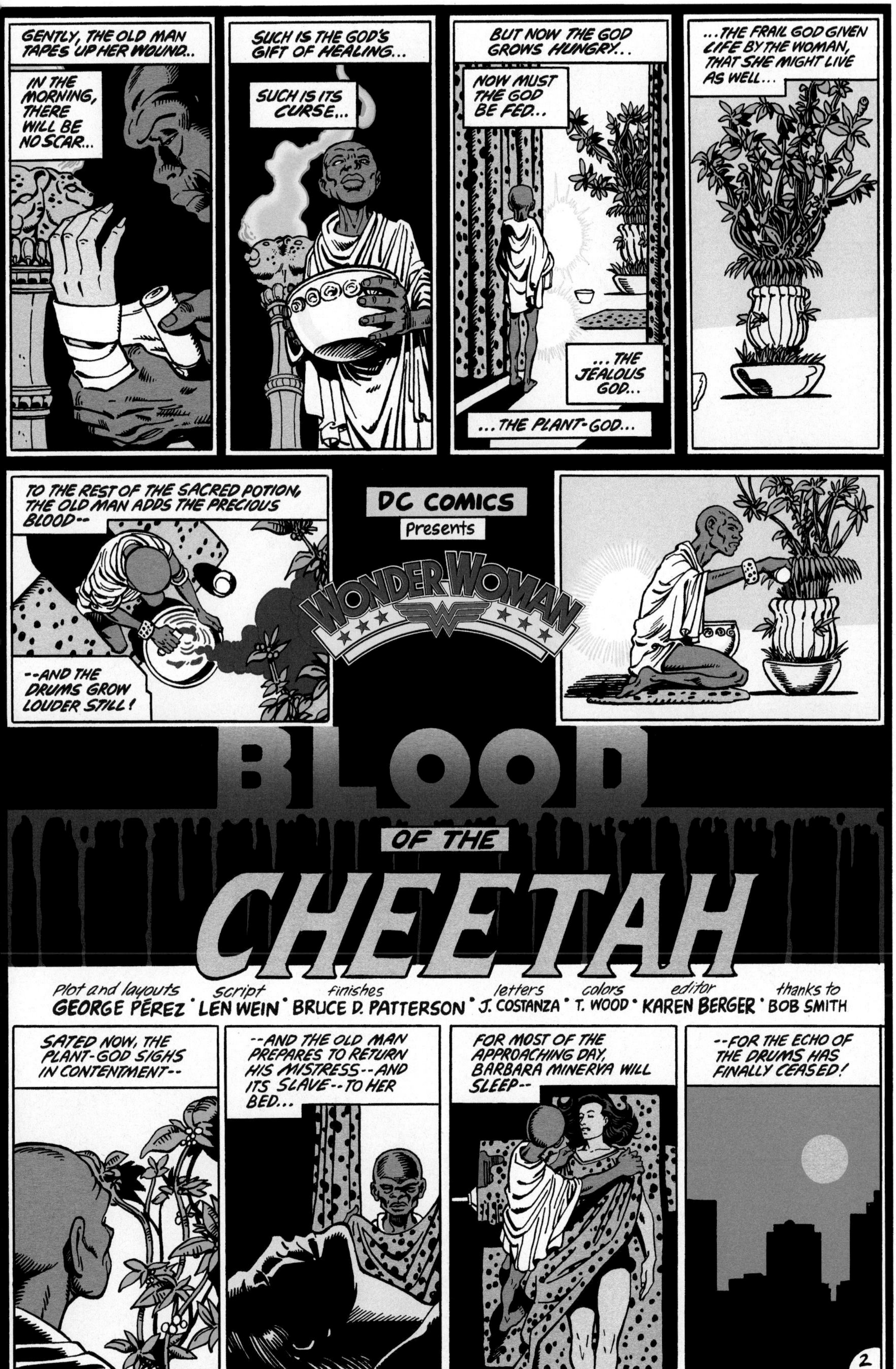
GENTLY, THE OLD MAN TAPES UP HER WOUND...
IN THE MORNING, THERE WILL BE NO SCAR...
SUCH IS THE GOD'S GIFT OF HEALING...
SUCH IS ITS CURSE...
BUT NOW THE GOD GROWS HUNGRY...
NOW MUST THE GOD BE FED...
...THE JEALOUS GOD...
...THE PLANT-GOD...
...THE FRAIL GOD GIVEN LIFE BY THE WOMAN, THAT SHE MIGHT LIVE AS WELL...
TO THE REST OF THE SACRED POTION, THE OLD MAN ADDS THE PRECIOUS BLOOD--
--AND THE DRUMS GROW LOUDER STILL!
DC COMICS
Presents
WONDER WOMAN
BLOOD
OF THE
CHEETAH
Plot and layouts GEORGE PÉREZ • script LEN WEIN • finishes BRUCE D. PATTERSON • letters J. COSTANZA • colors T. WOOD • editor KAREN BERGER • thanks to BOB SMITH
SATED NOW, THE PLANT-GOD SIGHS IN CONTENTMENT--
--AND THE OLD MAN PREPARES TO RETURN HIS MISTRESS--AND ITS SLAVE--TO HER BED...
FOR MOST OF THE APPROACHING DAY, BARBARA MINERVA WILL SLEEP--
--FOR THE ECHO OF THE DRUMS HAS FINALLY CEASED!
2

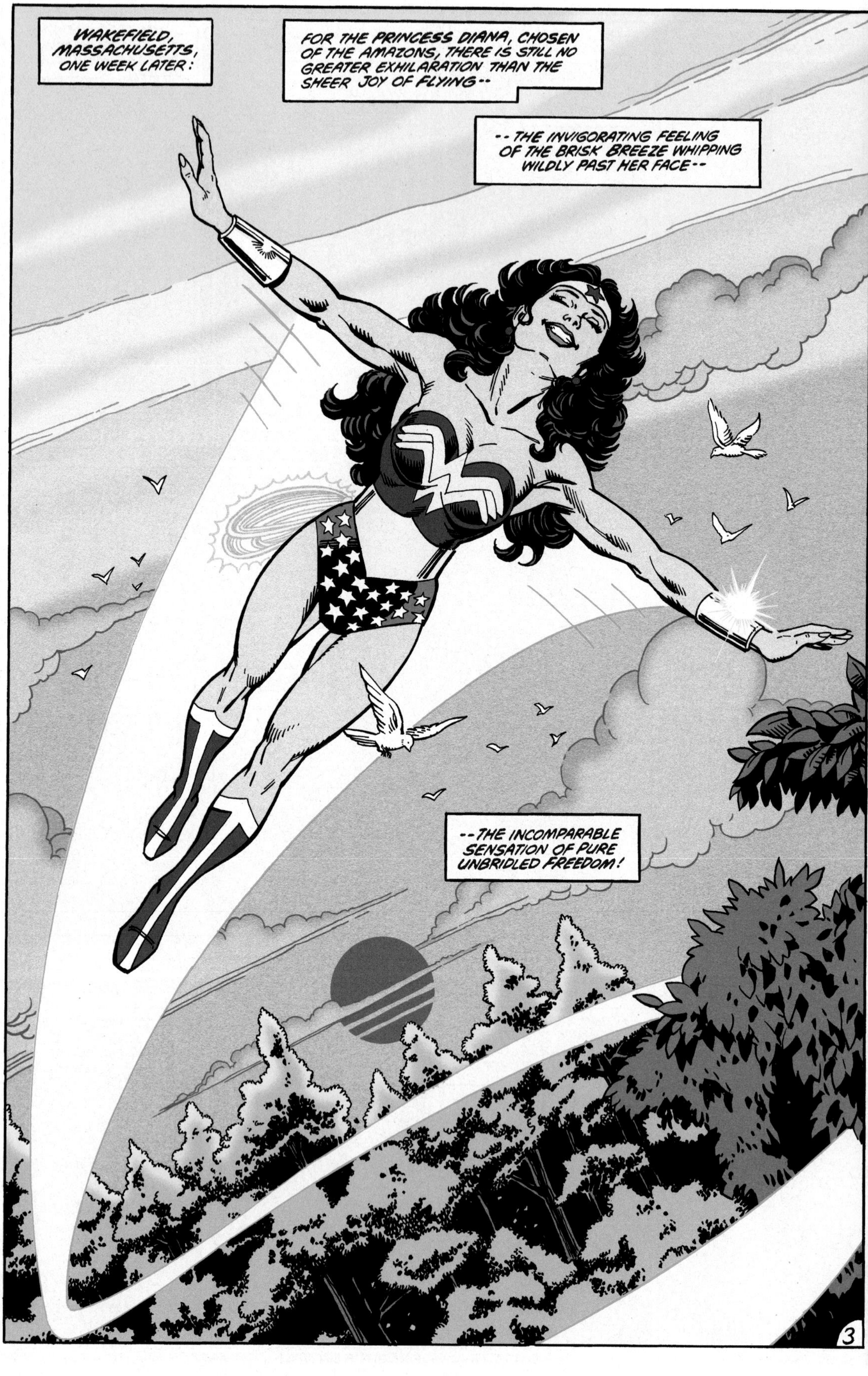
WAKEFIELD, MASSACHUSETTS, ONE WEEK LATER:
FOR THE PRINCESS DIANA, CHOSEN OF THE AMAZONS, THERE IS STILL NO GREATER EXHILARATION THAN THE SHEER JOY OF FLYING--
--THE INVIGORATING FEELING OF THE BRISK BREEZE WHIPPING WILDLY PAST HER FACE--
--THE INCOMPARABLE SENSATION OF PURE UNBRIDLED FREEDOM!
3

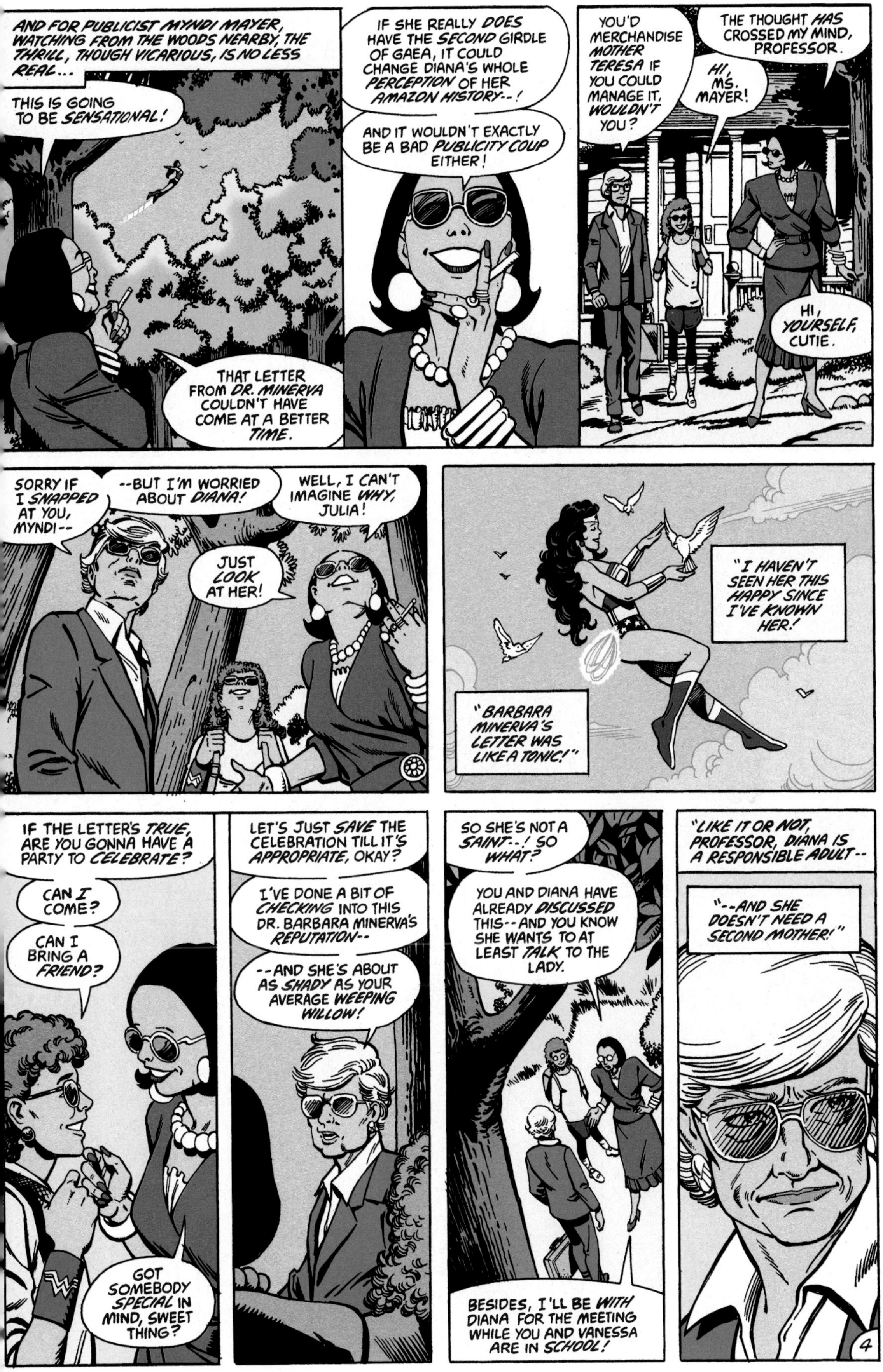
AND FOR PUBLICIST MYNDI MAYER, WATCHING FROM THE WOODS NEARBY, THE THRILL, THOUGH VICARIOUS, IS NO LESS REAL...
THIS IS GOING TO BE SENSATIONAL!
THAT LETTER FROM DR. MINERVA COULDN'T HAVE COME AT A BETTER TIME.
IF SHE REALLY DOES HAVE THE SECOND GIRDLE OF GAEA, IT COULD CHANGE DIANA'S WHOLE PERCEPTION OF HER AMAZON HISTORY--!
AND IT WOULDN'T EXACTLY BE A BAD PUBLICITY COUP EITHER!
YOU'D MERCHANDISE MOTHER TERESA IF YOU COULD MANAGE IT, WOULDN'T YOU?
THE THOUGHT HAS CROSSED MY MIND, PROFESSOR.
HI, MS. MAYER!
HI, YOURSELF, CUTIE.
SORRY IF I SNAPPED AT YOU, MYNDI--
--BUT I'M WORRIED ABOUT DIANA!
WELL, I CAN'T IMAGINE WHY, JULIA!
JUST LOOK AT HER!
"I HAVEN'T SEEN HER THIS HAPPY SINCE I'VE KNOWN HER!
"BARBARA MINERVA'S LETTER WAS LIKE A TONIC!"
IF THE LETTER'S TRUE, ARE YOU GONNA HAVE A PARTY TO CELEBRATE?
CAN I COME?
CAN I BRING A FRIEND?
GOT SOMEBODY SPECIAL IN MIND, SWEET THING?
LET'S JUST SAVE THE CELEBRATION TILL IT'S APPROPRIATE, OKAY?
I'VE DONE A BIT OF CHECKING INTO THIS DR. BARBARA MINERVA'S REPUTATION--
--AND SHE'S ABOUT AS SHADY AS YOUR AVERAGE WEEPING WILLOW!
SO SHE'S NOT A SAINT--! SO WHAT?
YOU AND DIANA HAVE ALREADY DISCUSSED THIS--AND YOU KNOW SHE WANTS TO AT LEAST TALK TO THE LADY.
BESIDES, I'LL BE WITH DIANA FOR THE MEETING WHILE YOU AND VANESSA ARE IN SCHOOL!
"LIKE IT OR NOT, PROFESSOR, DIANA IS A RESPONSIBLE ADULT--
"--AND SHE DOESN'T NEED A SECOND MOTHER!"
4

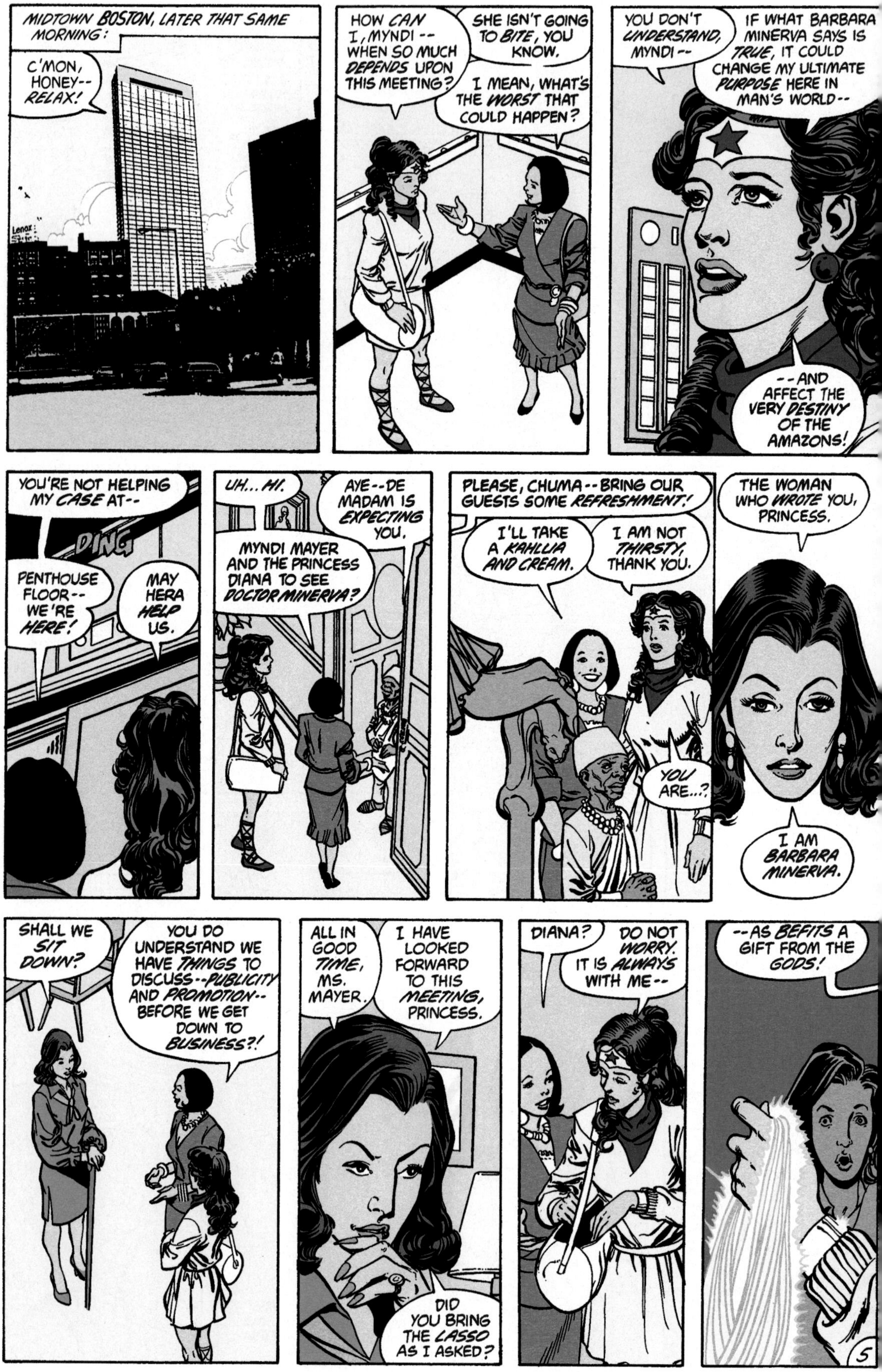
MIDTOWN BOSTON, LATER THAT SAME MORNING:
C'MON, HONEY-- RELAX!
HOW CAN I, MYNDI -- WHEN SO MUCH DEPENDS UPON THIS MEETING?
SHE ISN'T GOING TO BITE, YOU KNOW.
I MEAN, WHAT'S THE WORST THAT COULD HAPPEN?
YOU DON'T UNDERSTAND, MYNDI --
IF WHAT BARBARA MINERVA SAYS IS TRUE, IT COULD CHANGE MY ULTIMATE PURPOSE HERE IN MAN'S WORLD--
--AND AFFECT THE VERY DESTINY OF THE AMAZONS!
YOU'RE NOT HELPING MY CASE AT--
DING
PENTHOUSE FLOOR-- WE'RE HERE!
MAY HERA HELP US.
UH... HI.
AYE--DE MADAM IS EXPECTING YOU.
MYNDI MAYER AND THE PRINCESS DIANA TO SEE DOCTOR MINERVA?
PLEASE, CHUMA--BRING OUR GUESTS SOME REFRESHMENT!
I'LL TAKE A KAHLUA AND CREAM.
I AM NOT THIRSTY, THANK YOU.
YOU ARE...?
THE WOMAN WHO WROTE YOU, PRINCESS.
I AM BARBARA MINERVA.
SHALL WE SIT DOWN?
YOU DO UNDERSTAND WE HAVE THINGS TO DISCUSS--PUBLICITY AND PROMOTION-- BEFORE WE GET DOWN TO BUSINESS?!
ALL IN GOOD TIME, MS. MAYER.
I HAVE LOOKED FORWARD TO THIS MEETING, PRINCESS.
DID YOU BRING THE LASSO AS I ASKED?
DIANA?
DO NOT WORRY. IT IS ALWAYS WITH ME--
--AS BEFITS A GIFT FROM THE GODS!
5

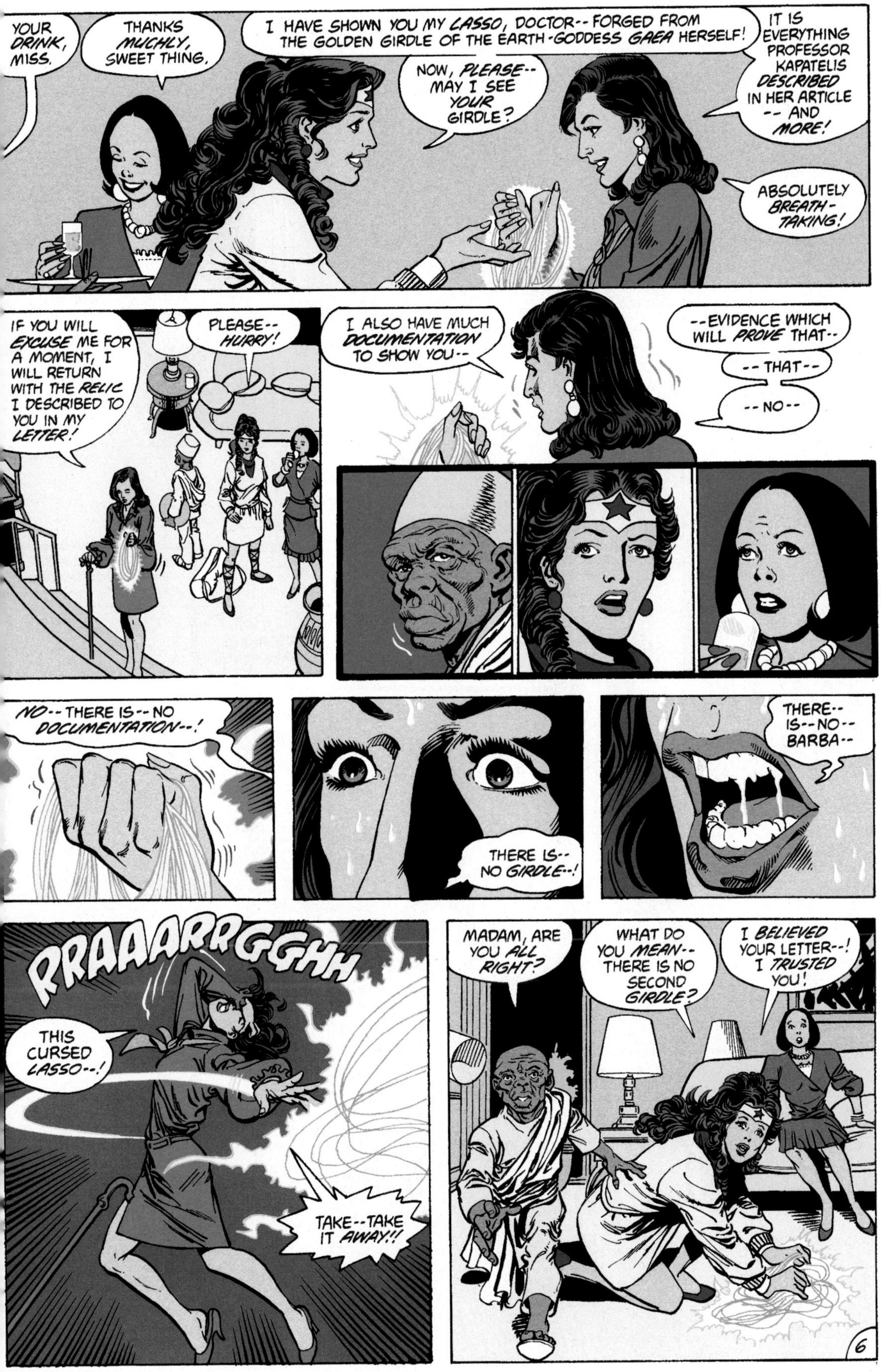
YOUR DRINK, MISS.
THANKS MUCHLY, SWEET THING.
I HAVE SHOWN YOU MY LASSO, DOCTOR-- FORGED FROM THE GOLDEN GIRDLE OF THE EARTH-GODDESS GAEA HERSELF!
NOW, PLEASE-- MAY I SEE YOUR GIRDLE?
IT IS EVERYTHING PROFESSOR KAPATELIS DESCRIBED IN HER ARTICLE -- AND MORE!
ABSOLUTELY BREATH-TAKING!
IF YOU WILL EXCUSE ME FOR A MOMENT, I WILL RETURN WITH THE RELIC I DESCRIBED TO YOU IN MY LETTER!
PLEASE-- HURRY!
I ALSO HAVE MUCH DOCUMENTATION TO SHOW YOU--
--EVIDENCE WHICH WILL PROVE THAT--
-- THAT --
-- NO --
NO-- THERE IS-- NO DOCUMENTATION--!
THERE IS-- NO GIRDLE--!
THERE-- IS--NO-- BARBA--
RRAAARRGGHH
THIS CURSED LASSO--!
TAKE--TAKE IT AWAY!!
MADAM, ARE YOU ALL RIGHT?
WHAT DO YOU MEAN-- THERE IS NO SECOND GIRDLE?
I BELIEVED YOUR LETTER--! I TRUSTED YOU!
6

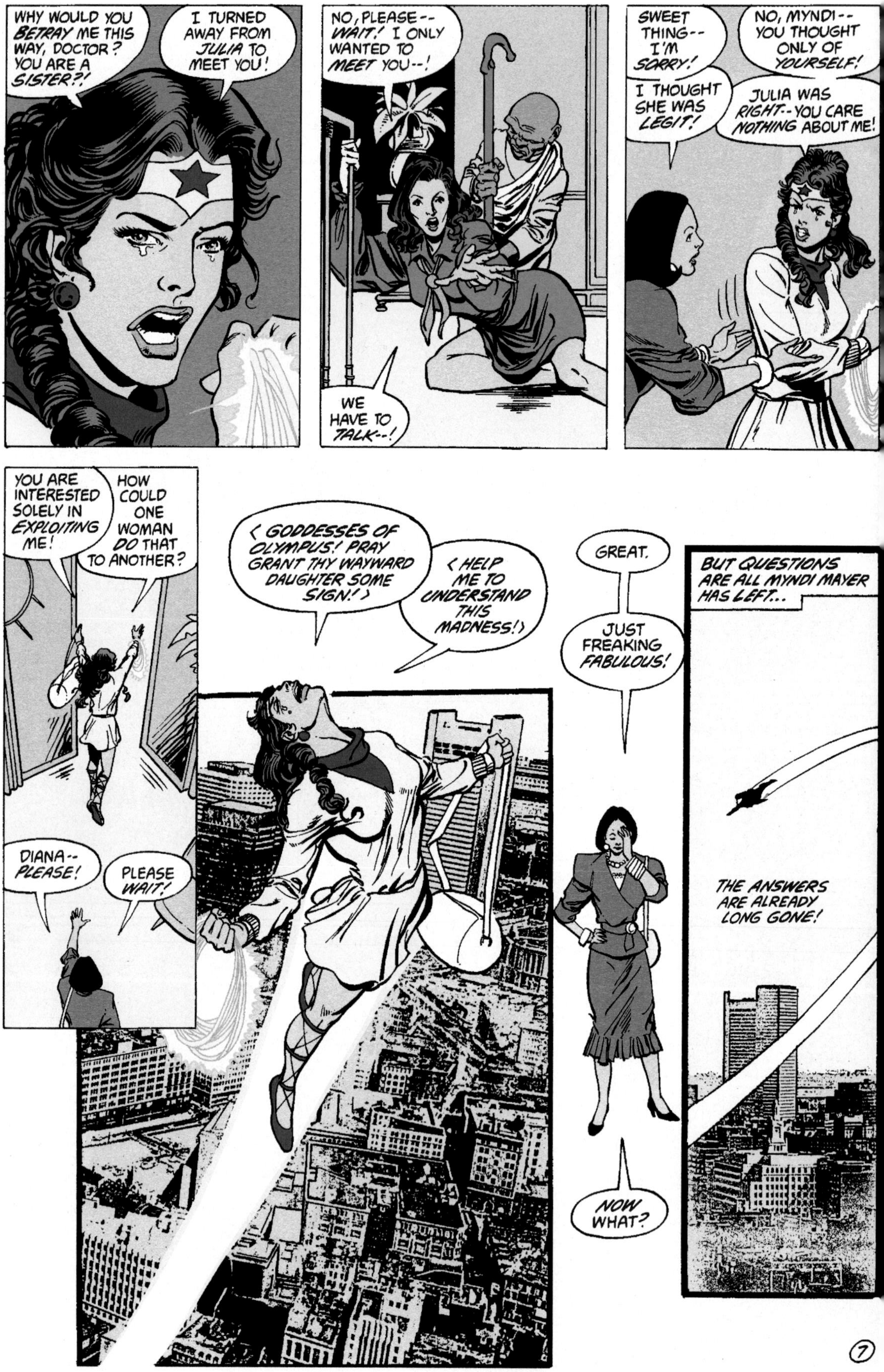
WHY WOULD YOU BETRAY ME THIS WAY, DOCTOR? YOU ARE A SISTER?!
I TURNED AWAY FROM JULIA TO MEET YOU!
NO, PLEASE-- WAIT! I ONLY WANTED TO MEET YOU--!
WE HAVE TO TALK--!
SWEET THING-- I'M SORRY!
I THOUGHT SHE WAS LEGIT!
NO, MYNDI-- YOU THOUGHT ONLY OF YOURSELF!
JULIA WAS RIGHT--YOU CARE NOTHING ABOUT ME!
YOU ARE INTERESTED SOLELY IN EXPLOITING ME!
HOW COULD ONE WOMAN DO THAT TO ANOTHER?
DIANA-- PLEASE!
PLEASE WAIT!
< GODDESSES OF OLYMPUS! PRAY GRANT THY WAYWARD DAUGHTER SOME SIGN! >
< HELP ME TO UNDERSTAND THIS MADNESS! >
GREAT.
JUST FREAKING FABULOUS!
NOW WHAT?
BUT QUESTIONS ARE ALL MYNDI MAYER HAS LEFT...
THE ANSWERS ARE ALREADY LONG GONE!
7

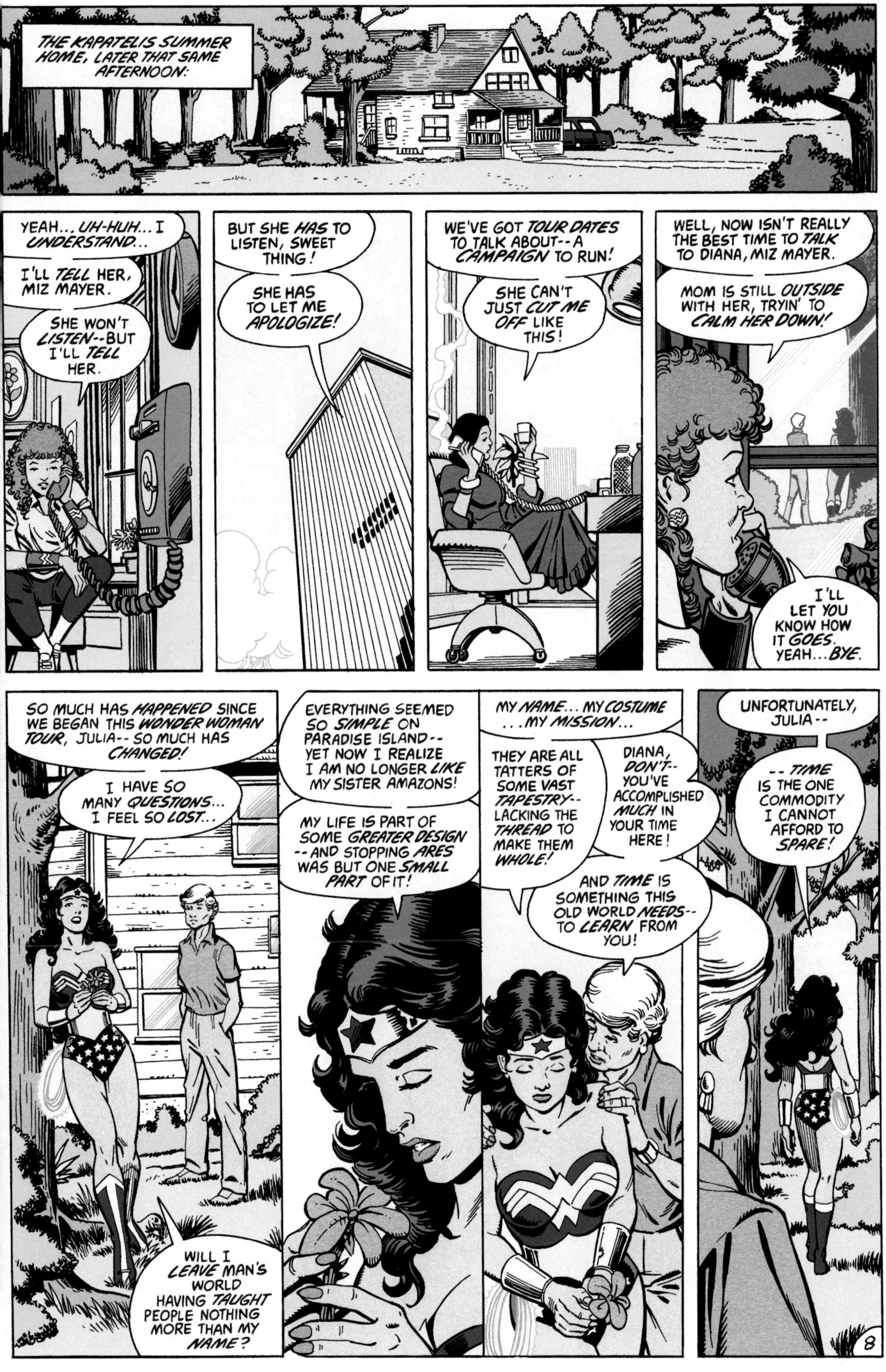
THE KAPATELIS SUMMER HOME, LATER THAT SAME AFTERNOON:
YEAH... UH-HUH... I UNDERSTAND...
I'LL TELL HER, MIZ MAYER.
SHE WON'T LISTEN--BUT I'LL TELL HER.
BUT SHE HAS TO LISTEN, SWEET THING!
SHE HAS TO LET ME APOLOGIZE!
WE'VE GOT TOUR DATES TO TALK ABOUT--A CAMPAIGN TO RUN!
SHE CAN'T JUST CUT ME OFF LIKE THIS!
WELL, NOW ISN'T REALLY THE BEST TIME TO TALK TO DIANA, MIZ MAYER.
MOM IS STILL OUTSIDE WITH HER, TRYIN' TO CALM HER DOWN!
I'LL LET YOU KNOW HOW IT GOES. YEAH... BYE.
SO MUCH HAS HAPPENED SINCE WE BEGAN THIS WONDER WOMAN TOUR, JULIA-- SO MUCH HAS CHANGED!
I HAVE SO MANY QUESTIONS... I FEEL SO LOST...
WILL I LEAVE MAN'S WORLD HAVING TAUGHT PEOPLE NOTHING MORE THAN MY NAME?
EVERYTHING SEEMED SO SIMPLE ON PARADISE ISLAND-- YET NOW I REALIZE I AM NO LONGER LIKE MY SISTER AMAZONS!
MY LIFE IS PART OF SOME GREATER DESIGN --AND STOPPING ARES WAS BUT ONE SMALL PART OF IT!
MY NAME... MY COSTUME ...MY MISSION...
THEY ARE ALL TATTERS OF SOME VAST TAPESTRY-- LACKING THE THREAD TO MAKE THEM WHOLE!
DIANA, DON'T-- YOU'VE ACCOMPLISHED MUCH IN YOUR TIME HERE!
AND TIME IS SOMETHING THIS OLD WORLD NEEDS-- TO LEARN FROM YOU!
UNFORTUNATELY, JULIA--
--TIME IS THE ONE COMMODITY I CANNOT AFFORD TO SPARE!
8

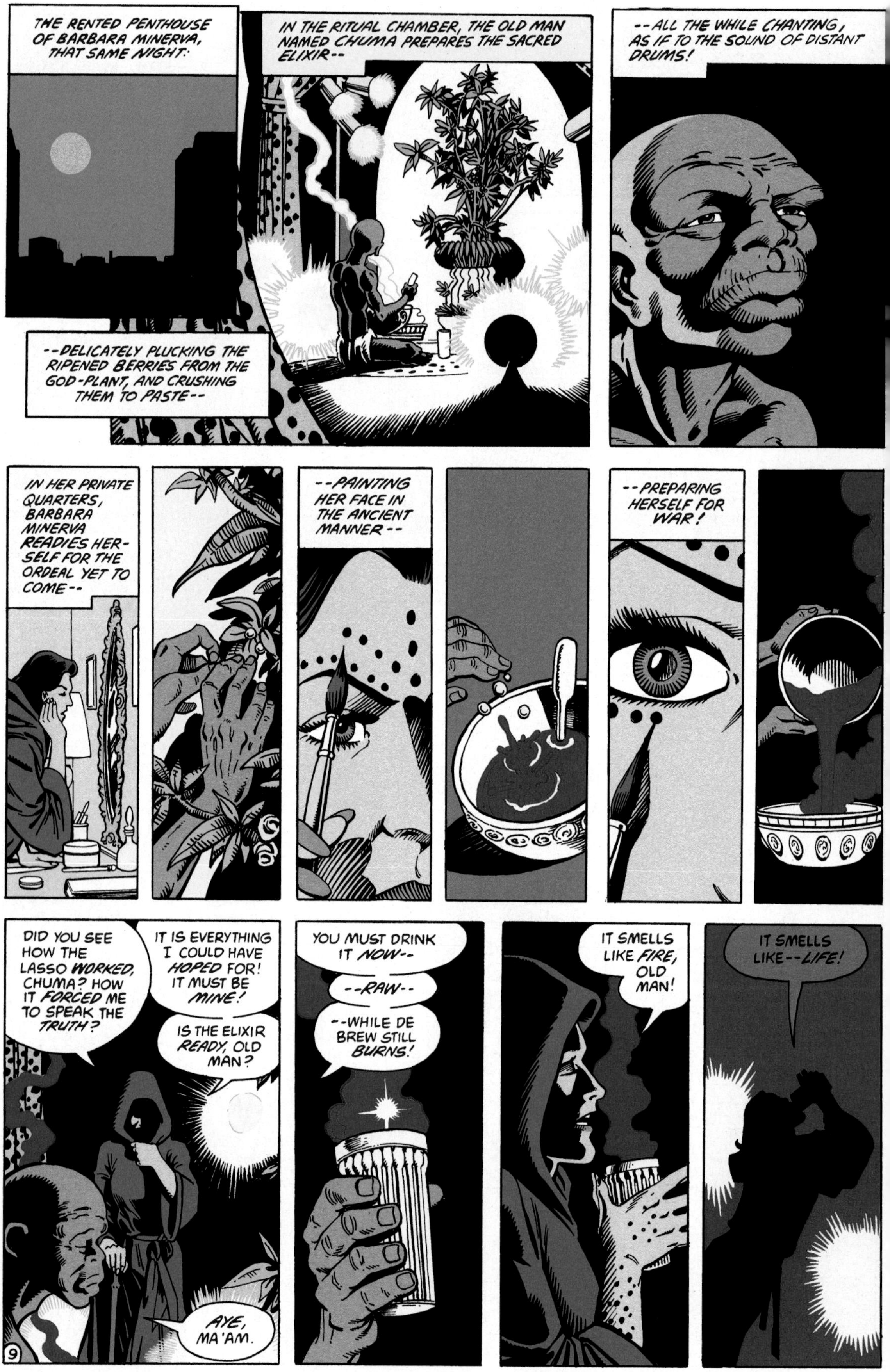

THE RENTED PENTHOUSE OF BARBARA MINERVA, THAT SAME NIGHT:
IN THE RITUAL CHAMBER, THE OLD MAN NAMED CHUMA PREPARES THE SACRED ELIXIR--
--DELICATELY PLUCKING THE RIPENED BERRIES FROM THE GOD-PLANT, AND CRUSHING THEM TO PASTE--
--ALL THE WHILE CHANTING, AS IF TO THE SOUND OF DISTANT DRUMS!
IN HER PRIVATE QUARTERS, BARBARA MINERVA READIES HER-SELF FOR THE ORDEAL YET TO COME--
--PAINTING HER FACE IN THE ANCIENT MANNER--
--PREPARING HERSELF FOR WAR!
DID YOU SEE HOW THE LASSO WORKED, CHUMA? HOW IT FORCED ME TO SPEAK THE TRUTH?
IT IS EVERYTHING I COULD HAVE HOPED FOR! IT MUST BE MINE!
IS THE ELIXIR READY, OLD MAN?
AYE, MA'AM.
9
YOU MUST DRINK IT NOW--
--RAW--
--WHILE DE BREW STILL BURNS!
IT SMELLS LIKE FIRE, OLD MAN!
IT SMELLS LIKE--LIFE!

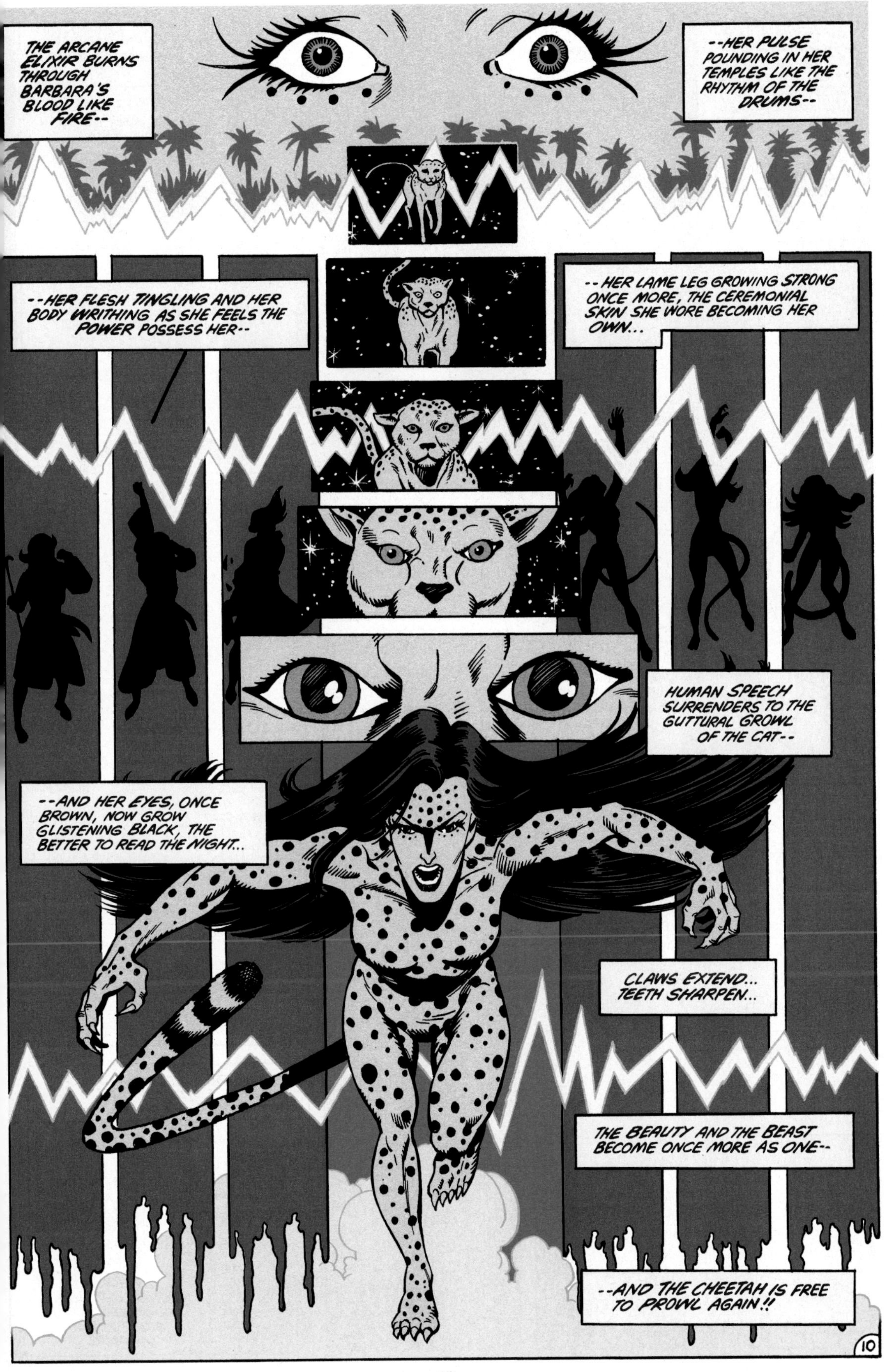
THE ARCANE ELIXIR BURNS THROUGH BARBARA'S BLOOD LIKE FIRE--
--HER PULSE POUNDING IN HER TEMPLES LIKE THE RHYTHM OF THE DRUMS--
--HER FLESH TINGLING AND HER BODY WRITHING AS SHE FEELS THE POWER POSSESS HER--
--HER LAME LEG GROWING STRONG ONCE MORE, THE CEREMONIAL SKIN SHE WORE BECOMING HER OWN...
HUMAN SPEECH SURRENDERS TO THE GUTTURAL GROWL OF THE CAT--
--AND HER EYES, ONCE BROWN, NOW GROW GLISTENING BLACK, THE BETTER TO READ THE NIGHT...
CLAWS EXTEND... TEETH SHARPEN...
THE BEAUTY AND THE BEAST BECOME ONCE MORE AS ONE--
--AND THE CHEETAH IS FREE TO PROWL AGAIN!!
10

HER CLAWS GOUGING HANDHOLDS IN THE BUILDING'S SHEER FACE, THE CHEETAH DESCENDS INTO THE DARKNESS--

--INTO THE CONCRETE JUNGLE THAT IS HER HUNTING GROUND--

LEAVING THE OLD MAN BEHIND TO *WAIT*--

--AND TO PONDER...

SHE BE THE *LAST* OF HER *KIND,* DAT ONE--

--AS HER *GOD* BE DE LAST OF ITS KIND--

--YET HER SURVIVAL BE IN DE HANDS OF A *FICKLE* GOD INDEED!

TANK YOU, ANCIENT ONE, FOR BRINGING DE CHEETAH *BACK* TO ME!

I PRAY YOU-- *KEEP HER SAFE!*

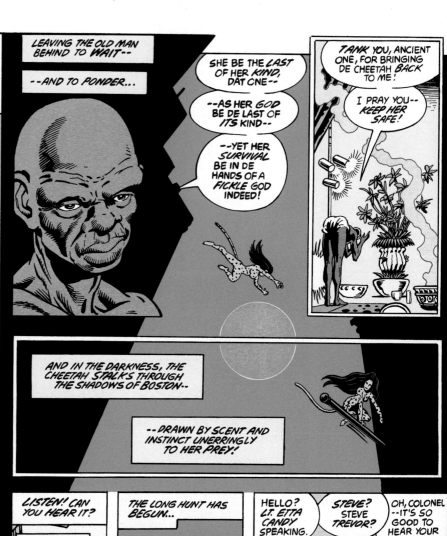

AND IN THE DARKNESS, THE CHEETAH *STALKS* THROUGH THE SHADOWS OF BOSTON--

--DRAWN BY SCENT AND INSTINCT UNERRINGLY TO HER PREY!

LISTEN! CAN YOU HEAR IT?

THERE ARE DRUMS IN THE NIGHT!

THE LONG HUNT HAS BEGUN...

BRINNNG BRINNNG

HELLO? LT. ETTA CANDY SPEAKING.

WHO--?

STEVE? STEVE TREVOR?

OH, COLONEL --IT'S SO GOOD TO HEAR YOUR *VOICE!*

...AND THE INVESTIGATION CONTINUES INTO THE *MYSTERIOUS DEATH* OF LOCAL CRIMINAL *TAMSYN McCONNELL...*

ANIMAL ATTACK

...WHO WAS *SLAIN* LAST WEEK, APPARENTLY BY SOME *WILD* ANIMAL...

11

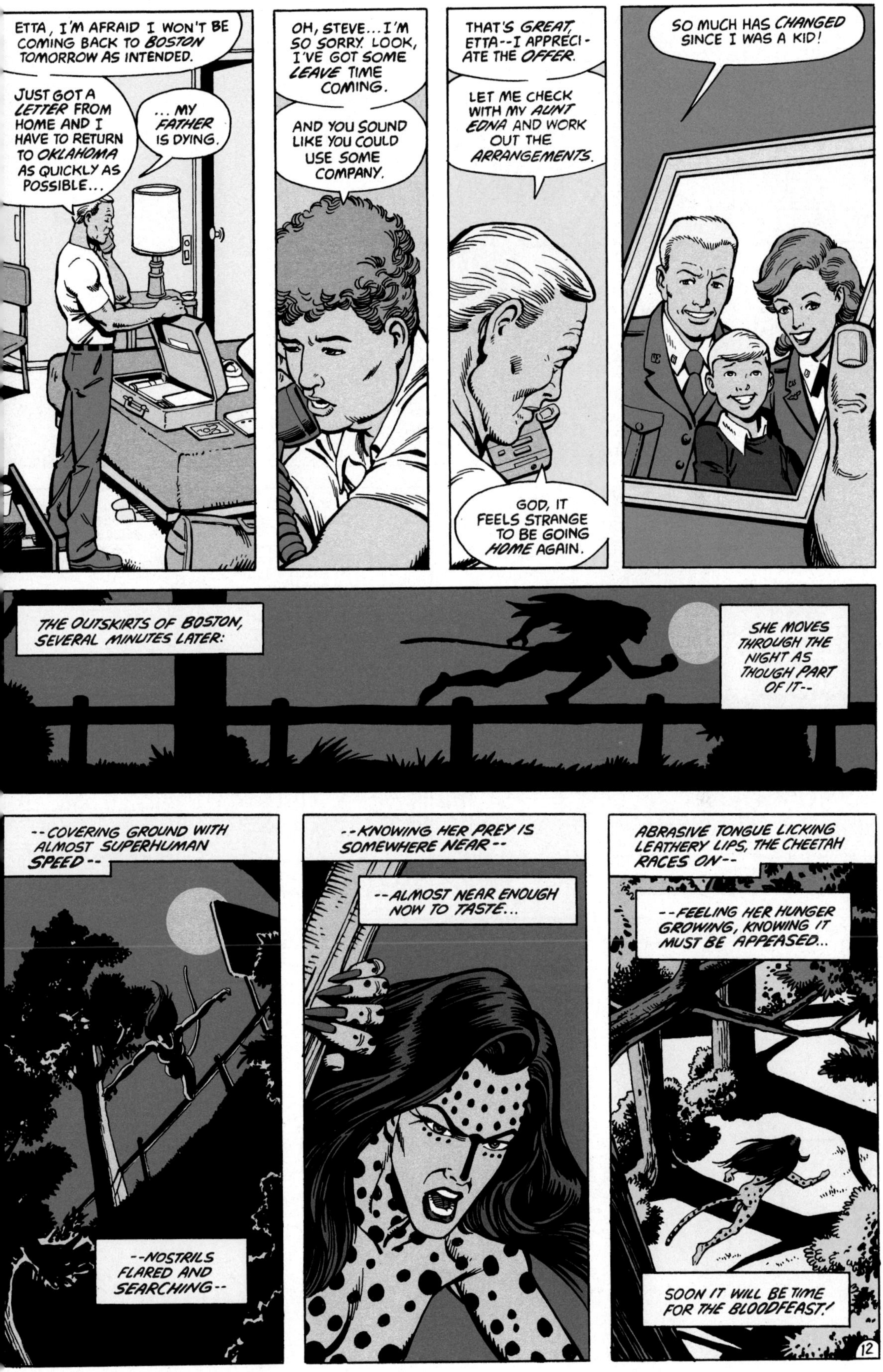
ETTA, I'M AFRAID I WON'T BE COMING BACK TO BOSTON TOMORROW AS INTENDED.
JUST GOT A LETTER FROM HOME AND I HAVE TO RETURN TO OKLAHOMA AS QUICKLY AS POSSIBLE...
... MY FATHER IS DYING.
OH, STEVE... I'M SO SORRY. LOOK, I'VE GOT SOME LEAVE TIME COMING.
AND YOU SOUND LIKE YOU COULD USE SOME COMPANY.
THAT'S GREAT, ETTA--I APPRECIATE THE OFFER.
LET ME CHECK WITH MY AUNT EDNA AND WORK OUT THE ARRANGEMENTS.
GOD, IT FEELS STRANGE TO BE GOING HOME AGAIN.
SO MUCH HAS CHANGED SINCE I WAS A KID!
THE OUTSKIRTS OF BOSTON, SEVERAL MINUTES LATER:
SHE MOVES THROUGH THE NIGHT AS THOUGH PART OF IT--
--COVERING GROUND WITH ALMOST SUPERHUMAN SPEED--
--NOSTRILS FLARED AND SEARCHING--
--KNOWING HER PREY IS SOMEWHERE NEAR--
--ALMOST NEAR ENOUGH NOW TO TASTE...
ABRASIVE TONGUE LICKING LEATHERY LIPS, THE CHEETAH RACES ON--
--FEELING HER HUNGER GROWING, KNOWING IT MUST BE APPEASED...
SOON IT WILL BE TIME FOR THE BLOODFEAST!
12

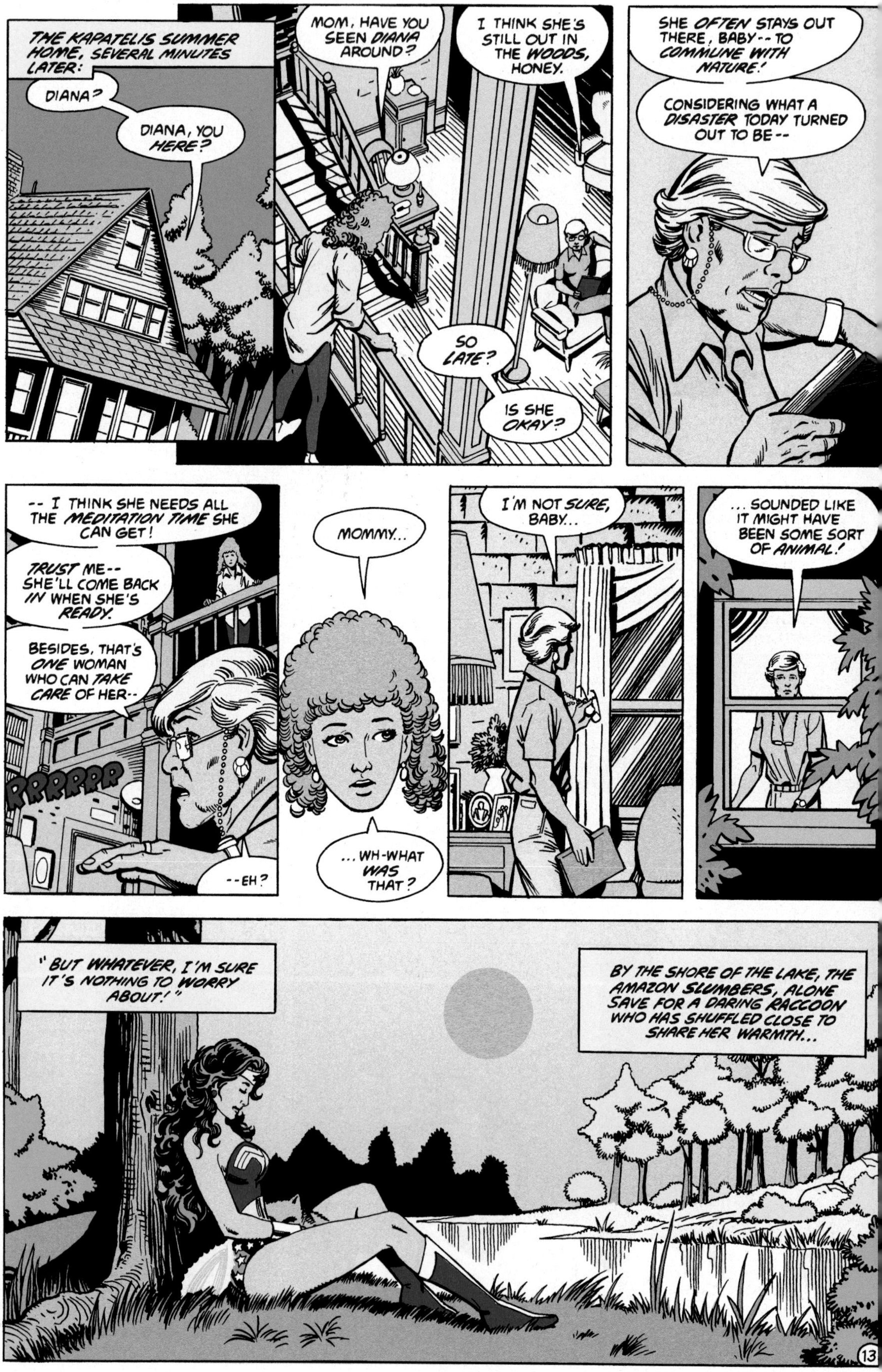
THE KAPATELIS SUMMER HOME, SEVERAL MINUTES LATER:
DIANA?
DIANA, YOU HERE?
MOM, HAVE YOU SEEN DIANA AROUND?
I THINK SHE'S STILL OUT IN THE WOODS, HONEY.
SO LATE?
IS SHE OKAY?
SHE OFTEN STAYS OUT THERE, BABY--TO COMMUNE WITH NATURE!
CONSIDERING WHAT A DISASTER TODAY TURNED OUT TO BE--
--I THINK SHE NEEDS ALL THE MEDITATION TIME SHE CAN GET!
TRUST ME--SHE'LL COME BACK IN WHEN SHE'S READY.
BESIDES, THAT'S ONE WOMAN WHO CAN TAKE CARE OF HER--
RRRRRR
--EH?
MOMMY...
...WH-WHAT WAS THAT?
I'M NOT SURE, BABY...
...SOUNDED LIKE IT MIGHT HAVE BEEN SOME SORT OF ANIMAL!
"BUT WHATEVER, I'M SURE IT'S NOTHING TO WORRY ABOUT!"
BY THE SHORE OF THE LAKE, THE AMAZON SLUMBERS, ALONE SAVE FOR A DARING RACCOON WHO HAS SHUFFLED CLOSE TO SHARE HER WARMTH...
13

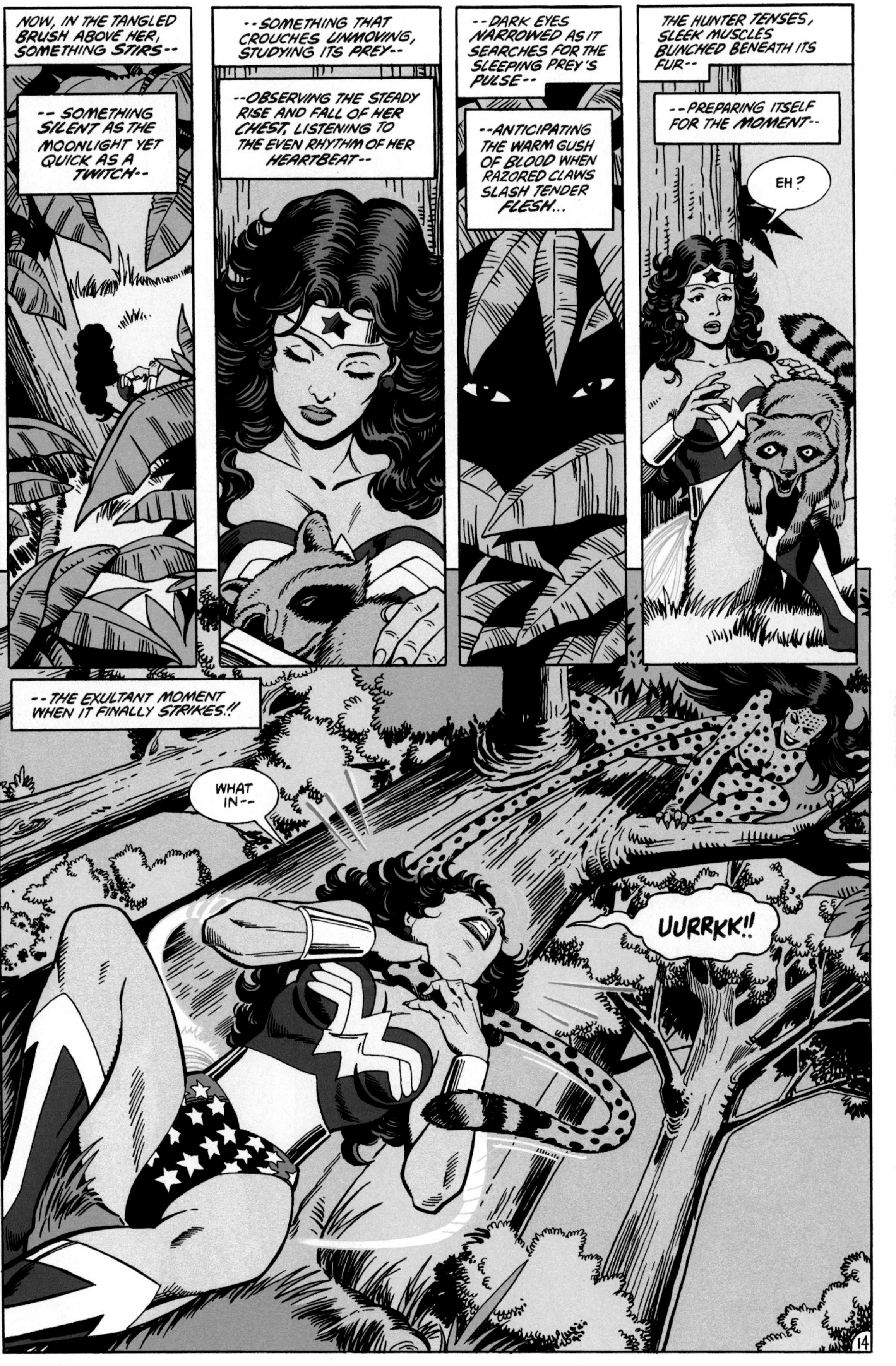

NOW, IN THE TANGLED BRUSH ABOVE HER, SOMETHING STIRS--
-- SOMETHING SILENT AS THE MOONLIGHT YET QUICK AS A TWITCH--
--SOMETHING THAT CROUCHES UNMOVING, STUDYING ITS PREY--
--OBSERVING THE STEADY RISE AND FALL OF HER CHEST, LISTENING TO THE EVEN RHYTHM OF HER HEARTBEAT--
--DARK EYES NARROWED AS IT SEARCHES FOR THE SLEEPING PREY'S PULSE--
--ANTICIPATING THE WARM GUSH OF BLOOD WHEN RAZORED CLAWS SLASH TENDER FLESH...
THE HUNTER TENSES, SLEEK MUSCLES BUNCHED BENEATH ITS FUR--
--PREPARING ITSELF FOR THE MOMENT--
EH?
--THE EXULTANT MOMENT WHEN IT FINALLY STRIKES!!
WHAT IN--
UURRKK!!
14

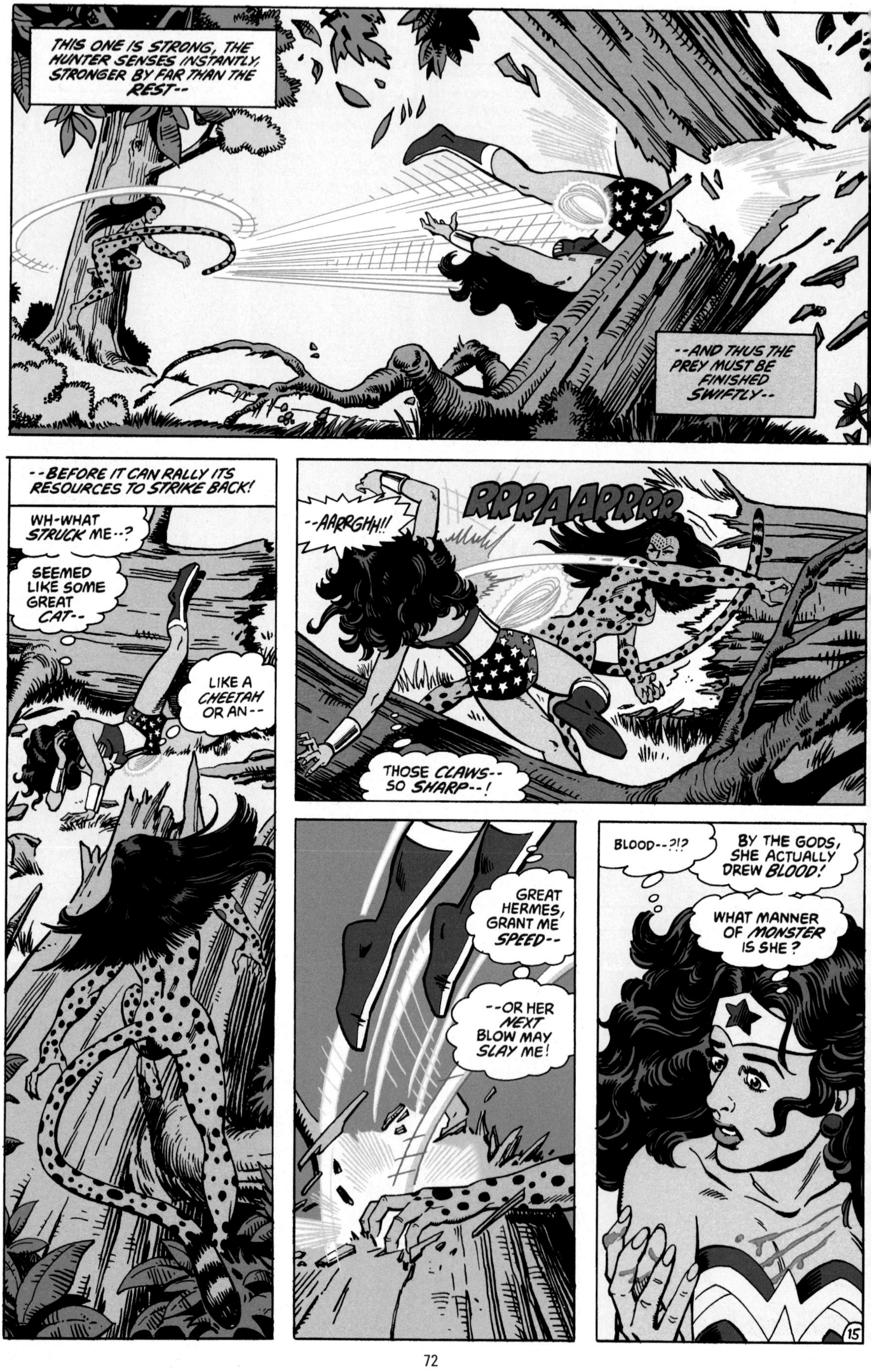
THIS ONE IS STRONG, THE HUNTER SENSES INSTANTLY, STRONGER BY FAR THAN THE REST--
--AND THUS THE PREY MUST BE FINISHED SWIFTLY--
--BEFORE IT CAN RALLY ITS RESOURCES TO STRIKE BACK!
WH-WHAT STRUCK ME--?
SEEMED LIKE SOME GREAT CAT--
LIKE A CHEETAH OR AN--
--AARGHH!!
RRRAAAPRRR
THOSE CLAWS-- SO SHARP--!
GREAT HERMES, GRANT ME SPEED--
--OR HER NEXT BLOW MAY SLAY ME!
BLOOD--?!?
BY THE GODS, SHE ACTUALLY DREW BLOOD!
WHAT MANNER OF MONSTER IS SHE?
15

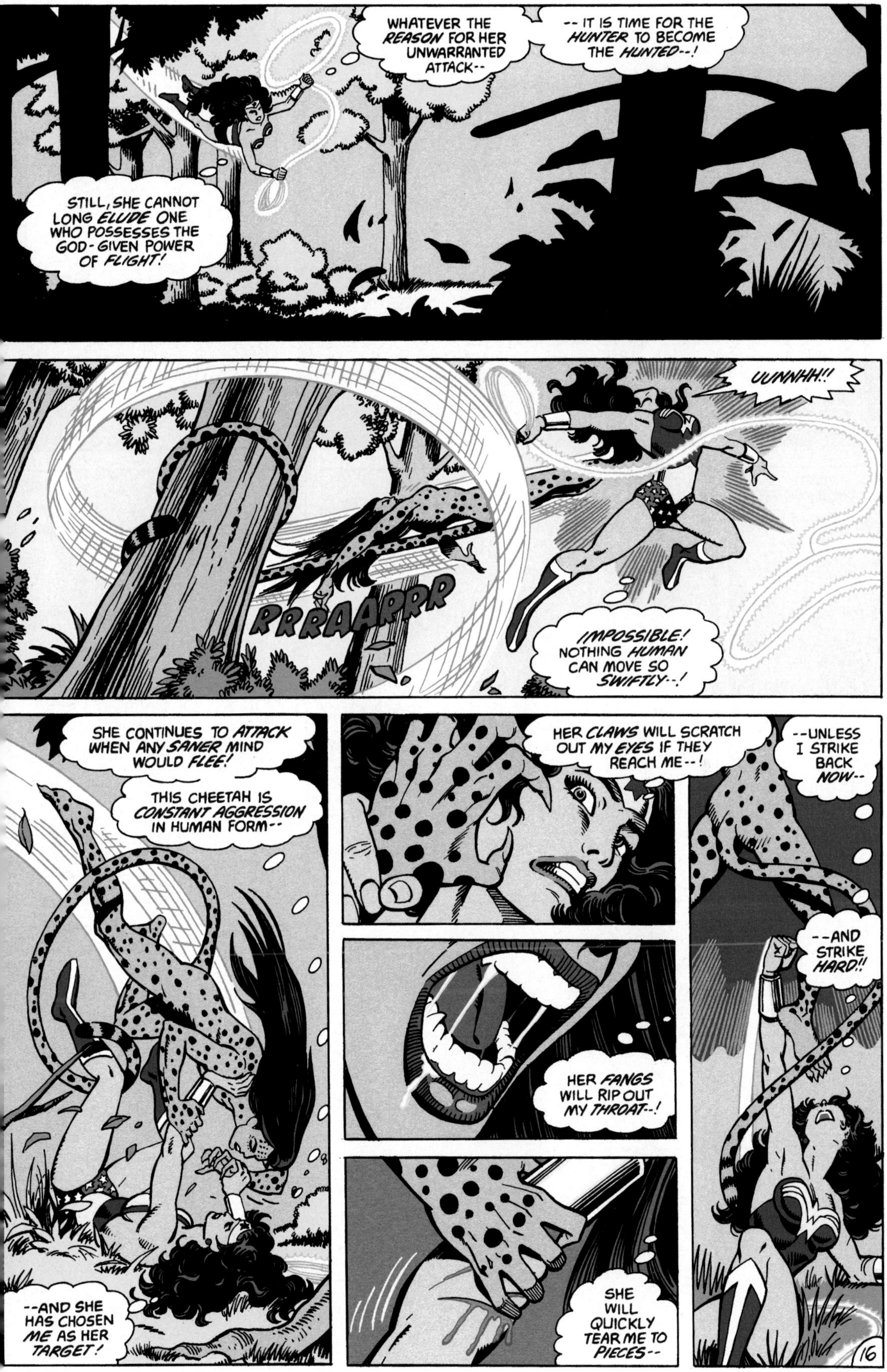
WHATEVER THE REASON FOR HER UNWARRANTED ATTACK--
-- IT IS TIME FOR THE HUNTER TO BECOME THE HUNTED--!
STILL, SHE CANNOT LONG ELUDE ONE WHO POSSESSES THE GOD-GIVEN POWER OF FLIGHT!
UUNNHH!!
RRRAARRR
IMPOSSIBLE! NOTHING HUMAN CAN MOVE SO SWIFTLY--!
SHE CONTINUES TO ATTACK WHEN ANY SANER MIND WOULD FLEE!
THIS CHEETAH IS CONSTANT AGGRESSION IN HUMAN FORM--
--AND SHE HAS CHOSEN ME AS HER TARGET!
HER CLAWS WILL SCRATCH OUT MY EYES IF THEY REACH ME--!
HER FANGS WILL RIP OUT MY THROAT--!
SHE WILL QUICKLY TEAR ME TO PIECES--
--UNLESS I STRIKE BACK NOW--
--AND STRIKE HARD!!
16

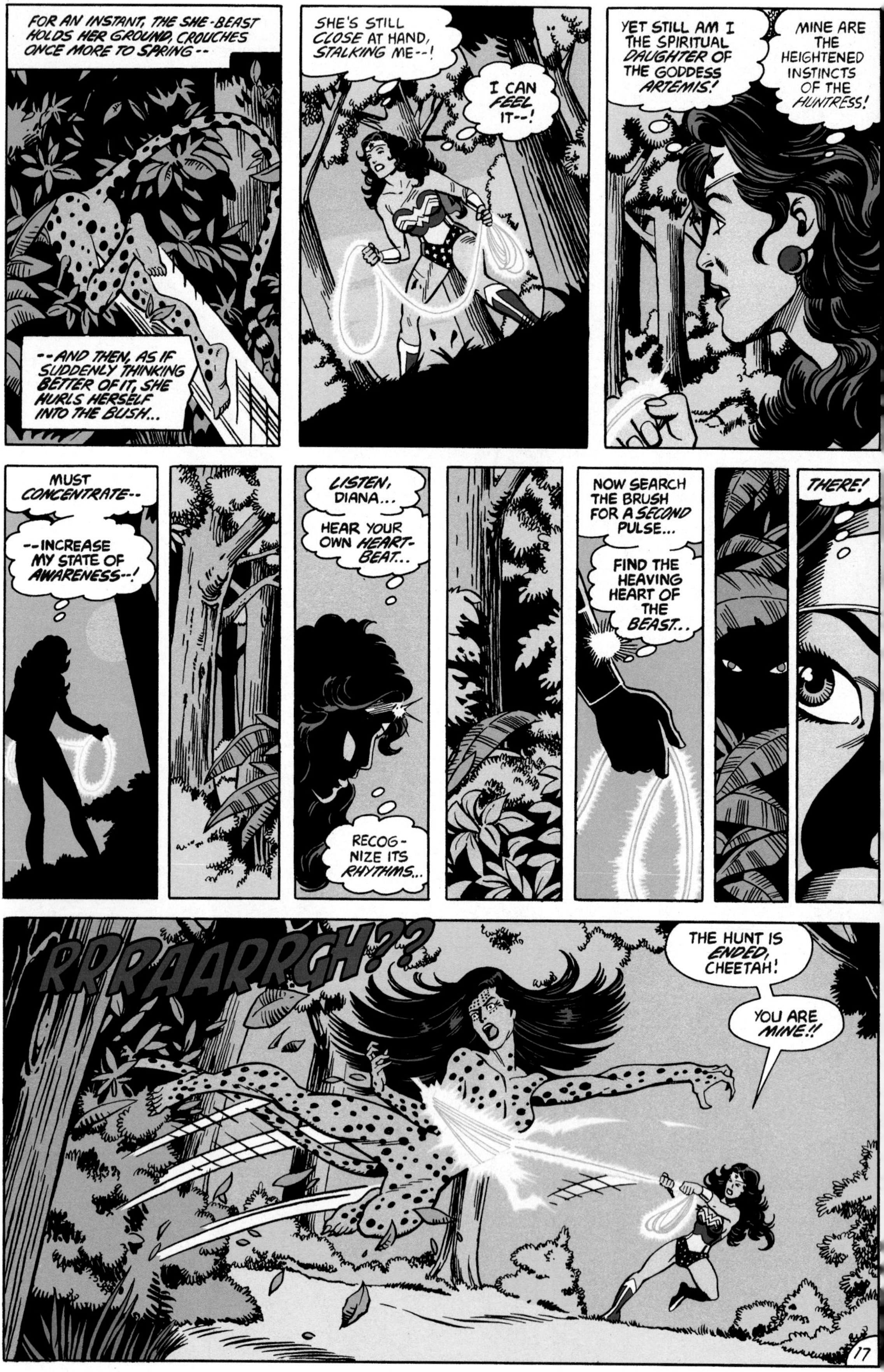
FOR AN INSTANT, THE SHE-BEAST HOLDS HER GROUND, CROUCHES ONCE MORE TO SPRING--
--AND THEN, AS IF SUDDENLY THINKING BETTER OF IT, SHE HURLS HERSELF INTO THE BUSH...
SHE'S STILL CLOSE AT HAND, STALKING ME--!
I CAN FEEL IT--!
YET STILL AM I THE SPIRITUAL DAUGHTER OF THE GODDESS ARTEMIS!
MINE ARE THE HEIGHTENED INSTINCTS OF THE HUNTRESS!
MUST CONCENTRATE--
--INCREASE MY STATE OF AWARENESS--!
LISTEN, DIANA...
HEAR YOUR OWN HEART-BEAT...
RECOG-NIZE ITS RHYTHMS...
NOW SEARCH THE BRUSH FOR A SECOND PULSE...
FIND THE HEAVING HEART OF THE BEAST...
THERE!
RRRAARRGH??
THE HUNT IS ENDED, CHEETAH!
YOU ARE MINE!!
17

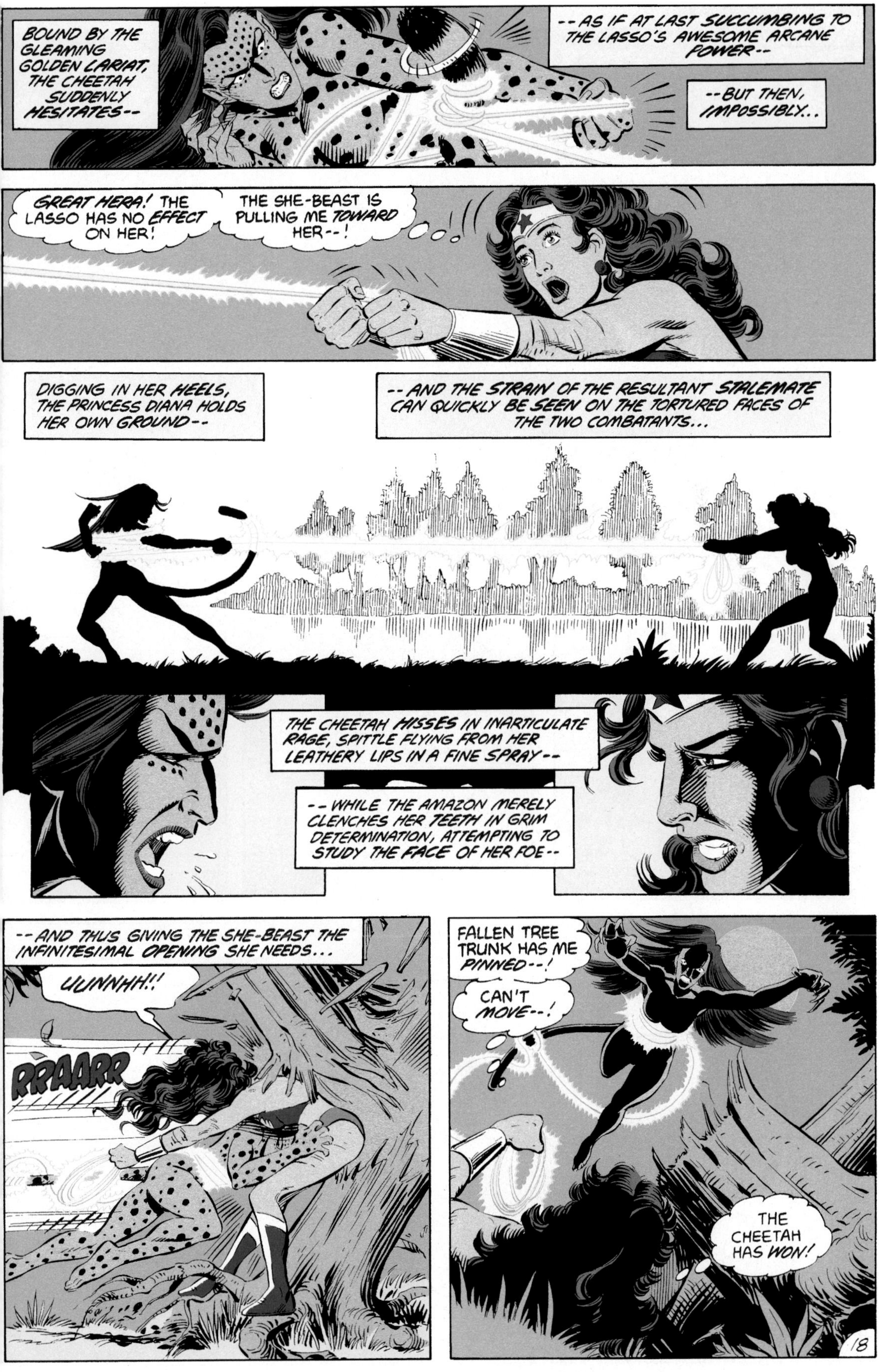
BOUND BY THE GLEAMING GOLDEN LARIAT, THE CHEETAH SUDDENLY HESITATES--
--AS IF AT LAST SUCCUMBING TO THE LASSO'S AWESOME ARCANE POWER--
--BUT THEN, IMPOSSIBLY...
GREAT HERA! THE LASSO HAS NO EFFECT ON HER!
THE SHE-BEAST IS PULLING ME TOWARD HER--!
DIGGING IN HER HEELS, THE PRINCESS DIANA HOLDS HER OWN GROUND--
--AND THE STRAIN OF THE RESULTANT STALEMATE CAN QUICKLY BE SEEN ON THE TORTURED FACES OF THE TWO COMBATANTS...
THE CHEETAH HISSES IN INARTICULATE RAGE, SPITTLE FLYING FROM HER LEATHERY LIPS IN A FINE SPRAY--
--WHILE THE AMAZON MERELY CLENCHES HER TEETH IN GRIM DETERMINATION, ATTEMPTING TO STUDY THE FACE OF HER FOE--
--AND THUS GIVING THE SHE-BEAST THE INFINITESIMAL OPENING SHE NEEDS...
UUNNHH!!
RRAARR
FALLEN TREE TRUNK HAS ME PINNED--!
CAN'T MOVE--!
THE CHEETAH HAS WON!
18

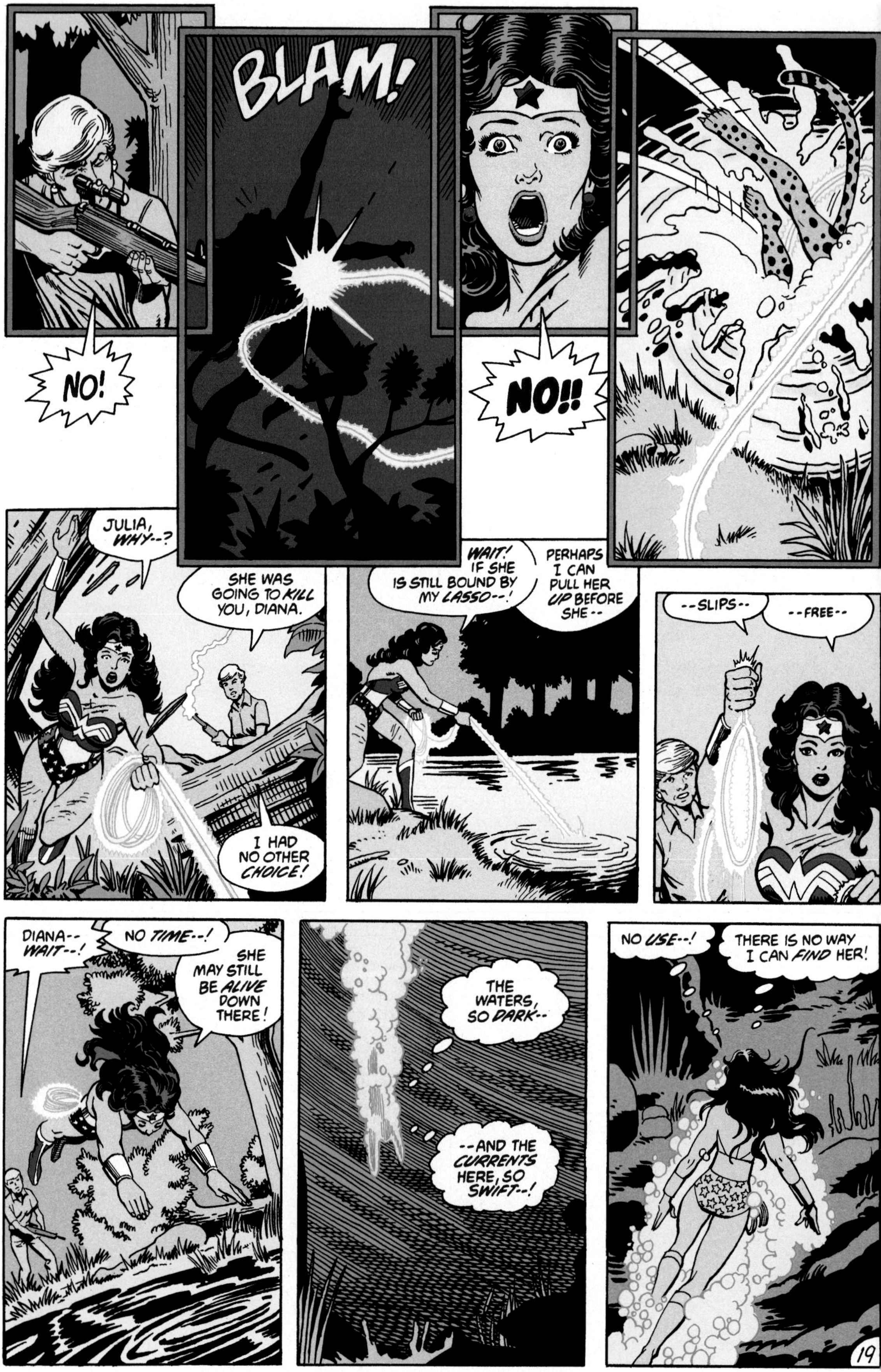
BLAM!
NO!
NO!!
JULIA, WHY--?
SHE WAS GOING TO KILL YOU, DIANA.
I HAD NO OTHER CHOICE!
WAIT! IF SHE IS STILL BOUND BY MY LASSO--!
PERHAPS I CAN PULL HER UP BEFORE SHE --
--SLIPS--
--FREE--
DIANA-- WAIT--!
NO TIME--!
SHE MAY STILL BE ALIVE DOWN THERE!
THE WATERS, SO DARK--
--AND THE CURRENTS HERE, SO SWIFT--!
NO USE--!
THERE IS NO WAY I CAN FIND HER!
19

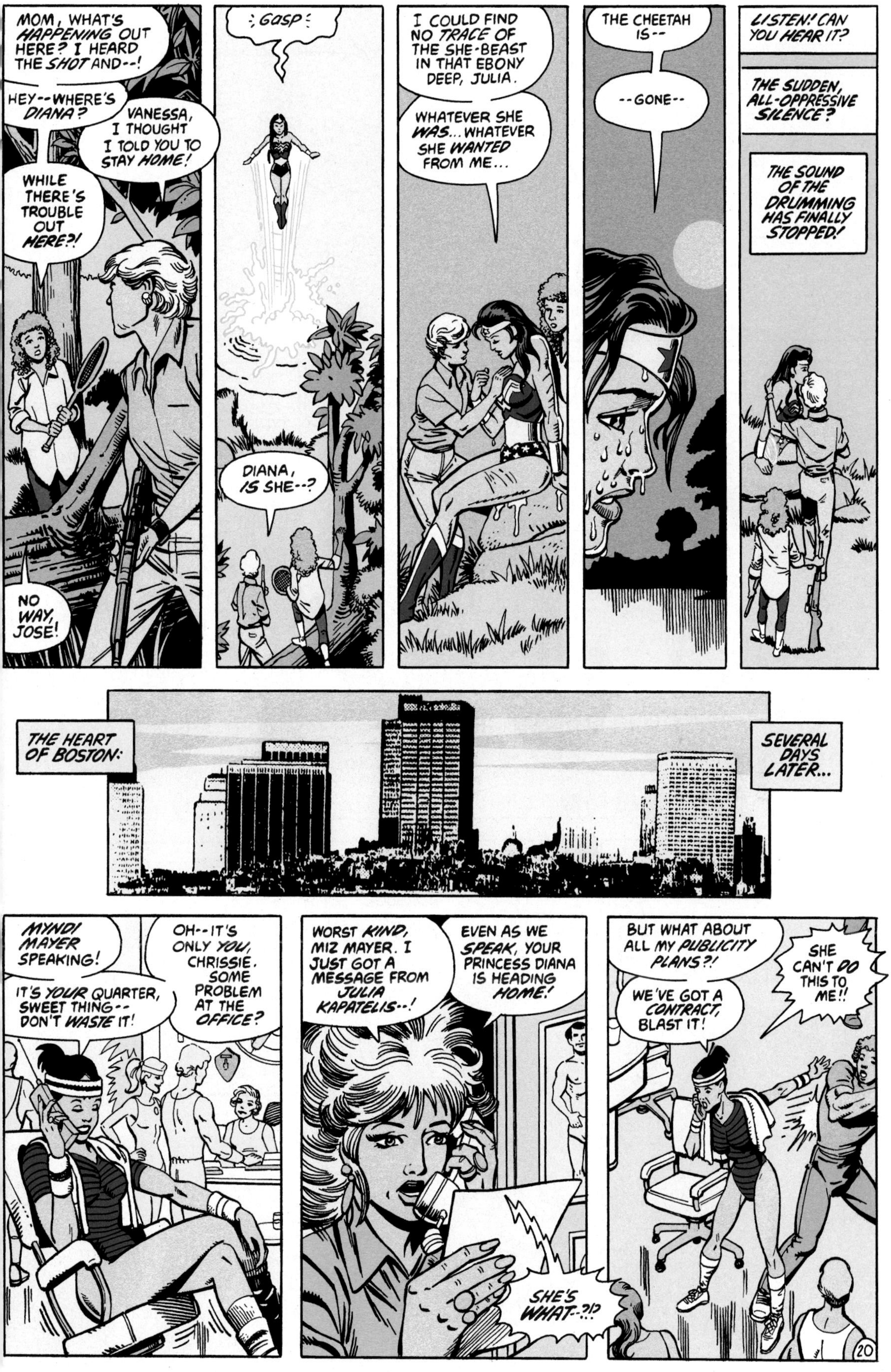
MOM, WHAT'S HAPPENING OUT HERE? I HEARD THE SHOT AND--!
HEY--WHERE'S DIANA?
VANESSA, I THOUGHT I TOLD YOU TO STAY HOME!
WHILE THERE'S TROUBLE OUT HERE?!
NO WAY, JOSE!
Gasp
DIANA, IS SHE--?
I COULD FIND NO TRACE OF THE SHE-BEAST IN THAT EBONY DEEP, JULIA.
WHATEVER SHE WAS... WHATEVER SHE WANTED FROM ME...
THE CHEETAH IS--
--GONE--
LISTEN! CAN YOU HEAR IT?
THE SUDDEN, ALL-OPPRESSIVE SILENCE?
THE SOUND OF THE DRUMMING HAS FINALLY STOPPED!
THE HEART OF BOSTON:
SEVERAL DAYS LATER...
MYNDI MAYER SPEAKING!
IT'S YOUR QUARTER, SWEET THING--DON'T WASTE IT!
OH--IT'S ONLY YOU, CHRISSIE. SOME PROBLEM AT THE OFFICE?
WORST KIND, MIZ MAYER. I JUST GOT A MESSAGE FROM JULIA KAPATELIS--!
EVEN AS WE SPEAK, YOUR PRINCESS DIANA IS HEADING HOME!
SHE'S WHAT--?!?
BUT WHAT ABOUT ALL MY PUBLICITY PLANS?!
WE'VE GOT A CONTRACT, BLAST IT!
SHE CAN'T DO THIS TO ME!!
20

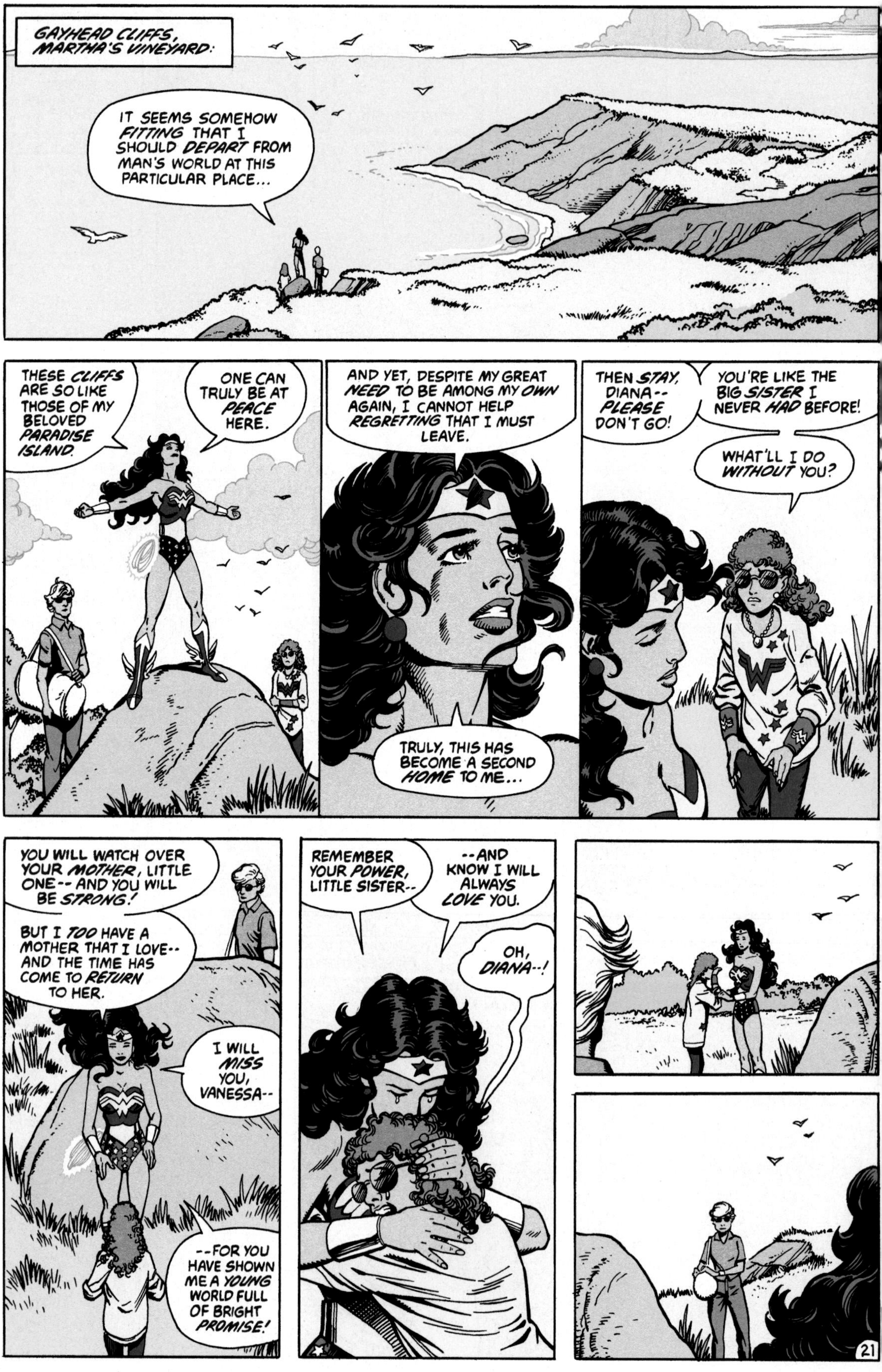
GAYHEAD CLIFFS, MARTHA'S VINEYARD:
IT SEEMS SOMEHOW FITTING THAT I SHOULD DEPART FROM MAN'S WORLD AT THIS PARTICULAR PLACE...
THESE CLIFFS ARE SO LIKE THOSE OF MY BELOVED PARADISE ISLAND.
ONE CAN TRULY BE AT PEACE HERE.
AND YET, DESPITE MY GREAT NEED TO BE AMONG MY OWN AGAIN, I CANNOT HELP REGRETTING THAT I MUST LEAVE.
TRULY, THIS HAS BECOME A SECOND HOME TO ME...
THEN STAY, DIANA-- PLEASE DON'T GO!
YOU'RE LIKE THE BIG SISTER I NEVER HAD BEFORE!
WHAT'LL I DO WITHOUT YOU?
YOU WILL WATCH OVER YOUR MOTHER, LITTLE ONE-- AND YOU WILL BE STRONG!
BUT I TOO HAVE A MOTHER THAT I LOVE-- AND THE TIME HAS COME TO RETURN TO HER.
I WILL MISS YOU, VANESSA--
--FOR YOU HAVE SHOWN ME A YOUNG WORLD FULL OF BRIGHT PROMISE!
REMEMBER YOUR POWER, LITTLE SISTER--
--AND KNOW I WILL ALWAYS LOVE YOU.
OH, DIANA--!
21

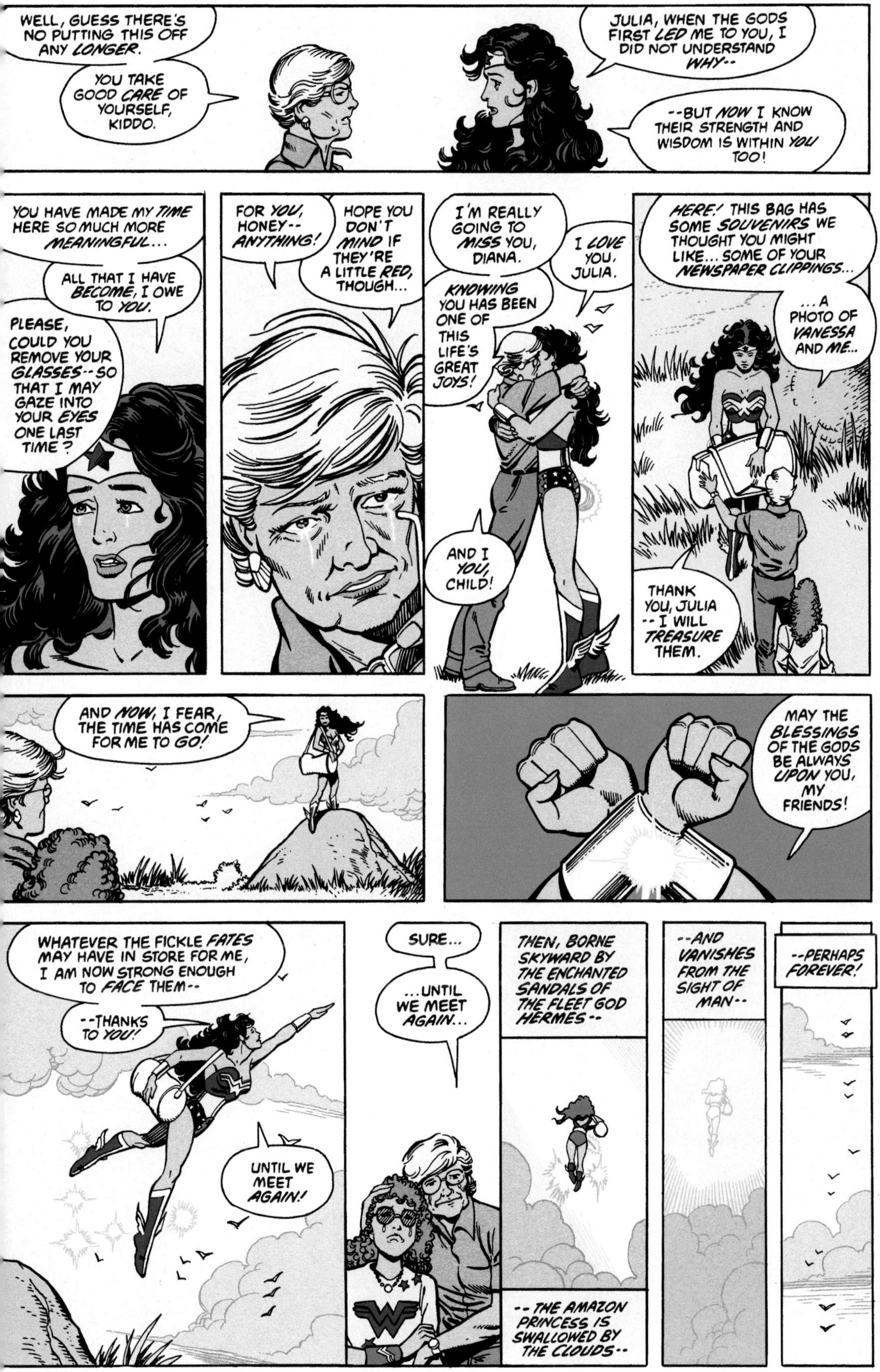
WELL, GUESS THERE'S NO PUTTING THIS OFF ANY LONGER.
YOU TAKE GOOD CARE OF YOURSELF, KIDDO.
JULIA, WHEN THE GODS FIRST LED ME TO YOU, I DID NOT UNDERSTAND WHY--
--BUT NOW I KNOW THEIR STRENGTH AND WISDOM IS WITHIN YOU TOO!
YOU HAVE MADE MY TIME HERE SO MUCH MORE MEANINGFUL...
ALL THAT I HAVE BECOME, I OWE TO YOU.
PLEASE, COULD YOU REMOVE YOUR GLASSES--SO THAT I MAY GAZE INTO YOUR EYES ONE LAST TIME?
FOR YOU, HONEY--ANYTHING!
HOPE YOU DON'T MIND IF THEY'RE A LITTLE RED, THOUGH...
I'M REALLY GOING TO MISS YOU, DIANA.
KNOWING YOU HAS BEEN ONE OF THIS LIFE'S GREAT JOYS!
I LOVE YOU, JULIA.
AND I YOU, CHILD!
HERE! THIS BAG HAS SOME SOUVENIRS WE THOUGHT YOU MIGHT LIKE... SOME OF YOUR NEWSPAPER CLIPPINGS...
...A PHOTO OF VANESSA AND ME...
THANK YOU, JULIA--I WILL TREASURE THEM.
AND NOW, I FEAR, THE TIME HAS COME FOR ME TO GO!
MAY THE BLESSINGS OF THE GODS BE ALWAYS UPON YOU, MY FRIENDS!
WHATEVER THE FICKLE FATES MAY HAVE IN STORE FOR ME, I AM NOW STRONG ENOUGH TO FACE THEM--
--THANKS TO YOU!
UNTIL WE MEET AGAIN!
SURE...
...UNTIL WE MEET AGAIN...
THEN, BORNE SKYWARD BY THE ENCHANTED SANDALS OF THE FLEET GOD HERMES--
--THE AMAZON PRINCESS IS SWALLOWED BY THE CLOUDS--
--AND VANISHES FROM THE SIGHT OF MAN--
--PERHAPS FOREVER!

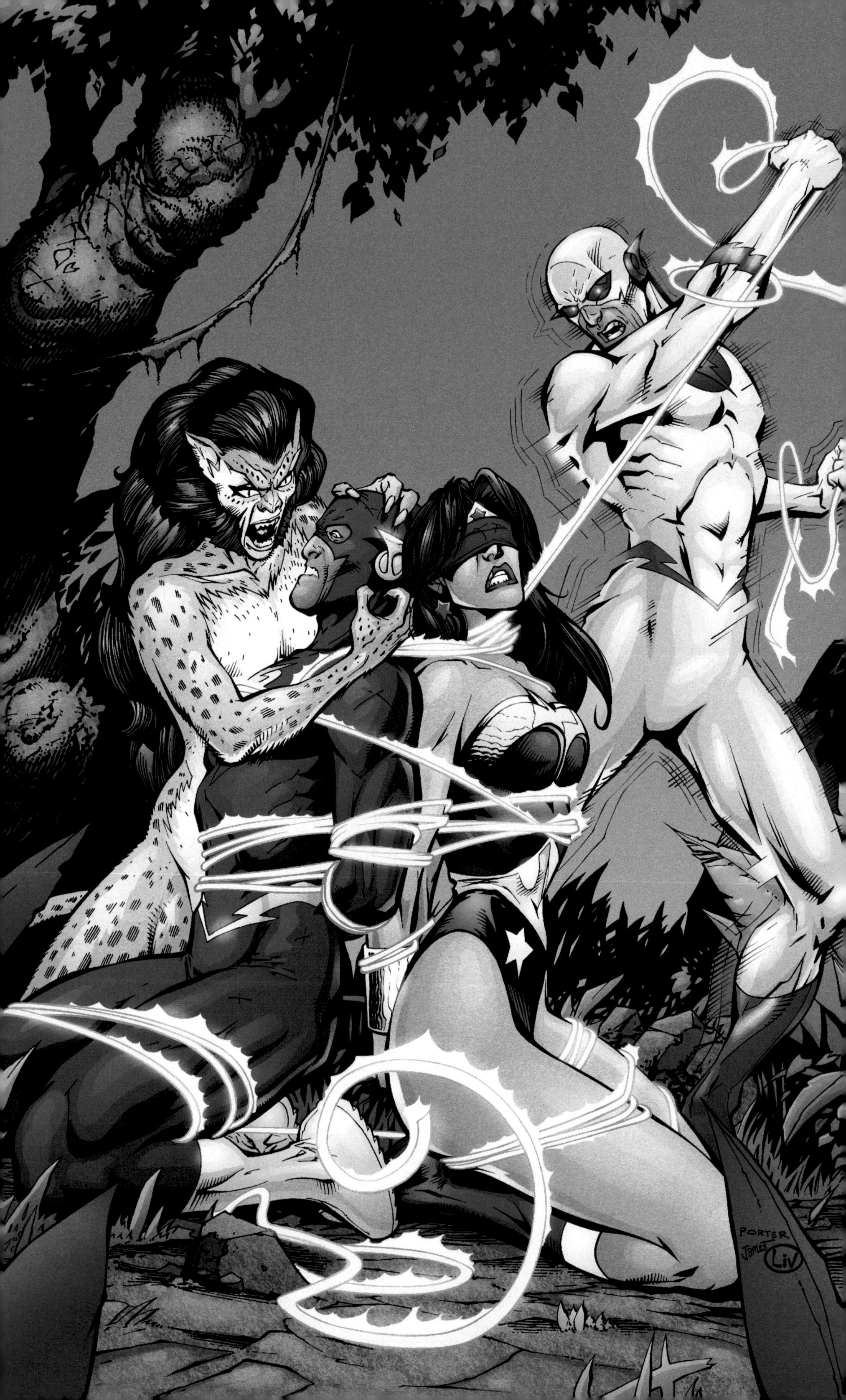
PORTER
James
Liv

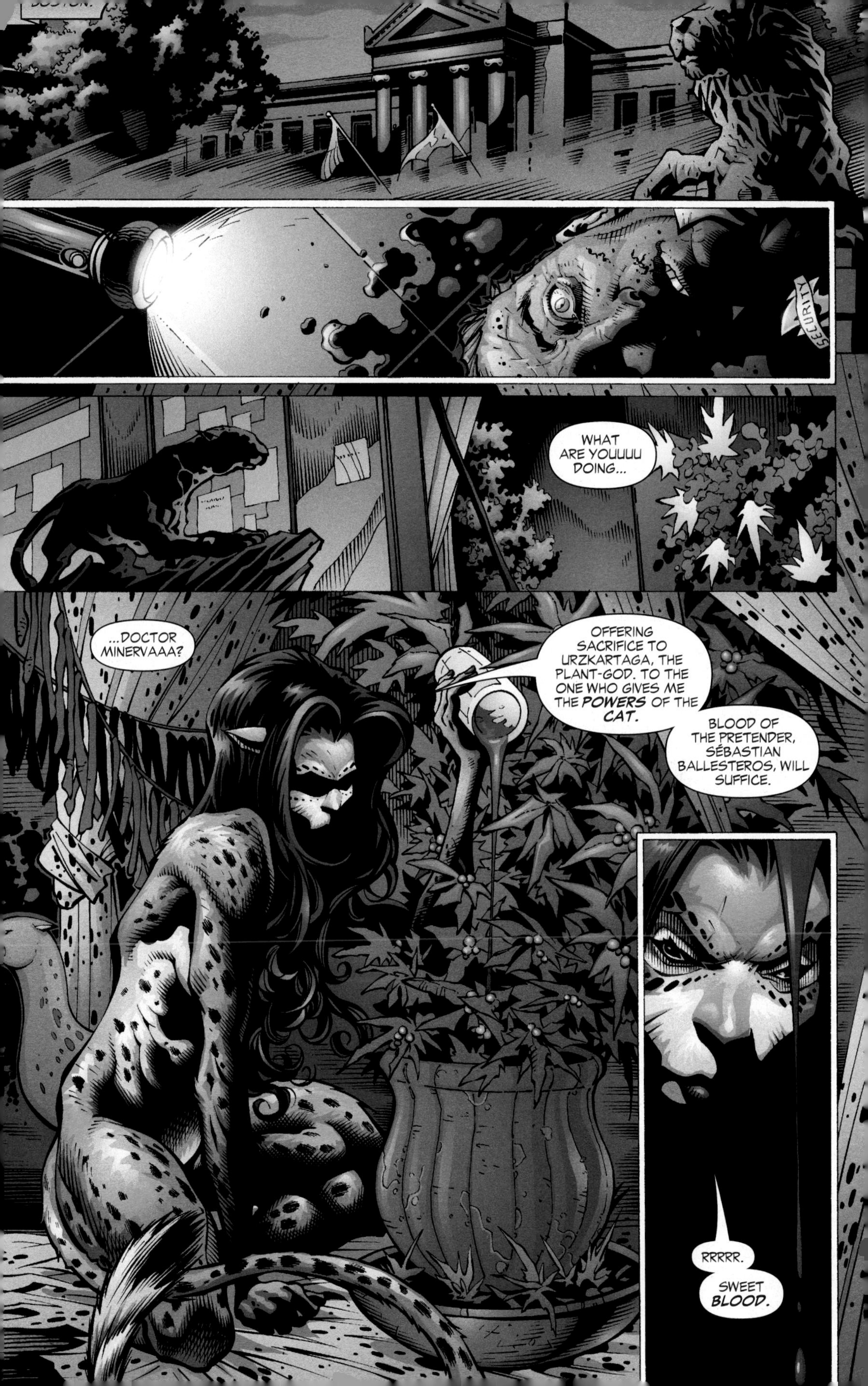
WHAT ARE YOUUUU DOING...
...DOCTOR MINERVAAA?
OFFERING SACRIFICE TO URZKARTAGA, THE PLANT-GOD. TO THE ONE WHO GIVES ME THE *POWERS* OF THE *CAT.*
BLOOD OF THE PRETENDER, SÉBASTIAN BALLESTEROS, WILL SUFFICE.
RRRRR.
SWEET *BLOOD.*

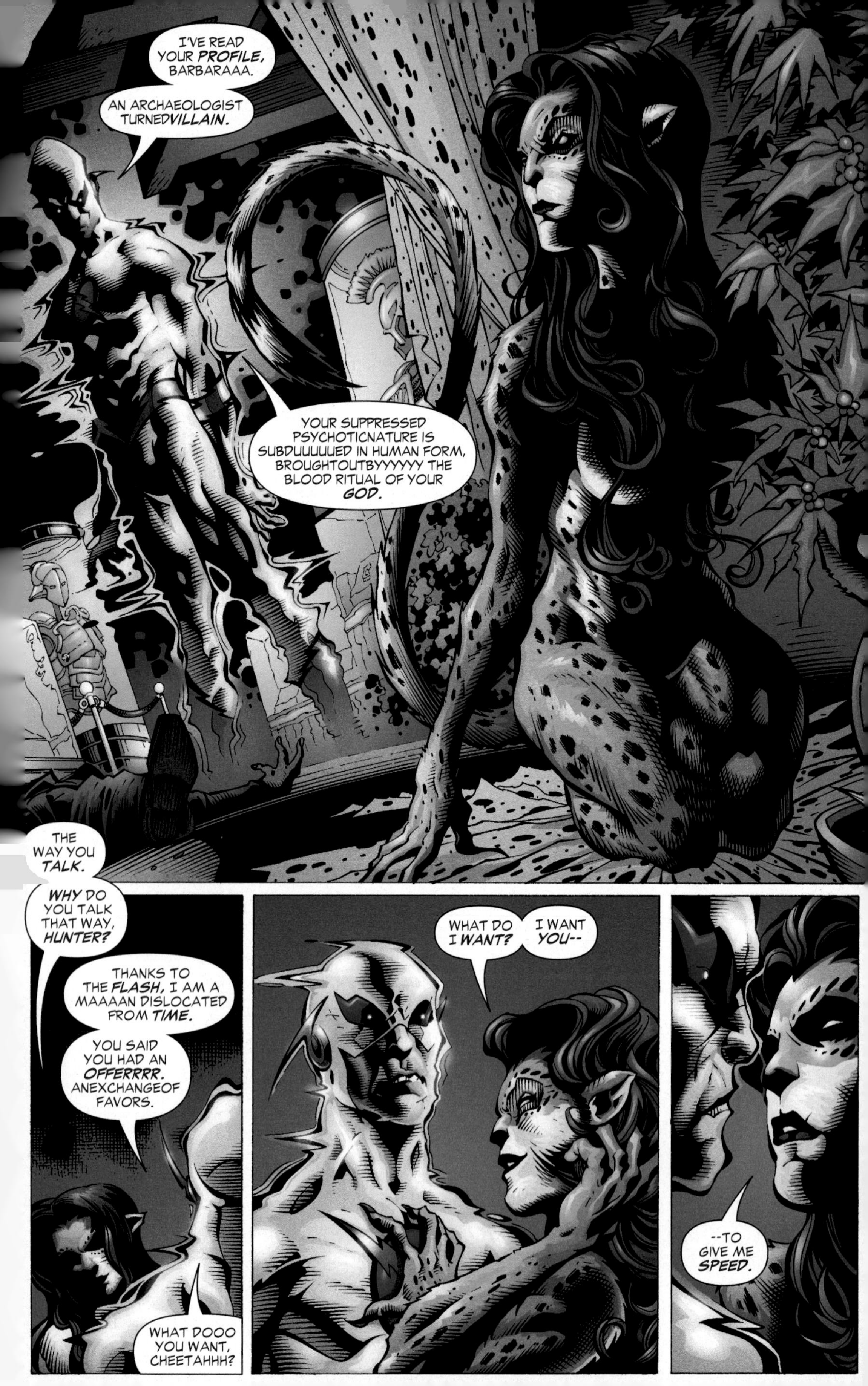

I'VE READ YOUR PROFILE, BARBARAAA.
AN ARCHAEOLOGIST TURNEDVILLAIN.
YOUR SUPPRESSED PSYCHOTICNATURE IS SUBDUUUUUED IN HUMAN FORM, BROUGHTOUTBYYYYYY THE BLOOD RITUAL OF YOUR GOD.
THE WAY YOU TALK.
WHY DO YOU TALK THAT WAY, HUNTER?
THANKS TO THE FLASH, I AM A MAAAAN DISLOCATED FROM TIME.
YOU SAID YOU HAD AN OFFERRRR. ANEXCHANGEOF FAVORS.
WHAT DOOO YOU WANT, CHEETAHHH?
WHAT DO I WANT?
I WANT YOU--
--TO GIVE ME SPEED.

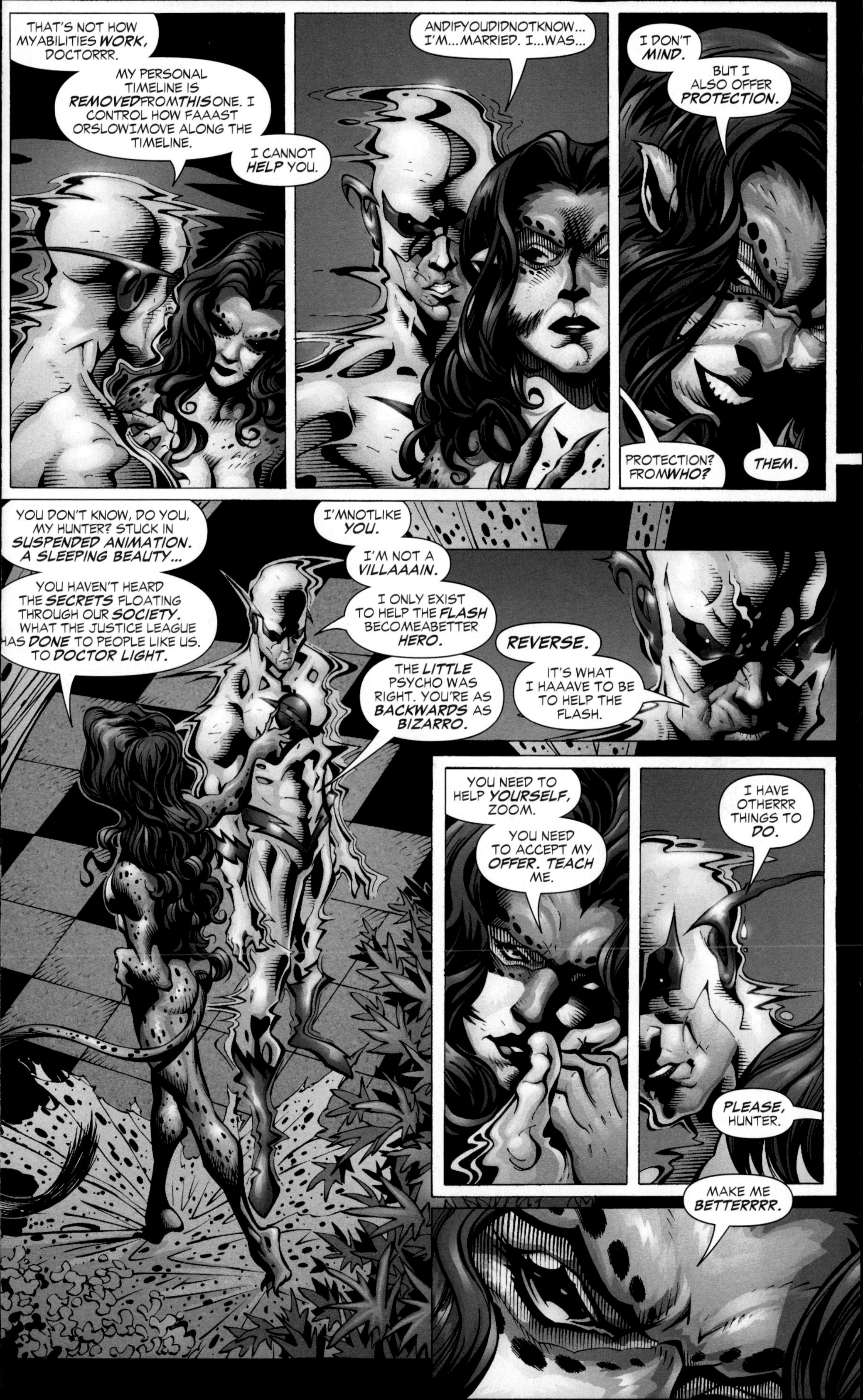
THAT'S NOT HOW MYABILITIES WORK, DOCTORRR.
MY PERSONAL TIMELINE IS REMOVEDFROMTHISONE. I CONTROL HOW FAAAST ORSLOWIMOVE ALONG THE TIMELINE.
I CANNOT HELP YOU.
ANDIFYOUDIDNOTKNOW... I'M...MARRIED. I...WAS...
I DON'T MIND.
BUT I ALSO OFFER PROTECTION.
PROTECTION? FROMWHO?
THEM.
YOU DON'T KNOW, DO YOU, MY HUNTER? STUCK IN SUSPENDED ANIMATION. A SLEEPING BEAUTY...
YOU HAVEN'T HEARD THE SECRETS FLOATING THROUGH OUR SOCIETY. WHAT THE JUSTICE LEAGUE HAS DONE TO PEOPLE LIKE US. TO DOCTOR LIGHT.
I'MNOTLIKE YOU.
I'M NOT A VILLAAAIN.
I ONLY EXIST TO HELP THE FLASH BECOMEABETTER HERO.
THE LITTLE PSYCHO WAS RIGHT. YOU'RE AS BACKWARDS AS BIZARRO.
REVERSE.
IT'S WHAT I HAAAVE TO BE TO HELP THE FLASH.
YOU NEED TO HELP YOURSELF, ZOOM.
YOU NEED TO ACCEPT MY OFFER. TEACH ME.
I HAVE OTHERRR THINGS TO DO.
PLEASE, HUNTER.
MAKE ME BETTERRRR.

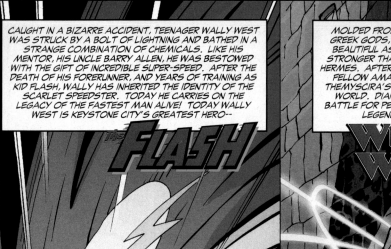

CAUGHT IN A BIZARRE ACCIDENT, TEENAGER WALLY WEST WAS STRUCK BY A BOLT OF LIGHTNING AND BATHED IN A STRANGE COMBINATION OF CHEMICALS. LIKE HIS MENTOR, HIS UNCLE BARRY ALLEN, HE WAS BESTOWED WITH THE GIFT OF INCREDIBLE SUPER-SPEED. AFTER THE DEATH OF HIS FORERUNNER, AND YEARS OF TRAINING AS KID FLASH, WALLY HAS INHERITED THE IDENTITY OF THE SCARLET SPEEDSTER. TODAY HE CARRIES ON THE LEGACY OF THE FASTEST MAN ALIVE! TODAY WALLY WEST IS KEYSTONE CITY'S GREATEST HERO--

THE FLASH

MOLDED FROM CLAY AND GIVEN LIFE BY THE GREEK GODS, PRINCESS DIANA WAS BORN AS BEAUTIFUL AS APHRODITE, WISE AS ATHENA, STRONGER THAN HERCULES AND SWIFTER THAN HERMES. AFTER WINNING A CONTEST AMONG HER FELLOW AMAZONS, DIANA WAS CHOSEN AS THEMYSCIRA'S AMBASSADOR TO THE OUTSIDE WORLD. DIANA ENTERED MAN'S WORLD TO BATTLE FOR PEACE AND JUSTICE AS THE MOST LEGENDARY AMAZON OF ALL--

WONDER WOMAN

TRUTH OR DARE PART 1

GEOFF JOHNS-WRITER   JUSTINIANO-PENCILLER
LIVESAY-INKER   WALDEN WONG-INKER-P 7, 18-22
PAT BROSSEAU-LETTERER   JAMES SINCLAIR-COLORIST
RACHEL GLUCKSTERN-ASST. EDITOR   JOEY CAVALIERI-EDITOR
SPECIAL THANKS TO GREG RUCKA

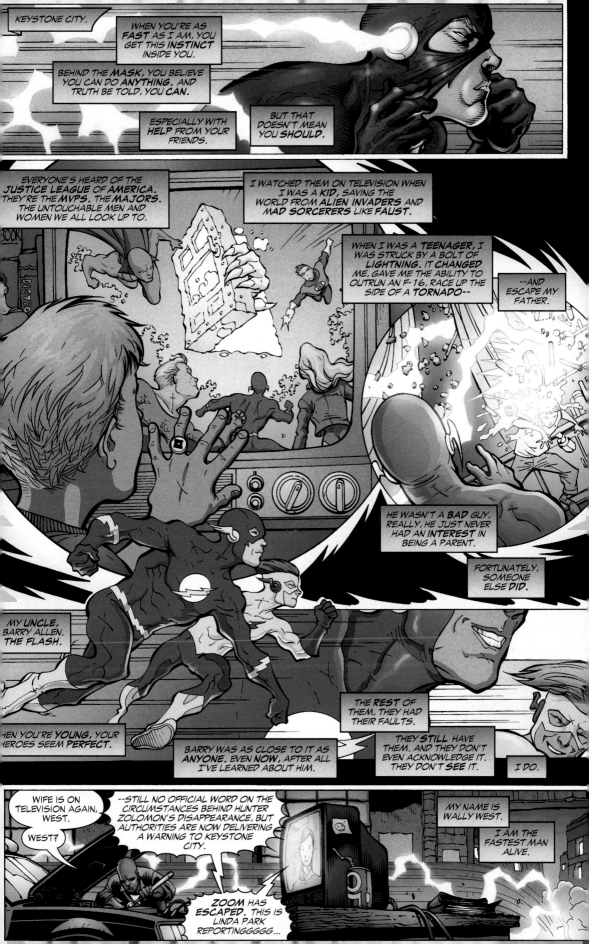

KEYSTONE CITY.

WHEN YOU'RE AS FAST AS I AM, YOU GET THIS INSTINCT INSIDE YOU.

BEHIND THE MASK, YOU BELIEVE YOU CAN DO ANYTHING. AND TRUTH BE TOLD, YOU CAN.

ESPECIALLY WITH HELP FROM YOUR FRIENDS.

BUT THAT DOESN'T MEAN YOU SHOULD.

EVERYONE'S HEARD OF THE JUSTICE LEAGUE OF AMERICA. THEY'RE THE MVPS. THE MAJORS. THE UNTOUCHABLE MEN AND WOMEN WE ALL LOOK UP TO.

I WATCHED THEM ON TELEVISION WHEN I WAS A KID, SAVING THE WORLD FROM ALIEN INVADERS AND MAD SORCERERS LIKE FAUST.

WHEN I WAS A TEENAGER, I WAS STRUCK BY A BOLT OF LIGHTNING. IT CHANGED ME, GAVE ME THE ABILITY TO OUTRUN AN F-16, RACE UP THE SIDE OF A TORNADO--

--AND ESCAPE MY FATHER.

HE WASN'T A BAD GUY, REALLY, HE JUST NEVER HAD AN INTEREST IN BEING A PARENT.

FORTUNATELY, SOMEONE ELSE DID.

MY UNCLE, BARRY ALLEN. THE FLASH.

THEN YOU'RE YOUNG, YOUR HEROES SEEM PERFECT.

BARRY WAS AS CLOSE TO IT AS ANYONE. EVEN NOW, AFTER ALL I'VE LEARNED ABOUT HIM.

THE REST OF THEM, THEY HAD THEIR FAULTS.

THEY STILL HAVE THEM. AND THEY DON'T EVEN ACKNOWLEDGE IT. THEY DON'T SEE IT.

I DO.

WIFE IS ON TELEVISION AGAIN, WEST.

WEST?

--STILL NO OFFICIAL WORD ON THE CIRCUMSTANCES BEHIND HUNTER ZOLOMON'S DISAPPEARANCE, BUT AUTHORITIES ARE NOW DELIVERING A WARNING TO KEYSTONE CITY.

ZOOM HAS ESCAPED. THIS IS LINDA PARK REPORTINGGGGG...

MY NAME IS WALLY WEST.

I AM THE FASTEST MAN ALIVE.

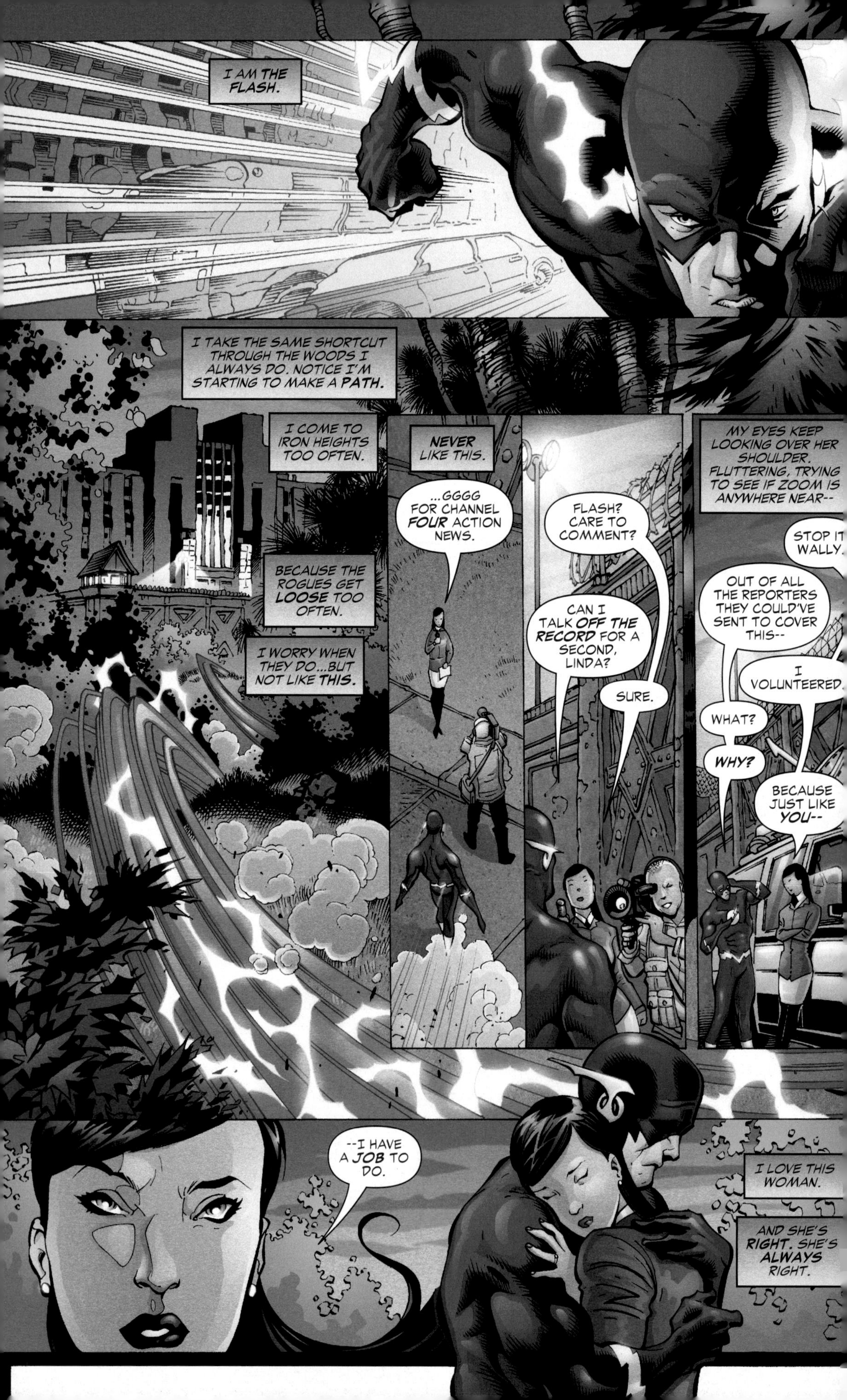

I AM THE FLASH.
I TAKE THE SAME SHORTCUT THROUGH THE WOODS I ALWAYS DO. NOTICE I'M STARTING TO MAKE A PATH.
I COME TO IRON HEIGHTS TOO OFTEN.
BECAUSE THE ROGUES GET LOOSE TOO OFTEN.
I WORRY WHEN THEY DO...BUT NOT LIKE THIS.
NEVER LIKE THIS.
...GGGG FOR CHANNEL FOUR ACTION NEWS.
FLASH? CARE TO COMMENT?
CAN I TALK OFF THE RECORD FOR A SECOND, LINDA?
SURE.
MY EYES KEEP LOOKING OVER HER SHOULDER. FLUTTERING, TRYING TO SEE IF ZOOM IS ANYWHERE NEAR--
STOP IT WALLY.
OUT OF ALL THE REPORTERS THEY COULD'VE SENT TO COVER THIS--
I VOLUNTEERED.
WHAT?
WHY?
BECAUSE JUST LIKE YOU--
--I HAVE A JOB TO DO.
I LOVE THIS WOMAN.
AND SHE'S RIGHT. SHE'S ALWAYS RIGHT.

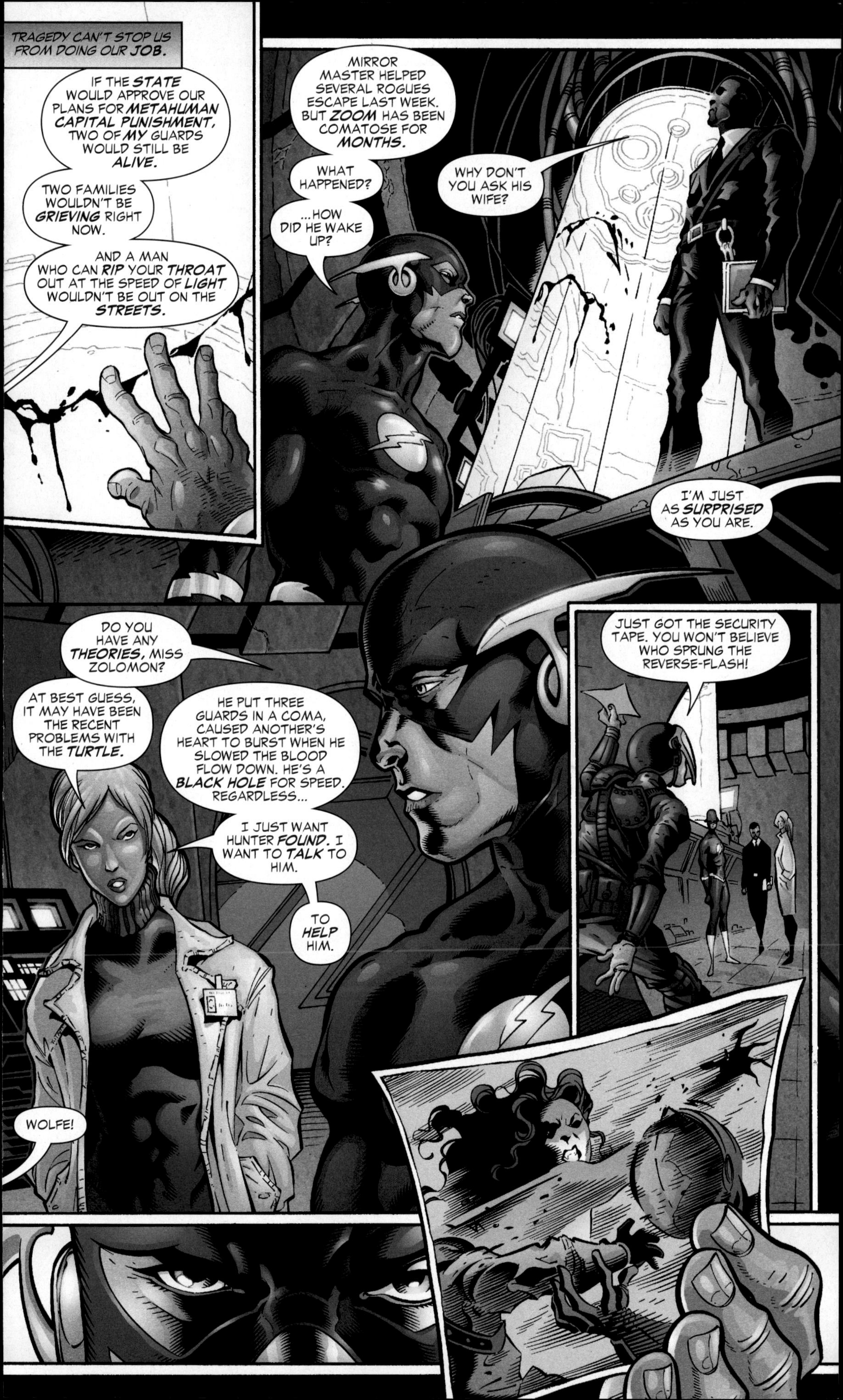
TRAGEDY CAN'T STOP US FROM DOING OUR JOB.
IF THE STATE WOULD APPROVE OUR PLANS FOR METAHUMAN CAPITAL PUNISHMENT, TWO OF MY GUARDS WOULD STILL BE ALIVE.
TWO FAMILIES WOULDN'T BE GRIEVING RIGHT NOW.
AND A MAN WHO CAN RIP YOUR THROAT OUT AT THE SPEED OF LIGHT WOULDN'T BE OUT ON THE STREETS.
MIRROR MASTER HELPED SEVERAL ROGUES ESCAPE LAST WEEK. BUT ZOOM HAS BEEN COMATOSE FOR MONTHS.
WHAT HAPPENED?
...HOW DID HE WAKE UP?
WHY DON'T YOU ASK HIS WIFE?
I'M JUST AS SURPRISED AS YOU ARE.
DO YOU HAVE ANY THEORIES, MISS ZOLOMON?
AT BEST GUESS, IT MAY HAVE BEEN THE RECENT PROBLEMS WITH THE TURTLE.
HE PUT THREE GUARDS IN A COMA, CAUSED ANOTHER'S HEART TO BURST WHEN HE SLOWED THE BLOOD FLOW DOWN. HE'S A BLACK HOLE FOR SPEED. REGARDLESS...
I JUST WANT HUNTER FOUND. I WANT TO TALK TO HIM.
TO HELP HIM.
JUST GOT THE SECURITY TAPE. YOU WON'T BELIEVE WHO SPRUNG THE REVERSE-FLASH!
WOLFE!

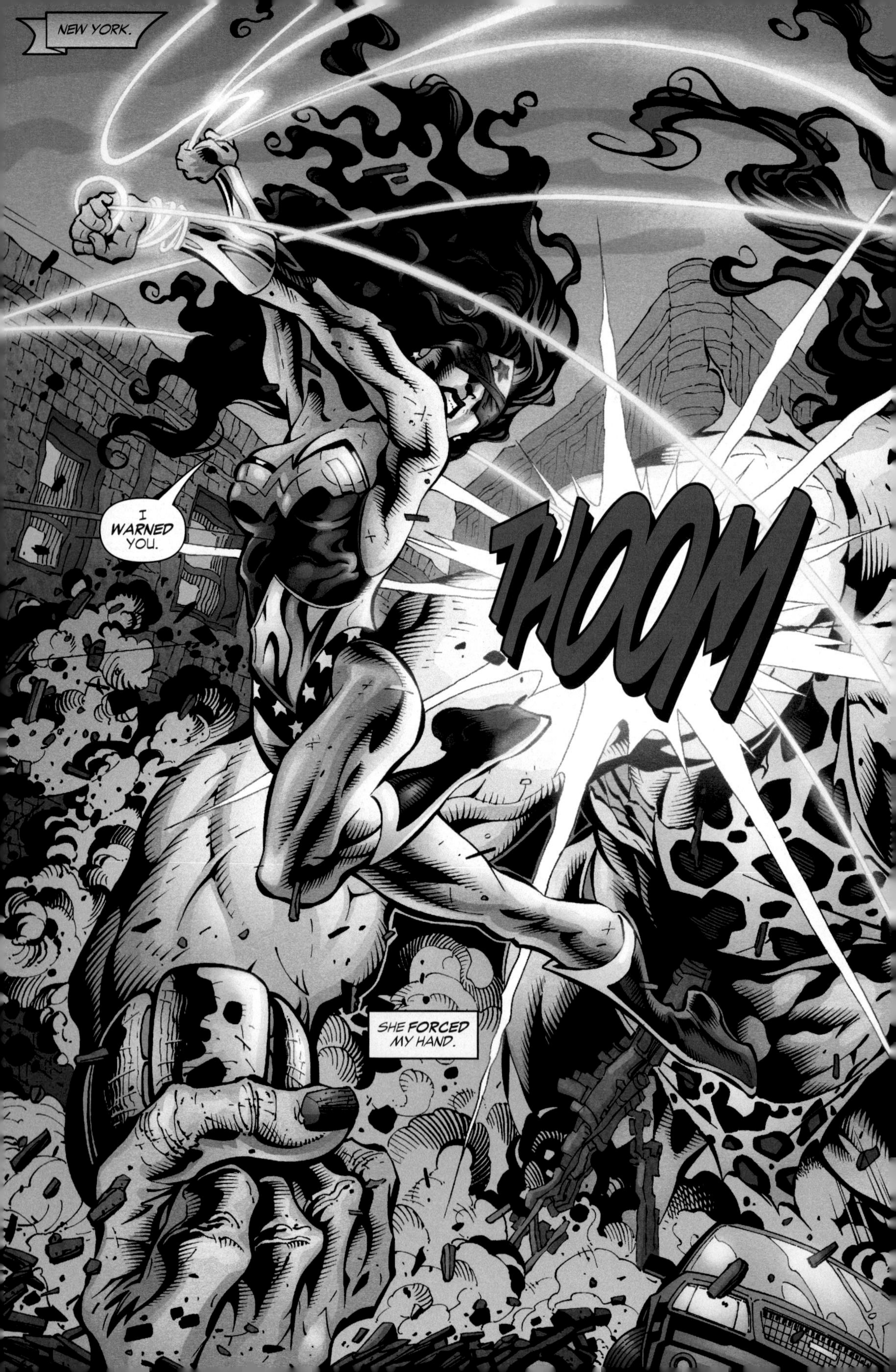
NEW YORK.
I WARNED YOU.
THOOM
SHE FORCED MY HAND.

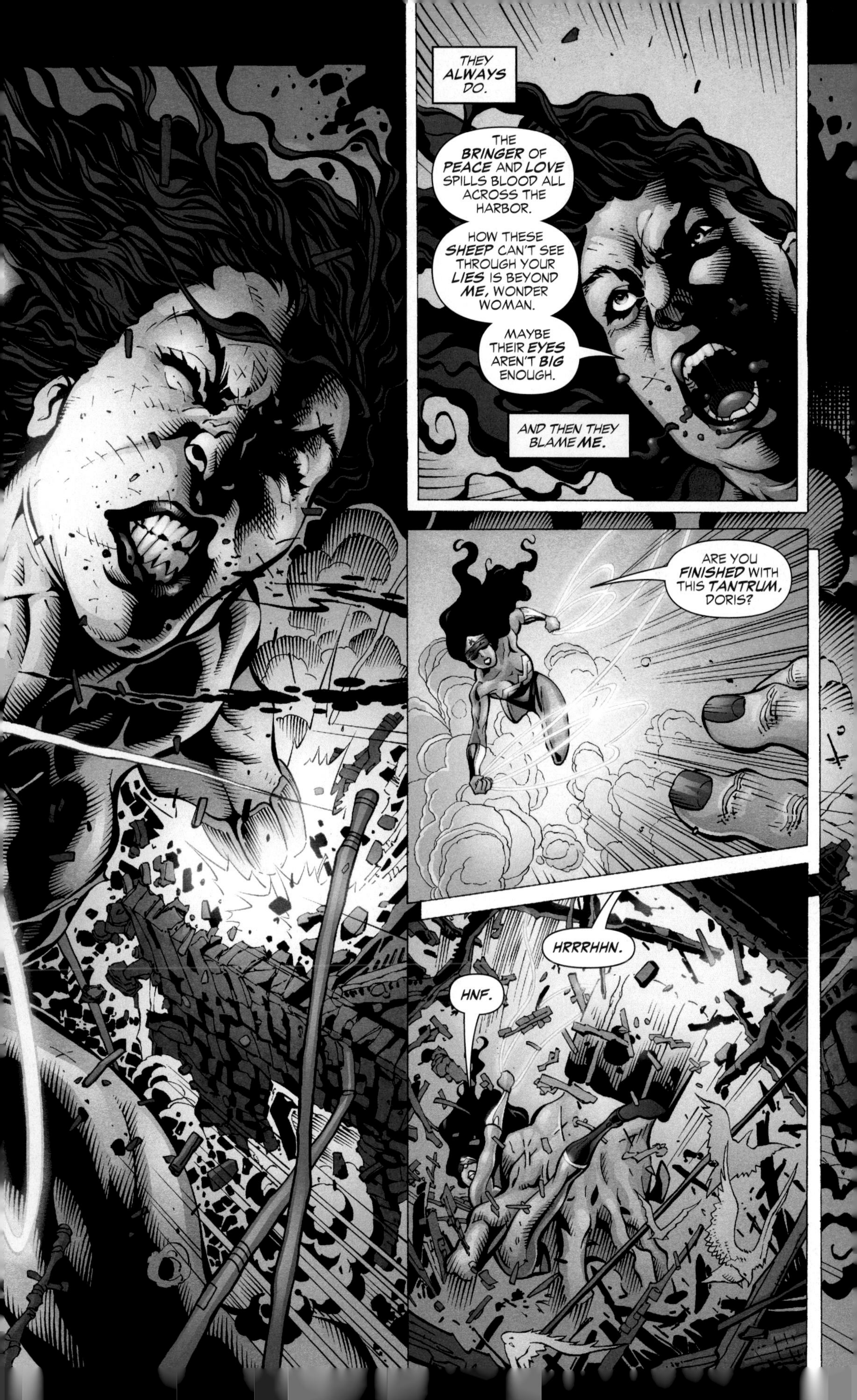
THEY ALWAYS DO.
THE BRINGER OF PEACE AND LOVE SPILLS BLOOD ALL ACROSS THE HARBOR.
HOW THESE SHEEP CAN'T SEE THROUGH YOUR LIES IS BEYOND ME, WONDER WOMAN.
MAYBE THEIR EYES AREN'T BIG ENOUGH.
AND THEN THEY BLAME ME.
ARE YOU FINISHED WITH THIS TANTRUM, DORIS?
HRRRHHN.
HNF.

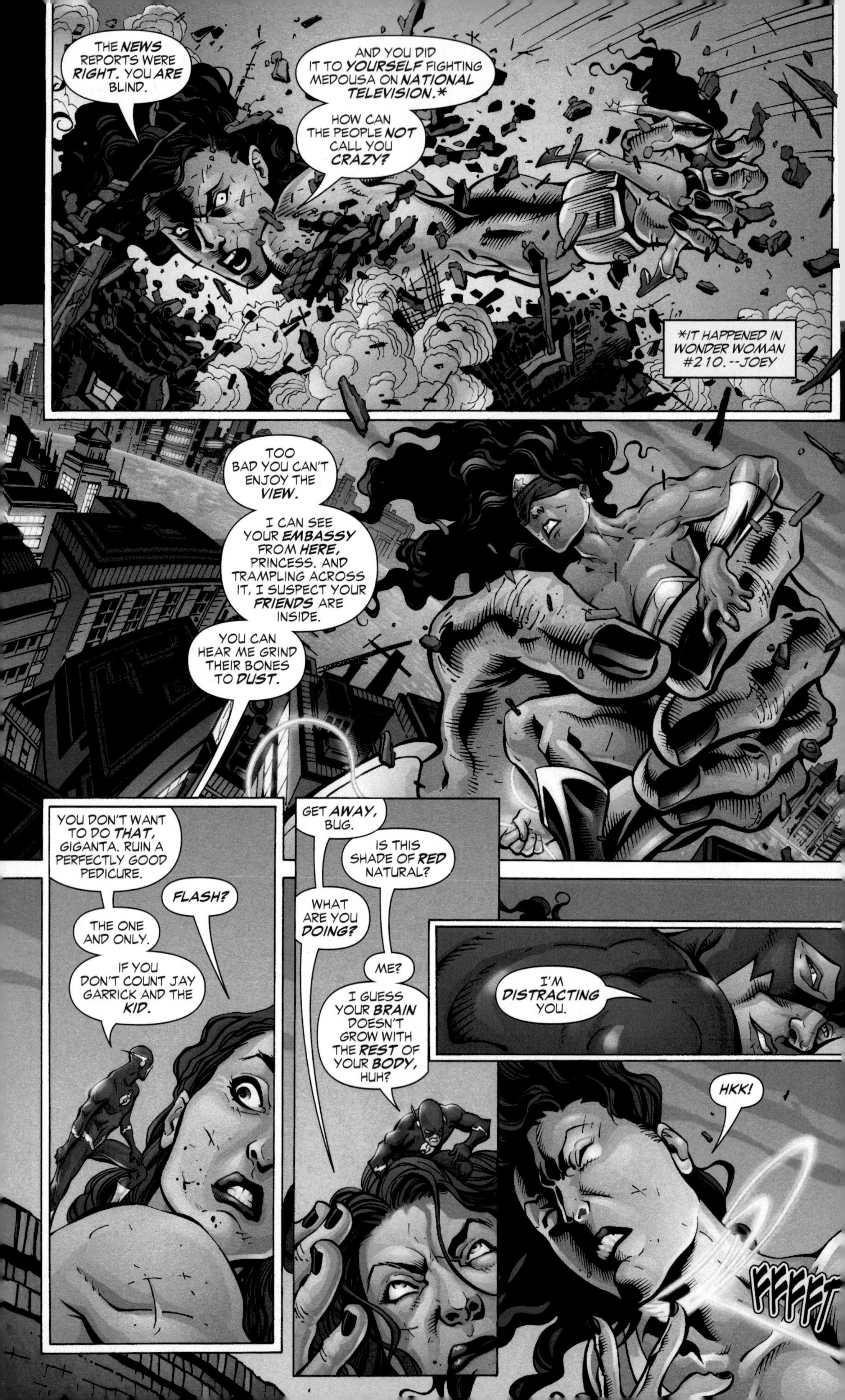
THE NEWS REPORTS WERE RIGHT. YOU ARE BLIND.
AND YOU DID IT TO YOURSELF FIGHTING MEDOUSA ON NATIONAL TELEVISION.*
HOW CAN THE PEOPLE NOT CALL YOU CRAZY?
*IT HAPPENED IN WONDER WOMAN #210.--JOEY
TOO BAD YOU CAN'T ENJOY THE VIEW.
I CAN SEE YOUR EMBASSY FROM HERE, PRINCESS. AND TRAMPLING ACROSS IT, I SUSPECT YOUR FRIENDS ARE INSIDE.
YOU CAN HEAR ME GRIND THEIR BONES TO DUST.
YOU DON'T WANT TO DO THAT, GIGANTA. RUIN A PERFECTLY GOOD PEDICURE.
FLASH?
THE ONE AND ONLY.
IF YOU DON'T COUNT JAY GARRICK AND THE KID.
GET AWAY, BUG.
IS THIS SHADE OF RED NATURAL?
WHAT ARE YOU DOING?
ME?
I GUESS YOUR BRAIN DOESN'T GROW WITH THE REST OF YOUR BODY, HUH?
I'M DISTRACTING YOU.
HKK!
FFFFT

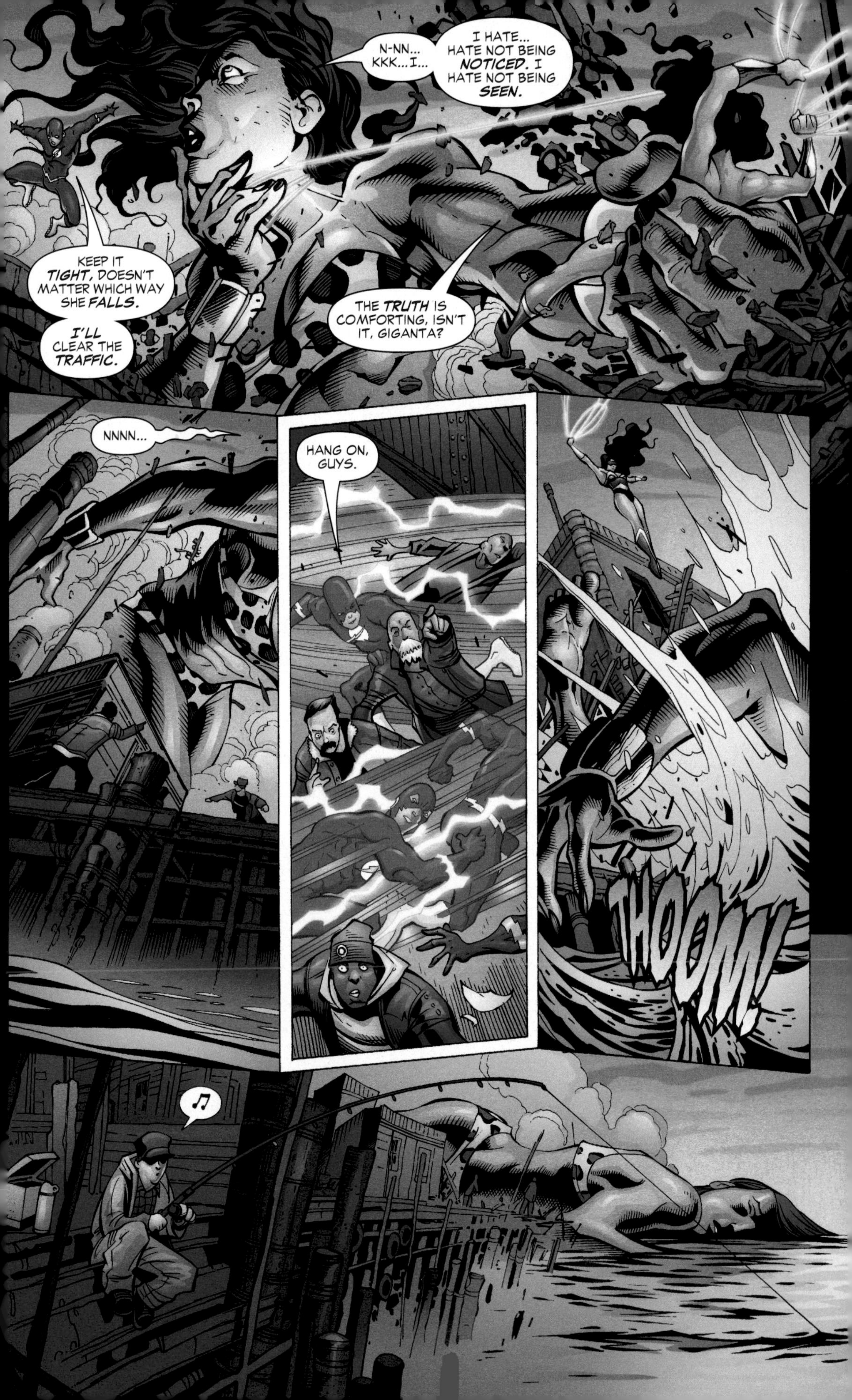
N-NN... KKK...I...
I HATE... HATE NOT BEING NOTICED. I HATE NOT BEING SEEN.
KEEP IT TIGHT, DOESN'T MATTER WHICH WAY SHE FALLS.
I'LL CLEAR THE TRAFFIC.
THE TRUTH IS COMFORTING, ISN'T IT, GIGANTA?
NNNN...
HANG ON, GUYS.
THOOM!
♫

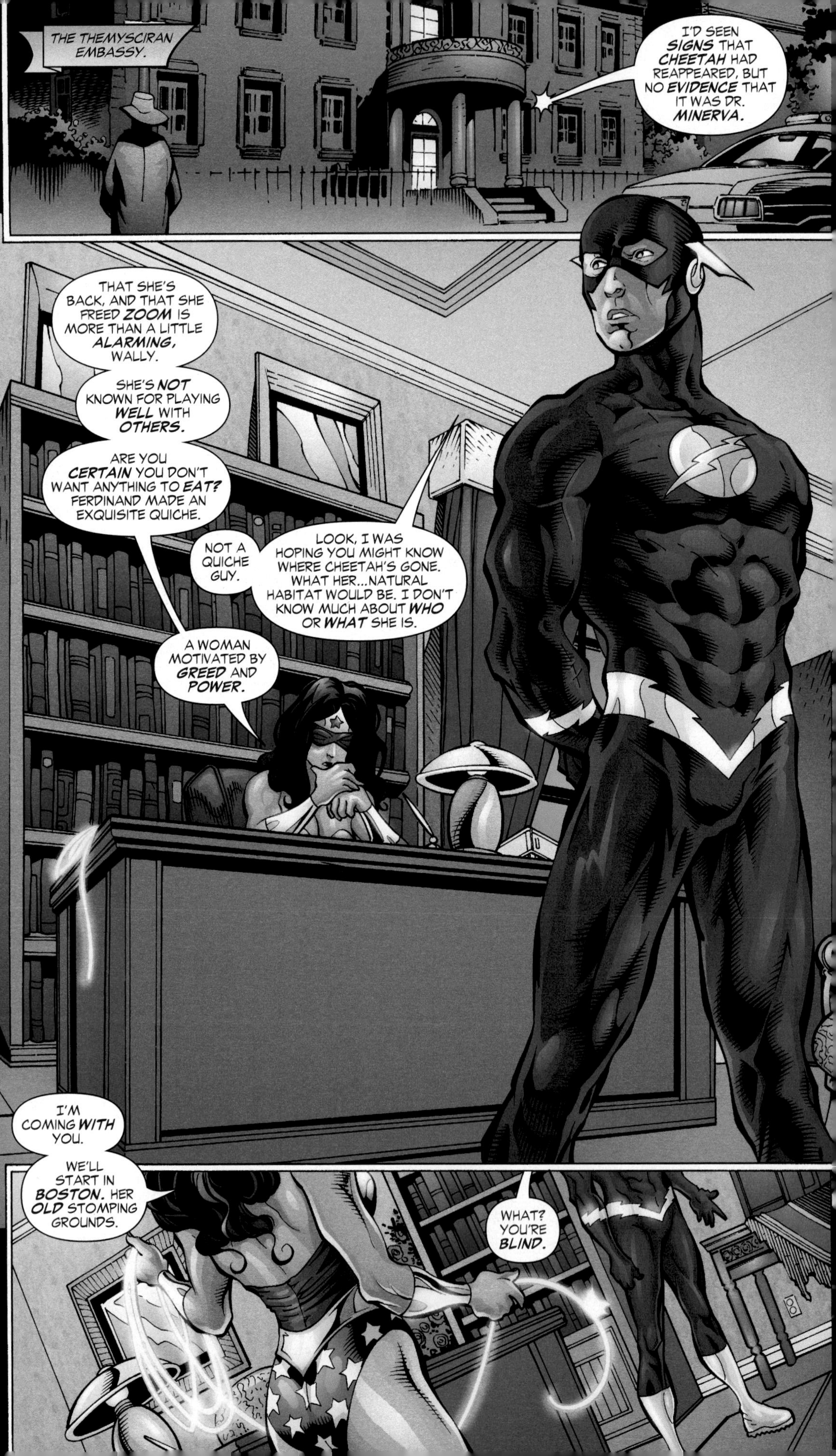
THE THEMYSCIRAN EMBASSY.
I'D SEEN SIGNS THAT CHEETAH HAD REAPPEARED, BUT NO EVIDENCE THAT IT WAS DR. MINERVA.
THAT SHE'S BACK, AND THAT SHE FREED ZOOM IS MORE THAN A LITTLE ALARMING, WALLY.
SHE'S NOT KNOWN FOR PLAYING WELL WITH OTHERS.
ARE YOU CERTAIN YOU DON'T WANT ANYTHING TO EAT? FERDINAND MADE AN EXQUISITE QUICHE.
NOT A QUICHE GUY.
LOOK, I WAS HOPING YOU MIGHT KNOW WHERE CHEETAH'S GONE. WHAT HER...NATURAL HABITAT WOULD BE. I DON'T KNOW MUCH ABOUT WHO OR WHAT SHE IS.
A WOMAN MOTIVATED BY GREED AND POWER.
I'M COMING WITH YOU.
WE'LL START IN BOSTON. HER OLD STOMPING GROUNDS.
WHAT? YOU'RE BLIND.

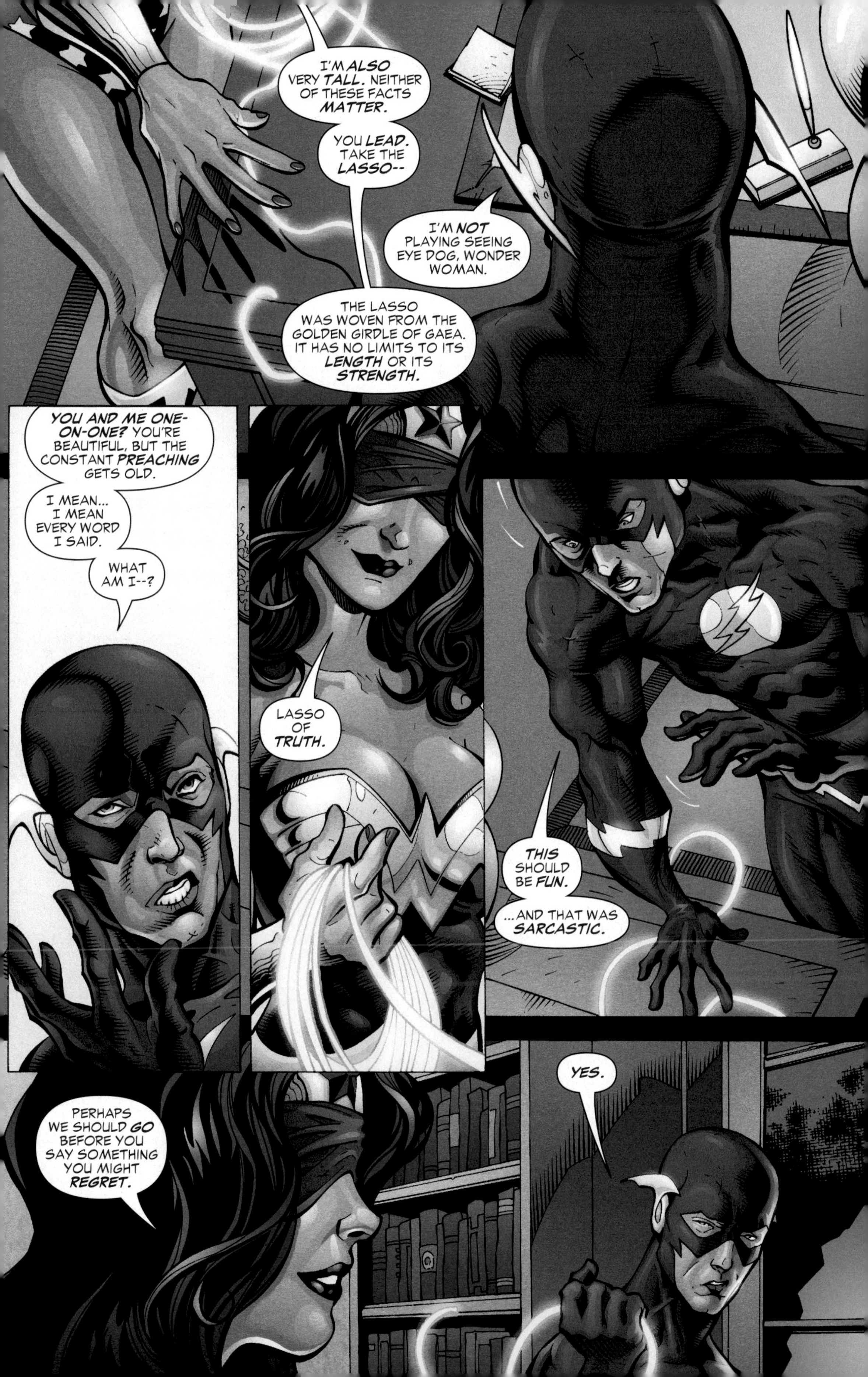
I'M ALSO VERY TALL. NEITHER OF THESE FACTS MATTER.
YOU LEAD. TAKE THE LASSO--
I'M NOT PLAYING SEEING EYE DOG, WONDER WOMAN.
THE LASSO WAS WOVEN FROM THE GOLDEN GIRDLE OF GAEA. IT HAS NO LIMITS TO ITS LENGTH OR ITS STRENGTH.
YOU AND ME ONE-ON-ONE? YOU'RE BEAUTIFUL, BUT THE CONSTANT PREACHING GETS OLD.
I MEAN... I MEAN EVERY WORD I SAID.
WHAT AM I--?
LASSO OF TRUTH.
THIS SHOULD BE FUN.
...AND THAT WAS SARCASTIC.
PERHAPS WE SHOULD GO BEFORE YOU SAY SOMETHING YOU MIGHT REGRET.
YES.

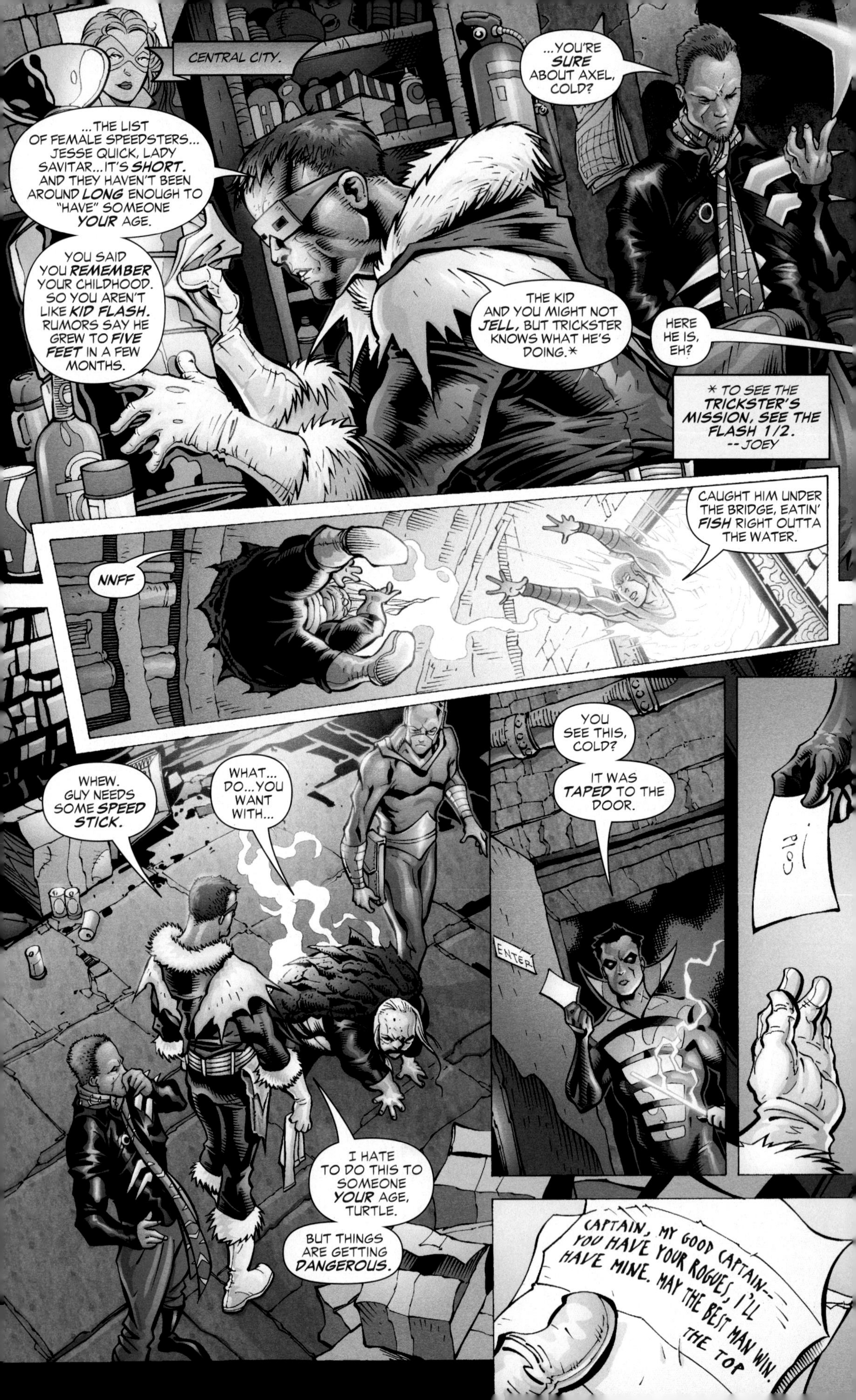
CENTRAL CITY.
...THE LIST OF FEMALE SPEEDSTERS... JESSE QUICK, LADY SAVITAR...IT'S SHORT. AND THEY HAVEN'T BEEN AROUND LONG ENOUGH TO "HAVE" SOMEONE YOUR AGE.
YOU SAID YOU REMEMBER YOUR CHILDHOOD. SO YOU AREN'T LIKE KID FLASH. RUMORS SAY HE GREW TO FIVE FEET IN A FEW MONTHS.
...YOU'RE SURE ABOUT AXEL, COLD?
THE KID AND YOU MIGHT NOT JELL, BUT TRICKSTER KNOWS WHAT HE'S DOING.*
HERE HE IS, EH?
* TO SEE THE TRICKSTER'S MISSION, SEE THE FLASH 1/2. --JOEY
CAUGHT HIM UNDER THE BRIDGE, EATIN' FISH RIGHT OUTTA THE WATER.
NNFF
WHEW. GUY NEEDS SOME SPEED STICK.
WHAT... DO...YOU WANT WITH...
I HATE TO DO THIS TO SOMEONE YOUR AGE, TURTLE.
BUT THINGS ARE GETTING DANGEROUS.
YOU SEE THIS, COLD?
IT WAS TAPED TO THE DOOR.
ENTER
COLD
CAPTAIN, MY GOOD CAPTAIN-- YOU HAVE YOUR ROGUES, I'LL HAVE MINE. MAY THE BEST MAN WIN.
THE TOP

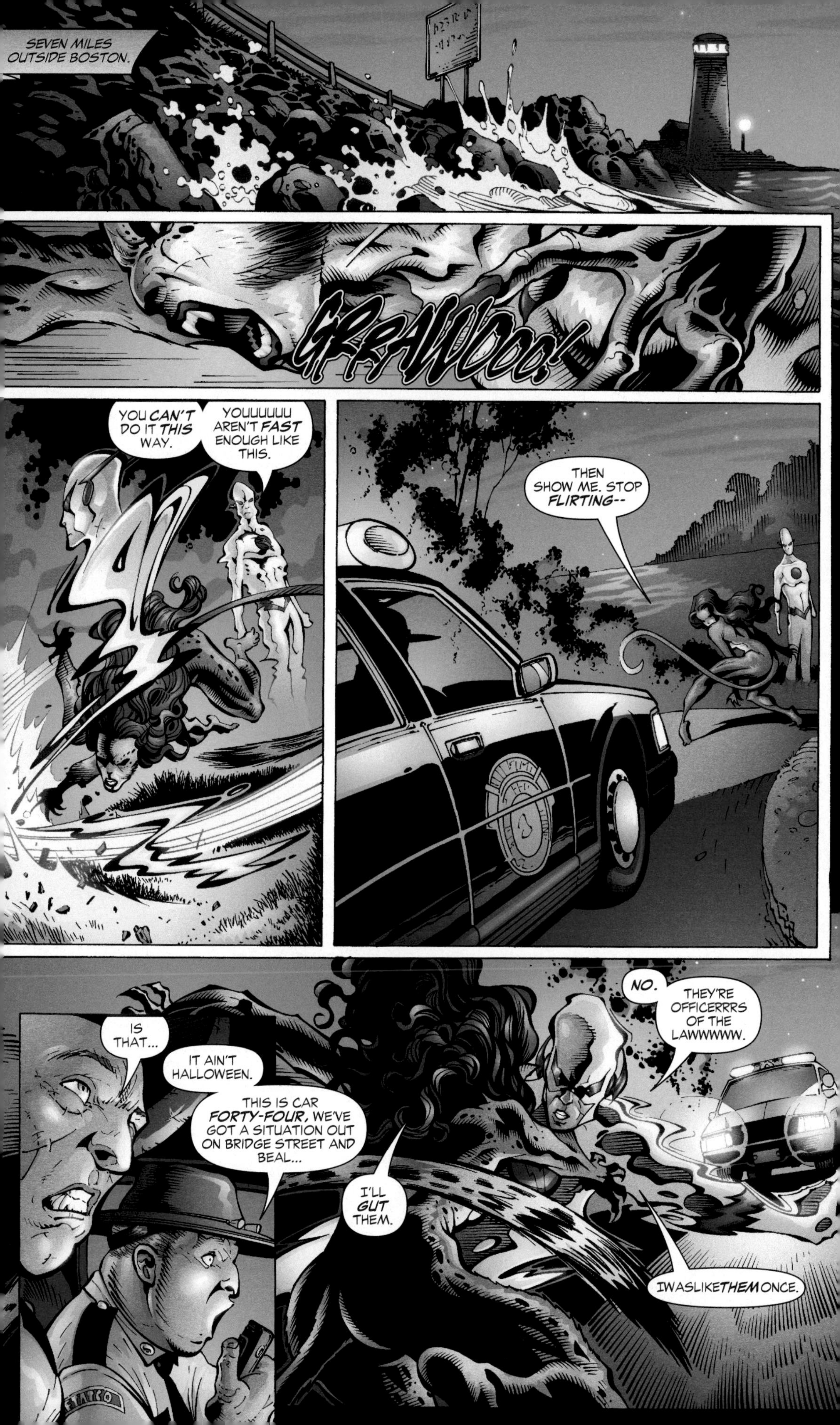
SEVEN MILES OUTSIDE BOSTON.
GRRAWOOO!
YOU CAN'T DO IT THIS WAY.
YOUUUUUU AREN'T FAST ENOUGH LIKE THIS.
THEN SHOW ME. STOP FLIRTING--
IS THAT...
IT AIN'T HALLOWEEN.
THIS IS CAR FORTY-FOUR, WE'VE GOT A SITUATION OUT ON BRIDGE STREET AND BEAL...
I'LL GUT THEM.
NO.
THEY'RE OFFICERRRS OF THE LAWWWWW.
IWASLIKETHEMONCE.

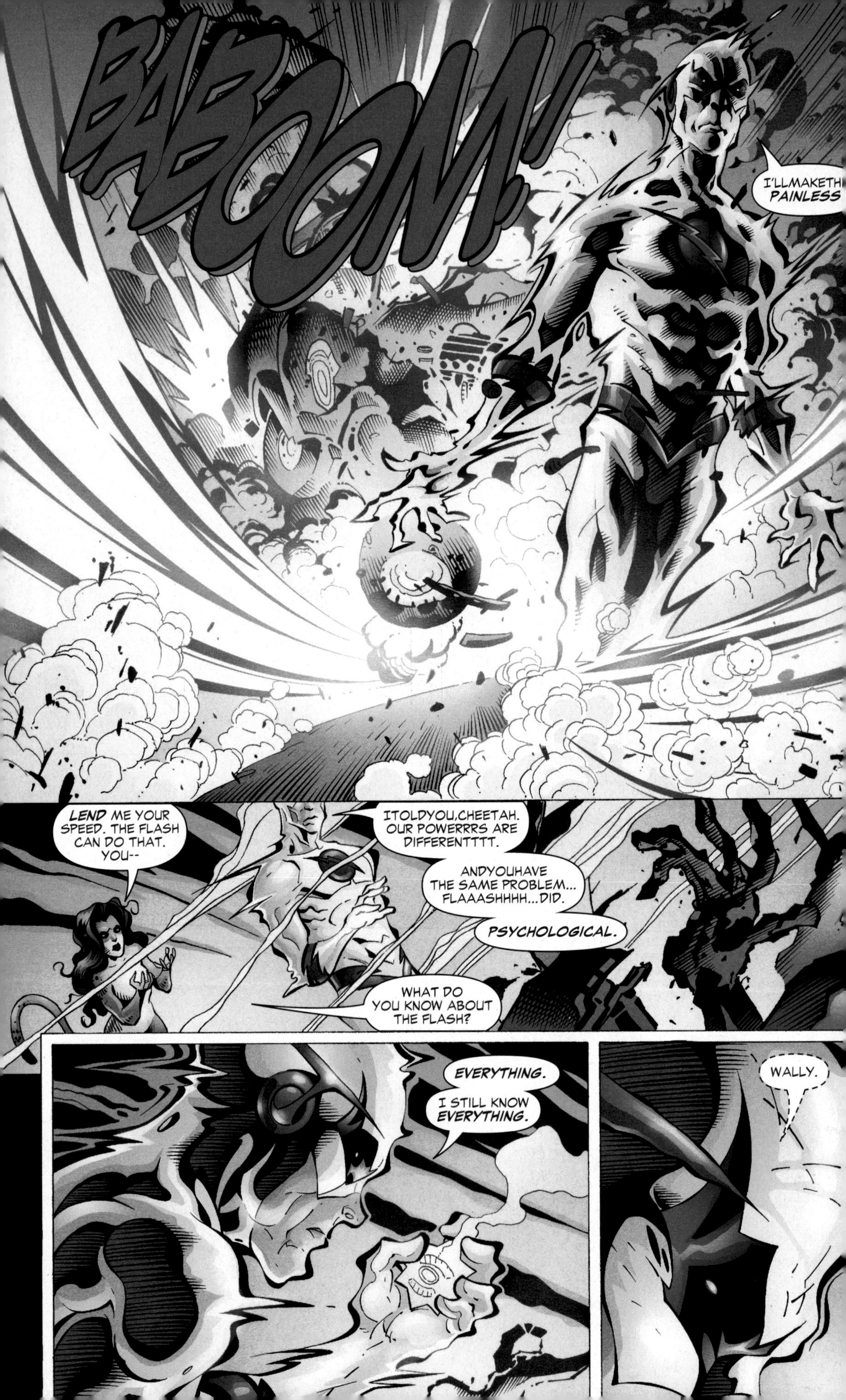

BABOOM!!
I'LLMAKETHI
PAINLESS
LEND ME YOUR SPEED. THE FLASH CAN DO THAT. YOU--
ITOLDYOU,CHEETAH. OUR POWERRRS ARE DIFFERENTTTT.
ANDYOUHAVE THE SAME PROBLEM... FLAAASHHHH...DID.
PSYCHOLOGICAL.
WHAT DO YOU KNOW ABOUT THE FLASH?
EVERYTHING.
I STILL KNOW EVERYTHING.
WALLY.

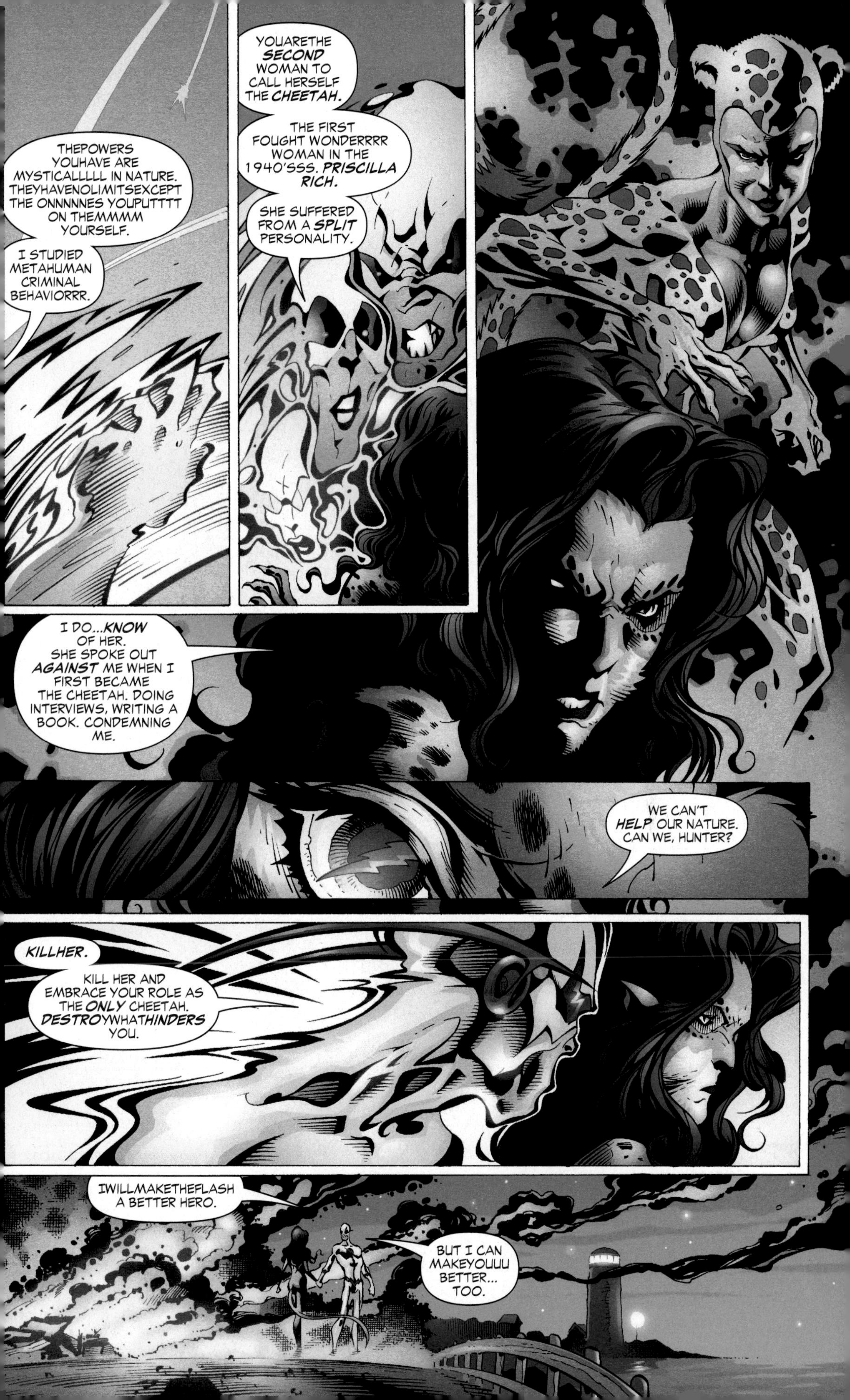
THEPOWERS YOUHAVE ARE MYSTICALLLLL IN NATURE. THEYHAVENOLIMITSEXCEPT THE ONNNNNES YOUPUTTTT ON THEMMMM YOURSELF.
I STUDIED METAHUMAN CRIMINAL BEHAVIORRR.
YOUARETHE SECOND WOMAN TO CALL HERSELF THE CHEETAH.
THE FIRST FOUGHT WONDERRRR WOMAN IN THE 1940'SSS. PRISCILLA RICH.
SHE SUFFERED FROM A SPLIT PERSONALITY.
I DO...KNOW OF HER. SHE SPOKE OUT AGAINST ME WHEN I FIRST BECAME THE CHEETAH. DOING INTERVIEWS, WRITING A BOOK. CONDEMNING ME.
WE CAN'T HELP OUR NATURE. CAN WE, HUNTER?
KILLHER.
KILL HER AND EMBRACE YOUR ROLE AS THE ONLY CHEETAH. DESTROYWHATHINDERS YOU.
IWILLMAKETHEFLASH A BETTER HERO.
BUT I CAN MAKEYOUUU BETTER... TOO.

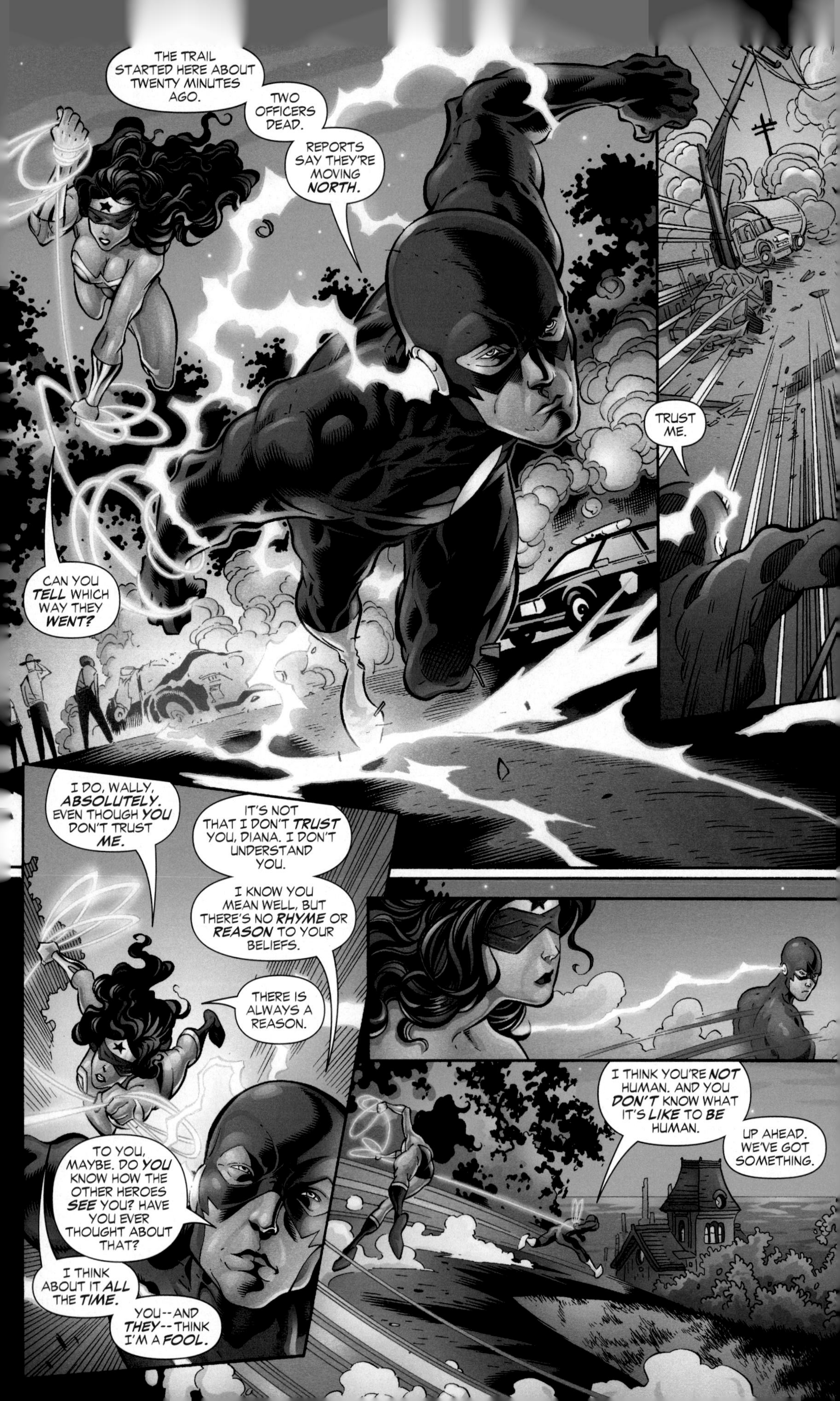
THE TRAIL STARTED HERE ABOUT TWENTY MINUTES AGO.
TWO OFFICERS DEAD.
REPORTS SAY THEY'RE MOVING NORTH.
CAN YOU TELL WHICH WAY THEY WENT?
TRUST ME.
I DO, WALLY, ABSOLUTELY. EVEN THOUGH YOU DON'T TRUST ME.
IT'S NOT THAT I DON'T TRUST YOU, DIANA. I DON'T UNDERSTAND YOU.
I KNOW YOU MEAN WELL, BUT THERE'S NO RHYME OR REASON TO YOUR BELIEFS.
THERE IS ALWAYS A REASON.
TO YOU, MAYBE. DO YOU KNOW HOW THE OTHER HEROES SEE YOU? HAVE YOU EVER THOUGHT ABOUT THAT?
I THINK ABOUT IT ALL THE TIME.
YOU--AND THEY--THINK I'M A FOOL.
I THINK YOU'RE NOT HUMAN. AND YOU DON'T KNOW WHAT IT'S LIKE TO BE HUMAN.
UP AHEAD. WE'VE GOT SOMETHING.

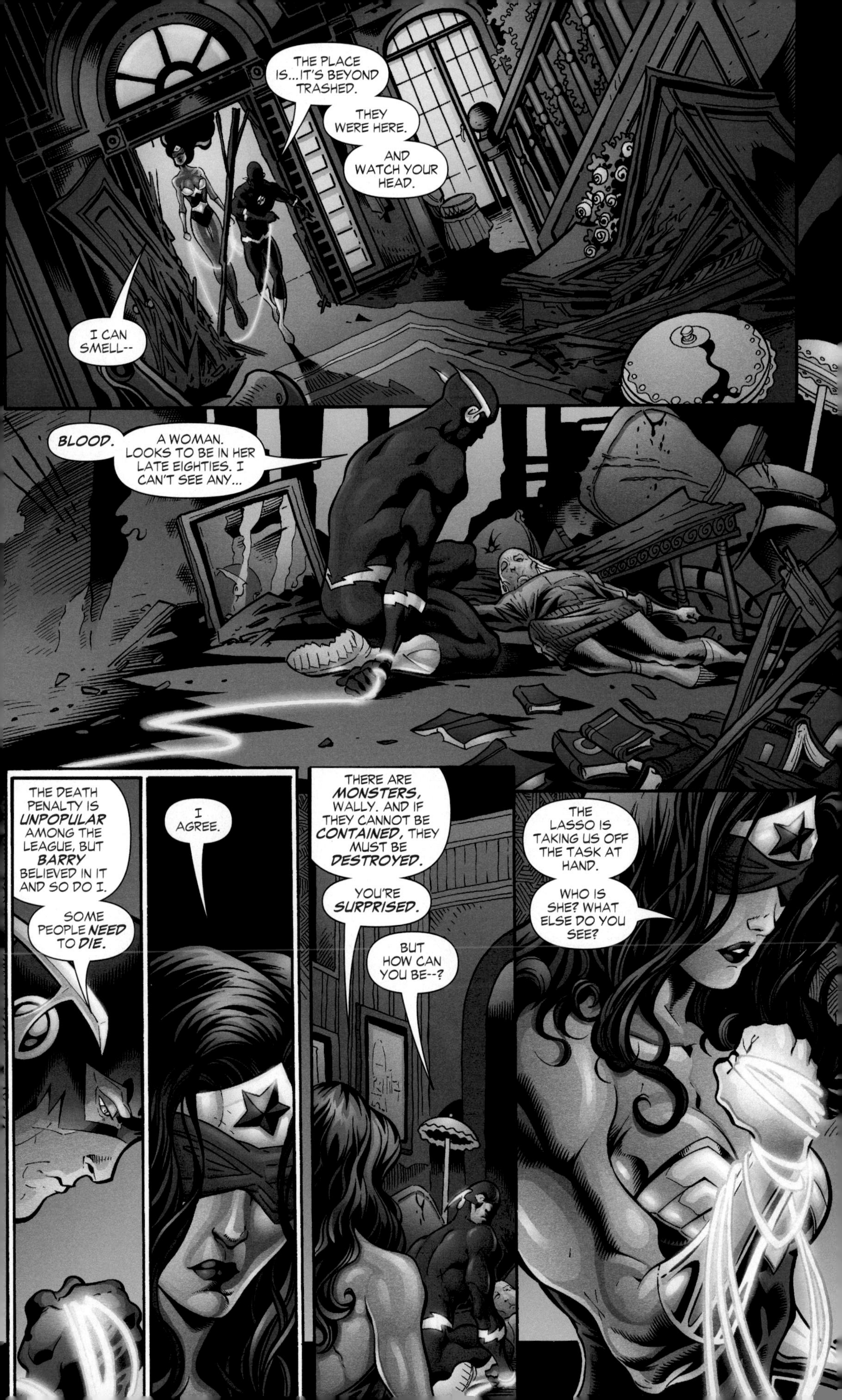
THE PLACE IS...IT'S BEYOND TRASHED.
THEY WERE HERE.
AND WATCH YOUR HEAD.
I CAN SMELL--
BLOOD.
A WOMAN. LOOKS TO BE IN HER LATE EIGHTIES. I CAN'T SEE ANY...
THE DEATH PENALTY IS UNPOPULAR AMONG THE LEAGUE, BUT BARRY BELIEVED IN IT AND SO DO I.
SOME PEOPLE NEED TO DIE.
I AGREE.
THERE ARE MONSTERS, WALLY. AND IF THEY CANNOT BE CONTAINED, THEY MUST BE DESTROYED.
YOU'RE SURPRISED.
BUT HOW CAN YOU BE--?
THE LASSO IS TAKING US OFF THE TASK AT HAND.
WHO IS SHE? WHAT ELSE DO YOU SEE?

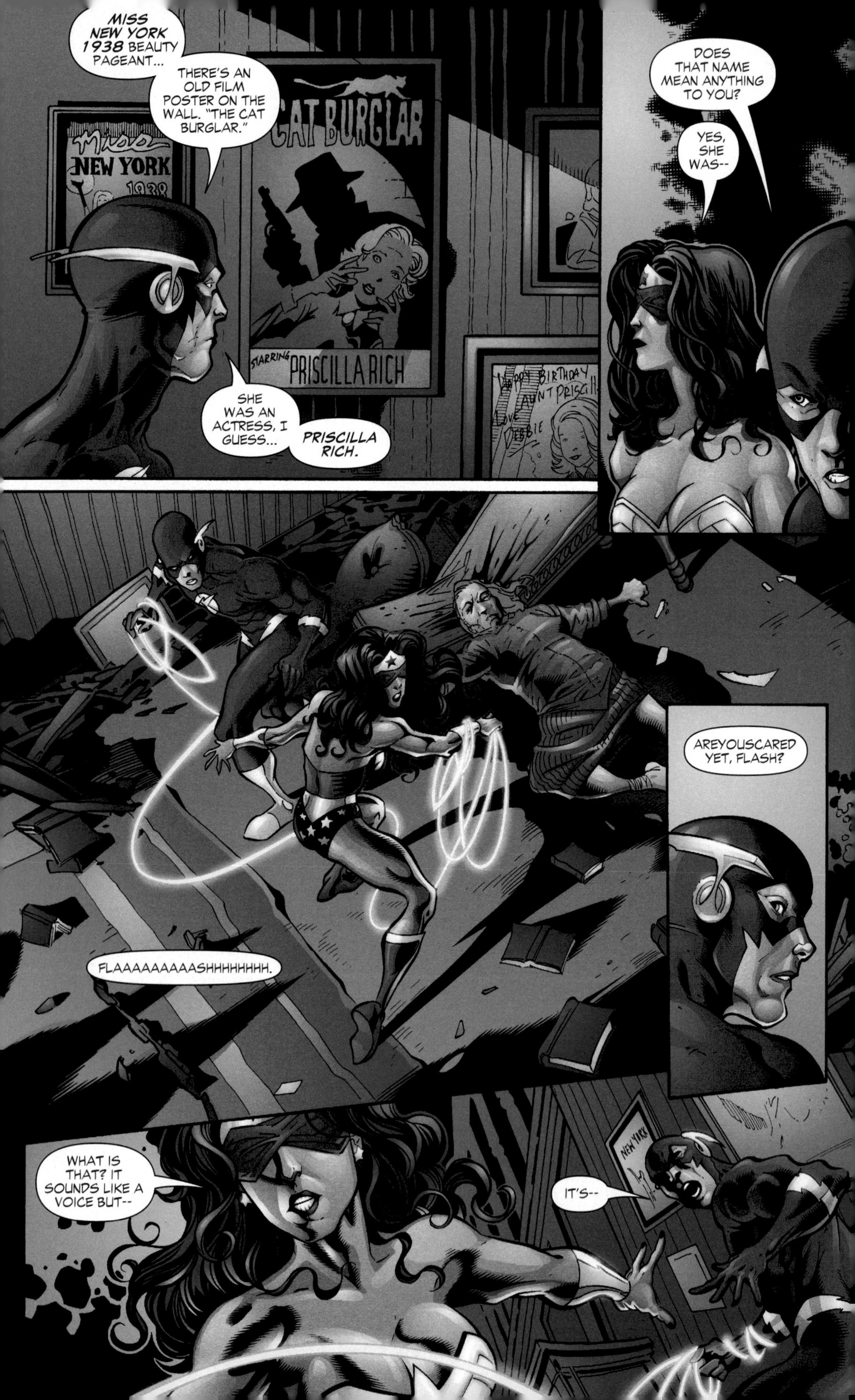
MISS NEW YORK 1938 BEAUTY PAGEANT...
THERE'S AN OLD FILM POSTER ON THE WALL. "THE CAT BURGLAR."
CAT BURGLAR
STARRING PRISCILLA RICH
MISS NEW YORK 1938
SHE WAS AN ACTRESS, I GUESS...
PRISCILLA RICH.
DOES THAT NAME MEAN ANYTHING TO YOU?
YES, SHE WAS--
AREYOUSCARED YET, FLASH?
FLAAAAAAAAASHHHHHHHH.
WHAT IS THAT? IT SOUNDS LIKE A VOICE BUT--
IT'S--

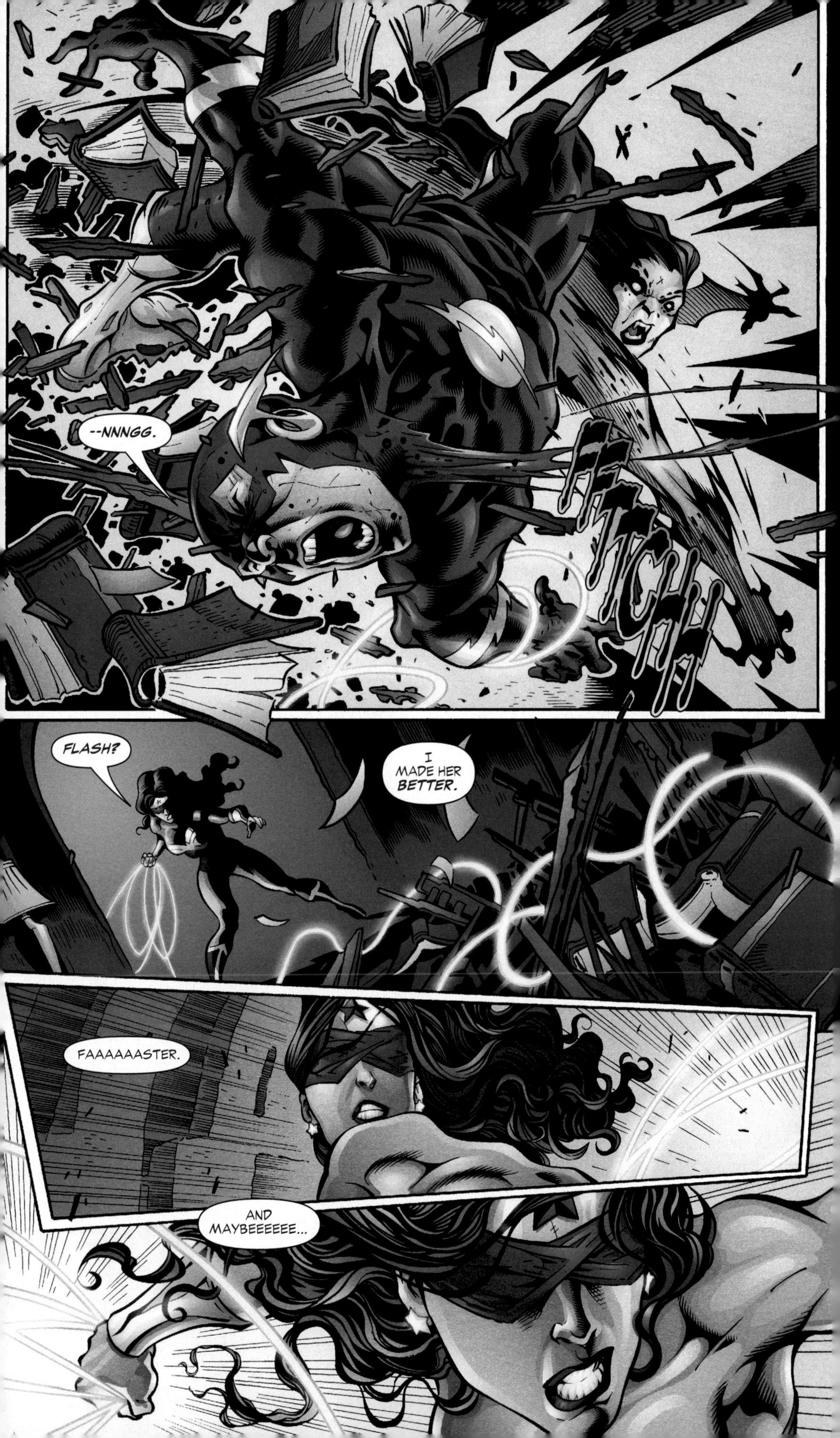

--NNNGG.
TTCHH
FLASH?
I MADE HER BETTER.
FAAAAAASTER.
AND MAYBEEEEEE...

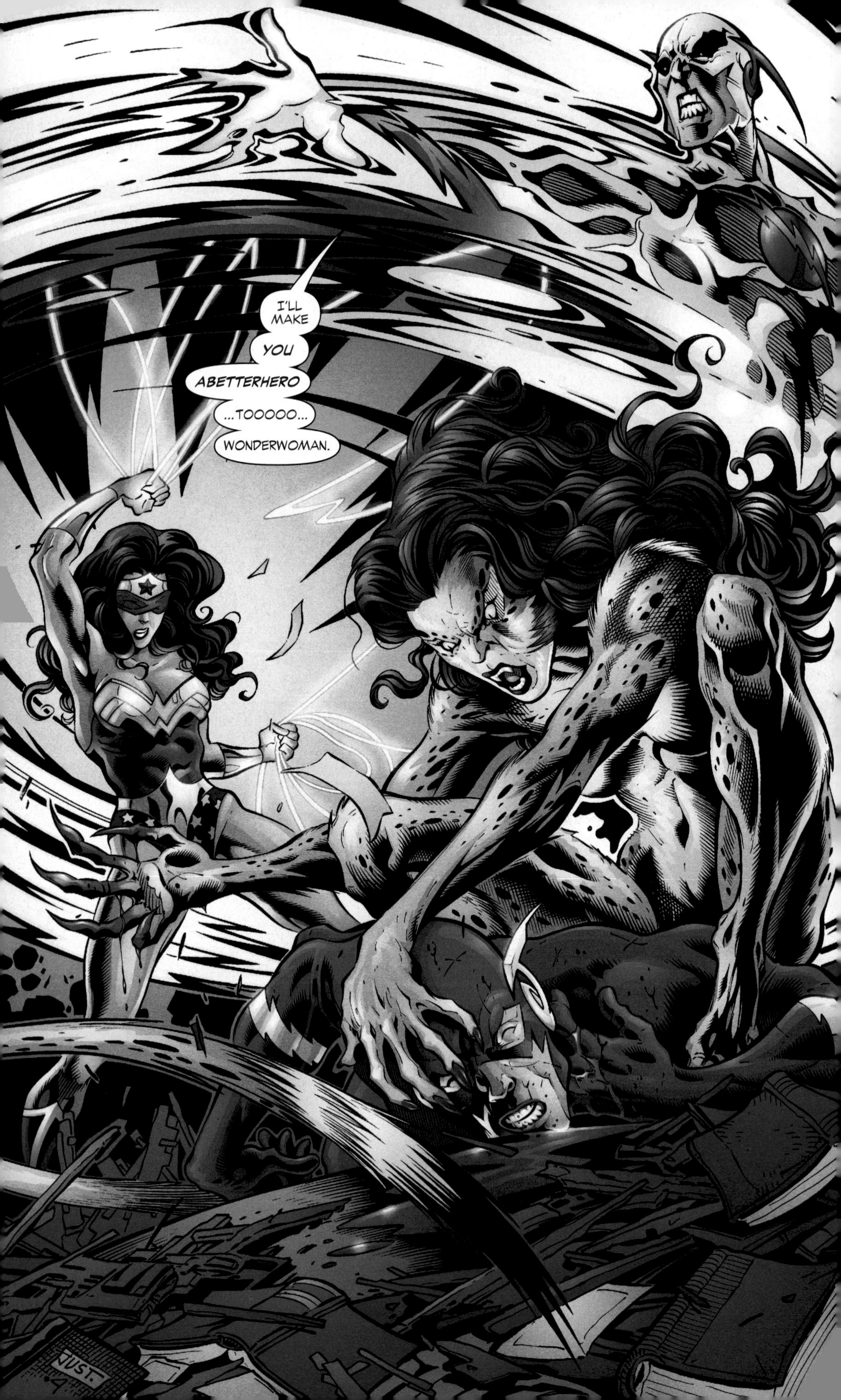
I'LL MAKE
YOU
ABETTERHERO
...TOOOOO...
WONDERWOMAN.
JUST.

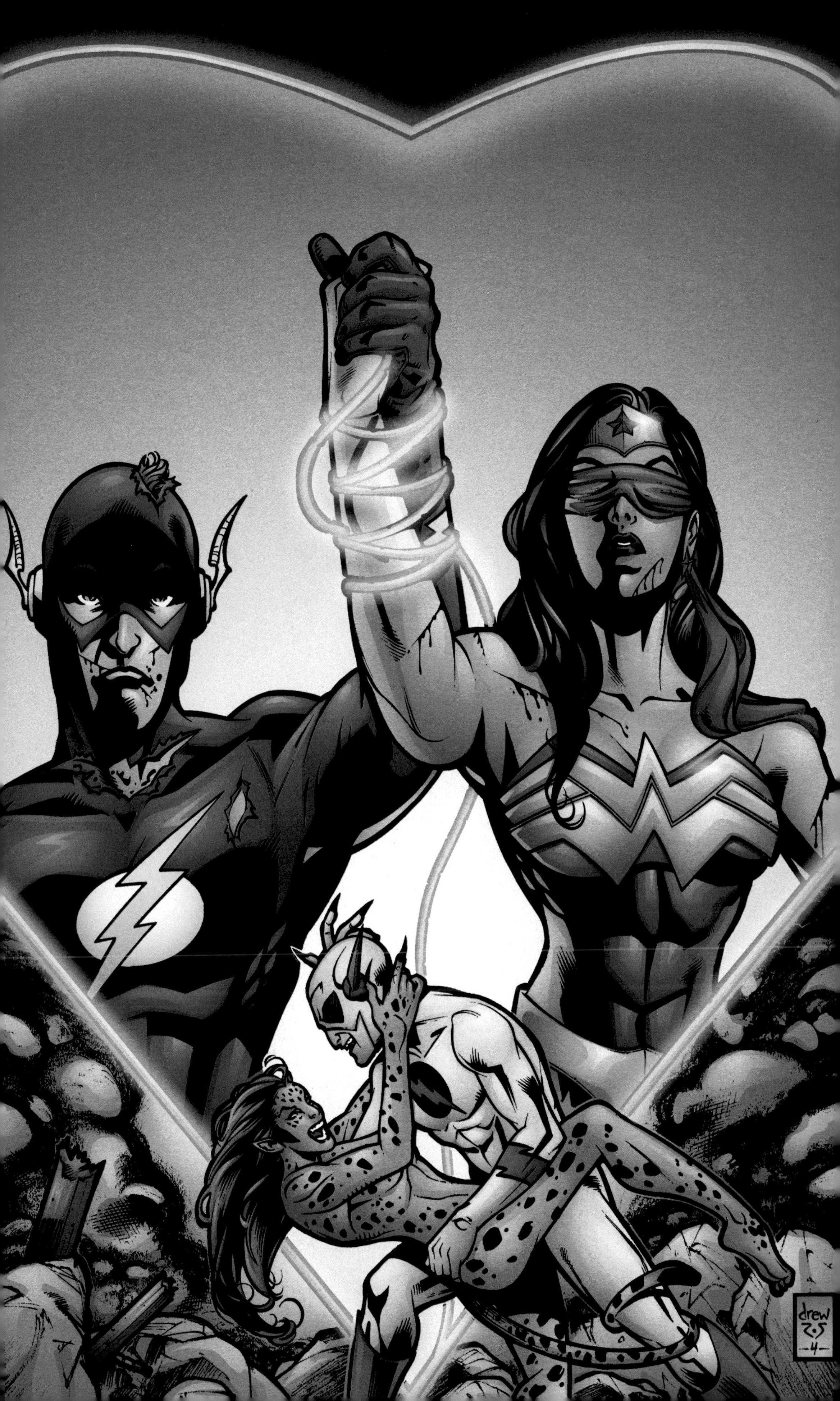
drew
2.5
-4-

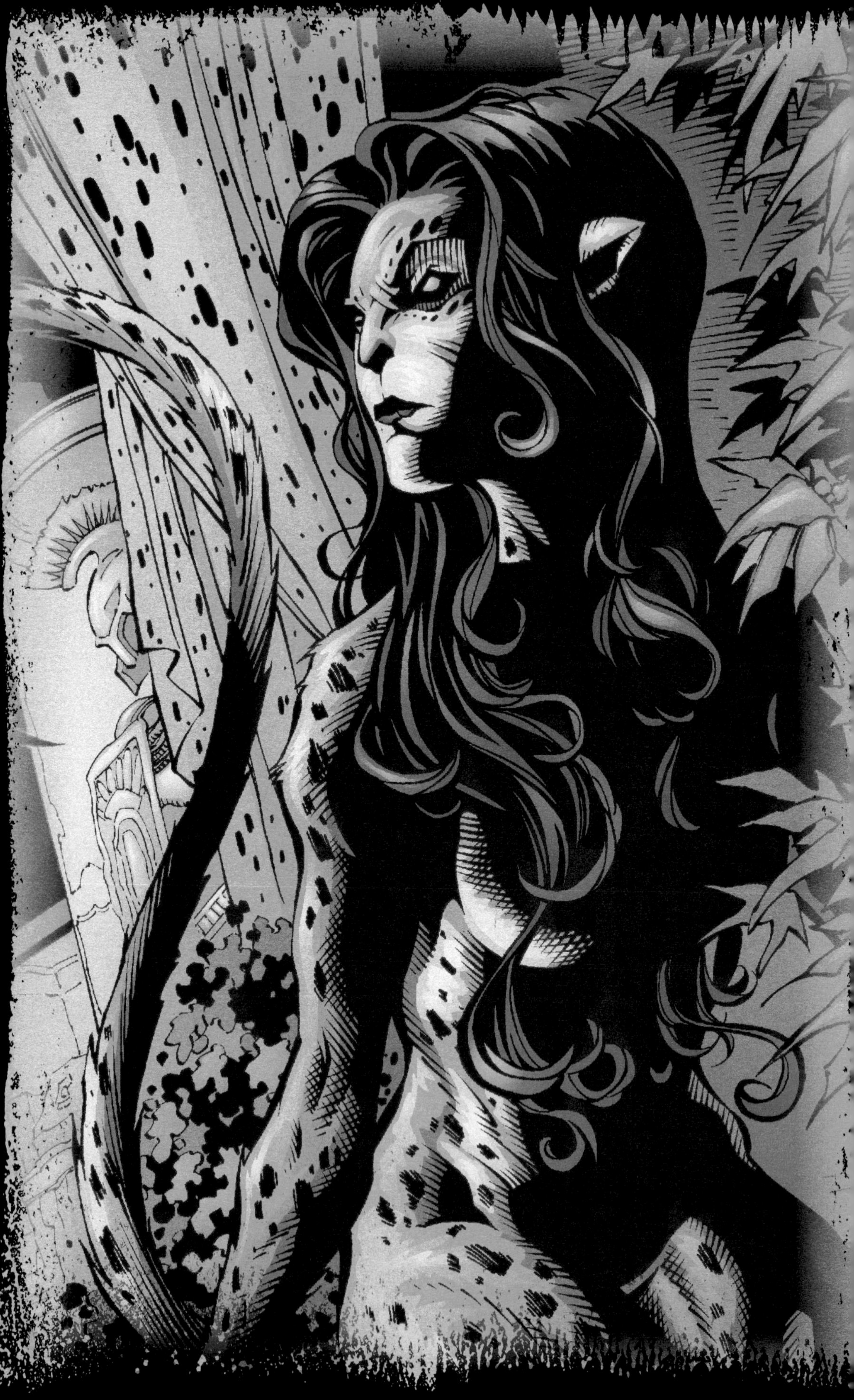

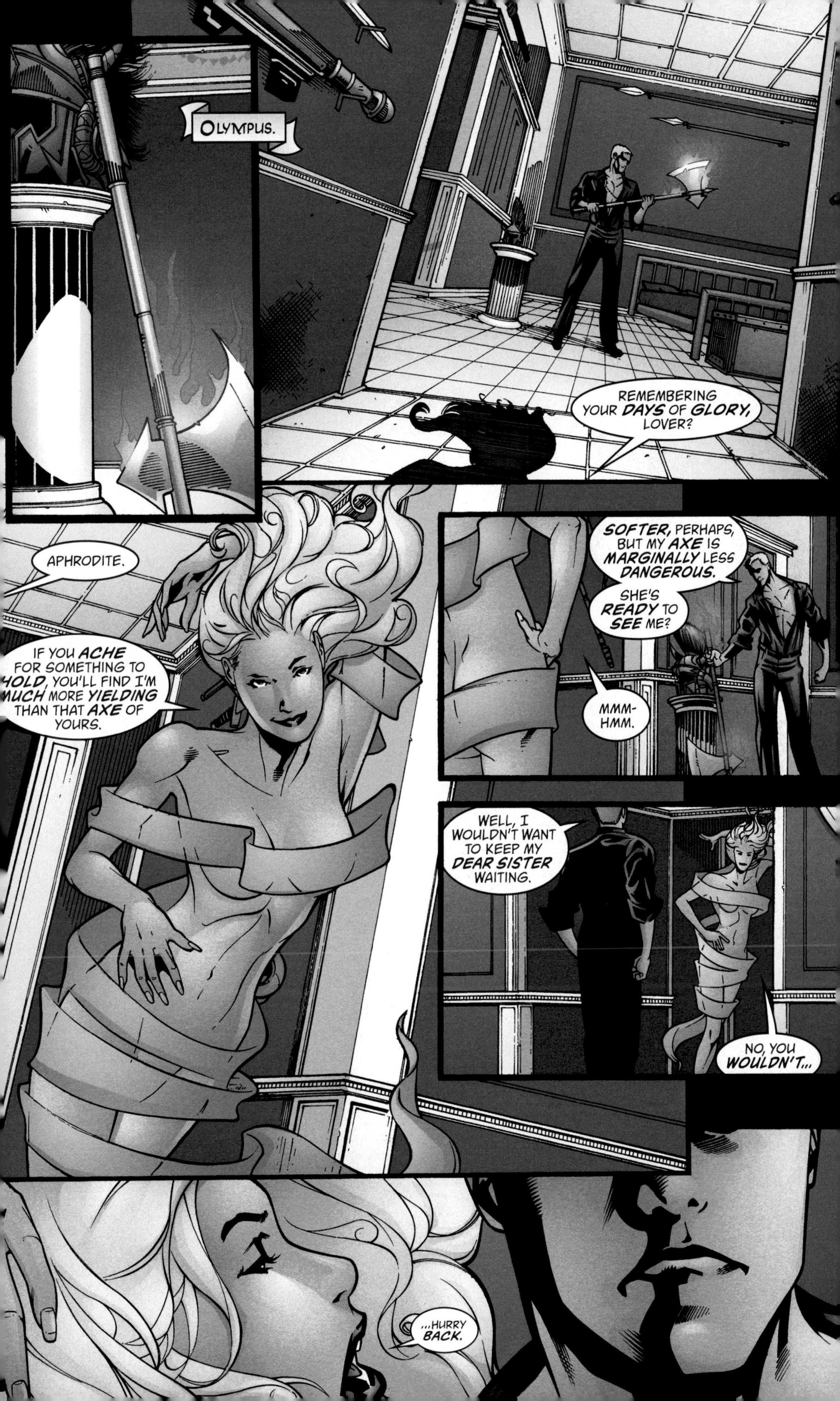
OLYMPUS.
REMEMBERING YOUR DAYS OF GLORY, LOVER?
APHRODITE.
IF YOU ACHE FOR SOMETHING TO HOLD, YOU'LL FIND I'M MUCH MORE YIELDING THAN THAT AXE OF YOURS.
SOFTER, PERHAPS, BUT MY AXE IS MARGINALLY LESS DANGEROUS.
SHE'S READY TO SEE ME?
MMM-HMM.
WELL, I WOULDN'T WANT TO KEEP MY DEAR SISTER WAITING.
NO, YOU WOULDN'T...
...HURRY BACK.

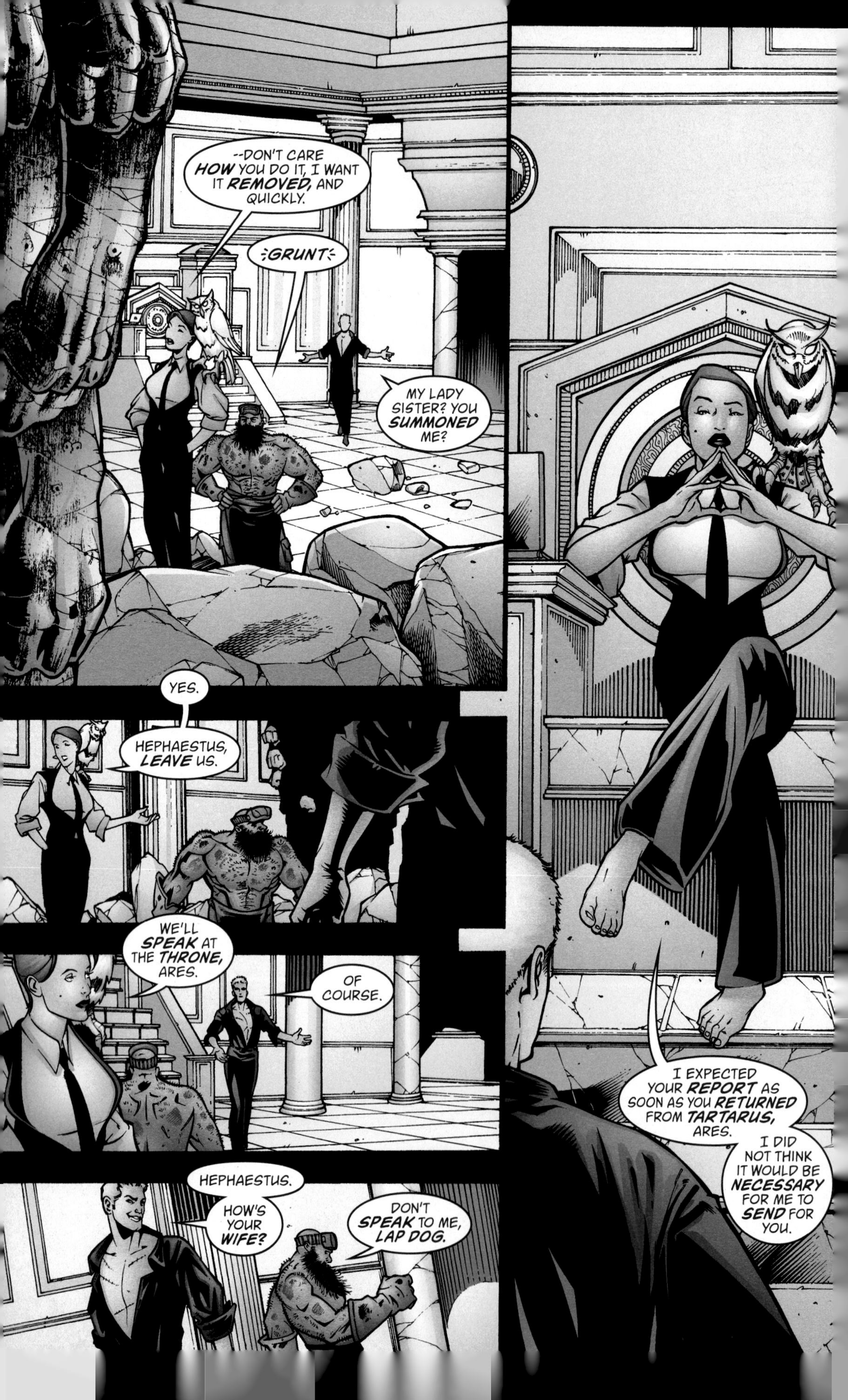
--DON'T CARE HOW YOU DO IT, I WANT IT REMOVED, AND QUICKLY.
GRUNT
MY LADY SISTER? YOU SUMMONED ME?
YES.
HEPHAESTUS, LEAVE US.
WE'LL SPEAK AT THE THRONE, ARES.
OF COURSE.
HEPHAESTUS.
HOW'S YOUR WIFE?
DON'T SPEAK TO ME, LAP DOG.
I EXPECTED YOUR REPORT AS SOON AS YOU RETURNED FROM TARTARUS, ARES.
I DID NOT THINK IT WOULD BE NECESSARY FOR ME TO SEND FOR YOU.

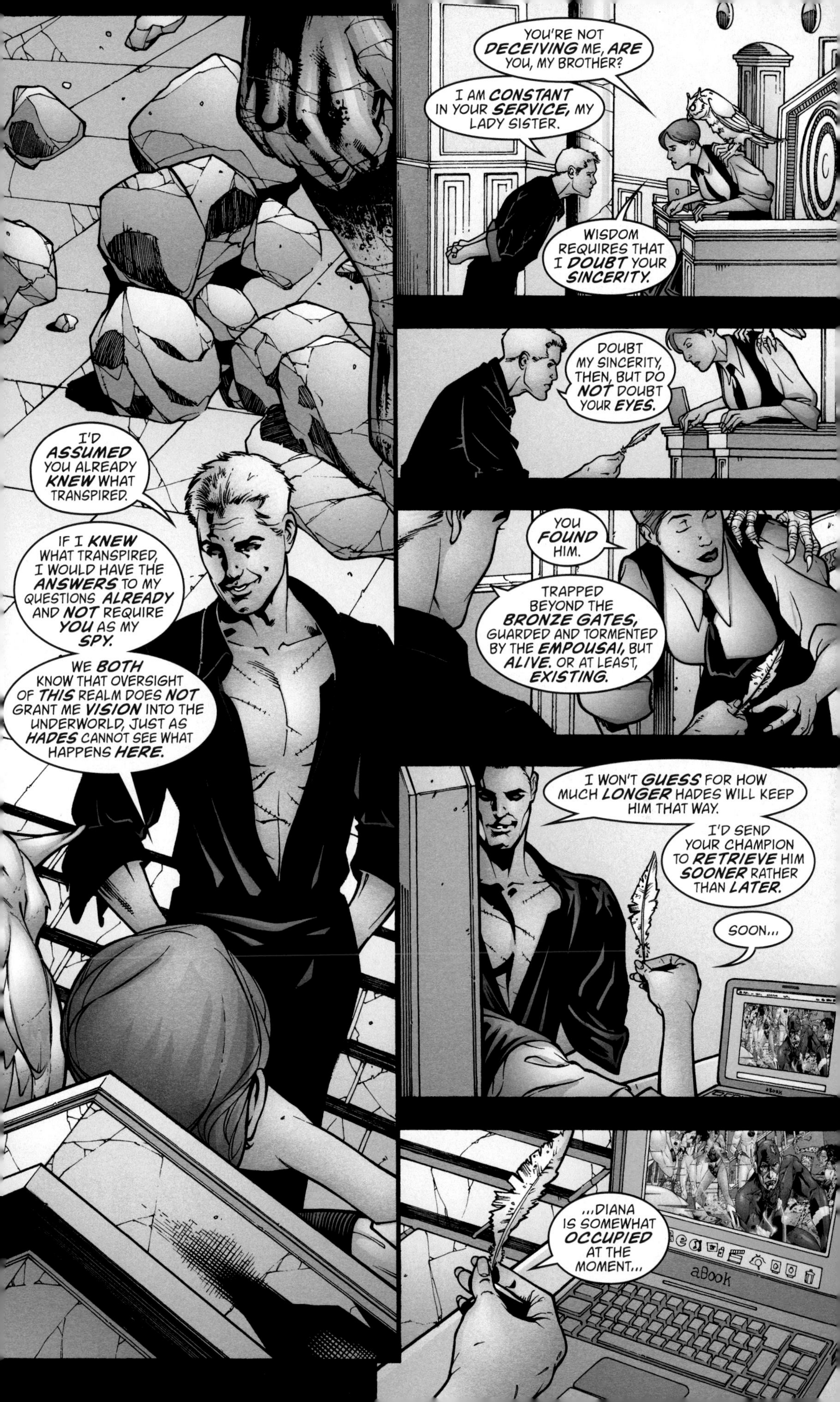
I'D ASSUMED YOU ALREADY KNEW WHAT TRANSPIRED.
IF I KNEW WHAT TRANSPIRED, I WOULD HAVE THE ANSWERS TO MY QUESTIONS ALREADY AND NOT REQUIRE YOU AS MY SPY.
WE BOTH KNOW THAT OVERSIGHT OF THIS REALM DOES NOT GRANT ME VISION INTO THE UNDERWORLD, JUST AS HADES CANNOT SEE WHAT HAPPENS HERE.
YOU'RE NOT DECEIVING ME, ARE YOU, MY BROTHER?
I AM CONSTANT IN YOUR SERVICE, MY LADY SISTER.
WISDOM REQUIRES THAT I DOUBT YOUR SINCERITY.
DOUBT MY SINCERITY, THEN, BUT DO NOT DOUBT YOUR EYES.
YOU FOUND HIM.
TRAPPED BEYOND THE BRONZE GATES, GUARDED AND TORMENTED BY THE EMPOUSAI, BUT ALIVE, OR AT LEAST, EXISTING.
I WON'T GUESS FOR HOW MUCH LONGER HADES WILL KEEP HIM THAT WAY.
I'D SEND YOUR CHAMPION TO RETRIEVE HIM SOONER RATHER THAN LATER.
SOON...
...DIANA IS SOMEWHAT OCCUPIED AT THE MOMENT...
aBook

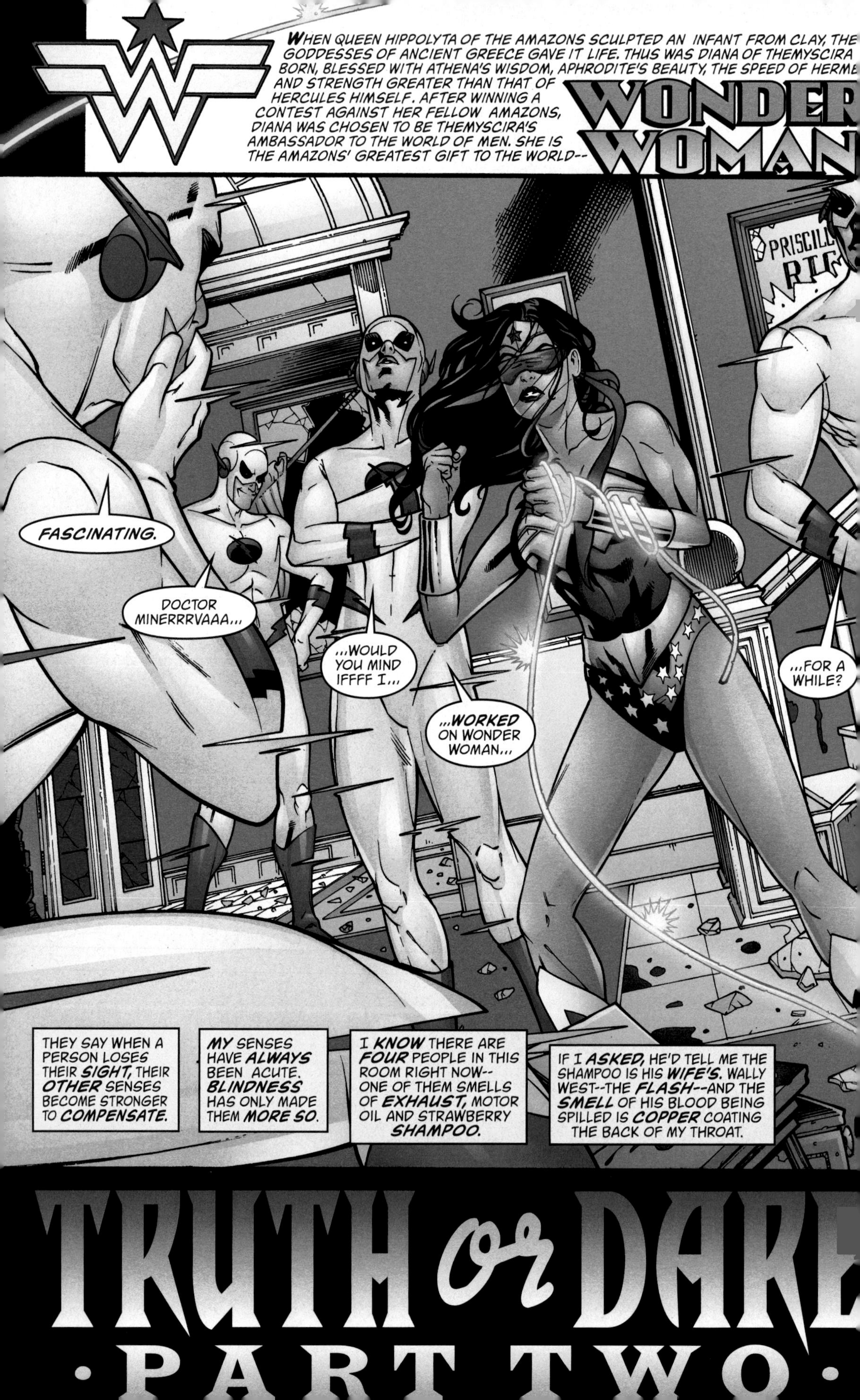
WHEN QUEEN HIPPOLYTA OF THE AMAZONS SCULPTED AN INFANT FROM CLAY, THE GODDESSES OF ANCIENT GREECE GAVE IT LIFE. THUS WAS DIANA OF THEMYSCIRA BORN, BLESSED WITH ATHENA'S WISDOM, APHRODITE'S BEAUTY, THE SPEED OF HERME AND STRENGTH GREATER THAN THAT OF HERCULES HIMSELF. AFTER WINNING A CONTEST AGAINST HER FELLOW AMAZONS, DIANA WAS CHOSEN TO BE THEMYSCIRA'S AMBASSADOR TO THE WORLD OF MEN. SHE IS THE AMAZONS' GREATEST GIFT TO THE WORLD--
WONDER WOMAN
FASCINATING.
DOCTOR MINERRRVAAA...
...WOULD YOU MIND IFFFF I...
...WORKED ON WONDER WOMAN...
...FOR A WHILE?
THEY SAY WHEN A PERSON LOSES THEIR SIGHT, THEIR OTHER SENSES BECOME STRONGER TO COMPENSATE.
MY SENSES HAVE ALWAYS BEEN ACUTE. BLINDNESS HAS ONLY MADE THEM MORE SO.
I KNOW THERE ARE FOUR PEOPLE IN THIS ROOM RIGHT NOW-- ONE OF THEM SMELLS OF EXHAUST, MOTOR OIL AND STRAWBERRY SHAMPOO.
IF I ASKED, HE'D TELL ME THE SHAMPOO IS HIS WIFE'S. WALLY WEST--THE FLASH--AND THE SMELL OF HIS BLOOD BEING SPILLED IS COPPER COATING THE BACK OF MY THROAT.
TRUTH or DARE
·PART TWO·

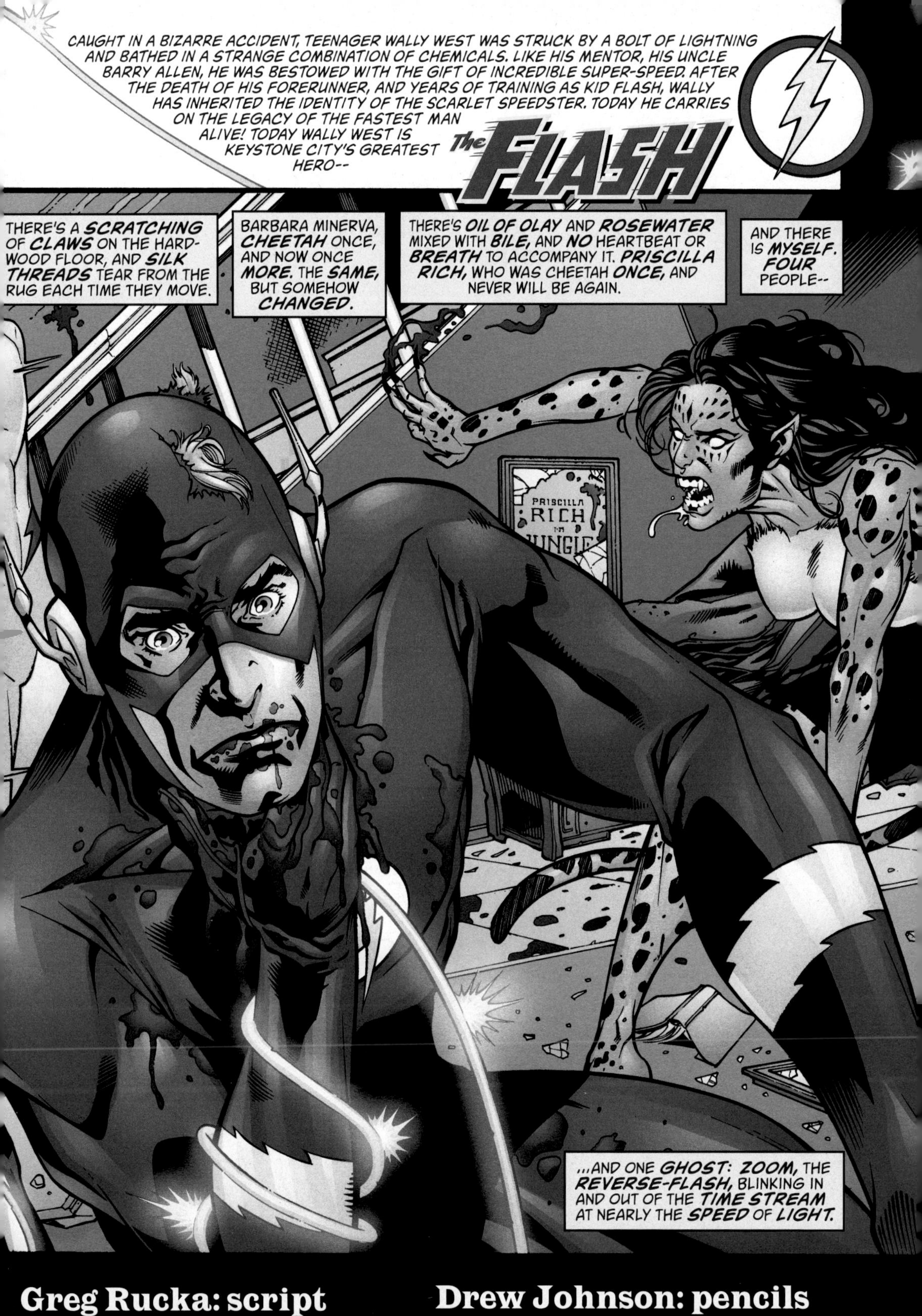
CAUGHT IN A BIZARRE ACCIDENT, TEENAGER WALLY WEST WAS STRUCK BY A BOLT OF LIGHTNING AND BATHED IN A STRANGE COMBINATION OF CHEMICALS. LIKE HIS MENTOR, HIS UNCLE BARRY ALLEN, HE WAS BESTOWED WITH THE GIFT OF INCREDIBLE SUPER-SPEED. AFTER THE DEATH OF HIS FORERUNNER, AND YEARS OF TRAINING AS KID FLASH, WALLY HAS INHERITED THE IDENTITY OF THE SCARLET SPEEDSTER. TODAY HE CARRIES ON THE LEGACY OF THE FASTEST MAN ALIVE! TODAY WALLY WEST IS KEYSTONE CITY'S GREATEST HERO--
The FLASH
THERE'S A SCRATCHING OF CLAWS ON THE HARDWOOD FLOOR, AND SILK THREADS TEAR FROM THE RUG EACH TIME THEY MOVE.
BARBARA MINERVA, CHEETAH ONCE, AND NOW ONCE MORE. THE SAME, BUT SOMEHOW CHANGED.
THERE'S OIL OF OLAY AND ROSEWATER MIXED WITH BILE, AND NO HEARTBEAT OR BREATH TO ACCOMPANY IT. PRISCILLA RICH, WHO WAS CHEETAH ONCE, AND NEVER WILL BE AGAIN.
AND THERE IS MYSELF. FOUR PEOPLE--
PRISCILLA RICH
...AND ONE GHOST: ZOOM, THE REVERSE-FLASH, BLINKING IN AND OUT OF THE TIME STREAM AT NEARLY THE SPEED OF LIGHT.

Greg Rucka: script **Drew Johnson: pencils**
Ray Snyder: inks **Richard & Tanya Horie: colors**
Todd Klein: letters **Ivan Cohen: editor**

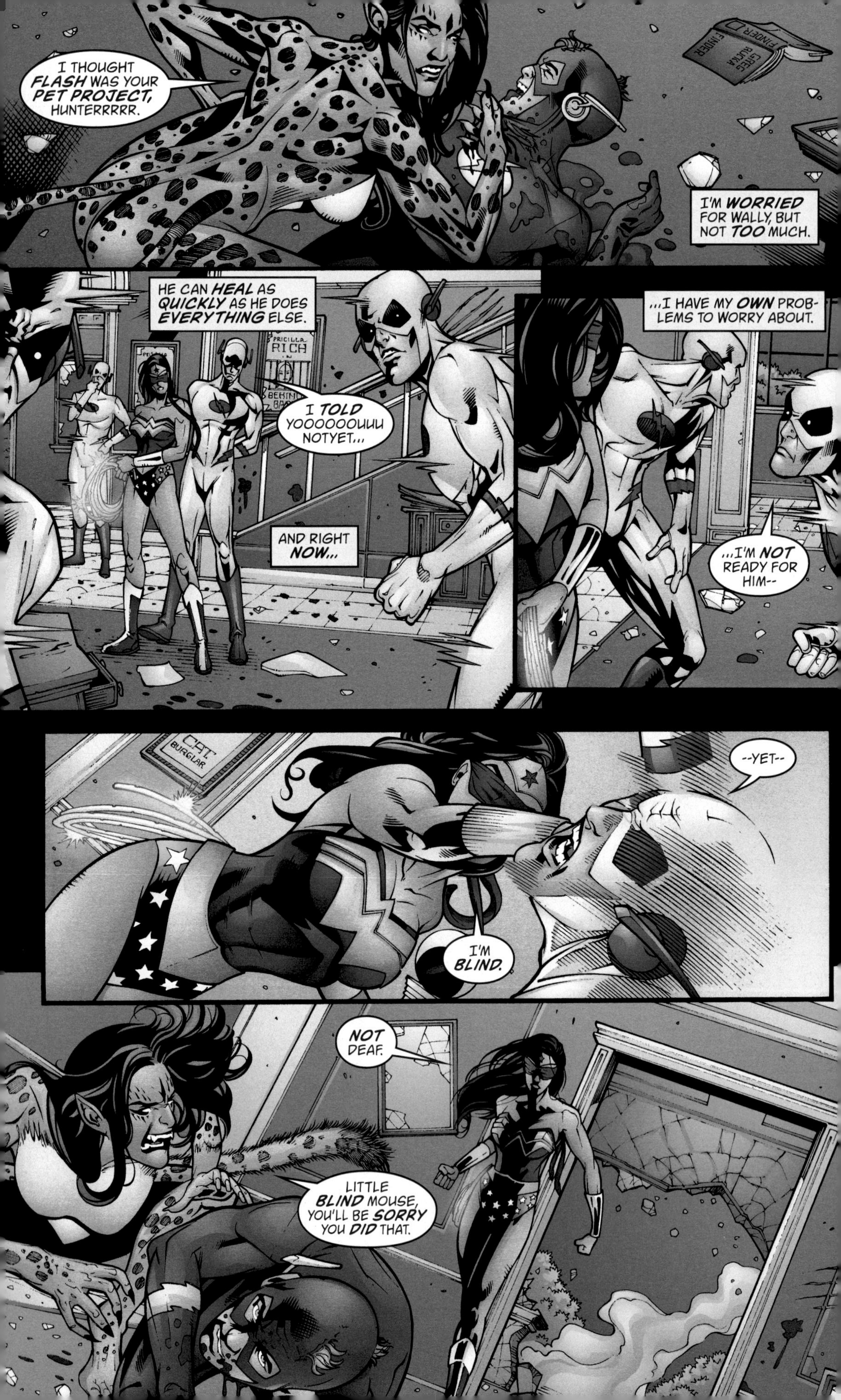

I THOUGHT FLASH WAS YOUR PET PROJECT, HUNTERRRRR.
I'M WORRIED FOR WALLY, BUT NOT TOO MUCH.
HE CAN HEAL AS QUICKLY AS HE DOES EVERYTHING ELSE.
PRICILLA RICH
I TOLD YOOOOOOUUU NOTYET...
AND RIGHT NOW...
...I HAVE MY OWN PROB-LEMS TO WORRY ABOUT.
...I'M NOT READY FOR HIM--
CAT BURGLAR
--YET--
I'M BLIND.
NOT DEAF.
LITTLE BLIND MOUSE, YOU'LL BE SORRY YOU DID THAT.

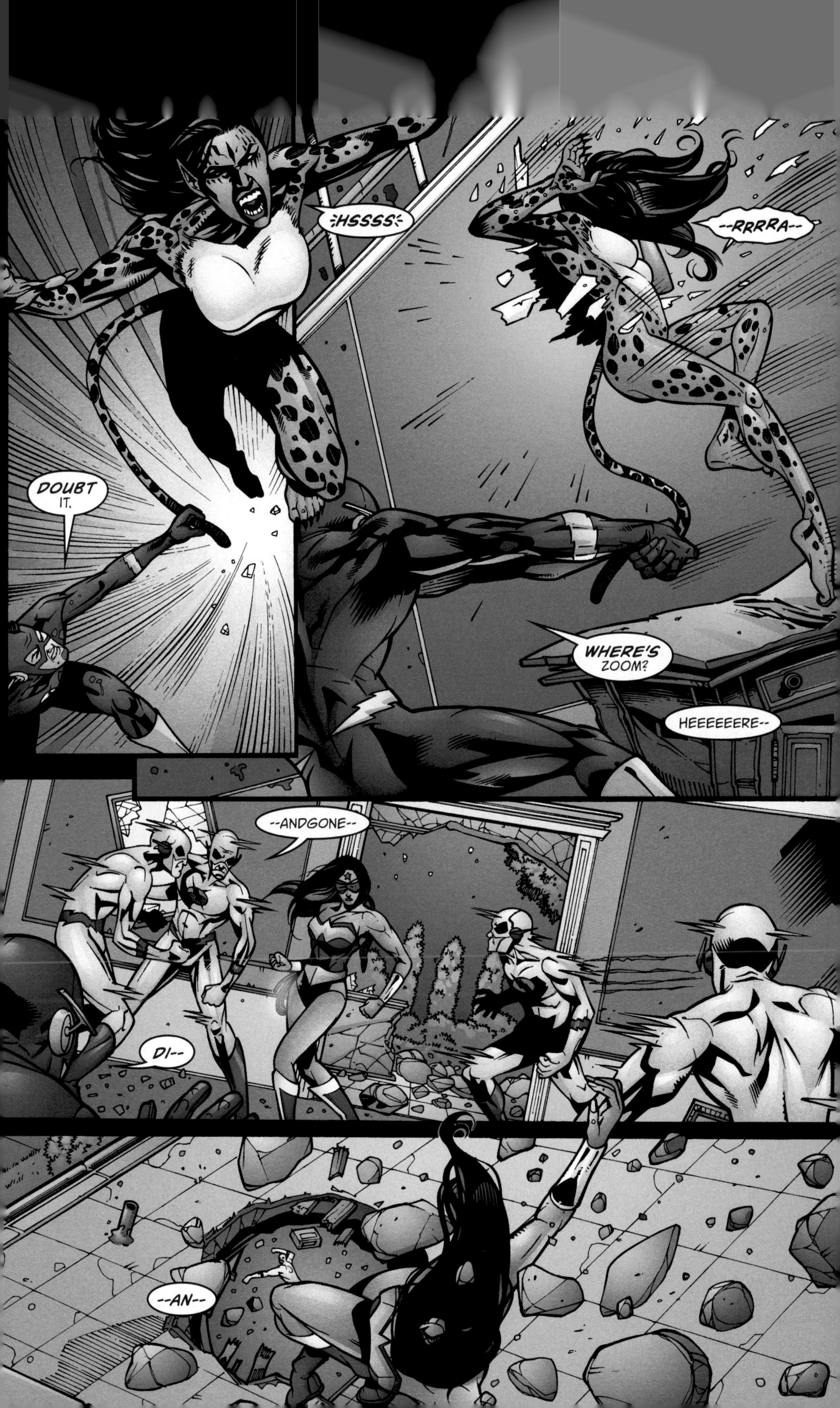

HSSSS
--RRRRA--
DOUBT IT.
WHERE'S ZOOM?
HEEEEEERE--
--ANDGONE--
DI--
--AN--

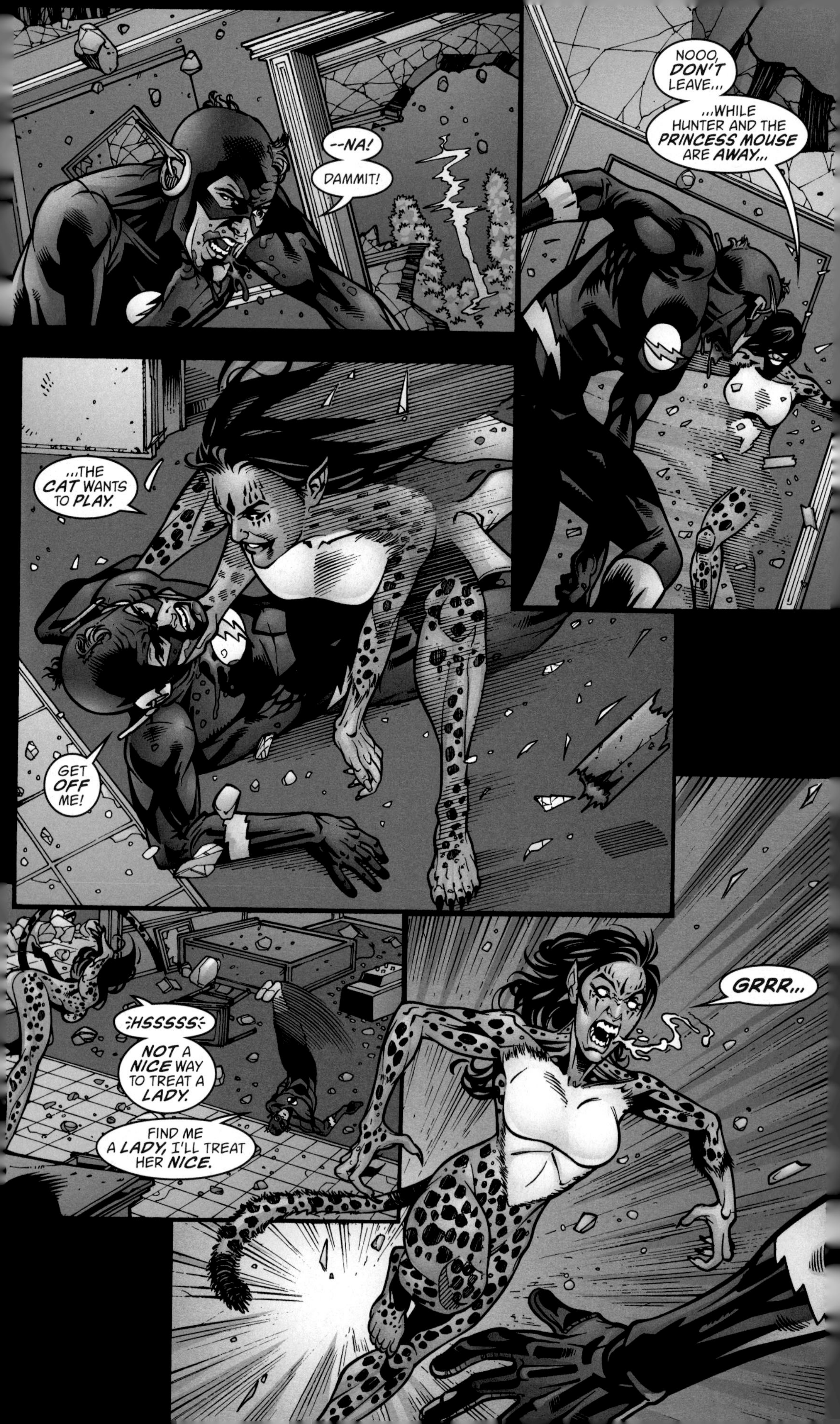
--NA!
DAMMIT!
NOOO, DON'T LEAVE...
...WHILE HUNTER AND THE PRINCESS MOUSE ARE AWAY...
...THE CAT WANTS TO PLAY.
GET OFF ME!
HSSSSS
NOT A NICE WAY TO TREAT A LADY.
FIND ME A LADY, I'LL TREAT HER NICE.
GRRR...

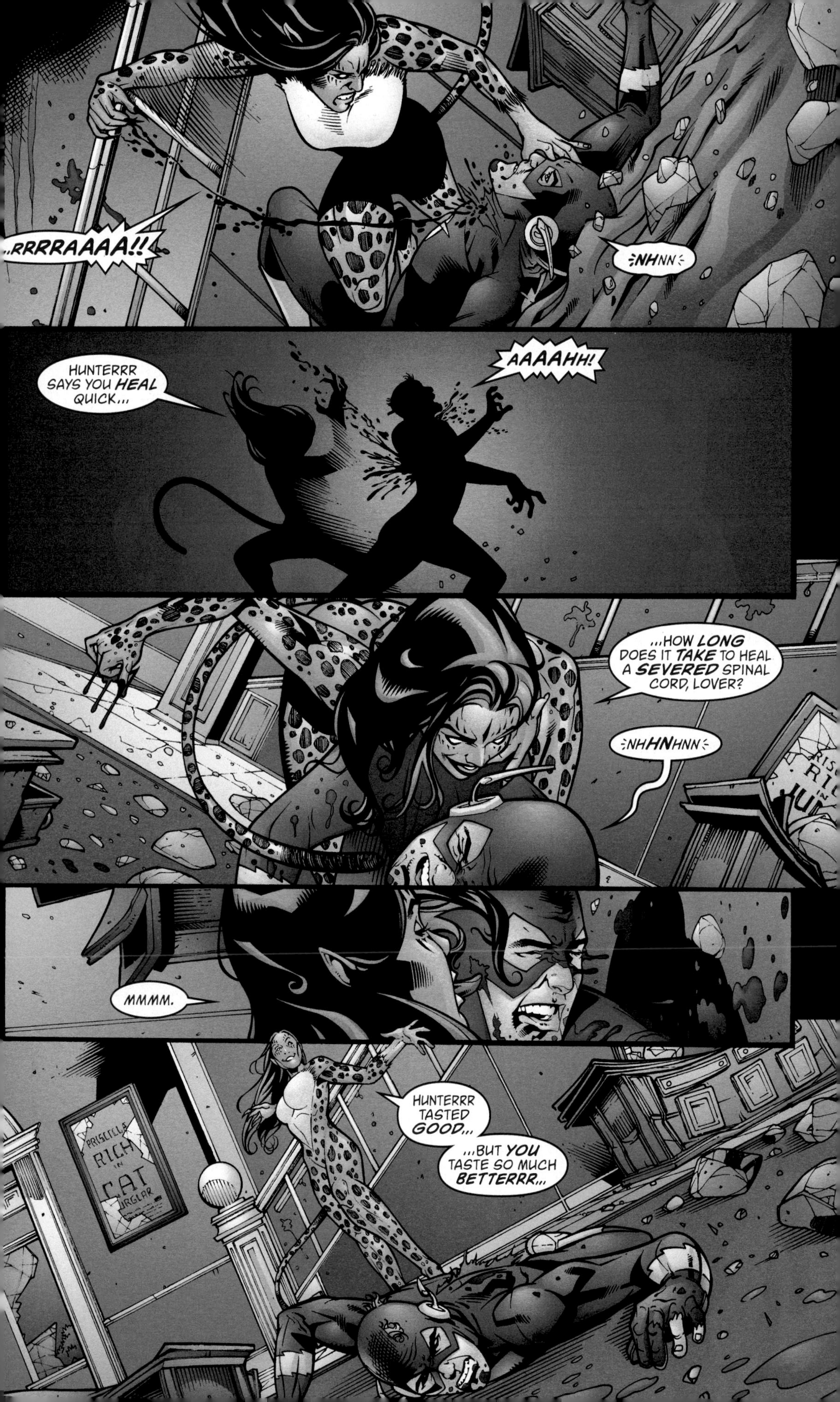
..RRRRAAAA!!
NHNN
HUNTERRR SAYS YOU HEAL QUICK...
AAAAHH!
...HOW LONG DOES IT TAKE TO HEAL A SEVERED SPINAL CORD, LOVER?
NHHNHNN
MMMM.
HUNTERRR TASTED GOOD...
...BUT YOU TASTE SO MUCH BETTERRR...
PRISCILLA RICH IN CAT BURGLAR

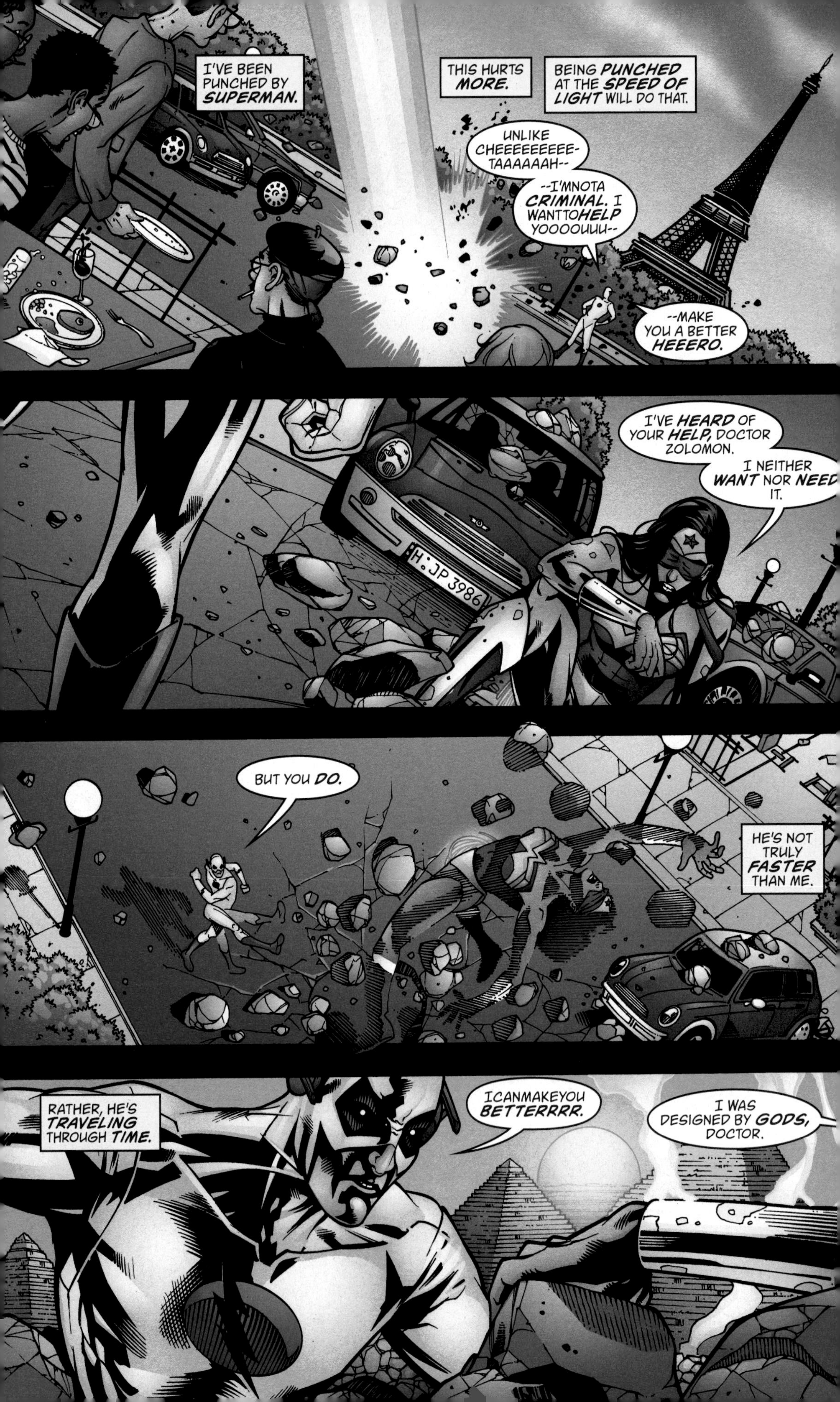

I'VE BEEN PUNCHED BY SUPERMAN.
THIS HURTS MORE.
BEING PUNCHED AT THE SPEED OF LIGHT WILL DO THAT.
UNLIKE CHEEEEEEEEE-TAAAAAAH--
--I'MNOTA CRIMINAL. I WANTTOHELP YOOOOUUU--
--MAKE YOU A BETTER HEEERO.
I'VE HEARD OF YOUR HELP, DOCTOR ZOLOMON.
I NEITHER WANT NOR NEED IT.
BUT YOU DO.
HE'S NOT TRULY FASTER THAN ME.
RATHER, HE'S TRAVELING THROUGH TIME.
ICANMAKEYOU BETTERRRR.
I WAS DESIGNED BY GODS, DOCTOR.

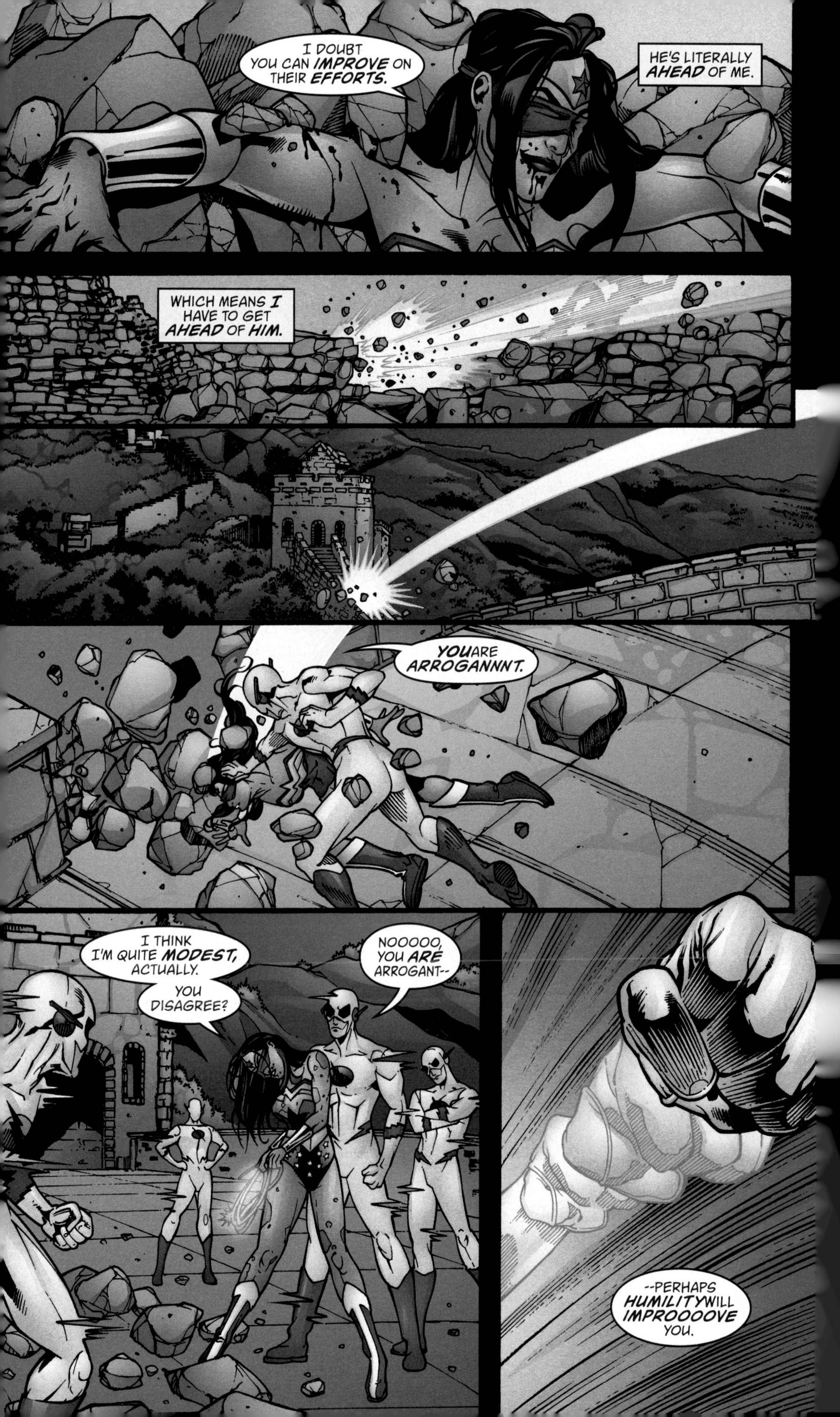
I DOUBT YOU CAN IMPROVE ON THEIR EFFORTS.
HE'S LITERALLY AHEAD OF ME.
WHICH MEANS I HAVE TO GET AHEAD OF HIM.
YOU ARE ARROGANNNT.
I THINK I'M QUITE MODEST, ACTUALLY.
YOU DISAGREE?
NOOOOO, YOU ARE ARROGANT--
--PERHAPS HUMILITY WILL IMPROOOOVE YOU.

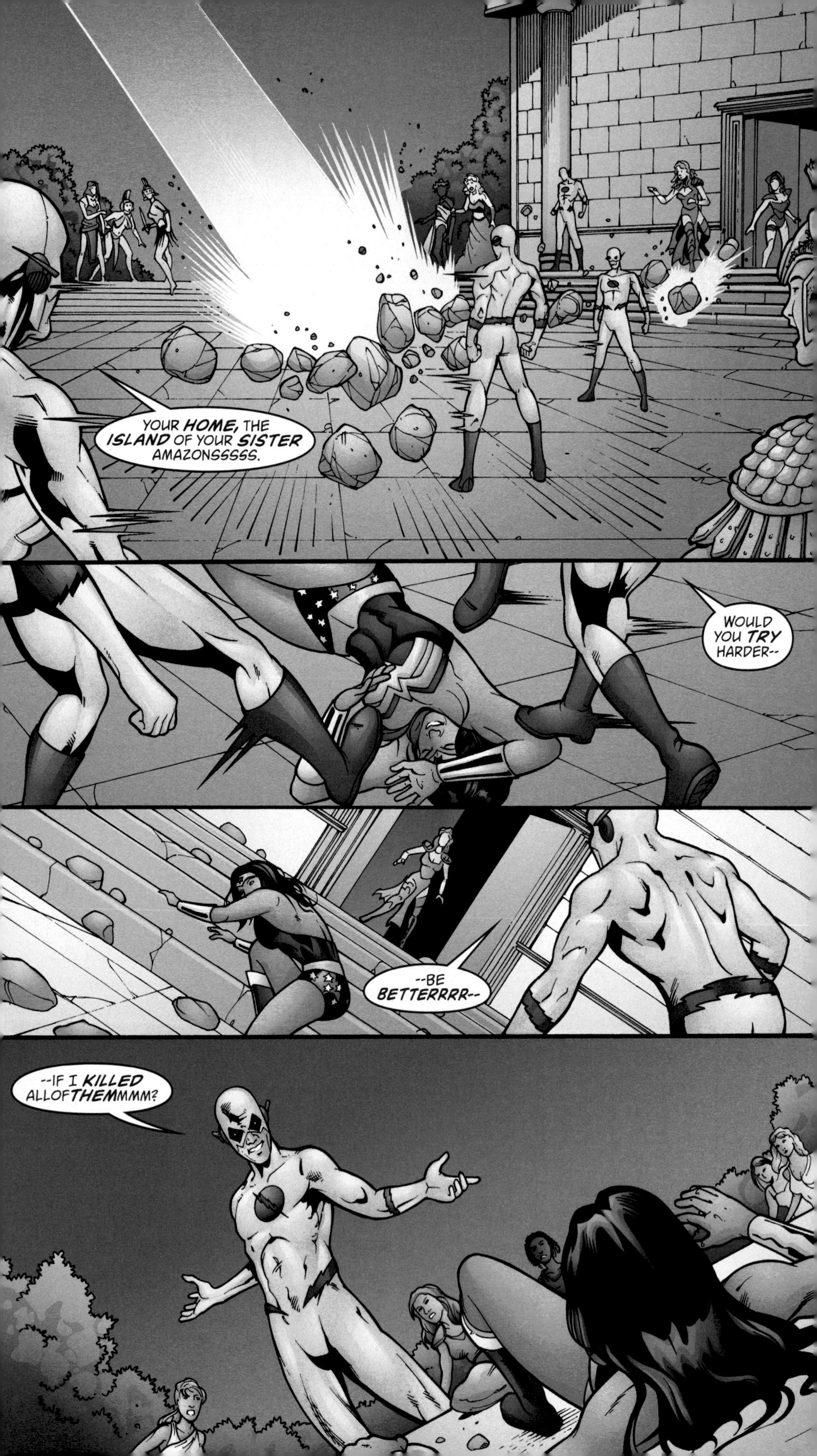

YOUR HOME, THE ISLAND OF YOUR SISTER AMAZONSSSSS.
WOULD YOU TRY HARDER--
--BE BETTERRRR--
--IF I KILLED ALLOFTHEMMMM?

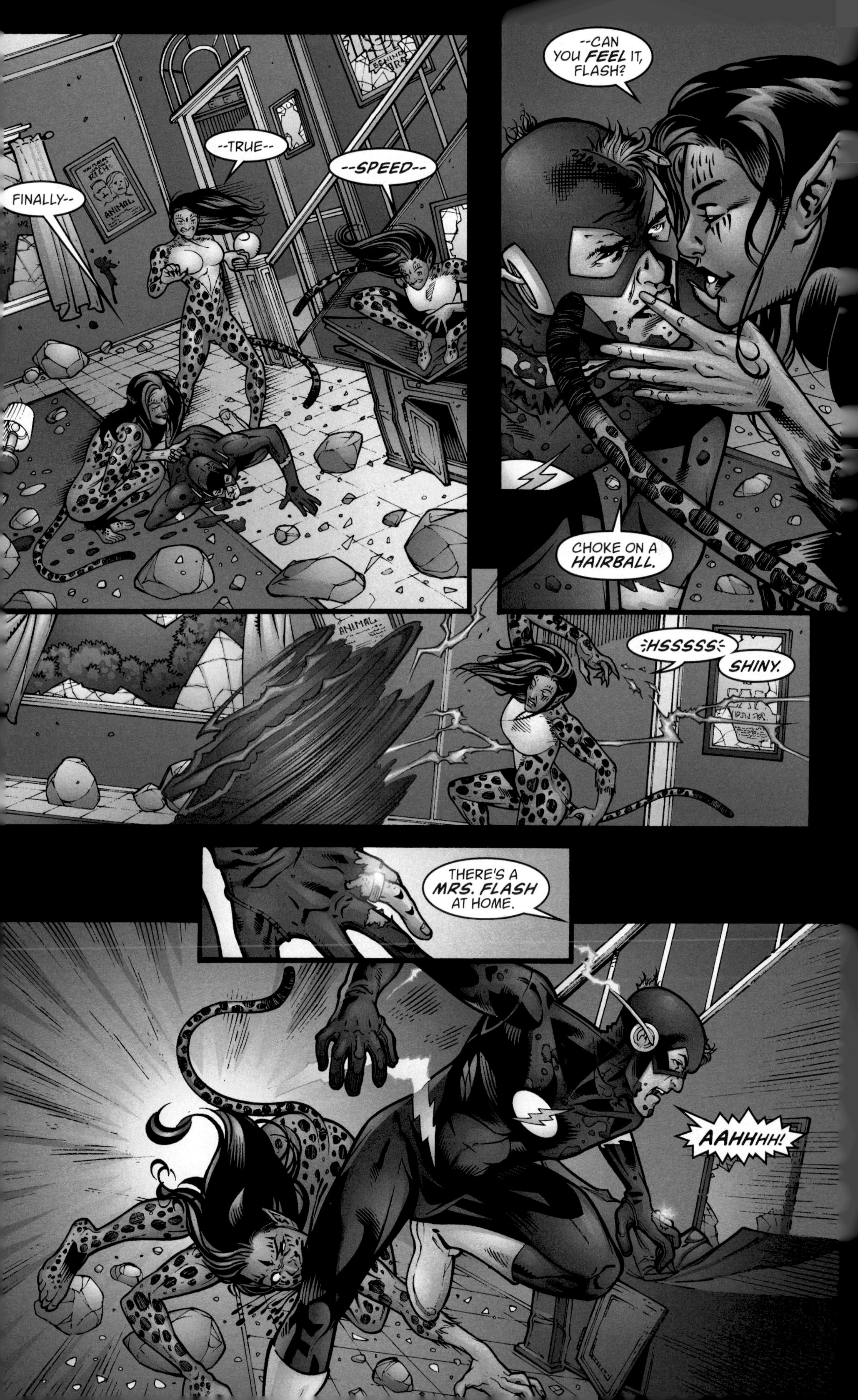
FINALLY--
--TRUE--
--SPEED--
--CAN YOU FEEL IT, FLASH?
CHOKE ON A HAIRBALL.
HSSSSS
SHINY.
THERE'S A MRS. FLASH AT HOME.
AAHHHH!

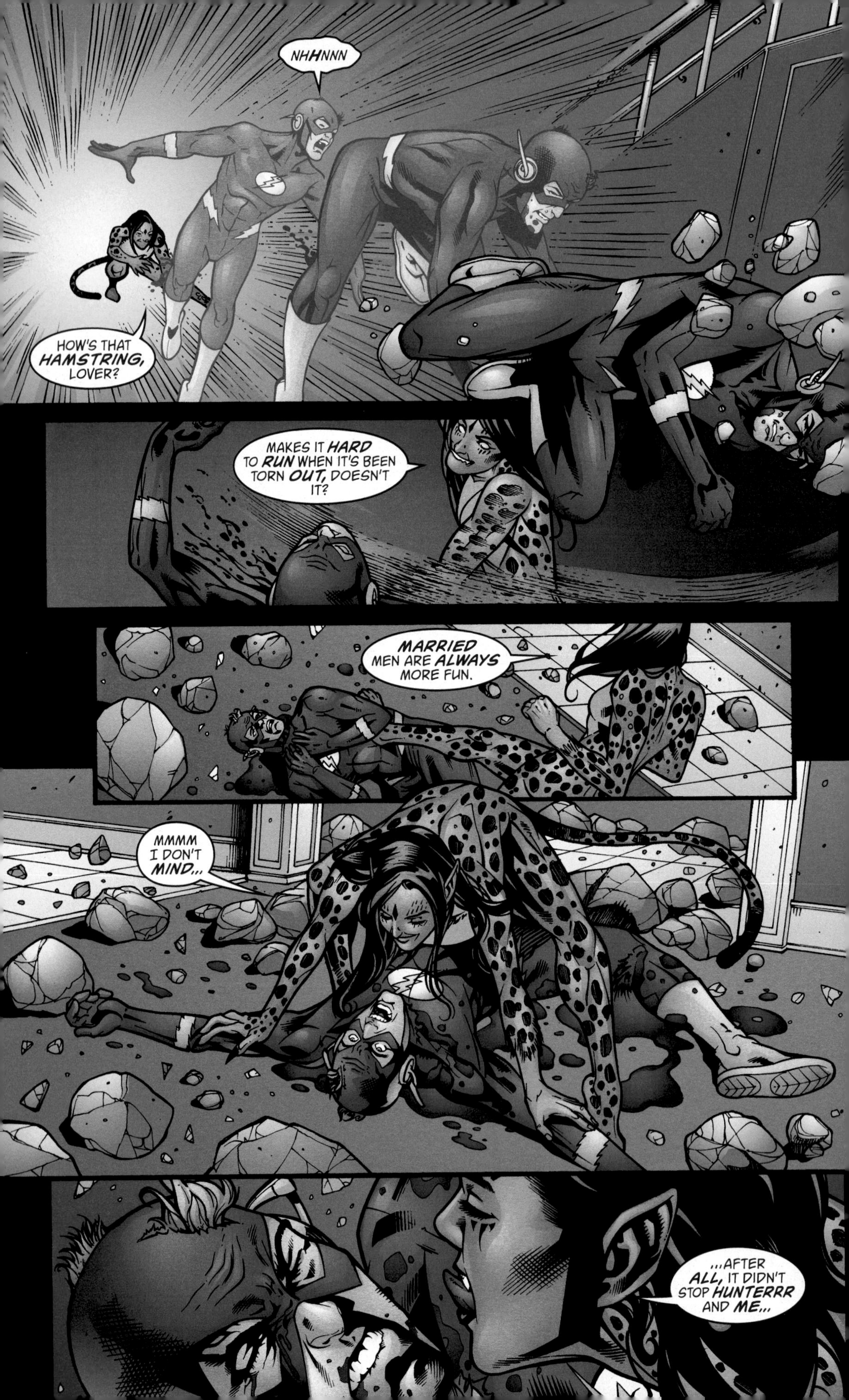
NHHNNN
HOW'S THAT HAMSTRING, LOVER?
MAKES IT HARD TO RUN WHEN IT'S BEEN TORN OUT, DOESN'T IT?
MARRIED MEN ARE ALWAYS MORE FUN.
MMMM I DON'T MIND...
...AFTER ALL, IT DIDN'T STOP HUNTERRR AND ME...

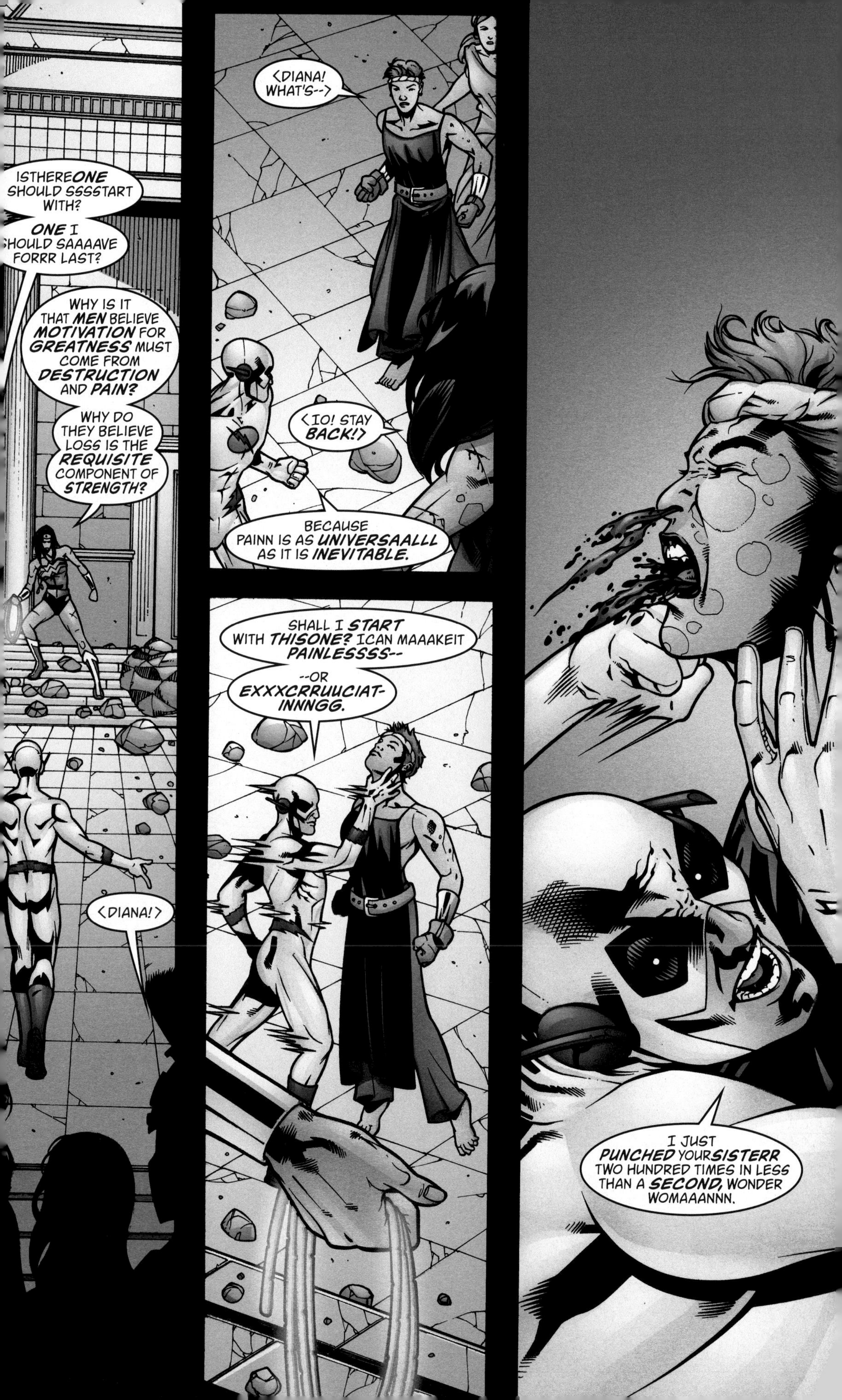
ISTHERE ONE SHOULD SSSSTART WITH?
ONE I SHOULD SAAAAVE FORRR LAST?
WHY IS IT THAT MEN BELIEVE MOTIVATION FOR GREATNESS MUST COME FROM DESTRUCTION AND PAIN?
WHY DO THEY BELIEVE LOSS IS THE REQUISITE COMPONENT OF STRENGTH?
<DIANA!>
<DIANA! WHAT'S-->
<IO! STAY BACK!>
BECAUSE PAINN IS AS UNIVERSAALLL AS IT IS INEVITABLE.
SHALL I START WITH THISONE? ICAN MAAAKEIT PAINLESSSS--
--OR EXXXCRRUUCIAT-INNNGG.
I JUST PUNCHED YOURSISTERR TWO HUNDRED TIMES IN LESS THAN A SECOND, WONDER WOMAAANNN.

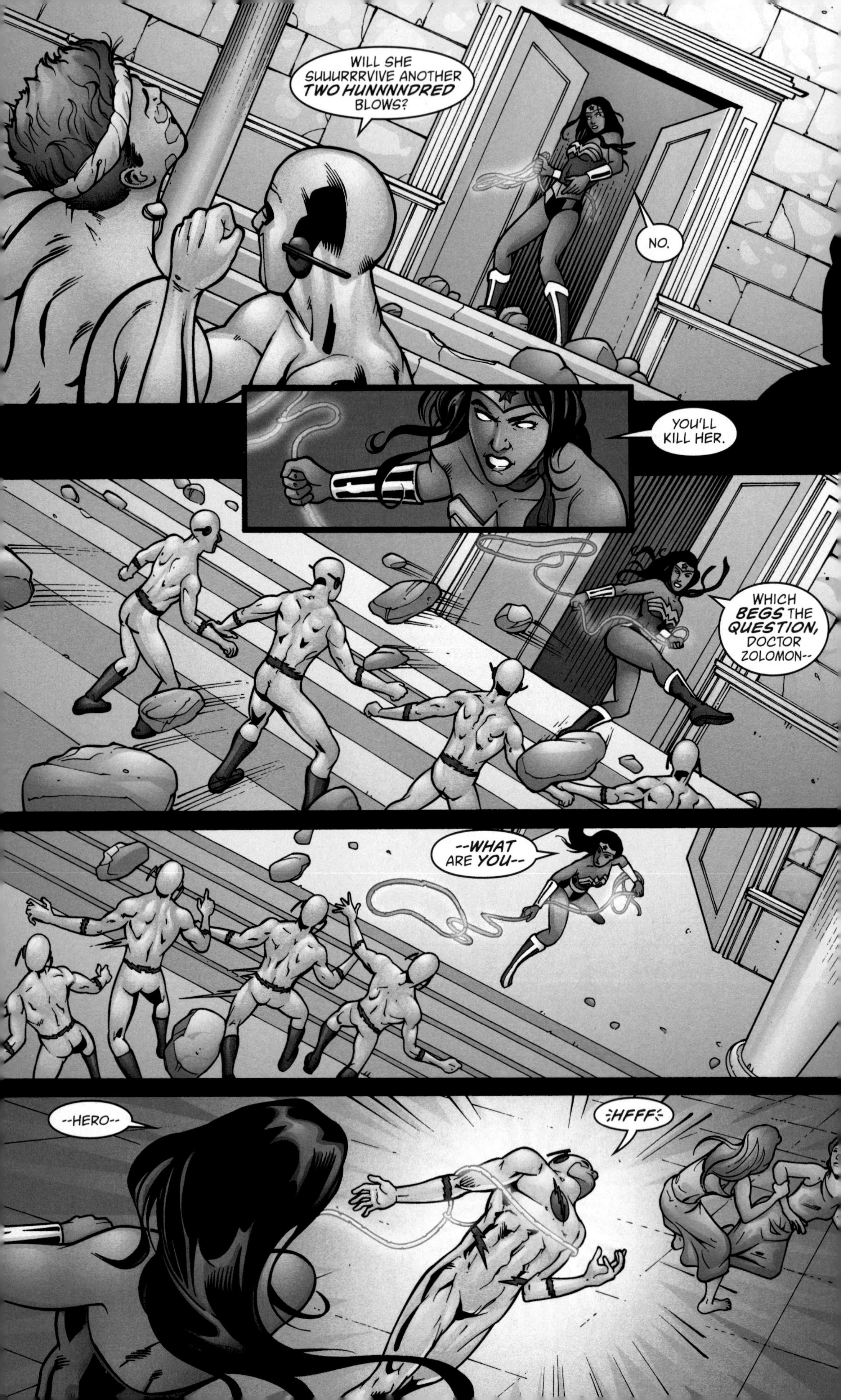
WILL SHE SUUURRRVIVE ANOTHER TWO HUNNNNDRED BLOWS?
NO.
YOU'LL KILL HER.
WHICH BEGS THE QUESTION, DOCTOR ZOLOMON--
--WHAT ARE YOU--
--HERO--
HFFF

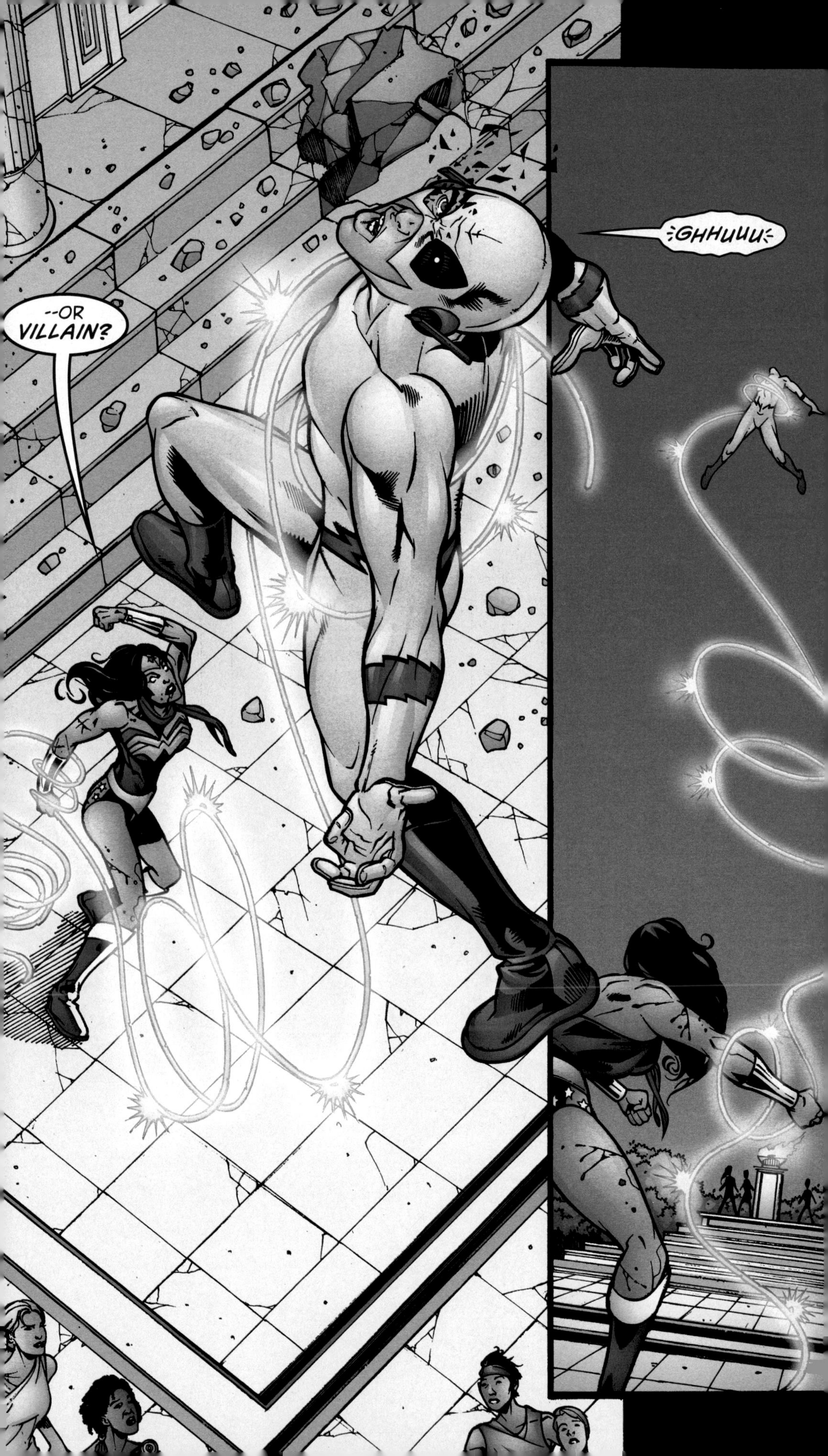
--OR VILLAIN?
GHHUUU

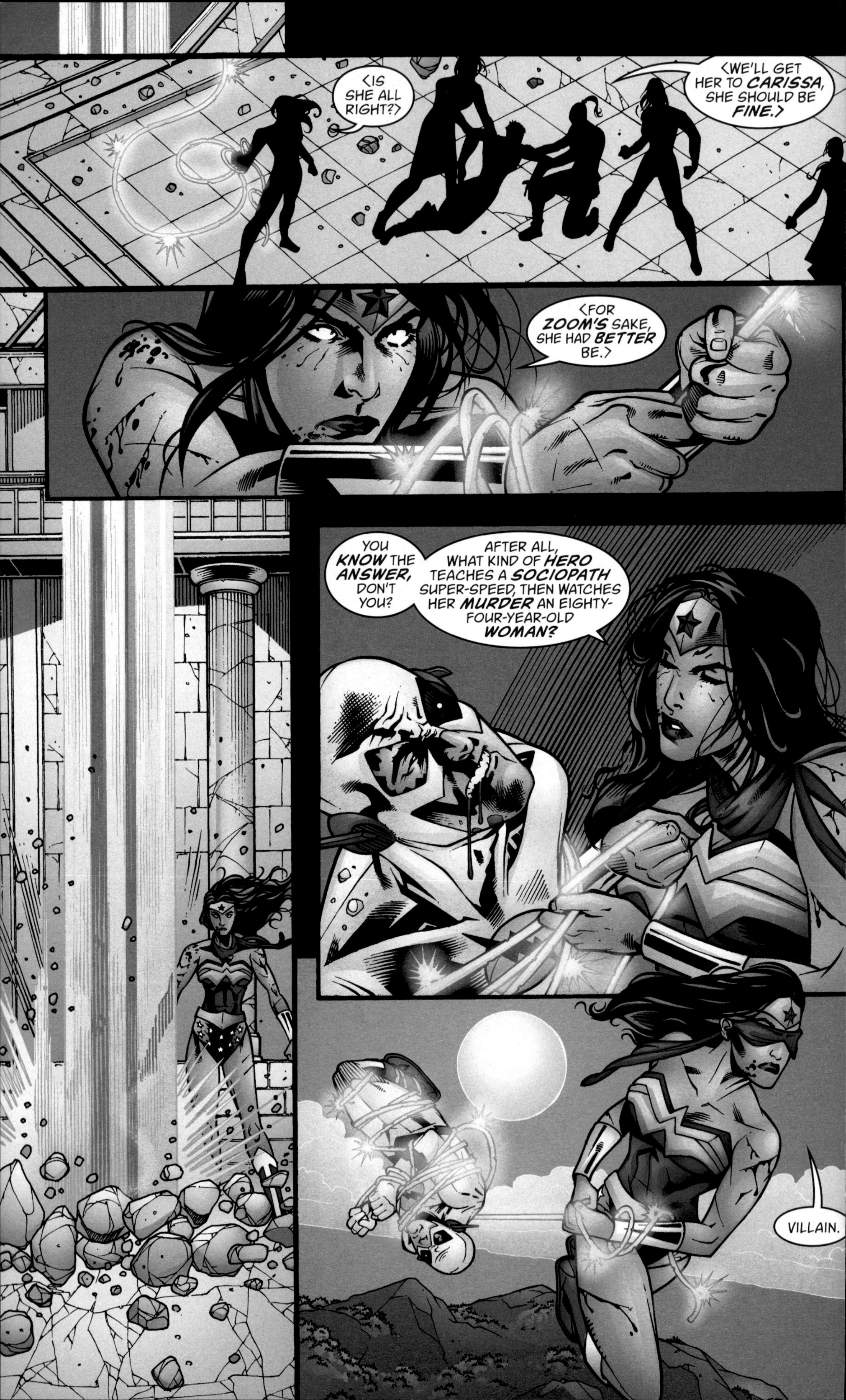
<IS SHE ALL RIGHT?>
<WE'LL GET HER TO CARISSA, SHE SHOULD BE FINE.>
<FOR ZOOM'S SAKE, SHE HAD BETTER BE.>
YOU KNOW THE ANSWER, DON'T YOU?
AFTER ALL, WHAT KIND OF HERO TEACHES A SOCIOPATH SUPER-SPEED, THEN WATCHES HER MURDER AN EIGHTY-FOUR-YEAR-OLD WOMAN?
VILLAIN.

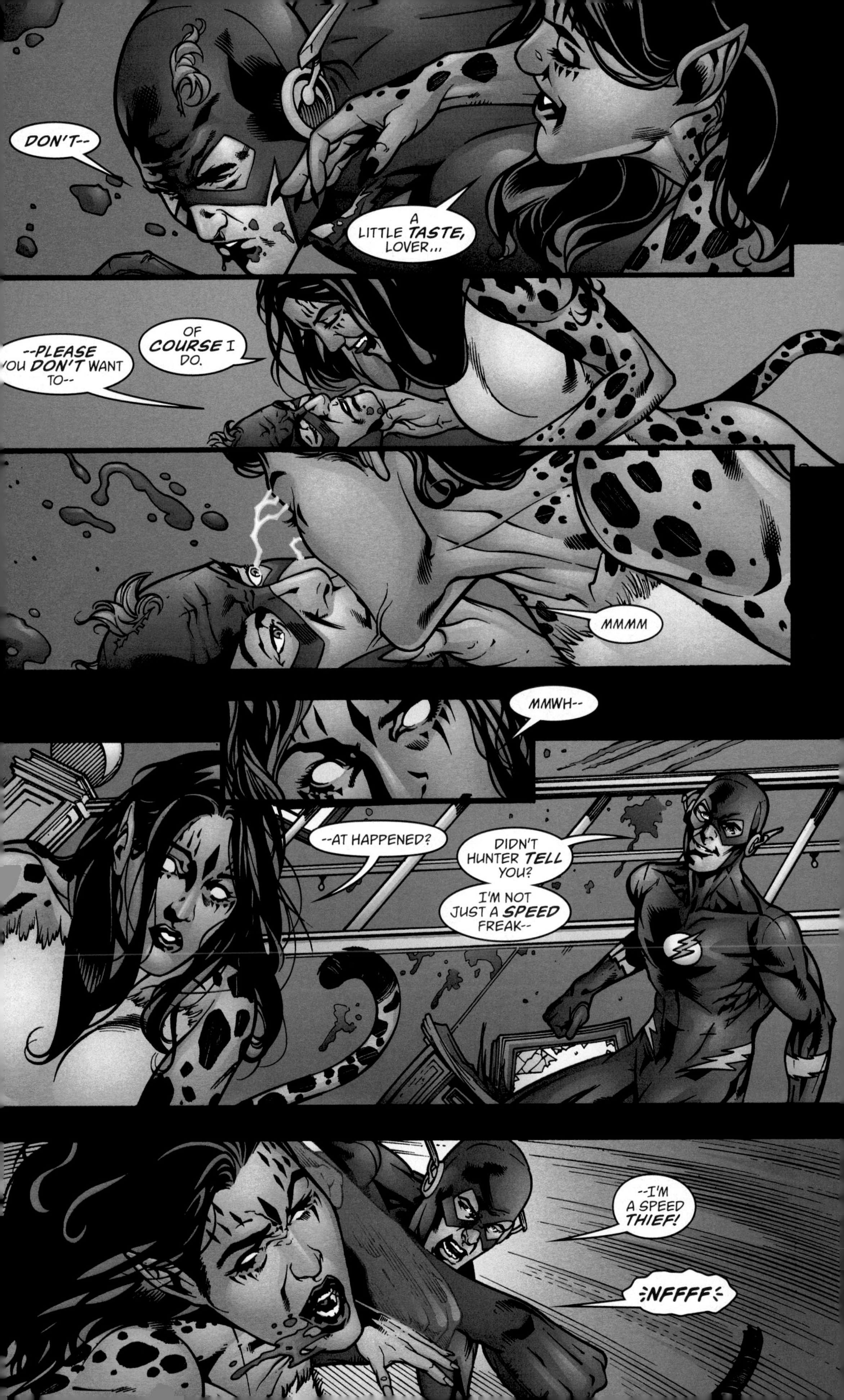
DON'T--
A LITTLE TASTE, LOVER...
--PLEASE YOU DON'T WANT TO--
OF COURSE I DO.
MMMM
MMWH--
--AT HAPPENED?
DIDN'T HUNTER TELL YOU?
I'M NOT JUST A SPEED FREAK--
--I'M A SPEED THIEF!
NFFFF

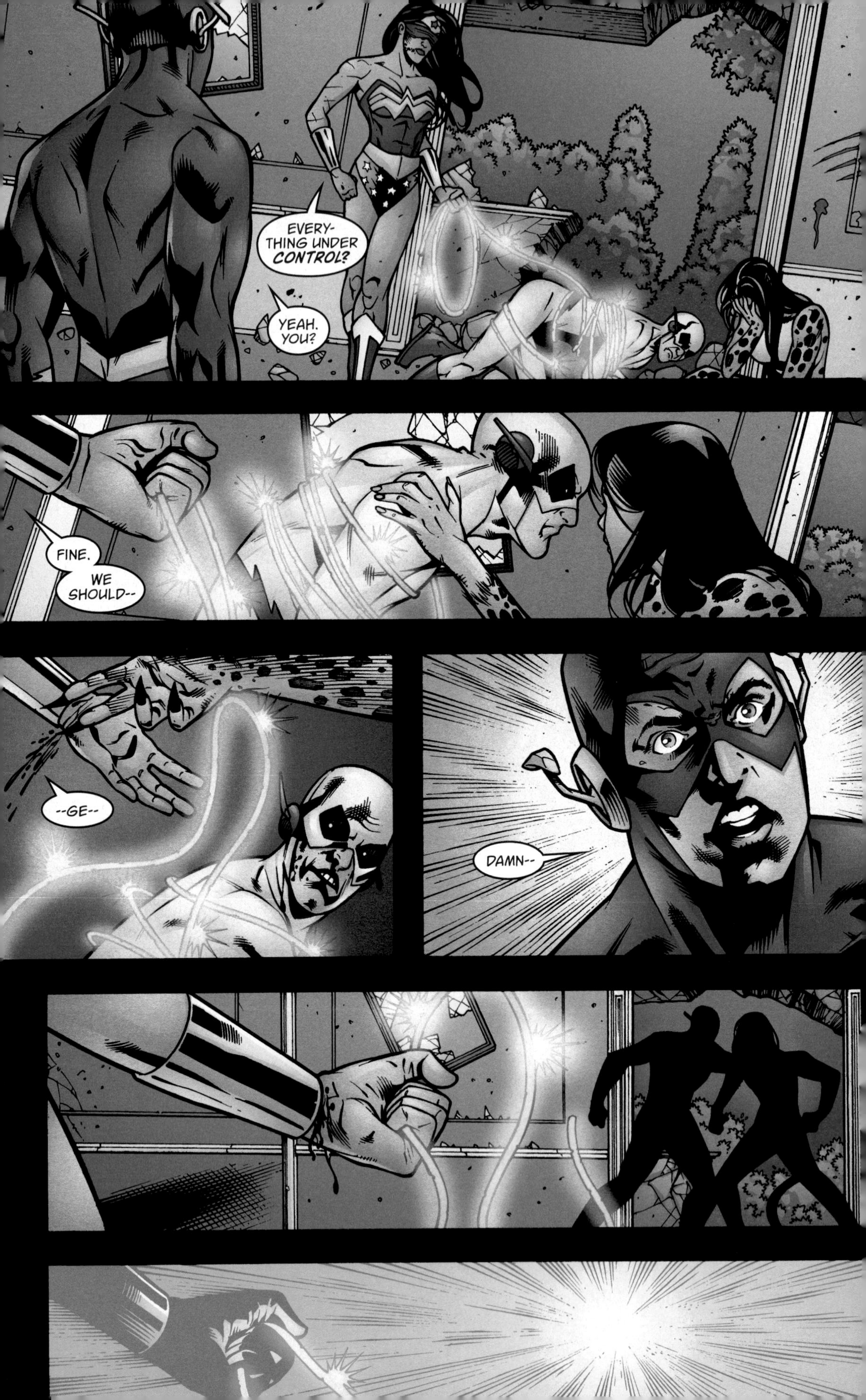
EVERY-THING UNDER CONTROL?
YEAH. YOU?
FINE.
WE SHOULD--
--GE--
DAMN--

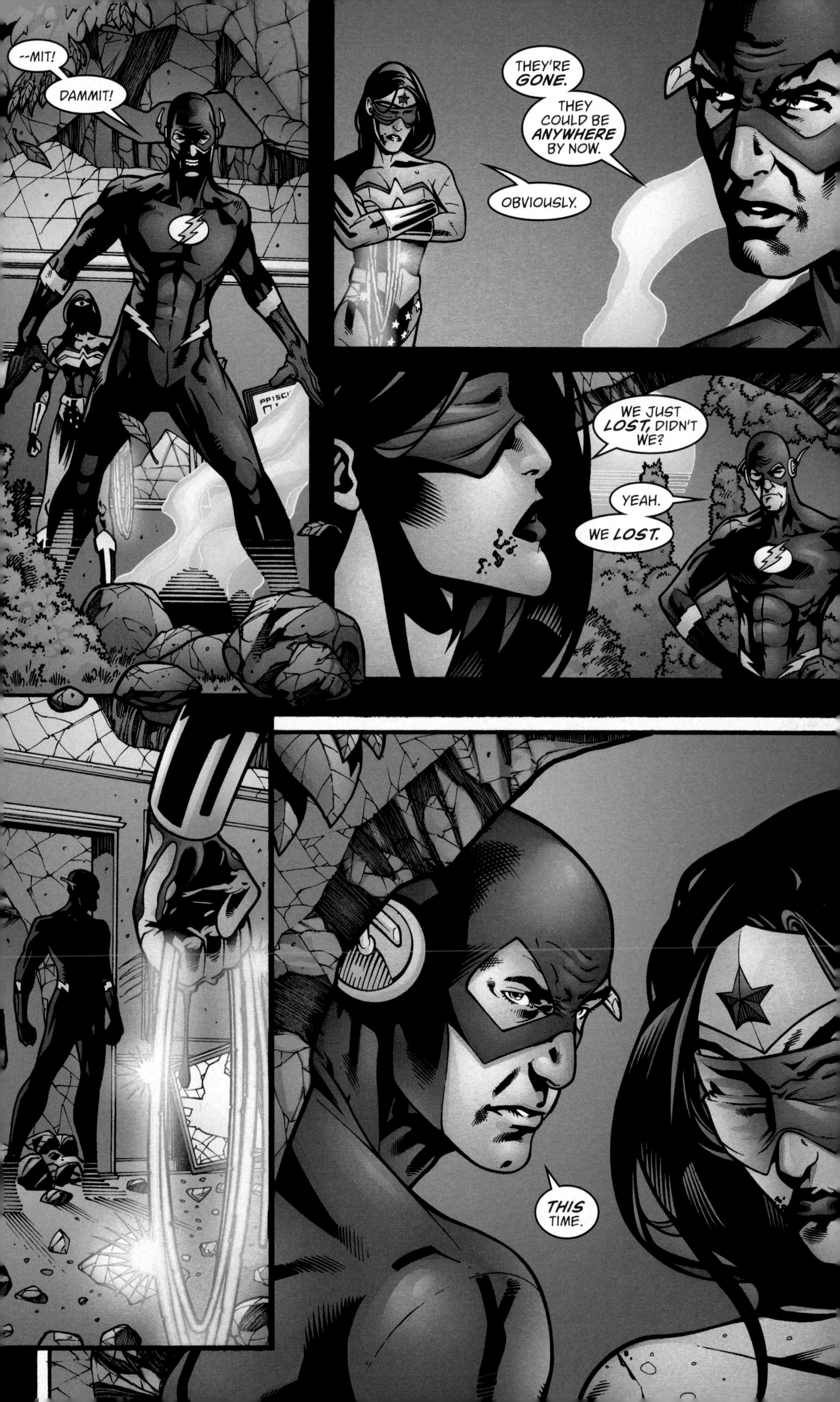
--MIT!
DAMMIT!
THEY'RE GONE.
THEY COULD BE ANYWHERE BY NOW.
OBVIOUSLY.
WE JUST LOST, DIDN'T WE?
YEAH.
WE LOST.
THIS TIME.

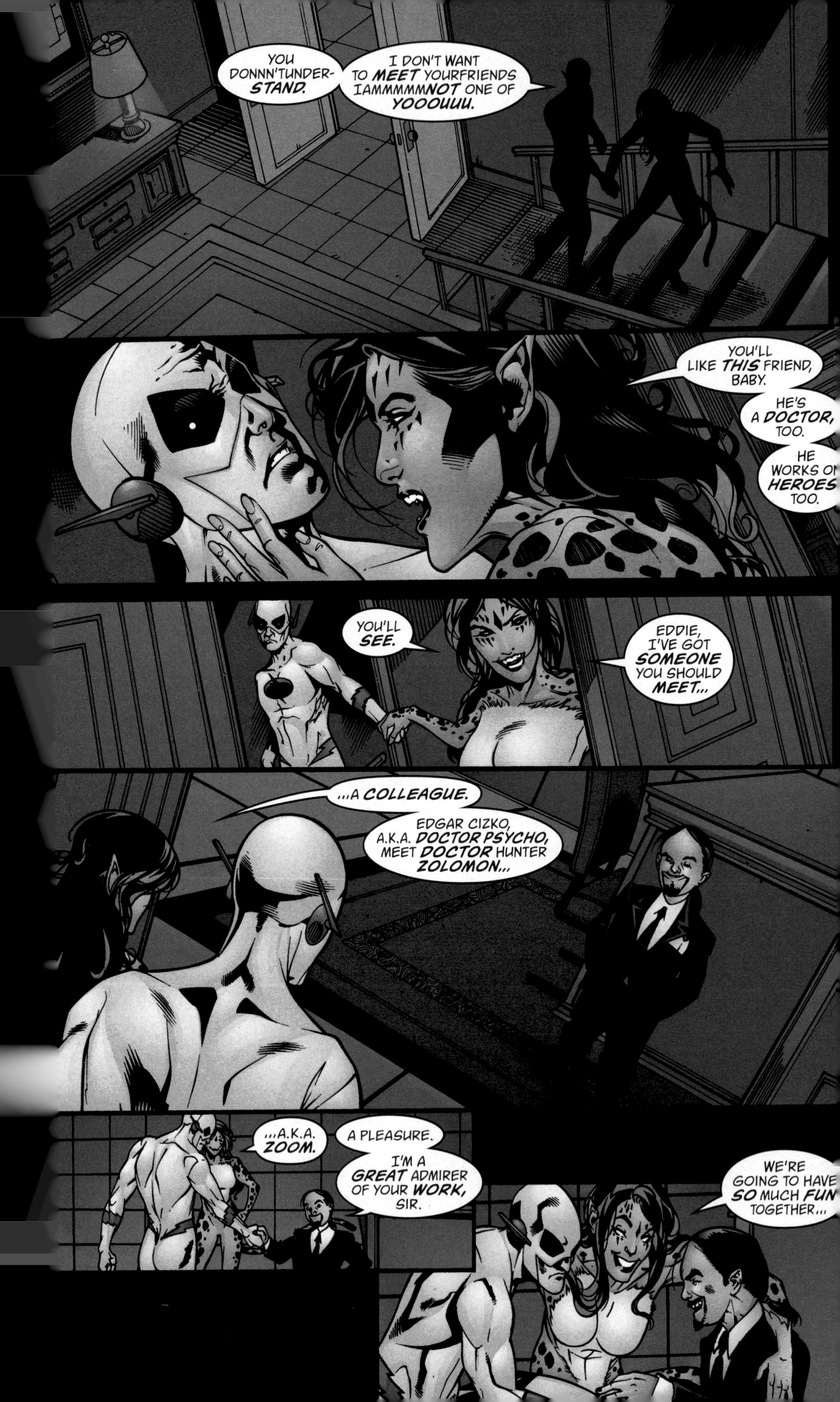

YOU DONNN'TUNDER-STAND.
I DON'T WANT TO MEET YOURFRIENDS IAMMMMMNOT ONE OF YOOOUUU.
YOU'LL LIKE THIS FRIEND, BABY.
HE'S A DOCTOR, TOO.
HE WORKS ON HEROES TOO.
YOU'LL SEE.
EDDIE, I'VE GOT SOMEONE YOU SHOULD MEET...
...A COLLEAGUE.
EDGAR CIZKO, A.K.A. DOCTOR PSYCHO, MEET DOCTOR HUNTER ZOLOMON...
...A.K.A. ZOOM.
A PLEASURE.
I'M A GREAT ADMIRER OF YOUR WORK, SIR.
WE'RE GOING TO HAVE SO MUCH FUN TOGETHER...

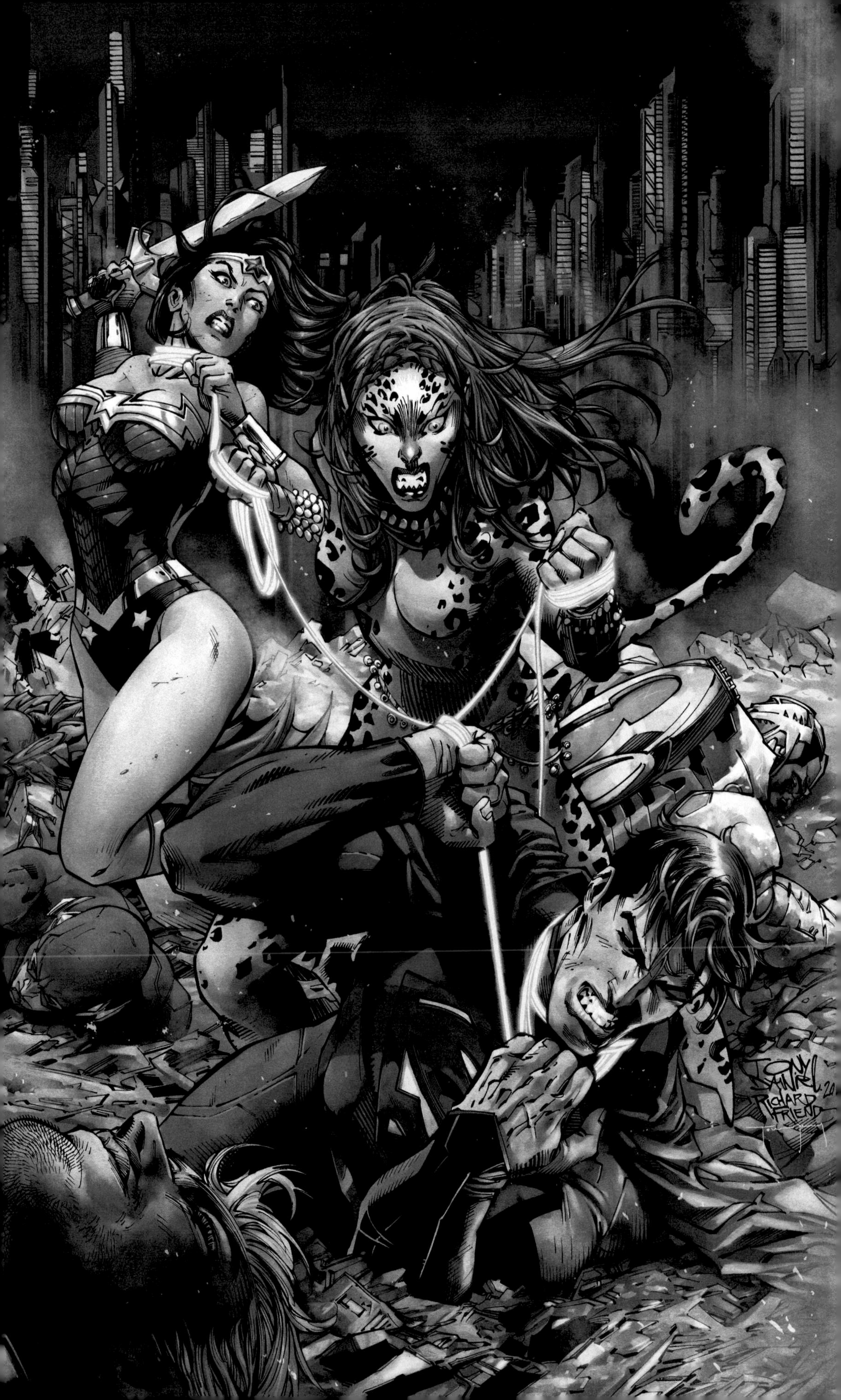
RICHARD FRIEND

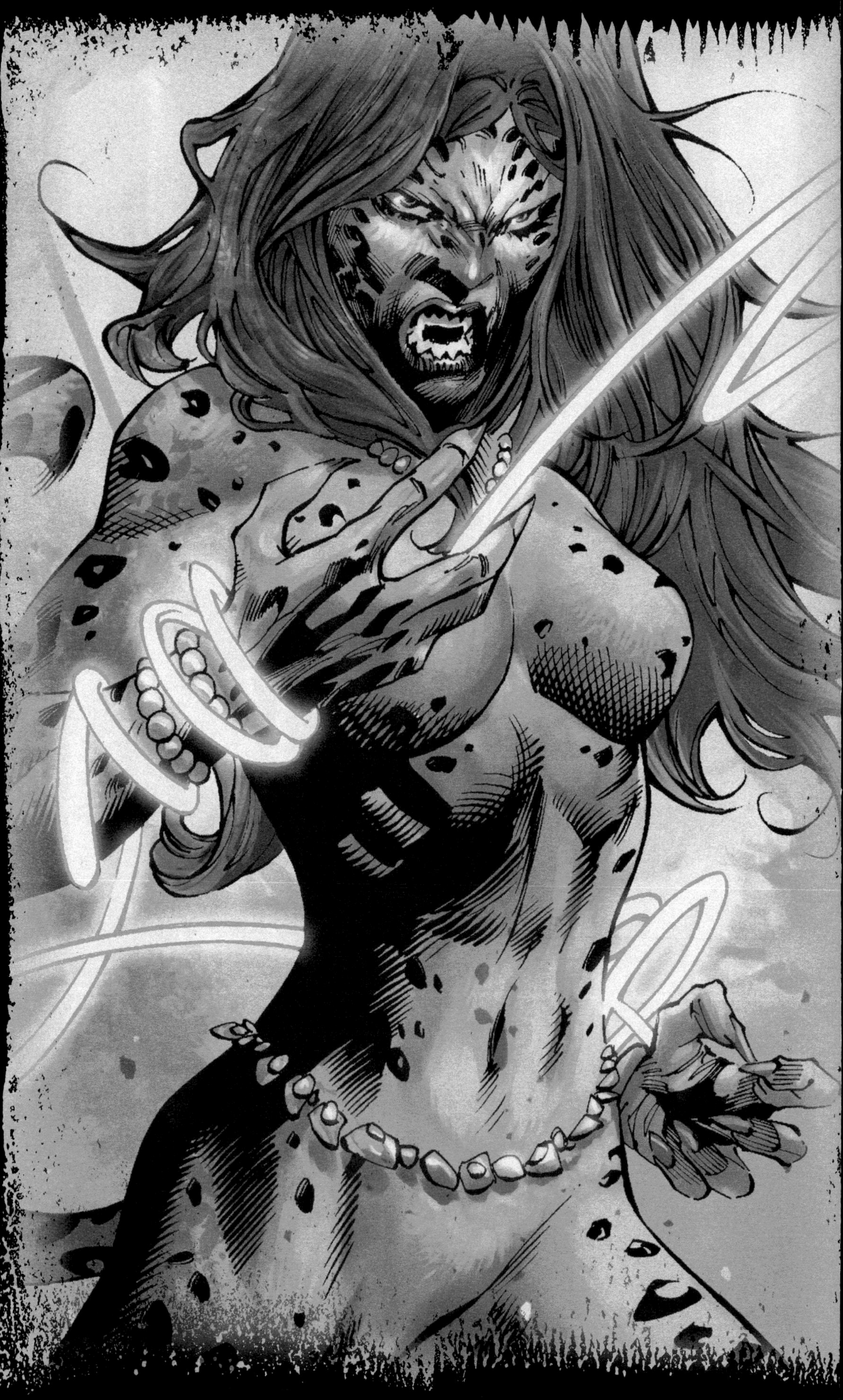

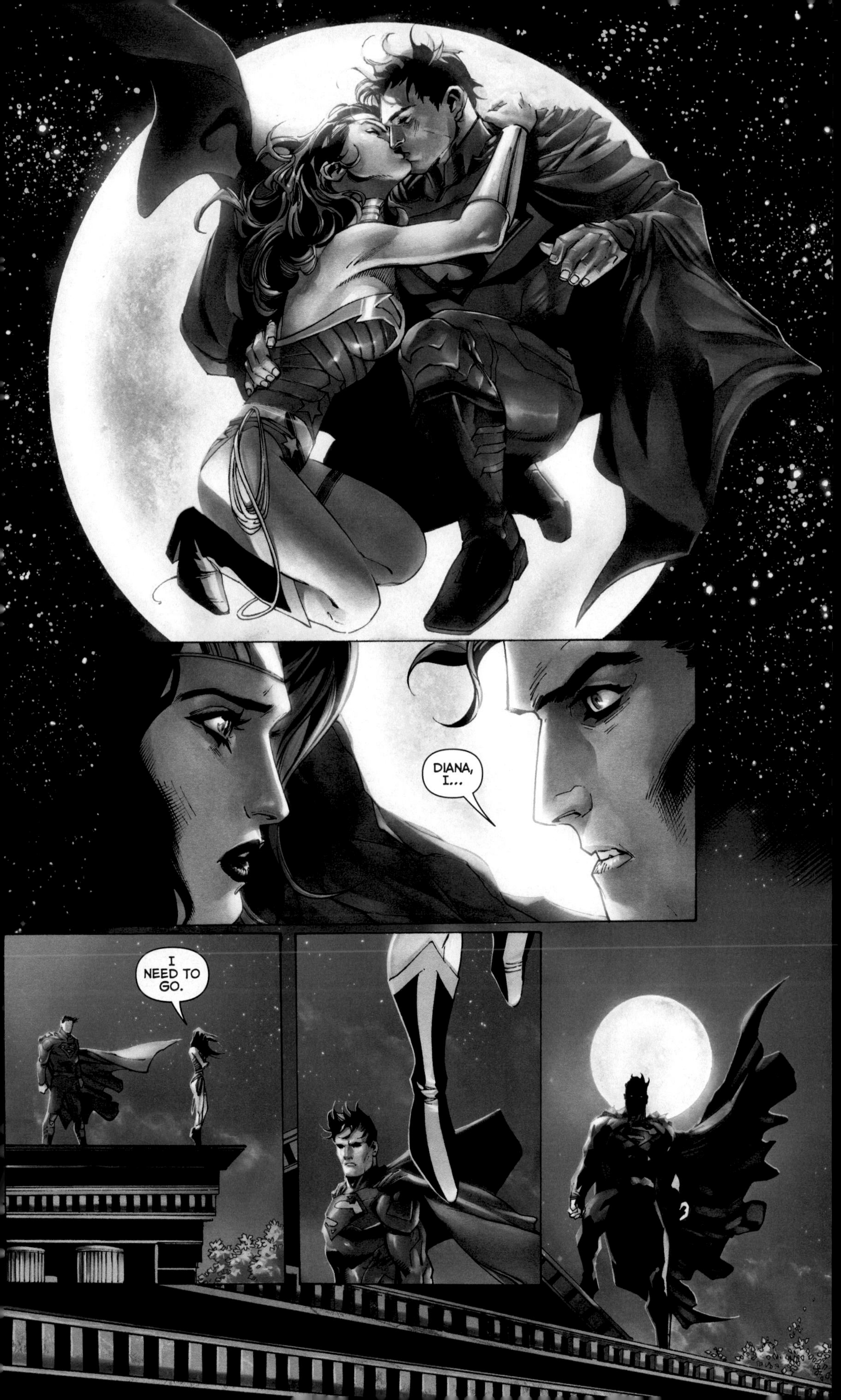
DIANA, I...
I NEED TO GO.

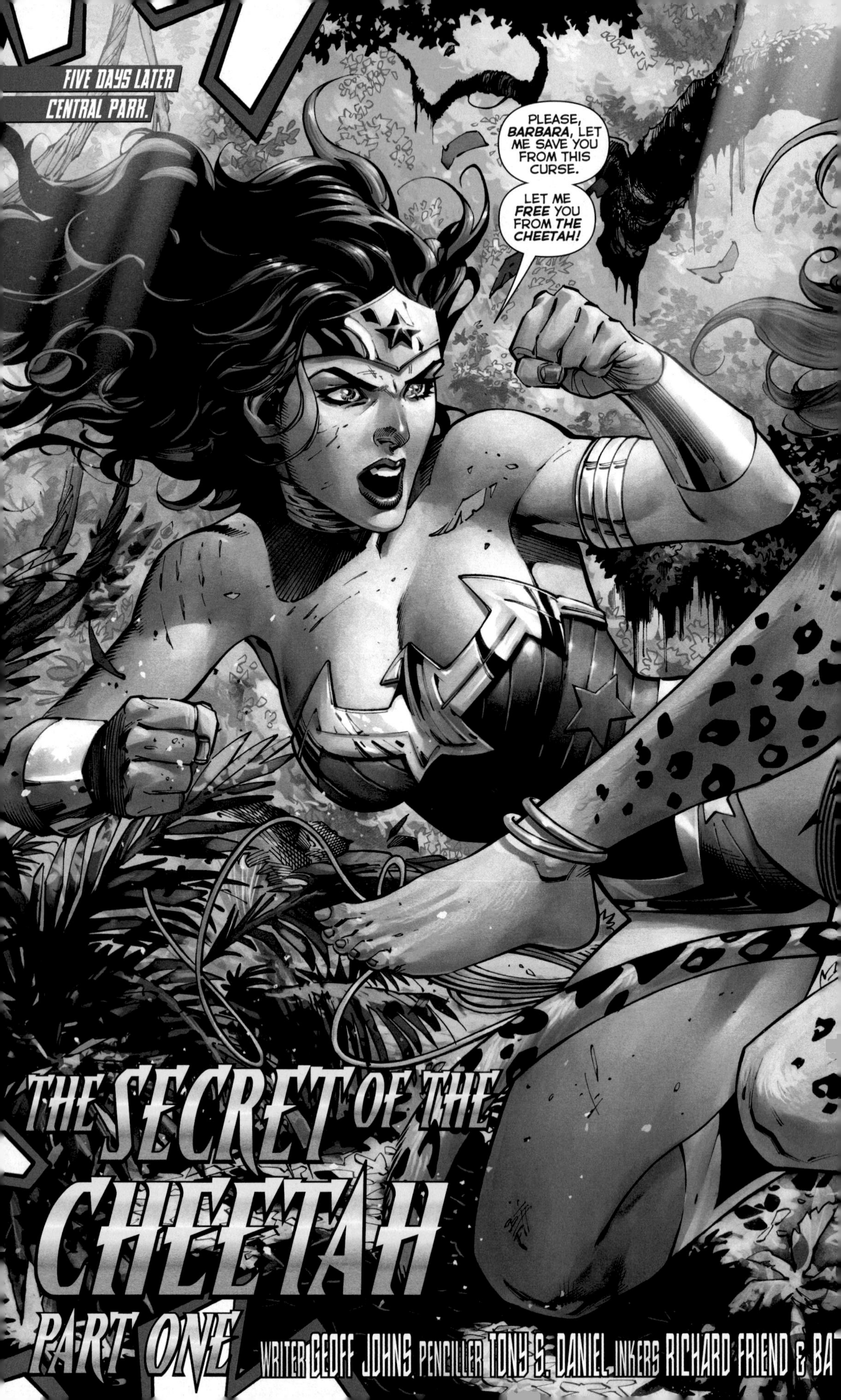
FIVE DAYS LATER
CENTRAL PARK.
PLEASE, BARBARA, LET ME SAVE YOU FROM THIS CURSE.
LET ME FREE YOU FROM THE CHEETAH!
THE SECRET OF THE CHEETAH
PART ONE
WRITER GEOFF JOHNS PENCILLER TONY S. DANIEL INKERS RICHARD FRIEND & BA

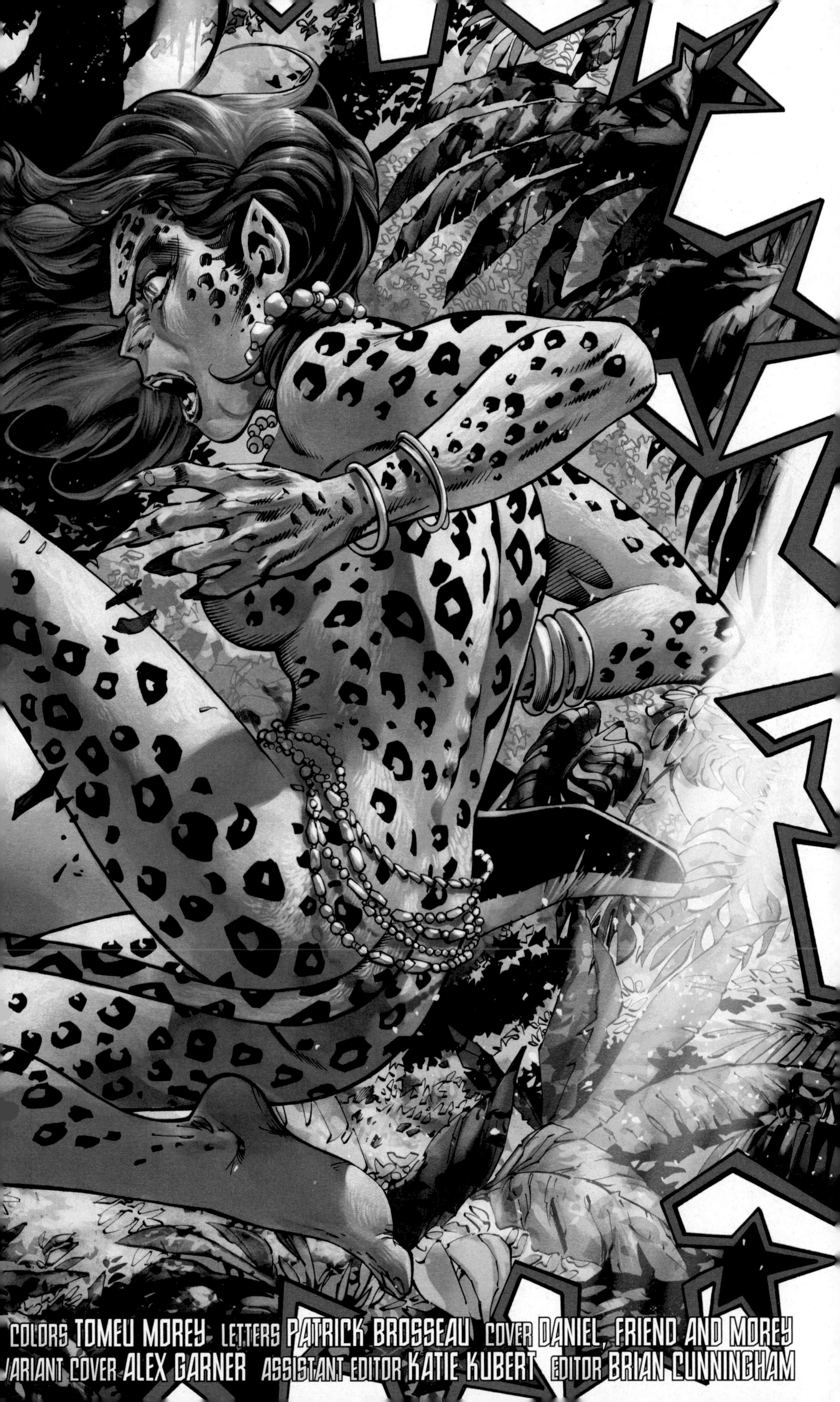

COLORS TOMEU MOREY LETTERS PATRICK BROSSEAU COVER DANIEL, FRIEND AND MOREY
/ARIANT COVER ALEX GARNER ASSISTANT EDITOR KATIE KUBERT EDITOR BRIAN CUNNINGHAM

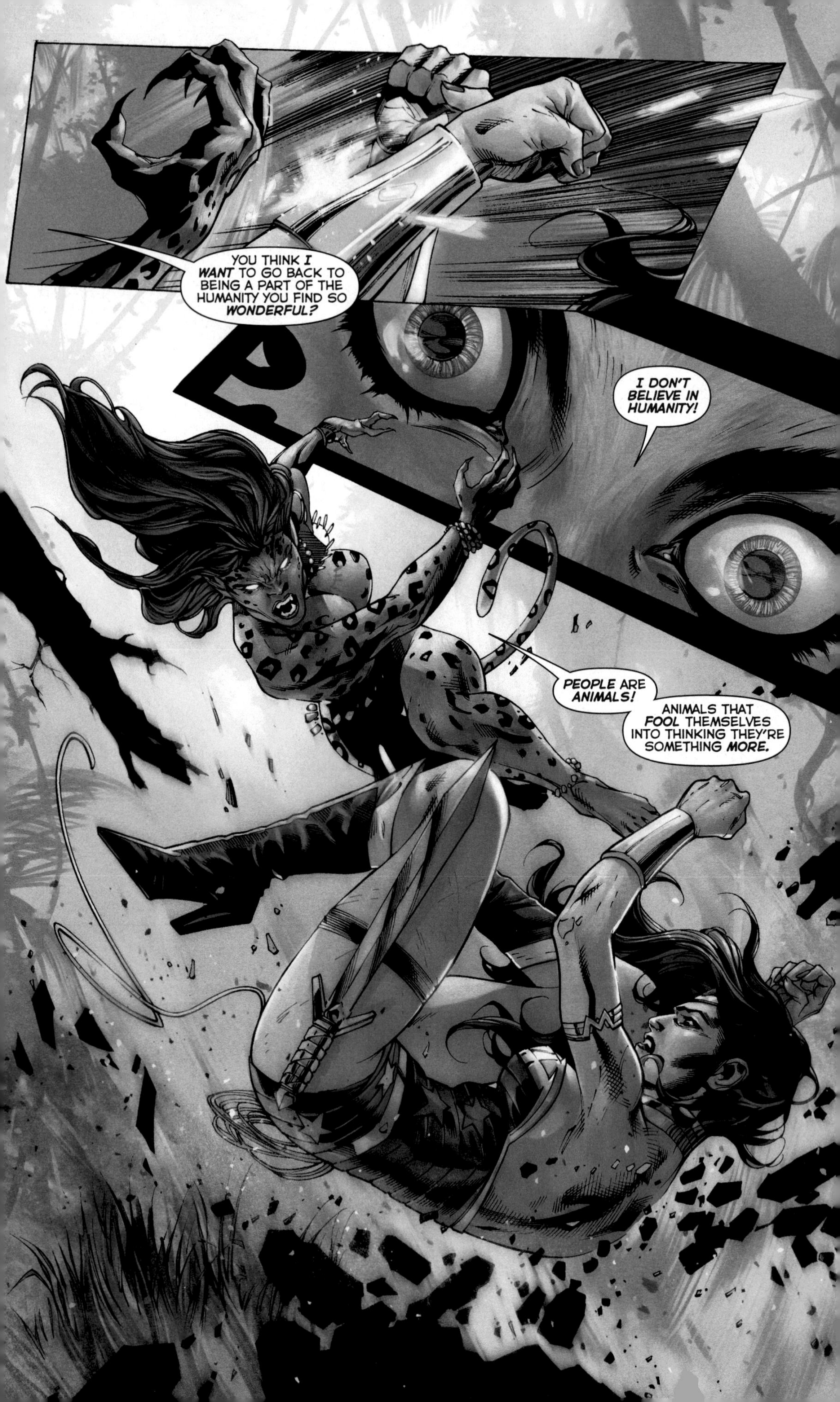

YOU THINK I WANT TO GO BACK TO BEING A PART OF THE HUMANITY YOU FIND SO WONDERFUL?
I DON'T BELIEVE IN HUMANITY!
PEOPLE ARE ANIMALS!
ANIMALS THAT FOOL THEMSELVES INTO THINKING THEY'RE SOMETHING MORE.

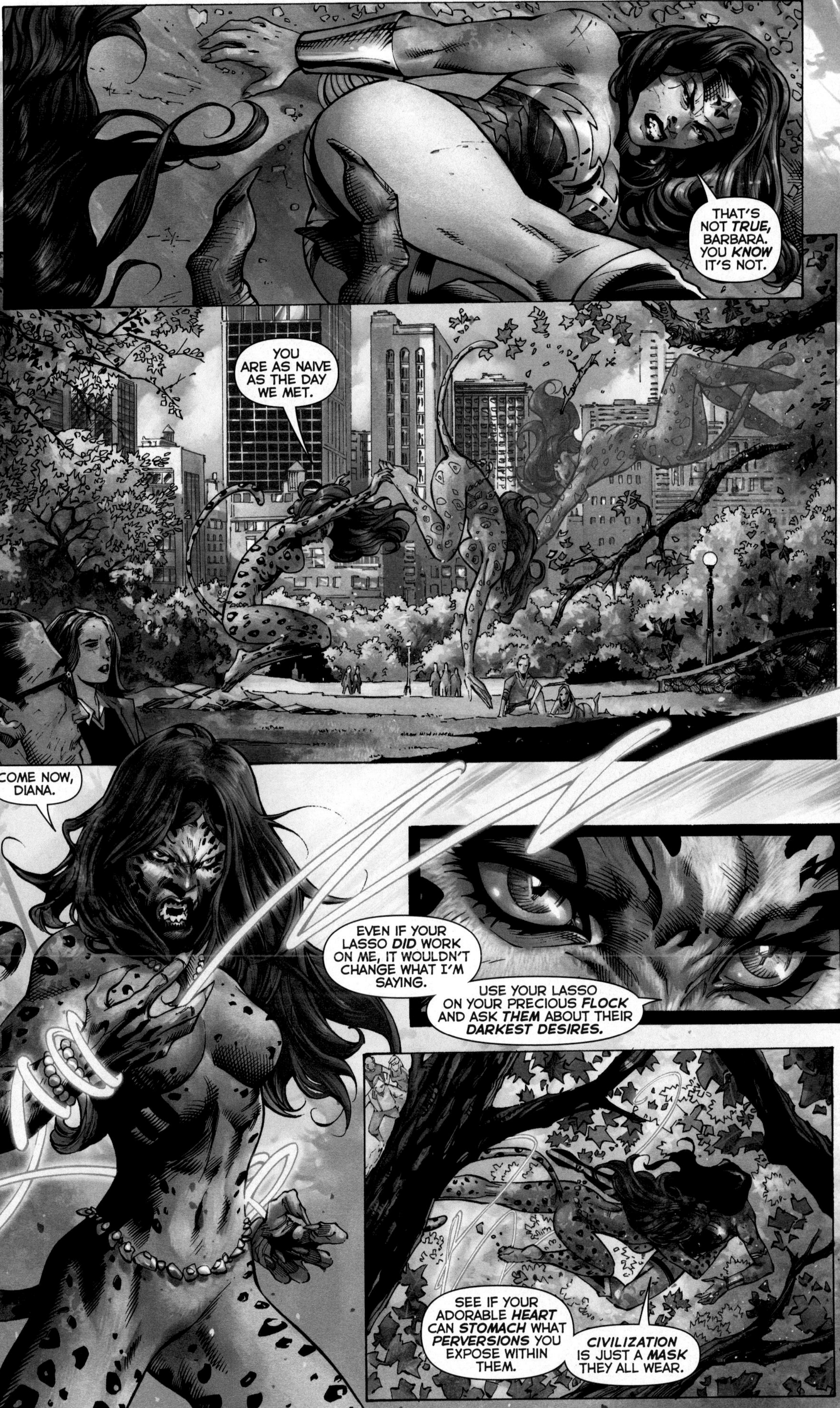
THAT'S NOT TRUE, BARBARA. YOU KNOW IT'S NOT.
YOU ARE AS NAIVE AS THE DAY WE MET.
COME NOW, DIANA.
EVEN IF YOUR LASSO DID WORK ON ME, IT WOULDN'T CHANGE WHAT I'M SAYING.
USE YOUR LASSO ON YOUR PRECIOUS FLOCK AND ASK THEM ABOUT THEIR DARKEST DESIRES.
SEE IF YOUR ADORABLE HEART CAN STOMACH WHAT PERVERSIONS YOU EXPOSE WITHIN THEM.
CIVILIZATION IS JUST A MASK THEY ALL WEAR.

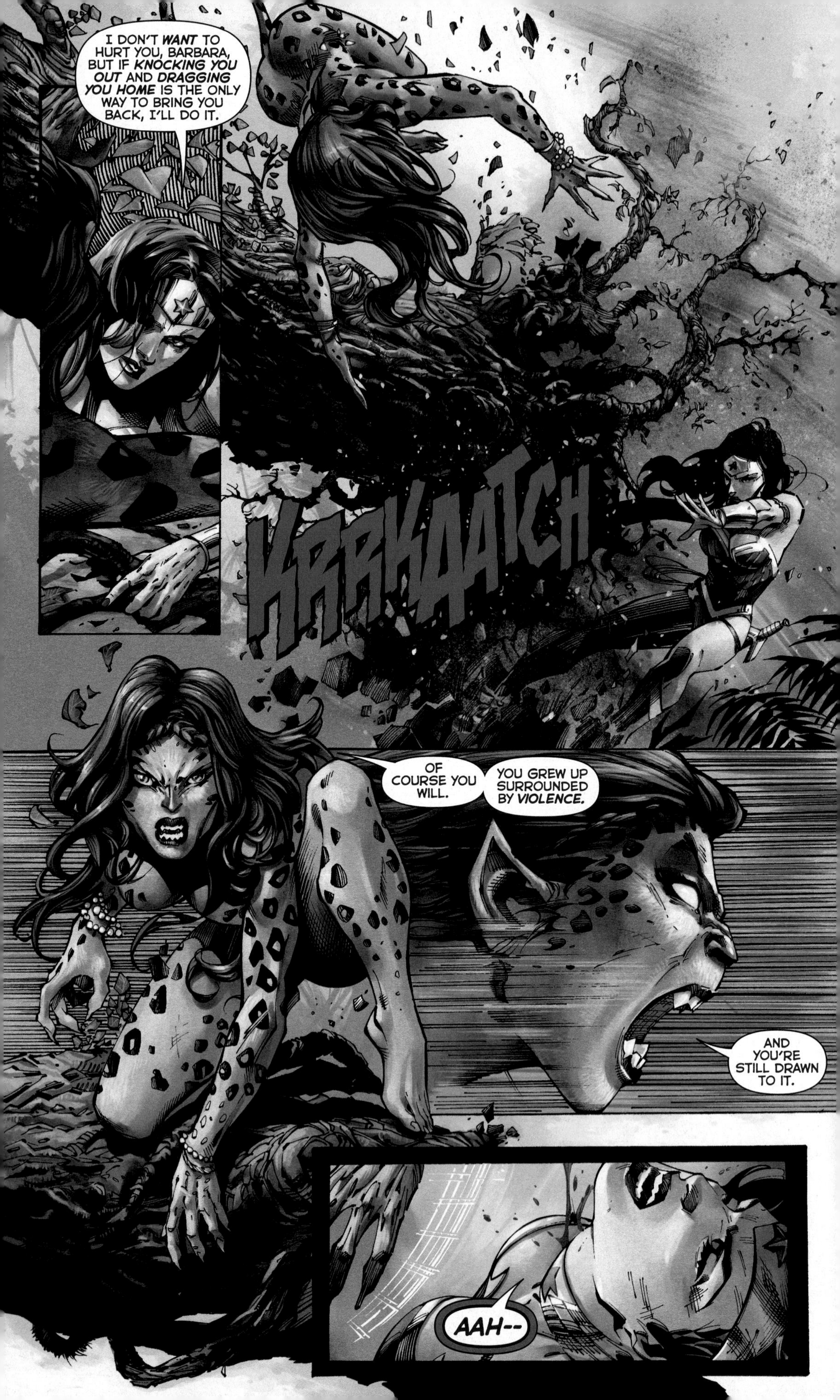
I DON'T WANT TO HURT YOU, BARBARA, BUT IF KNOCKING YOU OUT AND DRAGGING YOU HOME IS THE ONLY WAY TO BRING YOU BACK, I'LL DO IT.
KRRKAATCH
OF COURSE YOU WILL.
YOU GREW UP SURROUNDED BY VIOLENCE.
AND YOU'RE STILL DRAWN TO IT.
AAH--

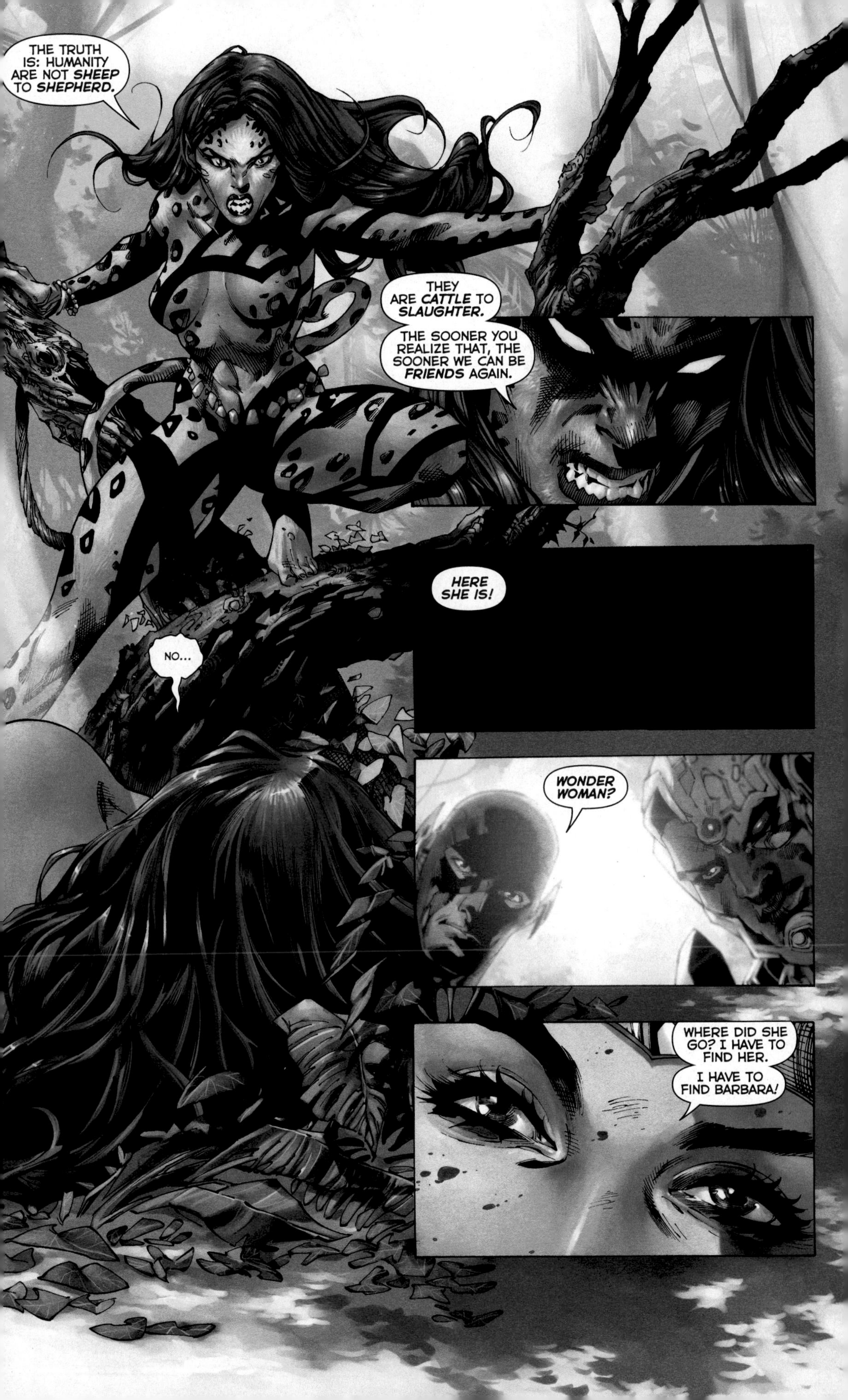
THE TRUTH IS: HUMANITY ARE NOT SHEEP TO SHEPHERD.
THEY ARE CATTLE TO SLAUGHTER.
THE SOONER YOU REALIZE THAT, THE SOONER WE CAN BE FRIENDS AGAIN.
HERE SHE IS!
NO...
WONDER WOMAN?
WHERE DID SHE GO? I HAVE TO FIND HER.
I HAVE TO FIND BARBARA!

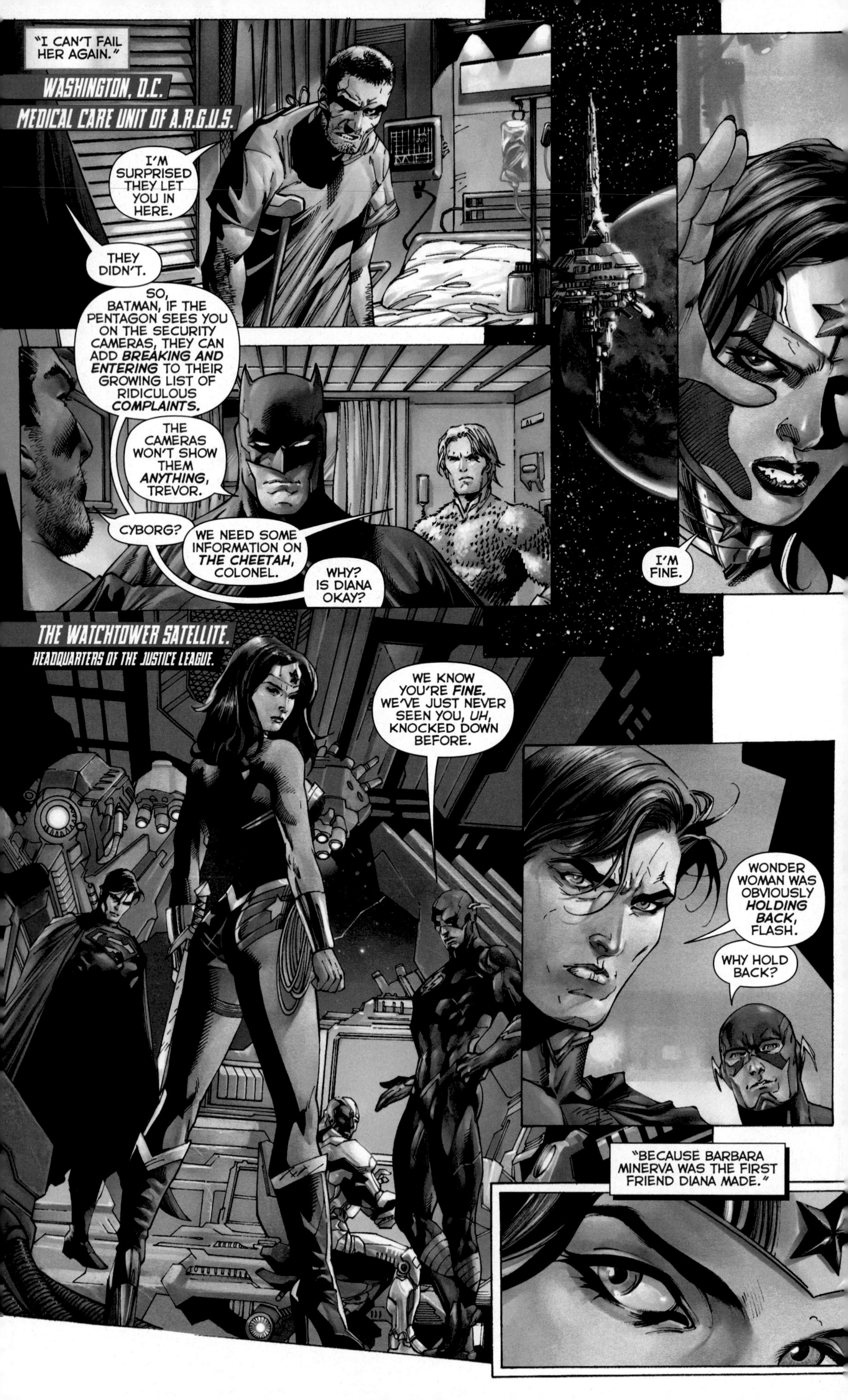
"I CAN'T FAIL HER AGAIN."
WASHINGTON, D.C.
MEDICAL CARE UNIT OF A.R.G.U.S.
I'M SURPRISED THEY LET YOU IN HERE.
THEY DIDN'T.
SO, BATMAN, IF THE PENTAGON SEES YOU ON THE SECURITY CAMERAS, THEY CAN ADD BREAKING AND ENTERING TO THEIR GROWING LIST OF RIDICULOUS COMPLAINTS.
THE CAMERAS WON'T SHOW THEM ANYTHING, TREVOR.
CYBORG?
WE NEED SOME INFORMATION ON THE CHEETAH, COLONEL.
WHY? IS DIANA OKAY?
I'M FINE.
THE WATCHTOWER SATELLITE.
HEADQUARTERS OF THE JUSTICE LEAGUE.
WE KNOW YOU'RE FINE. WE'VE JUST NEVER SEEN YOU, UH, KNOCKED DOWN BEFORE.
WONDER WOMAN WAS OBVIOUSLY HOLDING BACK, FLASH.
WHY HOLD BACK?
"BECAUSE BARBARA MINERVA WAS THE FIRST FRIEND DIANA MADE."

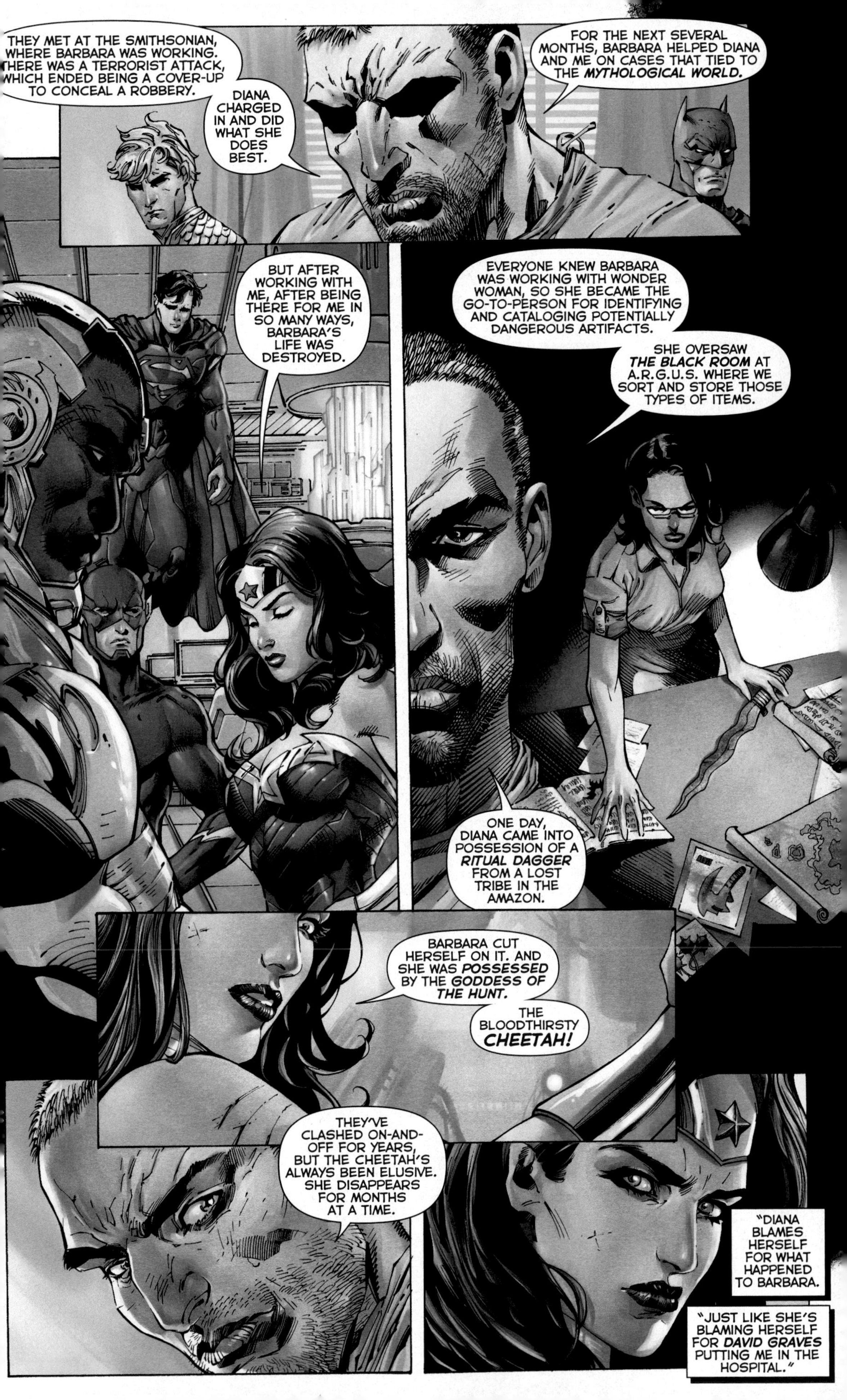
THEY MET AT THE SMITHSONIAN, WHERE BARBARA WAS WORKING. THERE WAS A TERRORIST ATTACK, WHICH ENDED BEING A COVER-UP TO CONCEAL A ROBBERY.
DIANA CHARGED IN AND DID WHAT SHE DOES BEST.
FOR THE NEXT SEVERAL MONTHS, BARBARA HELPED DIANA AND ME ON CASES THAT TIED TO THE *MYTHOLOGICAL WORLD.*
BUT AFTER WORKING WITH ME, AFTER BEING THERE FOR ME IN SO MANY WAYS, BARBARA'S LIFE WAS DESTROYED.
EVERYONE KNEW BARBARA WAS WORKING WITH WONDER WOMAN, SO SHE BECAME THE GO-TO-PERSON FOR IDENTIFYING AND CATALOGING POTENTIALLY DANGEROUS ARTIFACTS.
SHE OVERSAW ***THE BLACK ROOM*** AT A.R.G.U.S. WHERE WE SORT AND STORE THOSE TYPES OF ITEMS.
ONE DAY, DIANA CAME INTO POSSESSION OF A ***RITUAL DAGGER*** FROM A LOST TRIBE IN THE AMAZON.
BARBARA CUT HERSELF ON IT. AND SHE WAS *POSSESSED* BY THE *GODDESS OF THE HUNT.*
THE BLOODTHIRSTY ***CHEETAH!***
THEY'VE CLASHED ON-AND-OFF FOR YEARS, BUT THE CHEETAH'S ALWAYS BEEN ELUSIVE. SHE DISAPPEARS FOR MONTHS AT A TIME.
"DIANA BLAMES HERSELF FOR WHAT HAPPENED TO BARBARA.
"JUST LIKE SHE'S BLAMING HERSELF FOR ***DAVID GRAVES*** PUTTING ME IN THE HOSPITAL."

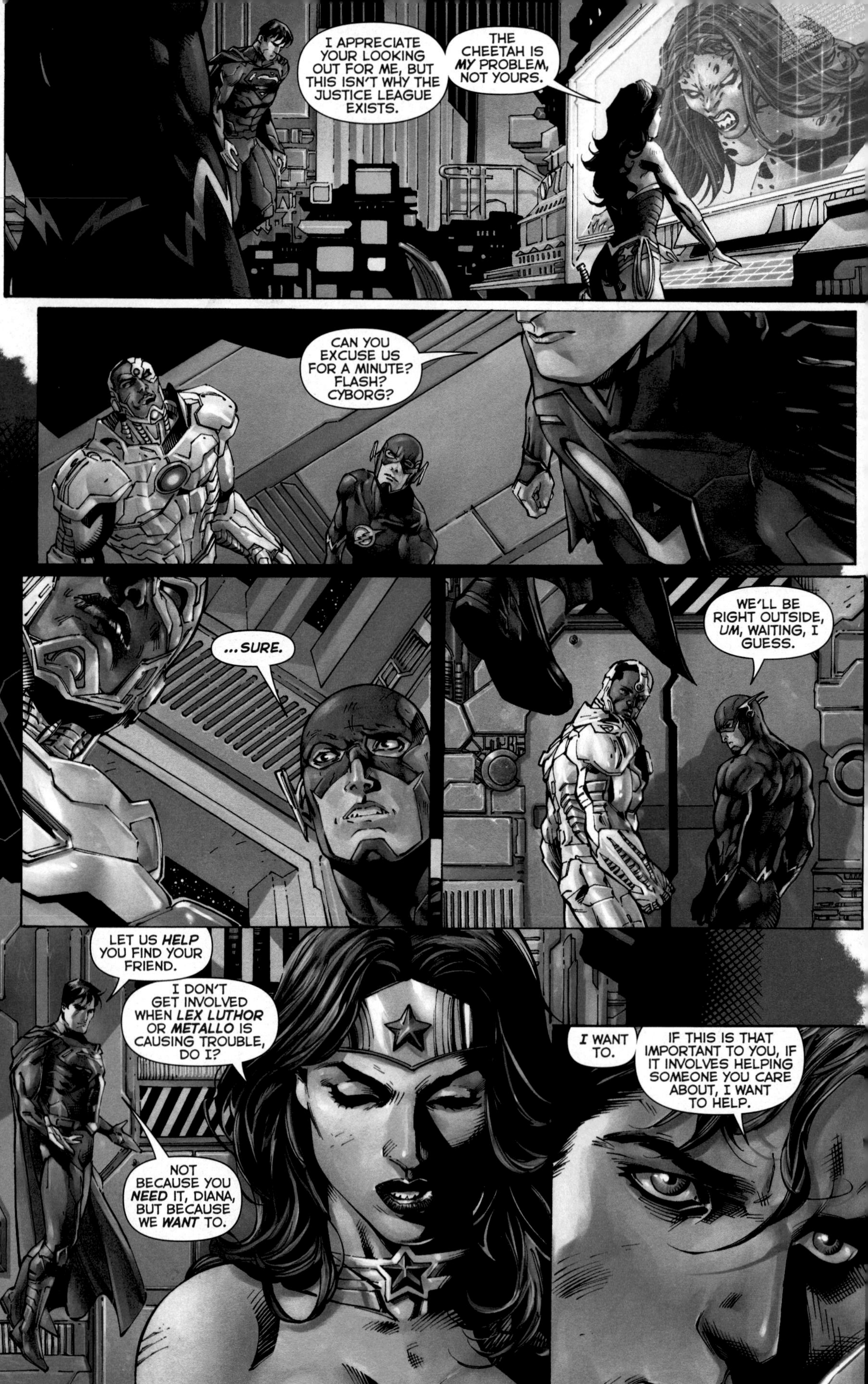
I APPRECIATE YOUR LOOKING OUT FOR ME, BUT THIS ISN'T WHY THE JUSTICE LEAGUE EXISTS.
THE CHEETAH IS *MY* PROBLEM, NOT YOURS.
CAN YOU EXCUSE US FOR A MINUTE? FLASH? CYBORG?
...SURE.
WE'LL BE RIGHT OUTSIDE, *UM*, WAITING, I GUESS.
LET US *HELP* YOU FIND YOUR FRIEND.
I DON'T GET INVOLVED WHEN *LEX LUTHOR* OR *METALLO* IS CAUSING TROUBLE, DO I?
NOT BECAUSE YOU *NEED* IT, DIANA, BUT BECAUSE WE *WANT* TO.
I WANT TO.
IF THIS IS THAT IMPORTANT TO YOU, IF IT INVOLVES HELPING SOMEONE YOU CARE ABOUT, I WANT TO HELP.

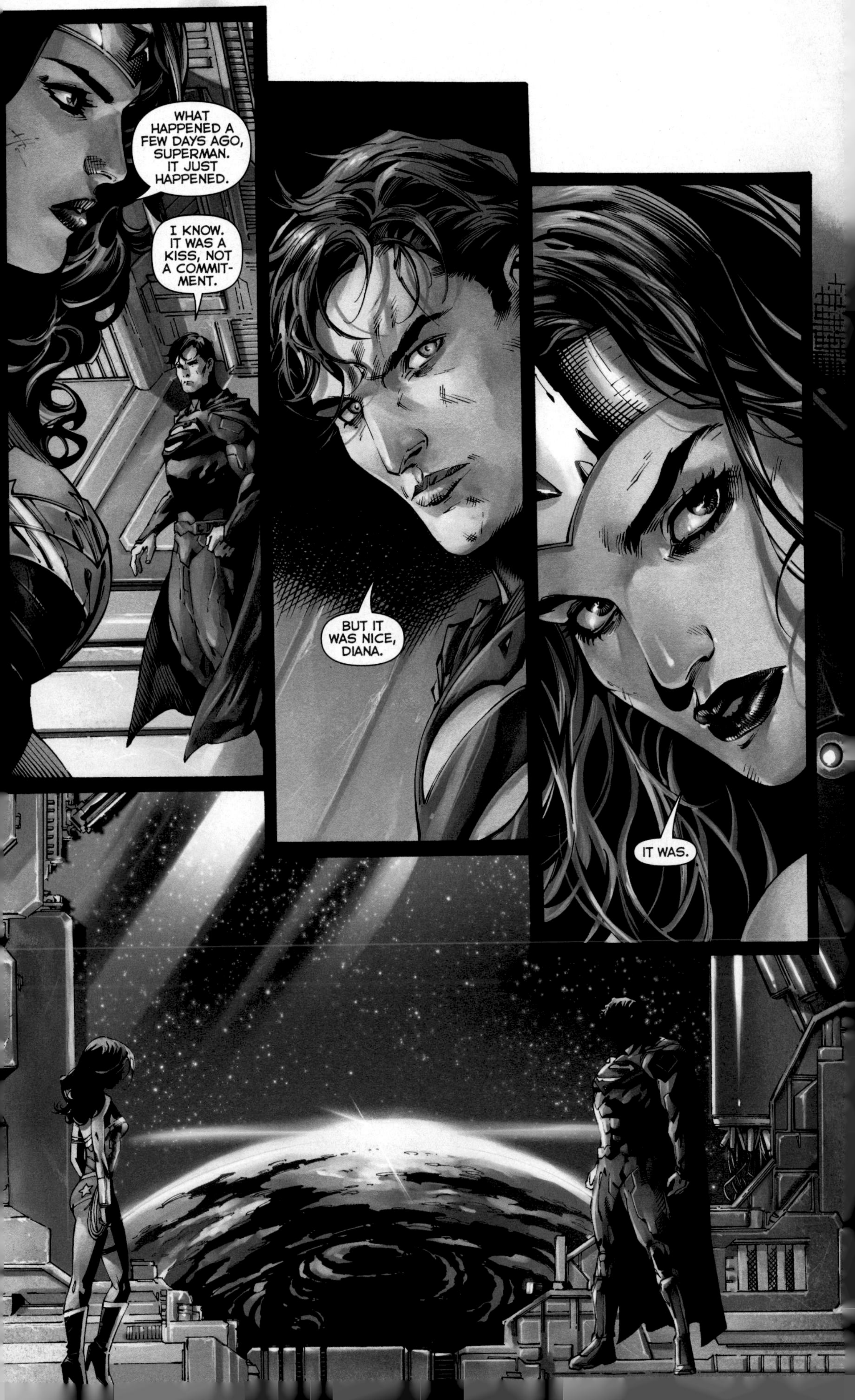
WHAT HAPPENED A FEW DAYS AGO, SUPERMAN. IT JUST HAPPENED.
I KNOW. IT WAS A KISS, NOT A COMMITMENT.
BUT IT WAS NICE, DIANA.
IT WAS.

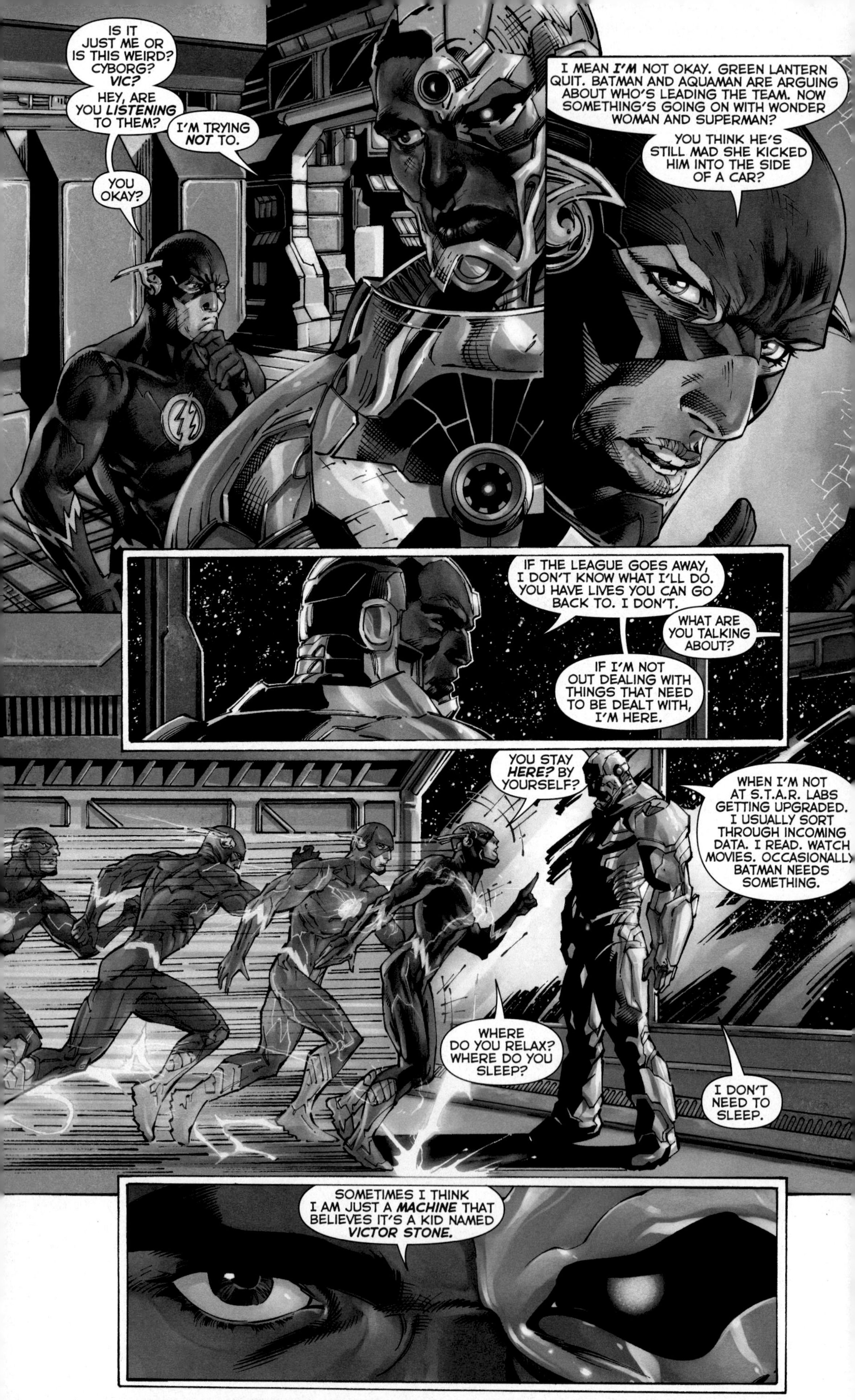
IS IT JUST ME OR IS THIS WEIRD? CYBORG? VIC?
HEY, ARE YOU LISTENING TO THEM?
I'M TRYING NOT TO.
YOU OKAY?
I MEAN I'M NOT OKAY. GREEN LANTERN QUIT. BATMAN AND AQUAMAN ARE ARGUING ABOUT WHO'S LEADING THE TEAM. NOW SOMETHING'S GOING ON WITH WONDER WOMAN AND SUPERMAN?
YOU THINK HE'S STILL MAD SHE KICKED HIM INTO THE SIDE OF A CAR?
IF THE LEAGUE GOES AWAY, I DON'T KNOW WHAT I'LL DO. YOU HAVE LIVES YOU CAN GO BACK TO. I DON'T.
WHAT ARE YOU TALKING ABOUT?
IF I'M NOT OUT DEALING WITH THINGS THAT NEED TO BE DEALT WITH, I'M HERE.
YOU STAY HERE? BY YOURSELF?
WHEN I'M NOT AT S.T.A.R. LABS GETTING UPGRADED, I USUALLY SORT THROUGH INCOMING DATA. I READ. WATCH MOVIES. OCCASIONALLY BATMAN NEEDS SOMETHING.
WHERE DO YOU RELAX? WHERE DO YOU SLEEP?
I DON'T NEED TO SLEEP.
SOMETIMES I THINK I AM JUST A MACHINE THAT BELIEVES IT'S A KID NAMED VICTOR STONE.

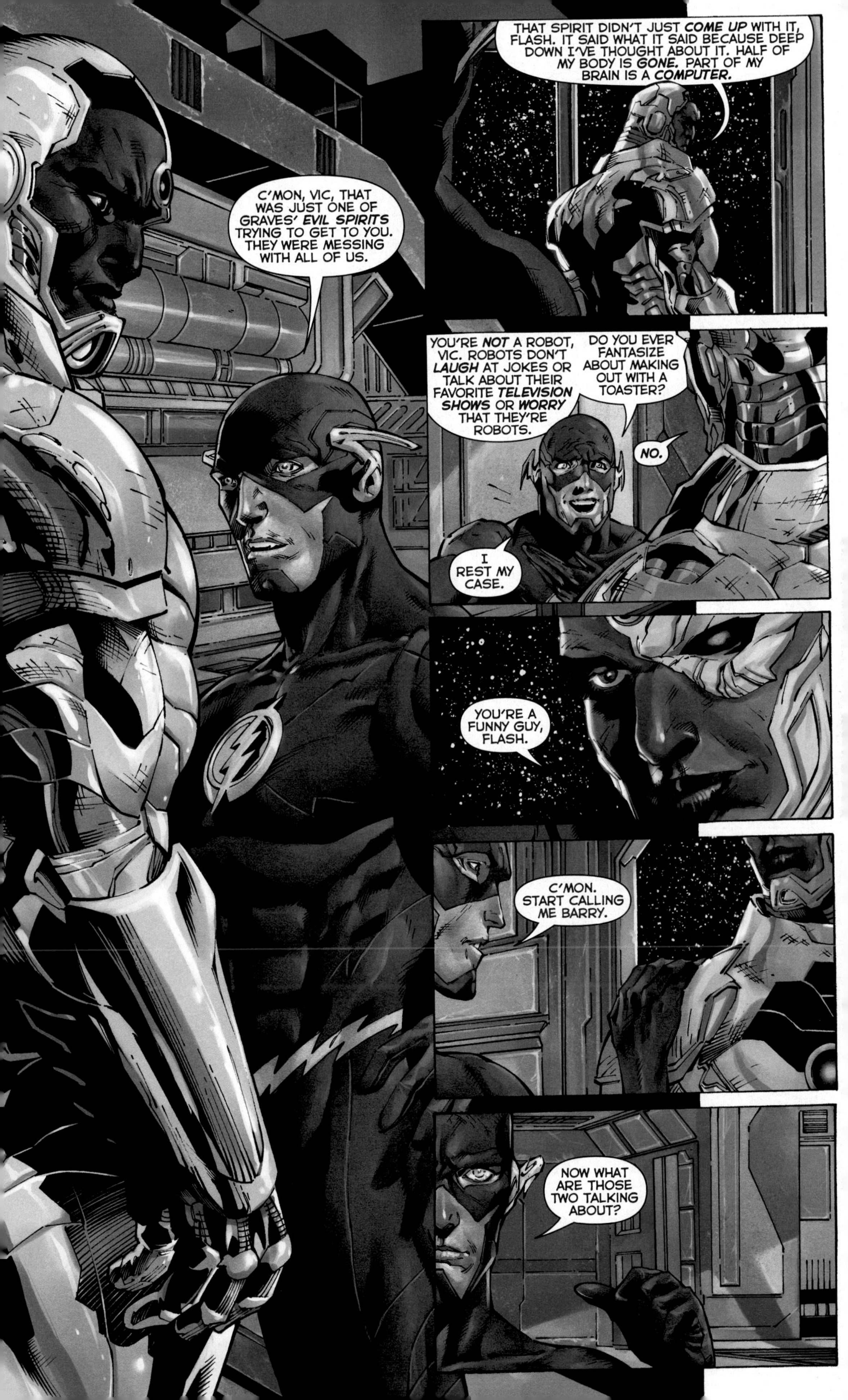

C'MON, VIC, THAT WAS JUST ONE OF GRAVES' EVIL SPIRITS TRYING TO GET TO YOU. THEY WERE MESSING WITH ALL OF US.
THAT SPIRIT DIDN'T JUST COME UP WITH IT, FLASH. IT SAID WHAT IT SAID BECAUSE DEEP DOWN I'VE THOUGHT ABOUT IT. HALF OF MY BODY IS GONE. PART OF MY BRAIN IS A COMPUTER.
YOU'RE NOT A ROBOT, VIC. ROBOTS DON'T LAUGH AT JOKES OR TALK ABOUT THEIR FAVORITE TELEVISION SHOWS OR WORRY THAT THEY'RE ROBOTS.
DO YOU EVER FANTASIZE ABOUT MAKING OUT WITH A TOASTER?
NO.
I REST MY CASE.
YOU'RE A FUNNY GUY, FLASH.
C'MON. START CALLING ME BARRY.
NOW WHAT ARE THOSE TWO TALKING ABOUT?

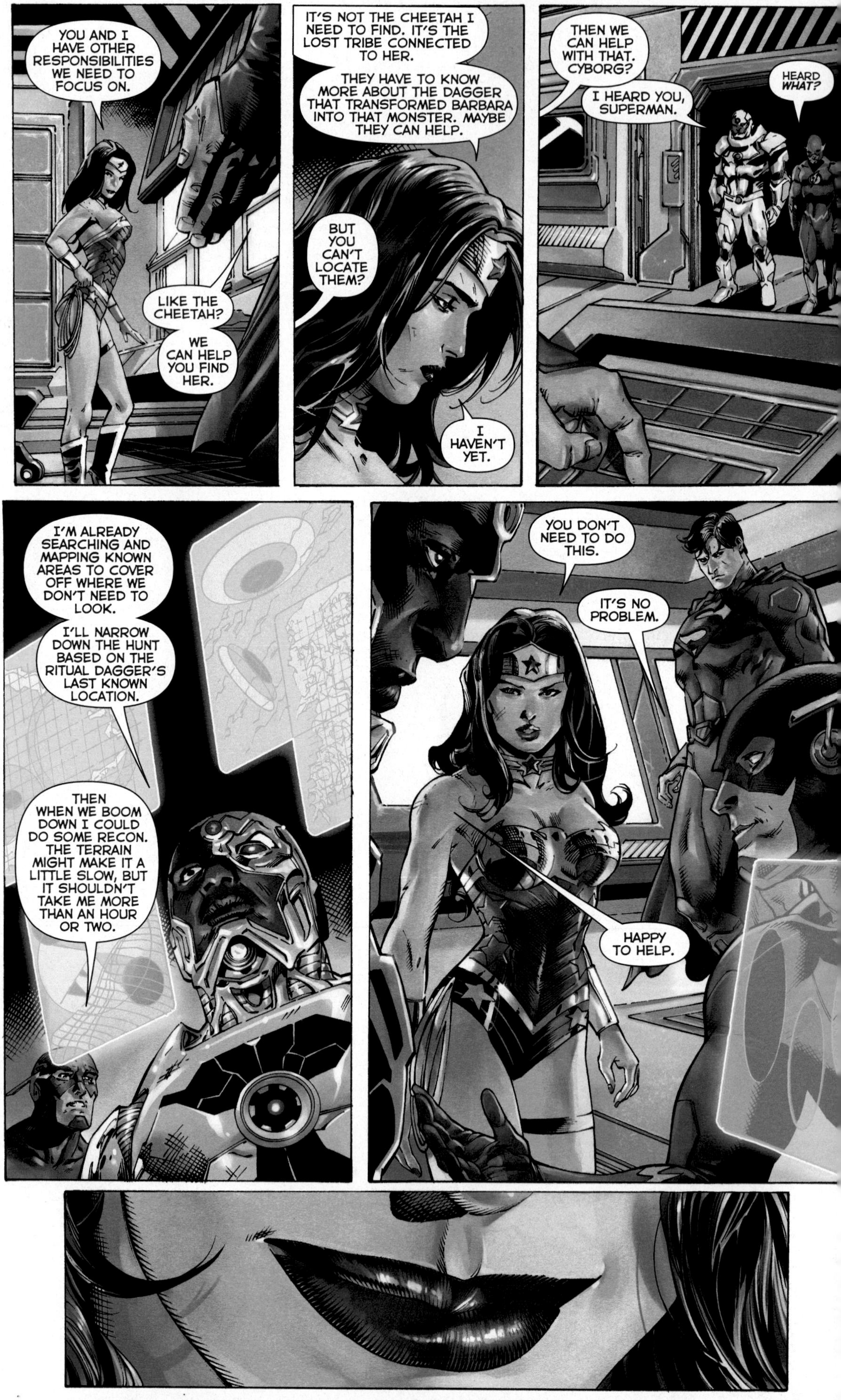

YOU AND I HAVE OTHER RESPONSIBILITIES WE NEED TO FOCUS ON.
LIKE THE CHEETAH?
WE CAN HELP YOU FIND HER.
IT'S NOT THE CHEETAH I NEED TO FIND. IT'S THE LOST TRIBE CONNECTED TO HER.
THEY HAVE TO KNOW MORE ABOUT THE DAGGER THAT TRANSFORMED BARBARA INTO THAT MONSTER. MAYBE THEY CAN HELP.
BUT YOU CAN'T LOCATE THEM?
I HAVEN'T YET.
THEN WE CAN HELP WITH THAT. CYBORG?
I HEARD YOU, SUPERMAN.
HEARD *WHAT?*
I'M ALREADY SEARCHING AND MAPPING KNOWN AREAS TO COVER OFF WHERE WE DON'T NEED TO LOOK.
I'LL NARROW DOWN THE HUNT BASED ON THE RITUAL DAGGER'S LAST KNOWN LOCATION.
THEN WHEN WE BOOM DOWN I COULD DO SOME RECON. THE TERRAIN MIGHT MAKE IT A LITTLE SLOW, BUT IT SHOULDN'T TAKE ME MORE THAN AN HOUR OR TWO.
YOU DON'T NEED TO DO THIS.
IT'S NO PROBLEM.
HAPPY TO HELP.

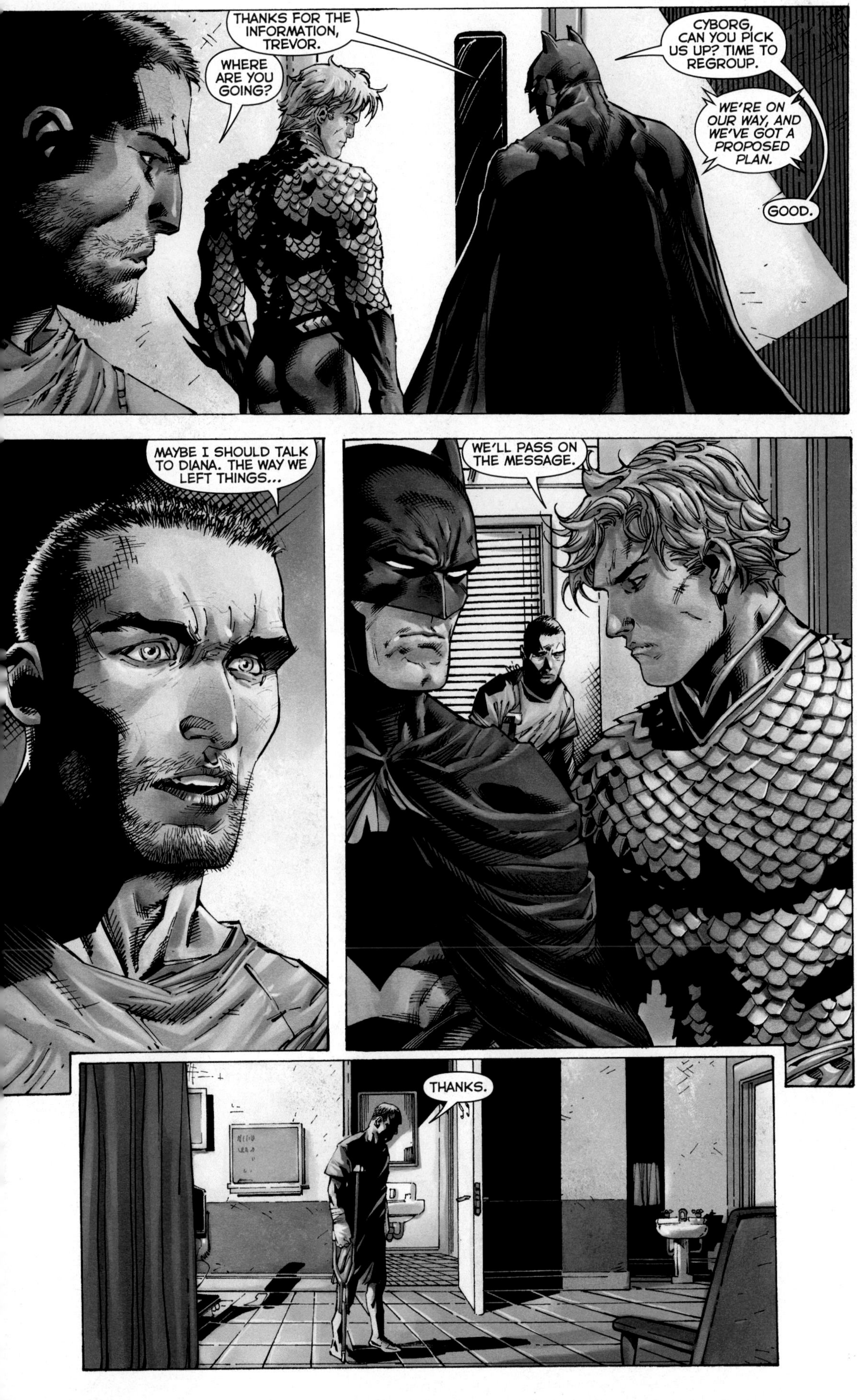
THANKS FOR THE INFORMATION, TREVOR.
WHERE ARE YOU GOING?
CYBORG, CAN YOU PICK US UP? TIME TO REGROUP.
WE'RE ON OUR WAY, AND WE'VE GOT A PROPOSED PLAN.
GOOD.
MAYBE I SHOULD TALK TO DIANA. THE WAY WE LEFT THINGS...
WE'LL PASS ON THE MESSAGE.
THANKS.

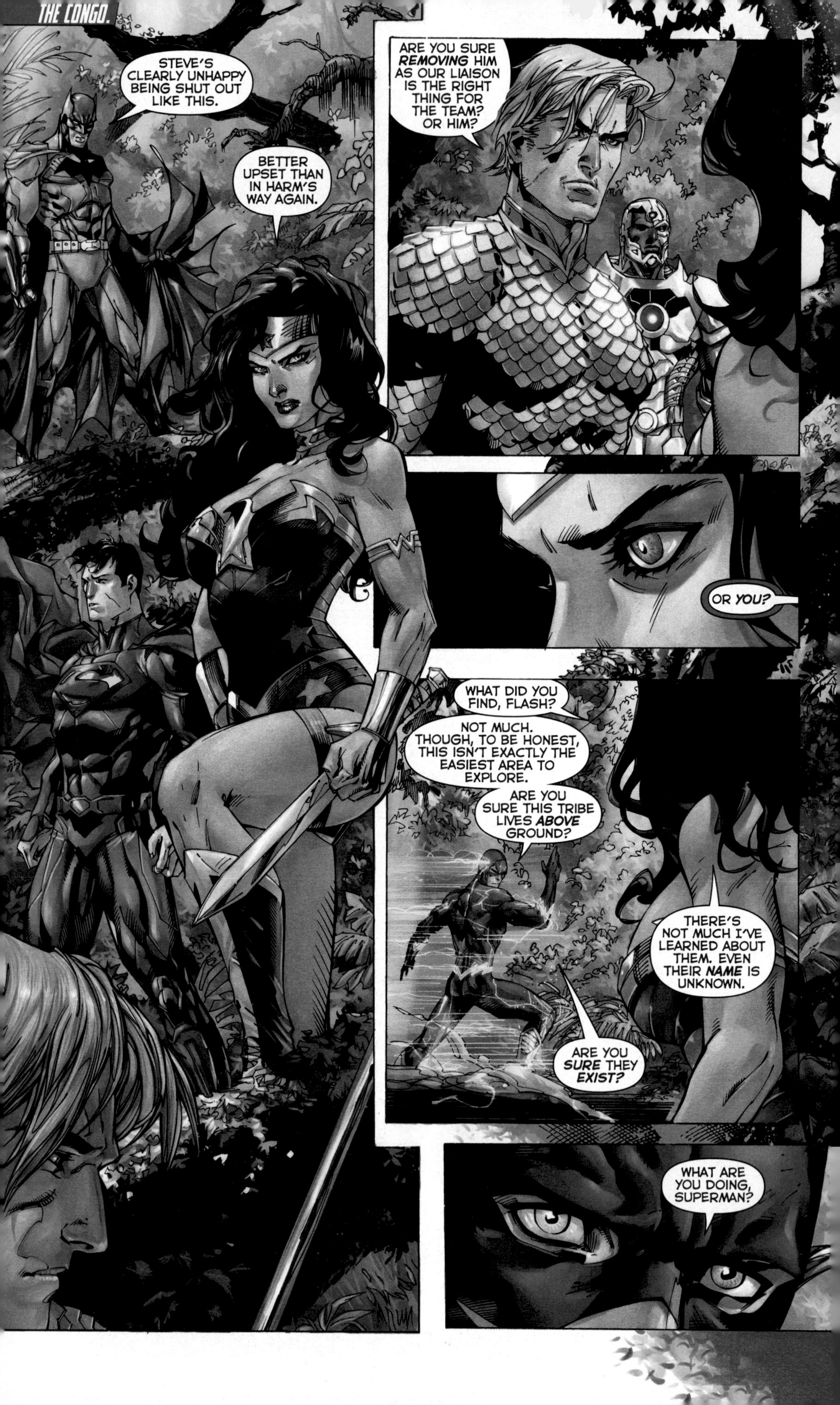
THE CONGO.
STEVE'S CLEARLY UNHAPPY BEING SHUT OUT LIKE THIS.
BETTER UPSET THAN IN HARM'S WAY AGAIN.
ARE YOU SURE REMOVING HIM AS OUR LIAISON IS THE RIGHT THING FOR THE TEAM? OR HIM?
OR YOU?
WHAT DID YOU FIND, FLASH?
NOT MUCH. THOUGH, TO BE HONEST, THIS ISN'T EXACTLY THE EASIEST AREA TO EXPLORE.
ARE YOU SURE THIS TRIBE LIVES ABOVE GROUND?
THERE'S NOT MUCH I'VE LEARNED ABOUT THEM. EVEN THEIR NAME IS UNKNOWN.
ARE YOU SURE THEY EXIST?
WHAT ARE YOU DOING, SUPERMAN?

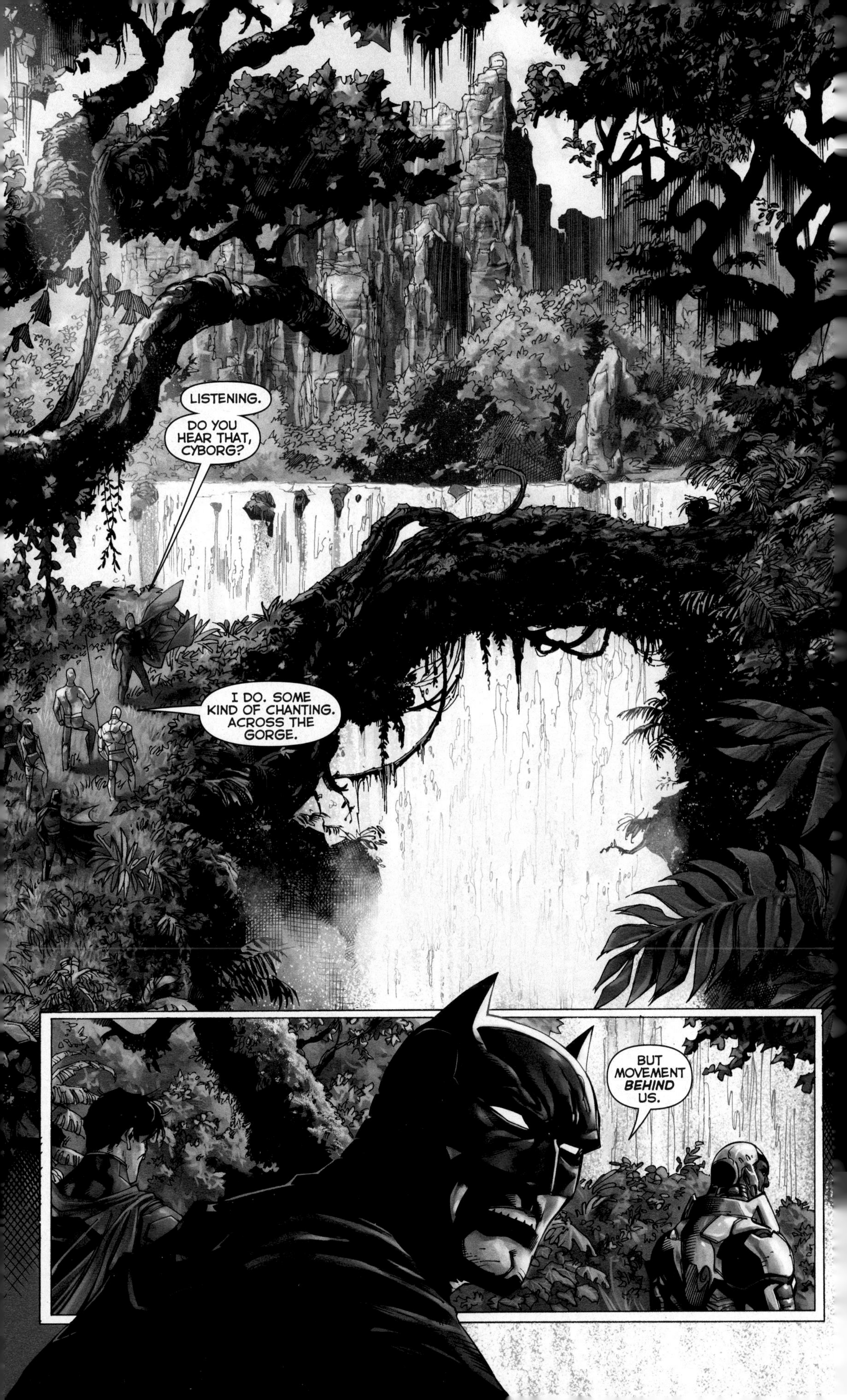
LISTENING.
DO YOU HEAR THAT, CYBORG?
I DO. SOME KIND OF CHANTING. ACROSS THE GORGE.
BUT MOVEMENT *BEHIND* US.

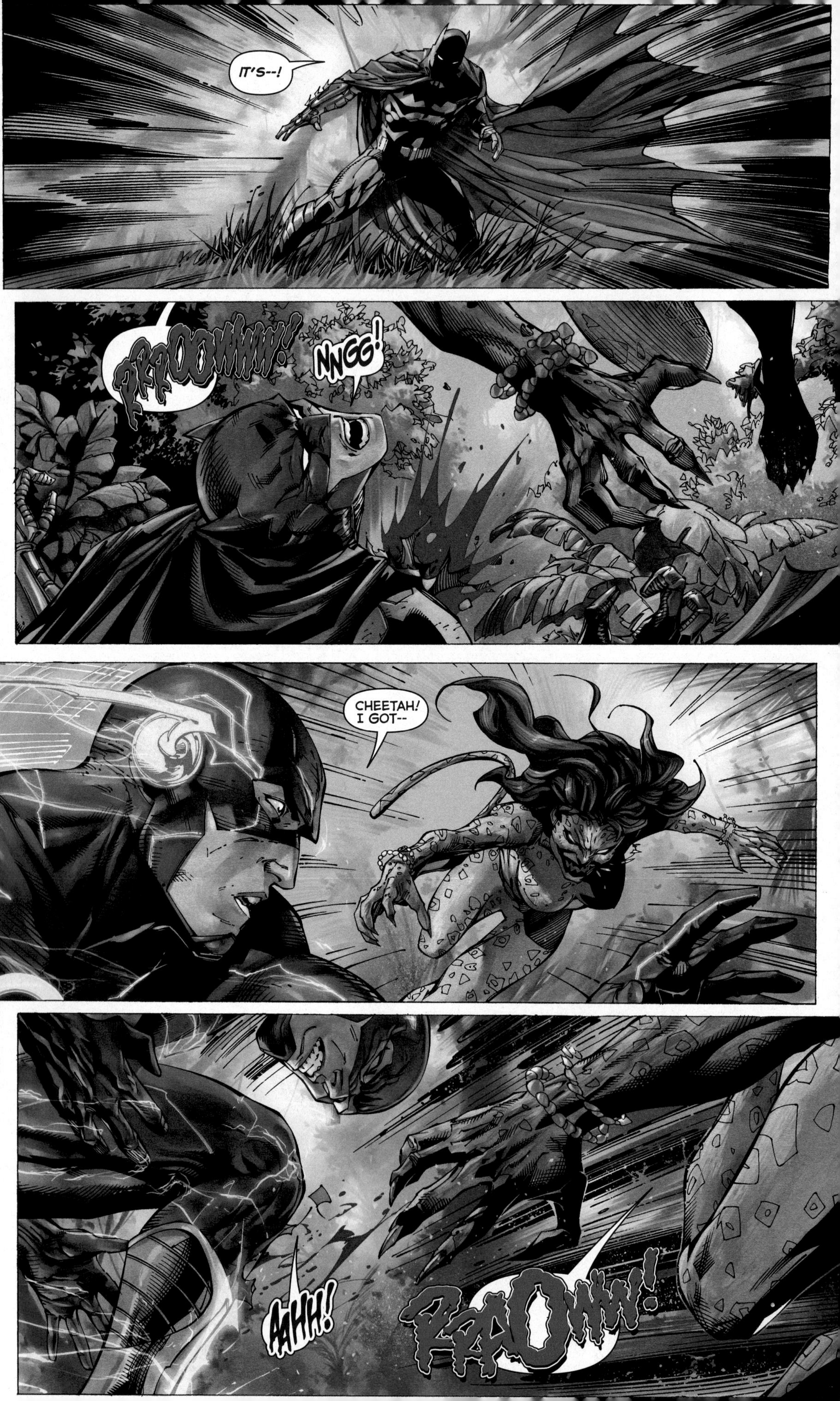
IT'S--!
RRROOWWW!
NNGG!
CHEETAH! I GOT--
AAHH!
RRAOWW!

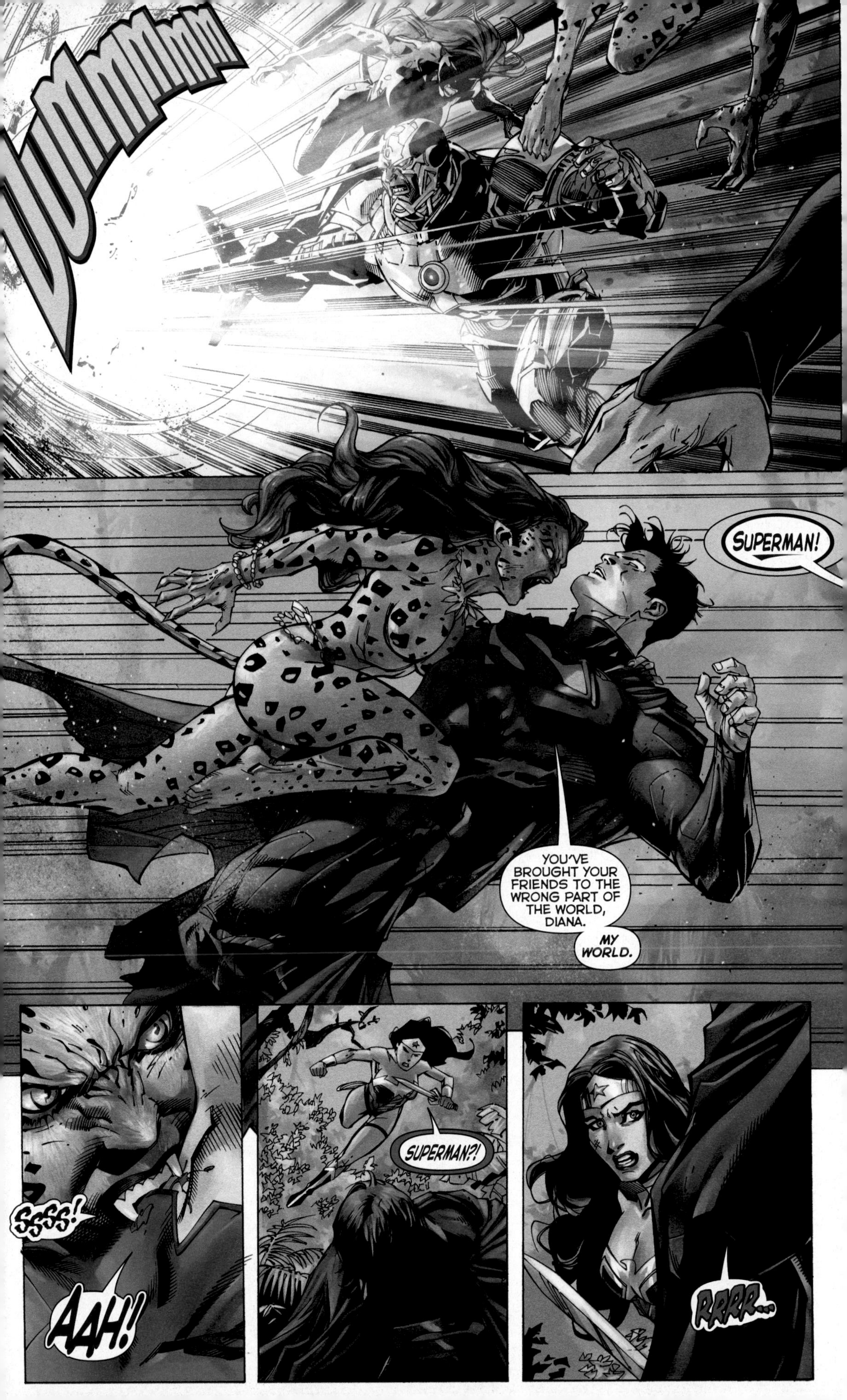

VUMMMMM
SUPERMAN!
YOU'VE BROUGHT YOUR FRIENDS TO THE WRONG PART OF THE WORLD, DIANA.
MY WORLD.
SSSS!
AAH!
SUPERMAN?!
RRRR...

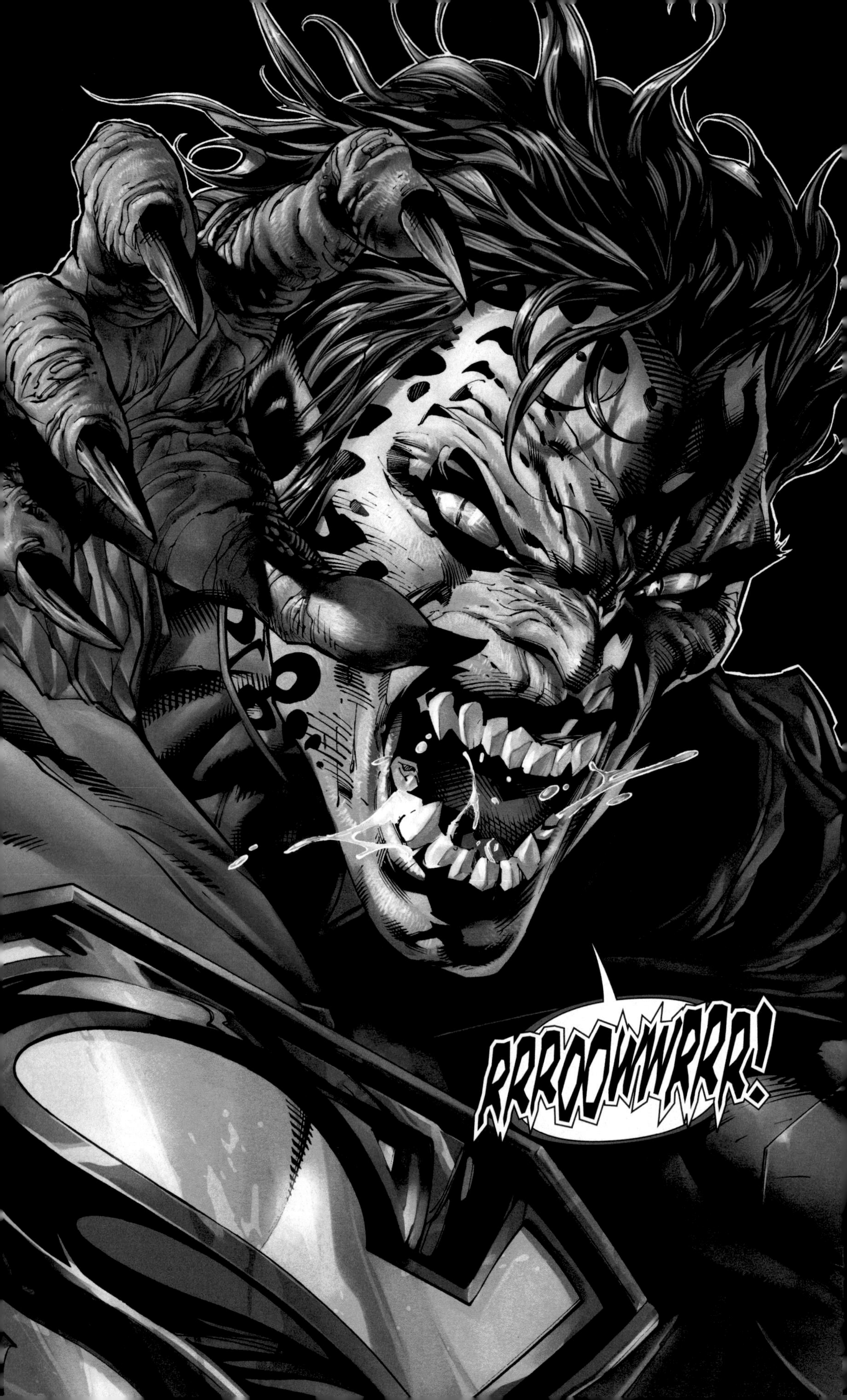
RRROOWWRRR!

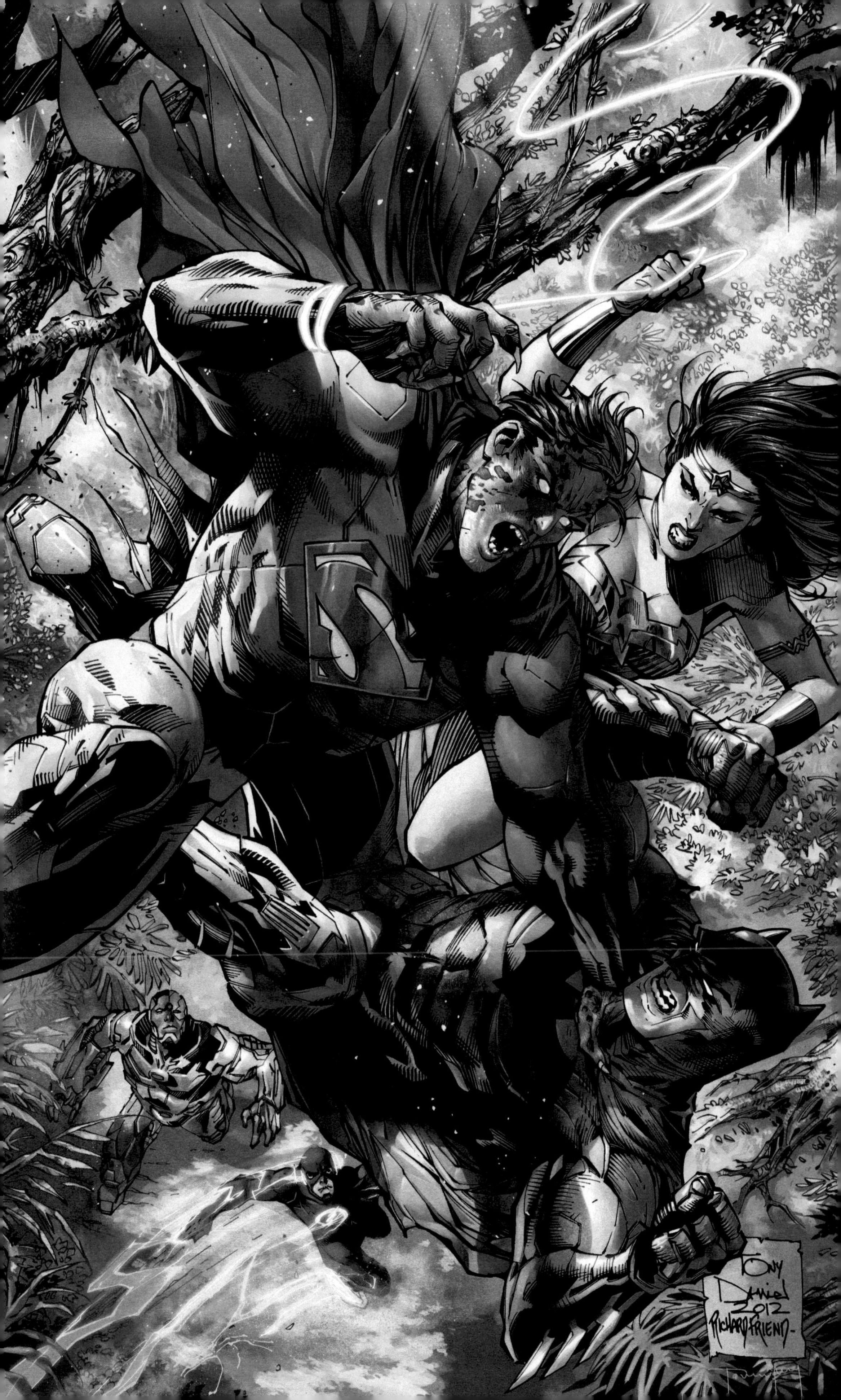
TONY DANIEL 2012
RICHARD FRIEND

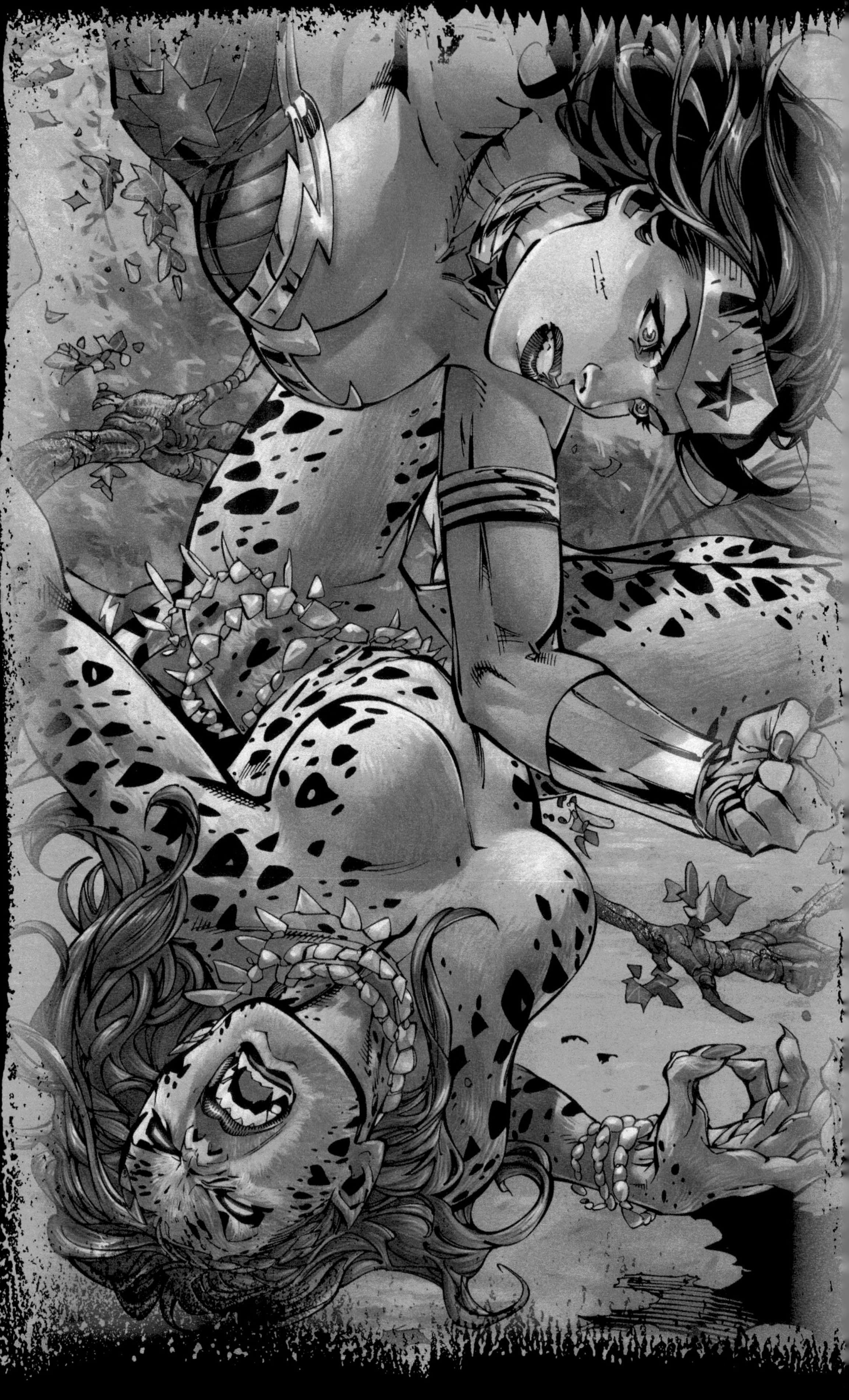

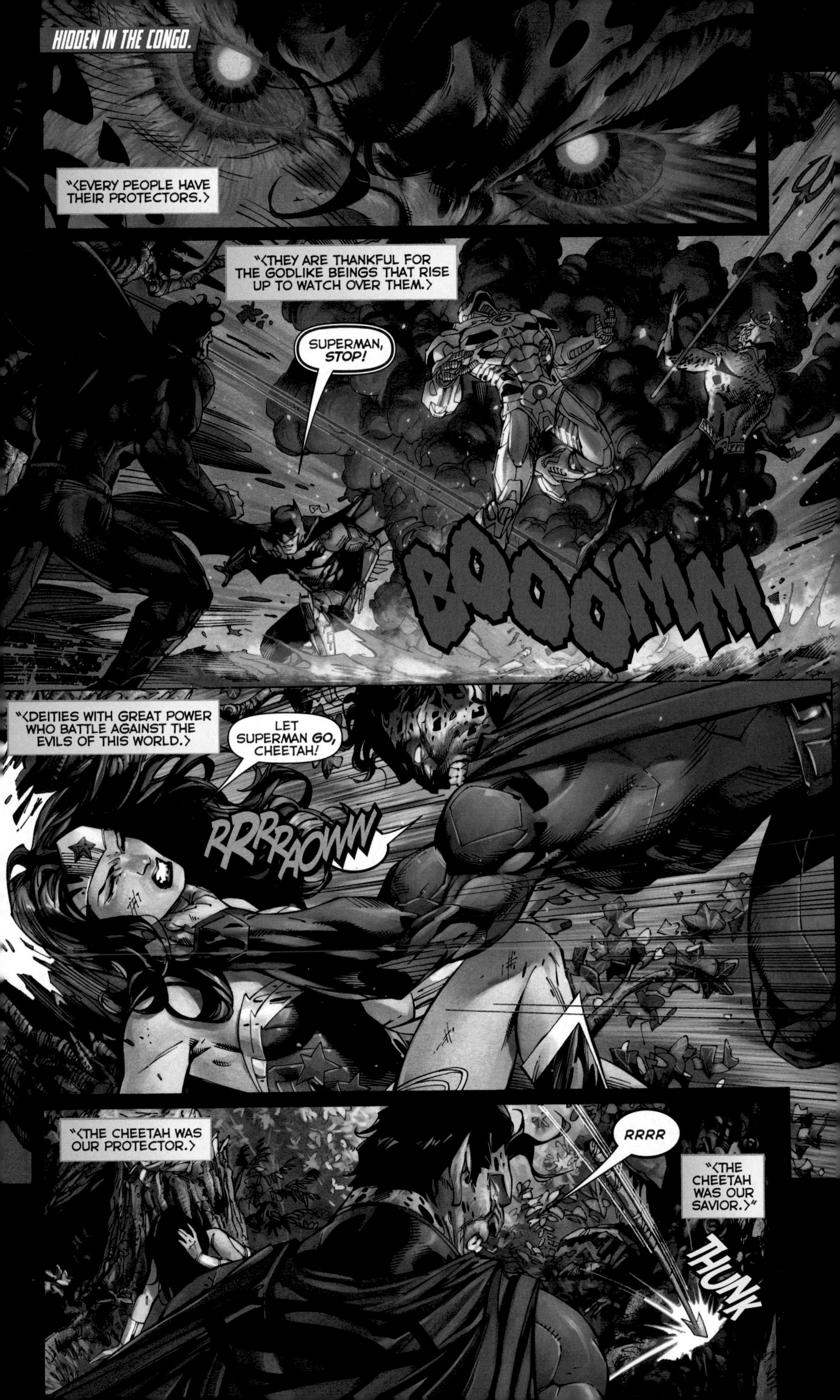
HIDDEN IN THE CONGO.
"<EVERY PEOPLE HAVE THEIR PROTECTORS.>
"<THEY ARE THANKFUL FOR THE GODLIKE BEINGS THAT RISE UP TO WATCH OVER THEM.>
SUPERMAN, STOP!
BOOOMM
"<DEITIES WITH GREAT POWER WHO BATTLE AGAINST THE EVILS OF THIS WORLD.>
LET SUPERMAN GO, CHEETAH!
RRRRAOWN
"<THE CHEETAH WAS OUR PROTECTOR.>
RRRR
"<THE CHEETAH WAS OUR SAVIOR.>"
THUNK

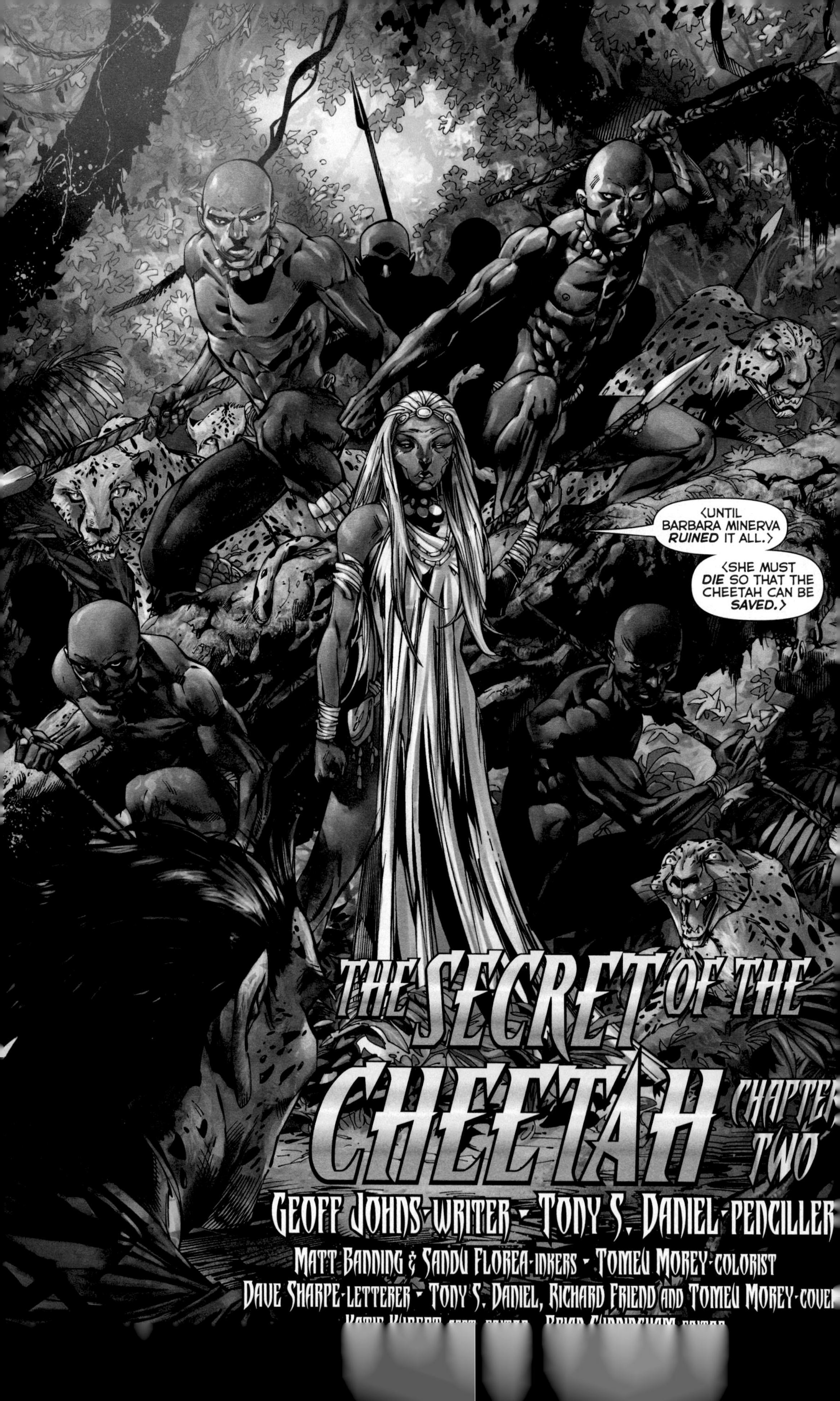

‹UNTIL BARBARA MINERVA RUINED IT ALL.›
‹SHE MUST DIE SO THAT THE CHEETAH CAN BE SAVED.›
THE SECRET OF THE CHEETAH
CHAPTER TWO
GEOFF JOHNS-WRITER - TONY S. DANIEL-PENCILLER
MATT BANNING & SANDU FLOREA-INKERS - TOMEU MOREY-COLORIST
DAVE SHARPE-LETTERER - TONY S. DANIEL, RICHARD FRIEND AND TOMEU MOREY-COVER

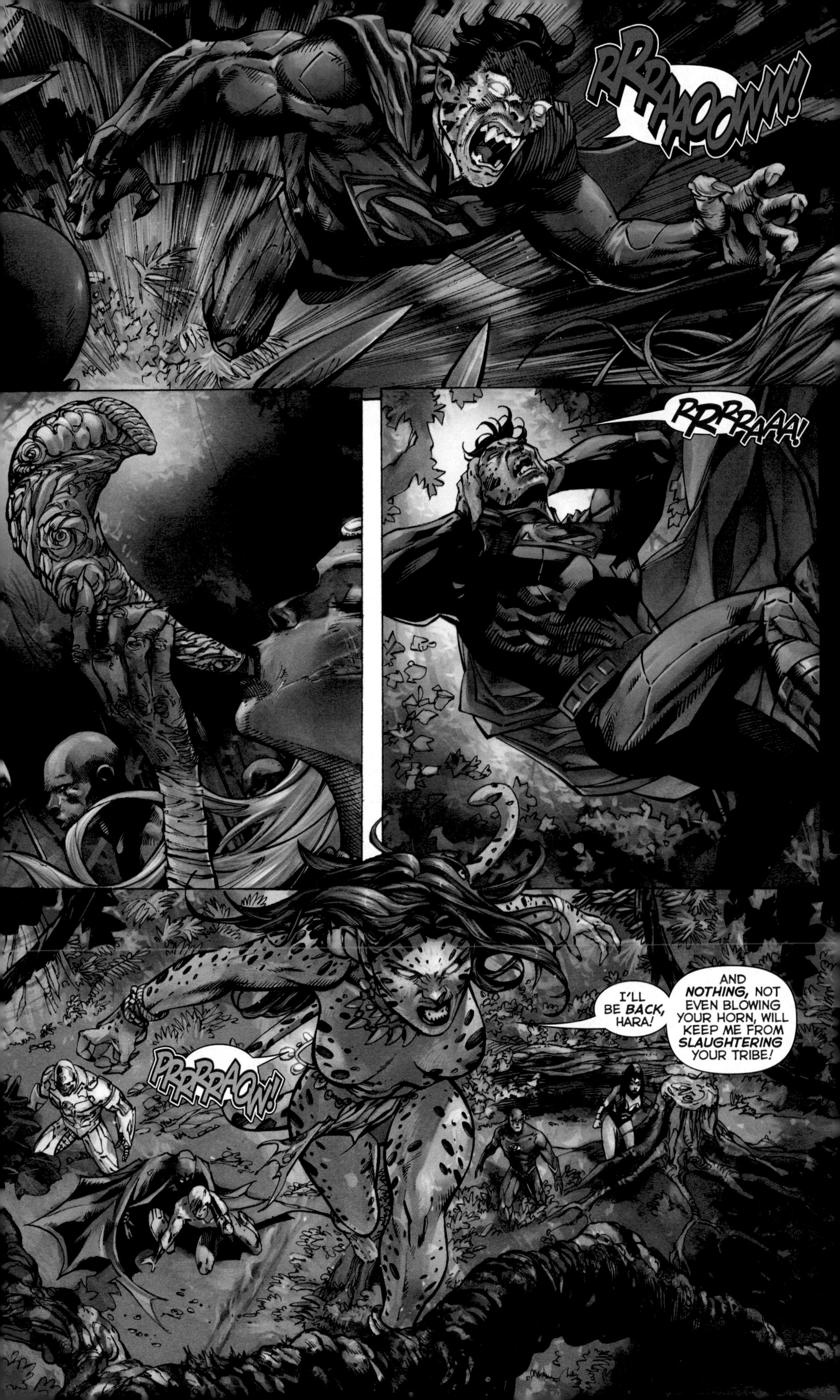
RRRAAOOWW!
RRRRAAA!
PRRRRAOW!
I'LL BE BACK, HARA!
AND NOTHING, NOT EVEN BLOWING YOUR HORN, WILL KEEP ME FROM SLAUGHTERING YOUR TRIBE!

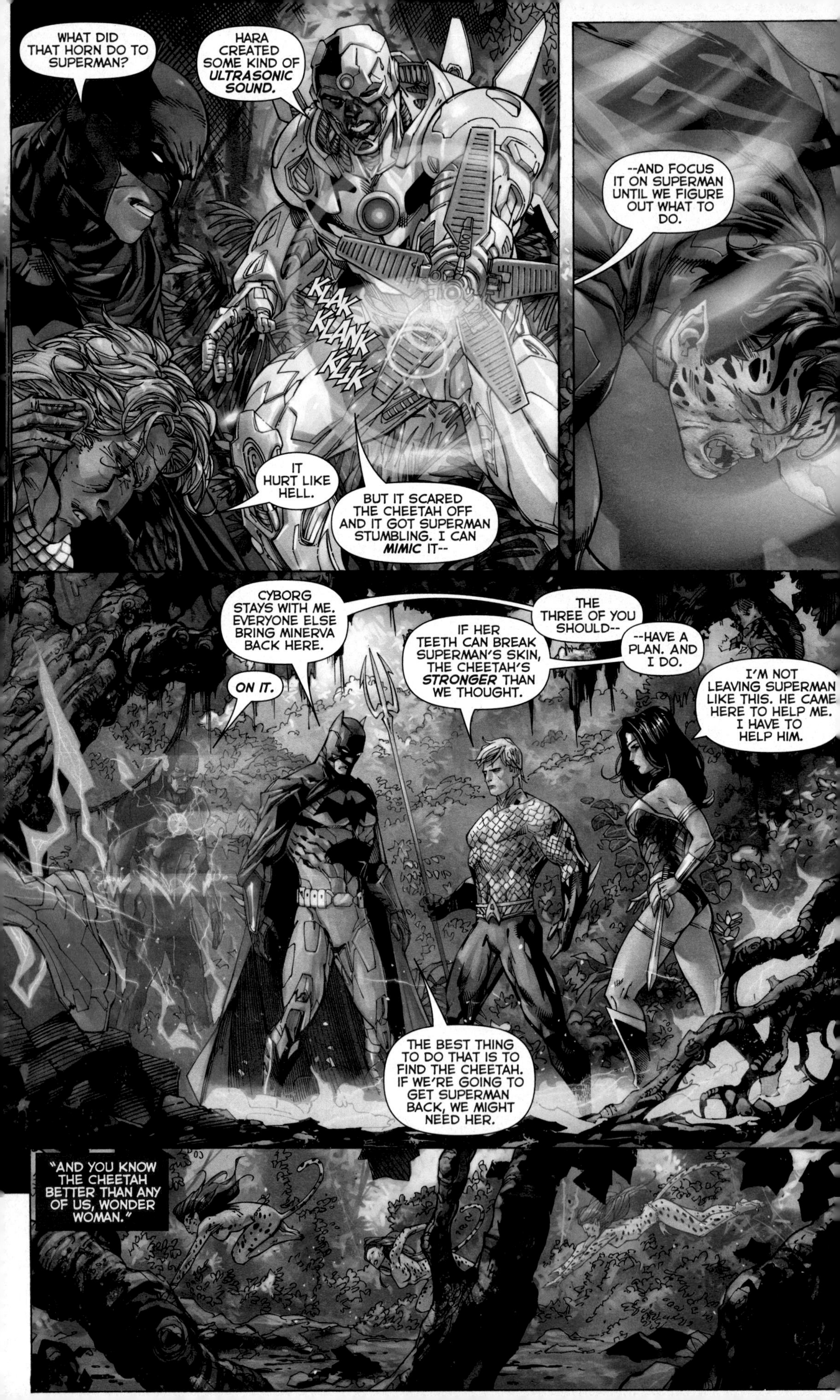
WHAT DID THAT HORN DO TO SUPERMAN?
HARA CREATED SOME KIND OF *ULTRASONIC SOUND.*
KLAK KLANK KLIK
IT HURT LIKE HELL.
BUT IT SCARED THE CHEETAH OFF AND IT GOT SUPERMAN STUMBLING. I CAN *MIMIC* IT--
--AND FOCUS IT ON SUPERMAN UNTIL WE FIGURE OUT WHAT TO DO.
CYBORG STAYS WITH ME. EVERYONE ELSE BRING MINERVA BACK HERE.
THE THREE OF YOU SHOULD--
IF HER TEETH CAN BREAK SUPERMAN'S SKIN, THE CHEETAH'S *STRONGER* THAN WE THOUGHT.
--HAVE A PLAN. AND I DO.
ON IT.
I'M NOT LEAVING SUPERMAN LIKE THIS. HE CAME HERE TO HELP ME. I HAVE TO HELP HIM.
THE BEST THING TO DO THAT IS TO FIND THE CHEETAH. IF WE'RE GOING TO GET SUPERMAN BACK, WE MIGHT NEED HER.
"AND YOU KNOW THE CHEETAH BETTER THAN ANY OF US, WONDER WOMAN."

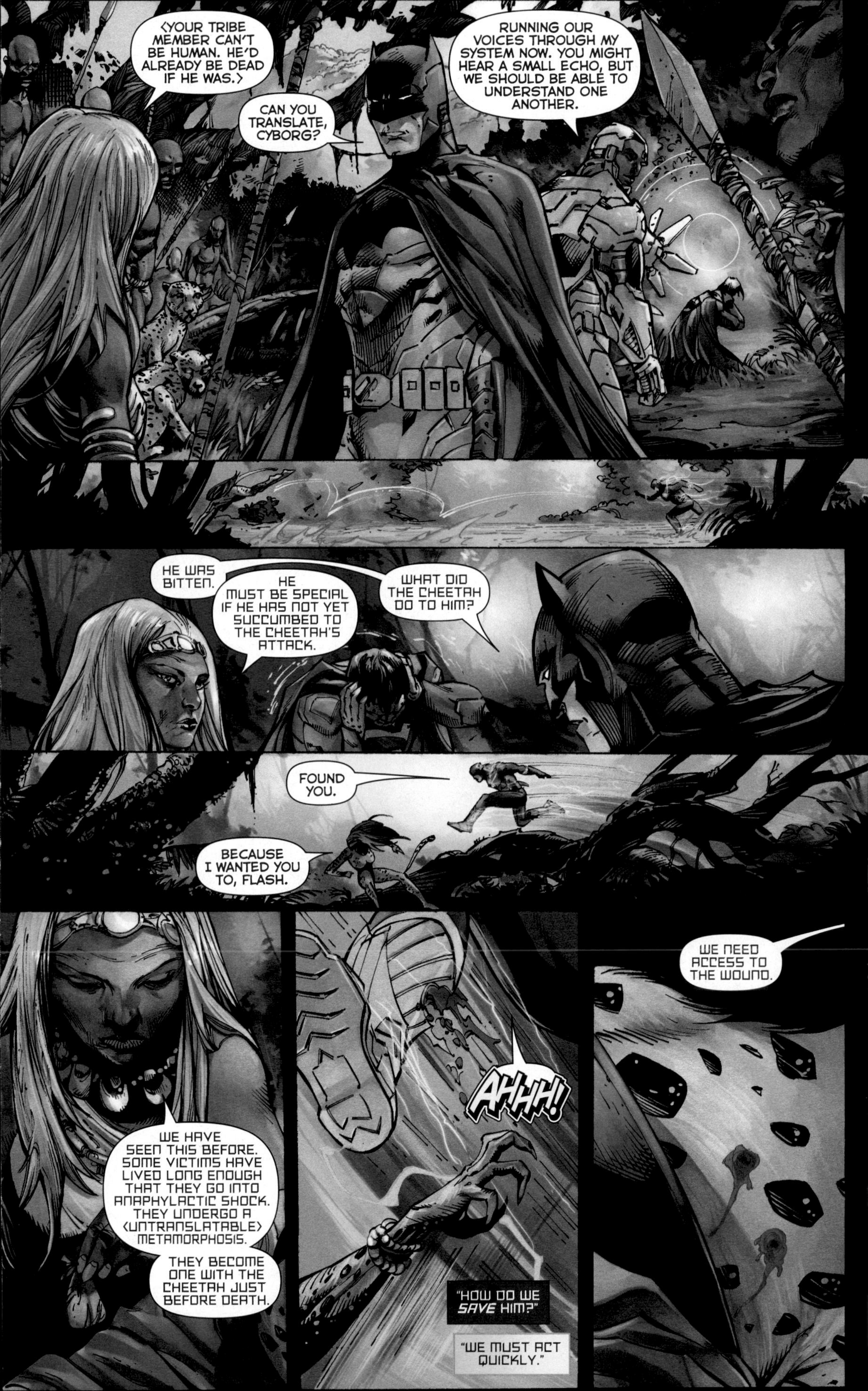

<YOUR TRIBE MEMBER CAN'T BE HUMAN. HE'D ALREADY BE DEAD IF HE WAS.>
CAN YOU TRANSLATE, CYBORG?
RUNNING OUR VOICES THROUGH MY SYSTEM NOW. YOU MIGHT HEAR A SMALL ECHO, BUT WE SHOULD BE ABLE TO UNDERSTAND ONE ANOTHER.
HE WAS BITTEN.
HE MUST BE SPECIAL IF HE HAS NOT YET SUCCUMBED TO THE CHEETAH'S ATTACK.
WHAT DID THE CHEETAH DO TO HIM?
FOUND YOU.
BECAUSE I WANTED YOU TO, FLASH.
WE HAVE SEEN THIS BEFORE. SOME VICTIMS HAVE LIVED LONG ENOUGH THAT THEY GO INTO ANAPHYLACTIC SHOCK. THEY UNDERGO A <UNTRANSLATABLE> METAMORPHOSIS.
THEY BECOME ONE WITH THE CHEETAH JUST BEFORE DEATH.
AHHH!
"HOW DO WE SAVE HIM?"
"WE MUST ACT QUICKLY."
WE NEED ACCESS TO THE WOUND.

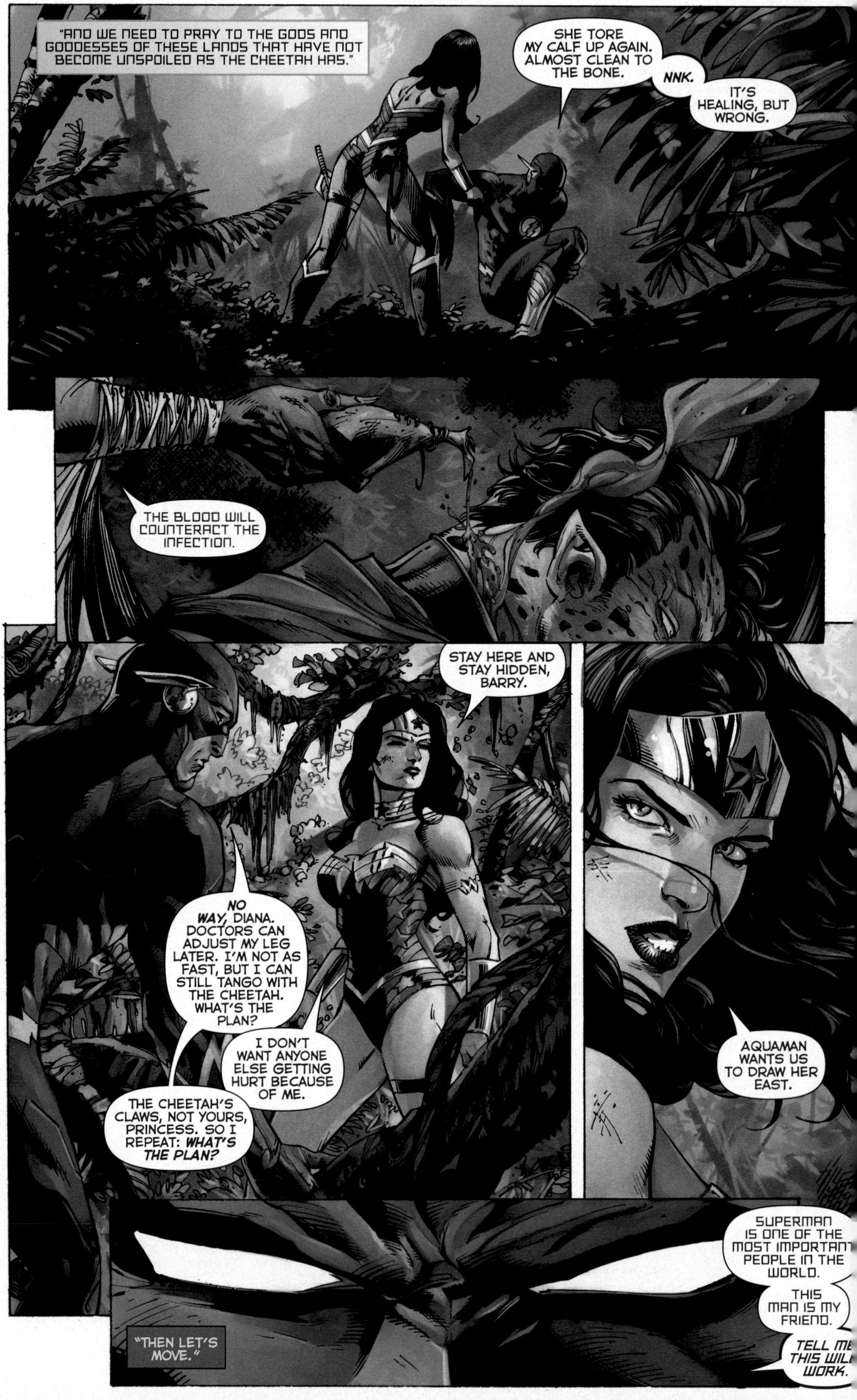
"AND WE NEED TO PRAY TO THE GODS AND GODDESSES OF THESE LANDS THAT HAVE NOT BECOME UNSPOILED AS THE CHEETAH HAS."
SHE TORE MY CALF UP AGAIN. ALMOST CLEAN TO THE BONE.
NNK.
IT'S HEALING, BUT WRONG.
THE BLOOD WILL COUNTERACT THE INFECTION.
STAY HERE AND STAY HIDDEN, BARRY.
NO WAY, DIANA. DOCTORS CAN ADJUST MY LEG LATER. I'M NOT AS FAST, BUT I CAN STILL TANGO WITH THE CHEETAH. WHAT'S THE PLAN?
I DON'T WANT ANYONE ELSE GETTING HURT BECAUSE OF ME.
THE CHEETAH'S CLAWS, NOT YOURS, PRINCESS. SO I REPEAT: WHAT'S THE PLAN?
AQUAMAN WANTS US TO DRAW HER EAST.
SUPERMAN IS ONE OF THE MOST IMPORTANT PEOPLE IN THE WORLD.
THIS MAN IS MY FRIEND.
"THEN LET'S MOVE."

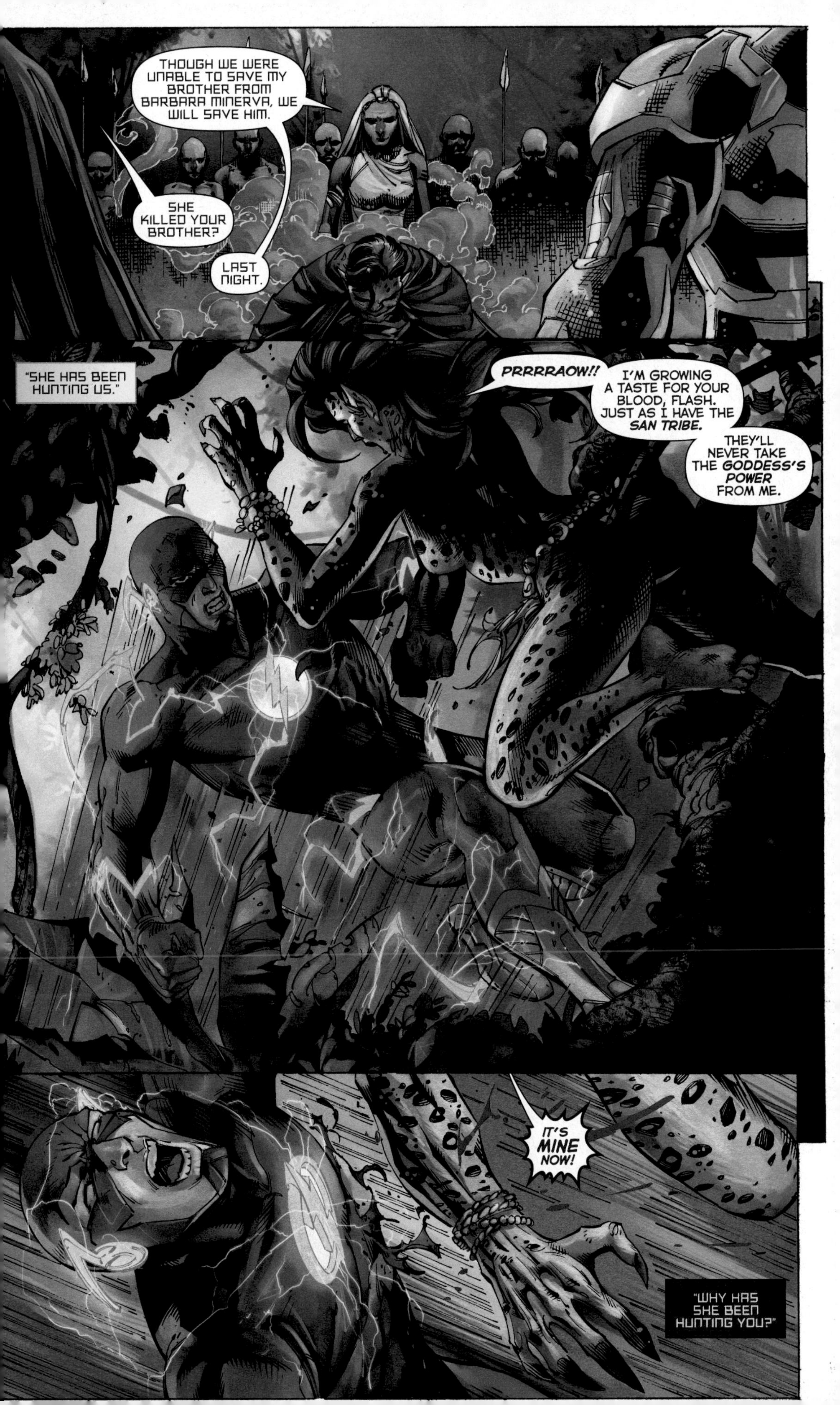
THOUGH WE WERE UNABLE TO SAVE MY BROTHER FROM BARBARA MINERVA, WE WILL SAVE HIM.
SHE KILLED YOUR BROTHER?
LAST NIGHT.
"SHE HAS BEEN HUNTING US."
PRRRRAOW!! I'M GROWING A TASTE FOR YOUR BLOOD, FLASH. JUST AS I HAVE THE SAN TRIBE.
THEY'LL NEVER TAKE THE GODDESS'S POWER FROM ME.
IT'S MINE NOW!
"WHY HAS SHE BEEN HUNTING YOU?"

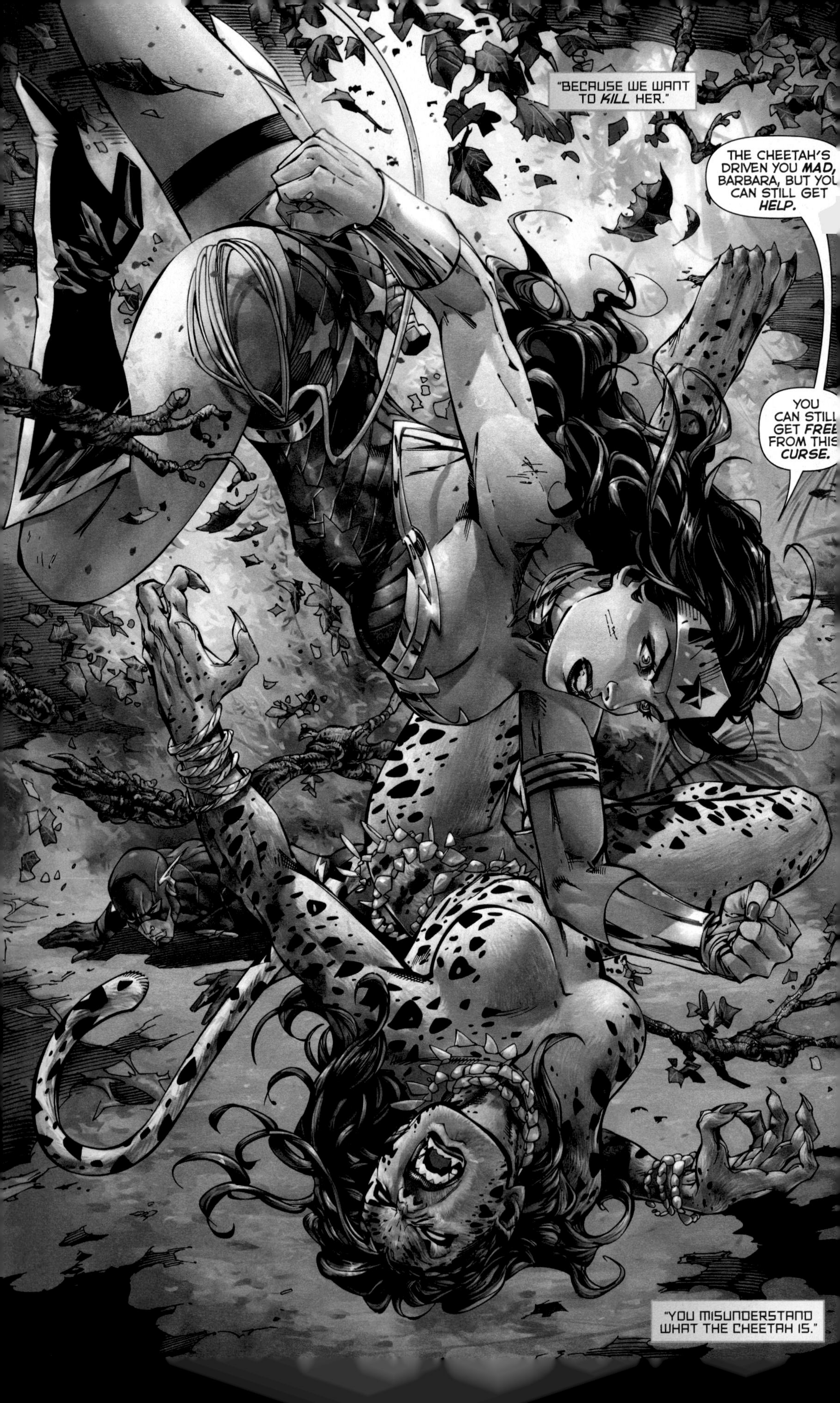
"BECAUSE WE WANT TO KILL HER."
THE CHEETAH'S DRIVEN YOU MAD, BARBARA, BUT YOU CAN STILL GET HELP.
YOU CAN STILL GET FREE FROM THIS CURSE.
"YOU MISUNDERSTAND WHAT THE CHEETAH IS."

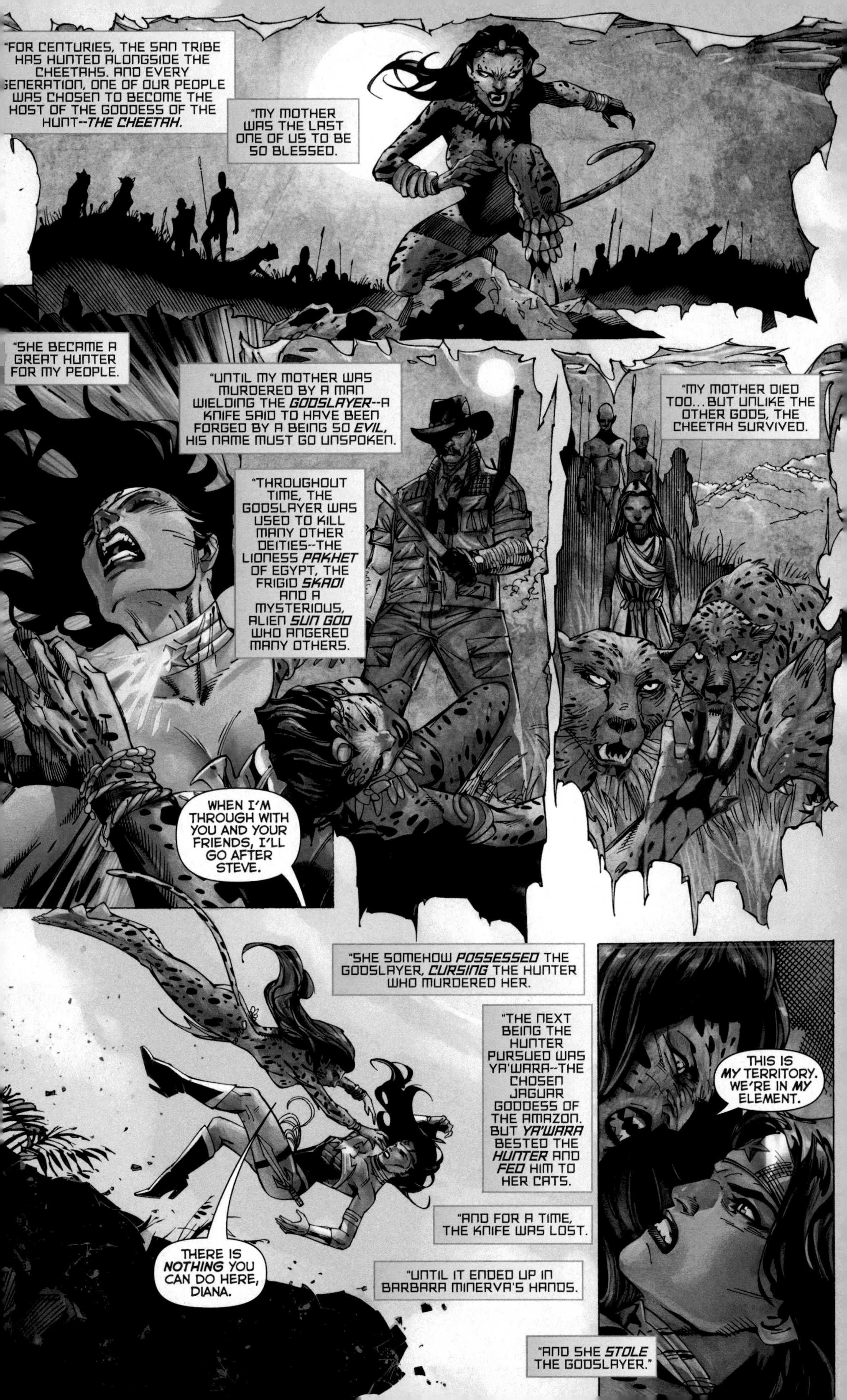

"FOR CENTURIES, THE SAN TRIBE HAS HUNTED ALONGSIDE THE CHEETAHS. AND EVERY GENERATION, ONE OF OUR PEOPLE WAS CHOSEN TO BECOME THE HOST OF THE GODDESS OF THE HUNT--THE CHEETAH.
"MY MOTHER WAS THE LAST ONE OF US TO BE SO BLESSED.
"SHE BECAME A GREAT HUNTER FOR MY PEOPLE.
"UNTIL MY MOTHER WAS MURDERED BY A MAN WIELDING THE GODSLAYER--A KNIFE SAID TO HAVE BEEN FORGED BY A BEING SO EVIL, HIS NAME MUST GO UNSPOKEN.
"THROUGHOUT TIME, THE GODSLAYER WAS USED TO KILL MANY OTHER DEITIES--THE LIONESS PAKHET OF EGYPT, THE FRIGID SKADI AND A MYSTERIOUS, ALIEN SUN GOD WHO ANGERED MANY OTHERS.
"MY MOTHER DIED TOO... BUT UNLIKE THE OTHER GODS, THE CHEETAH SURVIVED.
WHEN I'M THROUGH WITH YOU AND YOUR FRIENDS, I'LL GO AFTER STEVE.
"SHE SOMEHOW POSSESSED THE GODSLAYER, CURSING THE HUNTER WHO MURDERED HER.
"THE NEXT BEING THE HUNTER PURSUED WAS YA'WARA--THE CHOSEN JAGUAR GODDESS OF THE AMAZON. BUT YA'WARA BESTED THE HUNTER AND FED HIM TO HER CATS.
"AND FOR A TIME, THE KNIFE WAS LOST.
"UNTIL IT ENDED UP IN BARBARA MINERVA'S HANDS.
THERE IS NOTHING YOU CAN DO HERE, DIANA.
THIS IS MY TERRITORY. WE'RE IN MY ELEMENT.
"AND SHE STOLE THE GODSLAYER."

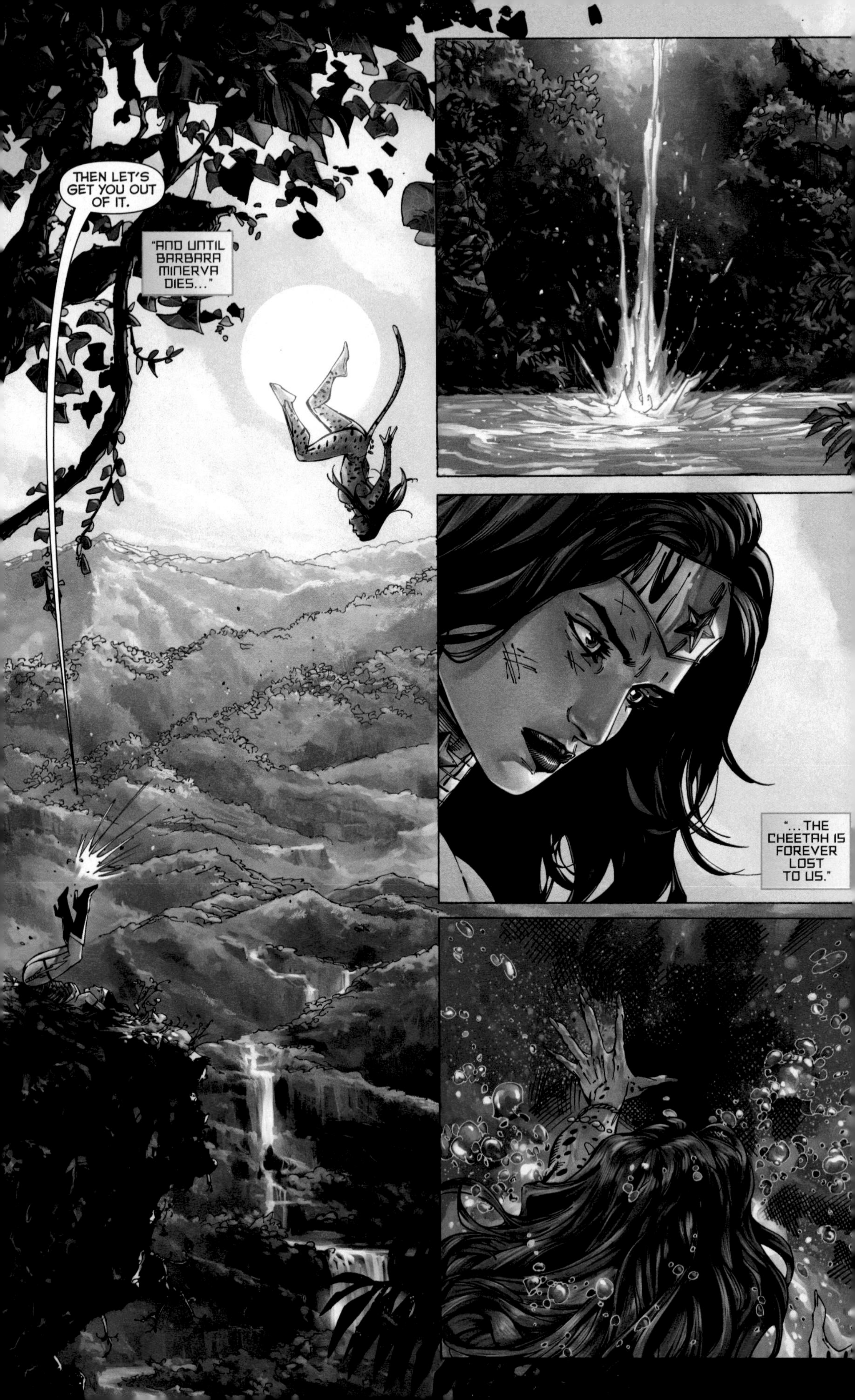
THEN LET'S GET YOU OUT OF IT.
"AND UNTIL BARBARA MINERVA DIES..."
"...THE CHEETAH IS FOREVER LOST TO US."

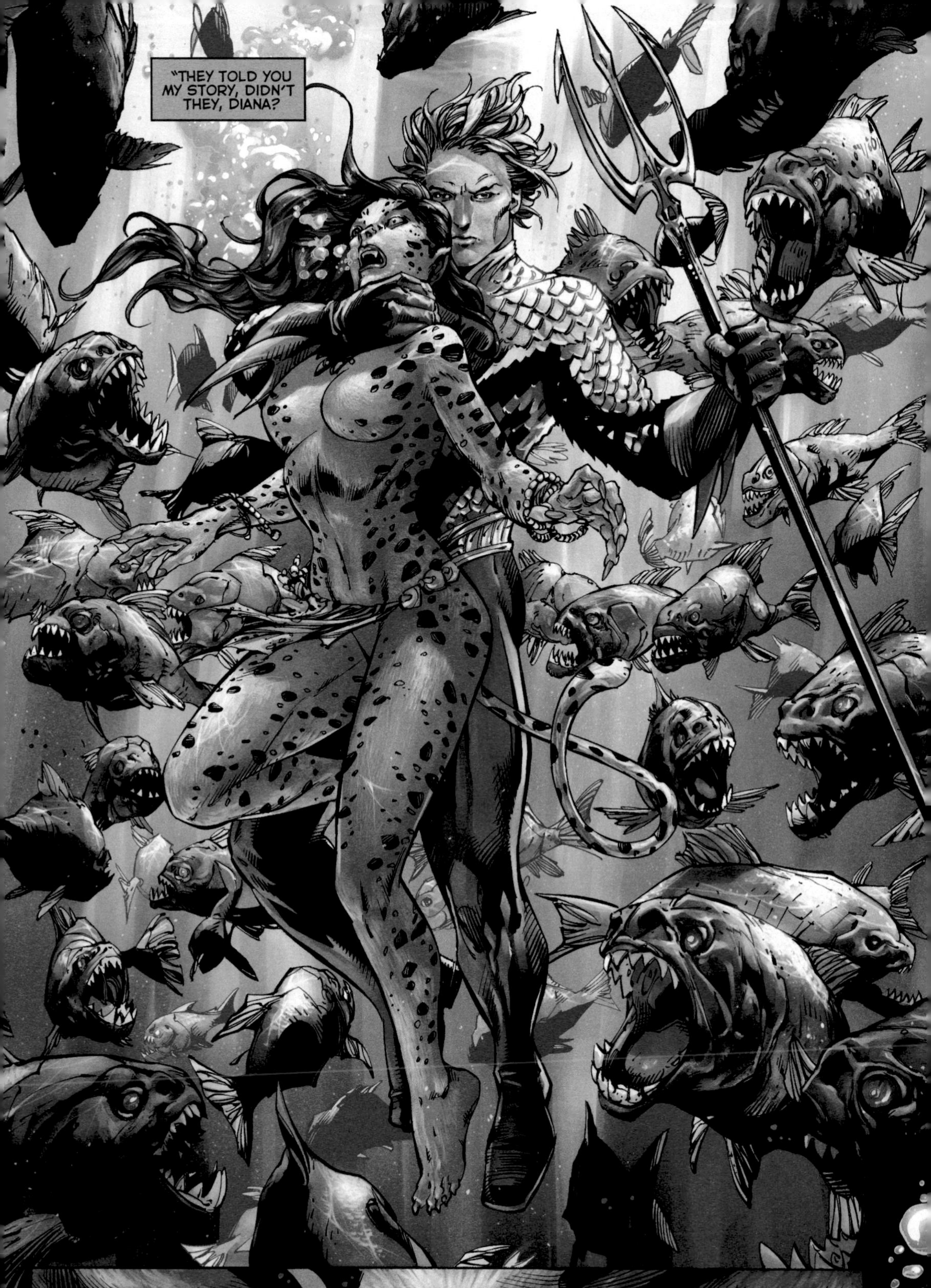
"THEY TOLD YOU MY STORY, DIDN'T THEY, DIANA?
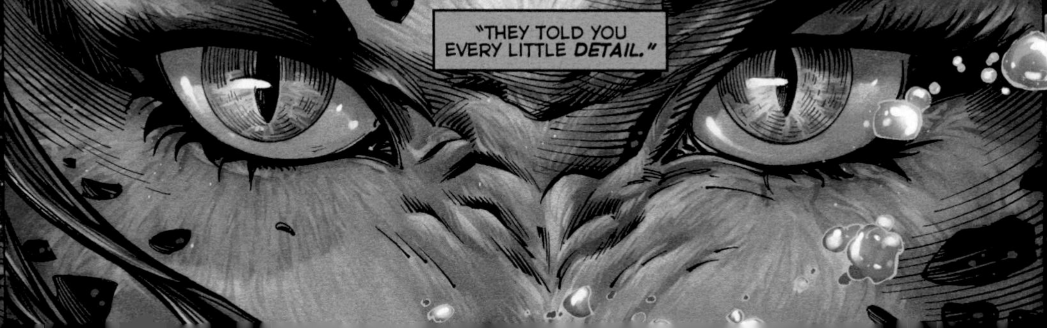
"THEY TOLD YOU EVERY LITTLE DETAIL."

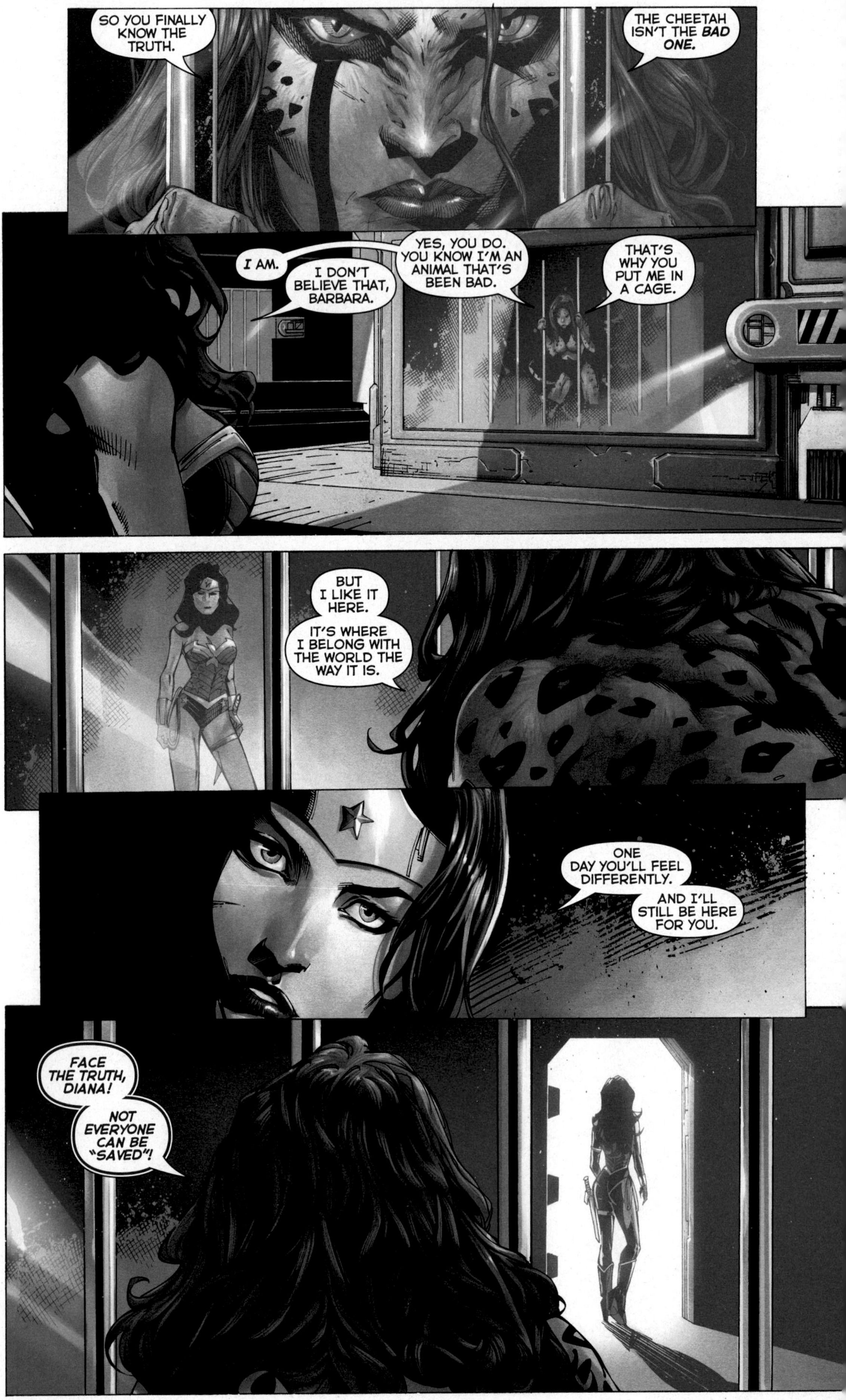
SO YOU FINALLY KNOW THE TRUTH.
THE CHEETAH ISN'T THE *BAD ONE.*
I AM.
I DON'T BELIEVE THAT, BARBARA.
YES, YOU DO. YOU KNOW I'M AN ANIMAL THAT'S BEEN BAD.
THAT'S WHY YOU PUT ME IN A CAGE.
BUT I LIKE IT HERE.
IT'S WHERE I BELONG WITH THE WORLD THE WAY IT IS.
ONE DAY YOU'LL FEEL DIFFERENTLY.
AND I'LL STILL BE HERE FOR YOU.
FACE THE TRUTH, DIANA!
NOT EVERYONE CAN BE "SAVED"!

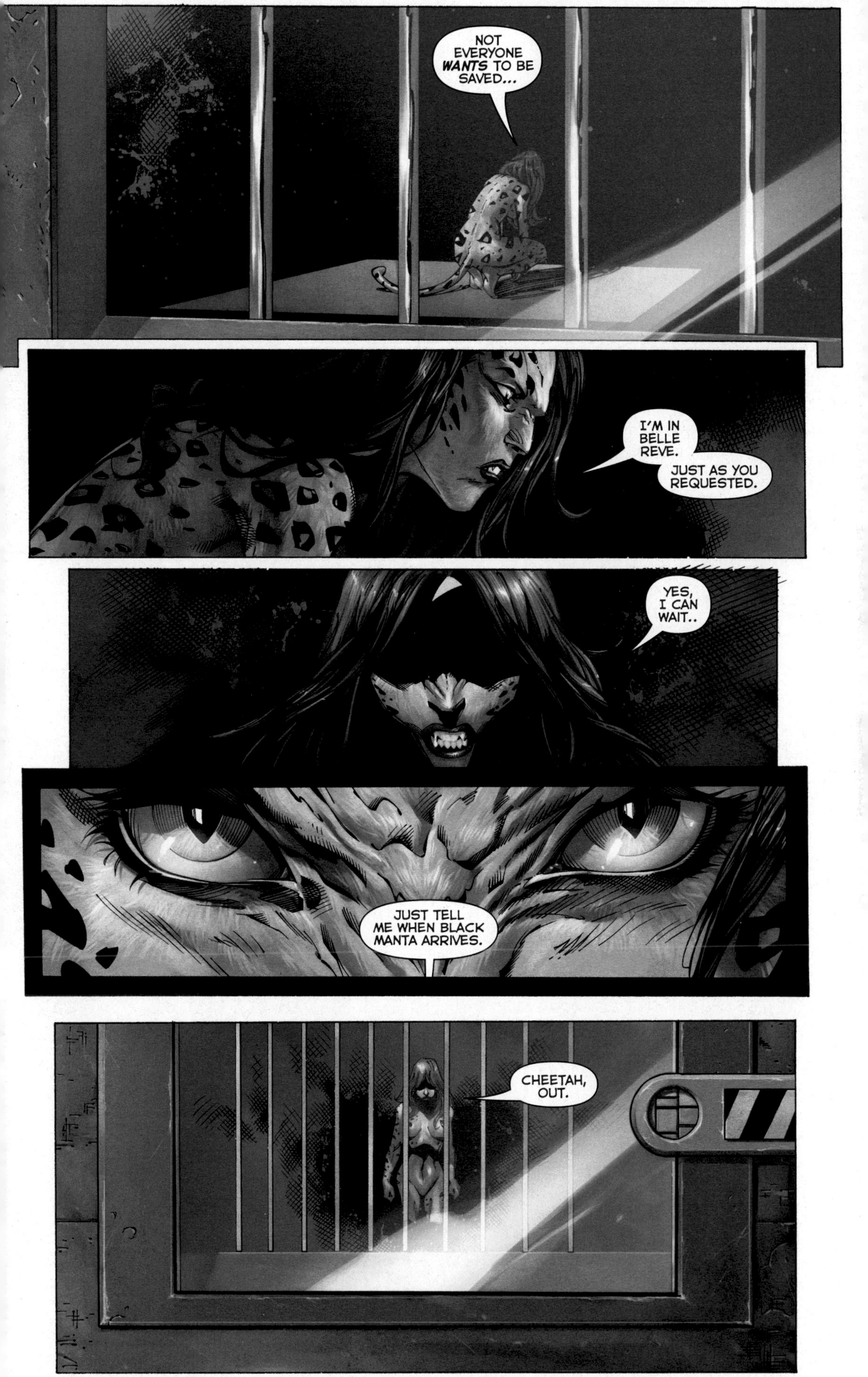
NOT EVERYONE WANTS TO BE SAVED...
I'M IN BELLE REVE.
JUST AS YOU REQUESTED.
YES, I CAN WAIT..
JUST TELL ME WHEN BLACK MANTA ARRIVES.
CHEETAH, OUT.

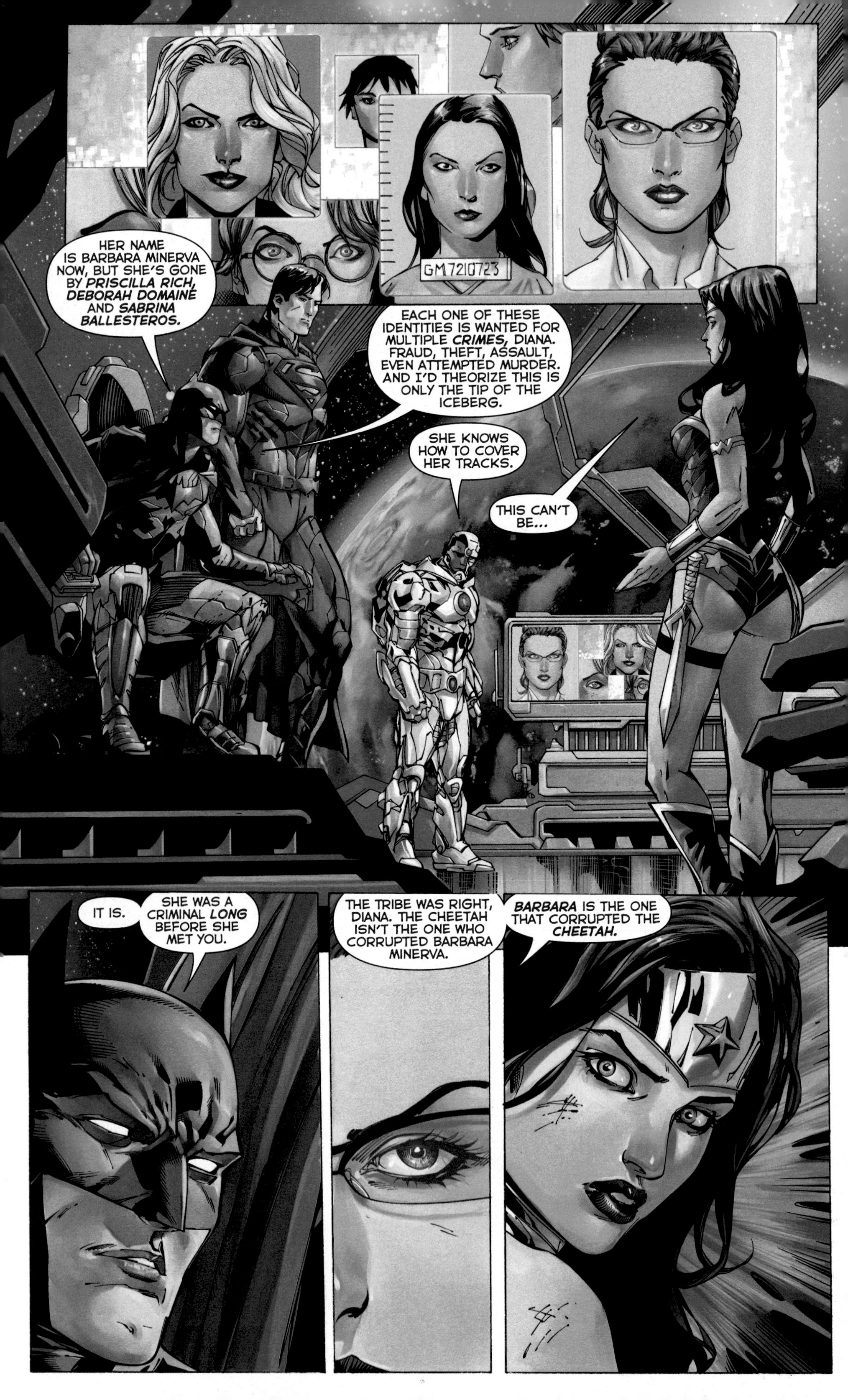
GM7210723
HER NAME IS BARBARA MINERVA NOW, BUT SHE'S GONE BY PRISCILLA RICH, DEBORAH DOMAINE AND SABRINA BALLESTEROS.
EACH ONE OF THESE IDENTITIES IS WANTED FOR MULTIPLE CRIMES, DIANA. FRAUD, THEFT, ASSAULT, EVEN ATTEMPTED MURDER. AND I'D THEORIZE THIS IS ONLY THE TIP OF THE ICEBERG.
SHE KNOWS HOW TO COVER HER TRACKS.
THIS CAN'T BE...
IT IS.
SHE WAS A CRIMINAL LONG BEFORE SHE MET YOU.
THE TRIBE WAS RIGHT, DIANA. THE CHEETAH ISN'T THE ONE WHO CORRUPTED BARBARA MINERVA.
BARBARA IS THE ONE THAT CORRUPTED THE CHEETAH.

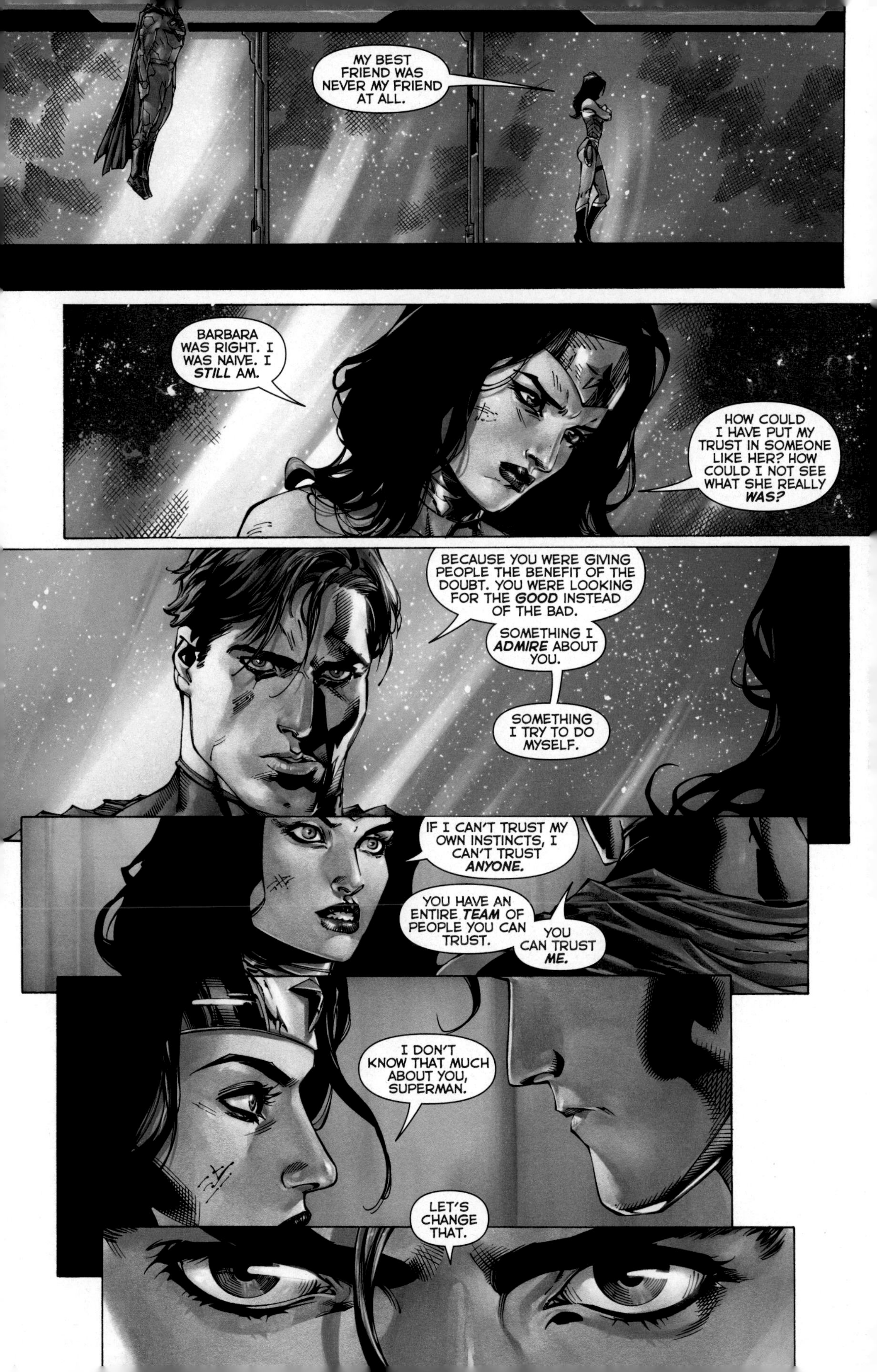
MY BEST FRIEND WAS NEVER MY FRIEND AT ALL.
BARBARA WAS RIGHT. I WAS NAIVE. I STILL AM.
HOW COULD I HAVE PUT MY TRUST IN SOMEONE LIKE HER? HOW COULD I NOT SEE WHAT SHE REALLY WAS?
BECAUSE YOU WERE GIVING PEOPLE THE BENEFIT OF THE DOUBT. YOU WERE LOOKING FOR THE GOOD INSTEAD OF THE BAD.
SOMETHING I ADMIRE ABOUT YOU.
SOMETHING I TRY TO DO MYSELF.
IF I CAN'T TRUST MY OWN INSTINCTS, I CAN'T TRUST ANYONE.
YOU HAVE AN ENTIRE TEAM OF PEOPLE YOU CAN TRUST.
YOU CAN TRUST ME.
I DON'T KNOW THAT MUCH ABOUT YOU, SUPERMAN.
LET'S CHANGE THAT.

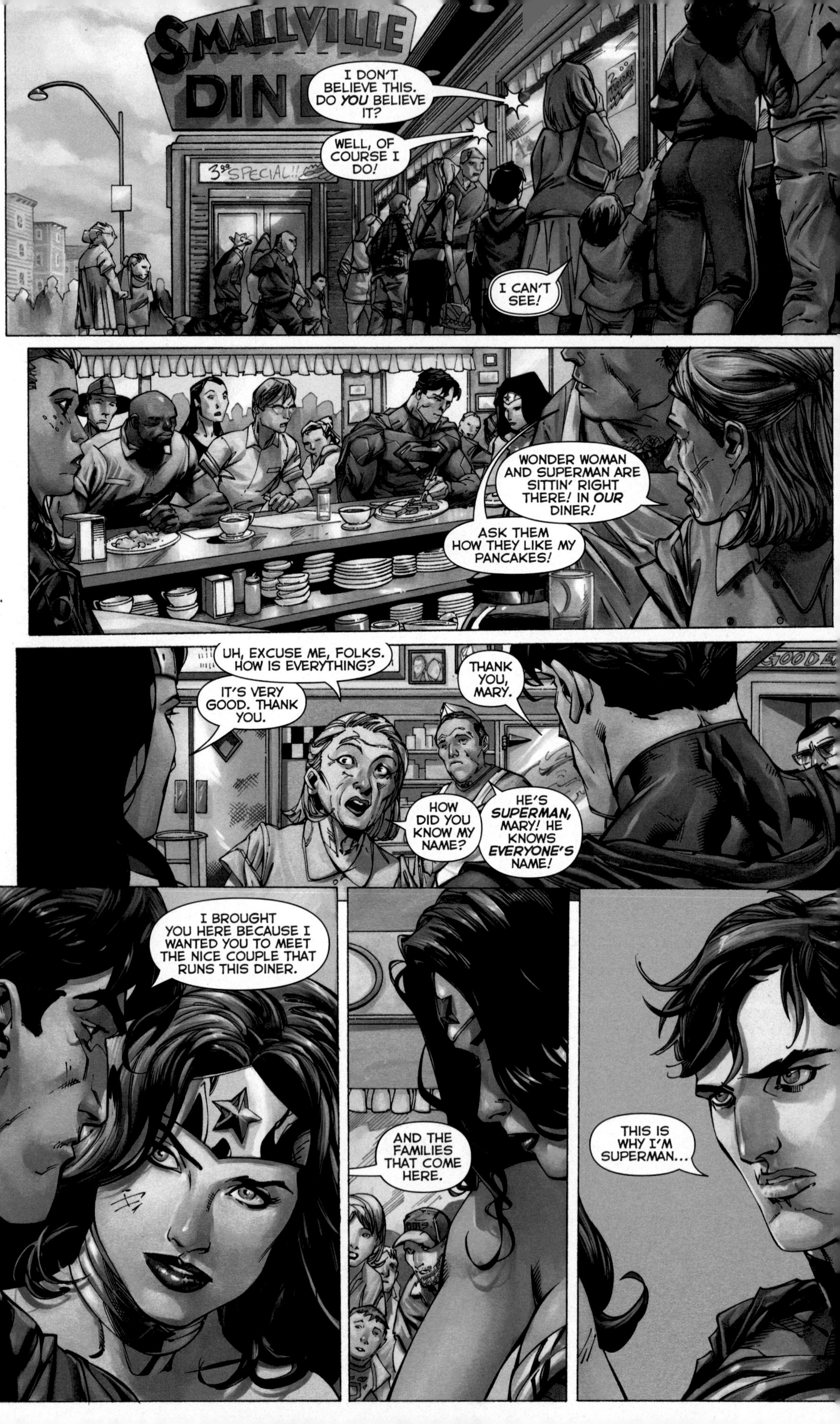
SMALLVILLE DIN
3.99 SPECIAL!!
I DON'T BELIEVE THIS. DO *YOU* BELIEVE IT?
WELL, OF COURSE I DO!
I CAN'T SEE!
WONDER WOMAN AND SUPERMAN ARE SITTIN' RIGHT THERE! IN *OUR* DINER!
ASK THEM HOW THEY LIKE MY PANCAKES!
UH, EXCUSE ME, FOLKS. HOW IS EVERYTHING?
IT'S VERY GOOD. THANK YOU.
THANK YOU, MARY.
HOW DID YOU KNOW MY NAME?
HE'S *SUPERMAN,* MARY! HE KNOWS *EVERYONE'S* NAME!
I BROUGHT YOU HERE BECAUSE I WANTED YOU TO MEET THE NICE COUPLE THAT RUNS THIS DINER.
AND THE FAMILIES THAT COME HERE.
THIS IS WHY I'M SUPERMAN...

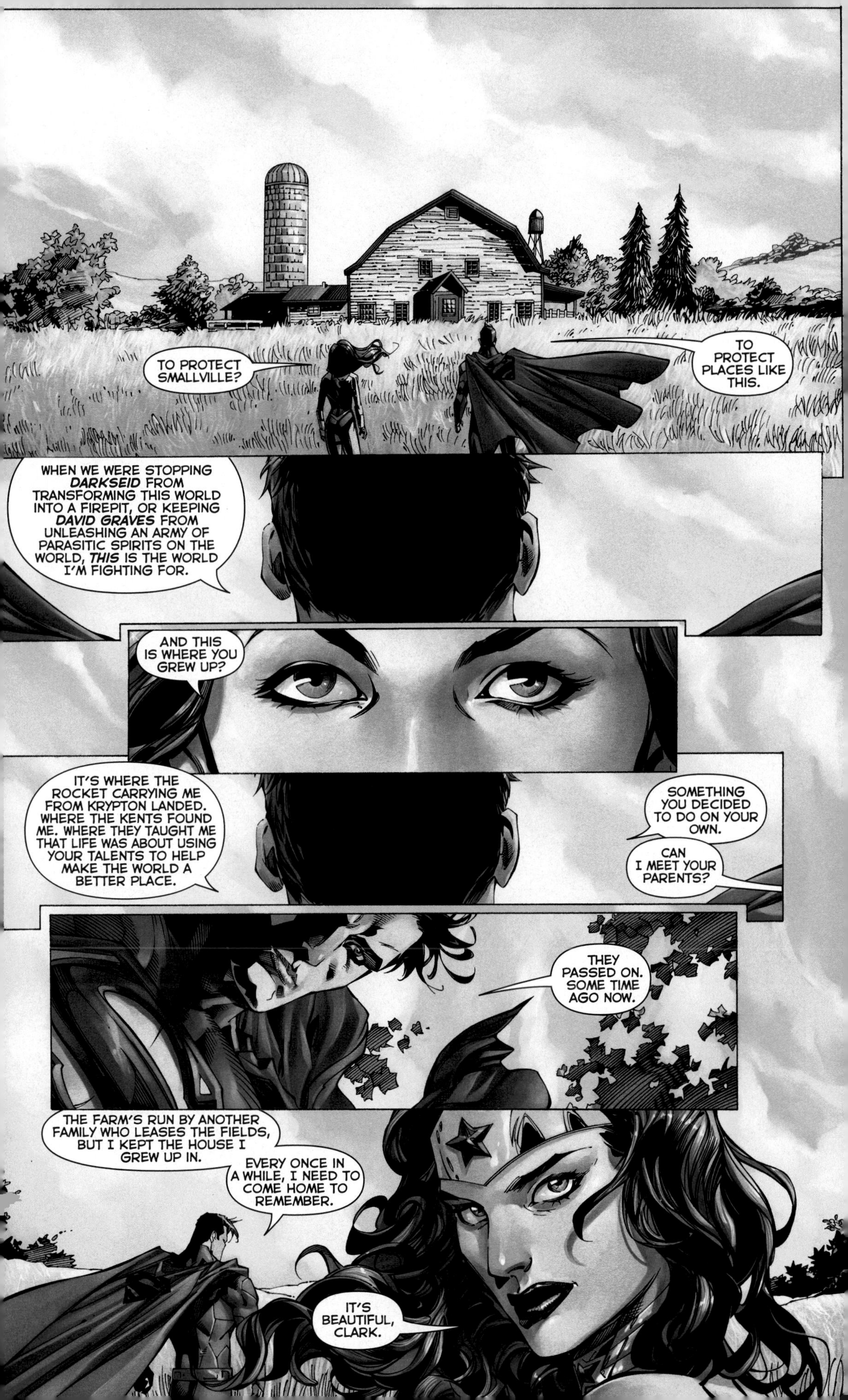
TO PROTECT SMALLVILLE?
TO PROTECT PLACES LIKE THIS.
WHEN WE WERE STOPPING DARKSEID FROM TRANSFORMING THIS WORLD INTO A FIREPIT, OR KEEPING DAVID GRAVES FROM UNLEASHING AN ARMY OF PARASITIC SPIRITS ON THE WORLD, THIS IS THE WORLD I'M FIGHTING FOR.
AND THIS IS WHERE YOU GREW UP?
IT'S WHERE THE ROCKET CARRYING ME FROM KRYPTON LANDED. WHERE THE KENTS FOUND ME. WHERE THEY TAUGHT ME THAT LIFE WAS ABOUT USING YOUR TALENTS TO HELP MAKE THE WORLD A BETTER PLACE.
SOMETHING YOU DECIDED TO DO ON YOUR OWN.
CAN I MEET YOUR PARENTS?
THEY PASSED ON. SOME TIME AGO NOW.
THE FARM'S RUN BY ANOTHER FAMILY WHO LEASES THE FIELDS, BUT I KEPT THE HOUSE I GREW UP IN.
EVERY ONCE IN A WHILE, I NEED TO COME HOME TO REMEMBER.
IT'S BEAUTIFUL, CLARK.

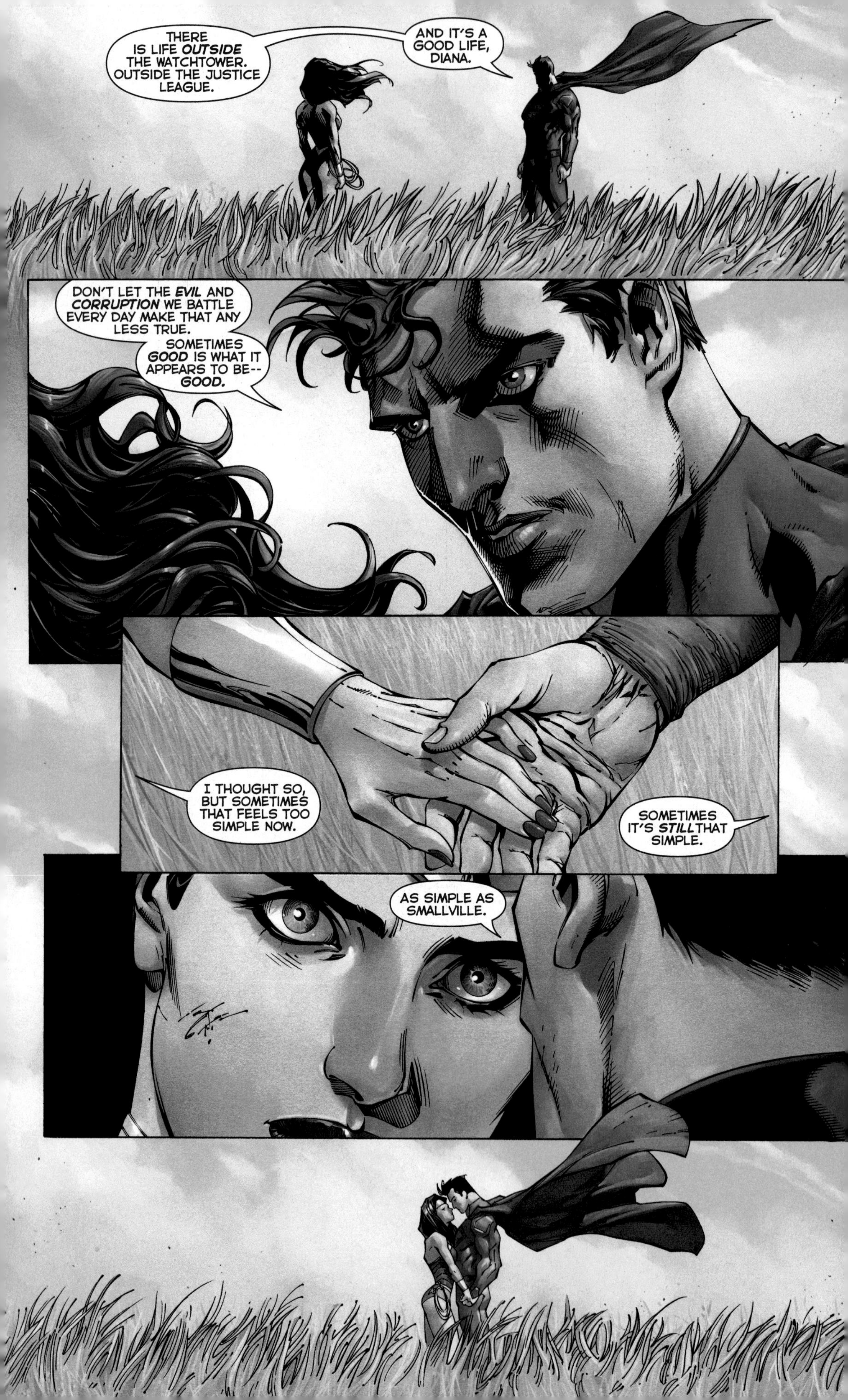
THERE IS LIFE OUTSIDE THE WATCHTOWER. OUTSIDE THE JUSTICE LEAGUE.
AND IT'S A GOOD LIFE, DIANA.
DON'T LET THE EVIL AND CORRUPTION WE BATTLE EVERY DAY MAKE THAT ANY LESS TRUE.
SOMETIMES GOOD IS WHAT IT APPEARS TO BE-- GOOD.
I THOUGHT SO, BUT SOMETIMES THAT FEELS TOO SIMPLE NOW.
SOMETIMES IT'S STILL THAT SIMPLE.
AS SIMPLE AS SMALLVILLE.

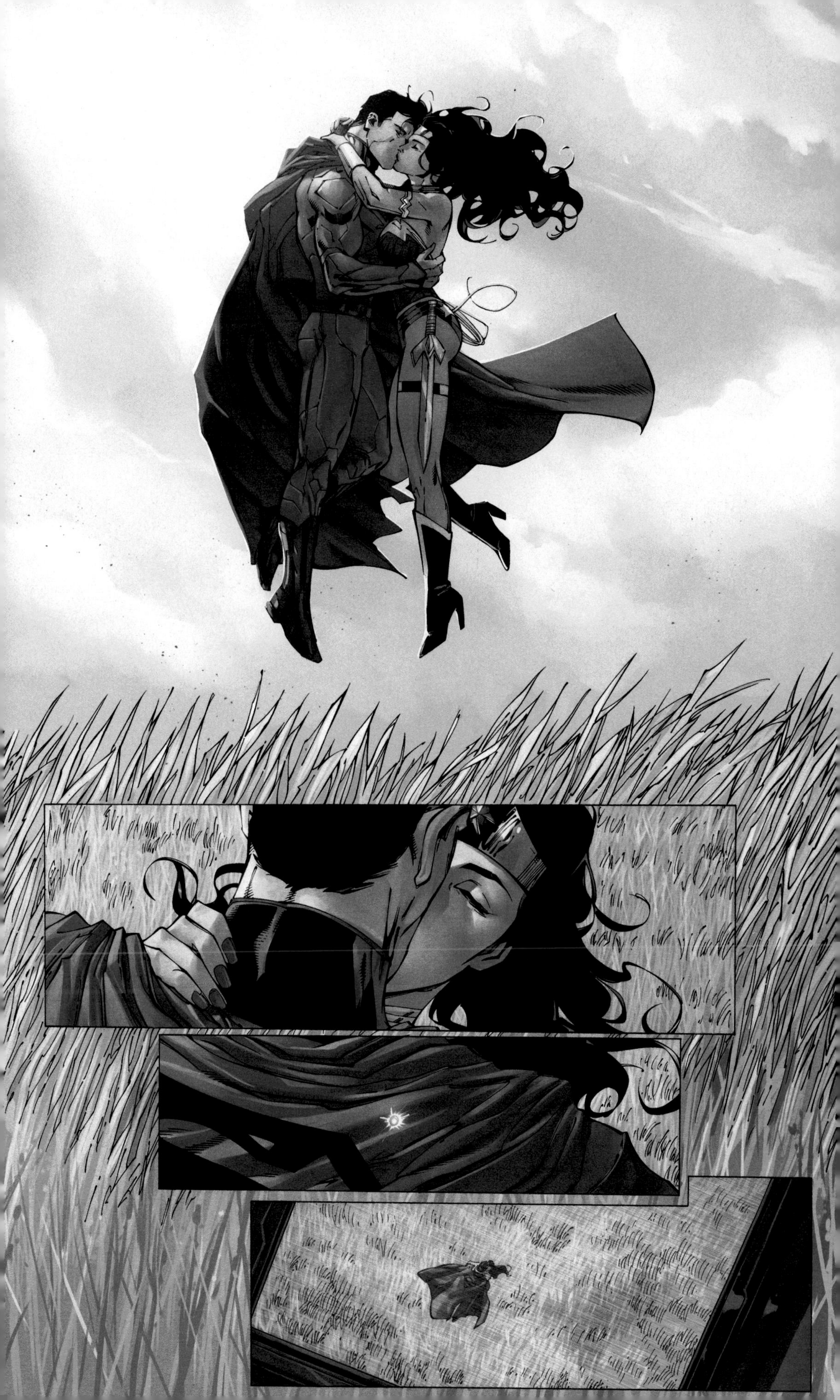

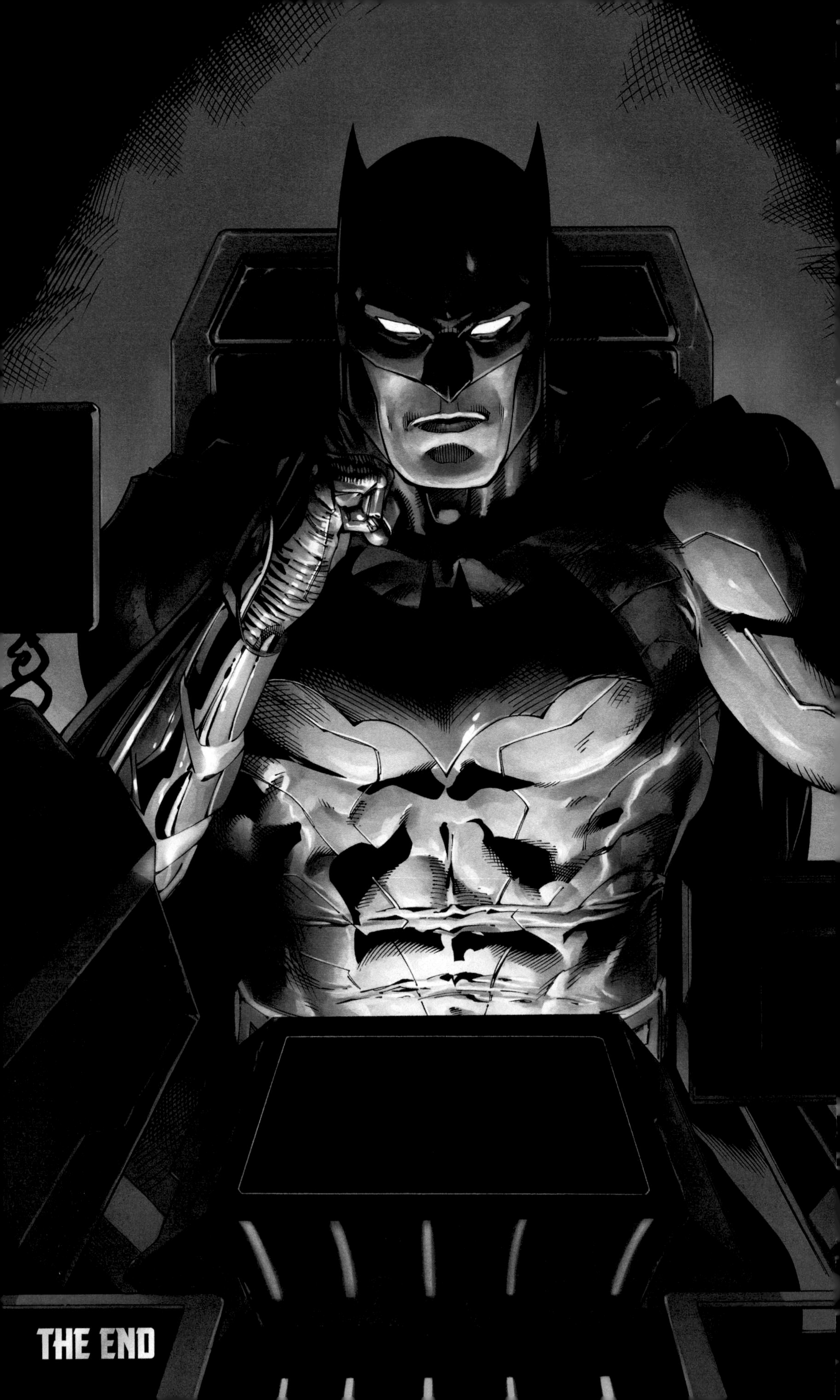
THE END

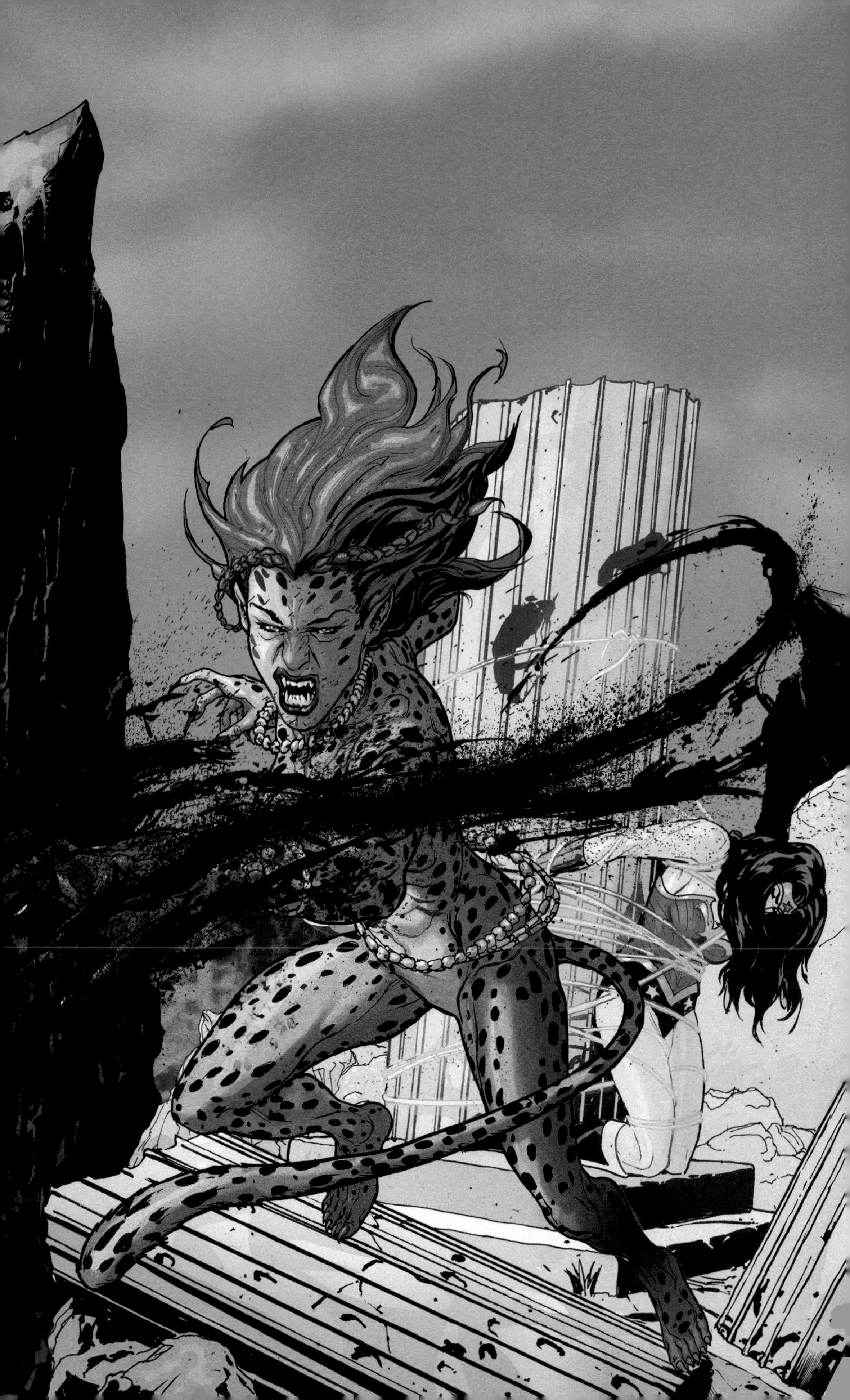

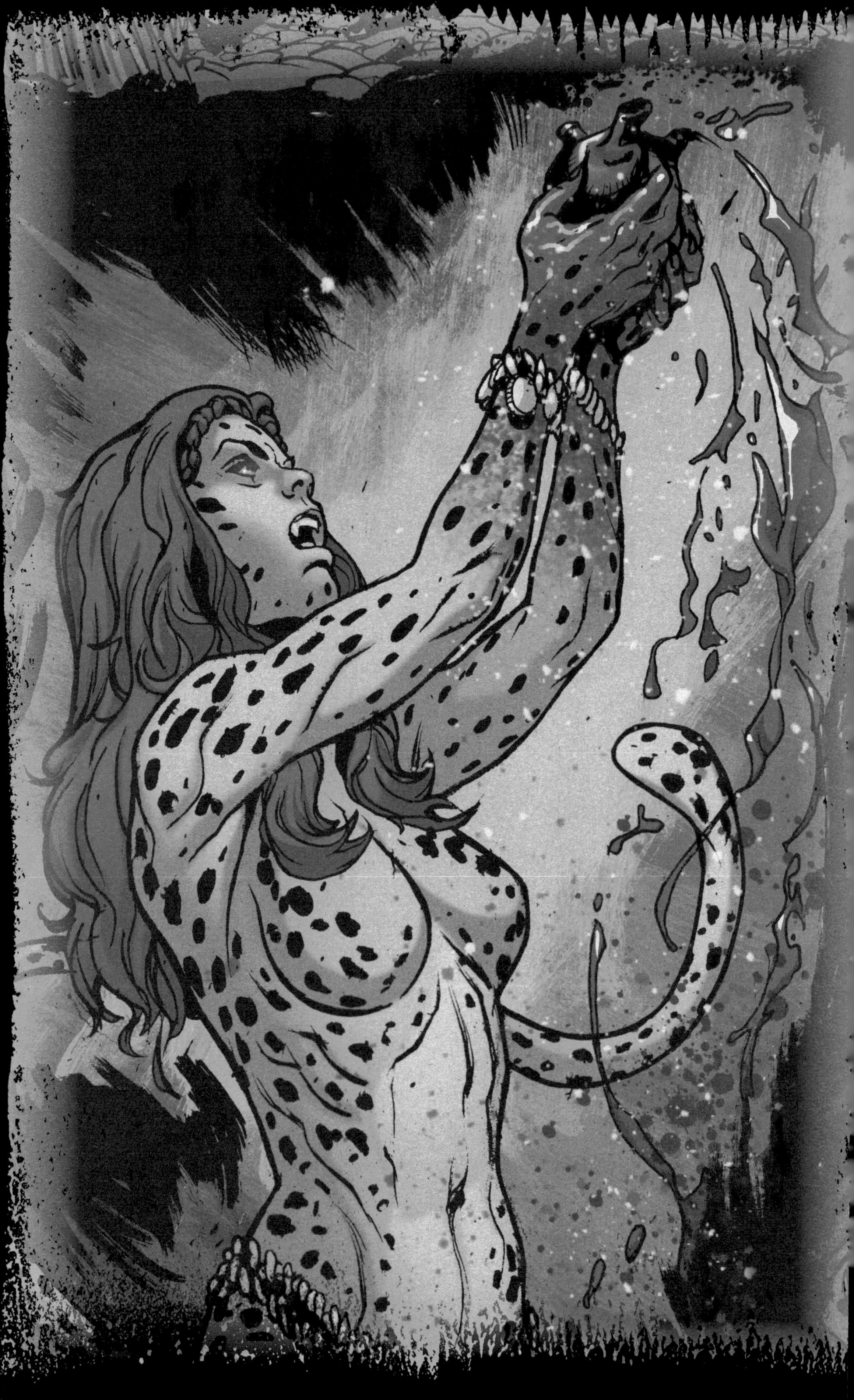

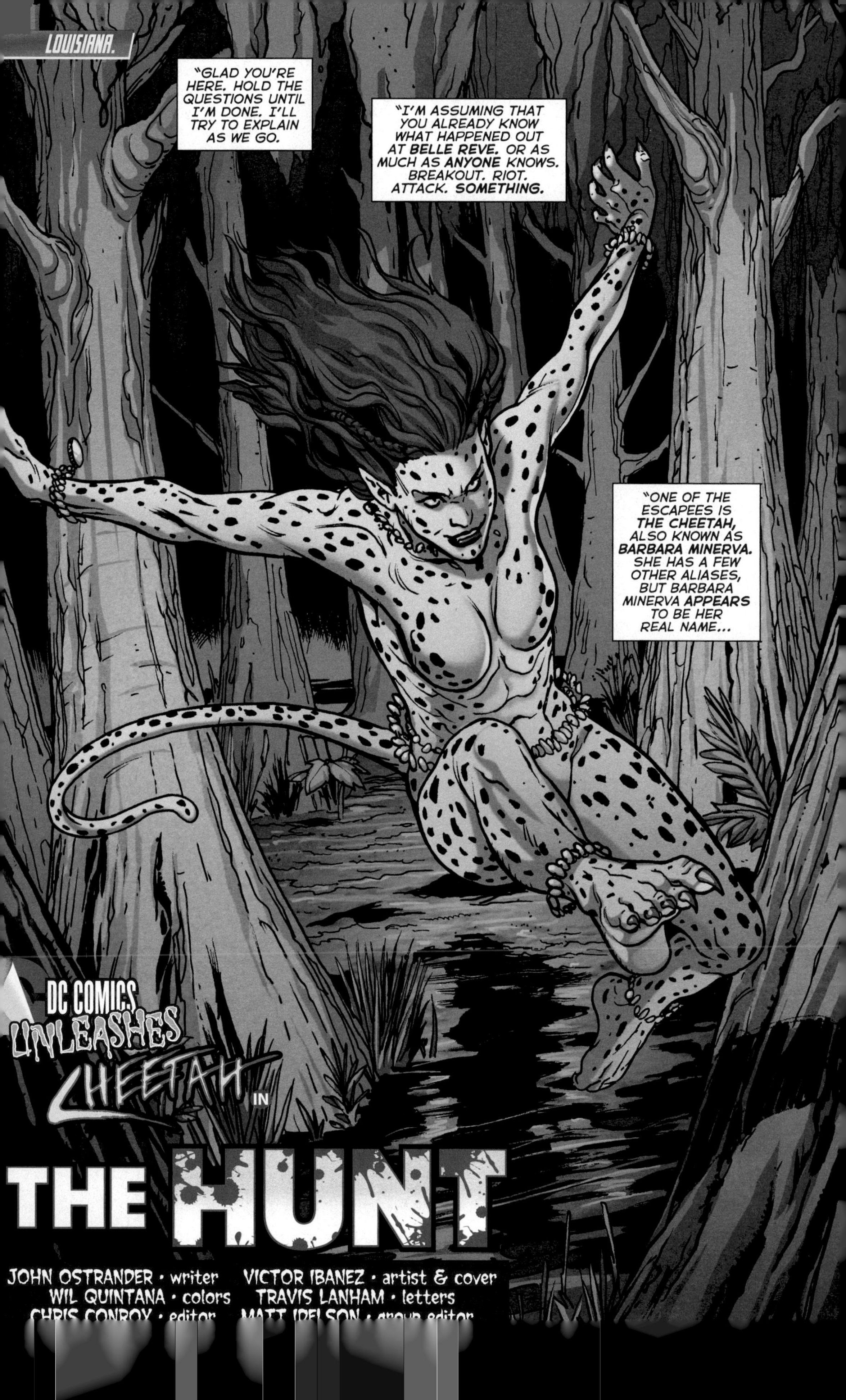

LOUISIANA.
"GLAD YOU'RE HERE. HOLD THE QUESTIONS UNTIL I'M DONE. I'LL TRY TO EXPLAIN AS WE GO.
"I'M ASSUMING THAT YOU ALREADY KNOW WHAT HAPPENED OUT AT BELLE REVE. OR AS MUCH AS ANYONE KNOWS. BREAKOUT. RIOT. ATTACK. SOMETHING.
"ONE OF THE ESCAPEES IS THE CHEETAH, ALSO KNOWN AS BARBARA MINERVA. SHE HAS A FEW OTHER ALIASES, BUT BARBARA MINERVA APPEARS TO BE HER REAL NAME...
DC COMICS UNLEASHES CHEETAH IN
THE HUNT
JOHN OSTRANDER • writer VICTOR IBANEZ • artist & cover
WIL QUINTANA • colors TRAVIS LANHAM • letters
CHRIS CONROY • editor MATT IDELSON • group editor

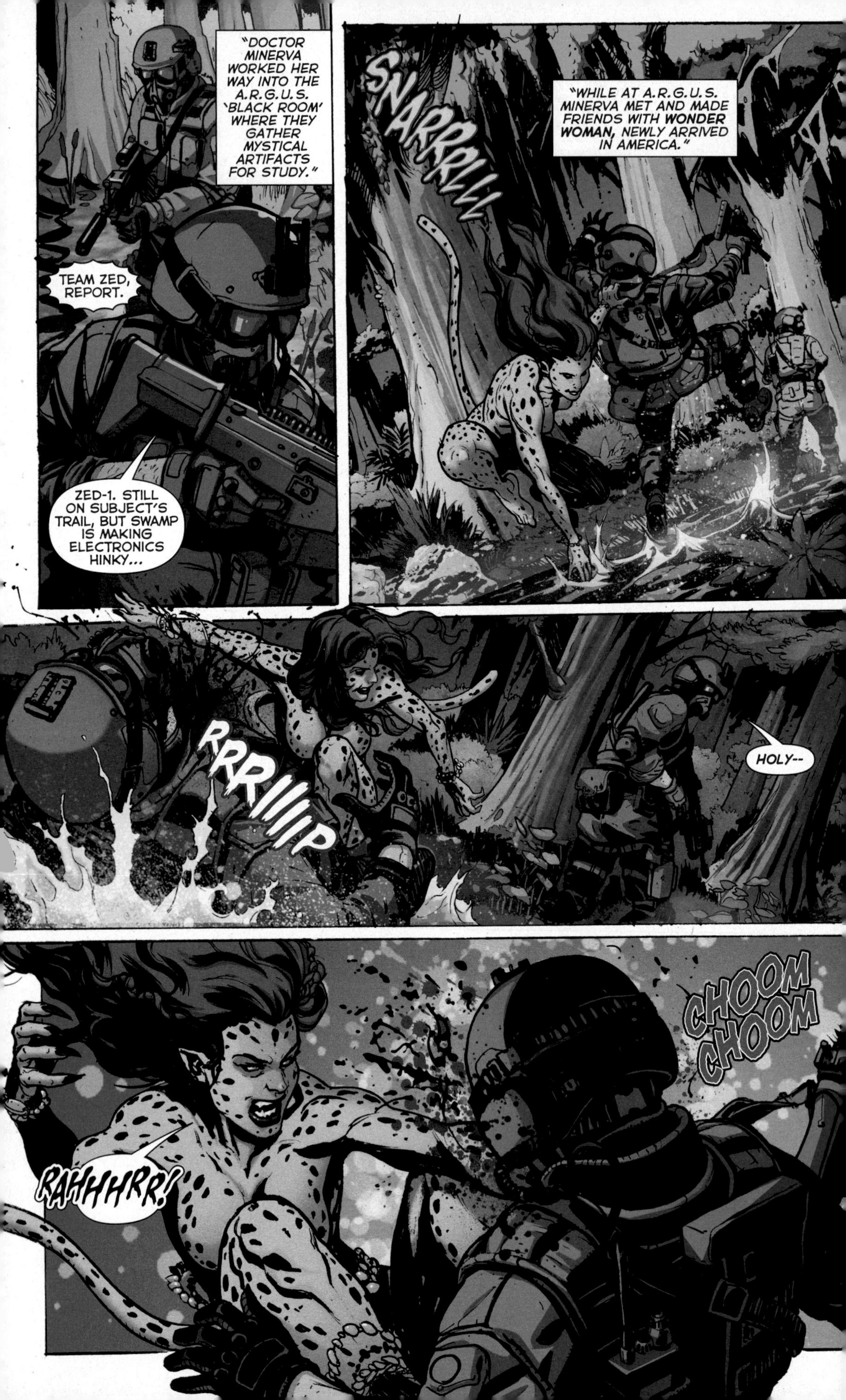
"DOCTOR MINERVA WORKED HER WAY INTO THE A.R.G.U.S. 'BLACK ROOM' WHERE THEY GATHER MYSTICAL ARTIFACTS FOR STUDY."
TEAM ZED, REPORT.
ZED-1. STILL ON SUBJECT'S TRAIL, BUT SWAMP IS MAKING ELECTRONICS HINKY...
SNARRRLLL
"WHILE AT A.R.G.U.S. MINERVA MET AND MADE FRIENDS WITH WONDER WOMAN, NEWLY ARRIVED IN AMERICA."
RRRIIIIIP
HOLY--
CHOOM CHOOM
RAHHHRR!

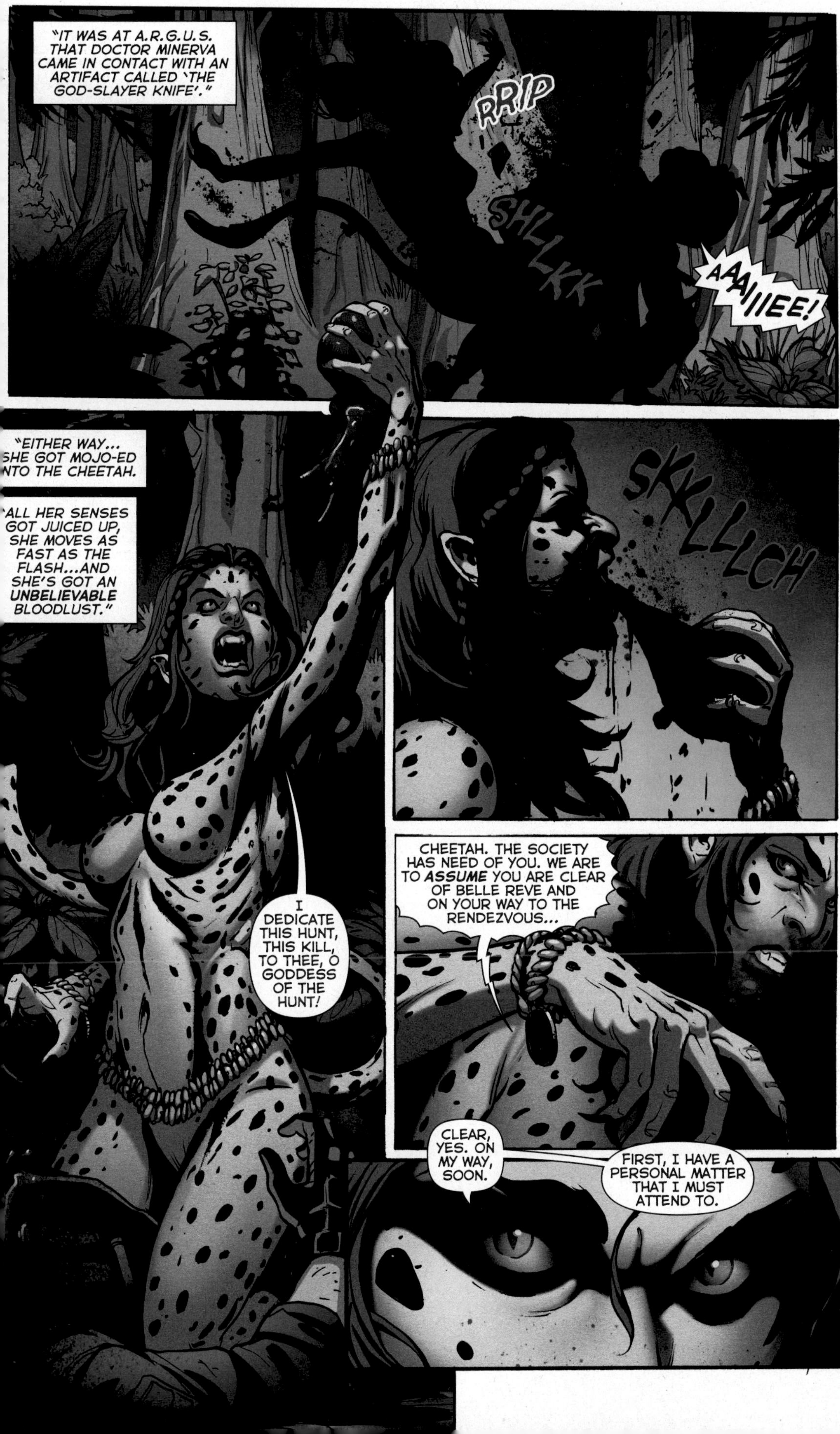
"IT WAS AT A.R.G.U.S. THAT DOCTOR MINERVA CAME IN CONTACT WITH AN ARTIFACT CALLED 'THE GOD-SLAYER KNIFE'."
RRIP
SHLLKK
AAAIIIEE!
"EITHER WAY... SHE GOT MOJO-ED INTO THE CHEETAH.
"ALL HER SENSES GOT JUICED UP, SHE MOVES AS FAST AS THE FLASH...AND SHE'S GOT AN UNBELIEVABLE BLOODLUST."
SKKLLLCH
I DEDICATE THIS HUNT, THIS KILL, TO THEE, O GODDESS OF THE HUNT!
CHEETAH. THE SOCIETY HAS NEED OF YOU. WE ARE TO ASSUME YOU ARE CLEAR OF BELLE REVE AND ON YOUR WAY TO THE RENDEZVOUS...
CLEAR, YES. ON MY WAY, SOON.
FIRST, I HAVE A PERSONAL MATTER THAT I MUST ATTEND TO.

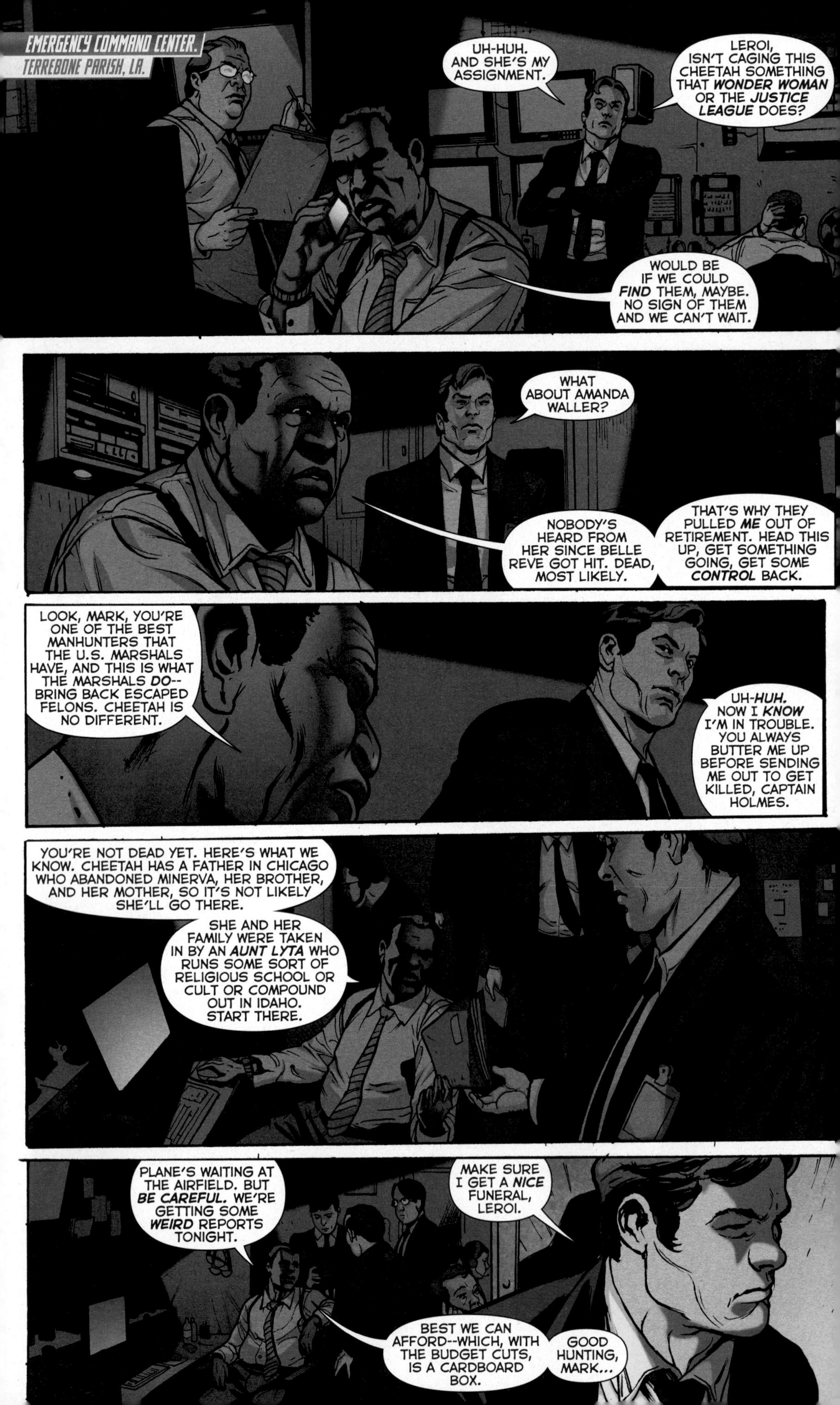
EMERGENCY COMMAND CENTER.
TERREBONE PARISH, LA.
UH-HUH. AND SHE'S MY ASSIGNMENT.
LEROI, ISN'T CAGING THIS CHEETAH SOMETHING THAT WONDER WOMAN OR THE JUSTICE LEAGUE DOES?
WOULD BE IF WE COULD FIND THEM, MAYBE. NO SIGN OF THEM AND WE CAN'T WAIT.
WHAT ABOUT AMANDA WALLER?
NOBODY'S HEARD FROM HER SINCE BELLE REVE GOT HIT. DEAD, MOST LIKELY.
THAT'S WHY THEY PULLED ME OUT OF RETIREMENT. HEAD THIS UP, GET SOMETHING GOING, GET SOME CONTROL BACK.
LOOK, MARK, YOU'RE ONE OF THE BEST MANHUNTERS THAT THE U.S. MARSHALS HAVE, AND THIS IS WHAT THE MARSHALS DO--BRING BACK ESCAPED FELONS. CHEETAH IS NO DIFFERENT.
UH-HUH. NOW I KNOW I'M IN TROUBLE. YOU ALWAYS BUTTER ME UP BEFORE SENDING ME OUT TO GET KILLED, CAPTAIN HOLMES.
YOU'RE NOT DEAD YET. HERE'S WHAT WE KNOW. CHEETAH HAS A FATHER IN CHICAGO WHO ABANDONED MINERVA, HER BROTHER, AND HER MOTHER, SO IT'S NOT LIKELY SHE'LL GO THERE.
SHE AND HER FAMILY WERE TAKEN IN BY AN AUNT LYTA WHO RUNS SOME SORT OF RELIGIOUS SCHOOL OR CULT OR COMPOUND OUT IN IDAHO. START THERE.
PLANE'S WAITING AT THE AIRFIELD. BUT BE CAREFUL. WE'RE GETTING SOME WEIRD REPORTS TONIGHT.
MAKE SURE I GET A NICE FUNERAL, LEROI.
BEST WE CAN AFFORD--WHICH, WITH THE BUDGET CUTS, IS A CARDBOARD BOX.
GOOD HUNTING, MARK...

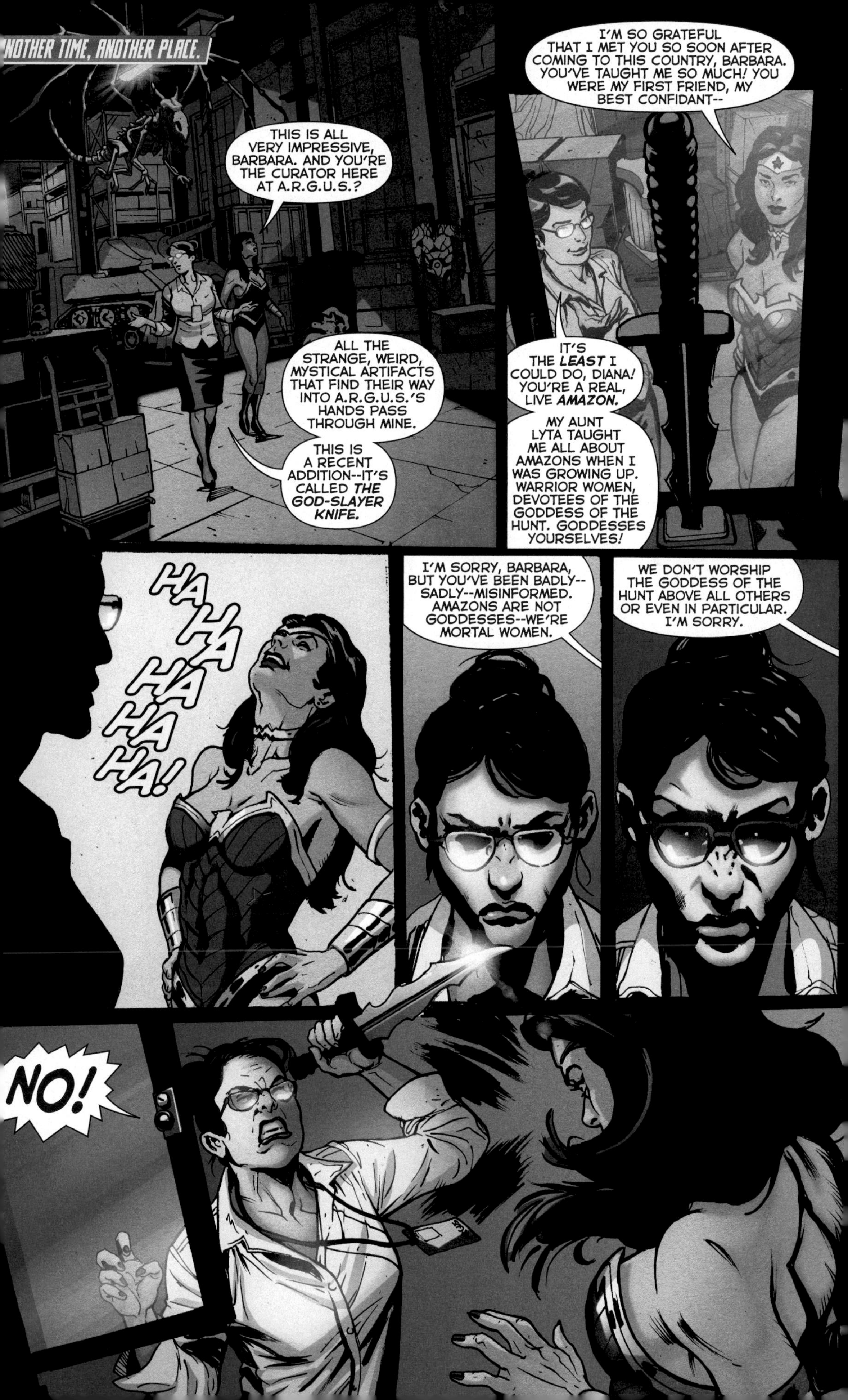

ANOTHER TIME, ANOTHER PLACE.
THIS IS ALL VERY IMPRESSIVE, BARBARA. AND YOU'RE THE CURATOR HERE AT A.R.G.U.S.?
ALL THE STRANGE, WEIRD, MYSTICAL ARTIFACTS THAT FIND THEIR WAY INTO A.R.G.U.S.'S HANDS PASS THROUGH MINE.
THIS IS A RECENT ADDITION--IT'S CALLED THE GOD-SLAYER KNIFE.
I'M SO GRATEFUL THAT I MET YOU SO SOON AFTER COMING TO THIS COUNTRY, BARBARA. YOU'VE TAUGHT ME SO MUCH! YOU WERE MY FIRST FRIEND, MY BEST CONFIDANT--
IT'S THE LEAST I COULD DO, DIANA! YOU'RE A REAL, LIVE AMAZON.
MY AUNT LYTA TAUGHT ME ALL ABOUT AMAZONS WHEN I WAS GROWING UP. WARRIOR WOMEN, DEVOTEES OF THE GODDESS OF THE HUNT. GODDESSES YOURSELVES!
HA HA HA HA HA HA!
I'M SORRY, BARBARA, BUT YOU'VE BEEN BADLY--SADLY--MISINFORMED. AMAZONS ARE NOT GODDESSES--WE'RE MORTAL WOMEN.
WE DON'T WORSHIP THE GODDESS OF THE HUNT ABOVE ALL OTHERS OR EVEN IN PARTICULAR. I'M SORRY.
NO!

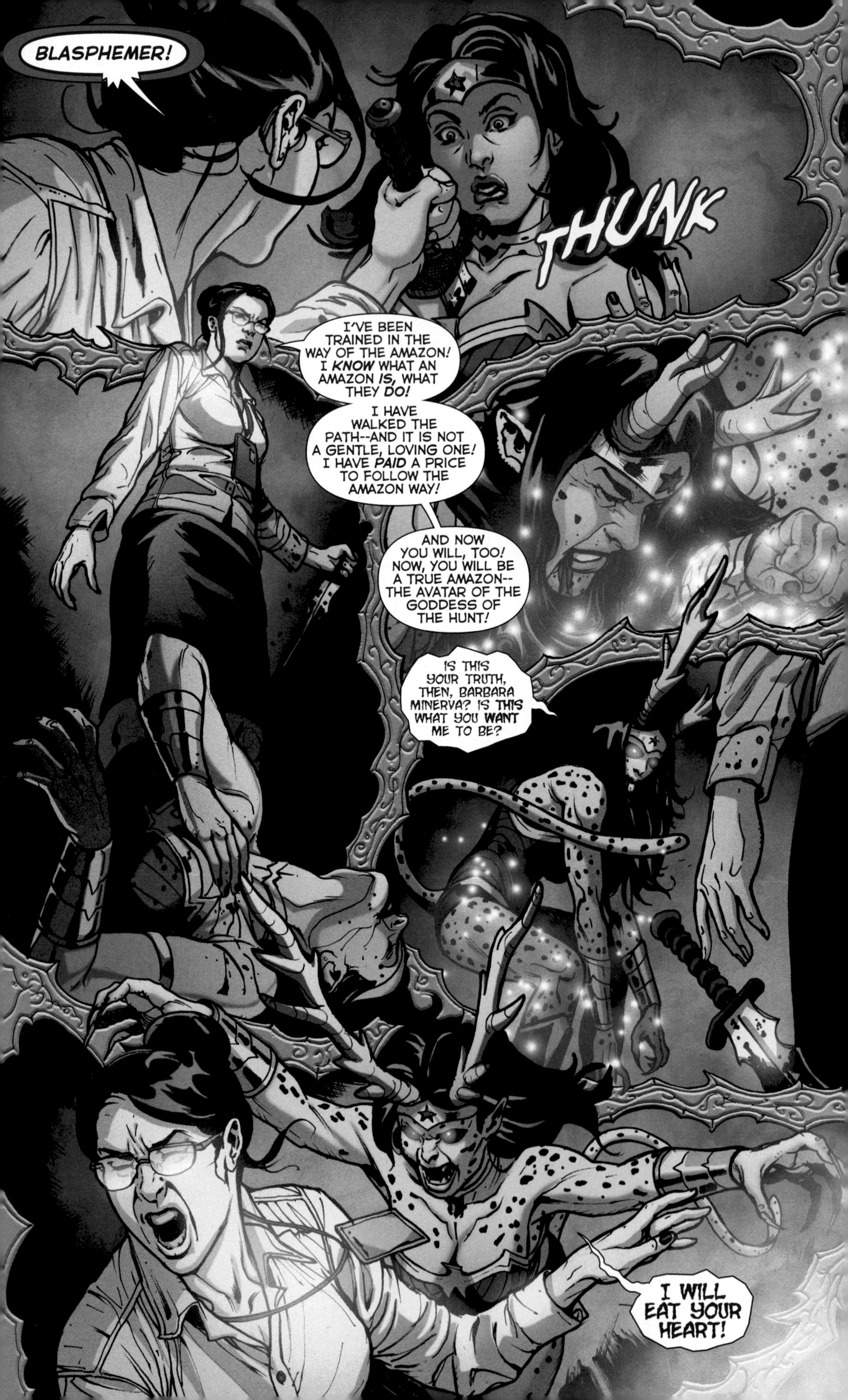
BLASPHEMER!
THUNK
I'VE BEEN TRAINED IN THE WAY OF THE AMAZON! I KNOW WHAT AN AMAZON IS, WHAT THEY DO!
I HAVE WALKED THE PATH--AND IT IS NOT A GENTLE, LOVING ONE! I HAVE PAID A PRICE TO FOLLOW THE AMAZON WAY!
AND NOW YOU WILL, TOO! NOW, YOU WILL BE A TRUE AMAZON-- THE AVATAR OF THE GODDESS OF THE HUNT!
IS THIS YOUR TRUTH, THEN, BARBARA MINERVA? IS THIS WHAT YOU WANT ME TO BE?
I WILL EAT YOUR HEART!

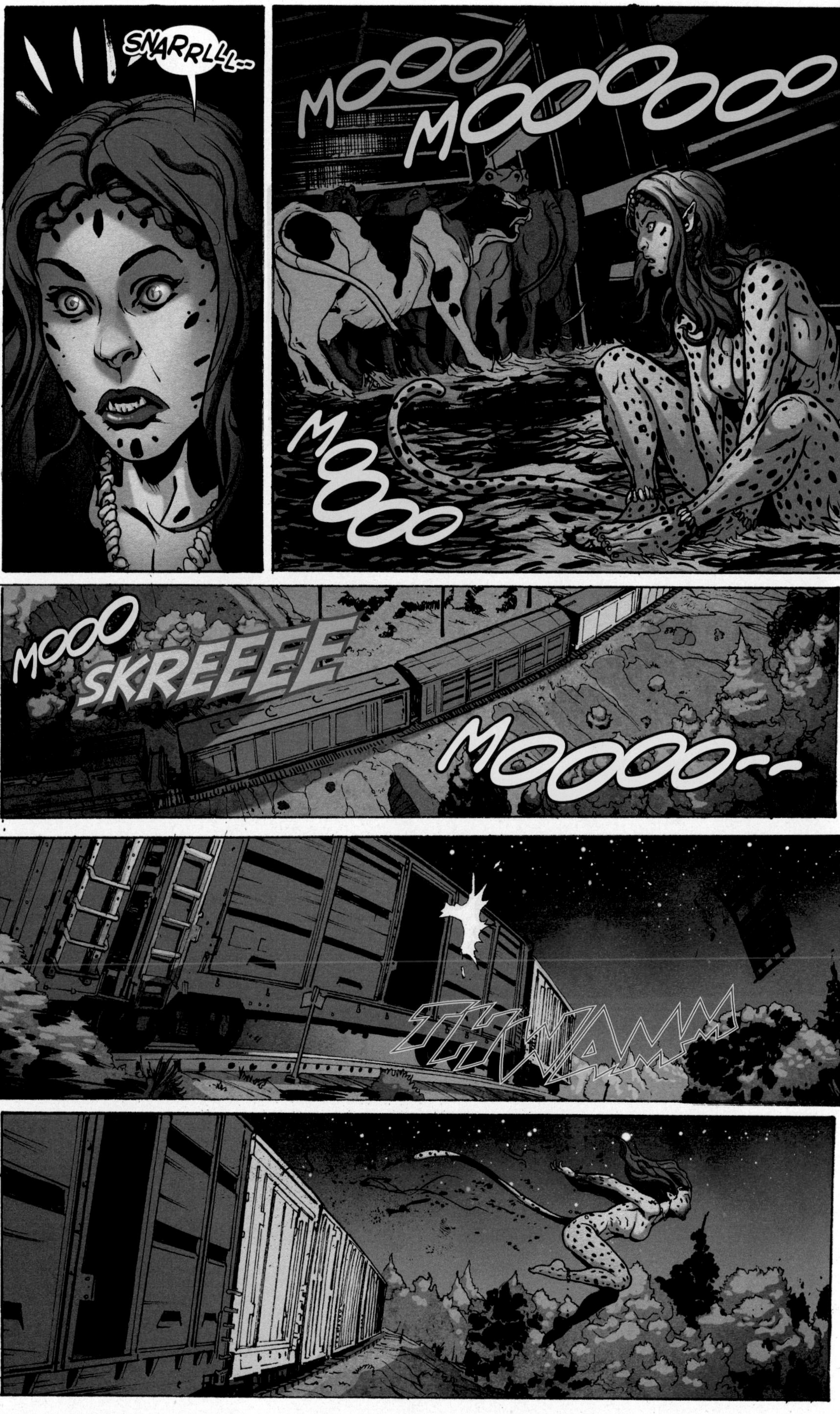
SNARRLLL--
MOOOO
MOOOOOOOO
MOOOO
MOOO
SKREEEE
MOOOO--
THWAMM

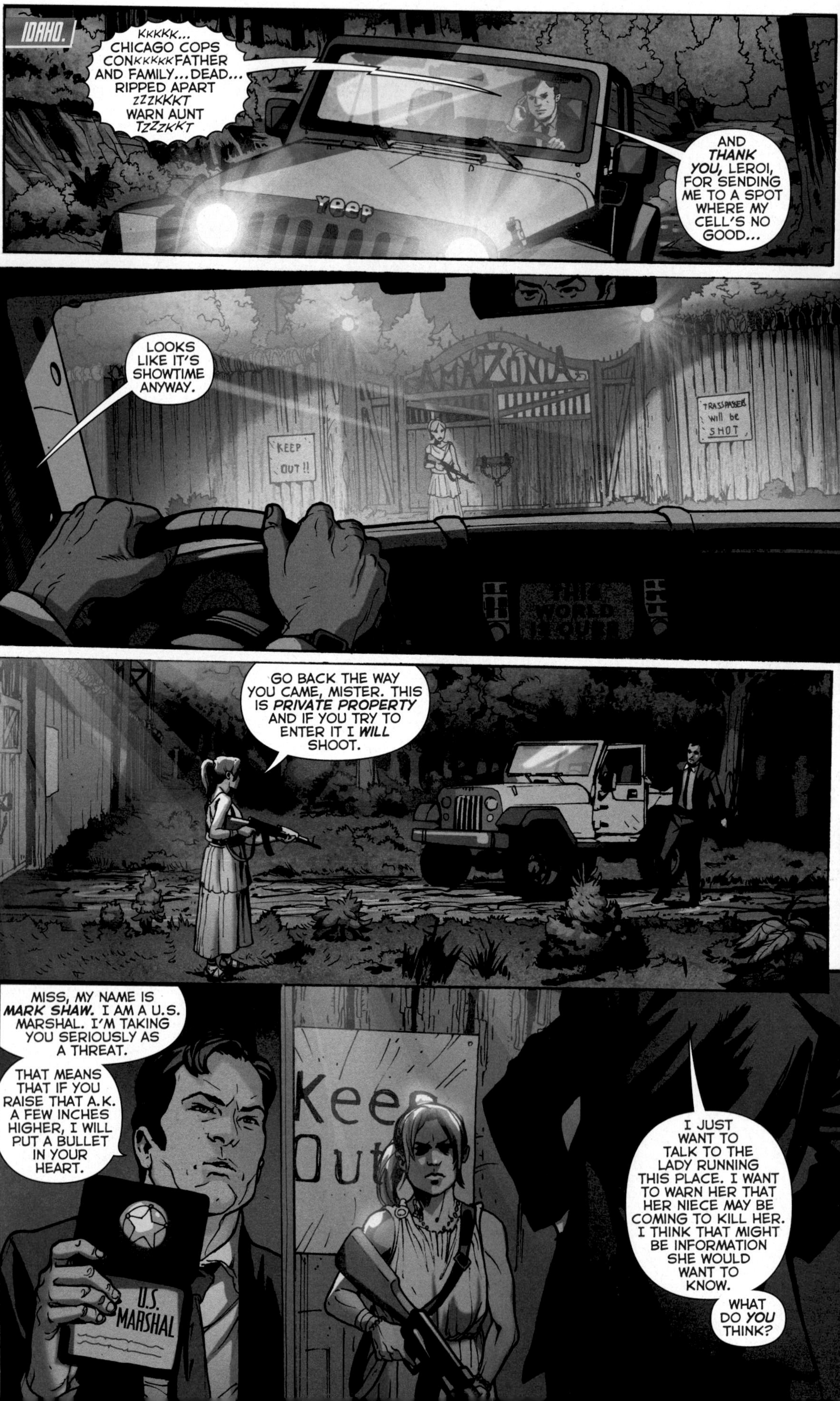
IDAHO.
KKKKK... CHICAGO COPS CONKKKKKFATHER AND FAMILY... DEAD... RIPPED APART ZZZKKKT WARN AUNT TZZZKKT
YEEP
AND *THANK YOU,* LEROI, FOR SENDING ME TO A SPOT WHERE MY CELL'S NO GOOD...
LOOKS LIKE IT'S SHOWTIME ANYWAY.
AMAZONIA
KEEP OUT!!
TRASSPASSERS will be SHOT
GO BACK THE WAY YOU CAME, MISTER. THIS IS *PRIVATE PROPERTY* AND IF YOU TRY TO ENTER IT I *WILL* SHOOT.
MISS, MY NAME IS *MARK SHAW.* I AM A U.S. MARSHAL. I'M TAKING YOU SERIOUSLY AS A THREAT.
THAT MEANS THAT IF YOU RAISE THAT A.K. A FEW INCHES HIGHER, I WILL PUT A BULLET IN YOUR HEART.
U.S. MARSHAL
I JUST WANT TO TALK TO THE LADY RUNNING THIS PLACE. I WANT TO WARN HER THAT HER NIECE MAY BE COMING TO KILL HER. I THINK THAT MIGHT BE INFORMATION SHE WOULD WANT TO KNOW.
WHAT DO *YOU* THINK?

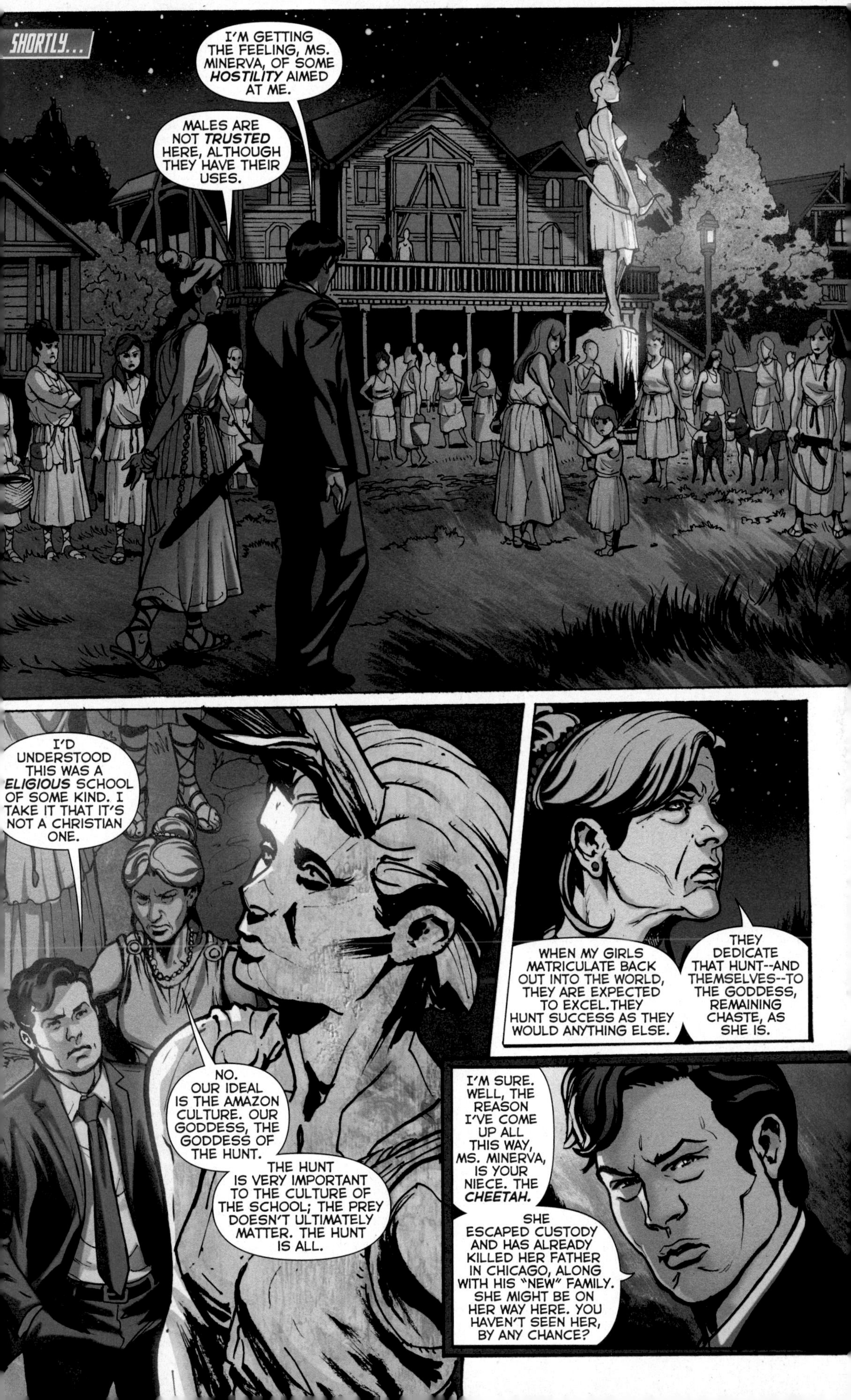
SHORTLY...
I'M GETTING THE FEELING, MS. MINERVA, OF SOME HOSTILITY AIMED AT ME.
MALES ARE NOT TRUSTED HERE, ALTHOUGH THEY HAVE THEIR USES.
I'D UNDERSTOOD THIS WAS A ELIGIOUS SCHOOL OF SOME KIND. I TAKE IT THAT IT'S NOT A CHRISTIAN ONE.
NO. OUR IDEAL IS THE AMAZON CULTURE. OUR GODDESS, THE GODDESS OF THE HUNT.
THE HUNT IS VERY IMPORTANT TO THE CULTURE OF THE SCHOOL; THE PREY DOESN'T ULTIMATELY MATTER. THE HUNT IS ALL.
WHEN MY GIRLS MATRICULATE BACK OUT INTO THE WORLD, THEY ARE EXPECTED TO EXCEL.THEY HUNT SUCCESS AS THEY WOULD ANYTHING ELSE.
THEY DEDICATE THAT HUNT--AND THEMSELVES--TO THE GODDESS, REMAINING CHASTE, AS SHE IS.
I'M SURE. WELL, THE REASON I'VE COME UP ALL THIS WAY, MS. MINERVA, IS YOUR NIECE. THE CHEETAH.
SHE ESCAPED CUSTODY AND HAS ALREADY KILLED HER FATHER IN CHICAGO, ALONG WITH HIS "NEW" FAMILY. SHE MIGHT BE ON HER WAY HERE. YOU HAVEN'T SEEN HER, BY ANY CHANCE?

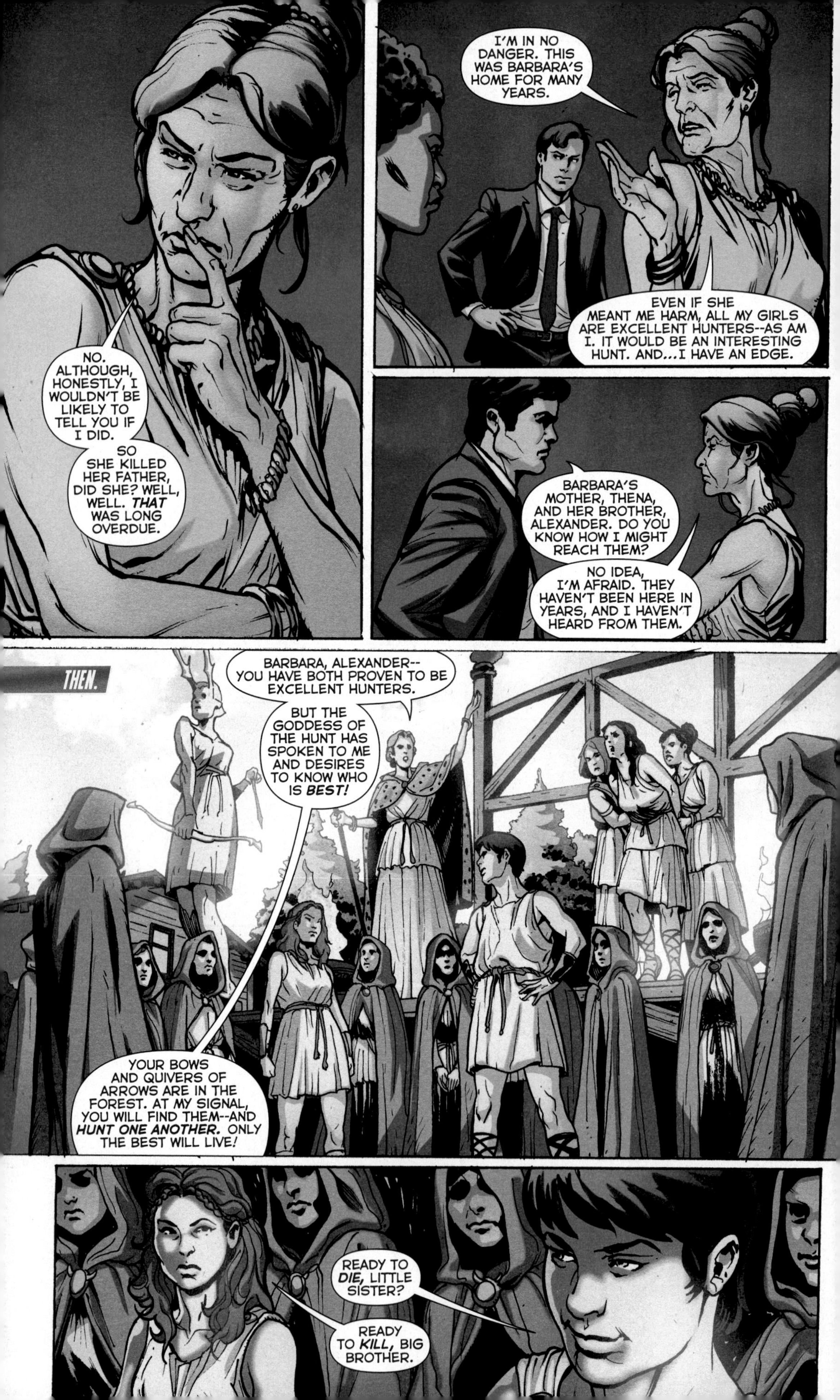

NO. ALTHOUGH, HONESTLY, I WOULDN'T BE LIKELY TO TELL YOU IF I DID.
SO SHE KILLED HER FATHER, DID SHE? WELL, WELL. *THAT* WAS LONG OVERDUE.
I'M IN NO DANGER. THIS WAS BARBARA'S HOME FOR MANY YEARS.
EVEN IF SHE MEANT ME HARM, ALL MY GIRLS ARE EXCELLENT HUNTERS--AS AM I. IT WOULD BE AN INTERESTING HUNT. AND...I HAVE AN EDGE.
BARBARA'S MOTHER, THENA, AND HER BROTHER, ALEXANDER. DO YOU KNOW HOW I MIGHT REACH THEM?
NO IDEA, I'M AFRAID. THEY HAVEN'T BEEN HERE IN YEARS, AND I HAVEN'T HEARD FROM THEM.
THEN.
BARBARA, ALEXANDER-- YOU HAVE BOTH PROVEN TO BE EXCELLENT HUNTERS.
BUT THE GODDESS OF THE HUNT HAS SPOKEN TO ME AND DESIRES TO KNOW WHO IS *BEST!*
YOUR BOWS AND QUIVERS OF ARROWS ARE IN THE FOREST. AT MY SIGNAL, YOU WILL FIND THEM--AND *HUNT ONE ANOTHER.* ONLY THE BEST WILL LIVE!
READY TO *DIE,* LITTLE SISTER?
READY TO *KILL,* BIG BROTHER.

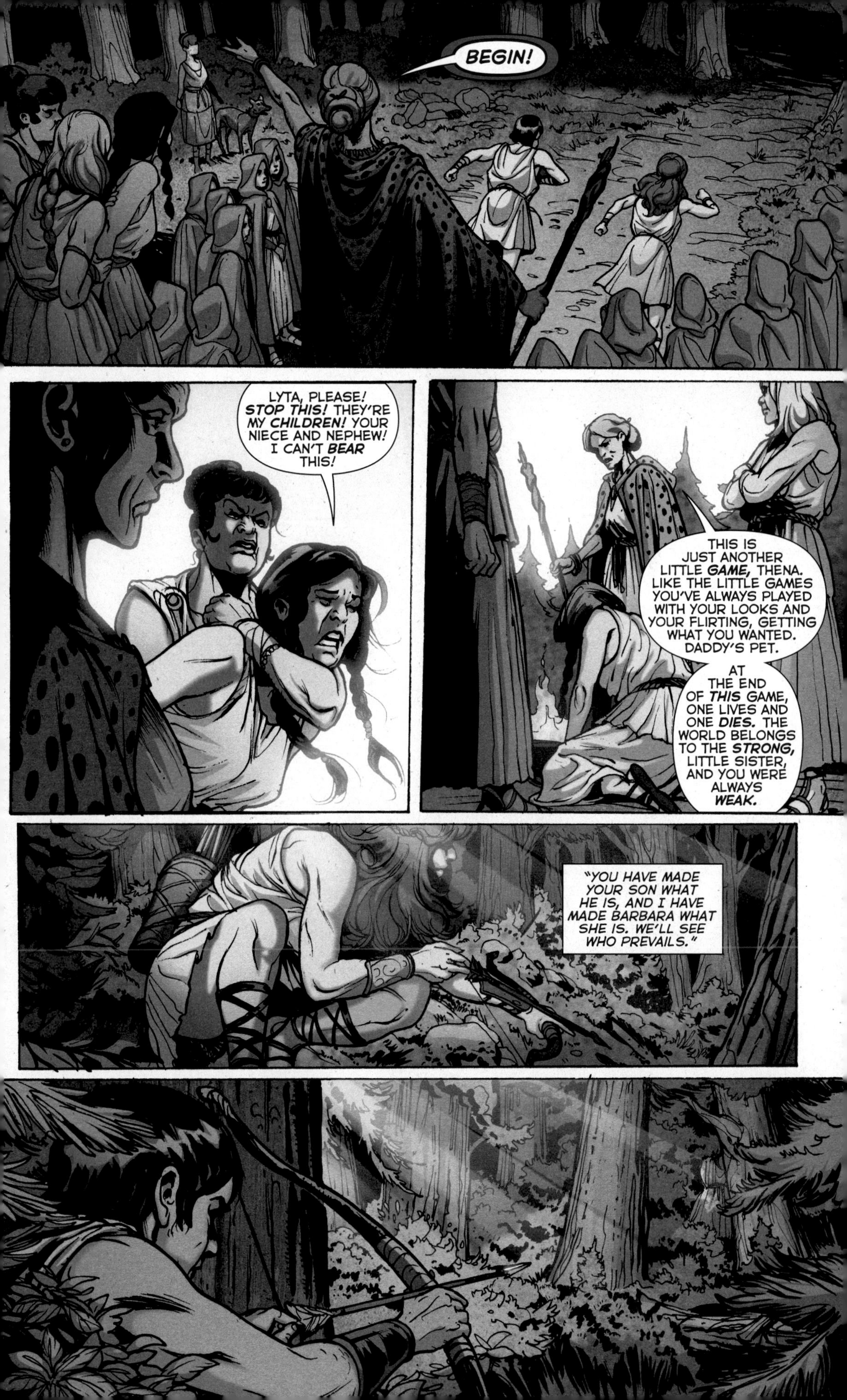
BEGIN!
LYTA, PLEASE! STOP THIS! THEY'RE MY CHILDREN! YOUR NIECE AND NEPHEW! I CAN'T BEAR THIS!
THIS IS JUST ANOTHER LITTLE GAME, THENA. LIKE THE LITTLE GAMES YOU'VE ALWAYS PLAYED WITH YOUR LOOKS AND YOUR FLIRTING, GETTING WHAT YOU WANTED. DADDY'S PET.
AT THE END OF THIS GAME, ONE LIVES AND ONE DIES. THE WORLD BELONGS TO THE STRONG, LITTLE SISTER, AND YOU WERE ALWAYS WEAK.
"YOU HAVE MADE YOUR SON WHAT HE IS, AND I HAVE MADE BARBARA WHAT SHE IS. WE'LL SEE WHO PREVAILS."

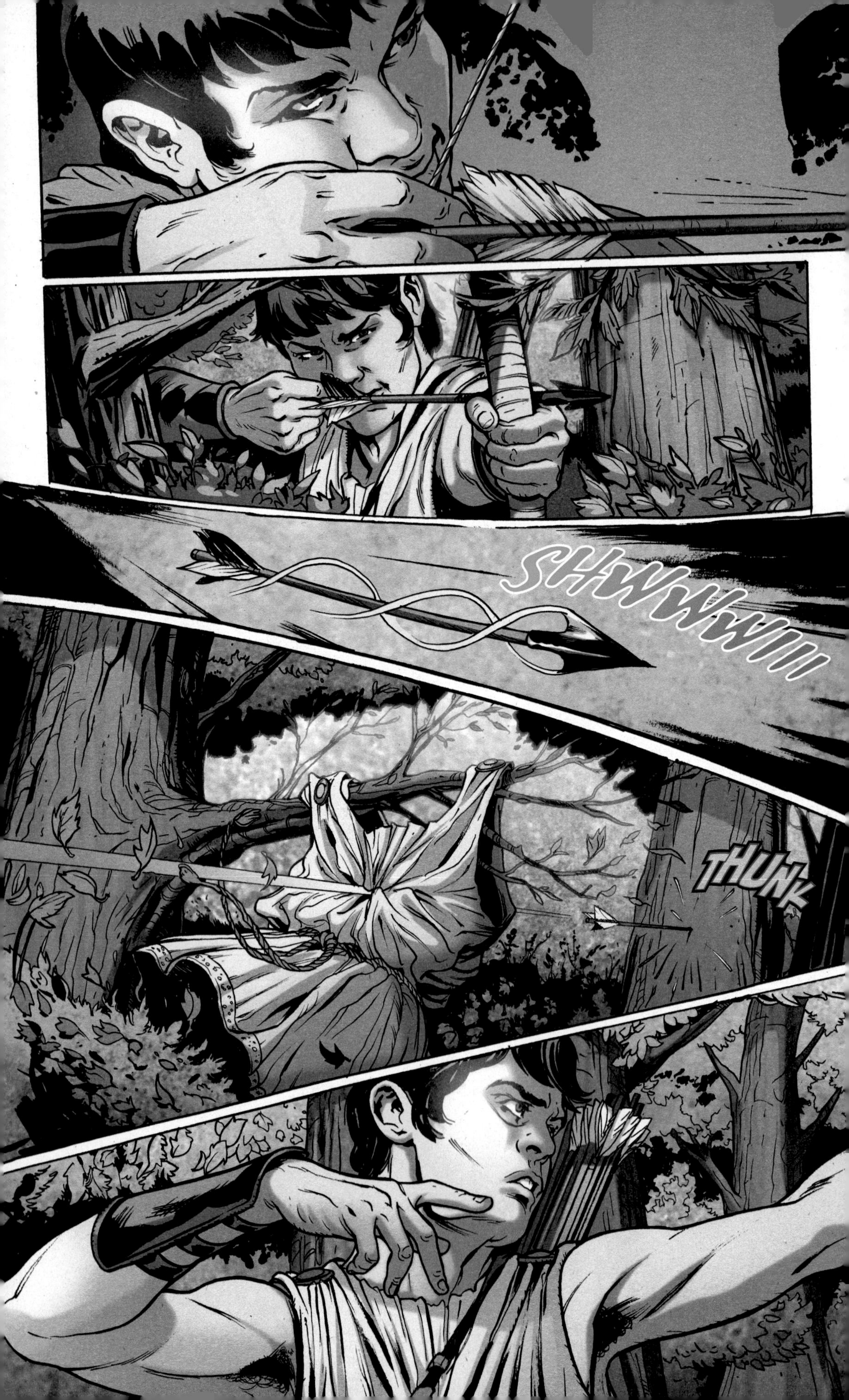
SHWWWIIII
THUNK

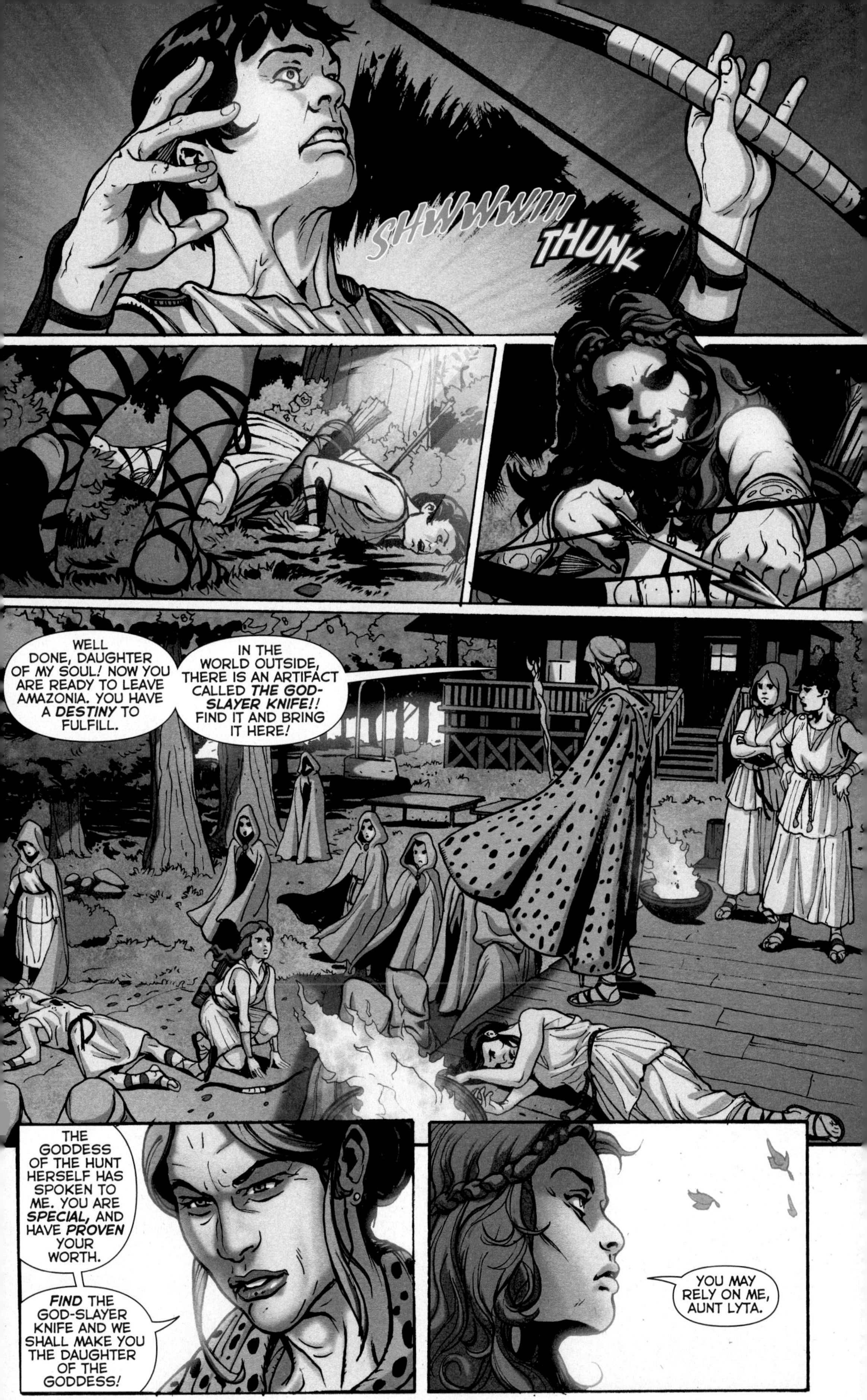
SHWWWIII
THUNK
WELL DONE, DAUGHTER OF MY SOUL! NOW YOU ARE READY TO LEAVE AMAZONIA. YOU HAVE A DESTINY TO FULFILL.
IN THE WORLD OUTSIDE, THERE IS AN ARTIFACT CALLED THE GOD-SLAYER KNIFE!! FIND IT AND BRING IT HERE!
THE GODDESS OF THE HUNT HERSELF HAS SPOKEN TO ME. YOU ARE SPECIAL, AND HAVE PROVEN YOUR WORTH.
FIND THE GOD-SLAYER KNIFE AND WE SHALL MAKE YOU THE DAUGHTER OF THE GODDESS!
YOU MAY RELY ON ME, AUNT LYTA.

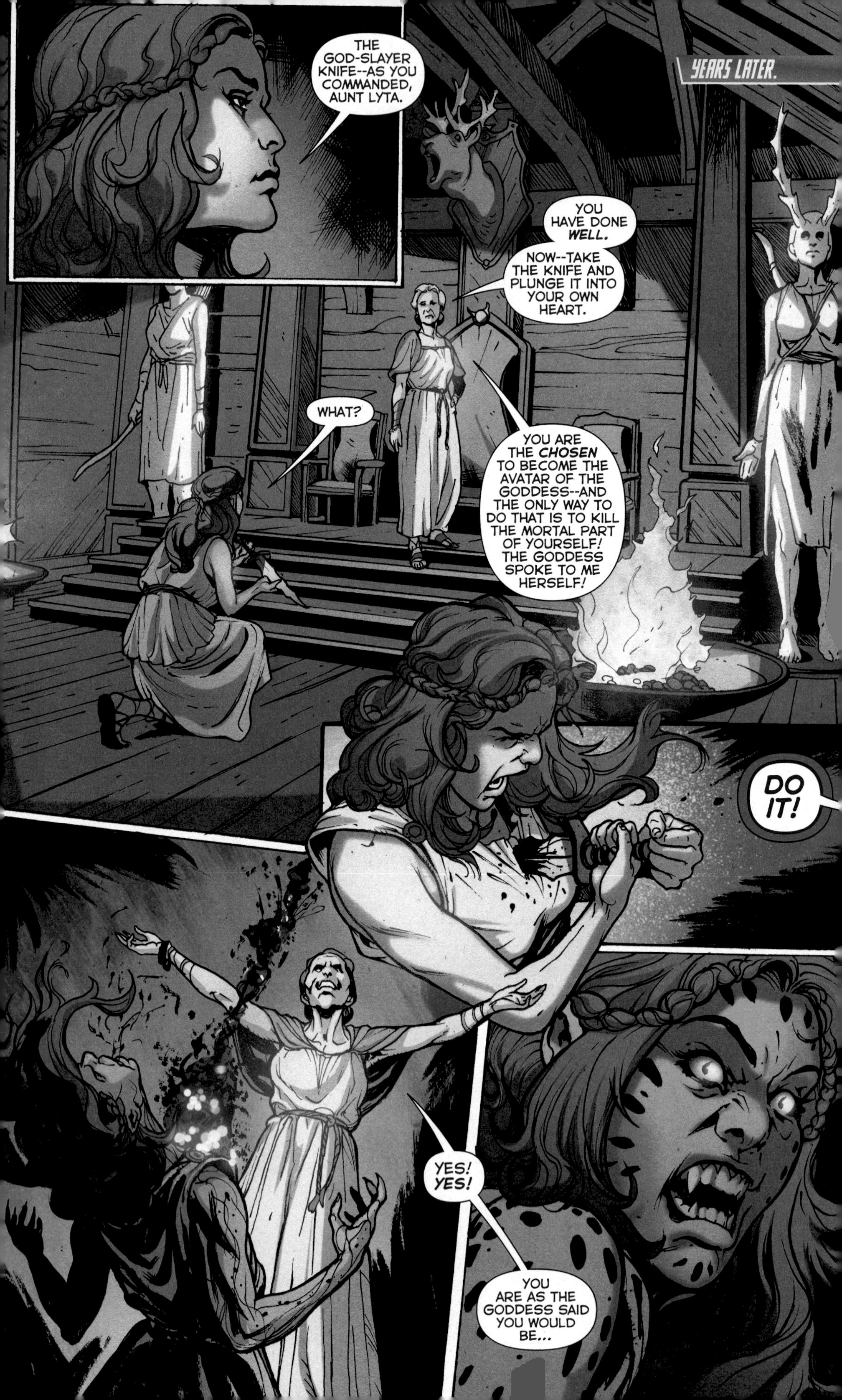
THE GOD-SLAYER KNIFE--AS YOU COMMANDED, AUNT LYTA.
YEARS LATER.
YOU HAVE DONE WELL.
NOW--TAKE THE KNIFE AND PLUNGE IT INTO YOUR OWN HEART.
WHAT?
YOU ARE THE CHOSEN TO BECOME THE AVATAR OF THE GODDESS--AND THE ONLY WAY TO DO THAT IS TO KILL THE MORTAL PART OF YOURSELF! THE GODDESS SPOKE TO ME HERSELF!
DO IT!
YES! YES!
YOU ARE AS THE GODDESS SAID YOU WOULD BE...

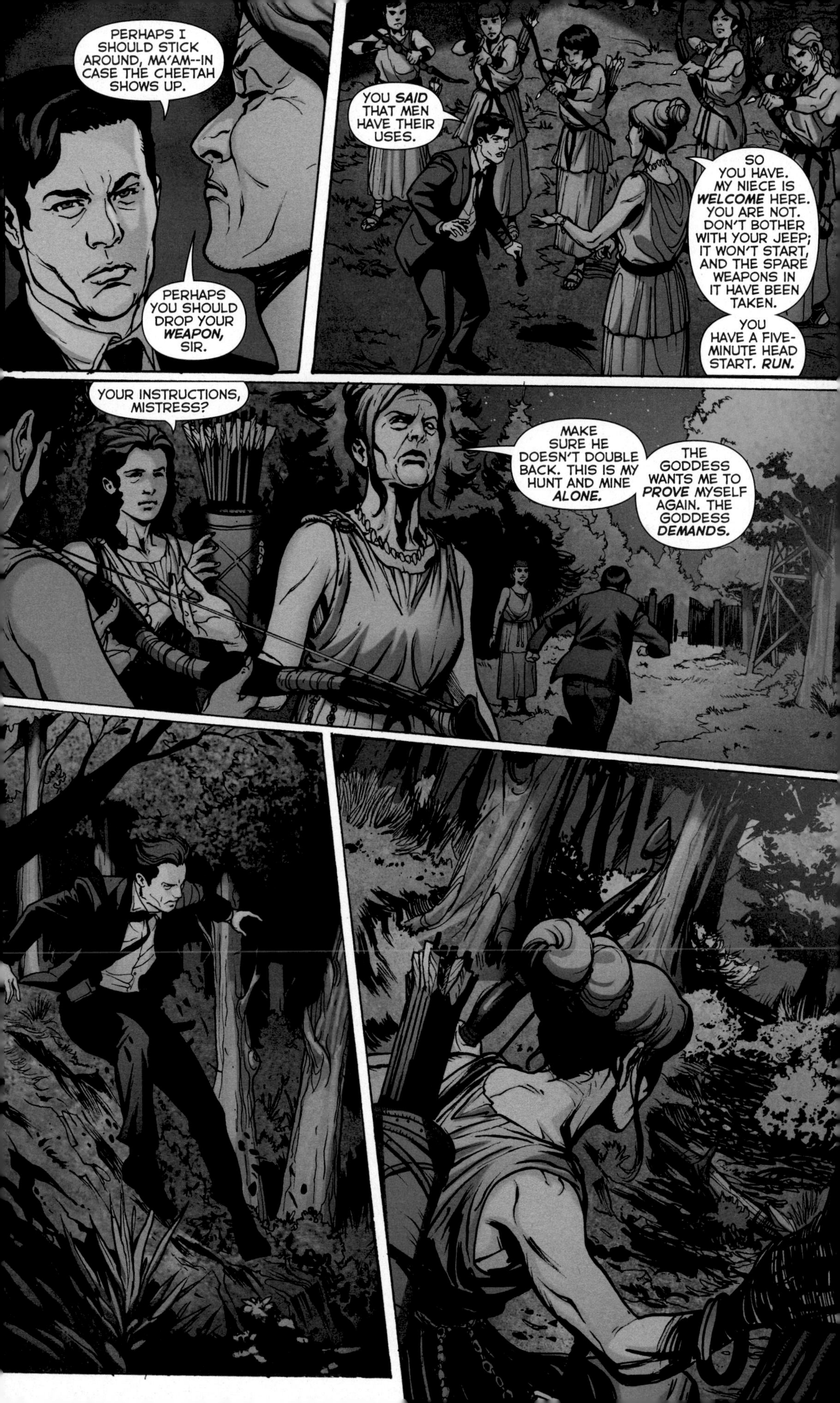
PERHAPS I SHOULD STICK AROUND, MA'AM--IN CASE THE CHEETAH SHOWS UP.
PERHAPS YOU SHOULD DROP YOUR WEAPON, SIR.
YOU SAID THAT MEN HAVE THEIR USES.
SO YOU HAVE. MY NIECE IS WELCOME HERE. YOU ARE NOT. DON'T BOTHER WITH YOUR JEEP; IT WON'T START, AND THE SPARE WEAPONS IN IT HAVE BEEN TAKEN.
YOU HAVE A FIVE-MINUTE HEAD START. RUN.
YOUR INSTRUCTIONS, MISTRESS?
MAKE SURE HE DOESN'T DOUBLE BACK. THIS IS MY HUNT AND MINE ALONE.
THE GODDESS WANTS ME TO PROVE MYSELF AGAIN. THE GODDESS DEMANDS.

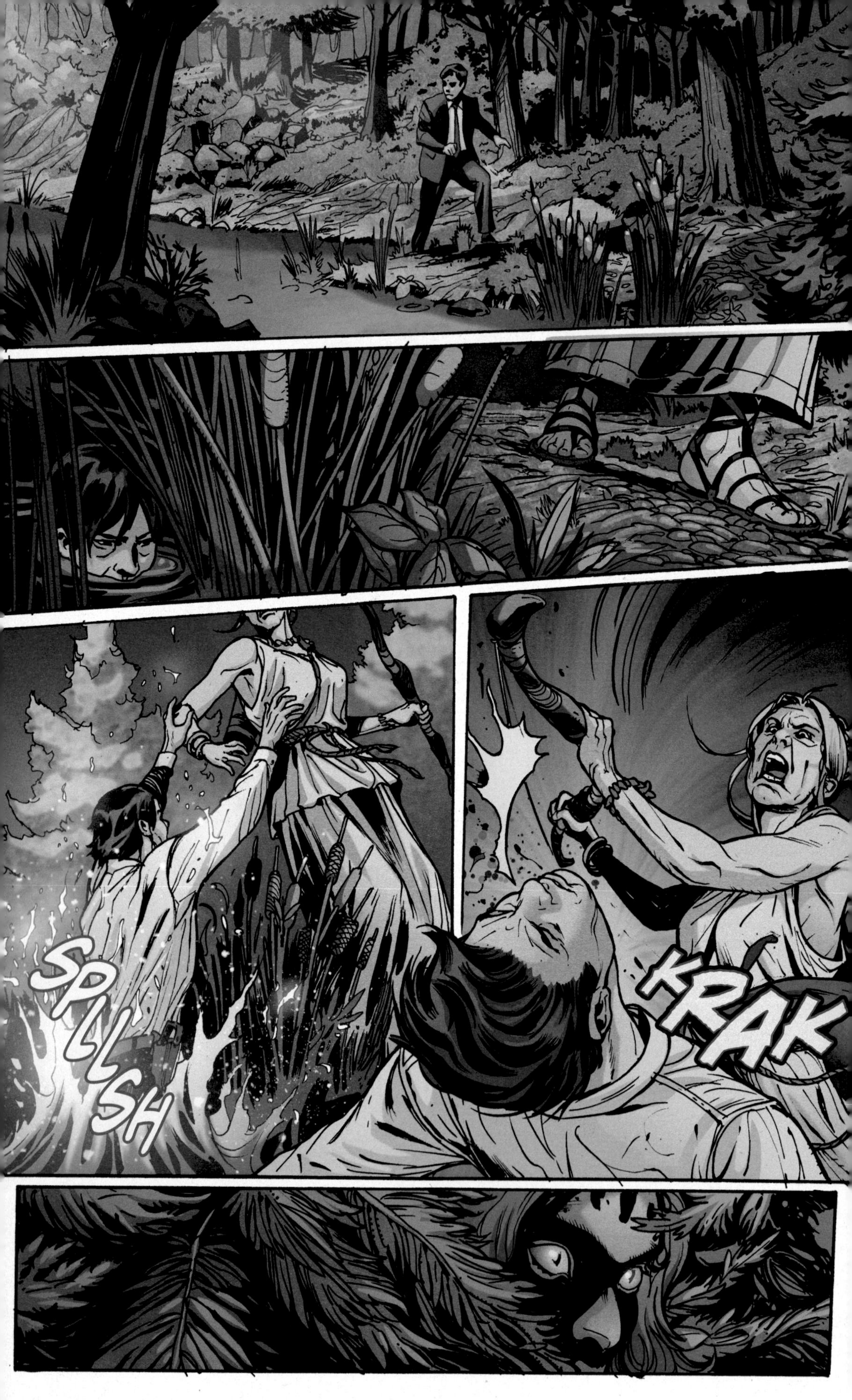

SPLLLSH
KRAK

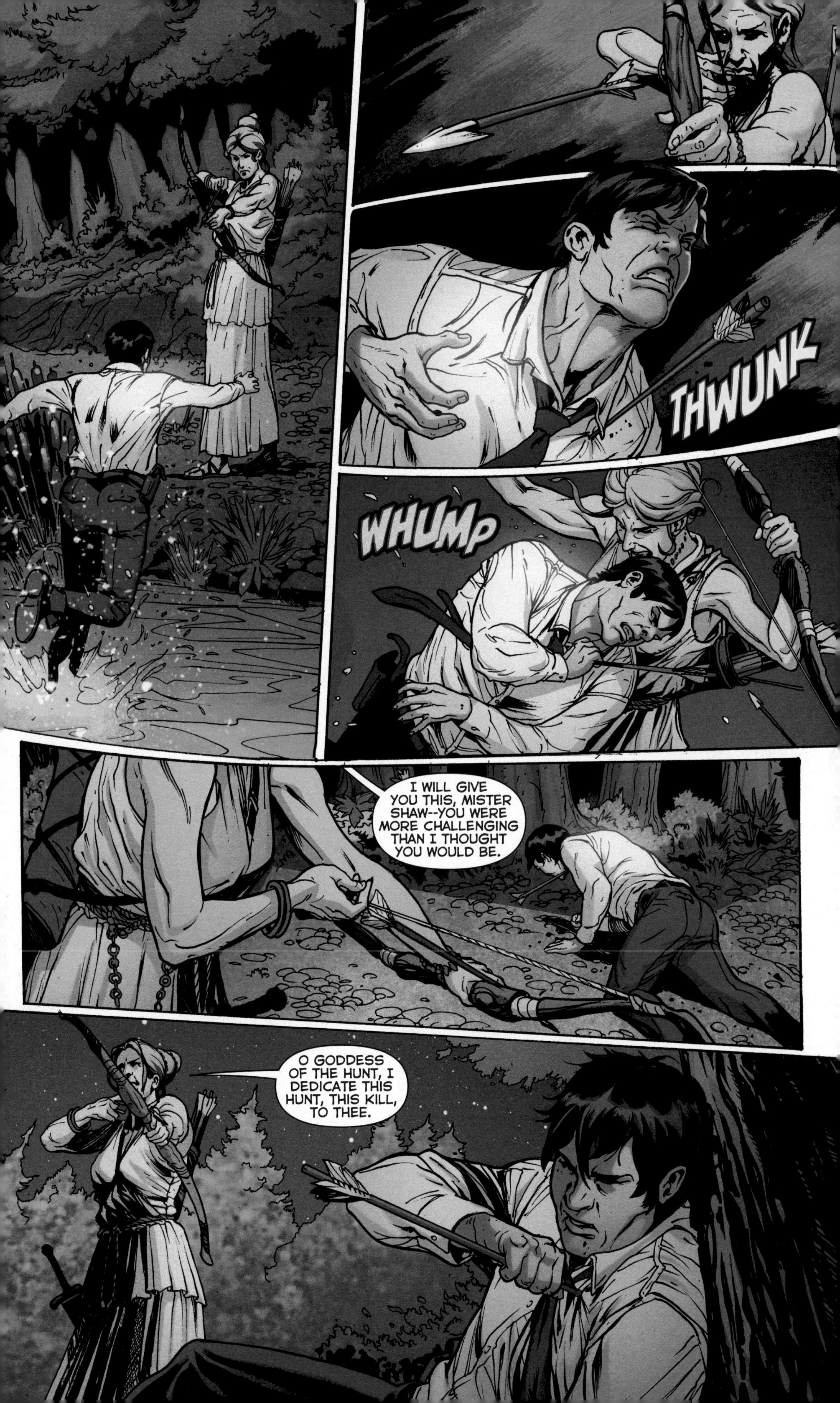
THWUNK
WHUMP
I WILL GIVE YOU THIS, MISTER SHAW--YOU WERE MORE CHALLENGING THAN I THOUGHT YOU WOULD BE.
O GODDESS OF THE HUNT, I DEDICATE THIS HUNT, THIS KILL, TO THEE.

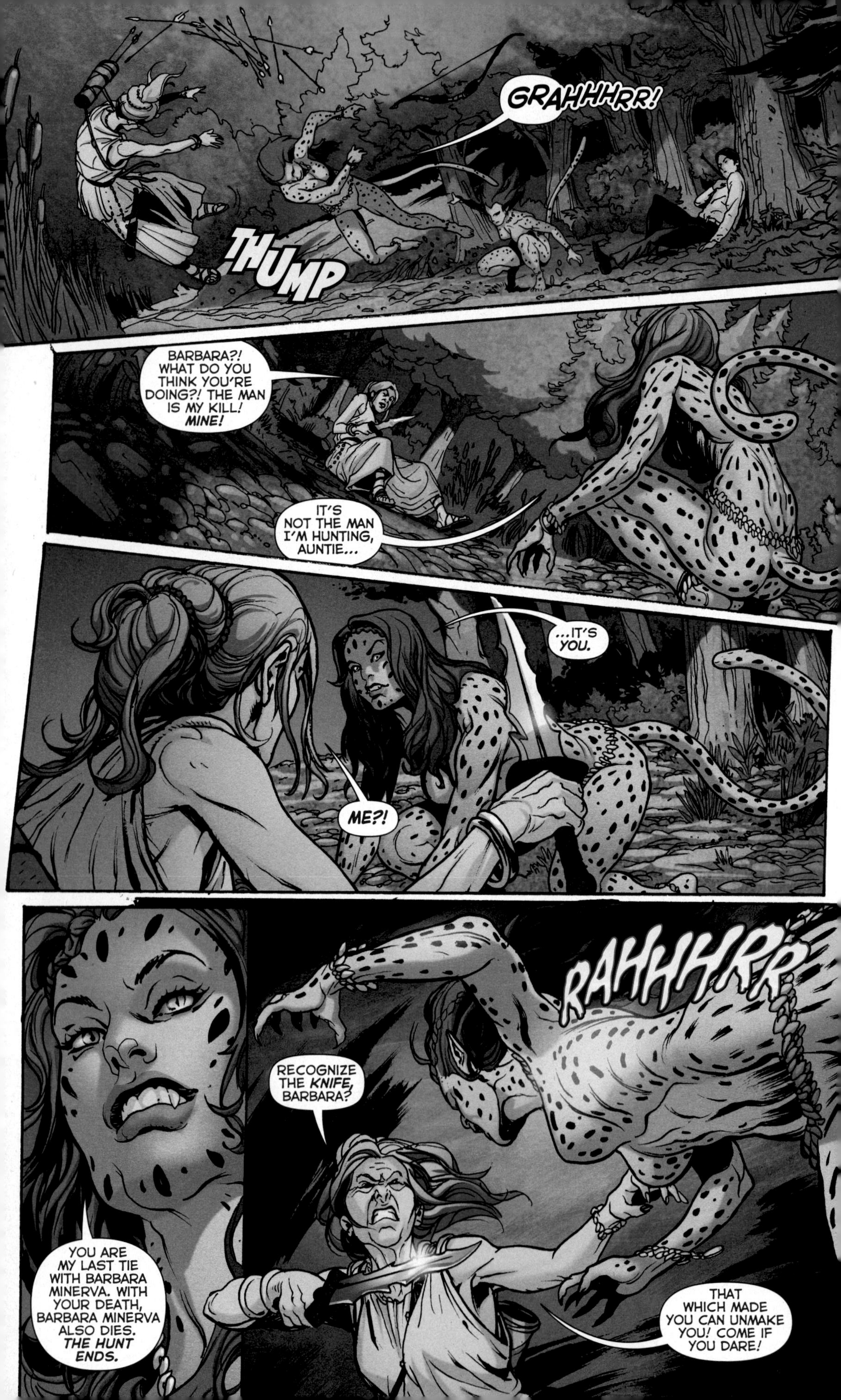
GRAHHHRR!
THUMP
BARBARA?! WHAT DO YOU THINK YOU'RE DOING?! THE MAN IS MY KILL! MINE!
IT'S NOT THE MAN I'M HUNTING, AUNTIE...
...IT'S YOU.
ME?!
RAHHHRR
RECOGNIZE THE KNIFE, BARBARA?
YOU ARE MY LAST TIE WITH BARBARA MINERVA. WITH YOUR DEATH, BARBARA MINERVA ALSO DIES. THE HUNT ENDS.
THAT WHICH MADE YOU CAN UNMAKE YOU! COME IF YOU DARE!

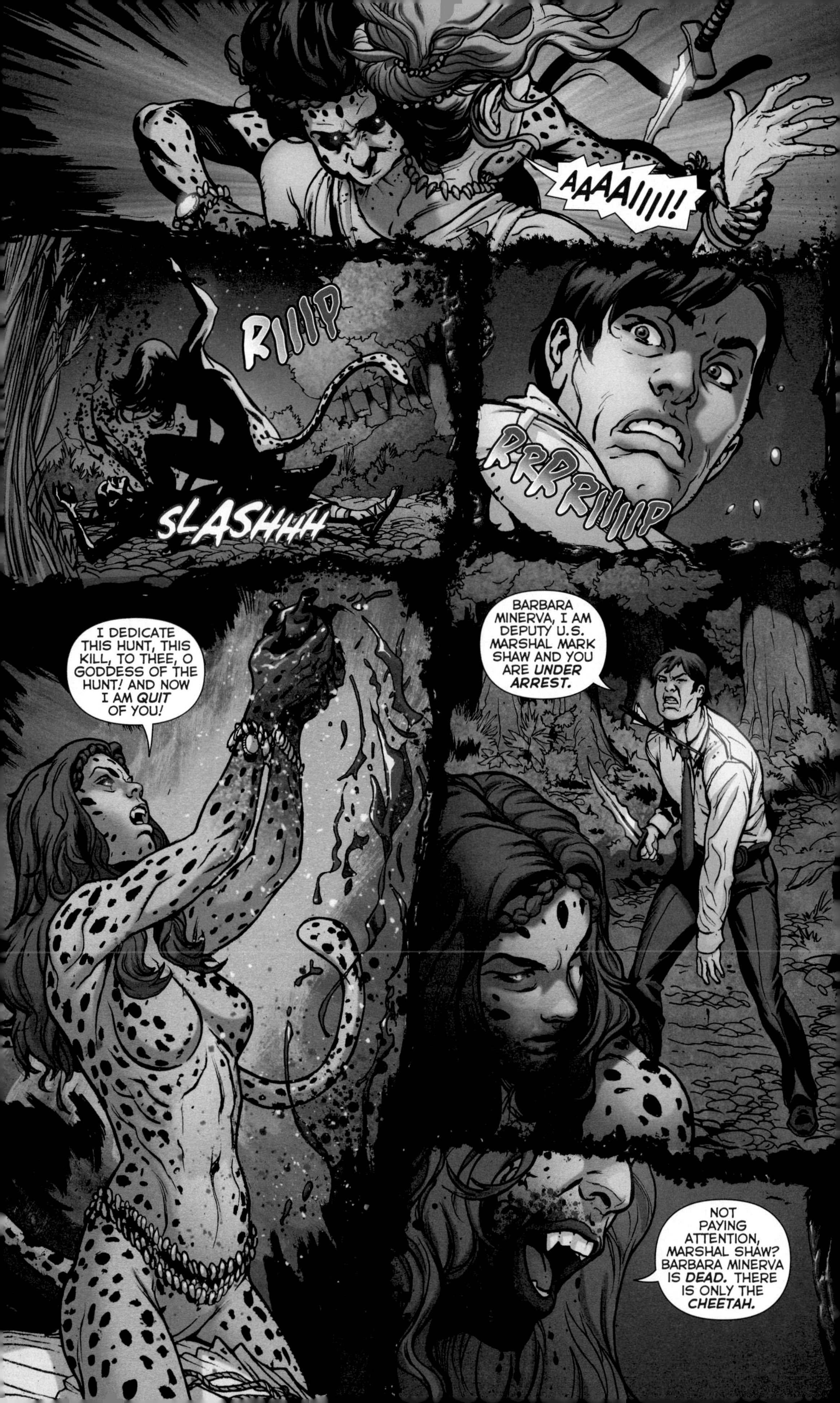
AAAAIIII!
RIIIP
SLASHHH
RRRRIIIIP
I DEDICATE THIS HUNT, THIS KILL, TO THEE, O GODDESS OF THE HUNT! AND NOW I AM *QUIT* OF YOU!
BARBARA MINERVA, I AM DEPUTY U.S. MARSHAL MARK SHAW AND YOU ARE *UNDER ARREST.*
NOT PAYING ATTENTION, MARSHAL SHAW? BARBARA MINERVA IS *DEAD.* THERE IS ONLY THE *CHEETAH.*

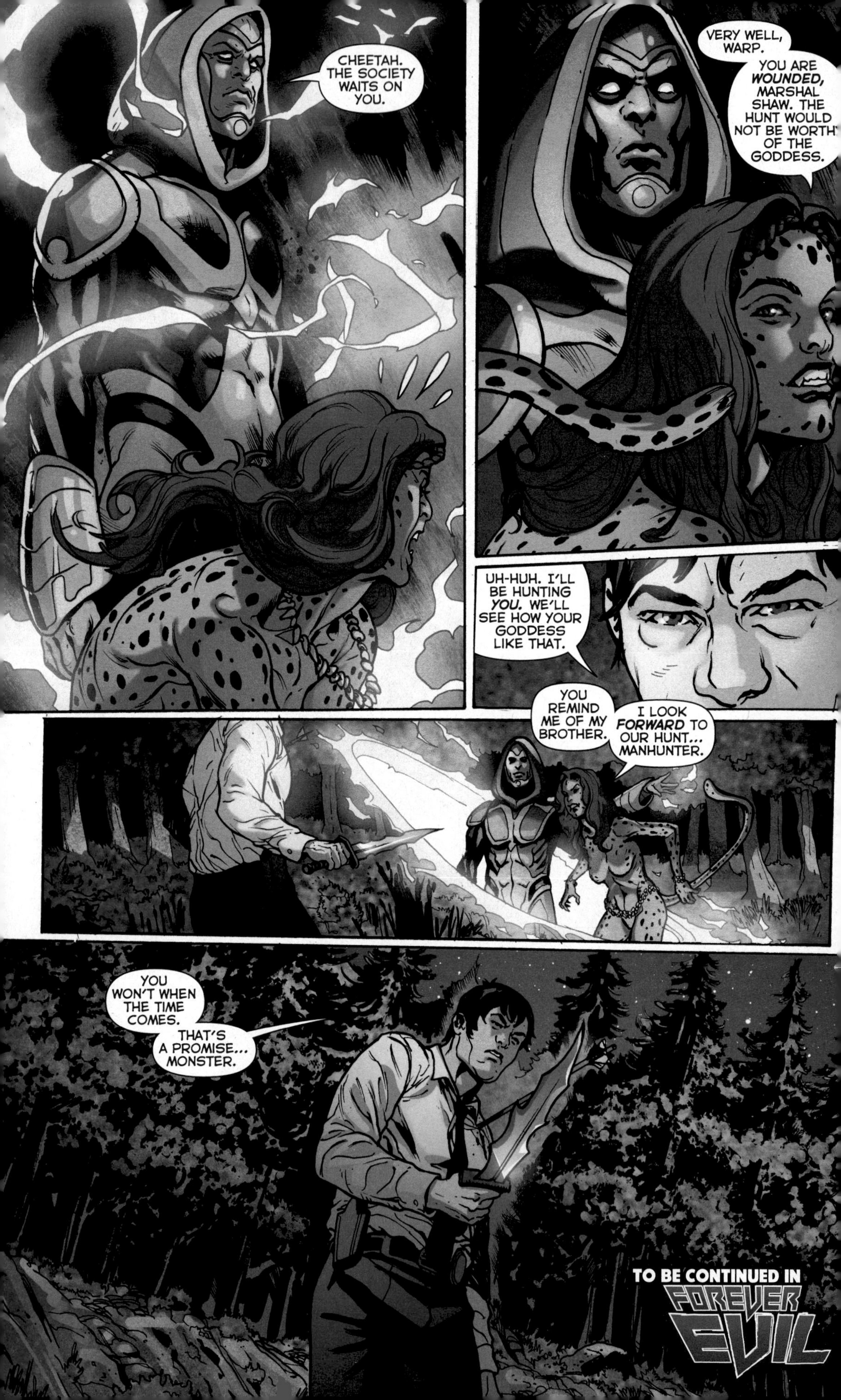
CHEETAH. THE SOCIETY WAITS ON YOU.
VERY WELL, WARP.
YOU ARE *WOUNDED,* MARSHAL SHAW. THE HUNT WOULD NOT BE WORTHY OF THE GODDESS.
UH-HUH. I'LL BE HUNTING *YOU.* WE'LL SEE HOW YOUR GODDESS LIKE THAT.
YOU REMIND ME OF MY BROTHER.
I LOOK *FORWARD* TO OUR HUNT... MANHUNTER.
YOU WON'T WHEN THE TIME COMES.
THAT'S A PROMISE... MONSTER.
TO BE CONTINUED IN
FOREVER EVIL

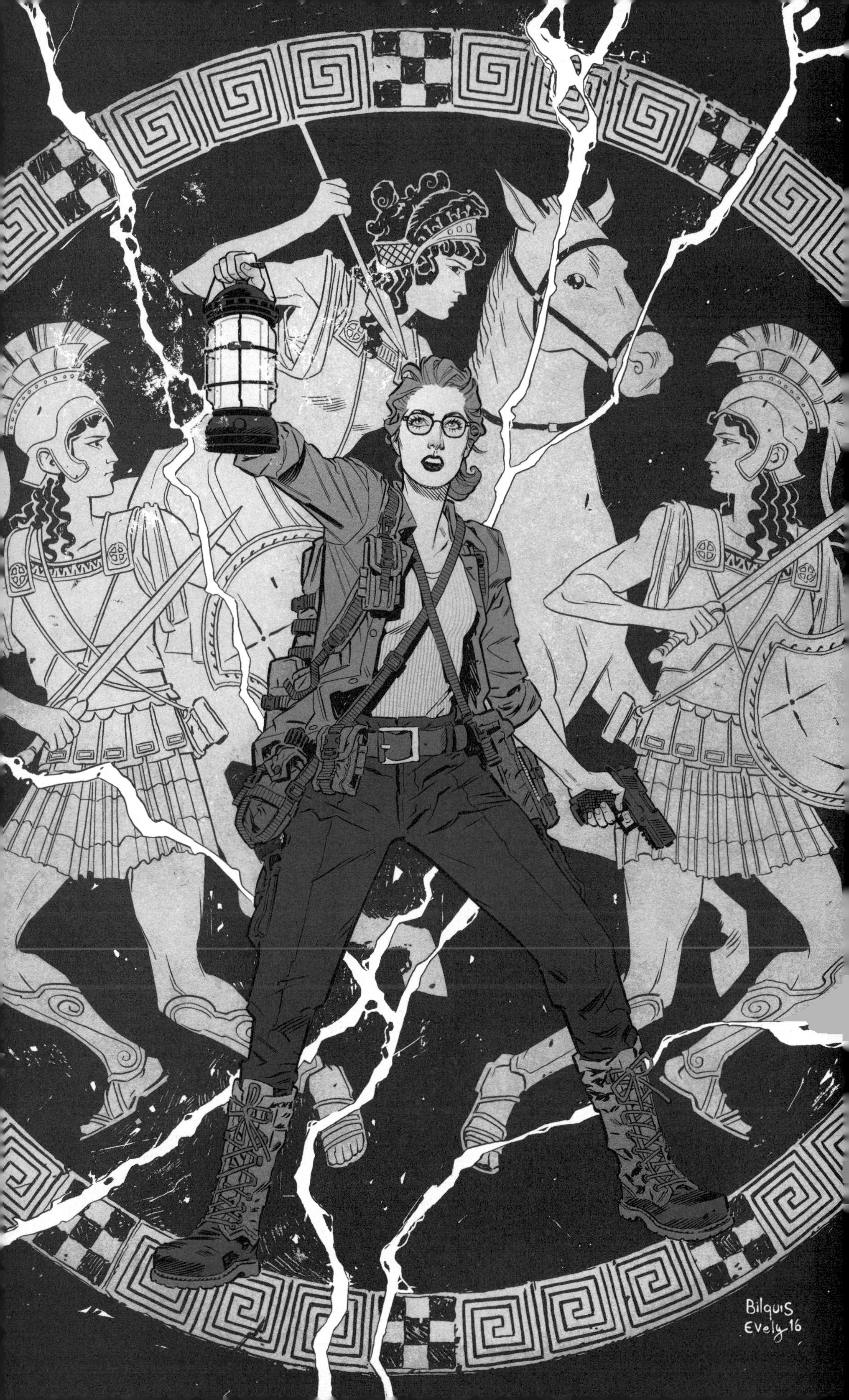
BILQUIS
EVELY 16

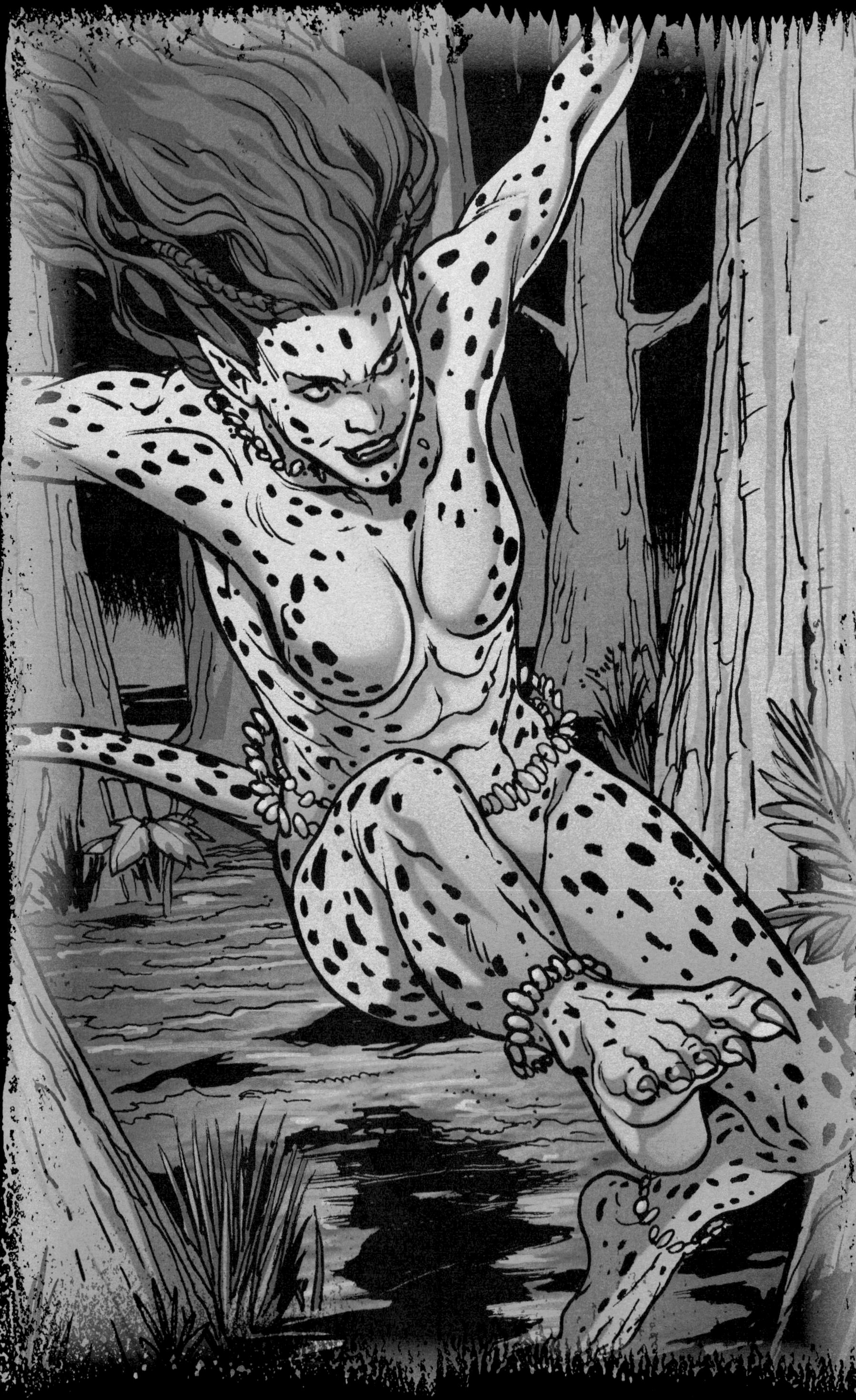

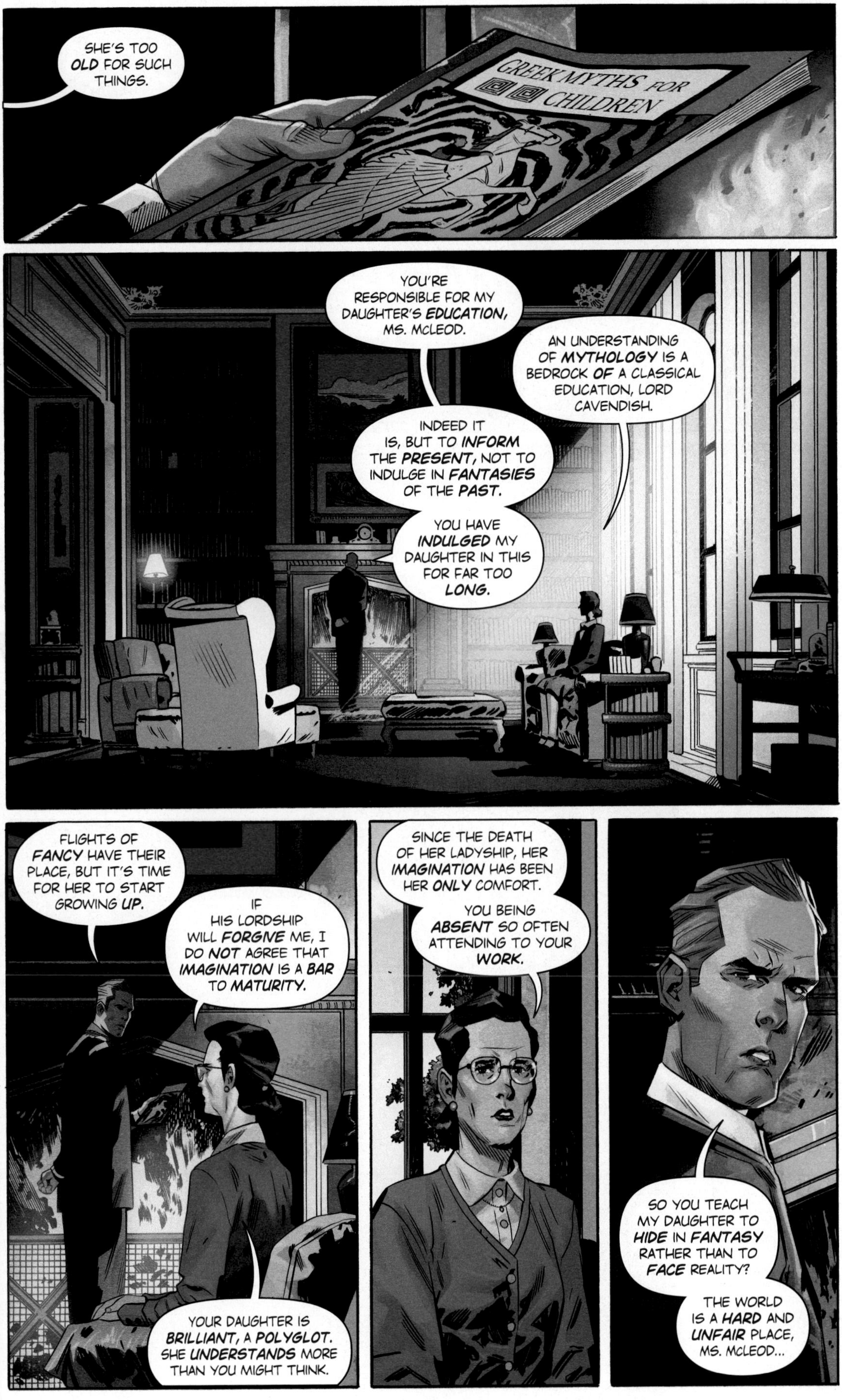
SHE'S TOO OLD FOR SUCH THINGS.
GREEK MYTHS FOR CHILDREN
YOU'RE RESPONSIBLE FOR MY DAUGHTER'S EDUCATION, MS. McLEOD.
AN UNDERSTANDING OF MYTHOLOGY IS A BEDROCK OF A CLASSICAL EDUCATION, LORD CAVENDISH.
INDEED IT IS, BUT TO INFORM THE PRESENT, NOT TO INDULGE IN FANTASIES OF THE PAST.
YOU HAVE INDULGED MY DAUGHTER IN THIS FOR FAR TOO LONG.
FLIGHTS OF FANCY HAVE THEIR PLACE, BUT IT'S TIME FOR HER TO START GROWING UP.
IF HIS LORDSHIP WILL FORGIVE ME, I DO NOT AGREE THAT IMAGINATION IS A BAR TO MATURITY.
YOUR DAUGHTER IS BRILLIANT, A POLYGLOT. SHE UNDERSTANDS MORE THAN YOU MIGHT THINK.
SINCE THE DEATH OF HER LADYSHIP, HER IMAGINATION HAS BEEN HER ONLY COMFORT.
YOU BEING ABSENT SO OFTEN ATTENDING TO YOUR WORK.
SO YOU TEACH MY DAUGHTER TO HIDE IN FANTASY RATHER THAN TO FACE REALITY?
THE WORLD IS A HARD AND UNFAIR PLACE, MS. McLEOD...

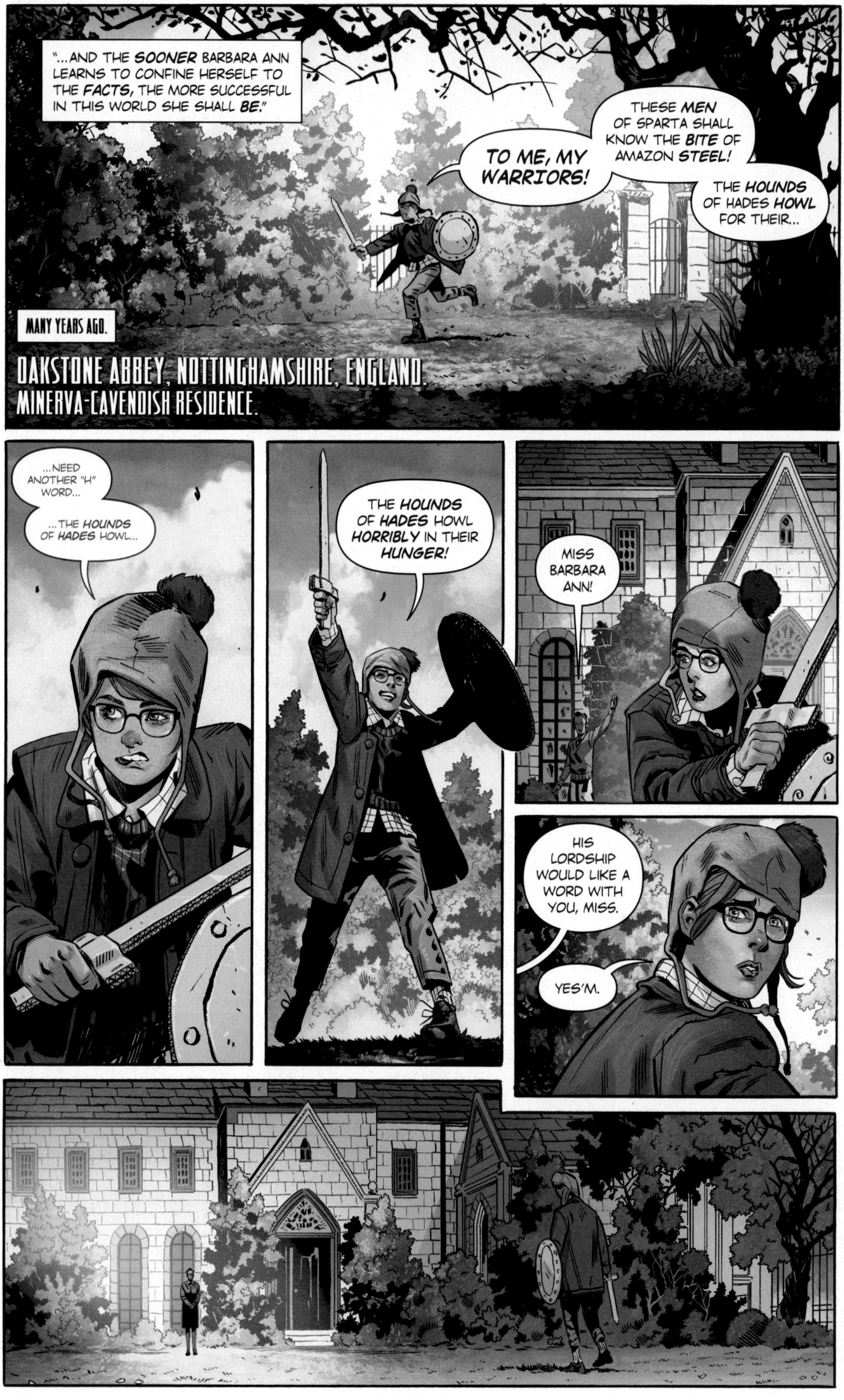

"...AND THE SOONER BARBARA ANN LEARNS TO CONFINE HERSELF TO THE FACTS, THE MORE SUCCESSFUL IN THIS WORLD SHE SHALL BE."
TO ME, MY WARRIORS!
THESE MEN OF SPARTA SHALL KNOW THE BITE OF AMAZON STEEL!
THE HOUNDS OF HADES HOWL FOR THEIR...
MANY YEARS AGO.
OAKSTONE ABBEY, NOTTINGHAMSHIRE, ENGLAND.
MINERVA-CAVENDISH RESIDENCE.
...NEED ANOTHER "H" WORD...
...THE HOUNDS OF HADES HOWL...
THE HOUNDS OF HADES HOWL HORRIBLY IN THEIR HUNGER!
MISS BARBARA ANN!
HIS LORDSHIP WOULD LIKE A WORD WITH YOU, MISS.
YES'M.

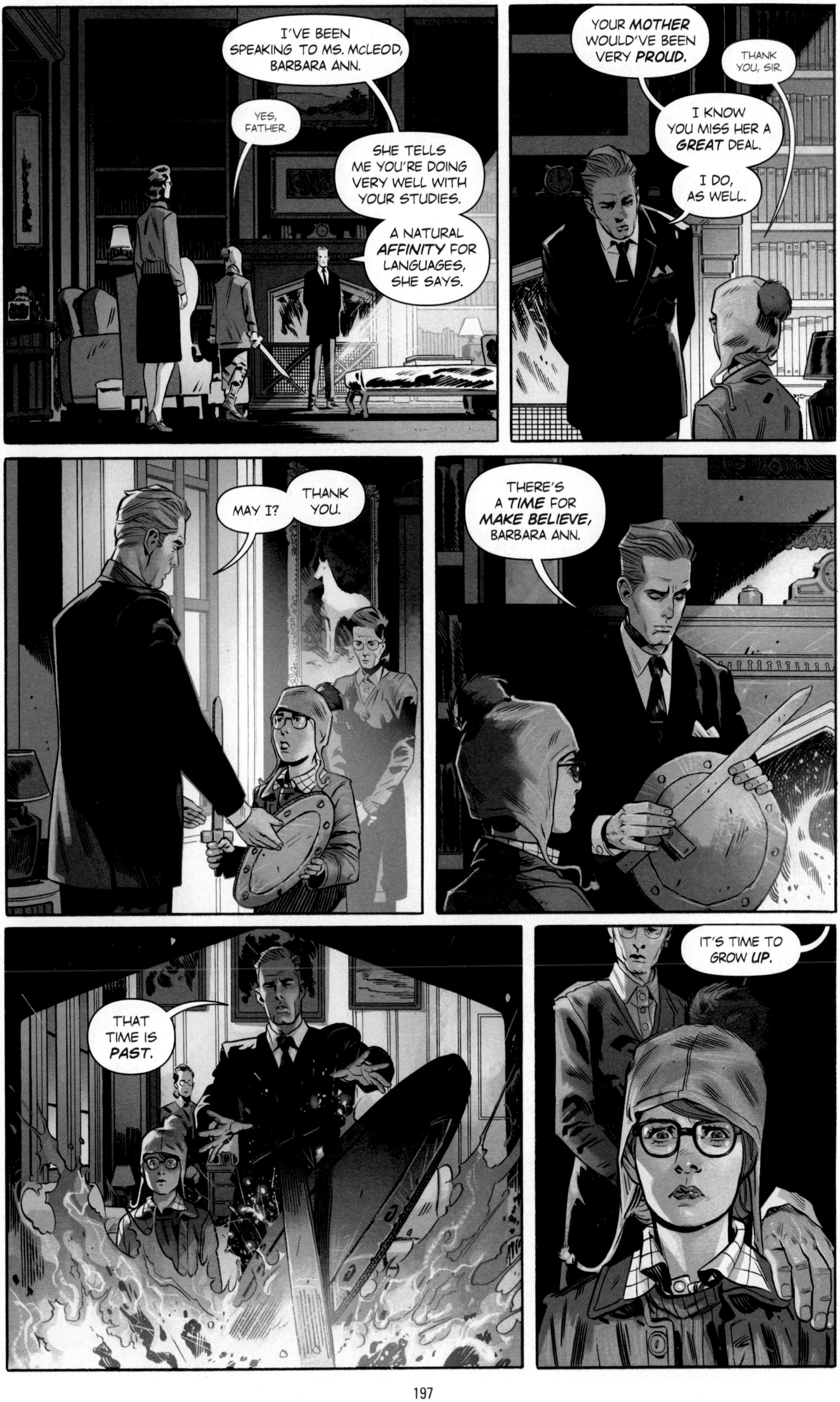
I'VE BEEN SPEAKING TO MS. McLEOD, BARBARA ANN.
YES, FATHER.
SHE TELLS ME YOU'RE DOING VERY WELL WITH YOUR STUDIES.
A NATURAL **AFFINITY** FOR LANGUAGES, SHE SAYS.
YOUR **MOTHER** WOULD'VE BEEN VERY **PROUD.**
THANK YOU, SIR.
I KNOW YOU MISS HER A **GREAT** DEAL.
I DO, AS WELL.
MAY I?
THANK YOU.
THERE'S A **TIME** FOR **MAKE BELIEVE,** BARBARA ANN.
THAT TIME IS **PAST.**
IT'S TIME TO GROW **UP.**

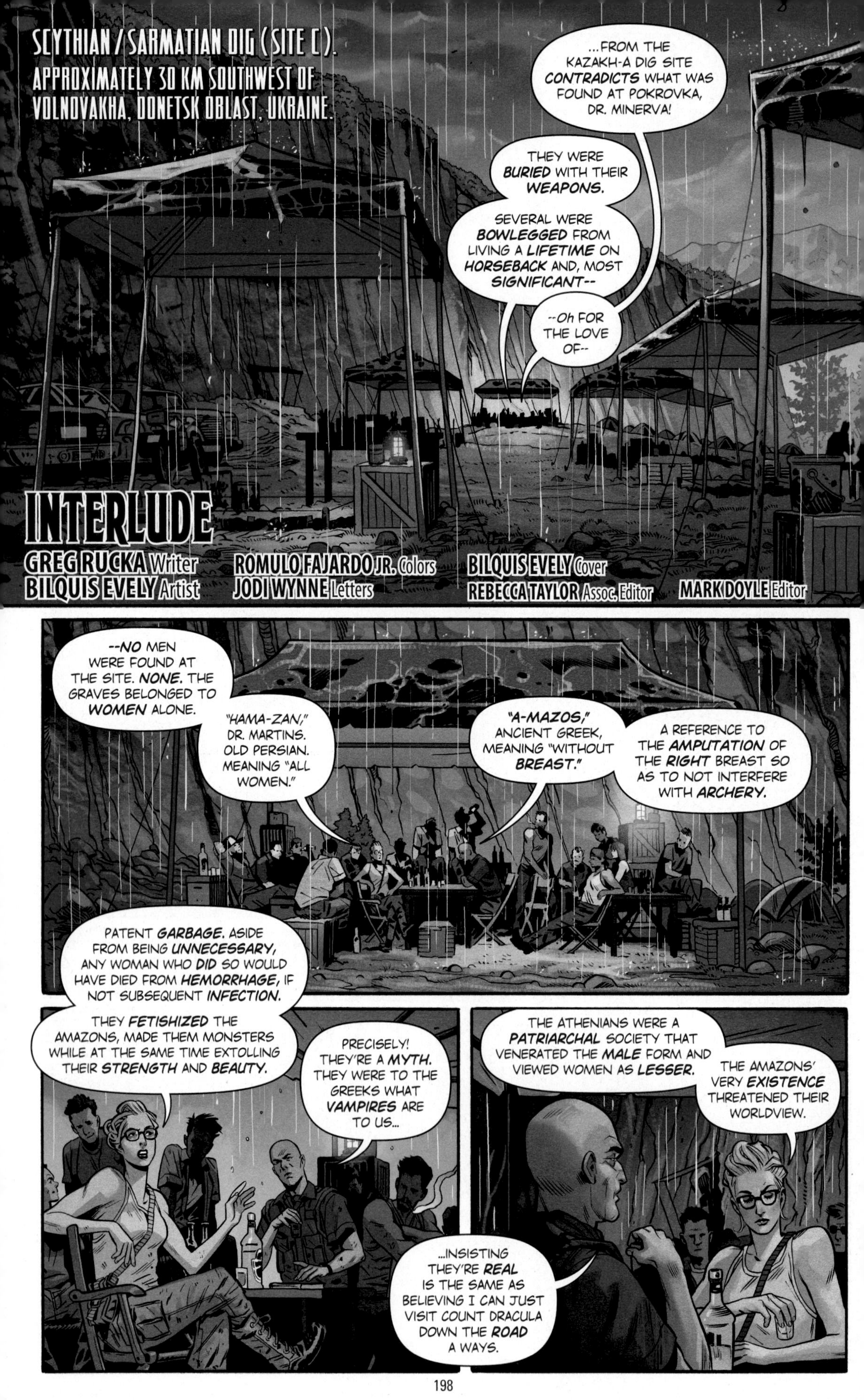
SCYTHIAN / SARMATIAN DIG (SITE C). APPROXIMATELY 30 KM SOUTHWEST OF VOLNOVAKHA, DONETSK OBLAST, UKRAINE.
...FROM THE KAZAKH-A DIG SITE CONTRADICTS WHAT WAS FOUND AT POKROVKA, DR. MINERVA!
THEY WERE BURIED WITH THEIR WEAPONS.
SEVERAL WERE BOWLEGGED FROM LIVING A LIFETIME ON HORSEBACK AND, MOST SIGNIFICANT--
--Oh FOR THE LOVE OF--
INTERLUDE
GREG RUCKA Writer
BILQUIS EVELY Artist
ROMULO FAJARDO JR. Colors
JODI WYNNE Letters
BILQUIS EVELY Cover
REBECCA TAYLOR Assoc. Editor
MARK DOYLE Editor
--NO MEN WERE FOUND AT THE SITE. NONE. THE GRAVES BELONGED TO WOMEN ALONE.
"HAMA-ZAN," DR. MARTINS. OLD PERSIAN. MEANING "ALL WOMEN."
"A-MAZOS," ANCIENT GREEK, MEANING "WITHOUT BREAST."
A REFERENCE TO THE AMPUTATION OF THE RIGHT BREAST SO AS TO NOT INTERFERE WITH ARCHERY.
PATENT GARBAGE. ASIDE FROM BEING UNNECESSARY, ANY WOMAN WHO DID SO WOULD HAVE DIED FROM HEMORRHAGE, IF NOT SUBSEQUENT INFECTION.
THEY FETISHIZED THE AMAZONS, MADE THEM MONSTERS WHILE AT THE SAME TIME EXTOLLING THEIR STRENGTH AND BEAUTY.
PRECISELY! THEY'RE A MYTH. THEY WERE TO THE GREEKS WHAT VAMPIRES ARE TO US...
THE ATHENIANS WERE A PATRIARCHAL SOCIETY THAT VENERATED THE MALE FORM AND VIEWED WOMEN AS LESSER.
THE AMAZONS' VERY EXISTENCE THREATENED THEIR WORLDVIEW.
...INSISTING THEY'RE REAL IS THE SAME AS BELIEVING I CAN JUST VISIT COUNT DRACULA DOWN THE ROAD A WAYS.

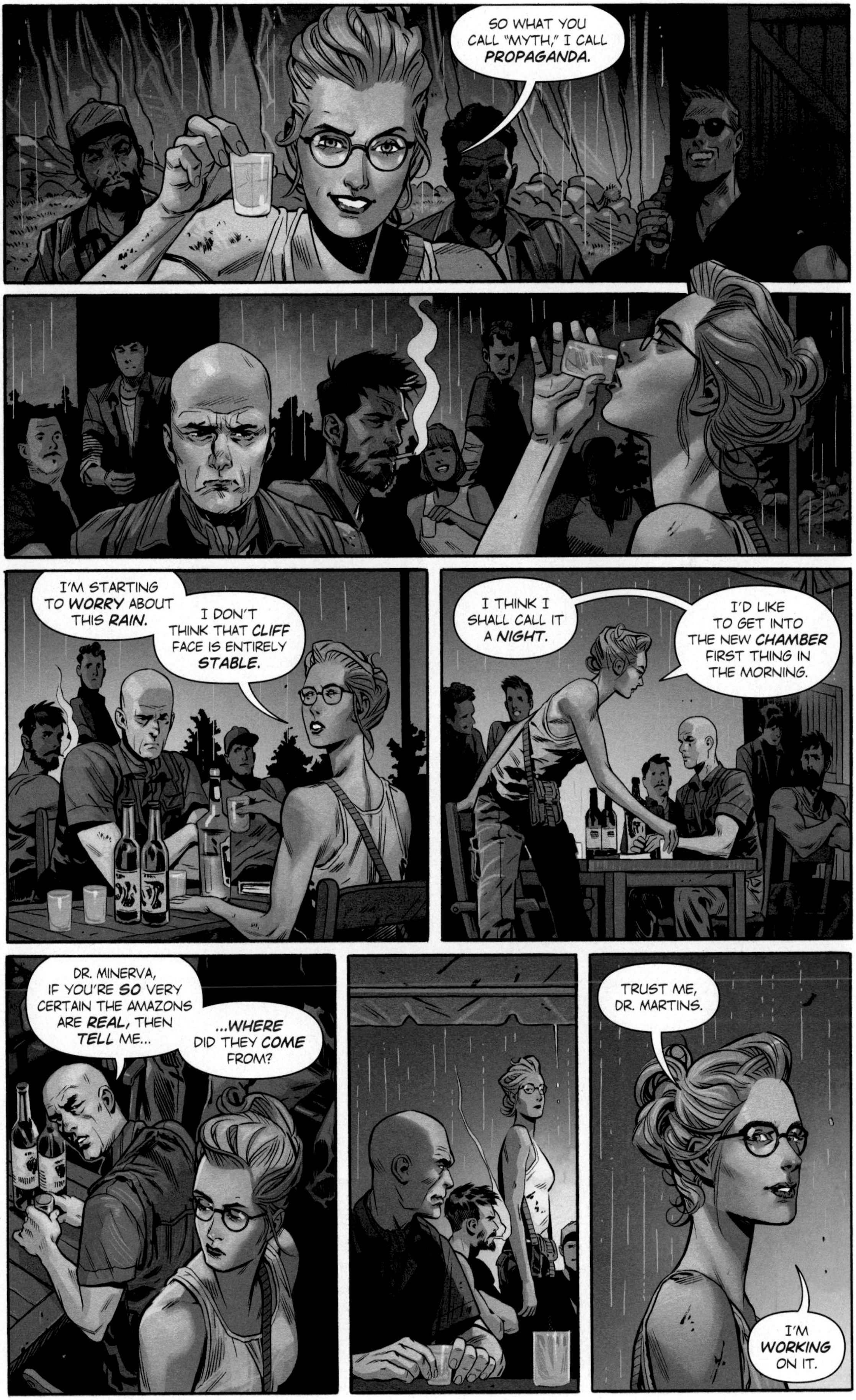
SO WHAT YOU CALL "MYTH," I CALL **PROPAGANDA.**
I'M STARTING TO **WORRY** ABOUT THIS **RAIN.**
I DON'T THINK THAT **CLIFF** FACE IS ENTIRELY **STABLE.**
I THINK I SHALL CALL IT A **NIGHT.**
I'D LIKE TO GET INTO THE NEW **CHAMBER** FIRST THING IN THE MORNING.
DR. MINERVA, IF YOU'RE **SO** VERY CERTAIN THE AMAZONS ARE **REAL,** THEN **TELL** ME...
...**WHERE** DID THEY **COME** FROM?
TRUST ME, DR. MARTINS.
I'M **WORKING** ON IT.

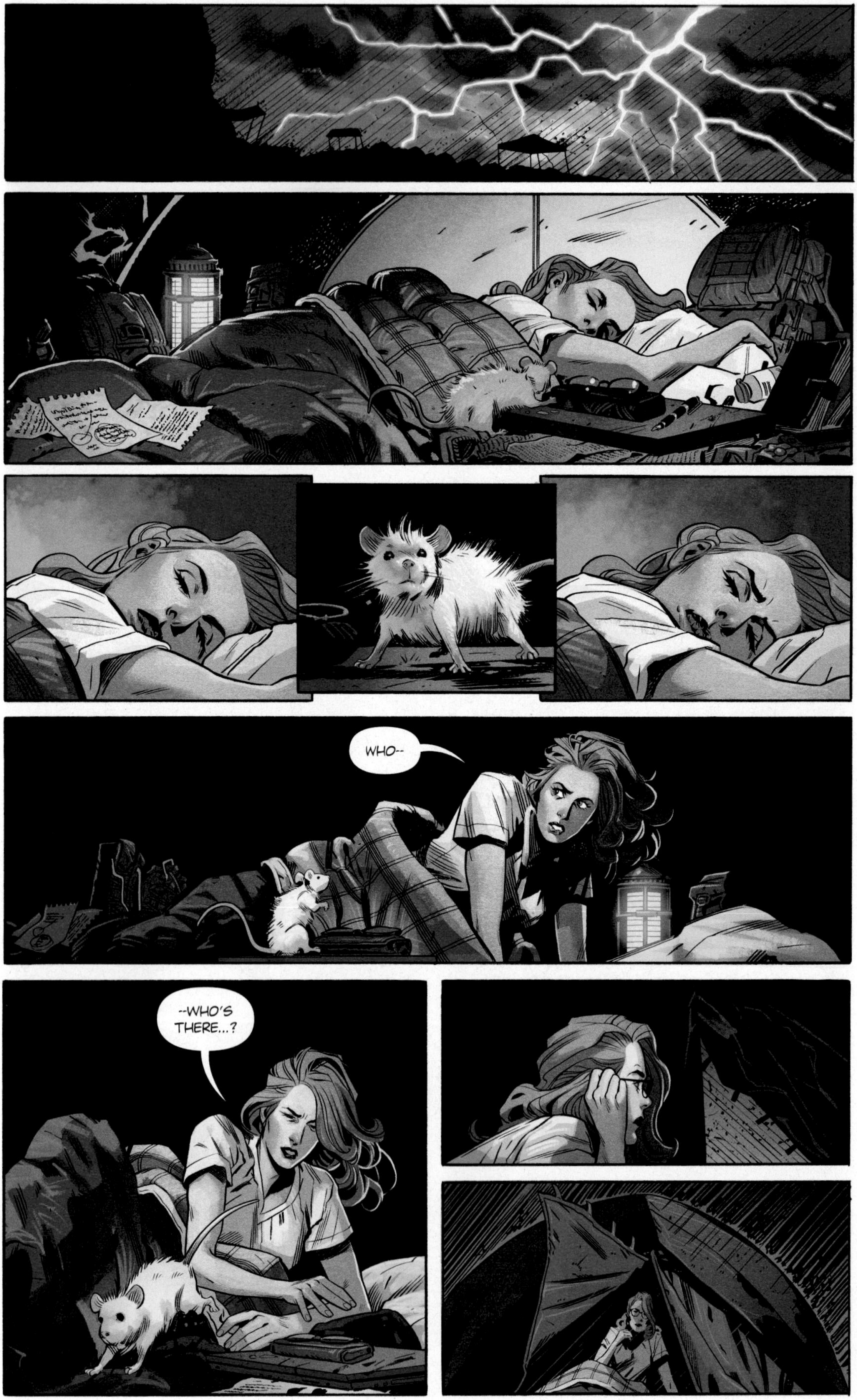
WHO--
--WHO'S THERE...?

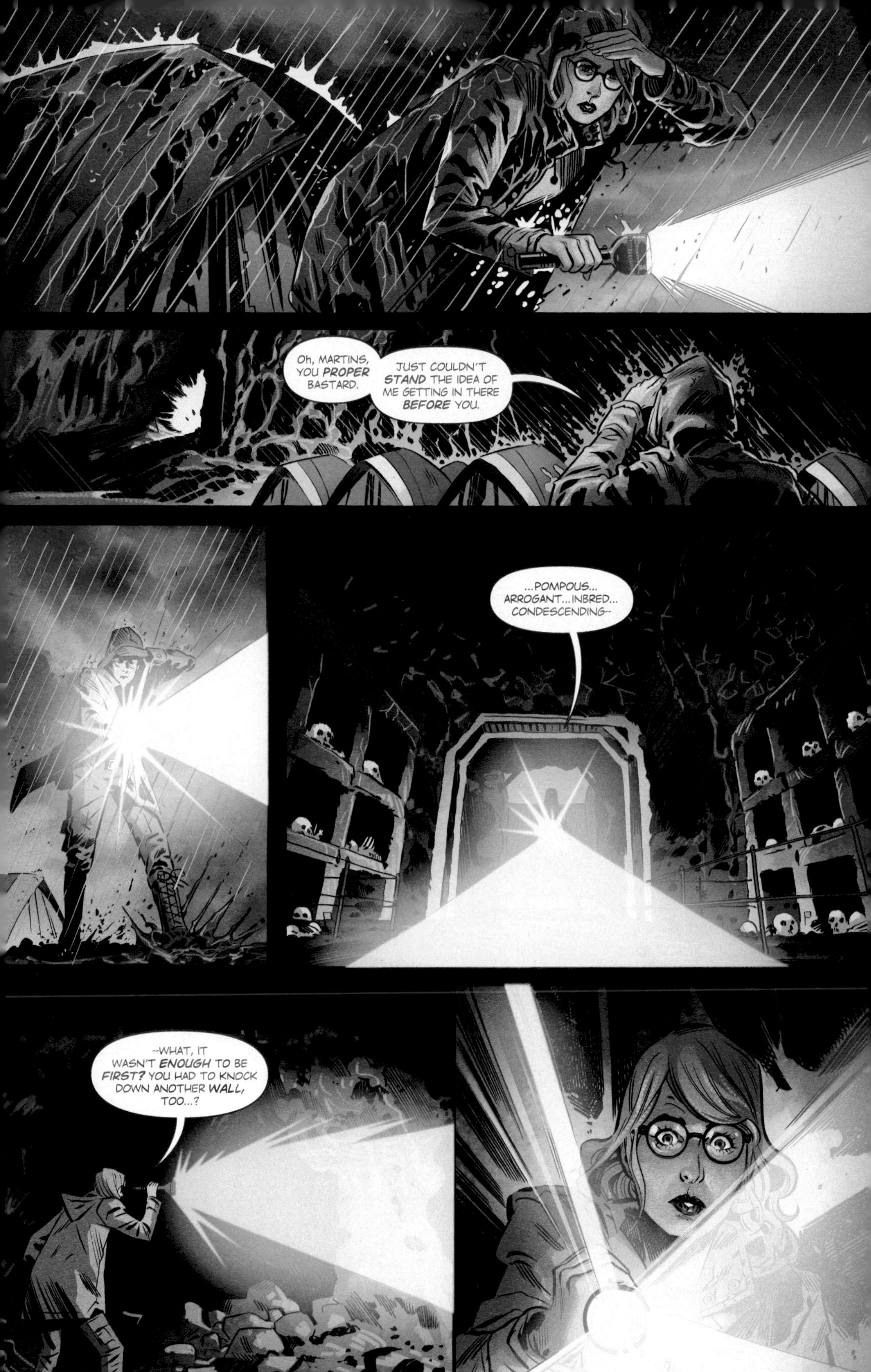
Oh, MARTINS, YOU PROPER BASTARD.
JUST COULDN'T STAND THE IDEA OF ME GETTING IN THERE BEFORE YOU.
...POMPOUS... ARROGANT...INBRED... CONDESCENDING--
--WHAT, IT WASN'T ENOUGH TO BE FIRST? YOU HAD TO KNOCK DOWN ANOTHER WALL, TOO...?

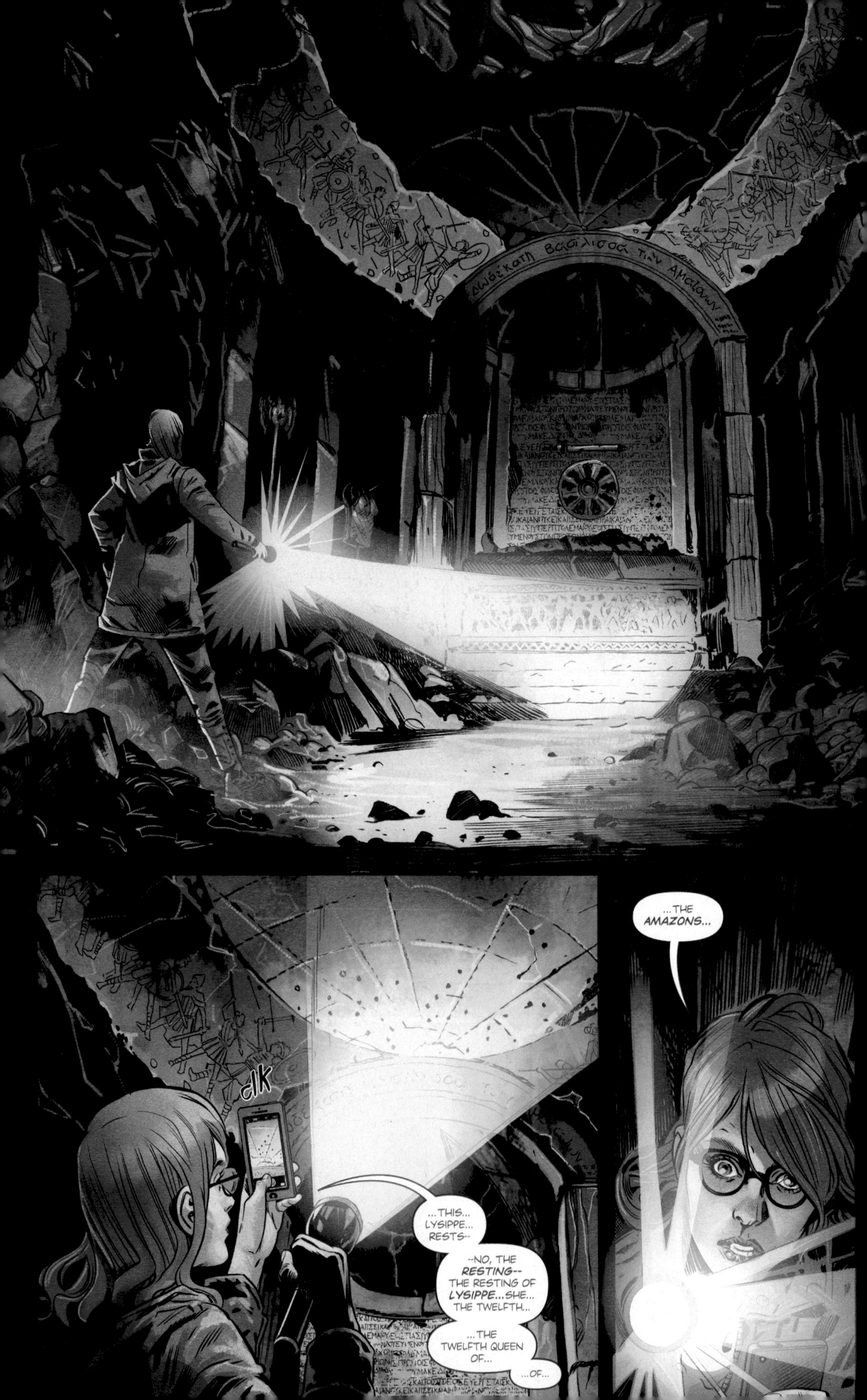
Δωδέκατη βασίλισσα των Αμαζόνων
clk
...THIS... LYSIPPE... RESTS--
--NO, THE *RESTING--* THE RESTING OF *LYSIPPE...*SHE... THE TWELFTH...
...THE TWELFTH QUEEN OF...
...OF...
...THE *AMAZONS...*

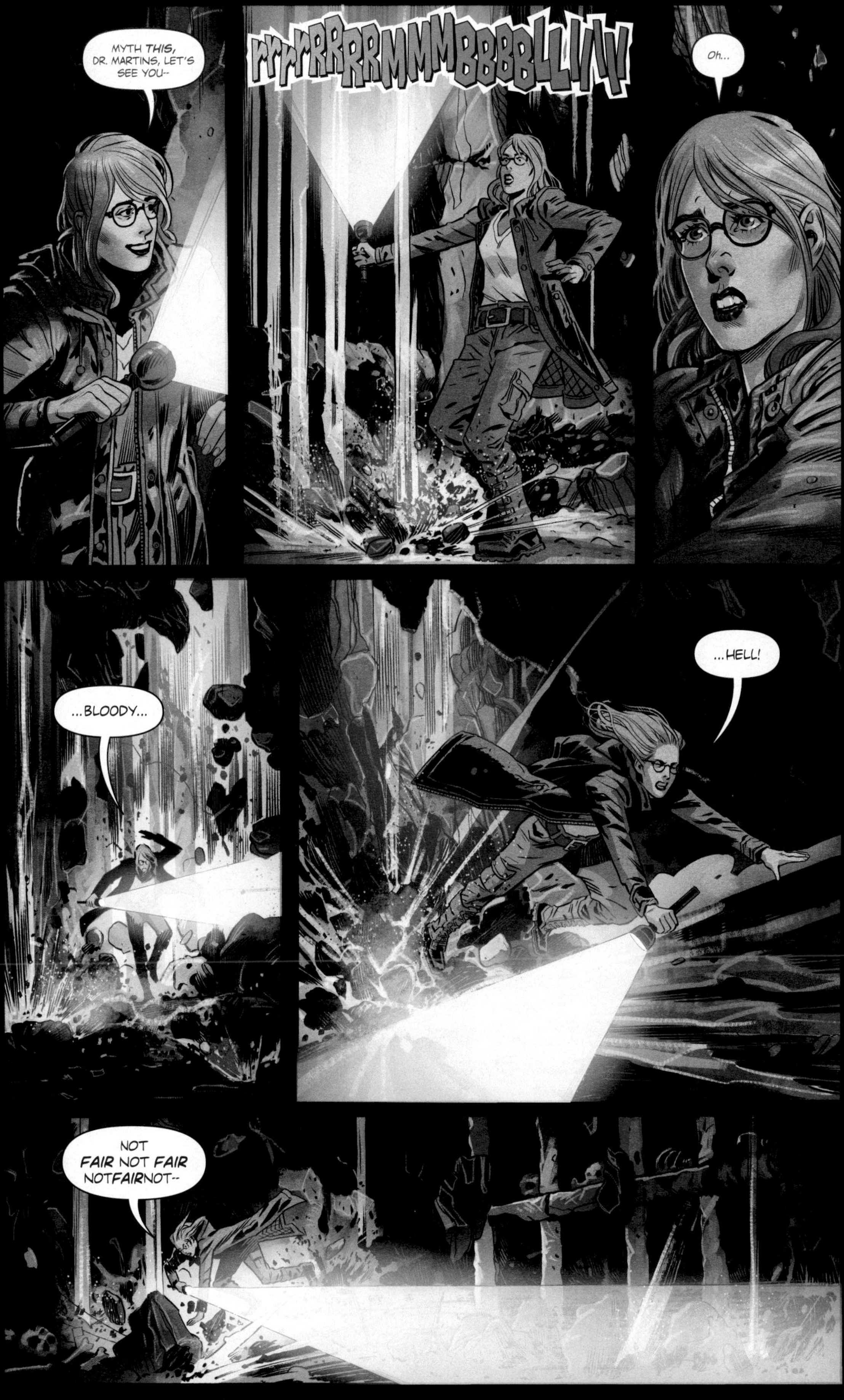
MYTH THIS, DR. MARTINS, LET'S SEE YOU--
rrrrRRRRMMMBBBBLLIIIV
Oh...
...BLOODY...
...HELL!
NOT FAIR NOT FAIR NOTFAIRNOT--

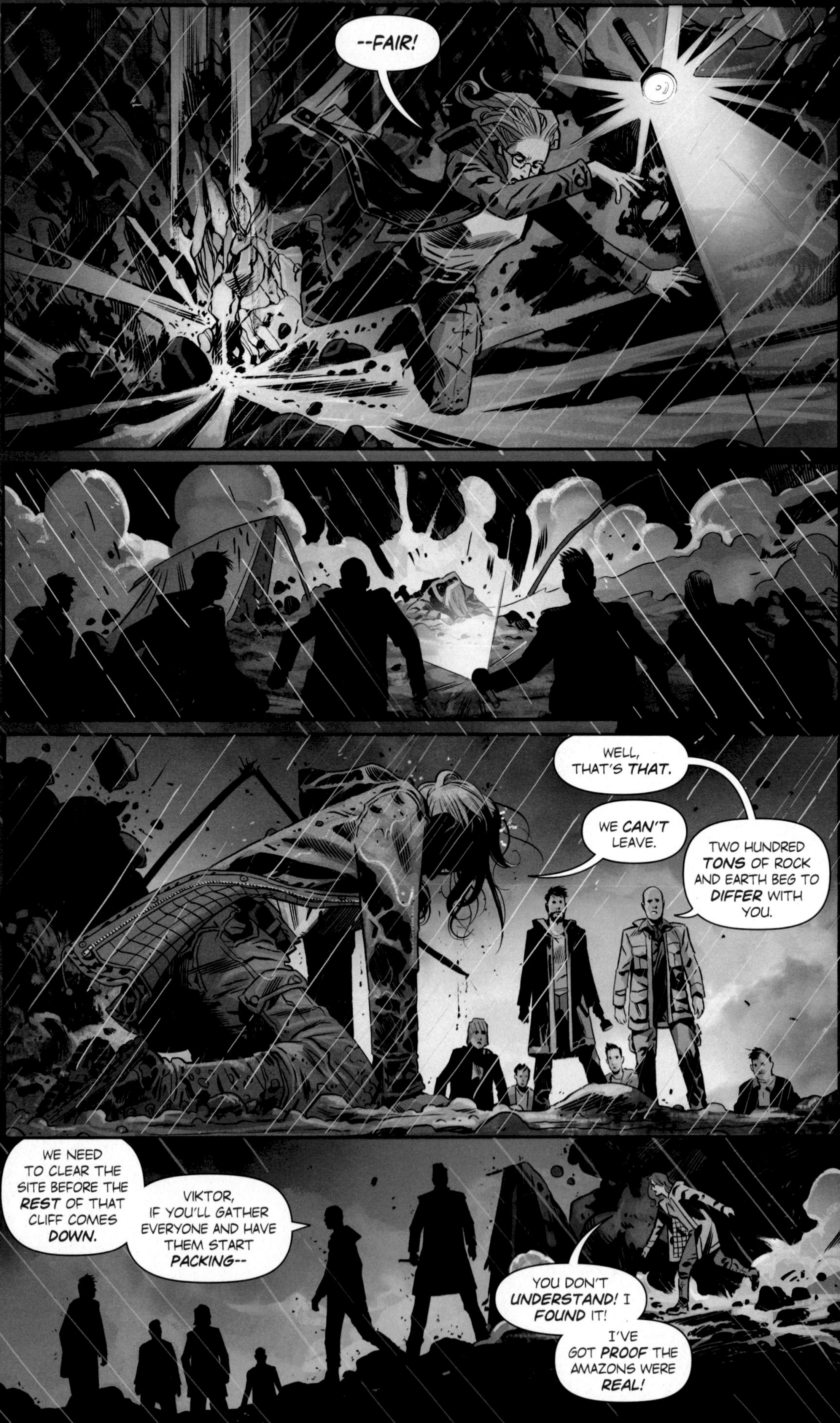
--FAIR!
WELL, THAT'S THAT.
WE CAN'T LEAVE.
TWO HUNDRED TONS OF ROCK AND EARTH BEG TO DIFFER WITH YOU.
WE NEED TO CLEAR THE SITE BEFORE THE REST OF THAT CLIFF COMES DOWN.
VIKTOR, IF YOU'LL GATHER EVERYONE AND HAVE THEM START PACKING--
YOU DON'T UNDERSTAND! I FOUND IT!
I'VE GOT PROOF THE AMAZONS WERE REAL!

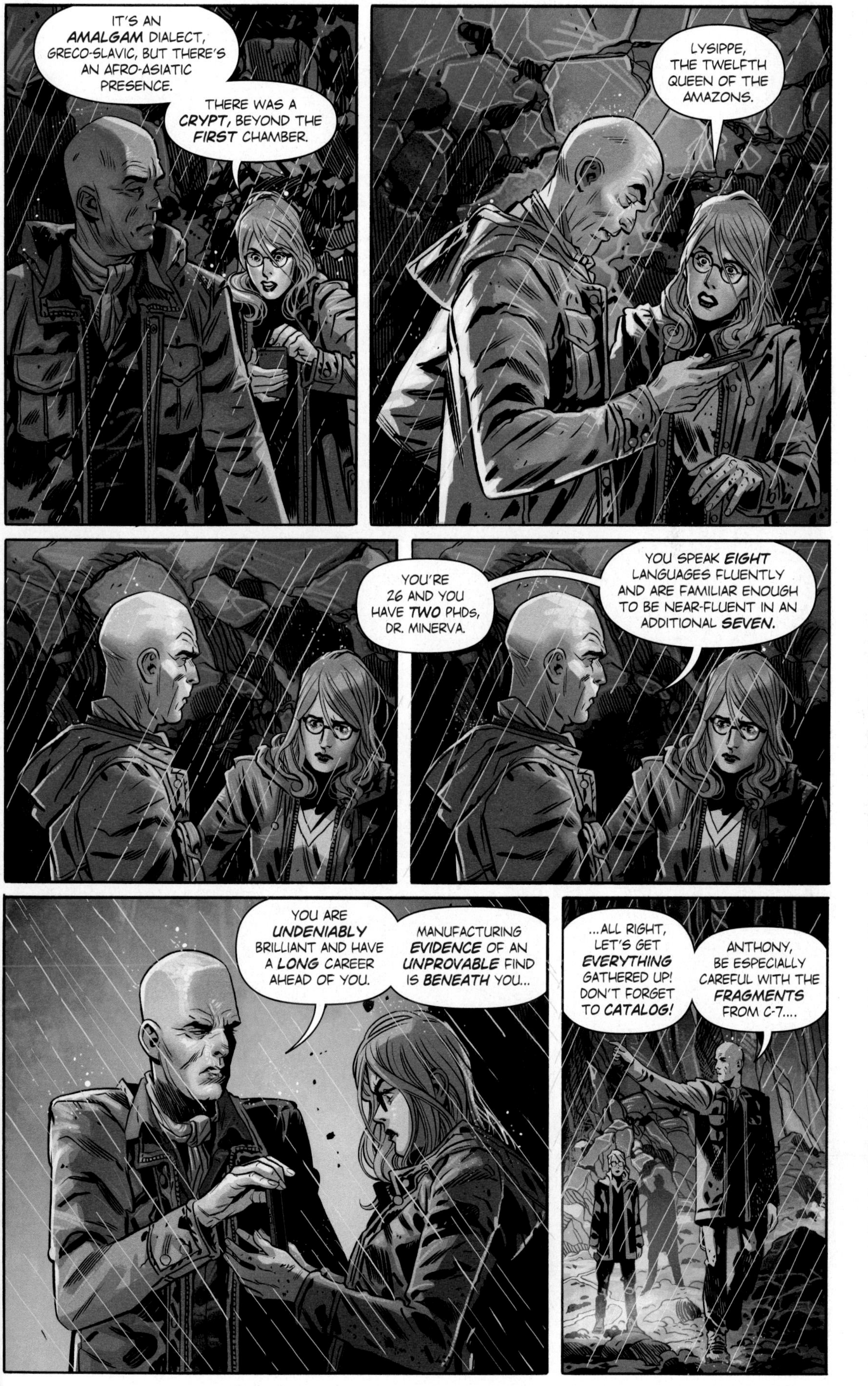
IT'S AN AMALGAM DIALECT, GRECO-SLAVIC, BUT THERE'S AN AFRO-ASIATIC PRESENCE.
THERE WAS A CRYPT, BEYOND THE FIRST CHAMBER.
LYSIPPE, THE TWELFTH QUEEN OF THE AMAZONS.
YOU'RE 26 AND YOU HAVE TWO PHDs, DR. MINERVA.
YOU SPEAK EIGHT LANGUAGES FLUENTLY AND ARE FAMILIAR ENOUGH TO BE NEAR-FLUENT IN AN ADDITIONAL SEVEN.
YOU ARE UNDENIABLY BRILLIANT AND HAVE A LONG CAREER AHEAD OF YOU.
MANUFACTURING EVIDENCE OF AN UNPROVABLE FIND IS BENEATH YOU...
...ALL RIGHT, LET'S GET EVERYTHING GATHERED UP! DON'T FORGET TO CATALOG!
ANTHONY, BE ESPECIALLY CAREFUL WITH THE FRAGMENTS FROM C-7....

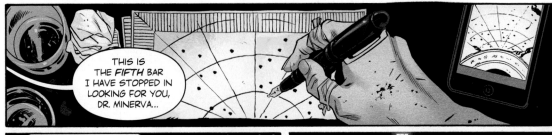

THIS IS THE *FIFTH* BAR I HAVE STOPPED IN LOOKING FOR YOU, DR. MINERVA...

...IT IS, PERHAPS, NOT THE *WISEST* THING? TO BE GETTING *DRUNK* ALL BY YOURSELF IN ODESSA?

I CAN CARE TAKE OF...

...I *MEAN*... I CAN *TAKE* CARE OF *MYSELF*, THANK YOU, VIKTOR.

THIS IS WHAT YOU SHOWED DR. MARTINS, IS IT? *LYSIPPE*, YOU *SAID*?

YOU *GOT* IT, BABY.

LYSIPPE LYSIPPE LYSIPPE. TWELFTH QUEEN OF THE AMAZONS. YOU KNOW WHAT *THAT* MEANS?

THERE'RE AT LEAST *ELEVEN* MORE TO *FIND*!

OOPS.

BUT THING IS, THE...THE *THING* IS, THE *SYMBOLS* ABOVE THE *OTHER* SYMBOLS THAT ARE *LETTERS*?

THOSE ARE *SYMBOLS.*

I JUST DON'T KNOW WHAT THEY MEAN YET.

VIKTOR?

...NO, YAKUVIC...

...VIKTOR YAKUVIC, THE LOCAL **FOREMAN**, YES...

...WELL, I BELIEVE HE STOLE MY **PHONE**, AND I'D LIKE TO GET IT **BACK**...

...YES, **THAT** PHONE, DR. MARTINS...

...YES ...YES--

--DR. MARTINS, IF YOU MIGHT **SHUT UP** FOR A MOMENT...

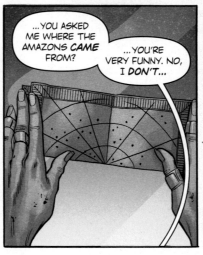

...YOU ASKED ME WHERE THE AMAZONS **CAME** FROM?

...YOU'RE VERY FUNNY. NO, I **DON'T**...

...BUT I MAY HAVE JUST DISCOVERED WHERE THEY **WENT**....

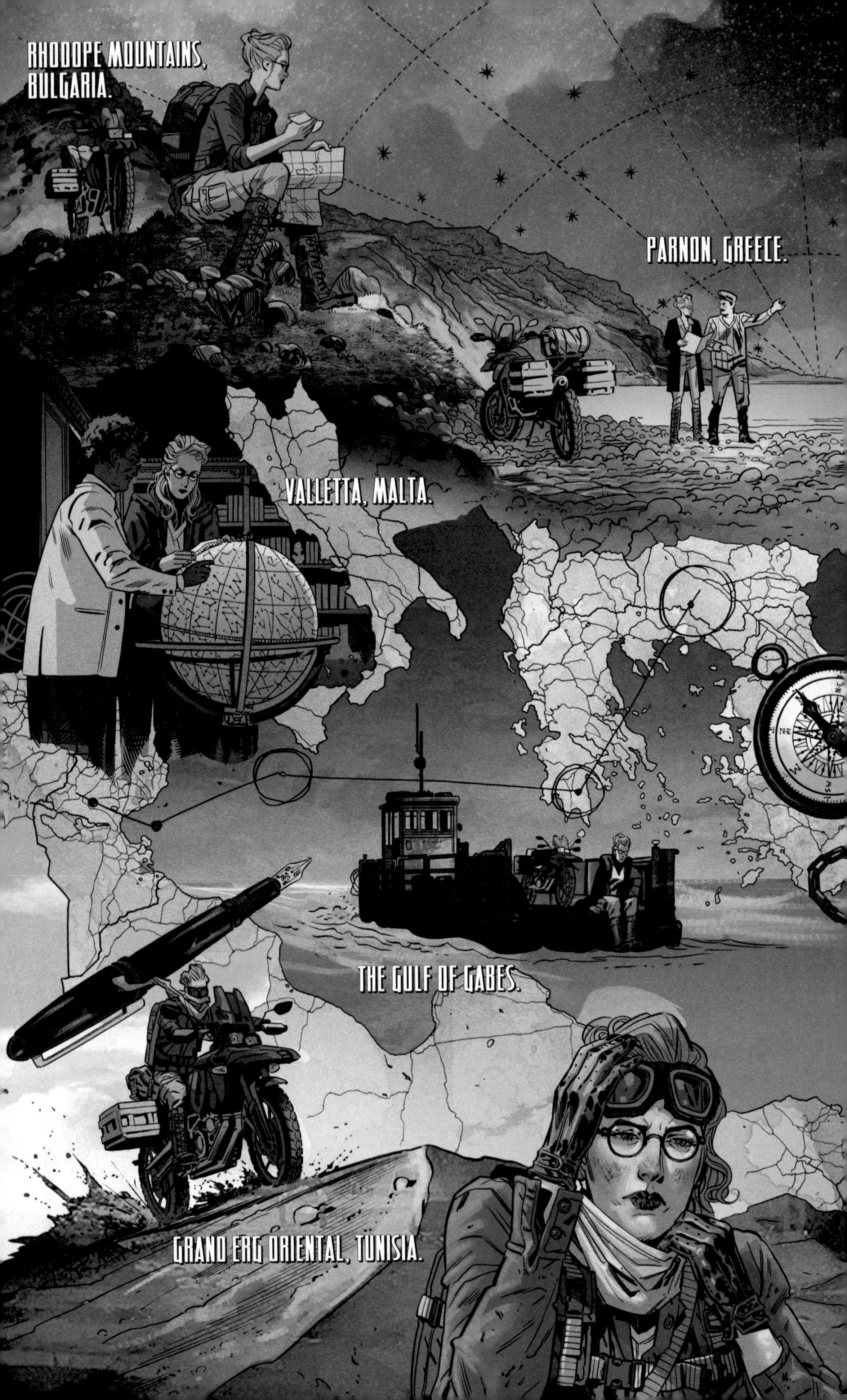
RHODOPE MOUNTAINS, BULGARIA.
PARNON, GREECE.
VALLETTA, MALTA.
THE GULF OF GABES.
GRAND ERG ORIENTAL, TUNISIA.

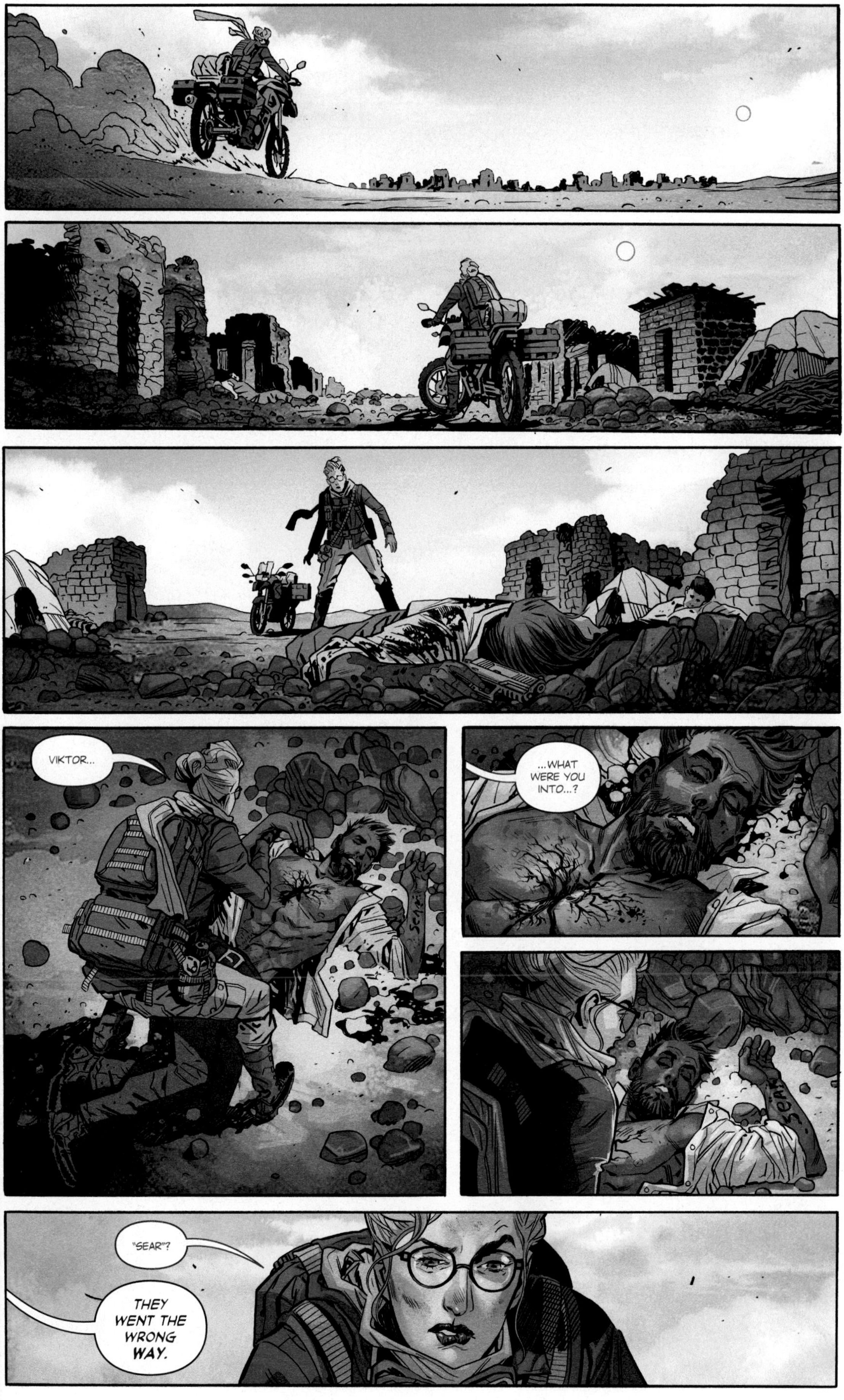
VIKTOR...
...WHAT WERE YOU INTO...?
"SEAR"?
THEY WENT THE WRONG WAY.

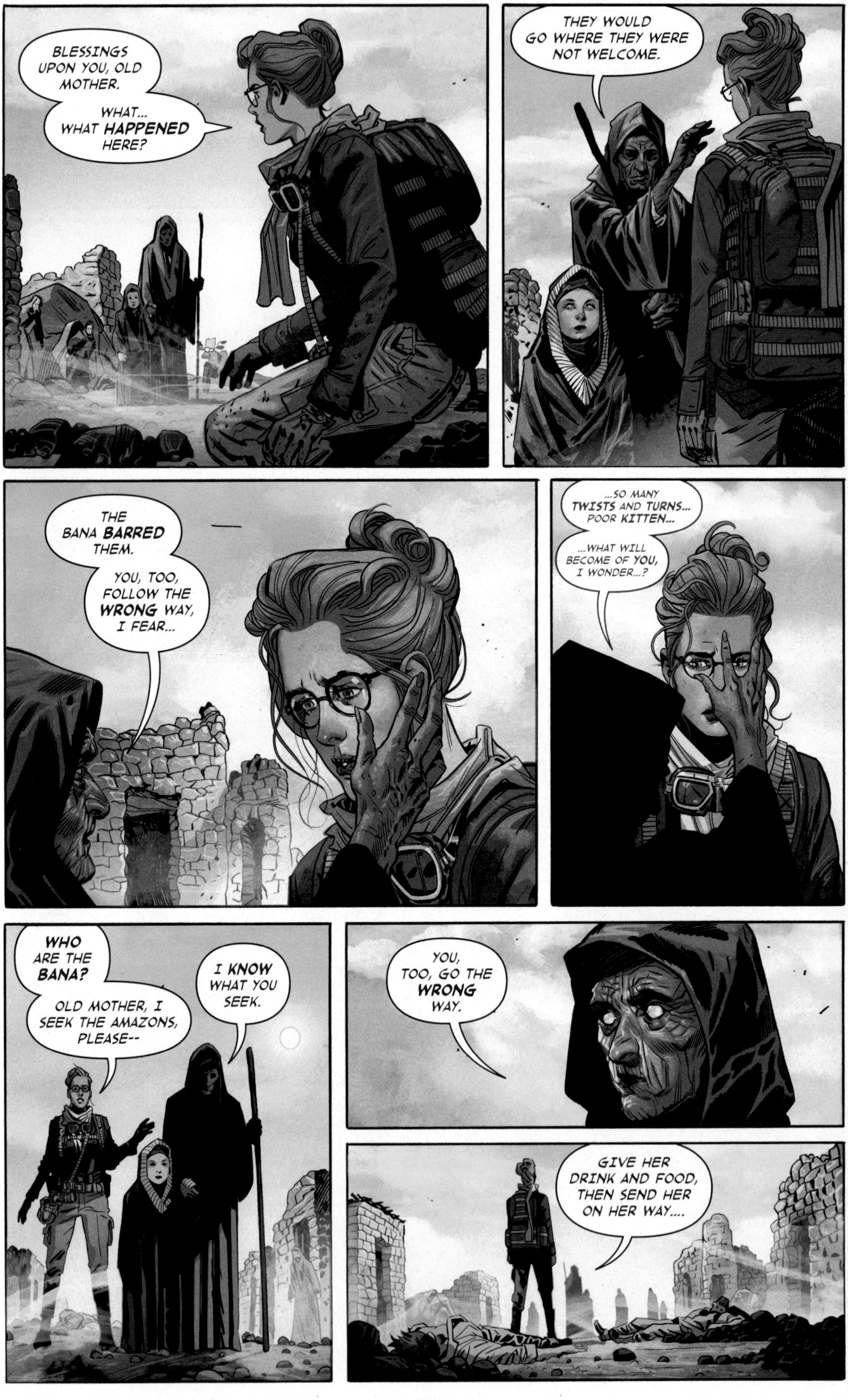
BLESSINGS UPON YOU, OLD MOTHER.
WHAT... WHAT HAPPENED HERE?
THEY WOULD GO WHERE THEY WERE NOT WELCOME.
THE BANA BARRED THEM.
YOU, TOO, FOLLOW THE WRONG WAY, I FEAR...
...SO MANY TWISTS AND TURNS... POOR KITTEN...
...WHAT WILL BECOME OF YOU, I WONDER...?
WHO ARE THE BANA?
OLD MOTHER, I SEEK THE AMAZONS, PLEASE--
I KNOW WHAT YOU SEEK.
YOU, TOO, GO THE WRONG WAY.
GIVE HER DRINK AND FOOD, THEN SEND HER ON HER WAY....

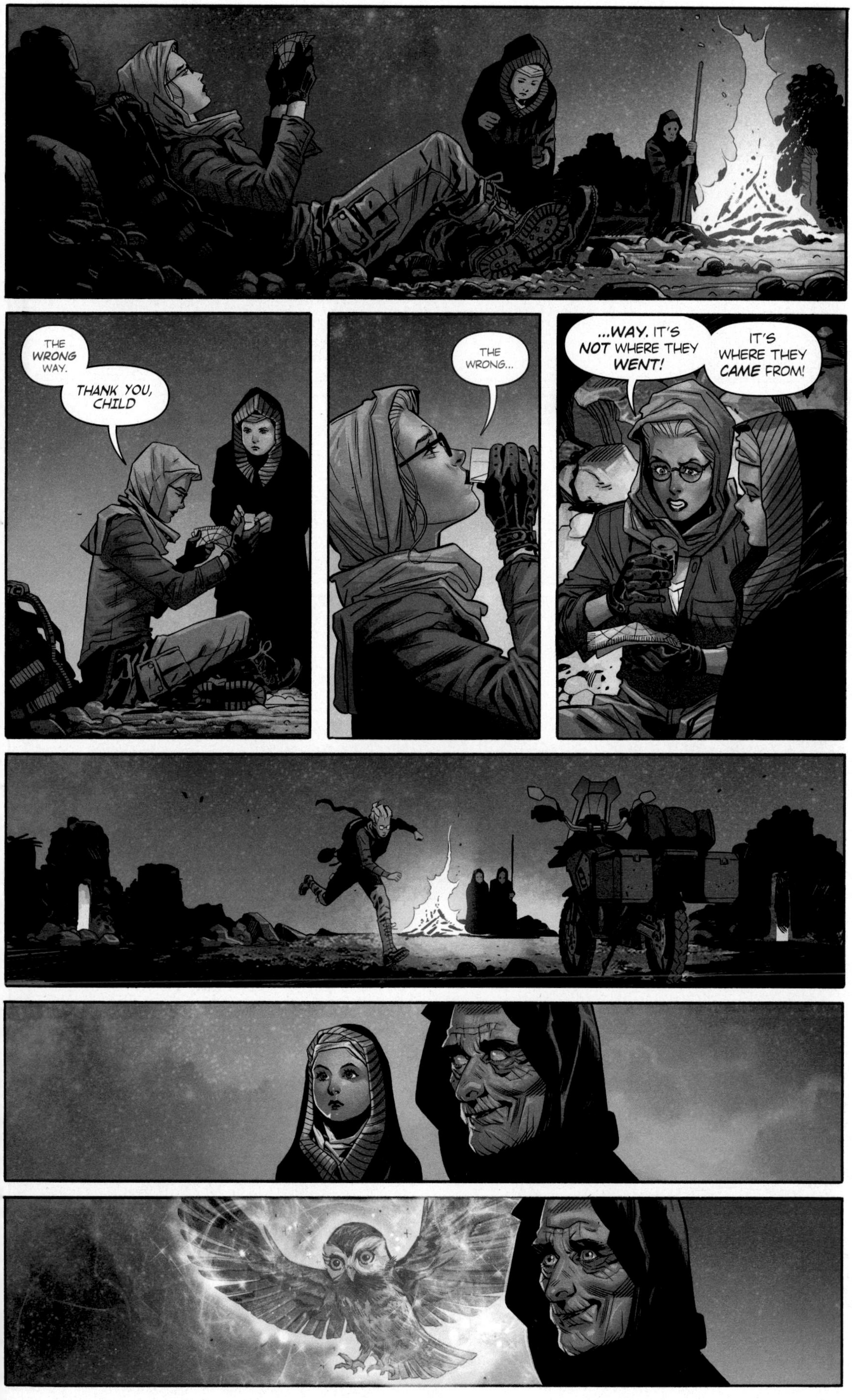
THE WRONG WAY.
THANK YOU, CHILD
THE WRONG...
...WAY. IT'S NOT WHERE THEY WENT!
IT'S WHERE THEY CAME FROM!

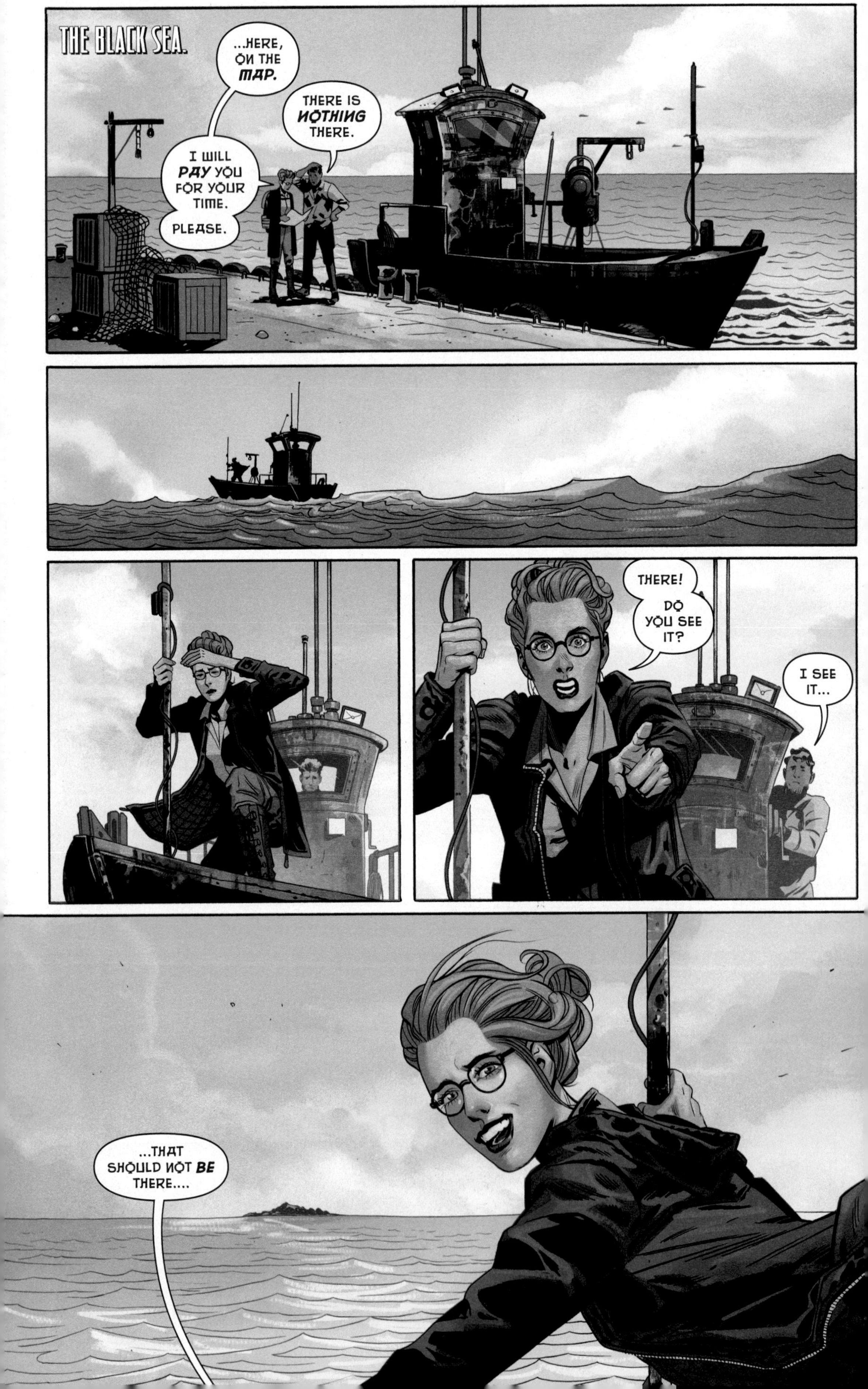
THE BLACK SEA.
...HERE, ON THE MAP.
THERE IS NOTHING THERE.
I WILL PAY YOU FOR YOUR TIME.
PLEASE.
THERE!
DO YOU SEE IT?
I SEE IT...
...THAT SHOULD NOT BE THERE....

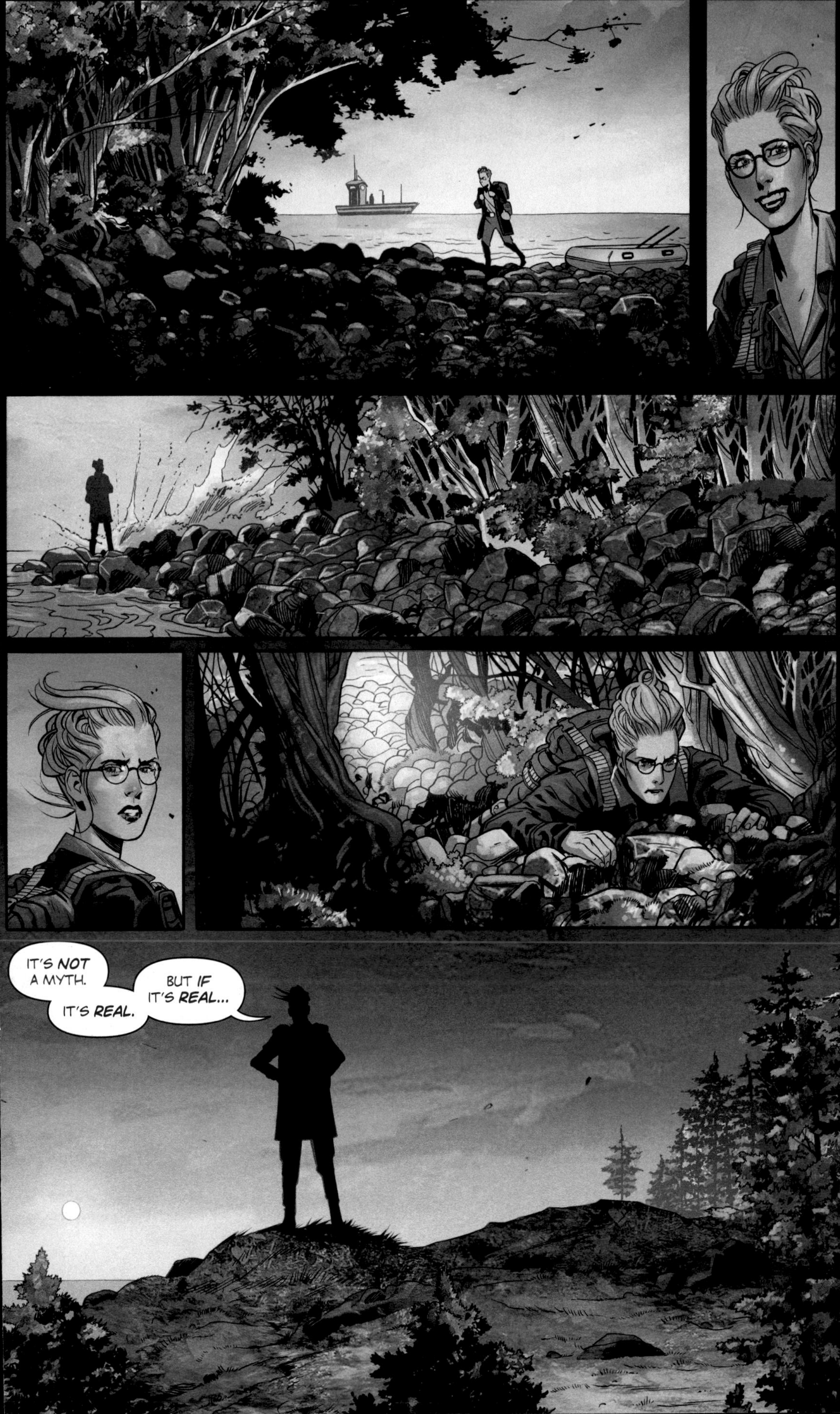
IT'S **NOT** A MYTH.
IT'S **REAL.**
BUT **IF** IT'S **REAL...**

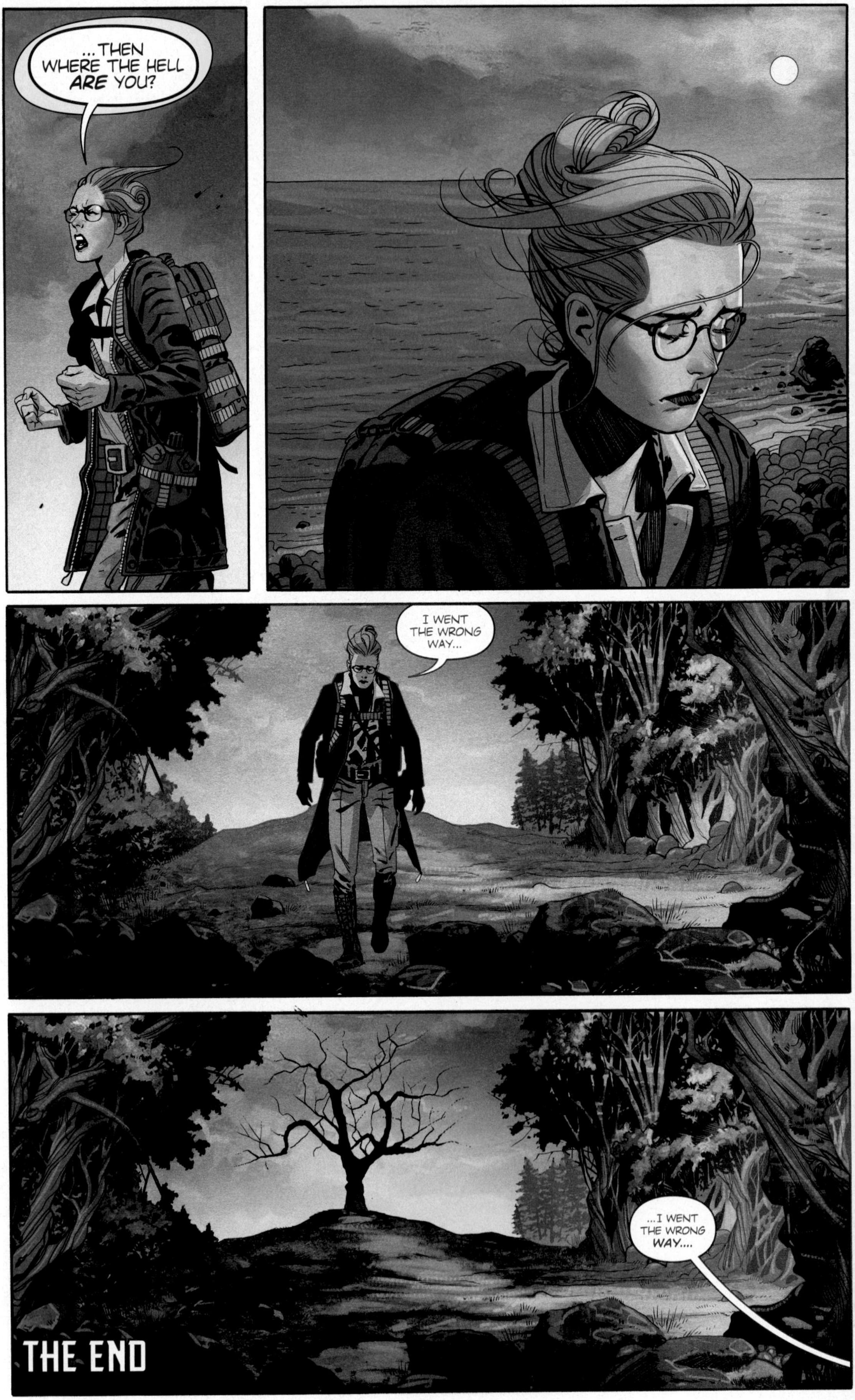
...THEN WHERE THE HELL ARE YOU?
I WENT THE WRONG WAY...
...I WENT THE WRONG WAY....
THE END

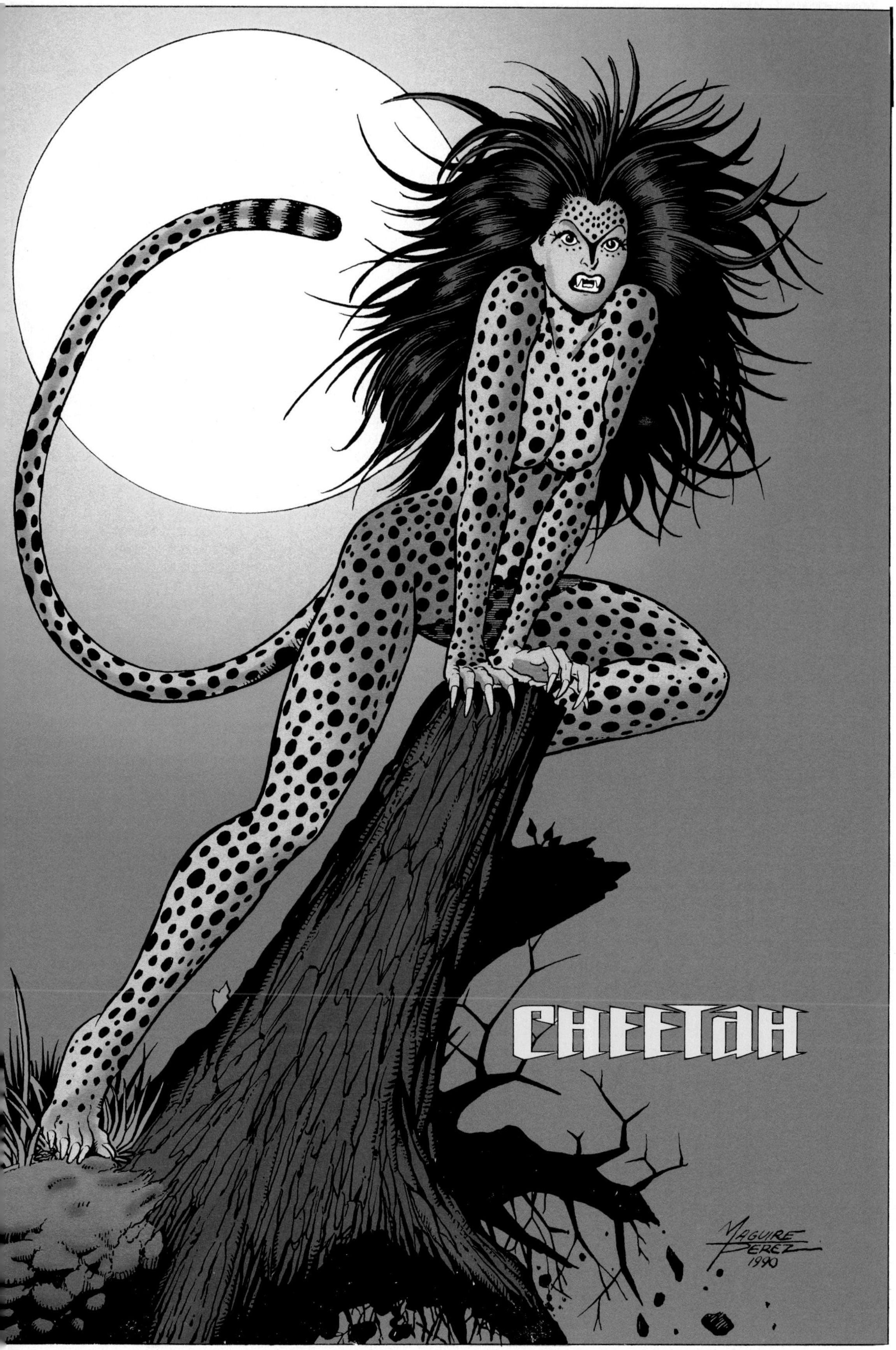
CHEETAH
MAGUIRE
PEREZ
1990

CHEETAH

Alter Ego: Barbara Ann Minerva
Occupation: Archaeologist, Treasure Hunter
Known Relatives: None
Group Affiliation: None
Base of Operations: Mobile

First Appearance: (as Barbara Ann)
WONDER WOMAN (second series) #7
(August, 1987); (as Cheetah)
WONDER WOMAN (second series) #9
(October, 1987)

Height: 5'9" **Weight:** 120 lbs.
Eyes: Brown **Hair:** Black

HISTORY

Barbara Ann Minerva had carved out a reputation as an archaeologist and treasure hunter, but at a great cost. On the one hand, she was responsible for countless important historical finds; on the other, her predatory ruthlessness made her willing to use any means at her disposal to achieve her goals.

Her final expedition took her through Africa toward the lost temple of Urzkartaga, home of a legendary tribe who reportedly worshipped a mystic cat-goddess who took the form of a human cheetah. Unbeknownst to Minerva and her companion, Dr. Leavens, the native priest who served as her guide had led the expeditionary party into a trap. Minerva's party was attacked by the people of Urzkartaga, who planned to use the explorers as blood sacrifices for the cat-god. Despite overwhelming odds, Minerva and Leavens escaped the ambush and later returned to the temple under cover of darkness. From their vantage point, they saw the sacrificial ceremony that revived and resuscitated Urzkartaga's cat-god, when, suddenly, another group of natives — a band armed with semi-automatic weapons — burst from the jungle to massacre the Urzkartagans, whose sacrifices had taken the lives of many of their own people. In the mêlée, the cat-god was killed and the temple razed, and Minerva found herself trapped within the temple's ruins along with the

native priest — Chuma — and the slain cat-god.

At Minerva's command, Chuma explained the ritual and history of the cat-god. Minerva, wishing to command the cat-god's power, demanded to be subjected to the ritual herself, even though part of the ritual required her to kill Leavens and drink his blood. Painted with sacred designs and dressed in the skin of the cat-god, she took the potion and became the Cheetah.

Because the ritual required its subject to be a virgin — a requirement Minerva could not meet — the Cheetah spell took its toll on her. In between doses of the rare elixir, prepared by her new companion, Chuma, Minerva's body became progressively weaker. Addicted to the power of the Cheetah, she was driven to hunting down victims to sacrifice in order to maintain her power.

Some time later, during the media blitz that accompanied Wonder Woman's arrival in America, Minerva read about Wonder Woman's golden lasso, forged from the legendary golden girdle of Gaea. Obsessed with the thought of owning such a valuable artifact, she vowed to make it her own. As the Cheetah, she attacked Wonder Woman but failed to capture her lasso; several months later, she used her power and influence to arrange for a band of captured alien invaders to steal it for her, then assumed her Cheetah form and killed them.

The subsequent turn of events surprised

even Minerva. The lasso itself compelled her to travel to Asia and drew her toward a hidden Egyptian mosque. There, she found the long-hidden second girdle of Gaea and took it for her own. By the time Wonder Woman traveled to Egypt and tracked Minerva down, the Amazon race whose mosque Minerva had defiled had gone after Minerva as well. In the ensuing three-way battle, Chuma was killed, and the girdle and lasso were regained by their respective owners.

In the aftermath of the battle, Minerva continued to be possessed by the spirit of the Cheetah but was severely weakened by her addiction to the elixir that gave her her powers, the secret of which died with Chuma. With her health slowly and continually ebbing, she is currently incarcerated, pending trial for several murders.

POWERS & WEAPONS

A deadly and powerful hand-to-hand combatant, the Cheetah is incredibly fast. She possesses superhuman strength and agility, acute night-vision, and razor-sharp claws that pierce flesh and stone with equal ease. She is also capable of using her prehensile tail as a weapon to strike out at or strangle her opponents.

text: MARK WAID/art: KEVIN MAGUIRE & GEORGE PÉREZ/colors: TOM McCRAW